MW00667062

The Red Rockets' Glare

Spaceflight and the Soviet Imagination, 1857–1957

The Red Rockets' Glare is the first academic study on the birth of the Soviet space program and one of the first social histories of Soviet science. Based on many years of archival research, the book situates the birth of cosmic enthusiasm within the social and cultural upheavals of Russian and Soviet history. Asif A. Siddiqi frames the origins of *Sputnik* by bridging imagination with engineering – seeing them not as dialectic, discrete, and sequential but as mutable, intertwined, and concurrent. Imagination and engineering not only fed each other but were also coproduced by key actors who maintained a delicate line between secret work on rockets (which interested the military) and public prognostications on the cosmos (which captivated the populace). *Sputnik*, he argues, was the outcome of both large-scale state imperatives to harness science and technology and populist phenomena that frequently owed little to the whims and needs of the state apparatus.

Asif A. Siddiqi is an assistant professor of history at Fordham University. He specializes in the social and cultural history of modern Russia and the history of science and technology. His work has been supported by the American Historical Association, the Smithsonian Institution, the Social Science Research Council, the National Science Foundation, and the American Academy of Arts & Sciences. His book, *Challenge to Apollo: The Soviet Union and the Space Race, 1945–1974* (2000), received a number of awards, including a citation by the *Wall Street Journal* as one of the best books written on space exploration. He received his doctorate from Carnegie Mellon University and currently lives in New York.

Cambridge Centennial of Flight

Editors:

John Anderson
Curator of Aerodynamics, National Air and Space Museum, and Professor Emeritus, Aerospace Engineering, University of Maryland

Von Hardesty
Smithsonian Institution

The series presents new titles dealing with the drama and historical impact of human flight. The Air Age began on December 17, 1903, with the epic powered and controlled flight by the Wright brothers at Kitty Hawk. The airplane rapidly developed into an efficient means of global travel and a lethal weapon of war. Modern rocketry has allowed heirs of the Wrights to orbit the Earth and to land on the Moon, inaugurating a new era of exploration of the solar system by humans and robotic machines. The Centennial of Flight series offers pioneering studies with fresh interpretative insights and broad appeal on key themes, events, and personalities that shaped the evolution of aerospace technology.

Also published in this series:
Scott W. Palmer, *Dictatorship of the Air: Aviation Culture and the Fate of Modern Russia*

Michael B. Petersen, *Missiles for the Fatherland: Peenemünde, National Socialism, and the V-2 Missile*

The Red Rockets' Glare

Spaceflight and the Soviet Imagination, 1857–1957

ASIF A. SIDDIQI
Fordham University

CAMBRIDGE
UNIVERSITY PRESS

CAMBRIDGE
UNIVERSITY PRESS

32 Avenue of the Americas, New York NY 10013-2473, USA

Cambridge University Press is part of the University of Cambridge.

It furthers the University's mission by disseminating knowledge in the pursuit of education, learning and research at the highest international levels of excellence.

www.cambridge.org
Information on this title: www.cambridge.org/9781107639324

First published 2010
First paperback edition 2013

A catalogue record for this publication is available from the British Library

Library of Congress Cataloguing in Publication data

Siddiqi, Asif A., 1966–
The red rockets' glare : spaceflight and the Soviet imagination, 1857–1957 / Asif A. Siddiqi.
p. cm. – (Cambridge centennial of flight)
Includes bibliographical references and index.
ISBN 978-0-521-89760-0 (hardback)
1. Astronautics – Soviet Union – History. 2. Science and state – Soviet Union – History. I. Title.
TL789.8.S65S489 2010
629.40947′09041 – dc22 2009033925

ISBN 978-0-521-89760-0 Hardback
ISBN 978-1-107-63932-4 Paperback

Contents

List of Illustrations and Tables

Illustrations

Tables

Acknowledgments

The research and writing for this book were made possible by the generous support of the following: the Smithsonian National Air and Space Museum's Guggenheim Short-Term Grant (2000), the National Science Foundation's Dissertation Improvement Grant (Award 1120239; 2001–2003), the Smithsonian National Air and Space Museum's A. Verville Fellowship (2002–2003), the Social Science Research Council's International Dissertation Research Fellowship (2002–2003), the American Historical Association's Fellowship in Aerospace History (2003–2004), and the Fordham Faculty Research Grant (2005–2006). In addition, I must thank the American Academy of Arts and Sciences for their generous support during my stay there in 2004–2005 as a visiting scholar.

Versions of three chapters were published in earlier forms and are credited to the following journals. Chapter 3 was published in an earlier version in *Osiris* 23 (2008): 260–288 under the title "Imagining the Cosmos: Utopians, Mystics, and the Popular Culture of Spaceflight in Revolutionary Russia" (© 2008 by the History of Science Society). Chapter 5 was published in an earlier version in *Technology and Culture* 44 (2003): 470–501 under the title "The Rockets' Red Glare: Technology, Conflict, and Terror in the Soviet Union" (© 2003 by the Society for the History of Technology). Chapter 6 was published in an earlier version in *Europe-Asia Studies* 56 no. 8 (2004): 1131–1156 under the title "Russians in Germany: Founding the Post-war Missile Programme" (© 2004 University of Glasgow).

I owe a huge debt of gratitude to David Hounshell. At every step of this project, David guided my writing, helping me shape the big questions while keeping a critical eye on the crucial details. Also at Carnegie Mellon, Wendy Goldman constantly challenged me to rethink Soviet history, to see it through new eyes. I benefited from her enormous knowledge as well as her boundless enthusiasm and encouragement. As scholars, I can think of no worthier role models than David and Wendy. I must also thank Jonathan Harris, who helped me eliminate inconsistencies in my writing and grounded me solidly in the institutional politics of postwar Soviet history.

Scott Sandage profoundly influenced my view on the relationship between history and language. I am still discovering the many things I learned under his tutelage. Others at Carnegie Mellon who provided invaluable guidance include Joe Trotter, Steve Schlossman, Ed Constant, and Naum Kats, as well as Gail Dickey, Natalie Taylor, and Dee Clydesdale. My peers in graduate school made this voyage more fun, both intellectually and otherwise, than I could have ever imagined. A special heartfelt thanks to Becky Kluchin, my fellow traveler in Pittsburgh, and also to Steve Burnett, Glen Asner, Jim Longhurst, Carl Zimring, and Jeff Suzik. I learned an incalculable amount from Carnegie Mellon's Cold War Science and Technology Studies Program, founded by David Hounshell and coordinated by Andy McIntyre.

At Fordham University, special thanks to my colleagues Ed Cahill, Nick Paul, Thierry Rigogne, Ebru Turan, David Myers, Mike Latham, Silvana Patriarca, Nancy Curtin, and Doron Ben-Atar. Also at Fordham, I want to thank Barbara Costa, April Acosta, and especially Esther Liberman-Cuenca for their help. I also acknowledge the support of fellow visiting scholars at the American Academy of Arts and Sciences, Hsuan Hsu, Chris Klemek, and Lisa Szefel, and James Carroll who directed the Visiting Scholars program at the Academy.

Roger Launius and Mike Neufeld at the Smithsonian's National Air and Space Museum provided indispensable help throughout this project. Without Roger's mentorship and guidance, I might never have come back to graduate school. Mike very kindly read the entire manuscript and provided useful comments.

I owe a huge debt of gratitude to Matthias Uhl, who helped me locate vast numbers of documents from Russian archives. In addition, conversations with the following scholars over many years (as well as a familiarity with their thought-provoking work) helped guide both my research and writing: Igor' Afanas'ev, James Andrews, Bill Barry, Irina Bystrova, Jonathan Coopersmith, Dwayne Day, Slava Gerovitch, Michael Gordin, Peter Gorin, Loren Graham, Michael Hagemeister, James Harford, Bart Hendrickx, Sergei Khrushchev, John Krige, Christian Lardier, John Logsdon, Vadim Lukashevich, Jonathan McDowell, Timofei Prygichev, Sonja Schmid, Frank Winter, and Ivan Zavidonov. A number of people helped with images. They include Cathy Lewis, Ron Miller, and Steven Zaloga.

At Cambridge University Press, a very special thanks to Von Hardesty, John Anderson, Frank Smith, and Eric Crahan for their generous support for this project. For their expert help with logistics, production, copyediting, and layout I should note the contributions of Marielle Poss, Emily Spangler, Jason Przybylski, Peter Katsirubas, and Susan Zinninger.

In Russia, I would like to acknowledge the staff members at the Russian State Archive of the Economy (S. I. Degtev and A. Nazarov), the Archive of the Russian Academy of Sciences (N. M. Sukhoruchkina), the State Archive of the Russian Federation (N. I. Abdulaeva), the Russian State Military Archive, and the Russian State Archive of Scientific-Technical Documentation. Working in Russia was a memorable experience owing to the many wonderful people I met there. I'd like to thank the friendly staff (particularly Irina Karapetiants) at the Russian State University of the Humanities (RGGU) for their generous help in setting up a temporary home in Moscow. Very special thanks to Dmitry Payson and Aleksei Kilichenko, both of whom helped with negotiating life in Moscow. Finally, a special note of gratitude to Soviet space program veterans and historians who agreed to sit for interviews or helped me in many untold ways. They include veterans B. E. Chertok, O. V. Gurko, N. S. Koroleva, V. A. Poliachenko, V. L. Ponomareva, S. N. Samburov, V. P. Savinykh, and the late V. S. Syromiatnikov. In the United States, I must acknowledge the Clark University Archives (Mott Linn), the National Security Archive at George Washington University, the Archives Division at the Smithsonian's National Air and Space Museum, and the NASA History Office Archives (Steve Garber, Nadine Andreassen, and Jane Odom).

On a personal note, I'd like to thank the whole Pittsburgh crew, all of whom have, it seems, moved on: Karen Barth, Jill Hochman, Heather Raphael, Kathy Robertson, and Tim Smith. Thanks to my friends in New York: Natalja Czarnecki, Joey Falcone, Sherri Islam, Mafruza Khan, Elizabeth Kosakowska, Shoma Lahiry, Sherry Lin, Amira Mittermaier, Rayaan Shums, and Sanjive Vaidya. Thanks as always to Mandar Jayawant in Ulan Bator. A special thanks to my childhood mentor, the late Fazlul Haque, who, I hope, would have been proud of me. Thanks to Godspeed You! Black Emperor for the soundtrack. Thank you and so much more to my best friend Karen Bell for guiding me to a career in academia.

Family members have been infinitely patient, inspiring, and generous. Thanks to Uncle, Auntie, Sarat, and Suzi for humoring me through all this, especially to Uncle whose enthusiastic spirit was so contagious and, I hope, lives on in these pages. Thanks to Rochona, Mohona, and David for their hospitality in both Philadelphia and New York. My father and my mother have been the best role models – this book is a small step in emulating their lofty standards of scholarship and intellectual rigor. Finally, this book is only partly mine, because, without Anoo, it would not exist. Through this entire process, from conception to birth, she has been a firm presence, helping to coax it into being. It is to her and to Sahil that I dedicate this. May a little part of him always dream of utopias.

Introduction

The history of the Soviet Union and the history of space exploration share a paradoxical quality: each is a history of possible futures. At times, both the Soviet project and the space program were grounded in deep-rooted expectations for new possibilities, utopian and pragmatic in nature. The coincident nature of these two projects – one largely social and the other broadly technological – has reinforced the notion that the Soviet space program was the outcome of forces that were deeply consistent with the aims and ideologies of the state. As a result, our understanding of the Soviet space program has been encumbered with a tone of inevitability, as if the effort inexorably sprang from a massive state infrastructure driven only by ideological considerations.

This perceived intersection of ideology, state intervention, and technology was embodied most potently in *Sputnik*, the world's first artificial satellite. In the days and weeks after *Sputnik's* October 4, 1957 launch, these connections provided a forceful narrative for the Soviet and Western media, the former seeking to create a new history of its cosmic enthusiasm, and the latter eager to use that history to highlight the crisis of Western power at the height of the Cold War. This first satellite, whose name in Russian meant "fellow traveler," fell from the heavens within a few weeks of its launch. Despite its early demise, *Sputnik* has remained in our collective imagination not only as a potent symbol of the political, social, and cultural possibilities of the late twentieth century but also as a metaphor for human aspirations and expectations for an exhilarating future.

Within the Soviet Union, the satellite and its successors invested the rising hopes of a new postwar "Sputnik generation" with a powerful icon.[1] Given the often conflicting hopes and disappointments of the Khrushchev era, the project of spaceflight was one of the few state policies that united all in its utopianism, heroism, and iconography. By the time cosmonaut Iurii Gagarin returned to Moscow after his historic flight into the cosmos in 1961, more people assembled in Red Square to welcome him than had for the parades celebrating victory in the Great Patriotic War. *Sputnik*, like

[1] Donald. J. Raleigh, *Russia's Sputnik Generation: Soviet Baby Boomers Talk About Their Lives* (Bloomington: Indiana University Press, 2006).

Gagarin, represented a powerful symbol for restoring Soviet pride in the aftermath of the economic, social, and political shocks of late Stalinism.[2]

Sputnik also served as potent evidence of the country's arrival as a superpower on the international stage. Five days after the launch, the front page of *Pravda* distilled its import down to a single headline: "A Great Victory in the Global Competition with Capitalism."[3] Loudly and often crudely, Nikita Khrushchev used the early successes in the Soviet space program to emphasize the political, social, technological, and ideological power of the modern Soviet Union. *Sputnik* also ensured serious consideration of Soviet claims – whether about science, or military power, or the economy. For years, many Western observers had disregarded Soviet assertions as crude propaganda, but the clear trail of the *Sputnik* satellite above the night skies of the American Midwest denuded the dismissive tenor of Westerners of its power, making clear once and for all that Soviet claims for global preeminence in science and technology rested on inarguable truths. There was also the unmistakable military connotation of *Sputnik*; implied in the many communiqués about the first satellite was the notion that any country capable of lobbing a satellite overhead could also deliver a nuclear bomb to the other side of the world. "Missile diplomacy" during the Khrushchev years depended to a large degree on the highly publicized successes of the early sputniks; the perceived Soviet mastery with rockets and space exploration fueled international confrontations of the early 1960s such as the Berlin and the Cuban Missile Crises.[4]

In the United States, *Sputnik* shocked a seemingly complacent society, secure in their new suburbs, vast highways, color televisions, and the highest peacetime budget in history. Launched on the same night that *Leave it to Beaver* premiered, *Sputnik* awoke a nation. Walter McDougall noted that "[n]o [single] event since Pearl Harbor set off such repercussions in public

[2] E. Iu. Zubkova, *Russia After the War: Hopes, Illusions, and Disappointments, 1945–1957* (London: M. E. Sharpe, 1998); Donald Filtzer, *Soviet Workers and Late Stalinism: Labour and the Restoration of the Stalinist System After World War II* (Cambridge, UK: Cambridge University Press, 2002).

[3] "Velikaia pobeda v mirnom sorevnovanii s kapitalizmom," *Pravda*, October 9, 1957.

[4] For Soviet perceptions of the "missile gap," see Sergei Khrushchev, *Nikita Khrushchev: Creation of a Superpower* (University Park, PA: Pennsylvania State University Press, 2000); Vladislav Zubok and Constantine Pleshakov, *Inside The Kremlin's Cold War: From Stalin to Khrushchev* (Cambridge, MA: Harvard University Press, 1996); Vladislav M. Zubok, *A Failed Empire: The Soviet Union in the Cold War from Stalin to Gorbachev* (Chapel Hill: University of North Carolina Press, 2007). For U.S. views, see Peter J. Roman, *Eisenhower and the Missile Gap* (Ithaca, NY: Cornell University Press, 1995); Christopher A. Preble, *John F. Kennedy and the Missile Gap* (DeKalb, IL: Northern Illinois University Press, 2004); Max Frankel, *High Noon: Kennedy, Khrushchev, and the Missile Crisis* (New York: Ballantine Books, 2004).

life."[5] A crisis of confidence washed over most of American society. The Eisenhower Administration produced legislation to create several new agencies, including the National Aeronautics and Space Administration (NASA). By the early 1960s, government-funded projects to improve the scientific and engineering expertise of the country vastly expanded. Believing that better education in Soviet Russia contributed to *Sputnik*, huge amounts of money poured into the American higher education system, making it a key component in the battles of the Cold War. These policies – the creation of new government agencies, increases in state-sponsored research and development, and the expansion and restructuring of higher education – significantly influenced America's political, social, and cultural trajectory in the Cold War.[6]

Historians have repeated a common narrative about the origins of *Sputnik*. It begins with the "patriarch" of Soviet cosmonautics, Konstantin Tsiolkovskii, who in 1903 mathematically substantiated that spaceflight was possible with the aid of liquid-propellant rockets. According to this deeply ingrained story, the Bol'sheviks recognized the value of Tsiolkovskii's work after the Russian Revolution, honored him with many awards, and declared him a national treasure. Inspired by Tsiolkovskii, young enthusiasts came together to build rockets. The Soviet government supported them, and in 1933 it sponsored the creation of a Reactive Scientific-Research Institute to build rockets. The institute produced remarkable scientific and technical results, gradually moving in parallel with the Germans until the Great Terror decimated the leaders of the effort. Historians believed that the rocketry effort was dealt a near-fatal blow and did not rebound until after the war, when Soviet engineers scoured Germany for the detritus of the Nazi rocket program. German engineering jump-started the Soviet rocketry program, and soon, Soviet designers under the charismatic Sergei Korolev began methodically building more powerful rockets. The designers convinced the Soviet government to use the new R-7 intercontinental ballistic missile to launch a satellite into space. The missile successfully inserted the

5 Walter McDougall, . . . *the Heavens and the Earth: A Political History of the Space Age* (New York: Basic Books, 1985), 142.

6 For only a small sampling of the literature on Sputnik's ramifications in the American milieu, see McDougall, *Heavens and the Earth*; Roger D. Launius, John M. Logsdon, and Robert W. Smith, eds., *Reconsidering Sputnik: Forty Years Since the Soviet Satellite* (Amsterdam: Harwood, 2000); Paul Dickson, *Sputnik: Shock of the Century* (New York: Walker & Co., 2001); Robert A. Divine, *The Sputnik Challenge: Eisenhower's Response to the Soviet Satellite* (New York: Oxford University Press, 1993); Stuart W. Leslie, *The Cold War and American Science: The Military-Industrial-Academic Complex at MIT and Stanford* (New York: Columbia University Press, 1993); Andrew Hartman, *Education and the Cold War: The Battle for the American School* (New York: Palgrave Macmillan, 2008); Zuoyue Wang, *In Sputnik's Shadow: The President's Science Advisory Committee and Cold War America* (New Brunswick, NJ: Rutgers University Press, 2008).

small metal ball known as *Sputnik* into orbit in late 1957, inaugurating the space era.

Most of the literature on *Sputnik* – which essentially replays this idealized narrative arc – has leaned on a number of unquestioned presuppositions. The most important of these is the conceit that the preamble to *Sputnik* was characterized by sustained symbolic and material support of cosmic ideas by the state, which began in the aftermath of the Russian Revolution of 1917. This assumption goes hand in hand with an understanding that the state's intervention into matters of rockets and space also took the form of indiscriminate violence during the Great Terror in the late 1930s as a result of which the Soviet drive to the cosmos was immeasurably hindered. The notion of the "noble" scientist runs through this story, particularly in the name of Sergei Pavlovich Korolev – the founder of the Soviet space program, whose dreams of the cosmos overcame the horrific injuries of Stalinism. The hagiographic trope of "triumph over adversity" has been a consistent thread in the narrative of the Soviet space program. By focusing on some key individuals such as Korolev and Nikita Khrushchev, the conventional histories obscure the contributions of hundreds of thousands who were as much responsible for *Sputnik* as the men at the apex.[7]

Scholars have revisited the history of the Soviet space program but none have situated the development of rocket technology in the broader context of Soviet social and cultural history.[8] Russian historians, although freed from Soviet-era constraints, have been mired in celebration and hagiography and have avoided critical contextual questions.[9] Social and cultural historians of the Soviet Union have, meanwhile, typically avoided the topic of space exploration, seeing in it fodder only for techno-buffs and unreconstructed Cold Warriors. Those who have studied this history have focused

[7] William Shelton, *Soviet Space Exploration: The First Decade* (New York: Washington Square Press, 1968); Michael Stoiko, *Soviet Rocketry: Past, Present, and Future* (New York: Holt, Rinehart & Winston, 1970); Nicholas Daniloff, *The Kremlin and the Cosmos* (New York: Knopf, 1972); Peter Smolders, *Soviets in Space* (New York: Taplinger, 1973); James E. Oberg, *Red Star in Orbit* (New York: Random House, 1981); James Harford, *Korolev: How One Man Masterminded the Soviet Drive to Beat America to the Moon* (New York: Wiley, 1997).

[8] Useful works include David Easton Potts, "Soviet Man in Space: Politics and Technology from Stalin to Gorbachev (Vols. I and II)," Georgetown University, PhD Dissertation, 1992; William P. Barry, "The Missile Design Bureaux and Soviet Piloted Space Policy, 1953–1974," University of Oxford, DPhil Dissertation, 1995; Asif A. Siddiqi, *Challenge to Apollo: The Soviet Union and the Space Race, 1945–1974* (Washington, DC: NASA, 2000).

[9] Ia. K. Golovanov, *Korolev: fakty i mify* (Moscow: Nauka, 1994); G. S. Vetrov, *S. P. Korolev i kosmonavtika: perve shagi* (Moscow: Nauka, 1994); Iu. P. Semenov, ed., *Raketno-Kosmicheskaia Korporatsiia "Energiia" imeni S. P. Koroleva* (Korolev: RKK Energiia, 1996); B. E. Chertok, *Rakety i liudi*, vols. 1–4 (Moscow: Mashinostroenie, 1994–1999); Iu. M. Baturin, ed., *Mirovaia pilotiruemaia kosmonavtika: Istoriia. Tekhnika. Liudi* (Moscow: RTSoft, 2005).

only on the halcyon days of the 1960s rather than the origins of Soviet cosmic aspirations.[10] Perhaps the most limiting factor was the dearth of archival sources, which were opened to scholars only after the collapse of the Soviet Union. Without primary sources, which conveyed the voices of the main actors, historians were unable to ask or answer difficult and nuanced questions about the space program.

Many have written about the Bol'shevik state's love affair with science and technology. A measure of technological utopianism had already emerged in Tsarist Russia at the turn of the century, but after the Bol'sheviks came to power in 1917, this fascination embodied a millenarian mantra.[11] This obsession with the power of science and technology to remake society was partly rooted in crude Marxism but much of it derived from the Bol'sheviks' own vision to remake Russia into a modern state, one which would compare and compete with the leading capitalist nations in forging a new path to the future. Here, the tools of capitalism – Ford's mass production, Taylor's scientific management, and the Wright Brothers' airplane – were value-neutral systems that could be relocated into a socialist context without the exploitative costs of capitalism; science and technology could, in this way, be de-linked from one ideology and connected to another.

The Bol'sheviks never adhered to a singular and sustained vision of the role of science and technology in building the new Soviet Union; on the contrary, the Party's approach was neither monolithic nor consistent. For example, in the 1920s, during the time of the New Economic Policy (NEP), the Bol'sheviks reluctantly embraced the old pre-Revolutionary scientific elite, conceding that their skills might be of use during a period of reconstruction. But by the 1930s, after the Cultural Revolution, Stalinist imperatives resulted in a backlash against the old intelligentsia who were seen as being divorced from the "real" problems of socialist construction. Instead, Party directives embraced a more populist stance on science and technology, "technology for the masses," in the words of a popular adage of the day.[12]

[10] Cathleen Susan Lewis, "A History of the Public and Material Culture of Early Human Spaceflight in the U.S.S.R.," George Washington University, PhD Dissertation, 2008; Asif A. Siddiqi, "Privatising Memory: The Soviet Space Programme Through Museums and Memoirs," in *Showcasing Space*, eds. Martin Collins and Douglas Millard (London: The Science Museum, 2005), 98–115; Slava Gerovitch, " 'New Soviet Man' Inside Machine: Human Engineering, Spacecraft Design, and the Construction of Communism," *Osiris* 22 (2007): 135–157.

[11] Richard Stites, *Revolutionary Dreams: Utopian Vision and Experimental Life in the Russian Revolution* (New York: Oxford University Press, 1989).

[12] For important works on the place of science and technology in the Soviet Union during the interwar years, see Kendall E. Bailes, *Technology and Society Under Stalin: Origins of the Soviet Technical Intelligentsia, 1917–1941* (Princeton: Princeton University Press, 1978); Robert A. Lewis, *Science and Industrialisation in the USSR* (New York: Holmes & Meier, 1979); Nicholas Lampert, *The Technical Intelligentsia and the Soviet State: A Study of Soviet Managers and Technicians, 1928–1935* (New York: Holmes & Meier, 1980).

Historians of Soviet and Russian science have, however, largely avoided the space program.[13] Two disciplinary considerations have kept them away. First, their primary concern has been the natural and physical sciences and not technology. Second, their interests led them to problems that exposed ideological "interference" in science rather than cases such as the space program that seemed to support rather than be distorted by official state discourses. During the Cold War, pioneering scholars of Soviet science such as David Joravsky and Loren Graham underscored the important relationship between ideology and Soviet science.[14] Yet most laypeople typically understood this connection within the Soviet context as discrete and unidirectional. For example, the "failures" of Soviet science, including the disastrous case of Lysenko and the ban on genetics research from 1948 to 1964, represented stark examples of the negative influence of ideology on science. Meanwhile, the successes of Soviet science were seen as exceptions where Soviet scientists succeeded despite the draconic and limiting structures imposed upon them.[15] The past decade-and-a-half of scholarship on Soviet science has completely overturned such views.[16] Besides returning agency to the scientific community and investing our understanding of the role of scientific and engineering practice under Stalin with deeper complexity and nuance, the most important achievement of this new literature has been to dislodge the perception that the Lysenko affair was emblematic of Soviet science as a whole.[17]

[13] For canonical works on Soviet and Russian science, see Zhores Medvedev, *Soviet Science* (New York: Norton, 1978); Alexander Vucinich, *Empire of Knowledge: The Academy of Sciences of the USSR (1917–1970)* (Berkeley: University of California Press, 1984); Loren R. Graham, *Science in Russia and the Soviet Union: A Short History* (Cambridge, UK: Cambridge University Press, 1993).

[14] David Joravsky, *Soviet Marxism and Natural Science, 1917–1932* (New York: Columbia University Press, 1961); Loren R. Graham, *Science, Philosophy, and Human Behavior in the Soviet Union* (New York: Columbia University Press, 1987).

[15] See, for example, Medvedev, *Soviet Science*; Valery N. Soyfer, *Lysenko and the Tragedy of Soviet Science* (New Brunswick, NJ: Rutgers University Press, 1994); Paul R. Josephson, *Totalitarian Science and Technology* (Atlantic Highlands, NJ: Humanities Press, 1996).

[16] Michael D. Gordin, Karl Hall, and Alexei B. Kojevnikov, eds., *Osiris, 2nd Series, Vol. 23 (Intelligentsia Science: The Russian Century, 1860-1960)* (Chicago: University of Chicago Press, 2008); Slava Gerovitch, *From Newspeak to Cyberspeak: A History of Soviet Cybernetics* (Cambridge, MA: MIT Press, 2002); Alexei B. Kojevnikov, *Stalin's Great Science: The Times and Adventures of Soviet Physicists* (London: Imperial College Press, 2004); Ethan Pollock, *Stalin and the Soviet Science Wars* (Princeton: Princeton University Press, 2006). See also the special issue of *Science in Context* 15 no. 2 (2002).

[17] Although written partly with the aim of making Soviet scientists agents of their own fate, Nikolai Krementsov's *Stalinist Science* (Princeton: Princeton University Press, 1997) helped to reinforce the centrality of the Lysenko episode in our understanding of Soviet science. For an excellent critique of this earlier school of thought, see Michael D. Gordin, "Was There Ever a 'Stalinist Science'?," *Kritika: Explorations in Russian and European History* 9 no. 3 (Summer 2008) 625–639.

If the relationship between science and the Soviet state (and indeed the lack of delineation between the two) has been a subject of much fresh inquiry, mass engagement with science and technology during Soviet times, including popular (and populist) enthusiasm for science, has, until very recently, been a marginalized field. Mass campaigns involving science and technology were, however, part and parcel of prevailing Soviet culture, especially in the interwar years. James Andrews' recent work on public science has underscored the ways in which public enthusiasm was not simply a result of structured state directives but had significant foundation in genuine mass interest in the powers of science and technology.[18] Lewis Siegelbaum and Scott Palmer have also explored specific dimensions of public engagement with science and technology, deepening our understanding of how Soviet scientific enthusiasm was a peculiar combination of the mundanely practical and the grandiosely symbolic.[19] This new work has not been monolithic. Where Siegelbaum sees automobile users as appropriating automotive technology in ways unanticipated by the state, Palmer sees the state as a more powerful force that exploited fascination with aviation to distract the populace from the earthly realities of the day.

Mass enthusiasm for science and technology in Soviet times had their own peculiarities, but they can be best understood as part of broader (usually) state-sponsored campaigns to encourage large segments of the population to invest their work and life with the transformative spirit of the Bol'shevik project. The most obvious touchstones here include Stakhanovism but there were many others, such as the celebration of new secular holidays and festivals, popular campaigns focused on atheism, stratospheric and arctic exploration, literacy initiatives, and industry-related programs such as the shock worker movement.[20] Historians who have investigated these phenomena have contended that mass enthusiasm for these causes were not cynically fostered by a monolithic state exerting power over a passive populace; they were the result of earnest "bottom-up" zeal that often mutated into forms at odds with the original intention of the campaigns.

[18] James T. Andrews, *Science for the Masses: The Bolshevik State, Public Science, and the Popular Imagination in Soviet Russia, 1917–1934* (College Station, TX: Texas A&M University Press, 2003).

[19] Lewis H. Siegelbaum, *Cars for Comrades: The Life of the Soviet Automobile* (Ithaca, NY: Cornell University Press, 2008); Scott W. Palmer, *Dictatorship of the Air: Aviation Culture and the Fate of Modern Russia* (New York: Cambridge University Press, 2006).

[20] Lewis H. Siegelbaum, *Stakhanovism and the Politics of Productivity in the USSR, 1935–1941* (Cambridge, UK: Cambridge University Press, 1988); Daniel Peris, *Storming the Heavens: The Soviet League of the Militant Godless* (Ithaca, NY: Cornell University Press, 1998); John McCannon, *Red Arctic: Polar Exploration and the Myth of the North in the Soviet Union, 1932-1939* (New York: Oxford University Press, 1998); Karen Petrone, *'Life Has Become More Joyous, Comrades': Celebrations in the Time of Stalin* (Bloomington: Indiana University Press, 2000); William Husband, *'Godless Communists': Atheism and Society in Soviet Russia, 1917–1932* (DeKalb, IL: Northern Illinois University Press, 2000).

This book builds upon both the recent scholarship on Soviet science and technology and the new literature on mass campaigns in the Soviet milieu. It is the first to revisit *Sputnik* by locating its birth within Soviet and Russian social and cultural history. Grounded in archival research, it recovers an alternate history of the birth of the Soviet space program, giving voice to those who were at the center in action but were consigned to the periphery in recollection. It is a story of utopian ideals, expansive imagination, and popular mobilization.

I reframe the birth of the Soviet space program by bridging *imagination* with *engineering* – seeing them not as dialectic, discrete, and sequential but as mutable, intertwined, and concurrent. Both imagination and engineering were necessary to attain the reality of space exploration. Russian imagining of the cosmos dated back to the late nineteenth century, a time when the first seeds of cosmic enthusiasm were sown in the broader literate public. This curiosity percolated into a burst of utopian fascination in the 1920s that inspired and then intersected with the practical realities of rocket engineering a decade later. Imagination and engineering not only fed each other but were coproduced by key actors who maintained a delicate line between secret work on rockets (which interested the military) and public prognostications on the cosmos (which captivated the populace). *Sputnik* was the outcome of both large-scale state imperatives to harness science and technology and populist phenomena that frequently owed little to the whims and needs of the state apparatus.

This book is also one of the first *social* histories of Soviet science and technology, one that describes the popular mobilization for science and technology rather than simply a story of state directives and elite communities. It contests accepted notions about the origins of the Soviet space program, about the history of Soviet science and technology, and more broadly, about the spaces for local initiative in Soviet society. I argue that the primary state institution typically associated with the advancement and sponsorship of Soviet science, the Academy of Sciences, was only marginally involved in the genesis and creation of one of the greatest public advertisements for Soviet science, their space program. Instead, the century-long origin of the Soviet space program provides evidence of a kind of "science from below," which later intersected with the military imperative to build rockets in giving birth to the space program.

The first major theme of this study centers on the state's relationship to the cause of space exploration. Undoubtedly, the launch of *Sputnik* would have been impossible without the vast state commitment to develop the intercontinental ballistic missile that inserted the satellite into orbit. But though the development of the ICBM is a fundamental part of the story of *Sputnik's* birth, Party and government leaders considered it first and foremost a strategic weapon to deter the United States; without the intervention of a small group of missile designers who were also active space enthusiasts, the two originating streams of utopian imagination and military engineering might not have intersected. In the received narrative of Soviet space history, the state appears as the central and indispensable agent in creating the Soviet space program, beginning with its grand and supposedly farsighted gestures in the 1920s and 1930s in elevating spaceflight as an important goal for the nation. In fact, Party and government officials had no interest in cosmic topics until the early 1950s.

That the state played an important role in every facet of Soviet life is inarguable, but as social and cultural historians have argued for decades now, agency also resided in the Soviet populace. All aspects of Soviet life at the height of Stalinism – such as work culture, urban life, family, mass campaigns, language, ritual, and aesthetics to name only a few – were defined by the outcome of negotiations between state actors and those outside the formal levers of power.[21] Not only did the state's attempt to legislate most public behavior frequently have unexpected outcomes, but the state could not intervene in all aspects of Soviet life, leaving key areas where the seemingly powerless were able to shape important phenomena.

During the Soviet era, the state also had a deep and abiding interest in the management of public opinion.[22] Mobilizing public attitudes in support of state imperatives was not, however, always easy or successful. In fact, as I show, at various times during the Soviet era – including at the height of Stalinism – it was possible for public opinion to mold state choices about science and technology, especially if those arguing on behalf of the public invoked the threat of foreign competition. For example, in the early 1950s, Soviet space enthusiast writers successfully elevated space exploration as a worthy goal for the Soviet Union in the backdrop of increasing American publications on the topic. In other words, the creation of a *popular* consensus about the place of science and technology in Soviet society was an important factor feeding state policy. Historians of Russian science, accustomed to focusing on elite scientific communities and their relationship to state ideologies, have largely missed these interactions, rendering invisible a key lever of influence on state science and technology policy.[23]

21 For a few recent examples, see Wendy Goldman, *Women, the State, and Revolution: Soviet Family Policy and Social Life, 1917–1936* (Cambridge, UK: Cambridge University Press, 1993); David Hoffman, *Peasant Metropolis: Social Identities in Moscow, 1929–1941* (Ithaca, NY: Cornell University Press, 1994); Lewis Siegelbaum and William Rosenberg, eds., *Social Dimensions of Soviet Industrialization* (Bloomington: Indiana University Press, 1993); Stephen Kotkin, *Magic Mountain: Stalinism as Civilization* (Berkeley: University of California Press, 1995); Matthew E. Lenoe, *Closer the Masses: Stalinist Culture, Social Revolution, and Soviet Newspapers* (Cambridge, MA: Harvard University Press, 2004).

22 See, for example, Sarah Davies, *Popular Opinion in Stalin's Russia: Terror, Propaganda, and Dissent, 1934–1941* (Cambridge, UK: Cambridge University Press, 1997).

23 Andrews' *Science for the Masses* was the first major work on the topic of science as a public phenomenon, although he stopped short of mapping the public discourse with formal scientific and technical work at the institutional level.

The gaps in the standard social history of Soviet science led me to the second major theme of my work, the social factors – specifically people involved in self-motivated activity – in enabling the project of spaceflight. These included, but were not limited to, amateur individuals without any formal education, members of semigovernmental mass voluntary societies, and science popularizers and journalists. My goal is to relocate the development of rockets and the advocacy of spaceflight in broader Soviet social and cultural history. By this, I mean not just the upheavals generally associated with Soviet science, but also, for example, the cultural explorations of the period of New Economic Policy (NEP), the social forces that led to the Great Terror, and post–World War II visions of technological utopianism.[24]

Beginning in the 1920s, disparate men and women joined together in urban centers across the Soviet Union to establish informal networks to exchange ideas on the possibility of space exploration. Despite complete (and understandable) indifference from the Soviet government, these networks flourished, leading to the formation of early amateur societies, circles (*kruzhki*), and exhibitions that played key roles in fostering the first widespread interest in space exploration among the Soviet populace. Space and rocketry activists reframed their rhetoric to adjust to prevailing social and political conditions. For example, in the early 1930s, they worked through mass voluntary societies and touted the advantages of "stratospheric" exploration; in the 1940s, they established a powerful network of rocket designers in Soviet-occupied Germany; and in the 1950s, defense industry designers on the "inside" formed an effective alliance with journalists on the "outside" to mobilize public opinion in support of a space program, once again despite a lack of interest from the government. In each case, the nature of the discourse generated or the type of rocket produced was neither predetermined nor inevitable but resulted from a complex play of social, political, and military factors; it was "socially constructed," in the parlance of historians of technology.[25]

[24] For literature on NEP, see Sheila Fitzpatrick, Alexander Rabinowitch, and Richard Stites, eds., *Russia in the Era of NEP: Explorations in Soviet Society and Culture* (Bloomington: Indiana University Press, 1991); Stites, *Revolutionary Dreams*; and Abbott Gleason, Peter Kenez, and Richard Stites, eds., *Bolshevik Culture: Experiment and Order in the Russian Revolution* (Bloomington: Indiana University Press, 1985). For the Great Terror, see J. Arch Getty and Roberta T. Manning, eds., *Stalin's Terror: New Perspectives* (New York: Cambridge University Press, 1993); J. Arch Getty and Oleg V. Naumov, eds., *The Road to Terror: Stalin and the Self-Destruction of the Bolsheviks, 1932–1939* (New Haven: Yale University Press, 1999); Wendy Z. Goldman, *Terror and Democracy in the Age of Stalin: The Social Dynamics of Repression* (New York: Cambridge University Press, 2007).

[25] For important works on the social construction of technology, see Wiebe E. Bijker, Thomas P. Hughes, and Trevor J. Pinch, eds., *The Social Construction of Technological Systems: New Directions in the Sociology and History of Technology* (Cambridge, MA: MIT Press, 1987); Merritt Roe Smith and Leo Marx, eds., *Does Technology Drive History? The Dilemma of Technological Determinism* (Cambridge, MA: MIT Press, 1995); Donald Mackenzie,

The networks of people that acted to implement the project of spaceflight included not only Soviet citizens but also foreigners. The role of foreign factors in the origin of *Sputnik*, particularly the tension between indigenous and appropriated knowledge, is the third major theme of this study. Many have studied the implications of technology transfer to Russia in the twentieth century, for the most part focusing on the Soviet adoption of foreign hardware in their civilian industry.[26] One of the largest transfers of technology in modern history occurred when the Allied powers plundered German industry in the aftermath of World War II. John Gimbel's work on the American exploitation of German know-how after the war underscored a more subtle form of technology transfer, what he called "intellectual reparations," which is the movement of skills and expertise across borders.[27] Recently, German historians have made use of Russian archives to detail German intellectual and material reparations that benefited the Soviet military industry. Matthias Uhl, in his *Stalins V-2*, described one of the most well-known but least understood episodes of Soviet exploitation of German technology, the use of captured German technology and expertise to help the nascent Soviet rocket program in the late 1940s.[28] Similarly, David Holloway's work on the Soviet atomic bomb contributed to an understanding of how espionage about the concurrent American effort affected indigenous Soviet work on a "big science" project.[29] Building on these works, I explore how foreign factors – material technology, intellectual reparations, intelligence, and international discourses – interacted with indigenous Soviet sources in promoting rocketry and spaceflight.

These three themes – the relationship between the state and the project of spaceflight, the mobilization of social and cultural forces in the cause of

Inventing Accuracy: A Historical Sociology of Nuclear Missile Guidance (Cambridge, MA: MIT Press, 1990); Wiebe Bijker, *Of Bicycles, Bakelites, and Bulbs: Toward a Theory of Sociotechnical Change* (Cambridge, MA: MIT Press, 1995); and Eda Kranakis, *Constructing a Bridge: An Exploration of Engineering Culture, Design and Research in Nineteenth Century France and America* (Cambridge, MA: MIT Press, 1997).

[26] George D. Holliday, *Technology Transfer to the USSR, 1928–1937 and 1966–1975: The Role of Western Technology in Soviet Economic Development* (Boulder, CO: Westview Press, 1979); Anthony Sutton, *Western Technology and Soviet Economic Development*, 3 vols. (Stanford, CA: Hoover Institution Press, 1968–1973). For lend–lease, see George C. Herring, *Aid to Russia, 1941–1946: Strategy, Diplomacy, the Origins of the Cold War* (New York: Columbia University Press, 1973). Albert L. Weeks, *Russia's Life-Saver: Lend-Lease Aid to the U.S.S.R. in World War II* (Lanham, MD: Lexington Books, 2004).

[27] John Gimbel, *Science, Technology, and Reparation: Exploitation and Plunder in Postwar Germany* (Stanford, CA: Stanford University Press, 1990).

[28] Matthias Uhl, *Stalins V-2: Der Technologietransfer der deutschen Fernlenkwaffentechnik in die UdSSR und der Aufbau der sowjetischen Raketenindustrie 1945 bis 1959* (Bonn: Bernard & Graefe-Verlag, 2001); Christoph Mick, *Forschen für Stalin: Deutsche Fachleute in der sowjetischen Rüstungsindustrie 1945–1958* (Munich: R. Oldenbourg, 2000).

[29] David Holloway, *Stalin and the Bomb: The Soviet Union and Atomic Energy, 1939–1956* (New York: Yale University Press, 1994).

spaceflight, and the role of foreign factors – are the lenses through which I explore the history of *Sputnik*. The book is neither a comprehensive history nor a chronological recounting of all the phenomena that culminated in the launch of *Sputnik* in 1957. Instead, I use the 100 years prior to the satellite to focus on a number of key episodes in the history, exploring those that answer important questions about the relationship between imagination and engineering and omitting episodes of technological work that do not significantly advance understanding of the creation of *Sputnik*. I have not, for example, described the experience of German specialists kidnapped and brought to the Soviet Union to work on their missile program, nor how the first Soviet intercontinental ballistic missile was built and tested in the mid-1950s.[30]

The book is organized roughly chronologically, beginning in the late nineteenth century with the birth of early popular fascination with the cosmos in Russian culture. It ends with the launch of *Sputnik* in 1957. In the introductory chapter, I show how the birth of "cosmonautics" in late imperial Russia was embodied in three traditions that were difficult to isolate: science fiction; theoretical work by lone individuals such as Tsiolkovskii; and popular science works published in journals and monographs. In describing each of these three seemingly distinct categories – first the history of Russian space fiction, then Tsiolkovskii's early biography and work on cosmonautics, and finally, the emergence of popular science in Russia – I show how the boundaries between categories of "public science" were frequently blurred. We also see during this period a fundamental shift in Russian popular thinking about the cosmos, as educated elites began to wrench cosmic discourses from the realm of folk traditions into the language of modern-day science.

The central actor in Chapter 2 is Konstantin Tsiolkovskii, whose fortunes were said to have dramatically improved after the Russian Revolution. My goal is not to challenge Tsiolkovskii's pioneering contribution to the theory of astronautics but to revisit claims about his relationship with the state. By reexamining Tsiolkovskii's biography, I reconstruct and reframe the various factors that contributed to the formation of a spaceflight *mentalité* in the post-Revolutionary eras. I describe the strategies that Tsiolkovskii and his supporters used to promote discourse on space travel in the face of little or no state support, specifically their formation of an informal, vibrant, and international network that existed outside the parameters of the "traditional" and elite scientific world. This was the first manifestation of a broad social phenomenon that entrenched the notion that cosmic travel was not simply an idea for an indefinite future but perhaps a more immediate prospect.

Chapter 3 focuses on the cultural dimensions of the "space fad" of the 1920s, which I locate as part of the utopian/dystopian explorations of

[30] I explore these issues elsewhere. Asif A. Siddiqi, "Germans in Russia: Cold War, Technology Transfer, and National Identity," *Osiris* 24 (2009): 120–143; Siddiqi, *Challenge to Apollo*, 128–138, 155–161.

NEP-era culture. In particular, the chapter explores the ways in which visions of space travel were characterized by fascinations with both technological modernity and mysticism. Individually or as part of amateur societies and collectives, Russians from all walks of life communicated their interest in space exploration through expression that spanned the gamut of literature, film, painting, exhibitions, pamphlets, posters, magazines, books, and philosophical tracts. Inspired by the Cosmist writings of the mysterious Nikolai Fedorov, some sought to achieve immortality through space exploration while others, energized by Bol'shevik fascination with modern technology, looked to a utopian and industrial future.

In Chapter 4, I describe the evolution of interest in spaceflight from utopian imagination to state-sponsored work to develop rockets. Between 1931 and 1933, popular enthusiasts of spaceflight organized the first practical research organizations dedicated to developing rockets. Most strikingly, young men such as glider pilot Sergei Korolev, the poverty-stricken Fridrikh Tsander, and Civil War veteran Mikhail Tikhonravov accomplished this goal without significant support from the state or a high level of technical expertise. Using money donated by a mass voluntary society (*Osoaviakhim*) and their own personal belongings such as melted silverware and broken tools, the activists built modest rockets that they flew in public spaces. This chapter shows how producing relatively innovative technology outside the traditional system of Soviet science represented a powerful counterexample to the increased centralization of Soviet research and development during the "Great Break." Soon, the amateurs skillfully sold their cause to the state, whose interests were primarily military in nature. High-level support, particularly from armaments chief Marshal Mikhail Tukhachevskii, led to the formation of a research institute, the world's first dedicated to developing rockets.

In 1938, during the height of the Great Terror, Soviet security services arrested and shot several rocket engineers; one man, the ambitious Sergei Korolev, was shipped off to the gold mines at Kolyma in eastern Siberia, where he nearly died from overwork and malnutrition. Historians have typically viewed this episode as part of the state's unilateral attack on the scientific and engineering community, repression that irrevocably stunted Russian rocket research. In Chapter 5, I reconstruct the events leading to the arrests and show how factions within the main rocket research institute clashed with each other throughout the 1930s over technical and professional issues; these conflicts were crucial factors in the arrests that engulfed the institute in 1938. My conclusions provide striking evidence of enormous social strain in the scientific community – as in many other parts of Soviet society – that fueled the terror, often with little control from the center.

Chapter 6 describes the Soviet excursion into Germany at the end of the Great Patriotic War when teams scoured through occupied areas to collect and study the detritus of the German wartime rocket weapons program.

Using declassified government documents, combat unit directives, local diaries, and memoirs, this chapter reconstructs the race to recover German technology and expertise before it fell into the hands of the other Allies. It shows how teams of Soviet engineers and soldiers formed a strong informal social network in Germany – frequently without the knowledge of the center – that served as the prototype of a systems approach to postwar Soviet innovation. Their success in forming an effective network to produce missiles strikingly illustrates the possibility of local, flexible, and dynamic management in the immediate postwar period. This network provided the foundation for the Soviet missile program, which, ten years later, evolved into the Soviet space program.

The first Soviet steps into the cosmos depended not only on the creation of popular awareness of the potential of space travel but also the very real creation of an intercontinental ballistic missile, one whose primary mandate had nothing to do with space but with deadly military requirements in the atomic age. In Chapter 7, I show how the path from the birth of the atomic program to a national commitment to produce the first Soviet ICBM was a long and circuitous one characterized by as much direction and willfulness as accident and abandoned routes. Although the cosmos was not strictly a part of this narrative – in official papers, ICBMs and satellites are not mentioned in the same breath until about 1955, well after the decision to build an ICBM – space exploration maintains a ghostly presence throughout the history of this rocket, insofar as the individuals who were responsible for conceiving an ICBM for Iosif Stalin and later Nikita Khrushchev were the same ones who had indulged in "fantasies" about space for over two decades.

In Chapter 8, I describe the rise of popular enthusiasm for space exploration in the postwar era, echoing the similar fascinations of the post-Revolutionary period. Here we see the full convergence of social and statist phenomena in support of space exploration, the former embodied by popular advocacy for space exploration and the latter by military missile development. The chapter shows how the primary advocates for space travel were missile designers – such as Korolev and Tikhonravov, who had worked together in the 1930s – laboring in anonymity within the defense industry. To bypass the curtain of secrecy, they formed a very effective alliance with popular science writers on the "outside," who shared with them a sincere belief in the inevitability and benefits of space technology. This coalition of space enthusiasts took advantage of the prevailing codes of *Zhdanovshchina* – a period of extreme nationalist sentiment – by canonizing the late Konstantin Tsiolkovskii as a great scientist in the Russian tradition, thus effectively legitimizing the cause of space exploration. Building on this momentum, they skillfully generated public statements on space exploration that were intended to alarm the American media. Then, using American statements in turn as evidence of a possible Cold War threat, the

Soviet activists successfully persuaded a disinterested Soviet government that space exploration was both a possibility and a necessity.

The final chapter, Chapter 9, is a microhistory of the launch of *Sputnik* itself, where I redirect my attention to the engineers, designers, technicians, and workers on the ground responsible for the event, providing a fresh perspective on the episode itself that avoids the typical hagiographical approaches centered only around Korolev and Khrushchev. The chapter underscores how workers involved in the creation of this object were largely unaware of the broader political import of their work. For them, *Sputnik* was no more special than the work they did before. *Sputnik* the satellite became *Sputnik* the event only *post facto*, when nostalgia imbued their work with a kind of gravitas that had been lacking before. As the state lay claim to the success of *Sputnik*, so was born the myth of the long Bol'shevik march to the cosmos.

1

A Space for Science and a Science for Space

> The correct path to solving the problem of flight beyond the atmosphere and interplanetary journeys has already been outlined; to the honor of Russian science, it was presented to humanity by a Russian scientist.[1]
>
> Iakov Perel'man, science popularizer, 1915

INTRODUCTION

"At first we inevitably have an idea, a fantasy, a fairy tale, and then come scientific calculations; finally execution crowns the thought," wrote Konstantin Eduardovich Tsiolkovskii, a wizened fifty-four-year-old schoolteacher in provincial Russia in 1911.[2] Tsiolkovskii's truism was both obvious and not entirely true in the case of Soviet space exploration. Obvious, because common sense tells us that such a progression, from to dreams to science to execution, might reasonably approximate trends in the history of science and technology. Not entirely true, because the sequential nature of the claim obscures parallel processes of dreams, science, and execution that characterized the birth of the science of space travel in modern Russia.

The science of space travel – known as "cosmonautics" in Russia and "astronautics" in the rest of the world – is a relatively new science. A lexicon to describe the discipline emerged only in the late 1920s when amateur societies in Europe and the Soviet Union began to exchange practical ideas on the possibility of space travel. Professionalization came much later, in the 1950s, as educational institutions in the United States and the Soviet Union offered specialized study on spaceflight, or its associated field, rocket engineering. In the Russian and Soviet contexts, the predisciplinary existence of cosmonautics is typically traced back to Tsiolkovskii, considered the "father" of Soviet space travel. His patriarchal status rests on the works he published between 1903 and 1914 in which he mathematically proved the possibility of reaching outer space by means of liquid-propellant rockets.

[1] Ia. Perel'man, *Mezhplanetnye puteshestviia* (Petrograd: P. P. Soikin, 1915), unnumbered introduction page.

[2] K. Tsiolkovskii, "Issledovanie mirovykh prostranstv reaktivnymi priborami," *Vestnik vozdukhoplavaniia* no. 19 (1911): 16–21.

Since the early 1930s, and especially after the early Soviet successes in space in the late 1950s, Soviet authorities singled out Tsiolkovskii as a classic example of native genius. Eulogizing Tsiolkovskii, however, posed some significant political problems because he had produced his most important works *before* the Revolution. On the one hand, they wished to trumpet Tsiolkovskii's achievements as part of a general focus on the possibilities inherent under the Soviet regime, but on the other hand, they sought to diminish the notion that useful science was possible under the imperial regime. They solved this problem by redefining Tsiolkovskii's work in relation to the state. According to this formulation, before the Revolution, the imperial government did not support Tsiolkovskii, and his valuable work went unrecognized, whereas after the Revolution, the farsighted Bol'sheviks discerned the value of space exploration, plucked Tsiolkovskii out of obscurity, and bestowed upon him the proper location in society that he deserved. The state's intervention inspired many to form cosmic societies, hold space-themed exhibitions, and eventually create a centralized rocket research establishment in the early 1930s. In this narrative, the state plays a crucial role in both the imperial and Bol'shevik eras, either in impeding (before 1917) or advancing (after 1917) the cause of cosmonautics. This rhetorical strategy, of redefining the origins of Soviet cosmonautics in relation to the state, in essence, marked 1917 as a saltation, an irrevocable turning point, an evolutionary leap in Soviet space exploration.

The *post facto* reformulation as 1917 as "year zero" masked an enormously important and overlooked dimension of the origins of cosmic discourse in modern Russia, the popularization of space exploration that began and achieved a critical mass in the last decades of the imperial era. Long before the notion of a demarcated field of "astronautics" existed in the public (or academic) imagination, many had speculated, predicted, and theorized on the possibility of space travel. Some scientific prognostications on cosmic flight existed on the margins of such established disciplines as aeronautics and astronautics, but most emerged almost entirely disconnected from the disciplinary norms of accepted science such as journals and conferences, appearing instead in the media of science fiction and popular science.

Beyond simply underscoring that the study and popularization of space exploration in modern Russian was a distinctly imperial-era phenomenon, recovering the "lost" roots of Russian cosmonautics, particularly the broad social, cultural, and scientific discourse that spanned from the 1880s to the early years of Bol'shevik rule, highlights the ways in which it evolved on the margins of accepted science, in a popular domain not dictated by elite scientists or the state. This "first wave" of mass interest in space travel, peaking during the Great War, was, in fact, made possible by a symbiotic relationship between three traditions: science fiction; theoretical work by lone individuals such as Tsiolkovskii; and popular science works published in journals and monographs. In describing each of these three seemingly distinct categories – first the history of Russian space fiction, then the development of spaceflight theory by Tsiolkovskii, and finally, the emergence of popular science in Russia – I show how the boundaries between these categories of public science were frequently blurred.[3] During this period before the Revolution, one was apt to find theorists dabbling in science fiction, science popularizers producing important theoretical works, and science fiction writers popularizing important theories. Tsiolkovskii's aphorism about fantasy, science, and execution provided a neat progression for later historians of the birth of the Soviet space program but in fact simplified and shortchanged the rich and complex space-themed discourses of the late imperial era.

FROM SCIENCE FICTION TO THE *ASTRONOMICHESKII ROMAN*

Meditations on the cosmos had been part of the cultural consciousness in Europe for centuries, propagated through myths, fantasy, and the supernatural. Written fictions of the seventeenth century such as Johannes Kepler's *Somnium* (*Dream*), Cyrano de Bergerac's *Voyage dans la Lune*, and Daniel Defoe's *The Consolidator* underscored a major shift in perceptions of the cosmos, from one of pondering its existence to one of voyages into the ether. In the Russian imagination, ruminations on the cosmos were largely utopian in nature, often with a folk or Slavic sensibility, and remained so until the collision between science and utopia in a number of scattered novels of the early nineteenth century. The famous Slavophil intellectual, V. F. Odoevskii, produced one of the first futuristic Russian works grounded in expectations of scientific discovery, the epistolary *4338 god* (*The Year 4338*). In contrast to other works of anticipatory wonder, Odoevskii's focus on science as a vehicle for social transformation drew much attention to the novel, which combined a Slavophil sensibility with Western science. Like many other utopian writings of the day, Odoevskii's work remained unpublished as a result of censorship, although it circulated in manuscript form among Russian intellectuals in the 1840s.[4]

Fictional anticipations that centered on the cosmos emerged in Russia in parallel with three broader social and cultural processes in the late nineteenth century: the rise and expansion of publishing concerns, the growth in literacy, and the beginnings of industrialization. Where works such as Odoevskii's novel had been furtively exchanged among readers, in the late imperial era, mass publishing and the intermittent relaxation of censorship brought the medium of technological anticipations directly to a newly

[3] For Soviet public science in general, see James T. Andrews, *Science for the Masses: The Bolshevik State, Public Science, and the Popular Imagination, 1917–1934* (College Station, TX: Texas A&M University Press, 2003).

[4] It was published in 1921 as V. F. Odoevskii, *4338 god: Peterburgskie pis'ma* (Moscow: Ogonek, 1921).

hungry urban populace. Following in Odoevskii's footsteps, many of these works – especially homegrown novels – often combined the mystical and folk traditions with a distinctly scientific and technological sheen and an appeal to utopian dreaming. New discoveries in chemistry, biology, physics, and, particularly, astronomy abetted a marked popular interest in a new medium, later known as *nauchnaia-fantastika* (literally "scientific fantasy") or science fiction.

The first popular awareness of the imagery and language of space travel in Russia came from translations of Jules Verne's novels, which, along with the fantasy works of other foreigners, flooded the Russian reading market in the late imperial era. Since the publication of Verne's first novel in Russia in 1864, the Frenchman had attained a kind of fame that cut across demographics: children and adults, Slavophils and Populists, Marxists and Tsarists, all read and praised his writing in glowing language. Established native writers such as Chekhov, Tolstoi, and Turgenev paid tribute to Verne as a master of the novel, giving Verne a legitimacy in Russia that many other foreign writers lacked. His popularity extended beyond those captivated by modern science and technology to the larger populace. As historian Richard Stites notes, in the late imperial era, Verne was "perhaps the most widely read foreign author of the age among Russians."[5] Beginning in 1906, Verne's complete works were published in an eighty-eight-volume set in Russian, a rare honor for a foreigner. Verne's two principal space-themed novels, *De La Terre à la Lune* (*From the Earth to the Moon*, 1865) and its sequel *Autour de la Lune* (*Around the Moon*, 1870) were published in Russia in the 1880s, inculcating a generation of young Russians for the first time with the possibility of space *travel* rather than the more sedentary occupation of astronomy.

Almost as popular was French astronomer Camille Flammarion, whose works served as prototypes for future Russians working across the boundaries of science, science popularization, and science fiction. Flammarion's initial claim to fame was through nonfiction works such as *La pluralité es mondes habite* (*The Plurality of Inhabited Worlds*, 1862) and *Astronomie populaire* (*Popular Astronomy*, 1880), where he indulged in speculation about the possibility and nature of life in other worlds. A steady stream of Russian versions of his novels in the 1890s included his most famous work of fiction, *La fin du monde* (*The End of the World*, 1893), a story about a comet colliding with the Earth that eventually leads to the death of the planet. To describe Flammarion's fiction, Russian publishers adopted the descriptor *astronomicheskii roman* (astronomical novel) for a special class of fiction devoted exclusively to meditations on the cosmos and space travel. Perhaps Flammarion's most lasting legacy in Russia involved Mars.

5 Richard Stites, *Revolutionary Dreams: Utopian Vision and Experimental Life in the Russian Revolution* (New York: Oxford University Press, 1989), 30.

Italian astronomer Giovanni Schiaparelli's observations of *canali* (channels) on Mars in the 1870s led a number of Europeans and Americans, including, most notably, the American astronomer Percival Lowell, to speculate on artificial formations, such as canals, on the surface of Mars. Excited by this possibility, Flammarion wrote frequently on the nature of life on Mars, reports widely publicized in Russia, thus launching a romance with Mars that would endure well into the 1920s in Russia.[6]

The works of Verne and Flammarion were part of a broader explosion in science fiction in late imperial Russia. Between 1890 and 1917, at least thirty *nauchnaia-fantastika* novels or novellas appeared in the Russian media, either as stand-alone monographs or serialized in journals. Although most of these works were foreign in origin – by authors such as Verne, Flammarion, H. G. Wells, Edgar Allan Burroughs, and others – the first homegrown exponents of science fiction emerged during this time, copying foreign works in form, content, and ideas, echoing a positivist and uplifting view on the role of technology in industrial society. In his seminal survey of the "utopian tradition of Russian science fiction," Darko Suvin called it a "tenuous" period in which "[t]he weight of industrial and scientific backwardness combined with the obtuse oppression of Tsarism was too great to allow a flowering of the genre."[7] Nevertheless, such generalizations obscure the diversity of the first wave of native Russian science fiction, both as a reaction to foreign works and in communicating the technological anticipations and anxieties of a profoundly transformative period in Russian history. Influenced particularly by Verne and Flammarion, at least half of these represented the new *astronomicheskii roman* genre.[8] B. Krasnogorskii's *Po volnam efire* (*On the Waves of Ether*, 1913) and the co-authored (with D. Sviatskii) *Ostrova efirnogo okeana* (*Islands in the Ether Ocean*, 1914) were fictions about space travel written in simplistic prose with an appeal to popularizing the latest discoveries in astronomy. Similarly, P. Infant'ev's *Na drugoi planete* (*On Another Planet*, 1901) and L. Afanas'ev's *Puteshestvie na Mars* (*Journey to Mars*, 1901) benefited from Flammarion's thoughts on extraterrestrial life as well as being cautionary tales about the costs of industrialization.[9]

6 Flammarion's most well-known comments on Mars were included in *La planète Mars et ses conditions d'habitabilité* [*The Planet Mars and Its Conditions of Habitability*] (Paris: Gauthier-Villars, 1892).

7 Darko Suvin, "The Utopian Tradition in Russian Science Fiction," *Modern Language Review* 66 no. 1 (1971): 139–159.

8 The count is based on the bibliography in A. F. Britikov, *Russkii sovetskii nauchno-fantasticheskii roman* (Leningrad: Nauka, 1970), 365–368.

9 B. Krasnogorskii, *Po volnam efira: astronomicheskii roman* (St. Petersburg: Rassvet, 1913); B. Krasnogorskii and D. Sviatskii, *Ostrova efirnogo okeana: astronomicheskii roman* (Petrograd: Rassvet, 1914); P. Infant'ev, *Na drugoi planete: povest' iz zhizni obitatelei Marsa* (Novgorod: Novgorodskaia gub. tipogr., 1901). The literary journal *Niva* serialized Afanas'ev's story in supplements to its January and April 1901 issues.

Imperial-era science fiction's continuity across the Revolutionary divide of 1917 was best underscored by one of the most well-read *astronomicheskii roman* of the late imperial period, Bol'shevik philosopher and intellectual Aleksandr Bogdanov's *Krasnaia zvezda* (*Red Star*), first published in 1908.[10] Bogdanov (a pseudonym for Aleksandr Malinovskii) had had a much-publicized split with Lenin, but his popularity in the 1920s, which rested on *Krasnaia zvezda* and *Inzhener Menni* (*Engineer Menni*, 1913), did not suffer. If *Krasnaia zvezda* received mixed reviews when first published, it was republished in 1918 and 1929 and sold quite well; a theatrical version played Moscow in 1920. On the surface, the story concerns an advanced socialist society on Mars as described by a Russian revolutionary visiting from Earth in the wake of the 1905 revolution. Some have interpreted the tale as an allegorical warning on the perils of how socialism could take on a distinctly totalitarian tenor if sufficiently militarized.[11] Others have seen it as a polemic on possible socialist utopias (of the Martian and terrestrial varieties) wrapped in the contemporary medium of the *astronomicheskii roman*.[12] If nothing else, Bogdanov's popular tale was firmly embedded in its peculiar temporal setting: The novel was clearly influenced by the influx of Western science and fiction about the space beyond our world, such as tales of canals popularized by Lowell, the works of Wells, and the growing strand of technological utopianism in Russia at the turn of the century.

No single person crossed the line between the theory, fiction, and popularization of space travel – and the divide of 1917 – with more ease than the Russian schoolteacher Konstantin Tsiolkovskii (see Figure 1). As a young man, he had been deeply influenced by the prolific science fiction in *fin-de-siècle* Russia, not only for its subject matter but also for its power as a communicative medium. Believing that "execution must be preceded by an idea, [and] precise calculation by fantasy," Tsiolkovskii approached fiction writing with the notion that it should have nothing to do with ordinary life; in other words, its only goal would be to advance and popularize serious scientific ideas, to stimulate action.[13] To a friend he wrote that "fantastic [novels] on the theme of interplanetary voyages raise new thoughts in the masses. Whoever studies these [ideas], would do useful things."[14]

10 A. A. Bogdanov, *Krasnaia zvezda: roman-utopiia* (St. Petersburg: Tvorchestvo khudozhestvennoi pechati, 1908).

11 Roy Medvedev was perhaps the most well-known historian to make this argument. *Let History Judge: The Origins and Consequences of Stalinism* (New York: Columbia University Press, 1989), 631.

12 Mark B. Adams, "'Red Star': Another Look at Aleksandr Bogdanov," *Slavic Review* 48 (Spring 1989): 3–15.

13 Quote from K. Tsiolkovskii, *Issledovanie mirovykh prostranstv reaktivnymi priborami (pereizdanie rabot 1903 i 1911 g. s nekotorymi izmeneniiami i dopolneniiami)* (Kaluga: K. E. Tsiolkovskii, 1926), 3.

14 ARAN, 555/4/10a/12–17 (January 24, 1935).

FIGURE 1. Konstantin Tsiolkovskii (1857–1935) was the first person to mathematically substantiate that space travel was possible by using the technology of liquid-propellant rockets. His early works on space travel represented a curious mix of science, popular science, and science fiction. Although ignored by state authorities for most of his life, he garnered a wide network of followers who followed his every word and untiringly promoted his cause of space exploration. [*Source*: Sergei Samburov]

With this credo, Tsiolkovskii produced three space fiction novels during his lifetime, all written in the imperial era; two were published in the 1890s and one in 1920.[15] In stilted language, Tsiolkovskii described a host of arcane technical ideas; the prose of these works suggests that a plot was a concession rather than a necessity. In them, he introduced a great many ideas such as the design of space stations, multistage rockets, spacesuits, life-support systems, and spacecraft takeoff and landing methods that became common to late-twentieth-century space exploration. The odd tension between his vision of the future – fantastic, unbelievable, and utopian – and the language that he used to communicate this vision – torpid, turgid, and inelegant – gave his fiction a strange tenor, one that firmly linked his fiction to popular science writing rather than creative literature. For example, the opening lines of "Dreams of the Earth and the Heavens . . . " suggest

[15] K. Tsiolkovskii, *Na lune* (Moscow: I. D. Sytin, 1893); K. Tsiolkovskii, *Grezy o zemle i nebe i effekty vsemirnogo tiagoteniia* (Moscow: A. N. Goncharov, 1895); K. Tsiolkovskii, *Vne zemli* (Kaluga: KOIPiMK, 1920). Portions of the latter novella were originally serialized in thirteen consecutive issues of the popular science journal *Priroda i liudi* [*Nature and People*] in 1918. Tsiolkovskii also published a short story "Bez tiazhest" ["Without Gravity"] in the same journal in 1914.

a science lesson more than an adventure: "If we walk continuously unimpeded and tirelessly, day and night, 'over land, over sea,' at the rate of 4.5 kilometers per hour, in a year's time, we shall have walked around the large circumference of the globe."[16] Despite his stated goal to be the "Chekhov of science," he openly stated that he had no interest in literary conventions; he in fact avoided calling his fiction "novels" because the word conveyed a worldly sensibility that he found uninteresting. Tsiolkovskii was not unaware of his limitations, but seemed to have little faith in the average reader. He wrote, "I understand very well that for example, [my story] *Vne zemli* (*Beyond the Earth*), is not good because it has many tedious places unintelligible to readers, yet it is understandable to me and strictly scientific."[17]

Early reviews of his early work were not kind – one reviewer saw Tsiolkovskii as a poor facsimile of Flammarion – but eventually these novellas accrued a reputation as scientifically solid and engaging works for youngsters.[18] Once Tsiolkovskii achieved national prominence near the end of his life in the early 1930s, the Bol'shevik government helped to reprint all of his works. Of his two pre-Revolutionary novels, *Na lune* (*On the Moon*) was republished in 1929, 1933, and 1934, whereas *Grezy o zemle i nebe i effekty vsemirnogo tiagoteniia* (*Dreams of the Earth and the Heavens and the Effects of Universal Gravitation*) was reissued in 1933 and 1934.[19] These novels were adopted by many amateur cosmic societies in the 1920s and early 1930s seeking to educate their members on the basics of space travel, especially because, as one such society member wrote to Tsiolkovskii at the time, the "demand for them was [so] great."[20] Tsiolkovskii's fiction also deeply influenced one of the most famous Soviet-era science fiction authors, Aleksandr Beliaev, who published widely in the 1930s and titled one of his novels after Tsiolkovskii. The popularity of these Tsiolkovskii's fiction prompted the *Molodaia gvardiia* (Young Guard) publishing house in the early 1930s to invite Tsiolkovskii as consultant to a project to "create a fantastic novel" on interplanetary travel by bringing together a team of specialists and authors.[21] Tsiolkovskii never participated in the project, although he left behind a number of unpublished and unfinished space fiction novels, many of which were finally issued in 1960 by no less an authority than the Academy of Sciences, an institution that had consistently ignored the scientist through most of his life.[22]

16 Tsiolkovskii, *Grezy o zemle*, 1.

17 ARAN, 555/4/17/36 (undated).

18 See the review of *Grezy o zemle* in the weekly *Nedelia* no. 18 (April 30, 1895): 574.

19 The latter was republished under the new title *Tiazhest' ischezla* [*Gravity Vanished*]. K. Tsiolkovskii, *Tiazhest' ischezla, fantasticheskii ocherk* (Moscow: Gosmashmetizdat, 1933).

20 ARAN, 555/4/356/2–3ob. (May 4, 1924).

21 ARAN, 555/3/141/1 (early 1930s).

22 K. Tsiolkovskii, *Put' k zvezdam* (Moscow: AN SSSR, 1960).

THE PATRIARCH OF COSMONAUTICS

Tsiolkovskii's life can be characterized by the persistent search for rational solutions to intractable problems. The seventh of ten children, he was born on September 17, 1857 in the village of Izhevskoe in the Riazan' region about 200 kilometers southeast of Moscow.[23] His father was a former forester of Polish descent who had served in a variety of low-level jobs in state bureaucracies; his mother was a homeworker of Tatar origin. After his father's retirement, the family remained poor. Tsiolkovskii's most resonant memories of childhood were his dreams of freedom from Earth's gravity. As he recalled, "[i]n my thoughts I would jump very high, [and] climb ropes and trees like a cat. I was dreaming of a total absence of gravity."[24] His early life was hampered by a bout of scarlet fever at age ten that not only left him nearly deaf but also ended his schooling. Isolated from his surroundings, Tsiolkovskii redirected his focus to modeling, devising experiments, and reading from his father's small library.

When he was sixteen, his father sent the boy to Moscow to expand his educational palette at a technical school. Upon arrival, Tsiolkovskii discovered that the technical school had reformed into a university that would no longer accept his credentials. Despite the setback, he decided to remain in the city. By his own account, Tsiolkovskii was somewhat of a lost villager in Moscow, and he was so poor that he suffered from malnutrition and deteriorating eyesight. He spent his time reading or conducting rudimentary experiments even as his general appearance grew so frightening that people in the streets would mock him for this tattered clothing and unkempt hair. Although his three-year stay in Moscow was physically demanding, Tsiolkovskii taught himself the basics of mathematics, physics, astronomy, and chemistry by using books from public libraries. It was during this short critical period that the young man first had thoughts of space travel, prompted in part by his obsession to overcome the bonds of gravity. Once, believing that he had devised a machine to take him to the heavens (an invention that he found later to be technically unfeasible), Tsiolkovskii was shaken to the core. He remembered: "I strolled about the Moscow streets and kept thinking of the great consequences of my discovery.... This night has been living in my memory since then; even 30 years after, in my night dreams I sometimes fly this machine to the stars, feeling the same delight as I experienced that unforgettable night."[25]

[23] In one of his self-written biographies, he notes that his mother gave birth to "no less than 13" children, at least three of whom died at birth. ARAN, 555/2/4/1–3 (May 1, 1928).

[24] K. Tsiolkovskii, "Moia zhizn' i rabot," in *K. E. Tsiolkovskii*, ed. N. A. Islent'ev (Moscow: Aeroflot, 1939), 17.

[25] Konstantin Tsiolkovskii, "The Autobiography of K. E. Tsiolkovskii," in *Interplanetary Flight and Communication, Vol. III, No. 7*, ed. N. A. Rynin (Jerusalem: Israel Program for Scientific Translations, 1971; originally published in 1931), 3.

Returning home, he taught mathematics to "backward" students at a school in provincial Borovsk for about a decade. In 1892, Tsiolkovskii, by then married, moved 150 kilometers southwest of Moscow to the small town of Kaluga, where he remained until the end of his life. Here, he taught at the women's diocesan school. Like many other large families in Kaluga, Tsiolkovskii's family lived in near-abject poverty. Most in Kaluga considered him an impoverished dreamer who had little understanding or indeed interest in the world outside his mind. Even as he rapidly accelerated the pace of his scientific investigations, he enjoyed very little support. He had few friends, and his near-deafness only exacerbated his isolation from social activity. Tsiolkovskii's work habits were idiosyncratic. He would hum incessantly through his waking hours, a habit compounded by his worsening hearing. Beyond reading and writing, his only other activities were bicycling or repairing a dilapidated motorbike. When visitors came to meet with him, he would sit in the living room with a cone-shaped object inserted into his ear to help his hearing. He was, in many ways, the archetype of the lone, eccentric amateur dabbling in science.

With the most minimal contact with the outside world, the young man began to write short works on scientific topics – such as on "The Theory of Gases" and "The Mechanics of Living Organisms" – sending them off to learned societies in St. Petersburg and Moscow, but eliciting little or no response. In Borovsk, he found himself strongly drawn to aeronautics, the new science of flight, an attraction that largely stemmed from his still formative philosophical view of an existence "beyond gravity." His thoughts moved quickly from aeronautics to flight beyond the Earth. In 1883, for example, Tsiolkovskii wrote "Free Space," a short unpublished monograph that indicated his first serious interest in the scientific principles behind spaceflight. Written in the form of a scientific diary, in this work he explored the movement of bodies in the absence of gravity and air, noting that "[i]f a man is a participant not only on Earth, but also in the heavens, then the influence of free space should be of special interest."[26]

Tsiolkovskii's growing interest in aeronautics was embodied in three different but interrelated directions: the idea of building a metallic dirigible (or airship), the concept of heavier-than-air flight, and modest experiments on aerodynamics. He persistently attempted to interest the elite scientific community in his proposal for a "metallic controlled aerostat," and wrote to both Nikolai Zhukovskii and Dmitrii Mendeleev for help, but was able to find few who would support him. Undeterred by indifference from the major scientific journals, he sustained his research with the help of local followers who believed that the true value of Tsiolkovskii's ideas on dirigibles

[26] "Free Space" was first published in 1954 as "Svobodnoe prostranstvo," in *K. E. Tsiolkovskii: sobranie sochinenii, tom vtoroi: reaktivnye letatel'nye apparaty*, ed. A. A. Blagonravov et al. (Moscow: AN SSSR, 1954), 25–68.

would be recognized if only the elite scientific community would give him a chance. His homemade experiments in aerodynamics – using a makeshift wind tunnel – yielded results interesting enough to cull a few articles in regional scientific journals such as the Odessa-based *Vestnik opytnoi fiziki i elementarnoi matematiki* (*Journal of Experimental Physics and Elementary Mathematics*). He used these publications to obtain a small grant of 470 rubles from the Imperial Academy of Sciences to conduct a further program of experiments. The Academy ultimately declined to publish his results, finding them inconclusive.[27] Without any further money, he abandoned experimentation, resorting to writing an endless stream of essays on aeronautics and the natural sciences, some of which he self-published as amateurish booklets. Although estranged from both the state and the established scientific community, Tsiolkovskii's name gained a certain level of currency among a technically minded audience as a rural Russian "inventor" of the (still unrealized) metallic dirigible.

Philosophically attracted to the notion of space exploration and deeply influenced by the proliferation of space-themed novels in print at the turn of the century, Tsiolkovskii turned his attentions to devising a mathematical understanding of space travel in the middle of the final decade of the nineteenth century. In a science fiction novel he began writing in 1896, he articulated the then-innovative idea that *rockets* could be used as a means for traveling from the Earth into outer space. He had been particularly inspired by *De La Terre à la Lune*, in which Verne's space-faring voyagers used a rocket to slow a vessel approaching the Moon. As Tsiolkovskii remembered in 1911, "it seems to me that the first seed of thought [of using rockets for space travel] was inspired by the well-known dreamer Jules Verne."[28] Soon after Tsiolkovskii began writing the novel, his ambitions outgrew the medium of fiction. As he later remembered, "many times I tried to write on the theme of 'interplanetary travel,' but in the end, attracted by considerations of precision, I ended up writing a serious [mathematical] work."[29]

Tsiolkovskii tackled the problem of space travel by rockets through two innovative approaches. First, he formulated the issue as a mathematical problem, and second, he rejected the use of powder-fueled rockets in favor of the then-unheard-of *liquid*-propellant rockets. In 1898 he began writing a mathematical piece, later entitled "Investigation of Cosmic Spaces by

[27] K. Tsiolkovskii, *Prostoe uchenie o vozdushnom korable i ego postroenii* (Kaluga: K. E. Tsiolkovskii, 1904), 14; Sergei Samoilovich, *Grazhdanin vselennoi* (Kaluga: GMIK im. K. E. Tsiolkovskogo, 1969), 17–22.

[28] K. E. Tsiolkovskii, "Issledovanie mirovykh prostranstv reaktivnymi priborami (1911–1912 gg.)," in *K. E. Tsiolkovskii: izbranne trudy*, eds. B. N. Vorob'ev and V. N. Sokol'skii (Moscow: AN SSSR, 1962), 167.

[29] K. Tsiolkovskii, "Tol'ko li fantaziia?," *Komsomol'skaia pravda*, July 23, 1935.

Reactive Devices," that set forth his basic propositions on the theory of rocket motion in space.[30]

Tsiolkovskii knew, as Jules Verne had described, that in order to escape the earth's gravitational pull, an object would have to reach a tremendous speed, an "escape velocity" of about eight kilometers per second. But how could one devise a mechanism that could impart such a high velocity to an object? After considering and then dismissing the use of balloons and powerful cannons long portrayed in the *astronomicheskii roman* genre, Tsiolkovskii argued that one plausible option was to use the "reaction principle" of the rocket, that is, where matter is ejected from a body, thus making it move. He argued that a rocket packed with liquid propellants would not only provide sufficient energy to accelerate a body to escape velocity, but also work in the vacuum of outer space. Tsiolkovskii developed an elegant mathematical model relating four variables: changing rocket speed, rocket mass, propellant mass, and the velocity of gas exiting from the rocket as a result of combustion of the propellants. His calculations showed how certain parameters – particularly gas exhaust velocity and the relative supply of propellants – could be altered for a rocket to reach escape velocity. He also illustrated the basic operating principles of a liquid-fuel rocket engine, selected the most efficient propellants (liquid oxygen and liquid hydrogen), suggested the use of pump-fed combustion chambers, and described how to cool the walls of a rocket engine by using the cold propellant itself.[31] Although unknown in the West for about thirty years, neither Western nor Russian historians now dispute that Tsiolkovskii's classic paper provided the first rigorous proof that space travel was physically possible.

Tsiolkovskii sent his two-part article to several established scientific journals, but when all declined to publish it, he appealed to the editor of *Nauchnoe obozrenie* (*Scientific Survey*), where he had already published a handful of articles in previous years.[32] *Nauchnoe obozrenie* had begun in 1894 as a popular science journal but had evolved by the turn of the century into a forum for Marxist and sometimes revolutionary thought. In the 1890s, when the journal still had a strong scientific bent, Tsiolkovskii – who had

[30] Tsiolkovskii's contemporary Aleksandr Fedorov also published a sixteen-page brochure, *Novyi printsip vozdukhoplavaniia, iskliuchaiushchii atmosferu kak opornuiu sredu* [*New Principles of Aeronautics, Excluding the Atmosphere as a Supporting Medium*] in 1896 in which he argued that a rocket did not require any support from the atmosphere to fly. Although Fedorov did not mention the cosmos or use any mathematics, his results influenced Tsiolkovskii's thinking. Tsiolkovskii, Issledovanie mirovykh prostranstv, 2.

[31] K. E. Tsiolkovskii, "Issledovanie mirovykh prostranstv reaktivnymi priborami," *Nauchnoe obozrenie* no. 5 (1903): 45–75.

[32] Handwritten notes in Tsiolkovskii's copy of "Issledovanie mirovykh prostranstv reaktivnymi priborami," *Nauchnoe obozrenie* no. 5 (1903): 45–75 stored in ARAN, 555/6/39/1–17.

no interest in Marxism let alone revolution – had established a good relationship with the journal's editor, Mikhail Filippov, a German-educated intellectual and sometime chemist. The journal came under increasing scrutiny from the Tsarist censors when Filippov published a number of political broadsides by dissident authors such as Lenin (under various pseudonyms), Georgii Plekhanov, and Aleksandra Kollontai. Unfortunately, Tsiolkovskii submitted his article for publication during this period. Originally slated for the February 1903 issue, the first part of Tsiolkovskii's article on space travel eventually appeared three months later in the May issue.[33] Unfortunately, only days after its publication, on June 12, journal editor Mikhail Filippov was found dead, apparently killed in a freak accident during a scientific experiment. His untimely death, as well as the Tsarist police's searches through Filippov's premises, put an end to the journal. The second part of Tsiolkovskii's article was never published in *Nauchnoe obozrenie*.

Russian and Western historians have made much of the fact that imperial police action ensured that few issues containing the key article were ever disseminated, which in turn seemed to explain why Tsiolkovskii's works were "ignored" during the imperial era. The evidence suggests otherwise; for example, a number of space enthusiasts later recalled that they had the issue in their possession or had seen the issue in their youth. Even the U.S. Library of Congress received the May 1903 issue.[34] If Tsiolkovskii's article was neglected, it may have had something to do with the audience of the journal. By 1903, the publication had become a popular forum dedicated to political and economic topics; few scientific-minded people read or followed the journal, having ceded their place to a much more politically oriented and often revolutionary demographic who saw in Tsiolkovskii's article little more than idle fantasy.

Apparently discouraged by the lack of a response, Tsiolkovskii for the time being abandoned further thoughts on space exploration and returned his energies to teaching and publishing, the latter focused on his beloved metallic airship. He continued to self-publish brochures that he distributed by himself to his small but curious hometown audience. His works on metallic airships

[33] Some have repeated an apocryphal story (based on the recollections of Filippov's son) that Tsiolkovskii's article was published only after a dispute with the state censor, who objected to it based on the premise that the piece was sacrilegious given its secular view of the heavens. Circumstantial evidence suggests that this was not so. Tsiolkovskii's article was delayed from the February to the May issue because the censor rejected *other* political articles in the journal as unsuitable. For the younger Filippov's recollections, see V. Filippov, "Pervye stat'i Tsiolkovskogo," *Literaturnaia gazeta*, June 27, 1963, 3.

[34] For a typical account of the "unavailability" of the May 1903 issue, see Samoilovich, *Grazhdanin vselennoi*, 70–71. F. A. Tsander, a space enthusiast, noted in 1924 that the issue was available in both the Lenin and Bol'shaia Rumiantsev Libraries in the 1910s. F. A. Tsander, "Doklad inzhenera F. A. Tsandera o svoem izobretenii," in F. A. Tsander, *Iz nauchnogo naslediia*, ed. A. F. Tsander (Moscow: Nauka, 1967), 37–38.

merited citations in important French journals such as *L'Aeronaute* and *Revue Scientifique*, which in turn prompted native Russian journals to pay more attention to the eccentric from Kaluga.[35] With his increasing corpus of work, Tsiolkovskii gained a modicum of respect, especially in his adopted hometown. In the years before the Great War, local societies there organized symposia to discuss Tsiolkovskii's metallic airship concepts and publicized many of his ideas in newspapers or journals.

In 1910, Tsiolkovskii's thoughts returned to space exploration, partly because of the rising national interest in aeronautics, reflected in the proliferation of dozens of new journals on flight. He had also felt that the original work had been published in "a careless manner" seven years earlier.[36] This time, he found a sympathetic publisher who was willing to issue his articles in a new journal, *Vestnik vozdukhoplavaniia* (*Journal of Aeronautics*), which catered to a growing audience in urban Russia that was fascinated by the possibilities of a relatively new arrival in Russia, the airplane.[37] Beginning late 1911, Tsiolkovskii published the second part in serialized issues of this (short-lived) journal, which unlike *Nauchnoe obozrenie* was completely apolitical.[38] Here he presented calculations on the energy necessary to overcome the Earth's gravitational pull and atmospheric resistance in order to "escape" beyond its field of control, and he ended with a long textual description of the sensations an observer might feel from rocket launch all the way up to space. Tsiolkovskii detailed elements of a life-support system as well as the foods that would be necessary to nourish this hypothetic cosmic traveler. He was not above appealing to the human imagination; echoing William Blake, he wrote,

> [t]o set foot on the soil of asteroids, to lift a rock with one's hand on the Moon, to place traveling stations in the ether of space, to cultivate living rings around Earth, the Moon, the Sun, to observe Mars at [close] distances, and to land on its satellite or even on its surface, what could be more mind-dazzling![39]

In ending the series of articles, he provided an exegesis on the final human migration to the stars: "In all likelihood, the better part of humanity will

[35] See, for example, "L'Aerostate Métallique Tziolkovski," *L'Aeronaute* 43 (October 8, 1910): 348.

[36] M. K. Tikhonravov, "Raboty K. E. Tsiolkovskogo po raketnoi tekhnike (vvodnaia stat'ia)," in K. E. Tsiolkovskii, *Trudy po raketnoi tekhnike*, ed. M. K. Tikhonravov (Moscow: Oborongiz, 1947), 13.

[37] Scott W. Palmer, *Dictatorship of the Air: Aviation Culture and the Fate of Modern Russia* (New York: Cambridge University Press, 2006), 11–75.

[38] The eight-part article had the title "Issledovanie mirovykh prostranstv reaktivnymi priborami." See *Vestnik vozdukhoplavaniia* no. 19 (1911): 16–21, no. 20 (1911): 29–32, nos. 21–22 (1911): 31–37, no. 2 (1912): 2–7, no. 3 (1912): 15–16, no. 5 (1912): 2–5, nos. 6–7 (1912): 6–9, and no. 9 (1912): 7–11.

[39] Tsiolkovskii, "Issledovanie mirovykh prostranstv reaktivnymi priborami (1911–1912 gg.)," 205.

never perish but will move from sun to sun as each one dies out in succession. Many hundreds of millions of years hence we may be living near a sun which today has not yet even flared up but exists only in the embryo."[40] Two years later, in 1914, Tsiolkovskii concluded his thoughts on space exploration with a self-published addendum in which he added more considerations on the use of different types of propellants for rocket engines in space as well as further descriptive passages on the experience of space travel, written in the form of diary.[41] His three-part meditation on the mathematics of space travel – published in 1903, 1911–1912, and 1914 – constituted an anomaly, an outlier in the geography of established fields such as astronomy and aeronautics. Although many in Europe and the United States had engaged in speculation on travel from the Earth into the heavens, none besides Tsiolkovskii had considered the actual mechanics of the process. In essence, Tsiolkovskii, the village eccentric, was founding a new field and discovering that there was no institutional scientific forum to put an imprimatur of gravitas on his work.

POPULAR SCIENCE

The Tsarist state understandably had no interest in sponsoring or disseminating work on space exploration, either by Tsiolkovskii or anyone. Instead, the medium of popular science, dependent on both private societies and publishing concerns, served as the principal domain for serious works on space exploration, although, admittedly, in both cases, cosmic exploration was a peripheral rather than a central topic of discourse.

The rise of scientific societies – especially ones that encouraged active participation of individuals without credentials from the Academy or the higher educational system – was one symptom of the rise of a middle class in imperial Russia.[42] If science was a profession for elite and educated individuals, popular science was a discursive space for the new bourgeois, a place where the content and meanings of science could be delineated in negotiation with state-sponsored narratives about the nature of "valid" science in Russian society.

The most obvious intellectual home for space travel were astronomical societies. Astronomy as a discipline with native practitioners came of age in Russia in the early nineteenth century. Strong support from successive imperial governments for astronomy facilitated the establishment of major

40 Ibid., 207.

41 K. E. Tsiolkovskii, *Issledovanie mirovykh prostranstv reaktivnymi priborami (dopol'nenie k I i II chasti truda togo zhe nazvaniia)* (Kaluga: K. E. Tsiolkovskii, 1914).

42 N. G. Filippov, *Nauchno-tekhnicheskie obshchestva rossii (1866–1917 gg.): uchebnoe posobie* (Moscow: MVSSO RSFSR, 1976); Joseph Bradley, "Subjects into Citizens: Societies, Civil Society, and Autocracy in Tsarist Russia," *American Historical Review* 107 (2002): 1094–1123.

observatories at Pulkovo (in 1839), Odessa (in 1870), Tashkent (in 1874), and Kazan' (1901); Loren Graham notes that the state "saw astronomy as a field where relatively small sums of money could bring considerable international acclaim."[43] For a brief period, between 1888 and 1895, the Pulkovo telescope was the largest refracting telescope in the world, a fact publicized by burgeoning astronomy societies that formed in the late nineteenth and early twentieth centuries in such cities as Nizhnii Novgorod, St. Petersburg, and Moscow. Although these originally formed as professional societies for the small astronomer community, eventually they opened their ranks to the interested public.

Probably the most well-known voluntary astronomy society was the Russian Society of Enthusiasts for the Study of the World (*Russkoe obshchestvo liubitelei mirovedeniia*, or ROLM), established in 1909 in St. Petersburg. The society was led by radical revolutionary Nikolai Morozov, who had recently emerged into public life after a twenty-two-year spell in Tsarist prisons for being a member of the People's Will terrorist organization.[44] Like Tsiolkovskii, Morozov was self-educated and shared an abiding belief in raising public interest in astronomy and space exploration through fiction and popular science; echoing Tsiolkovskii, Morozov's early ideas on space exploration were published as fictional works in popular science journals.[45] At Morozov's urging, the ROLM sponsored a number of lectures and functions on the topic of space travel in the 1910s. The society also had its own observatory, developed a program to study variable stars, and in 1912 began publishing its own journal, *Mirovedenie* (*Study of the Universe*), which was loosely styled on the format of popular science journals that had emerged in Russia in the late nineteenth century.

Compared to societies, publishing had a much deeper imprint on the creation of a popular consciousness on spaceflight in imperial Russia. Popular science publishing in Russia goes back to 1710, the time of Peter the Great, when the imperial government issued what may have been the first nonspecialized writing on the natural sciences, a small volume on geography with information on "the terrestrial globe and all its separate parts," which supported a distinctly Copernican view of the universe.[46] Through the mid-eighteenth century, the Imperial Academy of Sciences and the major

43 Loren R. Graham, *Science in Russia and the Soviet Union: A Short History* (Cambridge, UK: Cambridge University Press, 1993), 220–221.

44 V. V. Sobolev, ed., *Istoriia astronomii v rossii i sssr* (Moscow: Ianus-K, 1999), 563–564; V. K. Lutskii, *Istoriia astronomicheskikh obshchestvennykh organizatsii v sssr, 1881–1941 gg.* (Moscow: Nauka, 1982), 55–64. A similar society opened in Moscow in 1912 with the active participation of professional astronomers.

45 N. A. Morozov, "V mirovom prostranstve," *Sovremennyi mir* no. 1 (1908): 159–175; N. A. Morozov, *Na granitse nevedomogo: nauchnye polufantazii* (Moscow: Zveno, 1910).

46 E. A. Lazarevich, *S vekom naravne: populiarizatsiia nauki v Rossii: kniga, gazeta, zhurnal* (Moscow: Kniga, 1984), 9–13.

universities dominated the process of disseminating scientific ideas to the public at large. The Academy, for example, sponsored the publication of vast numbers of manuals, journals, calendars, and textbooks on the established natural sciences, particularly astronomy, history, and geography. The first popular science journals for a broad audience began appearing in the second quarter of the eighteenth century in connection with the rise of scientific societies and the coalescing of a distinct Russian middle-class sensibility. In these publications, authors typically presented information in an encyclopedic way with fact after fact, punctuated by the occasional illustration.

The most important qualitative change in popular science publishing occurred in the late nineteenth century with the acceleration of industrialization (and consequent popular interest in the aesthetics and mechanics of machines), the rise of private publishers interested in science popularization, and the formation of a unique identity of popular *journals* as distinct from monographs. The tenor of popular engagement with late-nineteenth-century science was also catalyzed by the predilection of established scientific luminaries – such as D. I. Mendeleev and K. A. Timiriazev – to join editorial boards of several major publishing houses that specialized in popular science publishing. Inspired by established scientists, a growing group of intelligentsia including V. V. Lunkevich, N. A. Rubakin, I. M. Sechenov, and E. N. Vodovozova embraced public science as a vocation, producing a spate of new textbooks for the coming generation of young Russians. By the first decades of the twentieth century, there were dozens of popular science journals flooding the market, many of them short lived, lasting three or four years. Their subject matter focused largely on aviation, biology, geography, or technology but the overriding theme was one of self-education.

If some private publishers in the late imperial era appeared and disappeared within a few years, some, such as the Soikin Company, established entire traditions. Soikin was the brainchild of Petr Petrovich Soikin (1862–1938), one of the most successful private publishers in late imperial Russia, and certainly the most prolific one dedicated to the popularization of science. Through its lifetime, the Soikin Company published 32 different popular science and fiction journals – with descriptive names such as *Priroda i liudi* (*Nature and People*), *Mir prikliuchenii* (*World of Adventure*), and *Vestnik znanii* (*Journal of Knowledge*) – and issued more than 80 million books that ingrained themselves into the collective imagination of several generations of Russian youth. Invisible in the received history of Russian space exploration, Soikin played an indispensable role in the formation of a space *mentalité* in both late imperial and early Bol'shevik Russia.

Soikin founded his business in 1885 as a modest printing press that issued small runs of journals or printed books for other publishers before he significantly expanded into a fully independent publisher in 1892. This was a period of great transformation for both publishing and reading in Russia – literacy rates gradually increased so that by 1914, about 40% of the Russian population were literate. Hand in hand, publishing changed dramatically as a result of new economic conditions and the use of efficient and higher quality printing presses; in 1860, Russian publishers issued only about 2,000 titles, a number that increased to 7,366 by 1887, and then nearly doubled to 11,548 by 1895; in other words, there was a five-order increase over thirty-five years. By the eve of the Great War, in 1910, Russia published nearly 30,000 individual monographs. An array of different publishers flooded the market – by 1908, there were at least 268 registered publishers – who introduced a more Western European and cosmopolitan flavor into literature, displacing the peasant-oriented and image-based *lubki* (folk prints) literature that had proliferated before. At the turn of the century, religious publications sponsored by the Tsarist government still outnumbered natural science works by about two to one, but there was far more diversity in the secular publishing market.[47]

Amid this growth and transformation, in 1889, the Soikin Company launched its most successful and long-lived journal, the weekly *Priroda i liudi*. Developed on the model of the French journal *La Nature*, which was also available in Russia, Soikin's domestic publication quickly eclipsed the French competitor. As originally envisioned, *Priroda i liudi* devoted its pages to five different categories of knowledge: historical and biographical information; science fiction devoted to "familiarizing readers with natures and peoples from all over the world, with the latest adventures in science, from the world underground, the abyss of the seas and the limitless expanse of the heavens"; geography and ethnography from across the world; popular descriptions of recent science; and the latest news on science, adventure, and exploration.[48] The heavily illustrated magazine was immensely popular among young, especially male, readers at the turn of the century, aided by a marketing strategy developed by Soikin that involved issuing supplements to the journal, which were essentially self-contained novels. These "supplement" novels were published as part of collections that readers sought to complete, under banners such as "Useful Library," "People's University" (a compendium of information on geology, geography, chemistry, botany, etc.), "Library for the Self-Educated," "Easy to Understand Philosophy," and "Knowledge for All." One supplementary series to *Priroda i liudi*, "Library of Novels. Adventures on Land and in Air," issued from 1890 to 1915, included translations of stories by many well-known European and American authors such as Arthur Conan Doyle, Alexandre Dumas, Rudyard Kipling, Robert Louis Stevenson, and Mark Twain. In 1912, Soikin

[47] Jeffrey Brooks, *When Russian Learned to Read: Literacy and Popular Culture, 1861–1917* (Princeton: Princeton University Press, 1985), 300, 307–308; Lazarevich, *S vekom naravne*, 164, 221–222.

[48] A. Admiral'skii and S. Belov, *Rytsar' knigi: ocherki zhizni i deiatel'nosti P. P. Soikina* (Leningrad: Lenizdat, 1970), 30–33.

published the complete works of Charles Dickens in forty-six volumes, doing the same the following year for James Fennimore Cooper.

Soikin was a major vehicle for bringing space exploration – in both its scientific and fantasy forms – to the masses during the imperial era. His publishing company facilitated and engendered an international exchange of information on the fantastic possibilities of space exploration by publishing a stream of foreign space-themed fiction, translated mostly from English or French. The most important Soikin publications in this regard were those by Jules Verne and H. G. Wells, but others, such as *Les Aventures Extraordinaires d'un Savant Russe* by French authors Henry de Graffigny and Georges Le Faure, about a team of French and Russian scientists who explore the solar system, were just as popular.[49]

Beyond fiction, Soikin's journals such as *Priroda i liudi* and *Mir prikliuchenii*, as well popular science journals issued by the larger publishing company of I. D. Sytin such as *Vokrug sveta* (*Around the World*), communicated a sensibility that blurred the distinction between science and its popularization. Tsiolkovskii's relationship with private presses like those of Soikin and Sytin was a case in point. In the early 1890s, Tsiolkovskii had published his first science fiction novel *Na lune* (*On the Moon*) through Sytin as a monograph "supplement" to *Vokrug sveta*. When he found it all but impossible to break into the world of elite science publishing, that is, journals sponsored by the Imperial Academy of Sciences, he turned to popular science journals as a way to publish serious scientific meditations. In the last decade of the nineteenth century, he published in the monthly *Nauka i zhizn'* (*Science and Life*) on a variety of topics and eventually established a relationship with *Nauchnoe obozrenie*, one of Soikin's banner popular science journals. Even as this journal moved into a political and revolutionary direction, Tsiolkovskii published a number of articles on astronomy and aerodynamics (e.g., "Continuity of Solar Radiation: Pressure Inside a Star (the Sun) and Its Compression in Connection with Material Elasticity"), often slotted between long expositions on Marxism and political economy. The "Soikin" name conferred upon his work a modicum of legitimacy in the absence of vetting through the Academy publication process.

Tsiolkovskii's isolated forays into the mathematical foundations of space travel might have languished in obscurity – and perhaps been forgotten – had it not been for popular science writers who were widely known, respected, and prolific in the science popularization genre. In fact, Tsiolkovskii's legacy – and the origins of spaceflight discourse in modern Russia – can

[49] Zh. Le For [G. Le Faure] and A. Grafin'i [H. de Graffigny], *Puteshestvie na Lunu* (St. Petersburg: P. P. Soikin, 1890); Zh. Le For and A. Grafin'i, *V nevedomykh mirakh. Vokrug solntsa. Neobychainye prikliucheniia russkogo uchenogo* (St. Petersburg: P. P. Soikin, 1891); G. Uells [H. G. Wells], *Pervye liudi na Lune* (St. Petersburg: P. P. Soikin, 1910). Other similar translations of space fiction included V. Fonviel' [Wilfrid de Fonvielle], *Na Marse* (St. Petersburg: P. P. Soikin, 1901).

neither be understood nor explained without exploration of the relationship between Tsiolkovskii and his two earliest "publicists," Vladimir Riumin and Iakov Perel'man. Beyond simply compensating for Tsiolkovskii's failings as a public communicator, these men played a fundamental role in the formation of popular attitudes toward space exploration in Russia during both the imperial and Bol'shevik eras.

Vladimir Riumin (1874–1937) was the first to bring Tsiolkovskii's scientific ideas into broader prominence during the 1910s. A graduate of a technological institute in Khar'kov, Riumin worked briefly as a teacher, first at a railway workers educational institution and then at a middle school for mechanics and technical education where he taught chemistry and physics. Beginning 1901, Riumin wrote an almost continuous stream of engineering text books on a variety of subjects on electricity, chemistry, minerals, and mathematics. His experience as an educator led him to found a monthly journal, *Elektrichestvo i zhizn'* (*Electricity and Life*), in 1910. As its editor, his goal was to make electricity "understandable to all," which he did by combining theoretical articles on electricity and magnetism with "useful advice" and instructions for amateurs for home experiments.

Riumin had been familiar with Tsiolkovskii's meditations on the construction of a metallic dirigible in the first decade of the twentieth century.[50] When the old man resumed publication of his abandoned series of articles on space travel in 1911–1912, Riumin found them especially interesting. In probably the first popular science article in Russia dedicated to the notion of space exploration, Riumin wrote a long synopsis of Tsiolkovskii's articles in 1912 in Soikin's banner journal *Priroda i liudi*. In the piece entitled "The Rocket into Cosmic Space," Riumin underscored the deep connections between the science, fiction, and popular science of cosmic travel:

> Who among us have not enthused over Jules Verne's fantastic novel "From the Earth to the Moon," and who knows that... Tsiolkovskii, has already provided the basis for the actual possibility of interplanetary [travel], not in the form of belle-lettrist work but rather in a solid work, grounded in mathematics?... With the gracious permission of the same K. E. Tsiolkovskii, I would like to popularize his original idea – outstanding in its boldness [and] to make it accessible to a wide circle of readers.[51]

Riumin's piece in *Priroda i liudi* – and others by him – represented the first salvo in a wave of popular articles on space exploration in the 1910s, a "first wave" that is all but forgotten. These works, published between 1912 and 1922, gave Russians their first taste that the fantasy of space travel – propagated in science fiction for decades – was not merely fodder for children and fans of adventure but could be part of the same vernacular of

[50] Riumin's first article on Tsiolkovskii was published in 1905 in the journal *Fizik-liubitel'* [*Physics Enthusiast*].

[51] V. V. Riumin, "Na rakete v kosmicheskoe prostranstvo," *Priroda i liudi* no. 36 (1912): 556–558.

FIGURE 2. Iakov Perel'man (1882–1942) was undoubtedly the most important Soviet popularizer of space exploration in the early twentieth century. His hundreds of articles and dozens of books on the topic profoundly influenced the shape and form of cosmic enthusiasm in the USSR. His greatest contribution may have been his promotion of Konstantin Tsiolkovskii as the "patriarch" of Soviet space exploration. [*Source*: Collection of Asif Siddiqi]

early-twentieth-century technological fascination – electricity, telephones, automobiles, airplanes, and other mechanical wonders. Articles on space exploration proliferated not only in popular science journals such as *Priroda i liudi* and *Elektrichestvo i zhizn'* but in publications with audiences unfamiliar with science or technology – *Sovremennoe slovo* (*The Modern Word*), *Svobodnoe slovo* (*The Free Word*), *Rech'* (*Conversation*), *Birzhevye vedomosti* (*Stockbroker Bulletin*), and *Novoe vremia* (*New Times*).[52]

IAKOV PEREL'MAN

The most prominent architect of this first wave of space popularization was Iakov Isidorovich Perel'man (1882–1942), arguably one of the most successful and well-known science popularizers in twentieth-century Russia (see Figure 2). He was enormously prolific: over a forty-year career that

[52] For a small sampling of articles by Riumin on space exploration, see "Reaktivnyye dvigatetali (fantaziia i deistvitel'nosti)," *Elektrichestvo i zhizn'* no. 1 (1913): 3–4; [using the pseudonym 'Pr. V.'] "Puteshestvie na lunu," *Elektrichestvo i zhizn'* nos. 7–8 (1913); "S zemli na lunu i dal'she! (griadushchaia vozmozhnost')," *Elektrichestvo i zhizn'* no. 6 (1914): 241–243; "S planety na planety," *Elektrichestvo i zhizn'* no. 10 (1915): 403–404. See also "Vozmozhny li puteshestviia na planety? (nauchnaia beseda Anri Grafin'i)," *Priroda i liudi* no. 13 (1916): 204–206.

crossed the divide of 1917, he wrote more than a thousand articles under several pseudonyms and published over 100 different books that were published in over 500 (often revised) editions. Conservative estimates suggest that more than 13 million Perel'man books were printed and sold in the Soviet Union alone, some as late as the 1980s. His books were translated into eighteen different foreign languages, spanning categories of popular science, "scientific-cognitive" (general knowledge), and textbooks, in the process creating an entirely new genre of science popularization in Russia, "science for entertainment" (*zanimatel'naia nauka*) that endures to this day.[53] But numbers convey only part of Perel'man's endurance and significance; his success in propagating a palatable idea of space exploration, one that combined the mathematics of Tsiolkovskii, the eloquence of Verne, and the utopianism of H. G. Wells, gave him a quality that cut across demographics.

With the possible exception of Tsiolkovskii, Perel'man was arguably the most important individual in creating and fostering the Russian romance with space exploration that began at the beginning of the twentieth century. Recovering his contributions from the periphery of Russian space history introduces a counterpoint to the largely technocentric narratives that have been passed down.

A child of Russian Jewish intelligentsia, Perel'man was an inquisitive child in his early age, growing up in the provincial town of Belostok on the Grodno region (now Bialystok in Belarus). After a struggle with financial penury, he managed to earn a degree from the St. Petersburg Forestry Institute in 1908, passing with honors. Earlier, as a way to earn extra money to feed himself, he had tried his hand at popular science writing, producing freelance articles for publisher Soikin's *Priroda i liudi* from 1901. Gaining confidence, upon graduation from the Forestry Institute, he decided to pursue writing as a full-time job, having already started serving as the secretary at *Priroda i liudi* from 1904.

Although Perel'man's principal reputation rests on his enormously prolific career after the Revolution, he established the archetype for his approach to science writing in the 500 odd articles and several books he wrote in the pre-Revolutionary period. Perel'man's aesthetic strategy emerged partly in response to his low opinion of the existing popular science genre in late imperial Russia, a class of writing that he believed was erroneous, oversimplified, sensationalist, and simply boring. He also felt that most science textbooks, as well as those on the burgeoning field of "technology" (*tekhniki*), were far too theoretical and divorced from the reality of daily life experiences. Perel'man convinced Soikin to sponsor the publication of a new book, *Zanimatel'naia*

[53] G. I. Mishkevich, *Doktor zanimatel'nykh nauk: zhizn' i tvorchestvo Iakova Isidorovicha Perel'mana* (Moscow: Znanie, 1986), 183–184. For a short biography, see ARAN, 4/14/207/1–2.

fizika (*Physics for Entertainment*), which was first published in 1913.[54] The response to the book, from both critics and consumers, was overwhelming, and it prompted Perel'man and Soikin to produce an entire series of books in the "entertainment" genre beginning in 1916: for algebra, arithmetic, astronomy, geometry, mathematics, and mechanics among others, published in dozens of editions over several decades.[55] The twenty-first Russian edition of *Physics for Entertainment* appeared in 1981, almost forty years after Perel'man's death. Following Perel'man's examples, nearly a dozen other authors also produced their own "entertainment" science series. Often written in the form of letters to the reader, these works incorporated the latest scientific theories, high-quality illustrations, and a penchant for flashy examples to communicate elementary laws and natural scientific ideas. They were also unabashedly enamored with modern science and technology, inheritors of a post-Enlightenment ethos that privileged the world view of reason and science as "truth," a kind of protective guard against the "irrationality" of the "old" world view of mysticism, superstition, and religion.

Perel'man also had a hand in disseminating foreign science fiction in Russia. Responding to his idea, publisher Soikin began issuing a free supplement, *Mir prikliuchenii* (*World of Adventure*), to the journal *Priroda i liudi* from 1910, a practice that continued for eighteen years, well into the Stalin period, and included titles by Wells, Doyle, Poe, and others. Perel'man not only chose which foreign novels were to be published for the series but also contributed to translating them for Russian audiences *and* writing introductions (or having prominent scientists write them) that provided a "scientific" counterpoint to the fictions of the narrative.[56] These novels fit completely in his world view of the close relationship between science, popular science, and science fiction. In an unpublished manuscript written near the end of his life, Perel'man noted,

> Who can rightfully claim to be the founder of science for entertainment? Here there can't be two opinions: this honor belongs to Jules Verne. He was not only a remarkable novelist and a creator of the science fantasy genre in literature but [also] the greatest master of scientific propaganda. He was the first to show that as it is necessary to popularize knowledge, [it is also necessary] to completely capture the attention of the reader, maintaining in them the most lively interest in the topic.[57]

[54] Ia. Perel'man, *Zanimatel'naia fizika* (kn. 1) (St. Petersburg: P. P. Soikin, 1913).

[55] The first editions, beginning 1916, were *Zanimatel'naia fizika* (kn. 2) (Petrograd: P. P. Soikin, 1916); *Zanimatel'naia geometriia* (1925); *Zanimatel'naia geometriia na vol'nom vozdukhe i doma* (1925); *Zanimatel'naia arifmetika* (1926); *Zanimatel'naia matematika* (1927); *Zanimatel'nye zadachi* (1928); *Zanimatel'naia matematika v rasskazakh* (1929); *Zanimatel'naia astronomiia* (1929); *Zanimatel'naia mekhanika* (1930); *Zanimatel'naia algebra* (1933); and *Zanimatel'nye zadachi i opyty* (Moscow: Detgiz, 1959). All first editions from 1925 to 1933 were published by Vremia in Leningrad.

[56] Mishkevich, *Doktor zanimatel'nykh nauk*, 29–30, 112–113.

[57] St. Petersburg Department of ARAN, 796/2/9/1–12 (1939).

Perel'man's principal contribution in the imperial era was to shift the public discourse of space travel from one of fantasy to plausibility. In the many articles on space exploration he wrote in the 1910s, he brought a distinctively "rational" sensibility that relied on measured and modest language – the language of "true" science – giving the idea of cosmic travel a sheen of respectability on par with any other established and professionalized science such as mathematics or astronomy. Yet at the same time, he considered the science fiction writers of the late nineteenth century as part of a single line of evolution on the thinking about cosmic travel; if there was a new shift in epistemology with the publication of Tsiolkovskii's works, it was only that where the early fiction writers had failed to envision the true means of propulsion in space, Tsiolkovskii had succeeded.

In a public lecture he gave to the Russian Society of Enthusiasts of the Study of the World (ROLM) in November 1913, Perel'man noted that "the success of aeronautics has not drawn [us] closer, and cannot draw us closer to the solution of questions of interplanetary travel." No previous individual, he argued, who had conceived of such ships – such as Jules Verne, H. G. Wells, or Kurd Lasswitz [Laßwitz] – had divined the correct solution to cosmic flight. Fortunately, now we had, Perel'man argued, a conception of a rocket vehicle proposed by Tsiolkovskii, which was "not the fabrication of a novelist, but a scientifically developed and deeply thought out technical idea, expressed with complete seriousness."[58] Perel'man's lecture was widely reported in media publications, and he even sent a copy of the transcript to Tsiolkovskii himself. Underscoring the intimate connection between the popular science of former and the theoretical science of latter, Perel'man's public pronouncement prompted Tsiolkovskii to further explore the mathematics of space travel. He wrote, "I have received your letter and article and read it with great pleasure. You raised a question dear to me, and I do not know how to thank you. As a result, I have once again studied rockets and done some new [work]."[59]

The notion that Tsiolkovskii was doing legitimate science, even as he was both ignored by the West and unappreciated by the Russian public, ran through the pages of probably the most important popular work on space exploration in the imperial era, Perel'man's first complete monograph on the topic, *Mezhplanetnye puteshestviia* (*Interplanetary Journeys*), issued by Soikin publishers in 1915. In this slim book, probably the first of its kind in the world dedicated to the science of space exploration, Perel'man

[58] Ia. I. Perel'man, "Mezhplanetnye puteshestviia," *Priroda i liudi* no. 8 (1914): 126–127. The original title of his lecture was "Interplanetary Travel: What Stages Could Hope to Achieve It in the Future."

[59] ARAN, 555/4/17/2–3 (December 9, 1913). Perel'man's lecture was reported in the following newspapers or journals: *Rech'* (November 22, 1913); *Sovremennoe slovo* (December 1, 1913, p. 3); *Birzhevye vedomosti*; *Novoe vremia*; and *Priroda i liudi* (no. 8, 1914).

summarized the various ways dreamers and authors through the centuries had imagined of traveling to space. Illustrated with eight finely produced drawings of space vehicles and flight to the planets, the book perfectly captured the zeitgeist of the early-twentieth-century Russian interest in space travel, the "greatest dream of humanity." Written in elegant prose with strong appeal to economy, Perel'man weaved together history, logic, and mathematics, and greatly helped to transform the idea of space travel from the realm of the absurd into turn-of-the-century technological anticipation. He made this note:

> There was a time when it was considered impossible to swim across the ocean; the current universal faith in the inaccessibility of celestial bodies is just as groundless as the belief of our ancestors in the unattainability of the antipodes. The correct path to solving the problem of flight beyond the atmosphere and interplanetary journeys has already been outlined; to the honor of Russian science, it was presented to humanity by a Russian scientist.[60]

The monograph drew a progressive but direct line from the cosmic dirigibles of H. G. Wells to the lunar spaceship of Jules Verne to Tsiolkovskii's theory of rocket flight through space. Nevertheless, even as they were part of the same fantastic and cognitive evolution of humanity's thinking on space exploration, Perel'man underlined how Tsiolkovskii had made a qualitative break. Having elaborated in several chapters on the imagination of Verne and Wells, in Chapter 9 Perel'man shifted the focus to Tsiolkovskii, framing the latter's contribution in relation to Newton rather than Verne:

> After so many disappointments, we finally approach the only truly developed project of interplanetary journeys – realized not yet today, but in more or less the near future. This project is developed by the Russian scientist K. E. Tsiolkovskii. . . . Here before us is no longer the fantasy of a novelist . . . but a deeply thought-out technical idea, expressed in complete seriousness. [The theory] points us to the only real way to accomplish flight beyond the atmosphere – a guided rocket.[61]

In the evolution of Russian imagining of space exploration, these exhortations were important for many reasons – for the first time, they began to link space exploration with the science of rocketry, two systems of knowledge that had hitherto had little or no overlap; also for the first time, they helped to advance the notion that space exploration could be conceived of as an idea separate from its origins in myth and fantasy, as part of already respectable and accepted epistemological notions grounded in Newtonian mechanics and astronomy; and finally, they introduced the notion that the self-educated village schoolteacher Tsiolkovskii was not a dilettante or amateur but a "scientist." The science of space exploration had found a place, albeit a small one, in Russian culture.

[60] Perel'man, *Mezhplanetnye puteshestviia*, unnumbered introduction page.
[61] Perel'man, *Mezhplanetnye puteshestviia*, 95.

CONCLUSIONS

The roots of cosmonautics in Russian do not date back to isolated data points, such as 1903 when Konstantin Tsiolkovskii published the first substantive mathematical meditations on the possibility of space exploration or 1917 after which the Bol'shevik government supposedly supported such utopian ideas. Although these temporal markers are undeniably important in the narrative of space exploration, their symbolic standing in the received history has effectively occluded antecedent and broader social, cultural, and literary phenomena that were equally important in facilitating a substantive shift in Russian thinking about the cosmos; if before, the cosmos was a place for fantasy and anticipation, for some at least, it became a real destination, visited with the help of science.

Tsiolkovskii's pre-Revolutionary works on space exploration were important catalysts to facilitate this evolution from fantasy to possibility, but they were by no means the most important factor in the origins of Russian fascination with space exploration. Through the late nineteenth century, Russian popular engagement with the idea of space exploration emerged through three different intersecting strands, that is, science fiction, the "scientific" works of Tsiolkovskii, and popular science. Necessary conditions for the emergence of distinct traditions of science fiction and popular science included the rise of a large and literate bourgeois class and the success of several influential private publishing concerns mired in a peculiarly Russian version of post-Enlightenment fascination with turn-of-the-century science and technology.

Here, Tsiolkovskii's theoretical contributions were no more critical than Jules Verne's early fiction that introduced the idea that rockets could be used for space exploration or Iakov Perel'man's numerous works legitimizing Tsiolkovskii's mathematics. None existed without the other, and they collectively represented a new kind of science, a science in search of a home. Without formal institutions, standards, or communicative media, the science of space travel existed within the overlapping and often indistinguishable discursive spaces of science fiction and popular science. Instead of emerging through existing legitimate disciplines such as astronomy or aeronautics, scientific and mathematical meditations on cosmic travel arose as part of an "extrascholarly" sensibility that was part theory, part fiction, and part popular science. Here, fiction represented the spectrum of imaginary possibilities, theory circumscribed the physical limits of this imagination, and popular science brought it to the public as a legitimate epistemology.[62] This process

[62] Others have noted permeable boundaries between science, science fiction, and popular science in entirely different contexts. See, for example, F. Mellor, "Between Fact and Fiction: Demarcating Science from Non-Science in Popular Physics Books," *Social Studies of Science* 33 (2003): 509–538; D. A. Kirby, "Science Consultants, Fictional Films and Scientific Practice," *Social Studies of Science* 33 (2003): 231–268.

helped create a new space where science could exist while also producing a new science where space could be understood. The pool of people engaged in and affected by this rich discourse was not large, but it was a new, distinct, and influential category of actors who would play even more critical roles in the 1920s as aspirations to visit the cosmos became a mass phenomenon in the Soviet Union, a process enabled by a vast, international, and informal network of correspondents spread across Europe and the United States with Konstantin Tsiolkovskii at its center.

2

"Grief and Genius"

Do we always have to get from foreigners what originated in our boundless homeland and died in loneliness from neglect?[1]

Aleksandr Chizhevskii, in the introduction to Tsiolkovskii's *The Rocket into Cosmic Space*, 1924

INTRODUCTION

Wednesday was an unusually cold day. The many Muscovites who had braved the chill for the annual May Day parade of 1935 wrapped themselves in layers of clothing and huddled close to retain warmth. Those who walked down ulitsa Tverskaia (Tver Street), the main thoroughfare leading to Red Square, passed by the nearly finished construction site at *Okhotnyi riad*, a station on the new Moscow underground subway system scheduled to open in two weeks. Once at the parade, the throngs heard the speeches of eminent personalities who extolled the virtues of the Soviet state. Near the end of the festivities, a new voice could be heard, evidently radioed from the provincial town of Kaluga. Weakened with age, the seventy-seven-year-old speaker's voice wavered between words and then grew in conviction as it echoed across the vast expanse:

Now comrades, I am firmly convinced that a dream of mine – space travel – for which I have given the theoretical foundations, will be realized. . . . I believe that many of you will be witnesses of the first journey beyond the atmosphere. In the Soviet Union we have many young pilots . . . [and] I place my most daring hopes in them. They will help to actualize my discoveries and will prepare the gifted builders of the first space vehicle. Heroes and men of courage will inaugurate the first airways: Earth to Moon orbit, Earth to Mars orbit, and still farther; Moscow to the Moon, Kaluga to Mars![2]

Konstantin Tsiolkovskii, who spoke these words, died later in the year and was canonized by the Soviet state as a great scientist and thinker. Since his

[1] Alexander Tshijewsky, "Anstatt eines Vorworts," in K. E. Tsiolkovskii, *Raketa v kosmicheskoe prostranstvo* (Kaluga: K. E. Tsiolkovskii, 1924), unnumbered preface page. The brochure was dated 1924, but the first copies came off the press in December 1923.

[2] "Osushchestvliaetsia drevneishaia mechta chelovechestva," *Pravda*, September 21, 1935.

death, and particularly in the postwar era, Soviet and Russian historians have gone to extraordinary lengths to elevate him into the pantheon of the history of science. With the support of state publishing houses, they have issued more than a thousand publications about him, including nearly twenty biographies and hundreds of monographs and articles.[3] During his lifetime, Tsiolkovskii published 148 separate works (monographs and articles); of the 600 works that remained unpublished at the time of his death, many have been posthumously published. Since 1966, dozens of scholars have gathered annually for the "Tsiolkovskii Readings" in the scientist's adopted hometown of Kaluga. Their published proceedings, nearing 100 volumes, present a life that has been scrutinized in every last detail.

This hagiographic approach to Tsiolkovskii's life has gone hand in hand with a second interpretative thread: Historians in both the east and the west have underlined the Soviet state's foresight in recognizing Tsiolkovskii's talents during his lifetime. The common touchstones of Tsiolkovskii's biography are his induction into the Socialist Academy of Social Sciences in 1918, the granting of a lifetime pension in 1921, and his national fame in the last years of his life. In the canonical work of Soviet-era space history, the *Kosmonavtika entsiklopediia* (*Cosmonautics Encyclopedia*) published in 1985, the authors note that "[w]ith [the coming of] Soviet power, the conditions for Tsiolkovskii's life and work radically changed. Tsiolkovskii was granted a personal pension and given the possibility for productive work."[4] Many used the previously noted May Day quotation as striking evidence of the Soviet state's sanction of Tsiolkovskii's message of cosmic travel at a time when no government in the West had even considered such an option.[5]

Western historians have also followed the same storyline, noting Tsiolkovskii's arc from obscurity under Tsarist rule to recognition under Soviet rule. William E. Burrows, in his award-winning 1998 synthesis, *This New Ocean*, notes, "the Bolsheviks, who were as afflicted by a national inferiority complex as most other Russians . . . grasped the fact that Tsiolkovskii's work

[3] For a bibliography of Tsiolkovskii's own works and also those about him, see T. Al'tman et al., eds., *Konstantin Eduardovich Tsiolkovskii (1857–1935): bibliograficheskii ukazatel'* (Kaluga: GMIK im. Tsiolkovskogo, 1983). For two Russian biographies, see A. A. Kosmodem'ianskii, *Konstantin Eduardovich Tsiolkovskii, 1857–1935* (Moscow: Nauka, 1987) and Sergei Samoilovich, *Grazhdanin vselennoi (cherty zhizni i deiatel'nosti Konstantina Eduardovicha Tsiolkovskogo)* (Kaluga: GMIK im. Tsiolkovskogo, 1969). The Kosmodem'ianskii book is the seventh revised edition of a work originally published in 1948.

[4] V. P. Glushko, ed., *Kosmonavtika entsiklopediia* (Moscow: Sovetskaia entsiklopediia, 1985), 437.

[5] For a Russian reference to the quotation, see A. A. Kosmodem'ianskii, "Mysli o K. E. Tsiolkovskom (kharakteristika otkrytii i tvorcheskogo stilya)," in *Iz istorii raketnoi tekhniki*, ed. A. A. Blagonravov (Moscow: Nauka, 1964), 81. For a Western reference, see William Shelton, *Soviet Space Exploration: The First Decade* (New York: Washington Square Press, 1968), 14–15. All these sources incorrectly list the year (1935) of the broadcast as 1933.

could be used to change the world under their own aegis and that it could bolster both [the] prestige of the Communist Party and of the nation."[6] Similarly, in 2002, a journalist noted in the Smithsonian's *Air & Space* magazine that "[i]n the years following the Bolshevik Revolution, [Tsiolkovskii] enjoyed the recognition and financial support of authorities anxious to tout the superiority of the Soviet system. His scientific works were widely published and popularized."[7] Authors routinely invoked the state's "discovery" and canonization of Tsiolkovskii as a metaphor for the Bol'sheviks' victory over the empire: Both opened up the infinite possibilities of the human condition.

That Tsiolkovskii was a pioneering theorist for the cause of spaceflight is incontestable. He also played an undeniably important role in the explosive interest in spaceflight in the Soviet Union during the 1920s. His works inspired groups of young students and workers who organized around the theme of space travel. The notion of Tsiolkovskii's preeminence, that is, that a Russian came before the American Robert Goddard or the German-Romanian Hermann Oberth, was important to his appeal. There was also a generational dimension to his significance: Young enthusiasts who paid homage to Tsiolkovskii in the 1930s – some of whom actually met him – later had impressive careers. Mikhail Tikhonravov, one of the founders of an amateur group of rocketry enthusiasts, visited Tsiolkovskii in his hometown of Kaluga in 1934. Twenty years later, he authored a report that led to the launch of the *Sputnik* satellite into space in 1957.[8] Many of the individuals who founded the Soviet space program in the 1950s owed their interest in space exploration to the public fascination with space travel in the 1920s, which was inextricably linked to Tsiolkovskii. Thus, because Tsiolkovskii's actions contributed to the origins of spaceflight discourse in the Soviet Union, it would be impossible to construct the latter without revisiting Tsiolkovskii's fate after the Revolution.

My goal in this chapter is not to challenge Tsiolkovskii's pioneering contribution to the theory of astronautics but to revisit claims about the relationship between the state and Tsiolkovskii. In particular, I hope to recover parts of this relationship that have been obscured or rewritten and to describe the consequences of that association (or lack thereof). I do this first by deconstructing one of the fundamental truisms about Tsiolkovskii's life, asserted repeatedly by historians, that the Bol'sheviks recognized and supported his contributions to spaceflight theory. Having underscored how little

6 William E. Burrows, *This New Ocean: The Story of the First Space Age* (New York: Random House, 1998), 42–43.

7 Anatoly Zak, "Konstantin Tsiolkovsky Slept Here," *Air & Space*, August/September (2002): 62–69.

8 M. K. Tikhonravov, "Takoe ne zabyvaetsia," in *V vospominaniiakh sovremennikov*, eds. V. S. Zotov et al. (Tula: Priokskoe knizhnoe izdatel'stvo, 1971), 82–85.

official support came his way, I describe the strategies that Tsiolkovskii and his supporters used to expand discourse on space travel in the face of little state support, specifically their formation of an informal, vibrant, and dynamic network that existed outside the parameters of the "traditional" and elite scientific world. This network was the crucial foundation upon which was built the edifice of the future Soviet space program.

SCIENCE AFTER THE REVOLUTION

The October Revolution had profound implications for the relationship between science and state in Russia. Given the Bol'sheviks' belief in the power of modern science and technology to improve social and economic conditions, it is not surprising that they had a very favorable attitude toward both the scientific community and the technical intelligentsia. Although Lenin and other high party officials considered most elite scientists bourgeois (and therefore ideologically suspect), they actively courted them because the new leaders wished to use the expertise of the scientific and technical community to stabilize the economy, especially during the years of the New Economic Policy (NEP). As a result, the government did much to improve the lives of scientists, such as providing food and fuel to the most needy.[9] Through the 1920s, the state allocated significant resources for scientific research, conferences, and publishing. In 1927, a state decree officially increased the salaries of all scientific workers. The government also established special honors such as the Lenin Prize to recognize the value of scientific work. Social backgrounds that would have been considered liabilities in other professions were frequently overlooked in the scientific profession because of the premium placed on scientific work.[10]

From the perspective of the scientific community, the most important change was the source of patronage: After the Revolution, no scientific work was funded by private sources, putting the elite scientific community effectively at the mercy of the new state. Most members of the Imperial Academy of Sciences greeted the October Revolution with marked hostility. During the anarchy of the Civil War and War Communism (the Russian economic system from 1918 to 1921, introduced by Lenin to combat the economic problems brought on by the Civil War), hundreds left the country while others who overtly supported the White Army were arrested. Many died from malnutrition or disease. Nevertheless, despite attacks from militant Bol'sheviks who considered the academy a remnant of the Tsarist system, the institution

[9] In December 1919, the *Sovnarkom* issued a decree, "On Improvement of Conditions for Scientific Specialists," that created a commission to oversee the process. G. A. Lakhtin, *Organizatsiia sovetskoi nauki: istoriia i sovremennost'* (Moscow: Nauka, 1990), 182–187.

[10] Nikolai Krementsov, *Stalinist Science* (Princeton: Princeton University Press, 1997), 17–18.

not only survived but thrived.[11] During the Civil War alone, over thirty new scientific institutions were created; scientists received "enormous support," allowing young scholars such as N. I. Vavilov (evolutionary theory), A. F. Ioffe, (physics), S. S. Chetverikov (genetics), N. K. Kol'tzov (biology), and others to initiate new innovative research.[12] The academy retained many of its former practices, such as its elitist pre-Revolutionary standards for entry into its membership. Historian Nikolai Krementsov argues that although the academy was "completely co-opted into the new system" by the end of the 1920s, its "[s]cientists enjoyed considerable authority and state support while preserving a high level of professional autonomy."[13] The academy's independence from Party directives was seriously compromised with a series of purges only in the late 1920s that cracked down on the old guard of intelligentsia.

By that time, as an alternative to the traditional academy system, the Bol'sheviks also created their "own" institution, the Socialist Academy of Social Sciences, formed by decree on July 13, 1918. Initially, the Socialist Academy focused on education in the social sciences but expanded in the mid-1920s into research into natural sciences, thus posing a direct threat to the supremacy of the Imperial Academy (renamed the USSR Academy in 1925). Many hardline Bol'sheviks believed that the Socialist Academy could be used to maintain strong ideological control over scientific research and eventually displace the older and more respected USSR Academy.[14] Unlike the latter, the new Socialist Academy placed less of a premium on degrees and titles, opening the door to many who might never have dreamed of entering the USSR Academy's ranks. For Tsiolkovskii, who had no formal education, the Socialist Academy presented the best chance for recognition from the scientific community after years of indifference during the Tsarist era.

"GENIUS AMONG THE MASSES"

In the many histories of the Soviet space program, both during and after the Soviet era, the Revolution plays a central role. State recognition of

[11] Vera Tolz, *Russian Academicians and the Revolution: Combining Professionalism and Politics* (London: St. Martin's Press, 1997); Alexander Vucinich, *Empire of Knowledge: The Academy of Sciences of the USSR, 1917–1970* (Berkeley: University of California Press, 1984); M. S. Bastrakova, *Stanovlenie sovetskoi sistemy organizatsii nauki, 1917–1922* (Moscow: Nauka, 1973).

[12] Zhores A. Medvedev, *Soviet Science* (New York: Norton, 1978), 10.

[13] Krementsov, *Stalinist Science*, 22.

[14] Michael David-Fox, *Revolution of the Mind: Higher Learning Among the Bolsheviks, 1918–1929* (Ithaca, NY: Cornell University Press, 1997), 192–253. The Socialist Academy of Social Sciences was renamed the Socialist Academy in 1922 and the Communist Academy in 1924. It was absorbed by the USSR Academy of Sciences in 1936.

Tsiolkovskii following 1917 served as surrogate for the notion that the new government patronized the idea of space exploration.[15] In this story, the first marker of state intervention is Tsiolkovskii's induction into the Socialist Academy in 1918. The second is the granting of a lifetime pension to Tsiolkovskii in 1921. This recognition seemed to indicate a new era of science in Russia, one that was not only less elite but also more visionary.

After the Revolution, even as Russian science was entering a transitional period, Tsiolkovskii remained insulated from the established scientific community. He had no contact with the USSR Academy and wrote mostly for the popular science audience rather than the more prestigious scientific elite. During the tumultuous year of 1917, Tsiolkovskii's single written comment about the events came in February, after the fall of the imperial regime, when he noted that "I greeted the Revolution with joy, with hope."[16] He wrote nothing about the Bol'shevik rise to power later in the year. Yet, after 1917, he made a concerted effort for recognition, motivated at least partially by financial considerations. His meager salary as a schoolteacher – his only regular source of income – afforded him barely enough to support a family that included two sons and two daughters (see Figure 3).[17]

Just two weeks after the public announcement of the establishment of the Socialist Academy, Tsiolkovskii sent a rambling handwritten letter in which he pleaded for a pension not only to pursue his research and writing, but also simply to feed himself and his family. Apart from cursory mention of his work on "scientific, technical, and social problems," he listed no qualifications or achievements. He described briefly the essence of an old science fiction story, "Beyond the Earth," recently published in the journal *Priroda i liudi* (*Nature and People*), saying that "[i]n the course of time, humanity would make use of the space around the Sun and disperse beyond the Earth." Rather opportunistically, Tsiolkovskii proposed that with the membership money, he would be able to finish a new work, a blueprint or constitution for the "ideal socialist reconstruction of humanity," which he noted was "rather close to the Soviet Constitution." If elected a member of the Academy, he promised to submit this important work in half a year so that it could be "published and disseminated" by the academy.[18] Less than a month later, the Socialist Academy sent Tsiolkovskii a letter informing him that it had formally approved his election as a junior member on August 25, 1918. The

[15] B. N. Vorob'ev and V. N. Sokol'skii, eds., *Pionery raketnoi tekhniki: Kibal'chich Tsiolkovskii Tsander Kondratiuk: izbrannye trudy* (Moscow: Nauka, 1964), 616.

[16] T. N. Zhelnina, *K. E. Tsiolkovskii (razvernutiia biokhronika zhizni i nauchnoi deiatel'nosti)* (Moscow: RAN, 1999), 73.

[17] Two of his children had already died – Leontii died from whooping cough in 1893 and Ignatii committed suicide in 1902. A third, daughter Mariia, lived with her husband from 1915 to 1929.

[18] GARF, 3415/1/44/417–418ob (July 30, 1918).

FIGURE 3. A picture of Tsiolkovskii's family from the early 1930s shows his wife, two daughters, and several grandchildren. Through much of the 1920s Tsiolkovskii and his family lived practically in destitute conditions, with barely enough to support his large extended family. Several of his offspring died young, although Tsiolkovskii expressed little remorse given his philosophical belief that death was nothing more than a transition from one state to another. [*Source*: Sergei Samburov]

honor came with a monthly salary of 300 rubles, roughly comparable to the average monthly wage of a factory worker.[19]

Due to poor health, Tsiolkovskii was unable to travel to Moscow to serve his term. He did, however, depend on money from the Socialist Academy; when it was late disbursing money in early 1919, he complained bitterly in a series of missives from Kaluga.[20] Unfortunately, the academy soon cut him off permanently; on July 1, 1919, less than one year after his election, the institution declined to re-elect him for another term, an event rarely mentioned by Russian space historians.[21] Tsiolkovskii's ejection from the Socialist Academy may have had to do with broader forces. As historian Michael David-Fox has noted, in 1919, the Socialist Academy underwent a crisis that resulted in a new charter and a "thoroughly revamped" membership. "Pacifist illusions" of the academy's first incarnation were abandoned

[19] GARF, 3415/1/44/419–419ob (August 26, 1918).
[20] GARF, 3415/1/44/429–429ob (January 16, 1919); GARF, 3415/1/44/430–430ob (March 22, 1919).
[21] ARAN, 555/3/4/1–2; GARF, 3415/1/44/431–32 (June 11, 1919).

in line with a new overwhelmingly Bol'shevik Marxist membership.[22] Tsiolkovskii, who was not a Marxist, let alone a Bol'shevik, did not fit into the picture. Tsiolkovskii's dismissal threw him once again into a near-destitute existence as the chaos of the Civil War began to rage throughout Russia.

Rejection from the Socialist Academy was followed by another difficult episode that remained hidden during the Soviet era because it undercut later claims of Bol'shevik recognition. On November 17, 1919, a month after the death of one of his sons (from peritonitis), two agents from the new Soviet secret police, the Extraordinary Commission (ChK or *Cheka*), showed up at his doorstep, took him to Moscow, and threw him in the notorious Lubianka prison. The *Cheka* had received information from a spy in Kiev, who himself had heard from captured White Guard sources that Tsiolkovskii was a member of a "rebel squad staff" and was providing agents of the Whites with information on the Red Army's plans on the eastern front. Although two interrogations and an in-depth investigation into the "Tsiolkovskii affair" led the *Cheka* agents to conclude that the scientist had nothing to do with the Whites, the police sentenced him to a one-year stay in a labor camp (for counter-revolutionaries) on the suspicion that he might be concealing an association with the Whites. Fortunately, before he could be sent to the camp, a high-ranking member of the *Cheka* ordered Tsiolkovskii's release, most likely because he found that Tsiolkovskii had been framed by a former associate who was "psychologically unstable." Tsiolkovskii was freed on December 2. Starving and in poor health, he wandered the streets of Moscow in search of the train station. When he arrived back in Kaluga two days later, his wife barely recognized him.[23]

Despite these hardships, Tsiolkovskii remained incredibly prolific through this period, writing numerous works on his favorite topic – metallic dirigibles – as well as on philosophy, astronomy, cosmology, and the future of humanity. The titles of a random selection of these works – "Why it's Difficult to Bring my Dirigibles to Life," "On Vesta: Conditions of Life on an Asteroid," "Stages of Humanity and Transformation of the Earth," and "Genius Among the Masses" – suggest a mind unencumbered by disciplinary boundaries. The latter essay was an a amplified version an earlier work written during the war, "Grief and Genius," which was a distillation of Tsiolkovskii's fascination with the role of "great men" (himself, of course,

[22] Michael David-Fox, "Symbiosis to Synthesis: The Communist Academy and the Bolshevization of the Russian Academy of Sciences, 1918–1929," *Jahrbücher für Geschichte Osteuropas* 46 no. 2 (1998): 219–243 (see p. 222). Tsiolkovskii was never a full member but a junior "competitor-member."

[23] GAKO, R-112/3/4/44; ARAN, 555/4/4/1–2 (May 4, 1920). Local trade union workers in Kaluga signed a petition on November 22, 1919, demanding that Tsiolkovskii be released because of his advanced age and poor health. For recent accounts of his arrest and incarceration, see Boris Sopel'niak, "13 dnei v podvalakh Lubianki," *Rodina* no. 9 (1994): 47–52; Zhelnina, *K. E. Tsiolkovskii*, 81–82.

one) in history in fostering social "progress," as well as the converse, that is, what kind of idealized social conditions lead to genius. With the exception of a handful of works, most of these writings remained unpublished. One of the few exceptions was the story *Vne zemli* (*Beyond the Earth*), which Tsiolkovskii published in Kaluga in August 1920 as a separate monograph. In wooden prose, Tsiolkovskii described how an international team of scientists built an Earth-orbiting spaceship on the one hundredth anniversary of the October Revolution. The names of the main heroes of the book probably reflected Tsiolkovskii's lack of literary imagination more than anything else: Franklin (from the United States), Newton (England), Laplace (France), Helmholtz (Germany), Galileo (Italy), and Ivanov (Russia) – a surrogate for himself. Although the story was one of the first post-Revolution science fiction novels published, the local Kaluga Society for the Study of Nature and Local Regions, not the state, financed its publication.[24]

If Tsiolkovskii did not receive much support from the government, he was fortunate to have dedicated followers such as the Kaluga Society and officials in the local Kaluga government. They persistently provided money to publish Tsiolkovskii's works and also publicized his contributions to aeronautics and the science of airship design. Both the society and the Kaluga *Guberniia* Economic Council (*Gubsovnarkhoz*) galvanized a network of supporters to petition the People's Commissariat of Enlightenment (*Narkompros*), the agency in charge of Soviet education and culture, to provide money for Tsiolkovskii's livelihood and work. Bolstered by renewed interest in his metal airship plans from the military, representatives from Kaluga went to Moscow to present their case to *Narkompros*, which, to their surprise, approved a 500,000 ruble award for Tsiolkovskii in August 1921. The order also specified that Tsiolkovskii's family be supplied with "an academic pension."[25] Because of hyperinflation during War Communism, prices had climbed to about 16,800 times the pre-World War II levels; Tsiolkovskii's half of a million rubles was an insignificant amount of money.

Narkompros forwarded the issue of the pension to the highest government body in the country, the Council of People's Commissars (*Sovnarkom*), who sent it down to the *Malyi sovnarkom* (Small Council of People's Commissars), a body established soon after the Revolution to deal with matters not considered important enough for the bigger *Sovnarkom*. On November 9, 1921, the *Malyi sovnarkom* issued a decree noting that, "[i]n view of the special contribution of the inventor-scientist, a specialist... in the field of scientific work on questions of aviation, K. E. Tsiolkovskii is named to

[24] Tsiolkovskii, *Vne zemli*. Tsiolkovskii began writing "Beyond the Earth" in 1896 and published a serialized and unfinished version in thirteen consecutive issues of the journal *Priroda i liudi* in 1918.

[25] GARF, 2306/1/511/13. Silvana Malle, *The Economic Organization of War Communism, 1918–1921* (Cambridge, UK: Cambridge University Press, 1985).

receive a lifetime pension of the sum of five hundred thousand rubles . . . per month."[26] Almost every biography of Tsiolkovskii prominently mentions this decree as evidence of Lenin's personal intervention to support the scientist, but the reality is that Lenin had nothing to do with the decision.[27]

There is incomplete evidence on whether Tsiolkovskii received any money from the central government. In November 1921, the same month the decree was issued, Tsiolkovskii quit his job as a teacher, partly as a result of his poor health and probably because of the expectation of a monthly pension. Three months later, he complained that he had not received any money from the government and was told that there was not an "appropriate fund" from which to allot money for the scientist. Tsiolkovskii and his family were close to starvation at this point, surviving on five loaves of bread per month.[28] Of his seven children, four died by 1923 as a result of health problems. Two further decrees, one from the Kaluga *Gubsovnarkhoz* in May 1922 and one from the national *Sovnarkhoz* in February 1923, again called for providing a monthly salary to Tsiolkovskii.[29] In the end, Tsiolkovskii received a paltry amount from the central government, but fortunately local Kaluga authorities provided him with an irregular stipend. Through much of the 1920s, Tsiolkovskii supported himself by augmenting the Kaluga stipend with sporadic subsidies from various aeronautics organizations interested in supporting his ideas for metallic airships or private individuals.

Although estranged from both the state and the established scientific community, Tsiolkovskii's name did achieve a certain level of currency among a technically minded audience. His scientific reputation and popularity rested, however, not so much on his contributions to rocketry and spaceflight – he published no journal articles on space exploration before 1930 – but on his numerous meditations on the science of building metallic dirigibles.

[26] GARF, R-130/5/291/4, 19 (November 9, 1921). N. D. Anoshchenko, an aide to the chief of *Glavvozdukhoflot* (Soviet Air Force), remembers a different sequence of events. He later claimed that Tsiolkovskii had written letters in the autumn of 1921 to him and N. I. Shabashev, another aide to the chief of *Glavvozdukhoflot*, with a plea for financial help. Impressed by Tsiolkovskii's qualifications, the two men, on behalf of *Glavvozdukhoflot* and *Aviadarm*, petitioned the USSR *Sovnarkom* for a lifetime pension and a scientist's salary for Tsiolkovskii. Anoshchenko claims it was this petition that led to the 1921 decree. N. D. Anoshchenko, "Priznanie prioreta," in *V vospominaniiakh sovremennikov*, 71–73.

[27] The topic of the pension award was among nineteen issues discussed during the meeting of the *Malyi sovnarkom* on November 9, 1921. GARF, R-130/5/291/1–20 (November 9, 1921). With regards to claims of Lenin's personal role, see, for example, M. F. Rebrov and A. V. Tkachev, *Moskva-kosmos* (Moscow: Moskovskii rabochii, 1983), 54–55; K. N. Altaiskii, "Tsiolkovskii o Lenine . . . ," in *Vperedi svoego veka*, ed. I. S. Korochentseva (Moscow: Mashinostroenie, 1970), 95–99. Lenin's signature was one of several on the decree but Lenin was not chairman (or even a member) of the *Malyi sovnarkom*.

[28] ARAN, 555/4/4/6 (February 4, 1922). "Five loaves of bread" is from ARAN, 555/2/4/1–3 (May 1, 1928). For Tsiolkovskii's summary of his lack of success in obtaining the pension, see ARAN, 4/14/198/129–30.

[29] GAKO, R-156/1/3631/12.

This distinction is crucial in understanding his relationship to the state in post-Revolutionary Russia, but it is rarely, if ever, mentioned in his posthumous biographies.[30] Between 1917 and his death in 1935, of the roughly 120 works (about forty monographs and eighty articles) he wrote and published, at least one-fourth were explicitly on the design and construction of metallic airships. By comparison, only one-eighth focused on rocketry or space exploration. The remainder were dominated by pseudo-mystical meditations on the physical and spatial future of humanity stemming from the philosophy of Cosmism; a smaller number were divided between aeronautics, physics, philosophy, political science, biology, evolution, linguistics, astronomy, and science fiction.

"THE FATE OF THINKERS"

The economic hardships that Tsiolkovskii faced in the aftermath of the Bol'shevik Revolution were not atypical for the average Soviet citizen. Civil War and famine decimated a generation of Russians and threw them into abject poverty. Thousands searched for food and work and lived destitute lives. However, among the scientific and technical intelligentsia, his experience was an anomaly; although the Civil War had taken a steep toll among scientific workers, the community as a whole rebounded very quickly after 1920, helped by generous support from the Bol'sheviks. Tsiolkovskii on the other hand, lay essentially adrift; his life's work remained in limbo, unrecognized beyond a small Russian audience, and his airship project was going nowhere. Pensions that the government promised were never delivered. Continuing poverty affected his health and that of his family. In January 1922, Tsiolkovskii's daughter Anna died from tuberculosis. A year later, in June 1923, his son Aleksandr committed suicide, the third of his offspring to pass away in four years.[31]

Given these circumstances, Tsiolkovskii could be forgiven for feeling bitter by what appeared in the daily edition of *Izvestiia* one morning in late October 1923. On page four under the rubric "News of Science and Technology," an anonymous author had written a short article, noting that a new book, "Rocket to the Planets" [sic] had just been published in Munich. The book's author, a Professor Hermann Oberth, had found that, using a "strict mathematical and physical path" and "with the aid of our modern technology, it is possible to achieve space velocity and overcome the forces of Earth's gravity." Dramatically (and incorrectly), the author declared that Oberth's

[30] In one biography published during Tsiolkovskii's life, thirty of sixty-three pages are devoted to airships and aeronautics. By comparison, thirteen pages are dedicated to rocketry and spaceflight. Ia. I. Perel'man, *Tsiolkovskii: ego zhizn', izobreteniia i nauchnye trudy* (Leningrad: GTTI, 1932).

[31] Zhelnina, *K. E. Tsiolkovskii*, 168–169.

book gave a theoretical foundation to the work of the "American professor Goddard, who recently presented a sensational plan to send a rocket to the Moon." The remainder of the article provided a fairly accurate synopsis of the book, noting that Oberth had touched on human spaceflight, artificial satellites around the earth capable of military action, and space travel to other planets. The author did not mention Tsiolkovskii or his works.[32]

Bitter that in his own country his contributions to spaceflight theory and rocketry had gone unrecognized, Tsiolkovskii entered into a struggle to establish his priority in the field. This was not the first time that he had had to do so, nor would it be the last, but it would have profound implications for the popularization of spaceflight in Soviet Russia.[33] Soon after *Izvestiia*'s brief note appeared in print, Tsiolkovskii's devotees wrote to uphold Russian priority in rocketry and spaceflight theory. Aleksandr Modestov, the erstwhile chairman of Kaluga's Association of Naturalists who had defended Tsiolkovskii's work on airships against critics, wrote a lengthy letter to *Izvestiia* that the newspaper published three weeks after the original piece on Oberth. In it, Modestov criticized *Izvestiia* for ignoring Tsiolkovskii's preeminence in this work, punctuating his narrative with references to publicists such as Riumin, Vorob'ev, and Perel'man who had done much in the pre-Revolutionary years to underscore the scientific validity of the Tsiolkovskii's work.[34] *V masterskoi prirody* (*In Nature's Workshop*) editor Iakov Perel'man, the active popularizer of spaceflight, also published a note in its next issue that underlined Tsiolkovskii's 1903 article as the very first contribution to "interplanetary flight with rocket-type apparatuses."[35] A local paper in Kaluga, *Kommuna* (Commune), made much the same point, adding that "after 20 years . . . European science is literally confirming the conclusions of our native scholar."[36]

[32] "Novosti nauki i tekhniki: neuzheli ne utopiia?," *Izvestiia VTsIK*, October 2, 1923. The author later revealed himself as "Engineer F. Davydov." The correct title of Oberth's book, published in June 1923, was *Die Rakete zu den Planetenräumen* (The Rocket into Interplanetary Space).

[33] In 1905, Tsiolkovskii had read in the newspaper *Birzhevye vedomosti* (*Stock Exchange Bulletin*) about a Swedish engineer who proposed the use of "reactive engines" on "flying mines" during battles. Tsiolkovskii wrote to the paper claiming priority for conceiving the rocket, although he emphasized that he was only interested in its peaceful applications. Later, in 1914, a Russian, K. E. Veigelin, published an article in *Priroda i liudi* giving priority to the French astronautics pioneer Robert Esnault-Pelterie for being the first to propose using liquid rockets to reach and explore space. Samoilovich, *Grazhdanin vselennoi*, 72, 80–81.

[34] A. P. Modestov, "Novosti nauki i tekhniki: izobretenie K. E. Tsiolkovskogo (pis'mo v redaktsiiu)," *Izvestiia VTsIK*, October 24, 1923.

[35] "Raketa k planetam," *V masterskoi prirody* no. 7 (1923): 61–62. In 1919, this journal published an article by Perel'man that may have been the first on space exploration published in Russia after the Revolution. "Za predely atmosfery," *V masterskoi prirody* nos. 5–6 (1919): 25–32.

[36] E. R., "Raketa k planetam," *Kommuna*, November 9, 1923.

Tsiolkovskii acted too. He decided to reissue his 1903 article (with some changes and corrections) as a thirty-two-page brochure under a new title, *Raketa v kosmicheskoe prostranstvo* (*The Rocket into Cosmic Space*), a deliberate alteration that reflected his need to counter Oberth's "Rocket into Interplanetary Space." His friends paid for the printing run and helped to edit the text. On November 12, 1923, just forty-one days after the original *Izvestiia* article, Tsiolkovskii sent the manuscript to the local Kaluga printers. In a new introductory essay entitled "The Fate of Thinkers or Twenty Years on Trial," Tsiolkovskii clumsily mixed bitterness with hubris, comparing his difficult struggle for recognition with the fortunes of such great scientists as Lamarck (mocked by the French Academy), Galileo (persecuted by the Catholic Church), Kepler (imprisoned), Bruno (burned at the stake), Darwin (denounced by the French Academy), Copernicus (delayed recognition), Gutenberg (who died in poverty), and others.[37] He waxed poetic that "European science" had finally confirmed what he had known for decades, that it was technically possible to achieve space travel. He cautioned that it would be decades before anybody ever broke through the atmosphere and centuries before the reality of flight to the Moon. But with his characteristic self-aggrandizing nature, Tsiolkovskii was not shy in emphasizing his future role, exclaiming that "the subject has been fired up, and I lit this fire!"[38] Not content simply to reach a Russian audience, Tsiolkovskii had his friend, the young intellectual Aleksandr Chizhevskii, write an introductory essay in German in which he lamented, "Do we always have to get from foreigners what originated in our boundless homeland and died in loneliness from neglect?"[39]

The printers formally issued the brochure on December 13, but because of paper shortages in Kaluga, they published only a few at the time; the whole run of a thousand copies appeared only in March 1924. Immediately, Chizhevskii took the lion's share of copies to Moscow; by the following month, these were either on sale in various bookstores in Moscow or in the hands of "editors and scholars" as gifts from Chizhevskii.[40] Because the copies were easily available, a vast array of Soviet publications made particular note of Tsiolkovskii in the mid-1920s, thus underscoring his contribution to the theory of space travel. These publications served as the principal sources of information that sustained and fed an informal, vibrant, and dynamic network of space enthusiasts that flourished outside the boundaries of the elite scientific community.

37 K. Tsiolkovskii, "Sud'ba myslitelei ili dvadtsat' let pod spudom," in *Raketa v kosmicheskoe prostranstvo*, IV–VI.

38 Ibid., V–VI.

39 Tshijewsky, "Anstatt eines Vorworts."

40 ARAN, 555/4/689/9 (April 6, 1924); ARAN, 555/4/689/23 (November 17, 1925).

ALTERNATIVE NETWORKS

Most members of the established Soviet scientific community, bolstered by significant financial commitments from the state, enjoyed the benefits of scientific equipment, foreign literature, travel abroad, and publishing. These activities created formal scientific networks that were reinforced by state-sponsored scientific conferences and congresses through the decade. Tsiolkovskii, a self-taught anomaly ignored by the state, could not make use of these established networks. His new mission to establish his priority as a theoretician of space exploration led him instead to use an alternative network of science – disconnected from the academy system – that fostered substantial exchange of information and useful debate on the possibility of space travel. The constituents of this network included voluntary scientific societies, laypersons with little or no qualifications, international correspondents (primarily in Germany), and influential popular science writers. The network's principal modes of communication were neither conferences nor meetings at research institutes but rather personal letters and privately financed publications.

Tsiolkovskii and the Societies

Tsiolkovskii communicated with several scientific societies in the 1920s. Most were registered with *Glavnauka*, the scientific department of *Narkompros*, but sustained themselves with a combination of state subsidies and private membership dues. None had strong ties with the established academic scientific system, and some, like the Association of (Self-Educated) Naturalists, were hostile to it. The association's members declared after its first meeting in October 1918 that it was a "vital necessity to unite... non-caste (*vnekastovykh*) toilers of science, who until recently, because of a caste scientific monopoly, could not systematically... do scientific work due to the absence of necessary condition[s] and material resources."[41] Although the association did not explicitly study space travel, through the 1920s, it helped bring Tsiolkovskii's name to a broader audience by sponsoring public dialogues over the scientific merits of his various airship designs. The new Moscow Society of Astronomy Enthusiasts (*Moskovskogo obshchestva liubitelei astronomii*, or MOLA) also sponsored a number of lectures on space travel and communicated with Tsiolkovskii. In 1925, the society, under the mistaken belief that the American rocket scientist Robert Goddard was

[41] ARAN, 4/14/198/73–74; The Association, which was supported by *Narkompros*, was dissolved in 1928 at the tail end of a struggle between *Glavnauka*, which had strongly supported pre-Revolutionary scientific societies, and the scientific-technical department of *Vesenkha*, which supported a more practical approach to science and technology. Andrews, *Science for the Masses*, 43–44.

coming to Moscow, wrote to Tsiolkovskii asking his advice on questions to ask the foreigner.[42] Another society, the pre-Revolutionary Russian Society of Amateur Enthusiasts for the Study of the World (ROLM), also focused its activities in promoting Tsiolkovskii's ideas on spaceflight. In 1923, a member of the ROLM's Odessa branch recommended Tsiolkovskii's works to a fifteen-year-old astronomy enthusiast named Valentin Glushko, who immediately wrote to the scientist to exchange books on space. The young man was so captivated by Tsiolkovskii's cause that he devoted his life to it; later he designed the rocket engines that propelled *Sputnik* into orbit in 1957.[43]

One of the most important nodes in Tsiolkovskii's network was the Moscow-based Zhukovskii Academy's Society for the Study of Interplanetary Communications (OIMS), which elected Tsiolkovskii as a member and frequently communicated with the old man in 1924 and 1925. Like other interplanetary societies of the period, its members studied his writings and treated him as the patron saint of their cause. They also helped to disseminate his word by purchasing copies of his books for the school library because the "demand for them was [so] great," thereby making his writings available to a generation of students at the Zhukovskii Academy."[44] Tsiolkovskii in turn advised them on how best to popularize ideas about spaceflight via lectures, journals, and even movies. Inspired by Tsiolkovskii, the society solicited articles for a journal named *Raketa* (*Rocket*) projected to include serious theoretical works on interplanetary travel and related fields such as astronomy, physics, chemistry, and aeronautics. Although the society never published the journal, members exchanged many of the articles submitted for it and engaged in substantive debate over them.[45]

Individuals

Tsiolkovskii communicated not only with such registered scientific societies but also with individuals. In his personal papers, there are several thousand letters from over 700 separate individuals from all walks of life. The list of self-identifiers included, among many others, "mining engineer," "anti-religious person," "metalworker," "judge," "telegraph supervisor,"

[42] ARAN, 555/3/135/3–3ob (December 10, 1925).

[43] V. P. Glushko, "Rozhdenie mechty i pervye shagi (avtobiograficheskii ocherk)," in V. P. Glushko, *Put' v raketnoi tekhnike: izbrannye trudy, 1924–1946* (Moscow: Mashinostroenie, 1977), 460–462.

[44] ARAN, 555/4/356/2–3ob (May 4, 1924).

[45] ARAN, 555/4/356/6–7 (May 21, 1924); ARAN, 555/3/102a/6 (June 4, 1924). For texts of the articles, see ARAN, 4/14/194/1–8, 15–25. The first issue would have featured eleven articles by Tsiolkovskii, Tsander, Kramarov, Vetchinkin, Mikhailov, Rezunov, Chernov, Perel'man, Sharonov, and Kaperskii. ARAN, 4/14/196/34–35ob.

"bookseller," "military official," and "amateur inventor."[46] Not all of the letters centered on spaceflight, but nearly all covered scientific or philosophical issues. Many people wrote to keep Tsiolkovskii abreast of scientific developments outside of his purview. For example, a Russian poet living in New York sent him cuttings from newspapers about the most modern airships in the United States.[47] In one memorable instance, Tsiolkovskii received over 200 letters from people offering information after he wrote an article in a newspaper about a meteor that might have streaked over the Moscow skies in May 1934.[48] A student circle at the Leningrad Polytechnical Institute wrote to ask him for copies of his books so that they could build their own rocket-plane.[49] School librarians wrote to him asking for copies of his self-published works, which were hard to find.[50]

Others wrote about scientific ideas: One writer agreed with Tsiolkovskii's thoughts on generating artificial gravity in space whereas another asked him to devote attention to forms of rocket propulsion in the future.[51] Many of these "scientific" letters were from individuals without any formal higher education who felt free to speculate – often intelligently – about interplanetary journeys, how to feed space travelers, or how to cool rocket engines; these were topics that would have been considered unworthy of elite science at the time. Although some correspondents doubted the veracity of his ideas, overall, the letters underscore both the advantages and pitfalls of unregulated scientific discourse: On the one hand, people felt free to discuss fruitful ideas that would have been ridiculed by members of the USSR Academy of Sciences, while on the other hand, their flights of fancy were sometimes full of misconceptions and often ridiculous. Remarkably, his papers contain no letters from within the academy's research network.

Tsiolkovskii and Self-Publishing

Apart from letters, Tsiolkovskii used the medium of self-publishing as a way to communicate and establish his priority in the new field of astronautics. In addition to the numerous publications on philosophy and natural sciences, Tsiolkovskii self-published seven short monographs on rocketry and space exploration between 1927 and 1932. Each contained thoughtful technical ideas on the design of rockets and spaceships, including meditations on

46 These letters are collected in the files between *delo* 35 and *delo* 743 (inclusive) in ARAN, f. 555, op. 4.

47 ARAN, 555/4/125/6 (February 10, 1931).

48 For these letters, see ARAN, f. 555, op. 4, d. 744 to 956a. The meteor allegedly flew over western Russia on May 14, 1934. Tsiolkovskii published an article on the incident in *Izvestiia* six days later.

49 ARAN, 555/4/226/2 (March 19, 1930).

50 ARAN, 555/3/199/13–13ob (November 30, 1929).

51 Letters from "I. G. G." and "Z. Kh." reproduced in K. Tsiolkovskii, *Stratoplan polureaktivnyi* (Kaluga: K. E. Tsiolkovskii, 1932), 29–30.

multistage rockets (which he called "rocket trains") and spaceplanes, that is, aircraft that could take off and fly straight into space.[52] Besides the technical content of these works, he included appendices in these monographs as a way of reasserting his priority in the absence of official recognition. In the appendices, he republished excerpts from older works as proof that his ideas on spaceflight dated back to the 1890s – even if they were casually mentioned in fiction.[53] In each of his publications, he provided his home address and invited readers' responses, which he would then publish in appendices of subsequent publications. In one case, he devoted an entire monograph, *Otkliki literaturnye* (*Literary Response*) to readers' views.[54] The balance of power in the communication between the so-called patriarch and his eager devotees obviously favored the former, but the process engendered insightful discussions about space travel, which, judging by the letters he published, generated enormous interest.[55] Tsiolkovskii privileged comments from abroad; votes of confidence from individuals in Germany, Austria, and England not only bolstered his claims for preeminence but also served as veiled statements to his domestic audience that even foreigners had recognized what the Soviet scientific establishment was unwilling to do. Tsiolkovskii most effectively expanded his network by including in his publications lists of "scientists working on the problem of space flight," with their full addresses. The strategy allowed readers to get in touch with each other, which not only expanded the network but also facilitated communication that bypassed the center.[56]

Tsiolkovskii Abroad

Just as prominent scientists working in the academy system might have contacts with foreign scientists, Tsiolkovskii's network extended overseas. For

[52] *Kosmicheskaia raketa. Opytnaia podgotovka* (Kaluga: K. E. Tsiolkovskii, 1927); *Kosmicheskie raketnye poezda. Reaktivnyi dvigatel'* (Kaluga: Sektsii nauchnykh rabotnikov, 1929); *Tseli zvezdoplavaniia* (Kaluga: K. E. Tsiolkovskii, 1929); *Novyi aeroplan. Za atmosferoi zemli. Reaktivnyi dvigatel'* (Kaluga: K. E. Tsiolkovskii, 1929); *Zvezdoplavateliam* (Kaluga: K. E. Tsiolkovskii, 1930); *Reaktivnyi aeroplan* (Kaluga: K. E. Tsiolkovskii, 1930); *Stratoplan polureaktivnyi.*

[53] For example, in 1926, he republished an excerpt from a science fiction story originally published in 1896, "Dreams of the Earth and Heavens," as an appendix to a larger theoretical work. "Slabaia tiazhest'. Otryvok iz moei knigi 'Grezy i zemle i nebe.' 1985 g.," in Tsiolkovskii, *Issledovanie mirovykh prostranstv* (1926), 118–125.

[54] K. E. Tsiolkovskii, *Otkliki literaturnye* (Kaluga: K. E. Tsiolkovskii, 1928). For appendices devoted to readers' responses in other monographs, see Tsiolkovskii, *Kosmicheskaia raketa*, 22–24; *Proshedshee zemli* (Kaluga: K. E. Tsiolkovskii, 1928), 17–21; *Liubov' k samomu sebe, ili istinnoe sebialiubie* (Kaluga: K. E. Tsiolkovskii, 1928), 33–39.

[55] See, for example, the many letters published in Tsiolkovskii, *Stratoplan polureaktivnyi*, 19–32.

[56] See, for example, "Uchenye, rabotaiushchie, nad problemnoi kosmicheskogo poleta," in Tsiolkovskii, *Issledovanie mirovykh prostranstv* (1926), 126–127.

many years, Aleksandr Shershevskii, a Russian citizen based in Germany who had written a number of popular articles on space travel in German, served as an intermediary between Tsiolkovskii and German enthusiasts. Shershevskii established contact with Oberth and even served briefly as the German's assistant during nascent rocketry experiments in the late 1920s. Shershevskii was not someone easy to like. Oberth described him as not only "the second laziest man [he had] ever met," but "a Russian emigrant... who lived... completely in filth. And fairly literally at that. I had the impression that, if one threw him against the wall, he would stick there."[57] Shershevskii's own countrymen evidently shared such views. One Soviet engineer, who knew him in the 1930s, remembered him as "a man in whom wide reading and an implausible talent for doing nothing – a kind of pathological laziness – was combined in the most astonishing way."[58] Despite these burdens, Shershevskii not only informed Tsiolkovskii about his standing in the nascent German space community, but he also disseminated Tsiolkovskii's works in that country.

Shershevskii's correspondence with Tsiolkovskii was the key medium by means of which the scientist found out whether the import of his early works on spaceflight had penetrated into the European zeitgeist. Shershevskii had written to Tsiolkovskii once – as early as 1921 – telling him about German interest in the topic. Later, after the publication of Oberth's book and subsequent German works in the mid-1920s, he wrote again to the scientist in early 1926 with news of Oberth and Goddard. Like many others taken by Tsiolkovskii's works, he had an almost religious fervor for the old man, calling him the "prophet of interplanetary communications." He regularly informed Tsiolkovskii of the German space community's rising curiosity about the Russian's work, telling the scientist that newspapers in Germany were " 'chirping' quite a bit about [Tsiolkovskii's] works" and that many "were preoccupied with such peculiar rumors" about Tsiolkovskii, including the sensational news that the scientist was about to "build a rocket in Moscow for 11 people."[59]

Because of his bilingual skills, Shershevskii served as the most important conduit for information between Tsiolkovskii and the German space community. He was, however, not the only link. In an exhaustive study of the contacts between Tsiolkovskii and German enthusiasts in the 1920s, Russian historian T. N. Zhelnina found that after 1920, Tsiolkovskii wrote fifty letters in response to no less than fifty-six letters from Germany. Most of the

57 Oberth quoted in Michael Neufeld, *The Rocket and the Reich: Peenemunde and the Coming of the Ballistic Missile Era* (Cambridge, MA: Harvard University Press, 1995), 10–11.

58 Boris V. Rauschenbach, *Hermann Oberth: The Father of Space Flight* (New York: West-Art, 1994), 65.

59 Tsiolkovskii published excerpts from Shershevskii's letters to him in one of his monographs. See K. E. Tsiolkovskii, *Um i strasti* (Kaluga: K. E. Tsiolkovskii, 1928), 21–24. See also ARAN, 555/4/698/22–22ob (November 8, 1926).

German letters (twenty of them) were from Shershevskii, with the remainder split between Robert W. E. Lademann (twelve) and Willy Ley (ten), two well-known popularizers of spaceflight in Germany.[60] In response, Tsiolkovskii actively tried to disseminate his works abroad. Between 1922 and 1934, he sent at least eighty copies of thirty-four different monographs to eighteen German addressees. Recipients, apart from the aforementioned, included spaceflight theoretician Walter Hohmann, "skeptic" Hans Lorenz, pyrotechnist and rocketry enthusiast Friederich Sander, and the automobile tycoon Fritz von Opel, as well as several libraries. With the notable exceptions of Lademann and Ley, few in the German or European space community read Russian. Because none of Tsiolkovskii's works was published in German during his lifetime, what these three said about Tsiolkovskii determined his standing abroad to a large degree.[61]

Did this network affect produce any substantive scientific breakthroughs? A few examples would seem to suggest so. For example, Tsiolkovskii had produced crude conceptions of multistage rockets in an early science fiction novella in the pre-Revolutionary years. However, he remained unconvinced of their efficacy until he read of Oberth's sophisticated work on the topic, passed on to him by Shershevskii in 1929. Tsiolkovskii immediately developed new mathematical ideas on multistage rockets that he presented in a self-published brochure, *Kosmicheskie raketnye poezda* (*Cosmic Rocket Trains*), issued the same year.[62] This monograph would have a profound imprint on the future Soviet space program because it was used as a starting point for conceptions of the rocket that put *Sputnik* into space. In his post-Revolutionary work, Tsiolkovskii also focused attention on determining the form of a vehicle that would lift off from the Earth and reach up to space. By the 1920s, he began to investigate extending the abilities of an airplane so it could fly *directly* into the cosmos. Again, the idea was not new. A Soviet engineer of Latvian origin named Fridrikh Tsander had started research on this idea as early as the first decade of the twentieth century, and he published an article on a "spaceplane" in 1924.[63] A German, Max Valier, also supported this technological option and, like Tsander, published on the idea in Germany in 1926. Tsiolkovskii had initially explored the idea in unpublished scribblings, but Tsander's meditations on the topic – as well

[60] T. N. Zhelnina, "K. E. Tsiolkovskii i pionery kosmonavtiki germanii," in *Trudy XXVII chtenii, posviashchennykh razrabotke nauchnogo nalslediia i razvitiiu idei K. E. Tsiolkovskogo (Kaluga, 15–18 Sentiabria 1992 g.): Sektsiia 'Issledovanie nauchnogo tvorchestva K. E. Tsiolkovskogo i istoriia aviatsiia i kosmonavtika'* (Moscow: IET AN SSSR, 1994), 3–55.

[61] On at least two occasions in 1927, Tsiolkovskii tried to publish his seminal 1926 monograph *Issledovanie mirovykh prostranstv reaktivnymi priborami* (Investigation of Cosmic Spaces with Reactive Devices) in Munich but failed. See Tsiolkovskii, *Um i strasti*, 23–24, 27; ARAN, 555/2/46/1–2; ARAN, 555/3/137/1–6; ARAN, 555/4/340/1–3.

[62] Tsiolkovskii, *Kosmicheskie raketnye poezda*.

[63] F. A. Tsander, "Perelety na drugie planety," *Tekhnika i zhizn'* no. 13 (1924): 15–16.

as Valier's ideas that were transmitted to Tsiolkovskii via his international network – prompted him to revisit the idea in the late 1920s.[64]

Other Nodes: Perel'man and Rynin

Beyond Tsiolkovskii, the two science popularizers Iakov Perel'man and Nikolai Rynin, both based in Leningrad, served as major nodes of Tsiolkovskii's alternative network. As the archetype of the popular science writer, Perel'man clearly grasped the science, wrote very clearly and succinctly, and believed in the power of modern science as a panacea for all social ills. After 1917, Perel'man continued and expanded his pre-Revolutionary work on popularizing science, extending his highly popular sciences "for entertainment" series into the Communist era. His unqualified technological enthusiasm perfectly aligned with the Bol'sheviks' visions of the role of science and technology in the new socialist state; the latter recruited him to write nearly two dozen math and physics text books for higher technical schools, and he played a major part in the introduction of the metric system into the Soviet educational system. In addition he continued his various editorial and writing duties. Already by the mid-1920s, Perel'man had written about a thousand articles and thirty books, which had had a total run of 1,300,000.

When the mass interest in spaceflight escalated sharply in 1924, Perel'man already had all the tools to disseminate his positivistic view of space exploration; by then, his classic *Mezhplanetnye puteshestviia* (*Interplanetary Voyages*) was in its *fifth* edition, the first having been published in 1915. As the editor of *Priroda i liudi* from 1901 to 1918 and *V masterskoi prirody* (*In Nature's Workshop*) from 1919 to 1924, and then as head of the mathematics and physics section of *Vestnik znaniia* (*Journal of Knowledge*) in the late 1920s, Perel'man was in an influential position to bring the news to the masses. His sixty plus articles and nearly twenty books (which included numerous editions) on spaceflight underscore his ability to communicate both the wonder and the science of the topic. He also wrote one of the very first biographies of Tsiolkovskii, published in 1932, before there was any state recognition of Tsiolkovskii's contribution to the theory of space travel. The book attached the descriptor, "patriarch" of astronautics, to Tsiolkovskii.[65] Perel'man's credo might be best be summarized by his comparison of two views on space travel in 1931, the first of which "consider[s] that such [flights] are absolutely unrealizable," and the second of which

[64] Shershevskii wrote to Tsiolkovskii about Valier's conception of a rocket-plane in 1926–1927. See ARAN, 555/4/698/25–30 (December 8, 1927); Tsiolkovskii, *Um i strasti*, 23. For Valier's publication on the topic, see Max Valier, "Vom Flugzeug zum Weltraumschiff," *Münchener Illustrierte Presse* no. 49 (1926): 1170.

[65] Perel'man, *Tsiolkovskii*, 8.

claims that spaceflight is "quite close to a solution." Perel'man noted that "[b]oth points of view are extreme, and far from reality."[66]

The other popularizer, Nikolai Rynin, came late to spaceflight but had better credentials. A prolific writer (he published more than 270 works), Rynin arrived at the topic as an established scholar in the field of aeronautics. He wrote a number of important textbooks in the pre-Revolutionary era that trained a generation of Soviet aeronautical engineers. Besides founding the discipline of engineering graphics in the Soviet Union, during his thirty years of teaching at the Leningrad Institute of Transportation Engineers and, after 1930, at the Leningrad Institute of Civil Aviation Fleet Engineers, Rynin popularized aviation in Russia. In 1908, he organized the country's first student aeronautics club and published a very popular journal for enthusiasts, *Aeromobil*. He also played an instrumental role in setting up civilian air transportation in the Soviet Union in the 1920s through surveying, designing, and studying the cost effectiveness of various burgeoning air routes.[67] Although he was aware of the general contours of the discourse from the 1910s, Rynin began writing about space travel only in the late 1920s in both scientific journals and daily newspapers such as *Izvestiia*, *Komsomol'skaia pravda*, *Krasnaia zvezda*, *Leningradskaia pravda*, and *Vecherniaia krasnaia gazeta*.

Beyond more than forty articles he wrote on spaceflight, Rynin's most enduring work is the nine-volume encyclopedia he produced on space exploration, *Mezhplanetnye soobshcheniia* (*Interplanetary Communications*). Published between 1928 and 1932, these volumes totaled 1,608 pages, constituting the most comprehensive works on the past, present, and future of space travel produced in the world until the 1950s. A British reviewer in 1956 called it "[a work] quite unchallenged."[68] Rynin described everything from myths and ancient stories about cosmic voyages (Volume 1) to the history of rocketry (Volume 4), and from the theory of rocket motion (Volume 5) to the mathematics of astronavigation (Volume 9). Unlike Perel'man, Rynin engaged in rigorous mathematical analyses of rocket and spacecraft technology. He devoted an entire volume to Tsiolkovskii and his works (Volume 7), which he held in particularly high esteem. Published in 1931, this volume provided the first serious analysis of Tsiolkovskii's space-related ideas.

Because Rynin was multilingual, he was able to keep abreast of information published in the West and then, via his encyclopedia, to disseminate

[66] Ia. Perel'man, "Sovremennoe sostoianie zvezdoplavaniia," *Vestnik znaniia* no. 7 (April 10, 1931): 367–368.

[67] These included *Kurs vozdukhoplavaniia* (Course in Aeronautics) in 1910 and *Teoriia aviatsii* (Theory of Aviation) in 1916. B. F. Tarasov, *Nikolai Alekseevich Rynin* (Moscow: Nauka, 1990).

[68] From G. V. Thompson's three-part review, still the best overview of the encyclopedia in the English language. "A Famous Russian Encyclopedia of Astronautics," *Journal of the British Interplanetary Society* 13 (1954): 193–202, 301–313; and 15 (1956): 82–91.

a massive amount of information on foreign achievements to Soviet audiences. Almost an entire generation of young Soviet space enthusiasts (many of whom later contributed to the USSR's postwar space program) read the complete translated works of Oberth, Goddard, Esnault-Pelterie, Hohmann, Valier, and Noordung in Rynin's encyclopedia. Similarly, Rynin kept Soviet readers well apprised of German developments, such as the founding of the famous German rocketry society *Verein für Raumschiffahrt* (VfR). Through correspondence, Rynin provided Soviet theorists of space exploration, particularly Tsiolkovskii, with his personal perspectives on how their work was being received both at home and abroad. Tsiolkovskii in turn sent out copies of encyclopedias to his correspondents abroad.[69]

Both Rynin and Perel'man also received information from Soviet readers that they passed on, either in publication or by letter, to others. In the final volume of his encyclopedia, Rynin underscored how he benefited through correspondence with more than 300 readers "from remote parts of the USSR, [who] suppl[ied] remarks and additions and often describ[ed] their own, valuable and interesting researches in the field of rocket propulsion and the history of interplanetary travel."[70]

The two men played key roles in expanding the network overseas. For example, both actively communicated with all the major figures in the field in Europe and the United States, including the reclusive Robert Goddard.[71] Using information from several letters from Goddard, often with long quotations from the American himself, Perel'man consistently tried to dispel some of the misconceptions in the Soviet media about Goddard's alleged Moon shot in the Soviet media (see Figure 4).[72] In several articles and books, Perel'man summarized American work on rocketry based upon his careful analysis of the various *Bulletins of the American Interplanetary Society* (formed in 1930) and letters from Goddard. In most of these accounts, Perel'man recognized and promoted Goddard as the most important American pioneer of rocketry.[73]

[69] See, for example, ARAN, 555/4/548/7 (June 20, 1926); ARAN, 555/4/548/14 (April 10, 1927); ARAN, 555/4/548/12 (April 30, 1927). On sending copies abroad, see ARAN, 555/3/200/6 (March 2, 1934); ARAN, 555/3/200/8 (March 6, 1934).

[70] N. A. Rynin, *Interplanetary Flight and Communication, Vol. III, No. 9: Astronavigation: Theory, Annals, Bibliography*, trans. by IPST staff (Jerusalem: Israel Program for Scientific Translations, 1971), 4. Originally published in 1932.

[71] For some of Rynin's correspondence with Goddard, see Esther C. Goddard and G. Edward Pendray, eds., *The Papers of Robert H. Goddard, Volume I: 1898–1924* (New York: McGraw-Hill, 1970), 575–577, 583, 585, 607–609.

[72] See quotation from Goddard in Ia. Perel'man, "Sostitsia li polet na lunu?," *Krasnaia gazeta*, October 17, 1925. For the "Goddard craze" in the Soviet Union, see Asif Siddiqi, "Deep Impact: Robert Goddard and the Soviet 'Space Fad' of the 1920s," *History and Technology* 20 (2004): 97–113.

[73] See, for example, articles by Perel'man: "V mire nauki: zvezdoplavanie na zapade," *Krasnaia gazeta*, July 24, 1929; "Novye opyty s raketami," *Krasnaia gazeta*, July 30, 1929; "Uspekhi

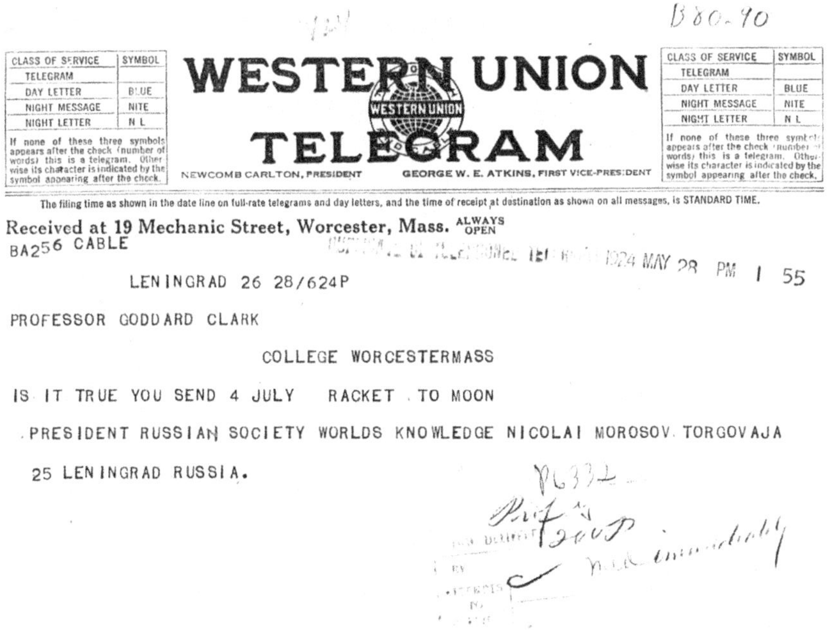

CLASS OF SERVICE | SYMBOL
TELEGRAM
DAY LETTER | BLUE
NIGHT MESSAGE | NITE
NIGHT LETTER | N L
If none of these three symbols appears after the check (number of words) this is a telegram. Otherwise its character is indicated by the symbol appearing after the check.

WESTERN UNION TELEGRAM

NEWCOMB CARLTON, PRESIDENT GEORGE W. E. ATKINS, FIRST VICE-PRESIDENT

The filing time as shown in the date line on full-rate telegrams and day letters, and the time of receipt at destination as shown on all messages, is STANDARD TIME.

Received at 19 Mechanic Street, Worcester, Mass. ALWAYS OPEN

BA256 CABLE 1924 MAY 28 PM 1 55

LENINGRAD 26 28/624P

PROFESSOR GODDARD CLARK

COLLEGE WORCESTERMASS

IS IT TRUE YOU SEND 4 JULY RACKET TO MOON

PRESIDENT RUSSIAN SOCIETY WORLDS KNOWLEDGE NICOLAI MOROSOV TORGOVAJA

25 LENINGRAD RUSSIA.

FIGURE 4. During the 1920s, space enthusiasts in the Soviet Union, Europe, and the United States exchanged information frequently. More often than not, by the time that information reached from one point to another, it was frequently garbled. Here we see a telegram from Nikolai Morozov to the American rocket pioneer Robert Goddard asking about an apocryphal rocket launch to the Moon on July 4, 1924. Goddard had no such plans. [*Source*: Clark University Archives]

Both Rynin and Perel'man also served as corresponding members of foreign space-enthusiast societies, particularly in Germany, Britain, and the United States. For example, Rynin's name appears on the donor lists of the German Rocket Society in 1929. Later, in 1931, Rynin corresponded with Noel Deisch of the American Interplanetary Society (AIS), who not only helped induct Rynin as a member of the AIS but also arranged for him to receive the *Bulletin of the American Interplanetary Society*, thus providing Soviet enthusiasts with direct information about American efforts in the early 1930s.[74]

zvezdoplavanie v Amerike," *Krasnaia gazeta*, April 15, 1930; "Novyi opyt s raketoi," *Krasnaia gazeta*, January 31, 1931; "Uspekhi zvezdoplavanie na zapade," *Krasnaia gazeta*, November 20, 1931.

74 For Rynin's contact with the AIS, see "Soviet Engineers Constructing Two Rockets," *Bulletin of the American Astronautical Society* no. 15 (January 1932): 1. For citations of Rynin's encyclopedia in the bulletin (which was renamed *Astronautics*), see "Rynin Completes New Rocket Index," *Astronautics* no. 23 (October 1932): 5; "Rocket and Astronautic Books," *Astronautics* no. 29 (September 1934): 4.

RECOGNITION

Remarkably, in spite of the vibrancy of the alternative network, Tsiolkovskii remained unrecognized by the Soviet government, underscoring the network's degree of independence from the state. Through most of the decade, Tsiolkovskii's spirits were low. In June 1926, in a letter to Nikolai Rynin, who had asked for his autobiography, Tsiolkovskii wrote, "even at the age of 68, I have not accomplished much and have not had any notable success."[75] The following year, still lacking official recognition, he wrote "I am plunging downhill, I am very tired, my courage declining and desire to live and work fading."[76] He frequently complained to friends about the difficulties of publishing as neither state nor private publishing houses expressed any interest in issuing his works.[77]

Then, quite rapidly, things changed. In the last three years of his life, from 1932 to 1935, Tsiolkovskii achieved national fame. Major newspapers covered his publications, state publishers issued his writings, and the government bestowed him important honors. Prior to Tsiolkovskii's death, even Stalin wrote to him. Seemingly, the recognition that Tsiolkovskii craved through much of his life finally came to him. A set of factors contributed to this sea change in Tsiolkovskii's fortunes. They included the persistent lobbying of his devotees in Kaluga, support by a major voluntary mass society, and the nationwide fascination with airships and rockets.

Although government money to ensure his and his family's livelihood was intermittent through the 1920s, his Kaluga devotees never gave up lobbying on his behalf. They drummed up support from influential members of *Osoaviakhim*, the mass society established by the Bol'sheviks to foster interest in aviation and chemistry, who petitioned the national Council of People's Commissars. In June 1928, the council agreed to give Tsiolkovskii a monthly pension of 225 rubles/month on the basis of his profession as an "inventor" of dirigibles who was infirm and in need of supporting four members of his family.[78]

Osoaviakhim's moderate support for Tsiolkovskii in 1928 proved critical for Tsiolkovskii's later recognition. By 1932, *Osoaviakhim* was championing the cause of exploring the stratosphere by means of both balloons and rockets. Its sudden interest had much to do with foreign achievements,

75 "The Autobiography of K. E. Tsiolkovskii," in N. A. Rynin, *Interplanetary Flight and Communication, Vol. III, No. 7: K. E. Tsiolkovskii: Life, Writings, and Rockets*, trans. by IPST staff (Jerusalem: Israel Program for Scientific Translations, 1971), 8. Original published in 1931.

76 A. Kosmodemiansky, *Konstantin Tsiolkovsky, 1857–1935* (Moscow: Nauka, 1985), 114.

77 See, for example, ARAN, 555/4/21/5 (June 21, 1925); ARAN, 555/4/17/12, 13, 17, 17a (January 9, 1932).

78 For a chronology of the events in 1927 and 1928 leading to this award, see ARAN, 555/2/60/1–26.

such as the popularity of the famed German airship and the explorations of Frenchman Auguste Piccard into the upper atmosphere via hot air balloons. Visits of the *Graf Zeppelin* to Moscow and Leningrad had caused a sensation in 1930–1931, and Soviet writers in the popular media were eager to claim that the sophisticated airships were nothing new because a Russian scientist had "invented" advanced models decades before.[79] This is precisely the strategy that *Osoaviakhim* took. As the mass society began turning attention in 1931–1932 to "conquering the stratosphere," Tsiolkovskii's ideas for a metallic airship and his writings on rockets found a welcome home. Simultaneously, the first two major biographies of Tsiolkovskii appeared in print, written by his network correspondents Rynin and Perel'man.[80] All of this serendipitously coincided with Tsiolkovskii's approaching seventy-fifth birthday in September 1932.

Four months before Tsiolkovskii's birthday, in May 1932, *Osoaviakhim* decided to commemorate the event as part of its broader stratosphere program and asked the Kaluga local government for ideas on how to go about doing such a thing. A Kaluga group, the Section of Scientific Workers, had already received permission from the Kaluga district committee (*raionnyi komitet*, or *raikom*) for a local celebration.[81] Stirred up by the new publicity about foreign exploits high in the air, the top leadership of *Osoaviakhim* ("the bureau of the presidium of the central council") met on July 1, 1932 to discuss plans for Tsiolkovskii's seventy-fifth birthday. The council recommended several ways to recognize his contributions to "reactive motion" and "dirigible construction"; among them was to ask the Communist Party to bestow upon him an award of "all-union" significance, to provide him with a lifetime monthly pension of 500 rubles, to publish his selected works for both specialized and popular audiences, and to support further work on his airships.[82] The topic of space travel was noticeably absent from any of these deliberations.

The effort began to snowball rapidly as *Osoaviakhim* allotted 16,000 rubles for the project, most of it to establish a stipend fund named after Tsiolkovskii for young students interested in science.[83] On October 17, 1932, about a month after Tsiolkovskii's actual birthday, *Osoaviakhim* hosted a reception in honor of the scientist. Tsiolkovskii, who was terrified of leaving

[79] B. N. Vorob'ev, "Professor Pikar na vysote 16.000 metrov," *Izvestiia*, June 9, 1931; "Soviets Building Dirigibles: Graf Visit Awakens Rivalry," *Washington Post*, April 18, 1931; N. Rynin, "Tekhnika poleta v stratosferu," *Izvestiia*, June 9, 1931; " 'Na shturm stratosfery': my gotovy otdat' svoi sily etomu delu!," *Tekhnika*, March 20, 1932.

[80] N. A. Rynin, *Mezhplanetnye soobshcheniia. Vyp. 7, Russkii izobretatel' i uchenyi Konstantin Eduardovich Tsiolkovskii. Ego biografiia, raboty i rakety* (Leningrad, 1931); Perel'man, *Tsiolkovskii*.

[81] Samoilovich, *Grazhdanin vselennoi*, 212–214.

[82] GARF, 8355/1/57/106–107 (July 1, 1932).

[83] GARF, 8355/1/58/68–70ob, 96 (September 16–20, 1932).

Kaluga, declined to show up, despite the best efforts to convince him otherwise. In his place, *Osoaviakhim* chief Robert Eideman and science writer Nikolai Rynin read speeches with much fanfare about airships and rockets at the Kolonn Hall at the Union House in Moscow.[84] On the same day, the Presidium of the government's Central Executive Committee formally approved the award of "Order of the Red Banner" – a common award for Soviet scientists – for Tsiolkovskii's for work in the "area of inventions, having great importance for the economic power and defense" of the country.[85] Tsiolkovskii reluctantly came to Moscow about a month later, on November 27, to accept the award from Communist Party chairman Mikhail Kalinin. Soon, Tsiolkovskii's name appeared in the mainstream press in the West; the *Washington Post* noted that he was an "airplane inventor" whose "achievements [were] said to have antedated [the] Wright Brothers."[86]

In the following years, Tsiolkovskii published many articles in the Soviet media, mostly on airships and rockets; the majority were rehashes of old ideas. State publishing houses finally published collections of his previous works, both fiction and nonfiction. Despite his resistance to Marxism as a tenable philosophy of social and economic order, in his later years, he began to soften his stance toward the Soviet government.[87] To a number of Party and government leaders, Tsiolkovskii served as a useful icon for the post-NEP era, largely because he was a self-taught savant, brought up almost entirely outside the imperial system of higher education, and thus a powerful weapon in the arguments against the still powerful but highly suspect scientific and technical intelligentsia who retained allegiances to the bourgeois sensibilities of the pre-Revolutionary era. By the mid-1930s, he was but one of many from the pre-Revolutionary era who were invoked as homegrown Russian heroes from a new "usable past" for the Stalinist era.[88] The many prominent articles about Tsiolkovskii from 1932 to 1935 all repeatedly emphasize his autodidactic background, the language of these tributes serving as not-so-veiled critiques of elite scientific community whose work was seen as increasingly at odds with the urgent matters at hand – to industrialize the Soviet Union.

Tsiolkovskii's rise to national prominence allowed him a part in the May Day parade in 1935, where a prerecorded speech was broadcast to Red Square. Quoted out of context after his death as evidence of Soviet support

84 Zhelnina, *K. E. Tsiolkovskii*, 141–142.

85 GARF, 3316/13/16/121 (October 17, 1932).

86 "Airplane Inventor Honored by Soviet," *Washington Post*, October 30, 1932. Probably the first Western reference to Tsiolkovskii was in "Rocket mortar," *Scientific American* no. 143 (1930): 141–142.

87 See for example, K. Tsiolkovskii, "Pobeda geroicheskikh liudei," *Kommuna*, June 28, 1935.

88 David Brandenberger, *National Bolshevism: Stalinist Mass Culture and the Formation of Modern Russian National Identity, 1931–1956* (Cambridge, MA: Harvard University Press, 2002), 43–45.

for the idea of spaceflight, the central theme of the speech was in fact, airships, described in metaphorical terms:

> Greetings! I picture to myself Red Square in the capital. Hundreds of steel dragonflies wave above the heads of the marching columns. Low flying dirigibles – the dream of my youth, the fulfillment of cherished imaginings, to some extent the result of my labors – go floating by. The air is thick with steel birds, and we have made that possible only now, when our party and government, all our industrious people, every worker of our Soviet Russia, have amicably applied themselves to the realization of mankind's most daring dream – conquest of the heights beyond the clouds. This is an unprecedented achievement! Nothing like it existed or could exist before. It is small wonder, therefore, that Soviet pilots have climbed higher than all others into the mysterious stratosphere.[89]

After further exhortations on Soviet aviation, Tsiolkovskii ended with his call for with a few words on cosmic travel.

After doctors diagnosed Tsiolkovskii with stomach cancer in the late summer of 1935, they operated on him, but few doubted that the scientist's days were numbered. In an unusual rush of publicity, newspapers throughout the country reported on an almost daily basis on the condition of his health. On September 13, the bedridden Tsiolkovskii allegedly had a famous letter sent to Stalin in which he praised the Bol'shevik Revolution and the "party of Lenin-Stalin" in uncharacteristically hyperbolic terms. He declared that "only October has brought recognition of the work of the self-educated; only Soviet power and the party of Lenin-Stalin has given me... aid." He bequeathed all his works to the Bol'shevik Party, the "genuine leaders of progress of human culture."[90] Stalin responded with a brief message that the main Moscow newspapers published simultaneously with Tsiolkovskii's letter.[91]

Tsiolkovskii died on the night of September 19. An outpouring of official media coverage followed. The next day, the Central Committee of the Bol'shevik Party issued a statement announcing "with great regret" the death of the "famous scientist in the area of dirigible construction."[92] Newspapers such as *Pravda*, *Izvestiia*, and *Vecherniaia moskva* dedicated full pages to covering every aspect of his life. Although most of the coverage focused on his contributions to airship design, the papers also carried pieces on his works on rocketry and spaceflight. Many popular science writers who had supported Tsiolkovskii through his life produced pieces that underlined his

[89] "Osushchestvliaetsia drevneishaia mechta chelovechestva."

[90] K. Tsiolkovskii, "TsK VKP(b) – vozhdiu naroda tov. Stalinu," *Izvestiia*, September 17, 1935.

[91] I. Stalin, "Znamenitmomu deiateliu nauki tovarishchu K. E. Tsiolkovskomu," *Izvestiia*, September 17, 1935.

[92] "Umer K. E. Tsiolkovskii," *Vecherniaia moskva*, September 20, 1935.

accomplishments.[93] Headlines from "Self-Educated Genius" to "Thinker and Dreamer" covered the gamut of his life.[94] Thousands showed up for his funeral in Kaluga, including representatives from the Party in Moscow.

Although Stalin did not personally acknowledge the proceedings, another famous Bol'shevik, Karl Radek, wrote a eulogy in *Izvestiia* that signaled a beginning more than an end: It used Tsiolkovskii as a prop in a sermon against the rise of fascism. Radek argued that Tsiolkovskii was a true communist, one who could never have been recognized by capitalist or fascist science.[95] Other writers explicitly connected the Bol'shevik revolution with Tsiolkovskii's rise from obscurity to success; one introduced the falsehood that "on Lenin's initiative [Tsiolkovskii] was awarded a personal pension."[96] These articles began the long process of rewriting Tsiolkovskii's life and redefining the relationship between the scientist and the state, all invoking Tsiolkovskii's final telegram that "only October" had brought him recognition, ironic given that Tsiolkovskii, who was known to have a very low opinion of Stalin, probably had nothing to do with his last telegram to Stalin; a journalist friend who was at his deathbed most likely fabricated this still-invoked letter.[97]

Tsiolkovskii's final three years as a nationally famous personality was a combination of substance and sham. On the one hand, he received a monthly pension from the government, he frequently published in official newspapers and journals, and he received awards; many invoked his name, in print and in speech, as a genius of Soviet science. Yet there was another less savory dimension to his standing. Despite such a sea change in his status, he remained a pariah to the mainstream scientific community. The USSR Academy of Sciences never invited him to become a member nor asked him to participate in any of its proceedings.[98] During his seventy-fifth birthday celebrations in 1932, the academy's Institute for the History of Science

93 *Izvestiia* carried full-page spreads on Tsiolkovskii two days in a row. "Konstantin Eduardovich Tsiolkovskii," *Izvestiia*, September 20, 1935; "Konstantin Eduardovich Tsiolkovskii," *Izvestiia*, September 21, 1935. The former included articles by both Perel'man and Rynin.

94 B. Reznikov, "Genial'nyi samouchka," *Pravda*, September 21, 1935; V. Semenov, "Myslitel' i mechtatel'," *Izvestiia*, September 21, 1935.

95 Karl Radek, "Znamenityi deiatel' nauki," *Izvestiia*, September 22, 1935.

96 O. Drozhzhin, "Patriarkh zvezdoplavaniia," *Vecherniaia moskva*, September 20, 1935; B. Vorob'ev, "Znamenityi deiatel' nauki," *Pravda*, September 20, 1935.

97 N. A. Maksimovskaia, "Novye arkhivnye materially k biografii K. E. Tsiolkovskogo," in *Trudy XXXI chtenii, posviashchennykh razrabotke nauchnogo nalsediia i razvitiiu idei K. E. Tsiolkovskogo (Kaluga, 17–19 sentiabria 1996 g.): Sektsiia 'issledovanie nauchnogo tvorchestva K. E. Tsiolkovskogo'* (Moscow: IIET RAN, 1999), 77–88.

98 During his life, Tsiolkovskii received only two letters from the USSR Academy of Sciences, both in 1932 in connection with the celebration of his seventy-fifth birthday. Although the academy congratulated him, it did not invite him to participate in its works. ARAN, 555/1932/66/100 (September 9, 1932); ARAN, 555/1932/66/110 (October 7, 1932).

and Technology hosted a session featuring papers on Tsiolkovskii, but the academy's elite scientists made their point clear in a harshly critical speech by one of their own.[99] If the government claimed publicly that Tsiolkovskii was a brilliant inventor of airships, it never seriously considered building any of his designs. In August 1932, a month before the government awarded him the Order of the Red Banner in honor of his seventy-fifth birthday, it quietly cancelled all work on his all-metal airship project. His scientific contributions were also publicly praised but privately denigrated. In a secret and comprehensive report to Stalin issued in June 1934 on the future development of airships in the Soviet Union, Iosif Unshlikht, the head of *Aeroflot*, dismissively mentioned Tsiolkovskii's ideas before moving on to concrete projects.[100] None of his airships were ever built.

CONCLUSIONS

The foundational myth of the Soviet space program has centered on the role of the Bol'sheviks in recognizing the value of space exploration, which they did by plucking Tsiolkovskii out of obscurity as soon as they came to power in 1917. The myth that the Bol'shevik Revolution changed Tsiolkovskii's fortunes, both personally and scientifically, originated almost immediately after his death. Later, in the post-World War II years, and especially after *Sputnik*, when the Academy of Sciences took great pains to promote Tsiolkovskii's contributions to rocket and spaceflight theory, scholars rewrote his life story. As cosmonauts began to explore space in the 1960s, Tsiolkovskii's contributions – and Bol'shevik recognition of it – became the most important element of the epic of space conquest; Marxism, Communism, and Leninism, it was said, had recognized the value of space exploration in the heady days after 1917.[101]

In reality, the one mark of continuity in Tsiolkovskii's life, from the time he began publishing in the 1890s to his death, was lack of state support for his ideas on space exploration. Tsiolkovskii languished in an often horrific state through the first fifteen years of Bol'shevik rule. When Party and state actors finally promoted and sponsored his work in the early 1930s, they deemphasized his works on the nebulous idea of space travel in favor of

99 The academy's Institute for the History of Science and Technology hosted the session on September 30, 1932 in Leningrad. Speakers included Nikolai Rynin (who gave a praising paper) and Academician Aleksei Krylov, who ridiculed Tsiolkovskii's ideas about space travel. N. A. Rynin, "K. E. Tsiolkovskii: ego zhizn' i raboty po aviatsii i reaktivnomu poletu: doklad," *Trudy instituta istorii nauki i tekhniki* 1, no. 2 (1934): 267–296; A. N. Krylov, *Moi vospominaniia* (Moscow: AN SSSR, 1945), 474–481.

100 RGVA, 4/14/1296/6–14 (June 15, 1934).

101 For a classic example, written at the height of *glasnost'*, see V. Lyndin, " 'Lish' oktiabr' prines priznanie . . . ' " [Only October Brought Me Recognition . . .], *Aviatsiia i kosmonavtika* no. 9 (1987): 42–43.

a more "grounded" notion of "conquering the stratosphere" connected to his work on airships. And, even that, they never took seriously. In looking back, we find that 1917, so touted as a defining turning point in the history of Soviet space exploration, was essentially a retroactively constructed one, an artificial marker of discontinuity that not only occluded the rich public discourse on space travel in the imperial era, but also helped to reinforce a before-and-after narrative useful for making the birth of the Soviet space program coterminous with the birth of the Soviet state. Both were now said to have emerged in a flash from the dustbin of the Tsarist era. The continuities of people (Tsiolkovskii, Perel'man), media (popular science journals), and claims (debates over Tsiolkovskii's priority as the first to develop the mathematical foundations for space travel) were erased from history.

Because the state never recognized Tsiolkovskii's unusual ideas on space travel (or indeed airships), he and his supporters sought out avenues of promotion and communication to advance Tsiolkovskii's claim of priority in the field, ones that did not rely on the government. These efforts were responding both to state neglect and to the well-publicized news of the activities of foreign enthusiasts, such as Hermann Oberth and Robert Goddard, who, it was claimed, had come to these ideas first. Fed by an increasing public appetite for cosmic ruminations, the outcome of this confluence of factors was the creation of a large, geographically disparate, and vibrant discursive network of scientific exchange that grew around Tsiolkovskii. The intersection of these phenomena, in 1924, signaled a much more substantive shift in the popular awareness of space exploration in Soviet society and culture than 1917. Through the late 1920s, Tsiolkovskii's struggle for recognition and priority in the field gained new urgency and invigorated a rich discourse played out in his own monographs, in the Soviet media, in letters passed between enthusiasts, and among science popularizers. The sustained dynamism of the network depended not only on Tsiolkovskii but also two other important nodes, journalists Nikolai Rynin and Iakov Perel'man, both of whom significantly expanded and deepened the level of scientific exchange.[102] Because of the vitality of this network, Tsiolkovskii's name for the first time was elevated to national prominence within the Soviet Union.

Scientific networks similar to Tsiolkovskii's network have a few historical parallels. Anthony F. C. Wallace, for example, investigated a similar communications network in early industrial United States, the "international fraternity of mechanicians," which worked without access to formal scientific networks or procedures but produced important technological innovations in the community of Rockdale, a cotton-manufacturing district in

[102] For the crucial importance of nodes in communications networks, see Albert-Laszló Barabási, *Linked: the New Science of Networks* (Cambridge, MA: Perseus, 2002).

Pennsylvania.[103] The vigor of Tsiolkovskii's network suggests that the conventional ways of understanding the history of science in Bol'shevik Russia – through the lens of the USSR Academy of Sciences – only communicates one part of the story, a tale of elite scientists educated at the most prestigious institutions in Russia. Tsiolkovskii, the cliché of the self-educated village genius, offers a striking counterexample of a person who made a difference despite consistent apathy from the established scientific community during his life. The power of Tsiolkovskii's network to generate discussion was most effectively underlined by the extent to which the idea of spaceflight seeped into popular culture during the era of the New Economic Policy. Fed by equal amounts technological utopianism and mysticism, and ignored completely by the state, a "space fad" in the 1920s inculcated a generation of young men and women with the idea that the destiny of the new Bol'shevik society lay beyond the Earth.

103 Anthony F. C. Wallace, *Rockdale* (New York: Knopf, 1978), 186–239.

3

Imagining the Cosmos

> By taking a pair of steps, I crossed over the threshold from one epoch to another, into the space [era].[1]
>
> Mikhail Popov, organizer of the world's first interplanetary exhibition, on what it felt like to step into the display hall, 1927

When the first young hero cosmonauts flew into space in the early 1960s, Soviet commentators repeatedly depicted them as emblematic of a modern and technologically sophisticated Russia, overtaking the West. And unlike American astronauts who thanked God for their successes, Soviet cosmonauts were explicitly atheistic; one of the first cosmonauts, the young German Titov, famously declared on a visit to the United States that during his seventeen orbits of the Earth, he had seen "no God or angels," adding that "no God helped build our rocket."[2] Such exclamations not only reinforced an alignment between space exploration and the Bol'shevik project, but also whitewashed inconvenient phenomena dating back to the 1920s when many Soviet space enthusiasts actively engaged with the idea of space travel in ways that did not conform to orthodoxies about the role of technology in post-Revolutionary society. These expressions emerged as part of the first Soviet "space fad," fed by Tsiolkovskii's ideas on space exploration and facilitated by his vast and informal network of contacts across the Soviet Union.

The artistic scope and diversity of the space fad was extraordinarily broad. With little or no support from the state, amateur and technically minded enthusiasts formed short-lived societies to discuss their interests and exchange information. Some put up impressive exhibitions displaying the visions of the major prognosticators of the day such as Tsiolkovskii, the American Robert Goddard, and the Romanian-German Herman Oberth. Advocates wrote in the popular media about the power of technology to improve and remake Russian society. On the cultural front, the science

[1] Sergei Samoilovich, *Grazhdanin vselennoi (cherty zhizni i deiatel'nosti Konstantina Eduardovicha Tsiolkovskogo)* (Kaluga: GMIK im. Tsiolkovskogo, 1969), 181.

[2] "Titov, Denying God, Puts His Faith in People," *New York Times*, May 7, 1962.

fiction of Aleksei Tolstoi, the paintings of the Suprematists and the *Amaravella* collective, and Iakov Protazanov's famous interplanetary movie *Aelita* all engaged mystical and spiritual ideas of the place of humanity in the cosmos. These embryonic artistic, philosophical, and cultural explorations were important not only because they underlined an interest in the power of modern science, but also because they disseminated ideas about space travel that were not simply about technology and/or modernization.

In a number of important ways, the space enthusiasts represented a counterexample to the more prominent elements of Soviet scientific and technical intelligentsia of the period.[3] They shared a few common traits. Both possessed a reverence for knowledge about the natural and material world. They exhibited an ambivalence between reason and faith, the former represented by an aspiration for modernization and the latter by a weakness for mysticism. Finally, although few of the space enthusiasts were revolutionary in the way that many Russian intelligentsia self-identified, the space obsessed saw themselves as the vanguard of a new era; the resistance they faced from public quarters for their utopian leanings emboldened their self-image as revolutionary and iconoclastic actors.

Yet, two major characteristics distinguished the *kosmopolity* from the burgeoning Soviet scientific and technical intelligentsia. First, the space obsessed could claim no formal education in the natural sciences; their "higher" knowledge was often the result of informal schooling or, at best, mediocre institutions. Second, they embraced an anti-elitist stance that led them to actively engage with the popular culture of the day. In fact, their very embrace of more popular and populist forms of communication contributed as much to their estrangement from the orthodox scientific community as their lack of formal educational identifiers, the autodidact Tsiolkovskii being the quintessential embodiment of this alienation. Revisiting the noise that these space enthusiasts generated – which spanned across the revolutionary divide of 1917 – opens a critical window into the discursive strategies used by marginal scientific actors in revolutionary Russia to advance seemingly outlandish scientific ideas. Theirs was the curious case of a demographic who strongly identified with the mainstream scientific and technical intelligentsia while being almost completely alienated from them.

Their cause, space exploration, was a small but important part of the wild cultural explorations of the New Economic Policy (NEP) era of the 1920s; it stemmed from both ideological oppositions and unions. Two intellectual strands contributed to the birth and sustenance of the 1920s space fad: technological utopianism and the mystical tradition of Cosmism. The former (seemingly modern, urban, international, materialist) clashed and

[3] For more on Russian and Soviet intelligentsia, see Michael D. Gordin, Karl Hall, and Alexei Kojevnikov, eds., *Osiris 23 (Intelligentsia Science: The Russian Century, 1860–1960)* (Chicago: University of Chicago Press, 2008).

meshed with the latter (superficially archaic, pastoral, Russian, spiritual), creating a complex ideological context for popular interest in spaceflight. If the language of technological utopianism has retained its place in the received history of Russian space travel, the role of Cosmism has been all but obscured. Recovering the "hidden" history of the Cosmist roots of Soviet space travel underscores how advocates of interplanetary flight from the early Bol'shevik era navigated the entire spectrum between extreme technology fetishism (such as the amateur student societies) and extreme occult fascinations (the Biocosmists). The most important bridge between these two seemingly contradictory world views was Konstantin Tsiolkovskii, the patriarch of Russian space travel.

TECHNOLOGICAL UTOPIANISM

Russian utopian thought, which has a history long predating Bol'shevism, Marxism, and indeed the nineteenth century, encompassed everything from overtly secular ideas to explicitly theological conceptions, and from monarchist ideals to anarchist visions. Already before the Revolution of 1917, Russian utopian philosophy incorporated both Marxist notions and twentieth-century modernist ideals of science and technology. The Revolution, however, allowed technological utopian visions to move from the wisp of dreams to the arena of *possibility*. After 1917, an ostensibly secular brand of millenarianism entered the picture.

The richest expressions of this meeting of sensibilities between utopia, technology, and possibility occurred during the NEP years when the country moved through rapid economic recovery that fostered what Sheila Fitzpatrick has called "an upsurge of optimism among the Bolshevik leaders."[4] Notwithstanding harsh conditions in the cities, urban population continued to grow through the 1920s as a result of peasant migration into the cities and massive demobilization following the end of the Civil War. Despite 1 million unemployed in 1924, wages finally began to rise the same year, and the standard of living for the average factory worker – someone like the tireless space crusader Fridrikh Tsander – began to improve noticeably. With urban renewal accelerating and the first fruits of the revolution appearing, people conjured up old dreams of utopia in new and experimental ways. In his indispensable study, *Revolutionary Dreams: Utopian Vision and Experimental Life in the Russian Revolution*, Richard Stites has described the many ways in which a wide spectrum of actors, from the poorest peasant to influential intelligentsia, invoked, debated over, wrote about, and often rejected utopia.[5] From ritual to religion, mannerisms to machines, and art

[4] Sheila Fitzpatrick, *The Russian Revolution*, 2nd ed. (Oxford, UK: Oxford University Press, 1994), 113.

[5] Richard Stites, *Revolutionary Dreams: Utopian Vision and Experimental Life in the Russian Revolution* (New York: Oxford University Press, 1989).

to architecture, utopian thought pervaded Soviet society at all levels. The utopian discussions of the period were not monolithic; in fact, their very contradictions and illogic often gave the social experimentation a rich and expansive tenor.

In the 1920s, technology played a major role in the social conjuring, debating, and enabling of utopias. Prominent voices of the scientific and technical intelligentsia, as well as Bol'shevik leaders, engaged in this discourse, and indeed, their pronouncements reflected the same types of tensions between naïveté and pragmatism emblematic of broader NEP culture. Lenin's fascination with the rapid electrification of Russia, industrial Taylorism, and the construction of modernized railroads in Russia were certainly all practical, but they also carried with them an underlying idea that technology itself was a possible panacea.[6] Beyond Lenin's oft-quoted phrase "communism equals Soviet power plus the electrification of the entire country," he had an almost evangelical view of the role of electricity, and technology in general, as if it had the power to transform nation and culture. H. G. Wells, after interviewing Lenin in 1920, wrote, "Lenin, [who] like a good orthodox Marxist, denounces all 'Utopians,' has succumbed at last to Utopia, the Utopia of electricians."[7] Even as Lenin underlined "the need to dream," he was also unforgiving of those who shied away from the harsh realities of practical action. In the pre-Revolutionary days, Lenin was consistently critical of utopian socialists as well as the Populists for their unrealistic goals.[8]

Lev Trotskii, another hardheaded revolutionary who few would characterize as being impractical, also spoke rather uncritically of the powers of science and technology. In his 1923 tract *Literature and Revolution*, Trotskii wrote that because of the Revolution, "[t]he shell of life will hardly have time to form before it will burst open again under the pressure of new technical and cultural achievements." Under the twin spell of science and utopia, Trotskii conjectured that advances in medicine would create a new "superman," able to "rise to the heights of an Aristotle, a Goethe, or a Marx."[9] Maksim Gor'kii, one of the most important cultural commentators of the day, who held Konstantin Tsiolkovskii in very high esteem, frequently

[6] For Lenin's personal role in plans for Soviet electrification, Taylorism, and railroads, see Jonathan Coopersmith, *The Electrification of Russia, 1880–1926* (Ithaca, NY: Cornell University Press, 1992), 153–155; Anthony Heywood, *Modernising Lenin's Russia: Economic Reconstruction, Foreign Trade and the Railway* (Cambridge, UK: Cambridge University Press, 1999).

[7] H. G. Wells, *Russia in the Shadows* (New York: George H. Doran, 1921), 158–159.

[8] The "need to dream" quotation is from V. I. Lenin, *Polnoe sobranie sochinenii: izdanie piatoe, t. 6* (Moscow: Gosudarstvennoe izdatel'stvo politicheskoi literatury, 1959), 171–172. For Lenin and utopianism, see Stites, *Revolutionary Dreams*, 41–46; Robert C. Tucker, "Lenin's Bolshevism as a Culture in the Making," in *Bolshevik Culture: Experiment and Order in the Russian Revolution*, eds. Abbott Gleason, Peter Kenez, and Richard Stites (Bloomington: Indiana University Press, 1985), 25–38.

[9] Leon Trotsky, *Literature and Revolution* (Ann Arbor: University of Michigan Press, 1975), 255.

spoke of technology as miraculous and a panacea to the world's ills; he coined the phrase "an area of miracles" to speak of the power of science.[10]

Stites and others have pointed to the Russian interest in aviation, which held a much broader fascination for the Soviet populace in the 1920s than spaceflight, as reflective of "a kinetic metaphor for liberation." Aviation represented a mixture of modernity and liberation that proved irresistible to many leading Bol'sheviks. They appropriated its symbolic meanings to encourage and inculcate ideas about a new world and used it to bridge the literal and metaphorical gaps between urban and rural masses.[11] Nevertheless, although flight served as a metaphor for liberation, and perhaps even emancipation, it had some basis in the reality of the 1920s; both in Soviet Russia and the rest of the developed world, most urban citizens had seen pictures or drawings of airplanes if not an actual machine flying over their heads.

The dream of spaceflight in the 1920s differed in two significant ways from the concurrent interest in aviation. First, spaceflight, which was also about liberation from the Earth, pushed the physical limits of emancipation beyond comprehension, past the boundaries of the visible skies. Second, spaceflight was entirely a discourse of fantasy: Voyages beyond the atmosphere had no precedent or template. Liberation and fantasy in one shape or other are common to most utopian dreams, but by extending liberation (into space) and pushing utopian speculations beyond reality (into fantasy), the spaceflight discourse was infused with a "universal" (in both senses of the word) appeal that aviation lacked. For a brief period in the 1920s, spaceflight was the most potent manifestation of the "fantasy of liberation," and indeed may be seen as a "liberation of fantasy." The speculations about spaceflight would not have been possible without the promise of new twentieth-century technology that made the utopias of liberation and fantasy attainable. As one single force – a combination of technology, fantasy, and liberation – spaceflight promised what aviation could only offer in part, total liberation from the signifiers of the past: social injustice, imperfection, gravity, and ultimately, the Earth.

COSMISM

Technology, fantasy, and liberation also figured prominently in a parallel set of ideas known as Russian Cosmism, which has fed into a nationalist discourse in current-day Russia. Cosmism resonated strongly in some Russian

[10] Bernice Glatzer Rosenthal, "Political Implications of the Occult Revival," in *The Occult in Russian and Soviet Culture*, ed. Bernice Glatzer Rosenthal (Ithaca, NY: Cornell University Press, 1997), 390.

[11] Scott W. Palmer, *Dictatorship of the Air: Aviation Culture and the Fate of Modern Russia* (New York: Cambridge University Press, 2006).

intellectual circles in the early twentieth century as a corpus of philosophical thought about the evolution of both humanity and the universe, and the relationship between the two. The philosophy influenced many famous Russian intellectuals in the 1920s. They included Bol'shevik ideologues, scientists, writers, philosophers, poets, artists, and architects who gathered in Moscow and Kaluga, Tsiolkovskii's hometown, to discuss its attributes. Cosmism's intellectual foundations comprised a hodgepodge of Eastern and Western philosophical traditions, theosophy, Pan-Slavism, and Russian Orthodox thinking.[12] The outcome was a nationalist and often reactionary philosophy that continues to attract the attention of many Russian intellectuals.

Tsiolkovskii served as a key contributor to the canon of Cosmism, but the most important world view that fed into twentieth-century Cosmism stemmed from the writings of Nikolai Fedorovich Fedorov (1828–1903), the eccentric philosopher whose works influenced many, including Dostoevskii, Gor'kii, and Tolstoi.[13] While working as a librarian at the Rumiantsev Library in Moscow, he developed his infamous *Filosofiia obshchego dela* (*Philosophy of the Common Task*), the most enduring and notorious of his many works.[14] Described by one Western biographer as "one of the most profound, comprehensive, and original ideas in the history of Russian speculation," Fedorov's doctrine, which was published after his death in 1906, was about "the common task" of all humanity, to resurrect the dead.[15] Fedorov's mission stemmed from a distinctly theocratic view of the universe in which he saw Christianity as primarily a religion of resurrection, an idea that attracted both Dostoevskii and Tolstoi. He believed that humanity's moral task was to emulate Christ and make bodily resurrection possible. Mass resurrection would finally eliminate the artificial boundaries among the "brotherhood" of humanity, that is, between previous and current generations. In other words, none of the ills of society could be solved without devising a solution to the inevitability of death. He argued that using all of the resources at its disposal, including science and technology, humanity

[12] For the best English-language meditation on Russian Cosmism as a historical process, see Michael Hagemeister, "Russian Cosmism in the 1920s and Today," in *The Occult in Russian and Soviet Culture*, 185–202.

[13] Those said to be influenced by Fedorov included writers (Dostoevskii, Gor'kii, Pasternak, Platonov, Tolstoi), political thinkers (Lunacharskii, Bogdanov), poets (Khlebnikov, Maiakovskii, Zabolotskii), painters (Filonov), architects (Mel'nikov), heliobiologists (Chizhevskii), and scientists (Vernadskii, Tsiolkovskii). For a description of the Moscow-based *Fedorovtsy* (supporters of N. F. Fedorov) in the 1920s, see Michael Hagemeister, *Nikolaj Fedorov: Studien zu Leben, Werk und Wirkung* (Munich: Sagner, 1989), 343–362.

[14] Fedorov devotees independently printed and distributed 480 copies of the original in 1906. A second volume was issued in 1913. His writings have been collected in *N. F. Fedorov: Sobranie sochinenii v chetyrekh tomakh*, 5 vols. (Vols. 1–4 and supplement), eds. A. G. Gacheva and S. G. Semenova (Moscow: Progress, 1995–2000).

[15] George M. Young, Jr., *Nikolai F. Fedorov: An Introduction* (Belmont, MA: Nordland, 1979), 7.

should engage in a quest to reassemble the corporeal particles lost in the "disintegration" of human death. In an ideal utopian setting ("as it ought to be"), Fedorov believed that there would be no birth and no death, only the progressive reanimation of the deceased millions from history.

Two aspects of Fedorov's "philosophy of the common task" related to Cosmism in general and to voyages into space in particular. First, to achieve his ultimate goal of "liberation from death," Fedorov called for restructuring human society and its natural environment, which for him included not only the Earth but also the entire universe. The idea of "regulating nature" by taking absolute control over it resonated deeply with the scientific and technical intelligentsia in the early post-Revolutionary era who, infected by Bol'shevik claims of remaking the social universe, were also interested in remaking the natural one.[16] Second, Fedorov believed that humans from Earth would have to travel into the cosmos – to the Moon, the planets, and stars – to recover disintegrated particles of deceased human beings that are spread throughout the universe. Once the bodies of the deceased were reconstituted (in forms that might not resemble humans), the resurrected would then settle throughout the universe. In his *Philosophy of the Common Task*, Fedorov wrote, "[The] conquest of the Path to Space is an absolute imperative, imposed on us as a duty in preparation for the Resurrection. We must take possession of new regions of Space because there is not enough space on Earth to allow the co-existence of all the resurrected generations."[17]

Fedorov's ideas of restructuring humanity and the cosmos, and especially the supreme role of science and technology in this transformation, anticipated Tsiolkovskii's writings, which are sprinkled with the Promethean urge to remake everything that surrounds us. Many historians have claimed that Fedorov inculcated Tsiolkovskii with his ideas about space travel; during his brief stay in Moscow as a teen in the 1870s, Tsiolkovskii had indeed met daily with Fedorov, who worked at a Moscow library. Fedorov played a critical role in supporting the young student in his struggle to learn more about the natural sciences. As Tsiolkovskii later remembered, "[i]t is no exaggeration to say that for me he took the place of university professors."[18] Nevertheless, those who suggest that Fedorov may have influenced Tsiolkovskii to

16 The famous Russian geochemist Vladimir Vernadskii, who shared these views (although he probably never heard of Fedorov), headed the Commission for the Study of the Natural Productive Forces (KEPS), a body whose goals encompassed such transformative projects as harnessing solar and electromagnetic forces for the good of Russian society. Kendall E. Bailes, *Science and Russian Culture in an Age of Revolutions: V. I. Vernadsky and His Scientific School, 1863–1945* (Bloomington: Indiana University Press, 1990).

17 Gacheva and Semenova, *N. F. Fedorov*; Jean Clair, "From Humboldt to Hubble," in *Cosmos: From Romanticism to the Avant Garde*, ed. Jean Clair (Munich: Prestel, 1999), 25; Young, *Nikolai F. Fedorov*, 182–183.

18 Konstantin Altaiskii, "Moskovskaia iunost' Tsiolkovskogo," *Moskva* no. 9 (1966): 176–192.

take up the cause of spaceflight are certainly mistaken. Tsiolkovskii himself maintained throughout his life that during his tenure of study under Fedorov, the two never discussed space travel although both had independently begun thinking of the possibility by this time.[19]

In parallel with his more technical writings, Tsiolkovskii issued numerous short monographs beginning in the late nineteenth century that touched on the philosophy of cosmic travel. These two strands, the technical and the philosophical, intertwined and influenced each other throughout his life, and although his philosophical writings are less well known, they form a corpus of work that easily exceeds in size his combined works on aeronautics, rocketry, and space travel.[20] He brought a messianic and transformative vision to the cause of spaceflight that mimicked some of Fedorov's ideas about immortality and cosmic unity. He also drew upon occult thought rooting back to German philosopher Carl du Prel, famous for drawing a link between cosmic and biological evolution, that is, that Darwinian natural selection acted on planetary bodies just as it acted on living organisms. In Tsiolkovskii's world view, the occult, theories of evolution, and Christianity existed without contradiction. At a fundamental level, Tsiolkovskii was a religious thinker whose life was an attempt to reconcile the scientific views of nature that seemed to contradict his strong faith in Christ. As such, he expended much energy explaining biblical events with the aid of modern-day science, a project that continues to engage many to the present day.

Like Fedorov, Tsiolkovskii believed that humanity's place in the universe depended on two related ideas, monism and panpsychism. He described both of these concepts in *Monizm vselennoi* (*Monism of the Universe*), a brochure he self-published in 1925 that was his most complete statement of cosmic philosophy. According to his version of monism, all matter in the universe, including organic matter, is made out of a single substance, has the same structure, and obeys the same set of laws. He explained panpsychism as the belief that all matter is made up of "atoms of ether," even smaller than "regular" atoms, which are in and of themselves *living organisms* or "happy

[19] The legend that Fedorov pointed Tsiolkovskii in the direction of space travel probably originated from scientist Viktor Shlovskii in his " 'K' in 'Kosmonavtika ot A do Ia'," *Literaturnaia gazeta*, April 7, 1971. See also V. E. L'vov, *Zagadochnyi starik: povesti* (Leningrad: Sov. pisatel', 1977). Many Western and Russian authors, without any evidence, make a direct causal connection between Fedorov and Tsiolkovskii.

[20] Especially through the 1920s, during the height of the "space fad," Tsiolkovskii's output on philosophical topics increased dramatically. He self-published such works as *The Wealth of the Universe* (1920), *The Origins of Life on Earth* (1922), *Monism of the Universe* (1925), *Reason for Space* (1925), *The Future of Earth and Humanity* (1928), *The Will of the Universe: Unknown Intelligent Forces* (1928), *Love for One Self or the Source of Egoism* (1928), *Intellect and Passion* (1928), *The Social Organization of Humanity* (1928), and *The Goal of Stellar Voyages* (1929). All of these works, and others unpublished during his lifetime, have been compiled into one volume. L. V. Golovanova, *K. E. Tsiolkovskii: Genii sredi liudi* (Moscow: Mysl', 2002).

atoms."[21] Tsiolkovskii's ideas were not original but deeply indebted to the theories of such German thinkers as Gottfried Leibniz and Ernst Haeckel. Tsiolkovskii believed that different living beings with differing abilities for expression result when these atoms combine in different ways. Because these ether atoms are indestructible, there is no such thing as true death because the atoms can be reconstituted in different combinations from the one that gave life to a specific human being.[22] This philosophy explained to a large degree Tsiolkovskii's surprising lack of sorrow when several of his children died.

For all their "progressive" ideas about the role of science and technology and human expansion of space, there was a darker side to Fedorov and Tsiolkovskii's vision. Fedorov's "common task" had a distinctly totalitarian tinge because it did not allow choice in the equation: He argued humans would *have* to participate in his project without exception. Tsiolkovskii's view of the search for human perfection also reflected his firm belief in eugenics; he advocated the extermination of imperfect plants and animal life and called for a "battle against the procreation of defective people and animals."[23] In a piece finished in 1918, he wrote that:

> I do not desire to live the life of the lowest races [such as] the life of a negro or an Indian. Therefore, the benefit of any atom, even the atom of a Papuan, requires the extinction also of the lowest races of humanity, and in an extreme measure the most imperfect individuals in the races.[24]

This view of space travel that combined the search for human perfection, racial purity, and occult thinking provided the fundamental impetus to Tsiolkovskii's more mathematically inclined meditations on rocket flight into outer space. Tsiolkovskii seamlessly combined his fascinations with technology and the occult into a fully formed *weltanschauung*. Yet to much of his audience in the 1920s – especially those young and technology-minded students who were inspired to dream of space travel – his goal of space travel fit nicely with prevailing Bol'shevik rhetoric connecting technology with modernity. The technophiles, in fact, believed that by avoiding Tsiolkovskii's mystical invocations, that they could construct a vision of space

[21] K. E. Tsiolkovskii, *Monizm vselennoi* (Kaluga: K. E. Tsiolkovskii, 1925).

[22] In *Volia vselennoi* (*Will of the Universe*), a brochure published in 1928 in Kaluga, Tsiolkovskii wrote, "Death is one of the illusions of a weak human mind. There is no death, for the existence of an atom in inorganic matter is not marked by memory and time – it is as if the latter does not exist at all." K. E. Tsiolkovskii, "Volia vselennoi," in Golovanova, *K. E. Tsiolkovskii*, 228–229.

[23] K. E. Tsiolkovskii, "Liubov' k samomu sebe, ili istinnoe sebialiuboe," in Golovanova, *K. E. Tsiolkovskii*, 396–402; Hagemeister, "Russian Cosmism in the 1920s and Today," 201–202.

[24] K. Tsiolkovskii, "Etika ili estestvennye osnovy nravstvennosti," in *K. E. Tsiolkovskii: kosmicheskaia filosofiia*, ed. V. S. Avduevskii (Moscow: URSS, 2001), 82.

travel that directly countered antiquated notions of the cosmos as part of an epistemology of superstition and folk tales. In forming societies to argue their cause, they saw in space travel a vehicle for creating a new world of machines and men.

TECHNOLOGICAL UTOPIANISM: THE COSMIC SOCIETIES

Most of the men and women who organized cosmic societies in the 1920s did so without any material support or encouragement from the state. They did, however, absorb official discourses on the role of technology as a panacea for all social ills in new, post-Revolutionary Russia. Space advocates saw in space exploration (and its corollary, rocketry) a manifestation of the cold hard power of rationality, science, and mathematics to move society ahead on the path of "progress" and "modernization."

Several technology-enraptured (and short-lived) societies coalesced during the period of the space fad. Of these, the most important and influential was the Moscow-based Society for the Study of Interplanetary Communications (*Obshchestva izucheniia mezhplanetnykh soobshchenii*, or OIMS), formed in 1924. It was not only the first in the world to effectively organize for the cause of space exploration, but also the first to build a domestic and international network around the idea. The history of the organization, a combination of serendipity, willful devotion, and eventual loss of momentum due to indifference from the state, illustrates the ways in which technological utopianism inspired a few to bring an esoteric idea to many.[25]

The Society emerged during the first intense wave of public fascination with spaceflight in the spring of 1924, set off by a story in the newspaper *Izvestiia* under the headline "Is Utopia Really Possible?" about the recently published meditations on spaceflight by the foreigners Oberth and Goddard.[26] Spurred to promote a Russian source for such ideas, the sixty-six-year-old Tsiolkovskii immediately republished his own pre-Revolutionary works on spaceflight. Almost overnight the Soviet media began to devote considerable attention to the cosmos. News and rumor of Oberth and Goddard's exploits, the publication of Aleksei Tolstoi's new space fiction novel *Aelita*, and the "Great Mars Opposition" of August 1924 – when Mars and Earth were closer to each other than they had been for hundreds of years – fed an explosion of public interest in space. In one lengthy *Pravda* article ("Voyage into Cosmic Space"), the author narrated the new history of space exploration, harking back to Leonardo da Vinci,

[25] For a detailed history, see Asif A. Siddiqi, "Making Spaceflight Modern: A Cultural History of the World's First Space Advocacy Group," in *The Societal Impact of Spaceflight*, eds. Steven J. Dick and Roger D. Launius (Washington, DC: NASA History Division, 2007), 513–537.

[26] "Novosti nauki i tekhniki: neuzheli ne utopiia?," *Izvestiia VTsIK*, October 2, 1923.

Cyrano de Bergerac, Jules Verne, and H. G. Wells. The history naturally culminated with the works of Tsiolkovskii, Oberth, and Goddard. Palpably excited by the optimism of the times, the writer concluded, "within a few years hundreds of heavenly ships will push into the starry cosmos."[27]

The media frenzy over space exploration in early 1924 might have faded away had it not been for some resourceful young men and women. In April 1924, about a dozen students at the prestigious Zhukovskii Military Air Engineering Academy's Military-Scientific Society (VNO) set up a "Section on Reactive Motion" to exchange ideas about rockets.[28] In compiling a list of goals, the section touched on all the key strategies that would characterize the ensuing space fad, from its technical side (building rockets) to outreach (lectures, publications, and book stores), to building a community (by interesting others in the same topics), to opening a channel to the West (by collecting media from overseas), and acknowledging the artistic medium as a possible way to educate and popularize (by branching into film).

The section first organized a public lecture. One of the section leaders, Morris Leiteizen, whose father was a famous pre-Revolutionary Bol'shevik, asked a family friend, Mikhail Lapirov-Skoblo, to do the honors. Lapirov-Skoblo, thirty-five years old and a rising member of the reconstituted post-Revolutionary technical intelligentsia, had been briefly acquainted with Lenin. After the latter's death, he served as deputy chairman of the Scientific-Technical Department of the Supreme Council of the National Economy (VSNKh or *Vesenkha*), a body tasked with supervisory duties over applied research and development in Soviet industry. He also headed *Pravda*'s department of science and technology.[29] Tsiolkovskii's recently published works so inspired Lapirov-Skoblo that he wrote the first well-researched essays on space travel in the post-Revolutionary era in *Pravda* and other publications.[30]

Lapirov-Skoblo's lecture, held on the evening of Friday, May 30, was a resounding success. Tickets sold out two days earlier; on the day of the talk, the organizers were forced to call for the police to control the mass of people who wanted to attend. Attendees eagerly bought up all the utopian literature on space travel on display – H. G. Wells' *War of the Worlds*,

27 M. Ia. Lapirov-Skoblo, "Puteshestviia v mezhplanetnye prostranstva," *Pravda*, April 15, 1924. For Goddard's prominent role in the space fad, see Asif A. Siddiqi, "Deep Impact: Robert Goddard and the Soviet 'Space Fad' of the 1920s," *History and Technology* 20 no. 2 (2004): 97–113.

28 The leading VNO student members included V. P. Kaperskii, M. G. Leiteizen, A. I. Makarevskii, M. A. Rezunov, and N. A. Sokolov-Sokolenok; ARAN, 4/14/197/32–33.

29 When Lenin supervised the formation of the State Commission for Electrification of Russia (GEOLRO) in 1920, he tapped Lapirov-Skoblo to represent the *Vesenkha* on GOELRO. For a biography, see ARAN, 4/14/197/30–30b.

30 For his other articles, both entitled "Puteshestviia v mezhplanetnye prostranstva," see *Molodaia gvardiia* no. 5 (1924) and *Khochu vse znat'* no. 3 (1924): 140.

Russian science fiction from Aleksei Tolstoi and Aleksandr Beliaev, and books by the popular science writer Iakov Perel'man. Lapirov-Skoblo's lecture, entitled "Interplanetary Communications (How Modern Science and Technology Solves this Question)," may have been the first exposition on space exploration in Russia that was open to the general public. His lecture was a typical example of the rhetoric of the technological utopian space advocates; he linked the idea of spaceflight with both modern technology and the future of a new Bol'shevik Russia, a nation that he believed had left behind its roots in tradition, backwardness, and peasant life. He concluded by calling on the Soviet populace to build rocket engines to "transform into reality the centuries old dream of flight into space."[31]

Following Lapirov-Skoblo's talk, section members invited the audience to sign up to form the core of a public society, thus opening up membership to laypeople outside the Zhukovskii Academy. Although the complete list of 179 names is lost, the surviving pages give a sense of these people. Of 121 names preserved, 104 were men. The majority of the members (68) were young, between the ages of twenty and thirty years. In terms of professions, a total of 96 members, that is, roughly 80%, were evenly split between students and workers. A smaller number identified themselves as "scientific workers," "writers," and "scientists and inventors."[32]

Grigorii Kramarov, elected to chair the new Society's "presidium," recalled forty years later that no one had any illusions that the Soviet Union would soon be sending men into space. He remembered that "in the work of the society [we] all saw one more possibility to aid the Motherland, to aid in the building of socialism." Instead of building rockets, the Society would bring science and technology to the masses. Its members were "convinced that the society's work would contribute to the preparation of cadres, who in the future would create the economic and scientific and technical base for solving the greatest problems."[33] They paid lip service to the notion that technology would improve social conditions in revolutionary Russia. In a speech to factory workers, Fridrikh Tsander, one of the principal activists in the Society, spoke of the many benefits from space travel such as "senior citizens [who] will find it much easier to maintain health in [space]," of the "inhabitants of Mars... [whose] inventions could help us to a great extent to become happy and well off," and of "[a]stronomy, [which] more than the other sciences, calls upon man to unite for a longer and happier life."[34] When critics attacked their views for being utopian, they responded by calling their

[31] For the transcript, see ARAN, 4/14/194/49–62. For recollections of attendees, see ARAN, 4/14/197/35–38; G. Kramarov, *Na zare kosmonavtiki: k 40-letiiu osnovaniia pervogo v mire obshchestva mezhplanetnykh soobshchenii* (Moscow: Znanie, 1965), 25–28.

[32] ARAN, 4/14/196/6–21; Kramarov, *Na zare kosmonavtiki*, 28.

[33] Kramarov, *Na zare kosmonavtiki*, 50.

[34] See Tsander, "Doklad inzhenera F. A. Tsandera a svoem izobretenii," in F. A. Tsander, *Iz nauchnogo naslediia* (Moscow: Nauka, 1967), 10–14.

FIGURE 5. Soviet space enthusiasts used street flyers to advertise lectures to attract large crowds. This one boldly announced a "debate" on the topic "Flight to Other Worlds" with talks promised from several astronomers and rocket pioneer F. A. Tsander. The event was one of many in 1924 focused on the perceived work of the American Robert Goddard and his alleged Moon rocket. The talk was held at an auditorium at the Physics Institute of the First University in Moscow at 8 p.m. on Saturday, October 4, 1924. Ticket prices were thirty kopecks. [*Source*: Collection of Asif Siddiqi]

opponents "conservative," thus locating supporters and detractors of space exploration within a binary world; one was either modern ("with science and technology") or one was traditional (against "progress").[35]

Through the year, the Society held numerous lectures and debates in Moscow, Leningrad, Khar'kov, Riazan', Tula, Saratov, and elsewhere, introducing the idea of space exploration to a huge audience beyond technology fetishists (Figure 5). But despite their many successes – including one near-riotous event in October 1924 when the Moscow horse militia had to be

[35] ARAN, 4/14/194/1–3.

called out to control unruly crowds interested in rumors of a rocket launch to the Moon in 1924 – lack of state support proved to be the Society's undoing. In late 1924, when the Society petitioned the administrative department of the Moscow city council to register the organization officially, the city council rejected the application on grounds that it had "insufficient scientific strength among its members."[36] The Society's members also had to deal with less committed members who were unable to sustain interest in the face of both the widespread poverty of the times and the possibility that space exploration was decades away. Society head Kramarov remembered that the most common question from the audience after each lecture was "How quickly would flight to the planets be accomplished?"[37] When it became clear that travel into space was years if not decades away, the "accidental members" dispersed quickly, leaving only a handful of the truly dedicated to pursue the cause. Eventually, even the faithful had to come down to the ground; most, such as Tsander, had little time to devote to activities that did not provide money for living. Valentin Chernov, for example, remembered later that his job as a violinist forced him to abandon the Society.[38] Like many utopians, the Society was unable to sustain a vision beyond the short term.

TECHNOLOGICAL UTOPIANISM: THE MEDIA

Dissemination of celebratory ideas about space travel during the NEP era depended greatly on the existence of vibrant popular scientific media, which maintained a deep continuity with the pre-Revolutionary practices in the dissemination of scientific knowledge. But where the treatment of cosmic topics in the imperial era was limited to a few scattered instances, the media in the 1920s was full of meditations on space exploration, benefiting from a massive increase in popular science publications. Publishers, both private and public, found that scientific titles were particularly popular among urban masses. Jeffrey Brooks notes that, "[p]ublishers had difficulty keeping up with the demand for works in popular science," which "comprised a fifth of [all] titles published from 1921–27."[39] Biweekly and

[36] ARAN, 4/14/197/19. Tsander later confirmed that the lack of "scientific workers" among members of the "board of directors," i.e., Tsander, Leiteizen, Kaperskii, Rezunov, Chernov, Serebrennikov, and Kramarov, was a source of dissension that contributed to the society's dissolution.

[37] Kramarov, *Na zare kosmonavtiki*, 56.

[38] Kramarov, *Na zare kosmonavtiki*, 51–52. Tsander, in his autobiography, notes that "the lack of published material and of spare time did not permit us to work intensively." See "Autobiography of Friedrich Arturovich Tsander, Mechanical Engineer," in N. A. Rynin, *Interplanetary Flight and Communication, Vol. II, No. 4: Rockets*, trans. T. Pelz (Jerusalem: Israel Program for Scientific Translations, 1971), 187. Originally published in 1929.

[39] Jeffrey Brooks, "The Breakdown in Production and Distribution of Printed Material, 1917–1927," in *Bolshevik Culture*, 159, 168–169.

monthly journals devoted to popular science were ubiquitous on newsstands by the mid-1920s, and they included both new and older publications with a panoply of descriptive titles such as *Tekhnika i zhizn'* (*Technology and Life*), *Tekhnika-molodezhi* (*Technology for Youth*), *V masterskoi prirody* (*In Nature's Workshop*), and *Znanie-sila* (*Knowledge Is Power*; see Figure 6).[40] The formerly private Leningrad-based publisher P. P. Soikin, which published the journals *Mir prikliuchenii* (*World of Adventure*) and *Vestnik znaniia* (*Journal of Knowledge*) in the 1920s, continued to play an influential role in the popularization of science through the second and third decades of the twentieth century; Soikin, in fact, remained one of the few imperial-era publishing concerns allowed to operate during the NEP years, although it was nationalized in 1918. In 1922, Soikin was recruited to serve on the publishing section of the *Vesenkha*, and he was allowed to continue with his pre-Revolutionary publishing activities, albeit with consideration of the state's interests.[41] Soikin carved out a dominating niche in the popular science market that remained unchallenged until the state publishing house in Leningrad completely absorbed his business in 1930. Circulation of *Vestnik znaniia*, one of Soikin's most popular monthlies, increased from 25,000 in 1925 to 75,000 by 1931.[42] The journal *Khochu vse znat'* (*I Want to Know All*), published by the Leningrad-based newspaper *Rabochei gazety* (*Working Gazette*), for example, set out to "[help] readers in developing a material understanding of the world" and to "familiarize readers with the newest achievements in modern science and technology," which would benefit the Revolution.[43] Such publications were widely available in bookstores such as Leningrad's "Nauka i znanie" (Science and Knowledge), one of the largest in the city, which catered exclusively to scientific and applied scientific titles. Its catalog in 1928 boasted around 7,000 titles from "all branches of [scientific and technical] knowledge."[44]

Space and space-related topics constituted a significant, although by no means major, slice of the popular science literature. The number of articles on spaceflight published between 1923 and 1932 (inclusive), the key years spanning the space fad, amounted to over 200 articles and over thirty books

[40] Popular science journals included *Bor'ba mirov* (*The World's Struggle*), *Khochu vse znat'* (*I Want to Know All*), *Krasnaia nov'* (*Red Virgin Soil*), *Mir prikliuchenii* (*World of Adventure*), *Nauka i tekhnika* (*Science and Technology*), *Pioner* (*Pioneer*), *Priroda i liudi* (*Nature and People*), *Tekhnika i zhizn'* (*Technology and Life*), *Tekhnika-molodezhi* (*Technology for Youth*), *Vestnik znaniia* (*Journal of Knowledge*), *V masterskoi prirody* (*In Nature's Workshop*), *Vsemirnyi sledopyt'* (*World Pathfinder*), and *Znanie-sila* (*Knowledge is Power*).

[41] A. Admiral'skii and S. Belov, *Rytsar' knigi: ocherki zhizni i deiatel'nosti P. P. Soikina* (Leningrad: Lenizdat, 1970).

[42] Publication runs are from the back pages of *Vestnik znaniia* in 1925 and 1931.

[43] Advertisement for *Khochu vse znat'* on the inside cover of various issues of *Vestnik znaniia*.

[44] From commercial advertisements on the back covers of various popular science magazines in 1928.

FIGURE 6. The proliferation of popular science magazines immensely helped the cause of space exploration in the 1920s. Here we see the very first cover story on space exploration in a popular journal, the March 1924 issue of *V masterskoi prirody* (*In Nature's Workshop*) whose editor was the famous science popularizer Iakov Perel'man. [*Source*: Collection of Asif Siddiqi]

(see Figure 7). Compared to the other pressing topics of the day, this output did not represent a great number, but that so many works on space exploration were published on such an arcane subject is in and of itself a striking result. By comparison, in the United States, only *two* nonfiction monographs on spaceflight appeared in the same period. Only in Germany, the single Western nation with a vocal spaceflight community, were there comparable levels of media attention.[45]

By the early 1930s, Soviet nonfiction monographs on space exploration all communicated a set of key themes, including the notion that the rocket

[45] Michael J. Neufeld, "Weimar Culture and Futuristic Technology: The Rocketry and Spaceflight Fad in Germany, 1923–1933," *Technology and Culture* 31 (October 1992): 725–752.

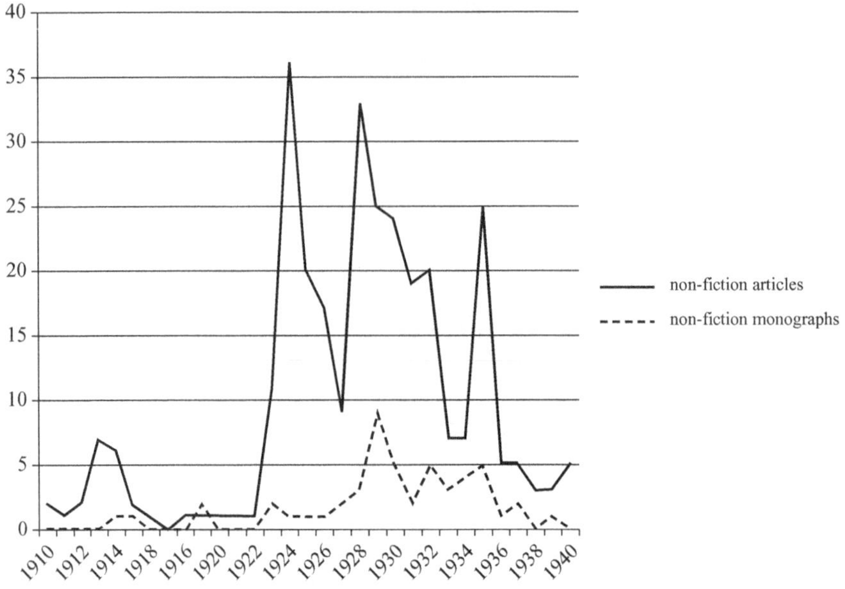

FIGURE 7. Graph of articles and monographs on space exploration published in the Russian and Soviet media, 1910–1940. The first peak (c. 1924) coincides with the fascination with cosmic themes generated by news of Oberth and Goddard. The second (c. 1928–29) resulted from media attention to German rocket exploits. Publications on space topics diminish sharply after 1932, excepting a brief interlude due to Tsiolkovskii's death in 1935.

was the only and obvious means to reach space, that space exploration was not fantasy but explicable by mathematics, and that the Soviet Union had a special stake in the future of space travel, especially given its priority (through Tsiolkovskii) in advancing its cause. Underlying all of these claims was the fundamental powerful of technology to transform the new socialist nation. Beyond these concerns, popular science writers were also actively engaged with their readers. The content of popular science media suggests that readers were not merely passive receptors of information on spaceflight. Brooks has noted that Soviet newspapers during the NEP era contained three spheres of discourse – an explanatory sphere, an interactive one, and an information one.[46] The dialogue over spaceflight in popular science journals echoed these divisions. Both *Nauka i tekhnika* (*Science and Technology*) and *Vestnik znaniia* had forums for interacting with its readers. The former, under the banner "Correspondence with Readers," published over two dozen responses to readers' letters per issue. Inquiries

[46] Jeffrey Brooks, "The Press and its Message: Images of America in the 1920s and 1930s," in *Russia in the Era of NEP: Explorations in Soviet Society and Culture*, eds. Sheila Fitzpatrick, Alexander Rabinowitch, and Richard Stites (Bloomington: Indiana University Press, 1991), 231–252.

and comments came from all over the country: Moscow, Rostov-on-Don, Voronezh, Leningrad, Krasnodar, Voznesensk, Khar'kov, Groznyi, Kiev, Taganrog, Belev, Donbass, and elsewhere. *Vestnik znaniia* had a similar section entitled "Living Communication," which published numerous editorial responses to readers' letters on various topics. The transformative, beneficial, and modernizing aspects of space travel were rarely, if ever, questioned in the exchange of ideas.

Many readers asked where to get materials on space, a service that the journals provided repeatedly, pointing out not only articles on space published in the journals' own pages but also elsewhere.[47] Some of the responses provided information whereas others clarified ambiguous topics. To comrade A. Semenov from Leningrad, for example, *Nauka i tekhnika* used a drawing to illustrate the changing distances between the planets. In some cases, the journal editors displayed a distinctly pedantic attitude to its readers, implying that lack of scientific and technical knowledge about space travel was indicative of ignorance about the modern world. For example, *Nauka i tekhnika* chastised comrade Pavliuchenko from Aleksandrovka for his "bewilderment" about movement through space in the absence of matter to push against.[48] On occasion, the journals acknowledged the "many numbers of questions to the Editors" on the topic; *Vestnik znaniia* claimed that numerous readers of the journal were dissatisfied with short articles on space travel and demanded complete books on the topic.[49] Some readers' communications required special attention. *Vestnik znaniia* returned comrade Iosifov's manuscript, "The Importance of the Planet and its Satellites in the Solar System," with several points explaining why his conclusions were "absolutely incorrect." In the same readers' section, comrade Goldenveizer conjectured about the unpleasant sensations space travelers might experience in a vessel, some of which had been discussed by Tsiolkovskii, Noordung, and others.[50] In one case, when one reader anticipated Fermi's paradox in relation to the possibility of space travel, *Vestnik znaniia* devoted a full article with responses from prominent writers, including Tsiolkovskii and Perel'man, to the question "Is Interplanetary Communications Possible?"[51]

[47] "Pred'iaviteliiu bileta avio-loterei ser. 008, No. 10220 (Baku)," *Nauka i tekhnika* no. 34 (August 19, 1927): 35; Ia. I. Perel'man, "Mezhplanetnye polety," *Vestnik znaniia* no. 4 (1928): 254; and "Tov. Miklashevskomu (Moskva)," *Nauka i tekhnika* no. 23 (June 9, 1928): 31.

[48] "Tov. A. Semenovu (Leningrad)," *Nauka i tekhnika* no. 47 (November 18, 1927): 28; "Tov. Pavliuchenko (d. Aleksandrovka)," *Nauka i tekhnika* no. 14 (April 7, 1928): 30. For an answer to a similar question, see "L'vovu," *Vestnik znaniia* no. 2 (January 25, 1931): 127.

[49] "Ot redkatskii," *Vestnik znaniia* no. 11 (1928): 551.

[50] I. T. Iosifovu" and "Podp. Goldenveizeru," *Vestnik znaniia* no. 19 (October 10, 1931): 1004.

[51] "Vozmozhny li mezhplanetnye soobshcheniia?," *Vestnik znaniia* no. 4 (1930): 152–153. Fermi's paradox describes the seeming contradiction of our galaxy being over several billion years old, and therefore possibly full of alien life forms, but humanity's lack of contact with them.

According to the writers, the answer was a resounding "yes," but only because modern science and technology would make it possible.

THE COSMOPOLITANS

Beyond societies and publishing, space advocates of the 1920s also used the medium of the *vystavka* or "display" to publicize their cause. Through exhibits, enthusiasts were able to let their visions run free in more creative ways than was possible by means of lectures or publications. By exposing the possibility of space travel for the first time to thousands, they served a very important role during the space fad. Unlike the technological utopians who organized or wrote, exhibition organizers represented a constituency that embraced certain mystical ideas about spaceflight. In their lexicon, Tsiolkovskii assumed near-messianic status in a cause that was equal amounts of fetishization of technology and speculation about human evolution. Recovering the history of the exhibitions underscores how, in the 1920s, the line between lunar aspirations and lunacy was often invisible and that the lexicon of technological utopians was frequently indistinguishable from those who were mystically minded.

In 1925, a group of spaceflight enthusiasts organized a small exhibition of spaceflight-related artifacts in Kiev.[52] Although the exhibit remained open for less than three months, its success prompted one of its organizers, Aleksandr Fedorov, to join up in 1927 with the Moscow-based Association of Inventors (*Assotsiatsiia izobretatelei-izobretateliam*, AIIZ) to open the world's first international exhibition on space travel.[53] The AIIZ, a forum for amateur enthusiasts to discuss their interests in science and technology, had recently created a "Sector for Propaganda and Popularization of Astronautics" to promote the cause of spaceflight.[54] The sector's leading members included a motley crew of self-described inventors: a pilot, a former convict, a student, a technician, a librarian, and Fedorov.[55] Obsessed with Tsiolkovskii, the idiosyncratic Fedorov found a shared cause in his fellow exhibition organizers, who seemed to see the old man in overtly evangelical terms; in one letter to Tsiolkovskii, Fedorov wrote that he considered himself "fortunate to work under the leadership of creative

52 ARAN, 4/14/195/10–12 (August 16, 1925).

53 The literal translation of AIIZ is "Association of Inventors to Inventors," but the society was commonly known as the Association of Inventors.

54 ARAN, 4/14/198/41. The precise word they used was *zvezdoplavaniia*, which literally translates as "stellar dynamics" in the same way that *vozdukhoplavaniia* means "aerodynamics." The closest English word is "astronautics," a term that Belgian writer J. J. Rosny invented. Other sections in the AIIZ included a "culture-propaganda" section and a language section for developing a universal language.

55 The "organizational committee" of the AIIZ's astronautics sector included G. A. Polevoi (an inventor and pilot), I. S. Beliaev (a former convict), A. S. Suvorov (a student), Z. G. Piatetskii (a technician), and O. V. Kholoptseva (a librarian). ARAN, 4/14/198/1–2.

great ideas, a thinker of our times and a preacher of great inconceivable truths!"[56]

Having organized the previous exhibition in Kiev, Fedorov suggested to the sector that it host a major exhibition of space artifacts in Moscow. The idea was to construct models of rockets and spacecraft conceived by the leading Soviet and foreign theoreticians of the day and display them with information for curious visitors. The association planned to display many of Tsiolkovskii's publications on spaceflight in one place – a library of sorts that they called the "smithy of all inventors."[57] The exhibition, which would also commemorate the tenth anniversary of the Great October Revolution, would be augmented by a publicity blitz on space travel, including lectures in dozens of locales in and around the capital city. The ragtag band of organizers united in their zealous belief in the power of "invention" and "inventors" and held up Tsiolkovskii as some sort of "prophet" of a new era, "superior even to Edison."[58]

Although Soviet-era accounts focused only on the organizers' fascination with modern technology, Fedorov and his associates were inspired not only by the products of modern engineering but also by a mystic calling. They referred to themselves as "cosmopolitans" (*kosmopoliti*), a derived word for "citizen of the universe" and their cause as "cosmopolitanism" (*kosmopolizma*).[59] Unlike many other technically minded popularizers of space exploration in the 1920s who carefully ignored Tsiolkovskii's spiritually oriented works about Cosmism and human destiny, the exhibition organizers embraced them, deifying Tsiolkovskii as a preacher, a visionary, the father of cosmopolitanism. They embraced the "master's" vision of animate matter and monism and believed in the importance of their efforts as part of a big evolutionary leap for all of humanity. In several effusive communications to Tsiolkovskii (the "first honorary captain rocket-mobilist") in late 1927, the organizers referenced Leibniz' world view on monism and underscored the power of inventors to "find the resources for human immortality" – the foundation of the Cosmist view of the universe.[60] Their rationale for space exploration had as much to do with equating technology with modernization as with a self-important and mystical notion of human destiny that harked back to the nineteenth century.

[56] ARAN, 555/4/641/1–5 (September 7, 1926).

[57] ARAN, 555/3/198/6–8 (February 5, 1927).

[58] ARAN, 555/3/199/5–6 (December 3, 1928).

[59] ARAN, 555/3/198/1–10b (January 21, 1927). Although nearly identical, the word *kosmopolizma* differed in meaning and etymology from the pejorative term *kosmopolitizm* that Party ideologues used in the late 1940s to describe a "decadent" and "bourgeois" lifestyle during the late Stalin years. The latter word was first introduced into public discourse in January 1949. *Kosmopoliti* was probably derived from the early-seventeenth-century French word "cosmopolite," as in a "citizen of the world."

[60] ARAN, 555/3/198/34–34ob (December 7, 1927); ARAN, 555/3/198/38–38ob (December 18, 1927).

FIGURE 8. A number of striking images exist of the space exhibition held in Moscow in 1927. A visitor entering the exhibit would first pass by the Tsiolkovskii section, which included a bust of the old man produced specifically for the event. The bust, placed on a pulpit, is surrounded by his various publications and models of rockets and spaceships. A framed sketch on the wall behind the bust shows Tsiolkovskii next to a dirigible. The whole arrangement suggests more a shrine than an exhibit, underscoring the near-religious fervor with which Tsiolkovskii's supporters believed in his cause. [*Source*: Ron Miller]

The exhibition, unimaginatively named the "World's First Exhibition of Models of Interplanetary Apparatus, Mechanisms, Instruments and Historical Materials," opened on April 24, 1927 not far from what is now Maiakovskii Square at number 68 (now 28) Tverskaia Street, one of Moscow's biggest thoroughfares (Figures 8 and 9). Open to the public for two months, the exhibition had an elaborately designed entrance with a huge display of an imagined planetary landscape placed behind a large pane of glass, designed and built by one Arkhipov. Part of the display, somewhat incorrectly called "Lunar Panorama," showed a hypothetical planet with orange soil and blue vegetation crisscrossed by straight canals. A giant silver rocket descended from the starry sky while a voyager in a spacesuit (made of plywood) stood at

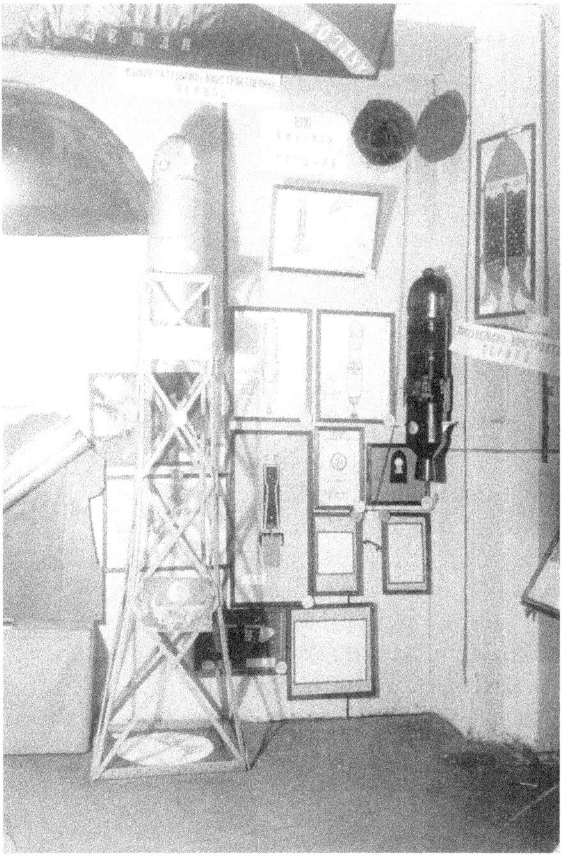

FIGURE 9. Another image from the space exhibition held in Moscow in 1927 shows "Goddard Corner," where models and drawings of Robert Goddard's rockets are depicted. The placard at the back notes that this is part of the "Inventor-Designer Period" of the history of space travel, exemplifying the ways in which Soviet enthusiasts of the time were already creating a master narrative of the history of space exploration. [*Source*: Ron Miller]

the edge of a crater. Organizer Mikhail Popov described the feeling of entering the exhibition: "By taking a pair [of] steps, I crossed over the threshold of one epoch to another, into the space [era]."[61]

Although state organs ignored the show, it succeeded resoundingly with the public. According to the organizers, in two months, between 10,000 and 12,000 people visited the exhibition. Visitors included school children, workers, service employees, artists, scientists, policemen, and such

[61] Samoilovich, *Grazhdanin vselennoi*, 181.

luminaries as poet Vladimir Maiakovskii.[62] Visitors, who were invited to record their impressions in a book of comments, were both effusive and candid. One person, who signed as "Gorev," wrote "[o]ur mind is not accustomed to all the 'wonderful and unknown' which was... seen and heard, as if in a dream, yet we understand that this is not a fantasy but a completely feasible idea supported by the achievements of science and engineering." Another person, an artist from the third state cinematographic studio, recommended that "[i]t would be desirable that our inventors achieve the first landing on the moon." One of the most captivated visitors was S. G. Vortkin, a reporter from the most important workers' news daily, *Rabochaia moskva*, who wrote, "I am going to accompany you on the first flight. I am quite serious about this. As soon as I heard what you had done, I tried in every way to make certain that you would take me with you. Please do not refuse my request."[63]

Beyond organizing an exhibition in 1927, the Association of Inventors also established a "language section" to develop a single universal language for the socialist future when men and women from all over the world would travel to space together. Like other social signifiers such as dress and titles, language was a central component of the transformations that demarcated pre-Revolutionary and post-Revolutionary modes of behavior.[64] In tune with ever changing conventions, Bol'shevik lexicon evolved over the 1920s and 1930s as words were discarded, adopted, or changed. Esperanto, the artificial language invented in the 1880s, was hugely popular in the Soviet Union in the 1920s. A world congress in Leningrad in 1926 helped Esperanto's cause; many believed that such an artificial language would facilitate connections across cultures and borders.[65] The Association members, unapologetically utopian minded, modeled their language on the same universal ideals of Esperanto, but they took it one step further: They meant universal in the literal sense. They called their new language "AO," apparently after a similarly named artificial language suggested by anarchists during the Civil War that consisted entirely of monosyllables.[66] Several members of the association changed their name to AO-derived words. For example, Ol'ga Kholoptseva, the woman who corresponded frequently with Tsiolkovskii about the 1927 exhibition, always signed off as "Efofbi."[67]

The Association members were undoubtedly influenced by one of the most popular science fiction novels of the era, V. D. Nikol'skii's *Cherez tysiachu*

62 ARAN, 4/14/198/38; ARAN, 4/14/198/11.

63 Comments from Rynin, *Interplanetary Flight and Communication, Vol. II, No.* 4, 205–206.

64 Michael S. Gorham, *Speaking in Tongues: Language Culture and the Politics of Voice in Revolutionary Russia* (DeKalb, IL: Northern Illinois University Press, 2003).

65 Peter Forster, *The Esperanto Movement* (The Hague: Mouton, 1982), 188–203.

66 Stites, *Revolutionary Dreams*, 135.

67 For several of these handwritten letters (mostly on postcards), see ARAN, f. 555, op. 3, d. 198.

let (*In a Thousand Years*), published in 1928, which not only featured a future planet busy with space travel, but citizens united by a single common language not unlike Esperanto.[68] Although he derisively wrote to the Association that "I somewhat doubt in the practicality of an artificial language," Tsiolkovskii himself invested much work in devising an artificial language. In 1927, he published a monograph on the subject and the following year patented a typewriter specifically for his "international" alphabet.[69] Perhaps the impulse to create a universal language was best summed up by Viktor Khlebnikov, the enigmatic Cubo-Futurist poet who, after the Revolution, called on all Soviet artists to "create a common graphic language, common to all the peoples of the third satellite of the sun, to devise graphic signs intelligible and acceptable throughout this inhabited star lost in space."[70] In Khlebnikov's view, which was not isolated, the revolution in space had no borders, encompassed multiple visions, and used one language.

SPACEFLIGHT IN ART AND CULTURE

The degree of popular Soviet fascination with space in the 1920s is also underlined by how deeply it resonated in the various art forms of the day. From literature to film to painting to poetry to architecture to language, clusters of artists produced works that reflected their belief that cosmic travel was an inevitable part of their future. A small sampling of this vast output, that is, Tolstoi's novel *Aelita*, Protazanov's movie of the same title, Malevich's Suprematist paintings, and the *Amaravella* group's artwork, highlights some of the key dimensions of this cultural discourse. On the surface, artists with a spiritually flavored view of the cosmos may have been disengaged from the modernist technologically minded utopians, but in fact they were linked to each other in a network united in the cause of space exploration. Like their more "scientifically" minded space enthusiast colleagues, the artists produced their populist work largely isolated from the elite Soviet scientific and technical intelligentsia of the NEP era.

Literature

The most widely disseminated media for communicating ideas about space exploration was *nauchnaia-fantastika*. Space fiction, which constituted about one-fifth of all Soviet science fiction in the post-Revolution period to

[68] V. Nikol'skii, *Cherez tysiachu let* (Leningrad: P. P. Soikin, 1928). Tsiolkovskii later reviewed this novel in *V boi za tekhniku* no. 2 (1934): 27–28.

[69] K. Tsiolkovskii, *Obshchechelovecheskaia azbuka, pravopisanie i iazyk* (Kaluga: K. E. Tsiolkovskii, 1927).

[70] Khlebnikov quoted in Larissa A. Zhadova, *Malevich: Suprematism and Revolution in Russian Art, 1910–1930* (London: Thames & Hudson, 1982), 56.

World War II, was remarkable for its disproportionate social resonance given the subgenre's relatively low numbers. To some degree, most of the space-related works reflected the same characteristics of the broader science fiction literature; in other words, almost all such works were technologically optimistic and can be divided into adventure stories (*krasnyi pinkerton* or "red detective") and future utopias. Stites' claim that "[Soviet] science fiction was a striking example of revolutionary discourse because of its total vision of communist life and its treatment of 'revolutionary dreams'" was also true for the smaller subset of space fiction.[71] Although the stories were less about social than technological revolution, the prevailing mood of revolution allowed the latter to be conflated with the former. The canon displayed distinct marks of continuity with pre-Revolutionary trends, partly because the literature on both sides of the divide benefited from the deep influence of foreign sources. Post-Revolutionary space fiction was distinguished largely by an often explicit sanction to the cause of socialism; such a concession reflected less an adeherence to Bol'shevik doctrine on the part of writers, almost all of whom were non-Party members, than their perception of the possible future convergence between technological utopia and socialist utopia.

Aleksandr Beliaev, often called the "Soviet Jules Verne," was probably the only Soviet writer to devote all his artistic output to the science fiction genre. Beliaev's novels focused on adventure, suspense, and technology, with the occasional satire, rather than socially relevant topics, but their immense popularity in the late 1920s and early 1930s suggests that his approach struck a nerve in the average science fiction reader. Part of his appeal might have been his unambiguous approach to storytelling in which he closely positioned his stories as parables on the struggle of communism versus capitalism, thus vocalizing his support for the Bol'sheviks. Beliaev's eagerness to provide narratives in support of the official position on the Revolution, that is, to write about the future of communism, is underlined by his appeal to *Narkompros* Commissar Anatolii Lunacharskii on what elements should underscore a science fiction novel set in an idealized classless society. The only answer he received, "the struggle of the old with the new," appears not to have satisfied him, and Beliaev instead fell upon old tropes to describe utopia. In his *Bor'ba v efire* (*Struggle in the Ether*, 1928), workers from a superindustrialized America, transformed into robots of the Taylor system, battled with Communists in space.[72] Although not critically acclaimed at the

[71] Stites, *Revolutionary Dreams*, 167–168. For general reviews of early Soviet science fiction, D. Suvin, "The Utopian Tradition of Russian Science Fiction," *Modern Language Review* 66 (1971): 139–159; A. F. Britikov, *Russkii Sovetskii nauchno-fantasticheskii roman* (Leningrad: Nauka, 1970); Patrick L. McGuire, *Red Stars: Political Aspects of Soviet Science Fiction* (Ann Arbor: UMI Research Press, 1985).

[72] Britikov, *Russkii Sovetskii nauchno-fantasticheskii roman*, 128; McGuire, *Red Star*, 12.

time, Beliaev has been evaluated less harshly in later years, perhaps because he provided such a boost to the genre of Soviet science fiction via his almost twenty novels. Packed with fantastic technology, lucid explanations, and compelling writing, Beliaev tried to achieve what he considered the goal of science fiction, "to serve humanism in the biggest, universal conception of this word."[73]

The most famous Soviet science fiction novel of the 1920s, Aleksei Tolstoi's *Aelita: Zakat Marsa* (*Aelita: Sunset of Mars*), first published in serialized form in 1922–1923, also remains the most famous *space* fiction work of the period.[74] It also perfectly encapsulated the contradictory themes of space advocacy in the 1920s. In the story, an engineer and a soldier voyage to Mars, where the latter incites a proletarian revolution among the bourgeois Martians. Aelita is the queen of Mars who falls in love with the Red Army soldier. On one level, the novel incorporates many elements of post-Revolutionary utopian science fiction: a bourgeois enemy, a socialist revolution, modern science and technology, adventure and romance borrowed from Edgar Rice Burroughs, and utopian dreaming. Yet, *Aelita*'s narrative also has hints of mysticism, especially ideas infused with theosophy and ancient anthrosophic ideas, not dissimilar to Fedorov and Tsiolkovskii's Cosmist views of the universe.[75] Defending his position from critics who blamed him for being too "emotional" in the novel, Tolstoi wrote, "Art – an artistic creation – appears momentarily like a dream. It has no place for logic, because its goal is not to find a cause for some sort of event, but to give in all its fullness a living piece of cosmos."[76] His use of the lexicon of panpsychism suggests a link to the mystical side of Tsiolkovskii and the Cosmists.[77]

Aelita, despite its invocation of space travel, or maybe because of its Cosmist overtones, was a novel less about looking forward than looking backward. Although regarded as the most important Soviet science fiction novel of the period, *Aelita*, Halina Stephan rightly claims, "concluded rather than inaugurated a literary tradition." Nevertheless, the technologically minded spaceflight enthusiasts of Tolstoi's day avoided the mysticism and found it forward-thinking because the novel was the first of the period that used a

[73] Britikov, *Russkii Sovetskii nauchno-fantasticheskii roman*, 113.

[74] The novel was originally published in three serialized parts in the journal *Krasnaia nov'*. In 1923, it was published as a stand-alone novel as *Aelita (Zakat Marsa)* (Moscow: Gosizdat, 1923).

[75] Halina Stephan makes a similar point: "Aleksei Tolstoi's *Aelita* and the Inauguration of Soviet Science Fiction," *Canadian-American Slavic Studies* 18 nos. 1–2 (1984): 63–75.

[76] Tolstoi quoted in Stephan, "Aleksei Tolstoi's *Aelita*," 72–73.

[77] See also Ian Christie, "Down to Earth: *Aelita* Relocated," in *Inside the Film Factory: New Approaches to Russian and Soviet Cinema*, eds. Richard Taylor and Ian Christie (London: Routledge, 1991), 97–98; Rosenthal, "Introduction," in *The Occult in Russian and Soviet Culture*, 25.

rocket for interplanetary travel. Members of the Moscow Society for the Study of Interplanetary Communications (OIMS) were so taken by Tolstoi's use of the rocket that they considered using the story to develop a film script – a project that was brought to fruition by others.

Film

The movie version of Tolstoi's *Aelita* appeared soon after publication of the print version and was directed by Iakov Protazanov, the Russian film director of pre-Revolutionary fame.[78] Released officially in September 1924 at the peak of the space fad, *Aelita* has since been hailed as the most important Soviet science fiction movie of the interwar era. It also contributed enormously to the popularization of spaceflight in Soviet culture in the 1920s; interest in the movie after its release drove up attendance numbers at interplanetary talks sponsored by space societies such as the OIMS. The film also established a new standard for Soviet cinema, if not in quality, then certainly in popularity and hype. Weeks of intense advertising campaigns in *Pravda* and *Kino-gazeta* (*Movie Gazette*) preceded its release, while airplanes dropped thousands of leaflets announcing the opening over Voronezh.[79] Tickets for the opening shows sold out, and the size of the crowd on opening night prevented even Protazanov from attending.

Protazanov, who like Tolstoi had only returned to the Soviet Union from exile to direct the film, engineered a significant transformation in Tolstoi's relatively conventional novel, producing a remarkable movie that not only mirrored and telescoped many prevailing social concerns of the NEP-era in movie form, but also critiqued Tolstoi's novel itself. With the help of scriptwriters Aleksei Faiko and Fedor Otsep, Protazanov reimagined Tolstoi's original account of the voyage to Mars as a dream in the mind of the protagonist Los'.[80] The so-called revolution on Mars – which occupies only one-fourth of the film – is riddled with ambiguities that do not demarcate strictly along bipolar lines (capitalist–communist, benevolent–exploitative); nothing is really what it seems. Here, Los' is not simply a one-dimensional

78 M. Aleinnikov, *Iakov Protazanov: o tvorcheskom puti rezhisera*, 2nd ed. (Moscow: Iskusstvo, 1957); M. Aleinnikov, *Iakov Protazanov* (Moscow: Iskusstvo, 1961); Ian Christie and Julian Graffy, eds., *Protazanov and the Continuity of Russian Cinema* (London: British Film Institute, 1993); Denise J. Youngblood, "The Return of the Native: Yakov Protazanov and Soviet Cinema," in *Inside the Film Factory*, 103–123.

79 The movie was produced by a new multinational company, *Mezhrabpom-Rus'*, a joint Russian–German company that combined *Mezhrabpom* (International Workers' Aid), a Berlin-based relief organization and *Rus'*, a Russian production company formed in 1918. Richard Taylor, *The Politics of the Soviet Cinema, 1917–1929* (Cambridge, UK: Cambridge University Press, 1979), 74.

80 Faiko and Otsep made changes to the original plot with Tolstoi's agreement. Aleinnikov, *Iakov Protazanov*, 32. Most Western sources incorrectly list his name incorrectly as "Otsen" instead of the correct "Otsep."

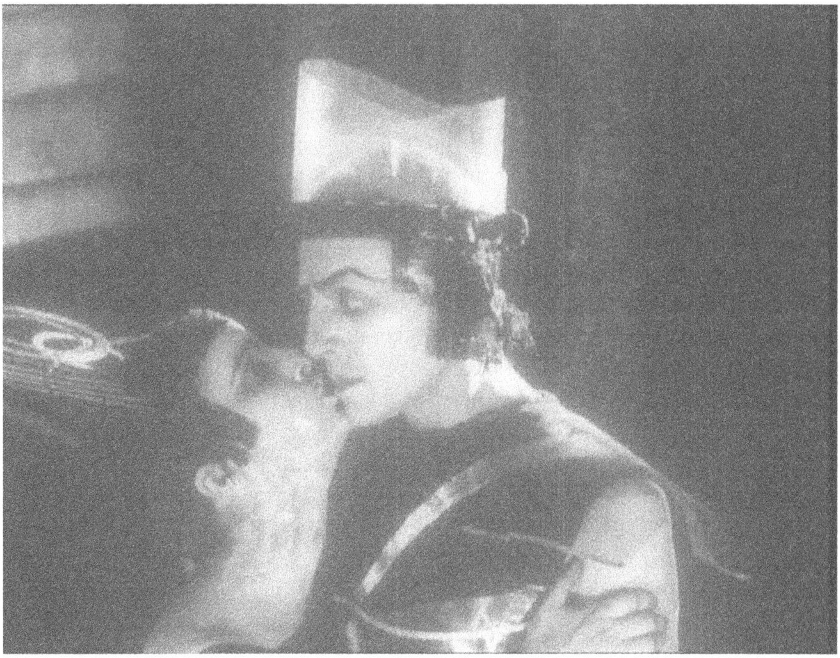

FIGURE 10. A still from Iakov Protazanov's famous 1924 movie shows Aelita (left), the queen of Mars, in a typically seductive pose. The movie was both highly influential and very controversial; it has come to be regarded as a seminal contribution to the era of Soviet silent films. For many space enthusiasts, the movie's sociopolitical dimensions were less important than the technologies of space travel depicted, which attracted many people to the idea of space exploration. [*Source*: Cathy Lewis]

caricature of the new Soviet man but rather one living in and mirroring the contradictory realities of NEP life.

In the movie *Aelita*, Protazanov's sought to produce an "impartial" work but the negative response surprised him. By and large, the state media criticized the film. In fact, the movie caused so much controversy that as late as 1928, newspapers and journals were still engaged in attacking the movie for being "alien to the working class," for its "petty bourgeois ending" because Los' returns to the domesticities of marriage, and for being "too Western."[81] Although many wrote off *Aelita* as a misstep in Protazanov's long career, it was an incredibly popular film; it did, after all, feature evocative acting, exotic scenes in interplanetary space, a glamorous princess, and women in provocative costumes (see Figure 10). Grigorii Kramarov, the head of the OIMS, later underscored how "the book and film played a

[81] Youngblood, "The Return of the Native," 111–112; Denise J. Youngblood, *Soviet Cinema in the Silent Era, 1918–1935* (Ann Arbor: UMI Research Press, 1985), 30–32.

significant role in strengthening interest towards interplanetary communications and contributed to the development of activities of our Society."[82] Among those deeply affected by the hoopla over *Aelita* was ten-year-old Vladimir Chelomei; forty-five years later, as a general designer of the Soviet space program, he named a new project of his, a huge space complex to send the first Soviet cosmonauts to Mars, *Aelita*.[83]

Aelita was one of two major motion pictures dealing with spaceflight in the interwar era. The other, *Kosmicheskii reis* (Space Voyage), was less celebrated and less popular, but it holds a special place in the history of Soviet cosmic culture because of Tsiolkovskii's involvement with the film. As a young film student, Vasilii Zhuravlev had decided that he would make a movie about spaceflight. In 1924, *Goskino*, the state film studio, acquired the rights of his script "The Conquest of the Moon by Mister Fox and Mister Trott" in order to make a major animated movie. Although only an animated short was made, Zhuravlev did not give up his ambition.[84] In 1932, with the help of the famed Sergei Eisenstein, for whom he worked, Zhuravlev signed a contract with the *Mosfil'm* studio to finance the project. Eisenstein had suggested that in order to make the movie as scientifically accurate as possible, Zhuravlev get in touch with Tsiolkovskii in Kaluga. Between 1933 and 1935, Zhuravlev's crew visited Tsiolkovskii three times to discuss how to accurately reproduce aspects of space travel on film. Zhuravlev also corresponded regularly by mail with Tsiolkovskii, who in the very brief period at the end of his life when he was adopted by the Soviet government as a national hero, was officially hired as a "scientific consultant" by *Mosfil'm*.[85] Zhuravlev later recalled that Tsiolkovskii "was very concerned that everything in the picture should be interesting and entertaining so that the film would in no case be a dry exposition of theoretical calculations."[86]

The movie, which came out in January 1936, four months after Tsiolkovskii's death, was not a big success. Its story and script, written by A. A. Filimonov, was rather wooden, and it involved a voyage from Moscow to the Moon in the summer of 1946 during which its protagonists, an academician, his young female assistant, and a boy, visit the hidden side of the Moon in their cumbersome spacesuits and leaden shoes. The movie was quickly forgotten, partly because it had been a silent film in an era of sound, but it did leave behind two important legacies. Zhuravlev's consultation with

[82] Kramarov, *Na zare kosmonavtiki*, 19–20.

[83] Asif A. Siddiqi, *The Soviet Space Race With Apollo* (Gainesville: University Press of Florida, 2003), 745–754.

[84] Nikolai Zhuravlev, "'Kosmicheskii reis' – skazka moego detstva," *Tekhnika-molodezhi* no. 10 (1987): 18–21. The animated short, called "Mezhplanetnaia revoliutsiia" (Interplanetary Revolution), was released in late 1924 just after *Aelita*, which it partly parodied.

[85] For Zhuravlev's letters to Tsiolkovskii, see ARAN, f. 555, op. 4, d. 232.

[86] V. Zhuravlev, "Shturm kosmosa," *Iskusstvo kino* no. 11 (1957): 91–97.

Tsiolkovskii paid dividends in that it was probably the very first science fiction film to accurately portray human movement in the zero gravity of outer space as well as the one-sixth gravity of the Moon.[87] Second, Tsiolkovskii, who was invigorated by participating in the movie – he wrote to Zhuravlev that "Cinema, this is the highest form of art" – left behind a remarkable document of his work on the movie, an "Album of Cosmic Voyages."[88] Tsiolkovskii produced this two-part work in 1933 to guide the makers of the film. The second part, composed of hand drawings, remains a striking example of his prescience. His sketches show with remarkable clarity the kind of activity space travelers would undertake. He illustrated astronauts doing acrobatics in zero gravity, conducting spacewalks outside a space station with tethers connecting them to their ship, using airlocks, sleeping in restrained sleeping bags, and looking out at the universe through common windows. He devised such technically elegant solutions as using shutters to control temperatures on spaceships, using hydroponic greenhouses to feed the crew, and strapping backpacks for spacewalking astronauts. Many of the drawings eerily mirror the actions of astronauts that are familiar to us today.[89] If Tsiolkovskii's scientific legacy is marred by his often mystical tracts about immortality and living molecules, the "Album of Cosmic Voyages" points to an equally important visionary quality that informed his character. It is a legacy of contradictions, like the entire corpus of artistic contribution to the Soviet space fad.

Art

Besides *Aelita*, both the novel and the film, other Russian works of art crossed the lines dividing technology and mysticism. Some scholars have claimed connections between the Russian avant-garde and Cosmism, arguing that the universal views of Nikolai Fedorov deeply influenced artistic personalities such as Kandinskii, Malevich, and Filonov.[90] But these connections were neither monolithic nor consistent. No single movement encapsulated the contradictions of the Soviet space fad better than did the Suprematists. Mentored by one of the legendary artists of the Russian avant-garde, Kazimir Malevich, the Suprematists exemplified the duality and ambiguity

[87] Iu. Soimenov, "Pervyi fil'm o kosmose," *Kryl'ia rodiny* no. 4 (1981): 36–37.

[88] ARAN, 555/4/10a/12–17 (January 24, 1935).

[89] "Al'bom kosmichceskikh puteshestvii (opisanie)," in *Rukopisnye materially K. E. Tsiolkovskogo v archive Akademii nauk sssr: nauchnoe opisanie*, eds. B. N. Vorob'ev and B. V. Levshin (Moscow: Nauka, 1966), 129–169.

[90] Iurii Linnik, *Russkii kosmizm i russkii avangard* (Petrozavodsk: Sviatoi ostrov, 1995); Michael Holquist, "Tsiolkovsky as a Moment in the Prehistory of the Avant-Garde," in *Laboratory of Dreams: The Russian Avant-Garde and Cultural Experiment*, eds. John E. Bowlt and Olga Matich (Stanford: Stanford University Press, 1996), 100–117.

of the space fad, cutting across not only mysticism (Cosmism) and science (space technology) but also the time and politics of the imperial and Bol'shevik eras.

Suprematism as an organized movement of Russian and Soviet artists developed in the mid-1910s by extending and rejecting many of the foundations of Cubism. It reached its peak right after the Revolution and then expanded into other media (principally architecture) in the 1920s before losing direction in the late 1920s. Malevich unveiled Suprematism at an exhibition of Futurist art in 1915, with works that in their geometric shapes and colors completely dispensed with representations of conventional space and perspective. The paintings acquired a peculiarly compelling nature by the juxtaposition of colors and shapes that conveyed a continuum of space and time rather than self-contained and defined objects or ideas. Malevich himself called his work the "non-objective world," that is, a perception of the environment's distilled spaciousness.[91]

Such an approach naturally led many Suprematist artists to eulogize first aviation and then ultimately the cosmos as the ultimate environment of spaciousness. In their paintings, such as Boris Ender's "Cosmic Landscape" (1923), space – both cosmic and otherwise – became an integral part of the composition instead of "filler" in more traditional artistic creations. Malevich expressed interest in both the most modern frontiers of art and science and technology, and he spent many years in pursuit of what he called the "science of art." He firmly believed in the power of technological "progress" and, like many other intellectuals of the day, supported the perfection of nature by means of artificial means. Malevich wrote, "I shall make my whole state comfortable and convenient, and, what is more, I shall convert other states and eventually the whole globe to my comfort and convenience."[92] His writings show an undeniably technologically utopian gloss, sprinkled with flirtations with anarchist ideas. Some have suggested that Malevich, like other many other Russian intellectuals, was captivated by mysticism and theosophy. For example, Kazus claimed Malevich was "the first Russian artist to take note of [Fedorov's views of the universe, and] placed [them] at the base of Suprematism."[93] Malevich's many writings and works, however, suggest that his works were attempts to merge some of the disparate ideological underpinnings of modernity and spiritualism, that is, technological utopianism and mysticism.

Malevich's interest in spatial ideas beyond Earth first manifested themselves after 1916. As he wrote to a friend, "Earth has been abandoned like

[91] Zhadova, *Malevich*, 49–50.

[92] Serge Fauchereau, *Malevich* (New York: Rizzoli, 1993), 27.

[93] Quotation from Igor A. Kazus, "The Idea of Cosmic Architecture and the Russian Avant-Garde of the Early Twentieth Century," in Clair, *Cosmos*, 194. See also, Igor Kazus, "Cosmic Architecture and the Russian avant-garde," *Project Russia* 15 (undated): 81–88.

a worm-eaten house. And an aspiration towards space is in fact lodged in man and his consciousness, a longing to break away from the globe of the earth."[94] Paintings at the time show geometric forms (usually squares or rectangles) with hollowed-out spaces and stretched drops of color, drenched in white light that highlighted things unimaginable on Earth, that is, without reference to any form of nature. There was literally no up or down. Malevich's engagement with spatial ideas in the cosmic sense reached a zenith in 1917–1918 during the height of the Revolutionary years and just after the first burst of invocations to space travel appeared in the media. In 1919, he explicitly articulated the notion that Suprematism itself could be part of the project of space exploration:

> Between [Earth and the Moon], a new Suprematist satellite can be constructed, equipped with every component, which will move along an orbit shaping its new track.... I have ripped through the blue lampshade of the constraints of color. I have come out into the white. Follow me, comrade aviators! Swim into the abyss. I have set up the semaphores of Suprematism. I have overcome the lining of the colored sky.... Swim! The white free abyss, infinity is before you.[95]

Some of Malevich's paintings from this period, such as "Suprematism" (1917) and "Drawing" (1918), depict objects not dissimilar to what we might today call space stations or futuristic cities in the cosmos. Malevich, of course, never alluded to them as such, and most certainly would not have known about such things given that few in the world had yet articulated similar ideas in print. Yet the paintings show a remarkable understanding of the basic concepts of space travel, particularly the idea of space stations, and predate similar artistic visions that were common in Soviet popular science journals and pulp fiction of the 1920s. Malevich's fascination with the cosmos peaked around 1918 with his attempts to achieve an absolute spaciousness with pure whiteness, a white light of infinity that he represented in perhaps his most extreme avant-garde experiment, "White Square on White" (1918).

Like Malevich's works, many of his protégés' works hinted at a Fedorovian or Cosmist view of space. The case of the Society of Easel Painters (OST), which included a number of Malevich protégés, perfectly encapsulated the tensions between technological utopianism and Cosmism in the Soviet space fad of the 1920s. Like many in the Soviet avant-garde, the OST were taken with the wonders of technology and believed that art should mirror and interpret technological advancement in both mechanistic and abstract ways. Artists such as Vladimir Liushin, who produced "Station for Interplanetary Communications" (1922), seemed wholly beholden to the

94 Quoted in Zhadova, *Malevich*, 124, n. 39.
95 Ibid., 57.

power of the machine to benefit society.[96] Yet Ivan Kudriashev, a Malevich protégé, eventually gravitated to a different view of the cosmos. Unlike other artists, Kudriashev had a direct connection to the space advocacy community: His father, a model builder, had been employed by Tsiolkovskii to build some of his conceptions. The younger Kudriashev accompanied his father on a visit to see the old man and translated Tsiolkovskii's technical terms for the model builder.[97] Kudriashev's philosophy, underlined in messianic essays about the expansion and settlement of humanity throughout the solar system, suggested a closer emotional affinity to Fedorov's mystic ideas than to earlier Suprematist works. Other Malevich followers, Lazar Lisitskii and Georgii Krutikov, explored a new type of architecture designed for "flying cities." These ideas stemmed not only from a fascination with space, but also the utilitarian view that because living space on the Earth was limited, one had to devise other spaces for habitation, a distinctively Fedorovian view of life.[98]

The most striking example of artistic fascination with space resulting from the meeting between the artistic avant-garde and the philosophy of Cosmism was in the work of the informal Soviet artists' group known as *Amaravella*. The self-contained contradictions characteristic of Russian Cosmist philosophy characterized their work: although they advocated a universal and cosmic consciousness to life and art, their art reflected deeply national influences (such as medieval Russian art) and their philosophy followed the tradition of an almost nationalist Russian approach to the cosmos, best underscored by many of Fedorov's followers. Superficially, they aspired to combine the most modern of both science and art, the progenitors of a long tradition during Soviet times, but on a deeper level, theirs was the lexicon of both "rational" and "irrational" science, of both modern and archaic art.

Petr Fateev, a thirty-two-year-old painter, formed and led the original *Amaravella* around 1922. It reached a stable membership of a few energetic and inspired artists such as Aleksandr Sardan, Sergei Shigolev, Viktor Chernovolenko, and Boris Smirnov-Rusetskii by 1927 and 1928 when the name *Amaravella* was coined, apparently derived by Sardan from a Sanskrit word meaning "bearing light" or "creative energy." The group, who operated as a commune, explored a remarkably wide range of ideas and approaches to art based on their nebulous philosophical ideas about cosmic harmony. Sardan, who was also a professional musician, produced compositions that

96 V. Kostin, *OST (Obshchestvo stankovistov)* (Leningrad: Khudozhnik RSFSR, 1976); John E. Bowlt, "The Society of Easel Artists (OST)," *Russian History/Histoire Russe* 9, Pts. 2–3 (1982): 203–226.

97 Kostin, *OST*, 24–26; Zhadova, *Malevich*, 129, n. 19.

98 S. Khan-Magomedov, "Proekt 'letaiushchego goroda'," *Dekorativnoe iskusstvo* no. 1 (1973): 30–36; Kazus, "The Idea of Cosmic Architecture and the Russian Avant-Garde of the Early Twentieth Century," in *Cosmos*, 196–197.

were combinations of sound, painting, and architecture. His works such as "Sound in Space" in 1920 and "Lunar Sonata" and "Cosmic Symphony" in 1925 tried to represent the "sound" of architecture through vivid colorful hues that aspired toward a cosmic (aural) harmony. Other works such as "Earth, Ocean, Space" (1922) and "Cosmic Motive" (late 1920s) addressed his philosophical views, some of them borrowed from eastern philosophies, whereas "From the Moon to Space Way" (1930) and "Earthly Beacon and Signals from Space" (1926) elucidated technical ideas. The group exhibited their works several times, including once in New York in 1927, when six of Sardan's paintings were displayed at an exhibition organized by the Russian avant-garde artist Nikolai Rerikh. Rerikh, in turn, served as a link to the "other" space advocate community, centered around Tsiolkovskii: He befriended Aleksandr Gorskii, an influential Cosmist and occultist who himself moved to Kaluga, Tsiolkovskii's adopted hometown, in the 1930s.[99]

LINKING COMMUNITIES: BIOCOSMISTS

At the very extreme of the continuum from technological utopianism to Cosmism were those who were fully engaged in a spiritual and sometimes occultish interest in space exploration. In the early 1920s, the most explicit mark of Cosmism's imprint emerged through scientific, cultural, and artistic icons such as Vladimir Vernadskii (the geochemist), Vladimir Zabolotskii (the poet), and Maksim Gor'kii (the writer) but also via short-lived groups such as the Anarchist-Biocosmists. The group (also known as the Biocosmist-Immortalists) coalesced in 1921 after the state's crackdown on anarchists following the funeral of famous Russian anarchist Petr Kropotkin. When the authorities arrested an anarchist group named the Universalists, a new collective, the Anarchist-Biocosmists, replaced them; adherents pledged their support to the Bol'sheviks but also announced their goal of initiating a social revolution "in interplanetary space."[100] The group, which had factions in both Moscow and Petrograd, briefly published a journal, *Bessmertie* (*Immortality*), under the banner "Immortalism and Interplanetarianism." In their manifesto, issued in 1921, they announced several goals, including victory over space ("not air navigation... but cosmic navigation"). They declared the two basic human rights to be the right to exist forever and the right to unimpeded movement in interplanetary space. Inspired by Fedorov's

99 Iurii Linnik, *Amaravella: Put' k pleiadam: russkie khodozniki-kosmisty* (Petrozavodsk: Sviatoi ostrov, 1995), 82–145; Iurii Linnik, "Amaravella," *Sever* no. 11 (1981): 108–114.

100 A. Sviator, "Biokosmicheskaia poetika," in *Literaturnye manifesty ot simvolizma do nashikh dnei*, ed. S. Dzhimbinov (Moscow: Izdatel'skii dom Soglasie, 2000), 305–314.

ideas, they wanted to abolish death, colonize the universe, and then resurrect those who had already died.[101] Just after Lenin's death, the Anarchist-Biocosmists published an official statement in *Izvestiia* arguing that all was not lost because the "[workers] and the oppressed all over the world can never reconcile itself with the fact of Lenin's death."[102]

Devotees of Cosmism and Fedorov's philosophy were connected to the technological utopian spaceflight community by means of a network that highlighted the fine line between science and mysticism. Tsiolkovskii, someone who was equally at ease writing about propellant masses as about victory over death, was naturally the most obvious and important link between the two sides.[103] There were other, more famous links. During the one-hundredth anniversary of Fedorov's birthday, Maksim Gor'kii, a devotee of Fedorov, famously declared in an interview in *Izvestiia* that "freedom without power over nature – that's the same as freeing peasants without land."[104] It is less well known that Gor'kii, who also believed in the search for immortality, considered Tsiolkovskii to be an important scientific and philosophical thinker. The writer had heard of Tsiolkovskii during his exile via the latter's 1925 work *Prichina kosmosa* (*Reason for Space*), a meditation on humanity's spiritual calling to go to space. Although Gor'kii intended to visit Tsiolkovskii in Kaluga upon his return to the Soviet Union in 1928, the two never met. Tsiolkovskii, however, sent Gor'kii many of his brochures on Cosmist philosophy, which evidently resonated deeply with the writer; Gor'kii sent a well-publicized congratulatory letter to the "interplanetary old man" (as he liked to call Tsiolkovskii) on his seventy-fifth birthday in 1932.[105]

Even at the very extreme of mysticism, people remained connected with the technological utopians. One well-known Biocosmist member, Leonid Vasil'ev, who was also a respected researcher of telepathy, maintained a friendship with Aleksandr Chizhevskii, the young intellectual and well-known Cosmist who wrote extensively on the relationship between cosmic factors (such as sunspots) and social activity on Earth. Chizhevskii lived in Kaluga briefly and later wrote a massive memoir on his relationship with

[101] "Deklarativnaia rezoliutsiia," *Izvestiia VTsIK*, January 4, 1922. The Biocosmists unsuccessfully tried to recruit such prominent scientists as Eugen Steinach and Albert Einstein. Michael Hagemeister, "Die 'Biokosmisten' – Anarchismus und Maximalismus in der frühen Sowjetzeit," in *Studia slavica in honorem viri doctissimi Olexa Horbatsch, Vol. 1, Pt. 1*, ed. G. Freidhof et al. (Munich: Sagner, 1983), 61–76; Hagemeister, "Russian Cosmism in the 1920s and Today," 195–196.

[102] A. Sviatogor, N. Lebedev, and V. Zikosi, "Golos anarkhistov," *Izvestiia VTsIK*, January 27, 1924.

[103] Tsiolkovskii also communicated with an international association, devotees of a philosophy similar to Russian Cosmism, known as the Association Internationale de Biocosmique (based in Lyon, France). ARAN, 555/3/200/12–13 (illegible but probably April 16, 1934).

[104] A. Gornostaev, "N. F. Fedorov," *Izvestiia*, December 29, 1928.

[105] ARAN, 555/4/183/1 (1932).

Tsiolkovskii.[106] Chizhevskii also holds a special place in the history of Soviet space exploration: He wrote the famous German-language introduction for Tsiolkovskii's 1924 monograph that effectively set off the Soviet space fad of the 1920s, enrapturing the technological utopians who wanted to build rockets to bring the Soviet Union into the modern world.

UTOPIA ABANDONED?

The political, social, and cultural climate dramatically changed in the Soviet Union between the beginning and end of the space fad. The combined repercussions of the Cultural Revolution, the First Five-Year Plan, and nationwide collectivization completely transformed much of Soviet society. For scientists and technical specialists, the Shakty trial and the Industrial Party affair redefined, with tragic consequences, the boundaries of "proper" behavior and expression. Party ideologues purged out of influential positions a huge numbers of old specialists, especially those with roots in pre-Revolutionary times.[107] They also removed "old influences" from the editorial boards of several popular science journals. The government absorbed P. P. Soikin's semiprivate publishing company, perhaps the most important promoter of space-related themes, and changed the profiles of several of its former journals. Although science popularization still remained a very important project for Bol'sheviks, the tenor of outreach changed. The journal *Priroda i liudi*, for example, changed its name to *Revoliutsiia i priroda* (*Revolution and Nature*) to reflect the explicitly utilitarian, socialist, and applied nature of its message. Its stated goal was now to popularize "technology for the masses." Similarly, the elite Academy of Sciences, although disconnected from the populist space fad, underwent a process of "Bol'shevization" that significantly limited its independent voice in matters of science so that it could refocus attention to applied rather than fundamental science.[108]

The rise of the state (both government and Party) as a ubiquitous and inescapable force in society at the turn of the 1930s profoundly affected the indigenously maintained space fad. In particular, the Bol'shevik Party's effort to realign scientific and technical work in the country for socialist reconstruction proved decisive. After an explosion of media attention at the

[106] A. L. Chizhevskii, *Na beregu vselennoi: gody druzhby s Tsiolkovskim: vospominaniia* (Moscow: Mysl', 1995).

[107] Kendall E. Bailes, *Technology and Society Under Stalin: Origins of the Soviet Technical Intelligentsia, 1917–1941* (Princeton: Princeton University Press, 1978).

[108] Michael David-Fox and György Péteri, eds., *Academia in Upheaval: Origins, Transfers, and Transformations of the Communist Academic Regime in Russia and East Central Europe* (Westport, CT: Bergin & Garvey, 2000); James T. Andrews, *Science for the Masses: The Bolshevik State, Public Science, and Popular Imagination* (College Station, TX: Texas A&M University Press), 130–134.

turn of decade, by 1933, the space fad was nearly over. The metamorphosis was striking. In 1931, the press published nearly two dozen articles on spaceflight, in 1932, less than a dozen, and the following year – when there were no private popular science journals left – no more than a handful. The same journals that had popularized utopian discussions about space travel now devoted more attention to technical knowledge applicable to workers on the shop floor. Linking science to industrial productivity marginalized many seemingly outlandish ideas such as space exploration. Societies, exhibitions, media, and art on the topic either disappeared or mutated into new forms.

A few spaceflight supporters from the 1920s were casualties of the Great Terror, although it is important to underscore that none suffered because of their advocacy of space travel. Cosmist philosopher N. A. Setnitskii lost his life in the late 1930s, whereas Tsiolkovskii's friend Aleksandr Chizhevskii was arrested in 1940 and eventually spent sixteen years in domestic exile. In 1939, the *Narodnyi komissariat vnutrennikh del*, or NKVD [People's Commissariat of Internal Affairs], shot the Society for the Study of Interplanetary Communications' former secretary, Morris Leiteizen, the son of an old Bol'shevik who was friends with Lenin. Mikhail Lapirov-Skoblo, one of the earliest advocates for spaceflight in the 1920s, also fell to the purges. After a very distinguished career as a vocal spokesperson for the Soviet scientific and technical intelligentsia, he was arrested in 1937, sentenced in 1941, and died in confinement in 1947 while working at a battery factory.[109]

Artists and writers also fell during the upheavals of the Cultural Revolution and the Great Terror. During the former, the Suprematists came under attack from the Association of Russian Revolutionary Painters as part of a general move to discredit the artistic avant-garde.[110] Similarly, the Proletarian Writers' Association launched a campaign that stigmatized the genre of science fiction, calling the style a distraction to the problems at hand. By 1936, the government included *Aelita* on its list of banned movies; the NKVD arrested some science fiction writers in the late 1930s while the government removed even Jules Verne from children's literature. Soviet science fiction did not recover from the resultant consequences until the Khrushchev era.[111]

[109] Semenova, "Russkii kosmizm," *Svobodnaia mysl'* no. 17 (1992): 81–97 (see 96–97); Roy Medvedev, *Let History Judge: The Origins and Consequences of Stalinism*, rev. ed. (New York: Columbia University Press, 1989), 444; "Lapirov-Skoblo Mikhail Iakovlevich," in E. N. Shoshkov, *Repressirovannoe ostekhbiuro* (St. Petersburg: NITs Memorial, 1995), 137.

[110] Fauchereau, *Malevich*, 31–33.

[111] McGuire, *Red Stars*, 13–15; Peter Kenez, *Cinema and Soviet Society, 1917–1953* (Cambridge, UK: Cambridge University Press, 1992), 144; Britikov, *Russkii Sovetskii nauchno-fantasticheskii roman*, 137.

Most space advocates, however, survived. They successfully embraced the discursive shift from indefinite utopia to definitive industrialization by changing their strategies. Popularizers and enthusiasts altered their lexicon rather than changing their vision. Many, for example, refocused their attention from rockets flying in space to the purer engineering problem of "reactive motion." Through the 1920s, interplanetary travel had always been connected to the development of reactive motion, that is, with rocket and jet engines. In the early 1930s, however, activists and enthusiasts disconnected reactive motion from interplanetary travel and connected it with more realistic goals that were part of the prevailing state culture of aviation. Although most space advocates never stopped aiming for outer space, they now redefined the problem into smaller chunks, the first step being "conquering the stratosphere" by using the principle of reactive motion. Stratospheric flight literally and metaphorically lowered the ceiling of ambition, situating the original idea of space exploration within prevailing aviation culture. Reactive motion implied a real engineering problem with real solutions; it also held immediate utility because such a principle could be used to propel airplanes. Many in Europe had already demonstrated the possibility. The limits of possibility moved downward from the cosmos to the clouds.

CONCLUSIONS

From the perspective of the Soviet state, the space fad was of no importance. During its existence, no major party or government official was involved in the activities of either the technological utopians or the mystically minded space advocates. The relatively loose controls over social, cultural, and economic activity during NEP allowed the ideas of space activists to flourish without notice or support from the party and the government. Trotskii's single public comment on the space fad was derisive and cautionary. In a section on proletarian culture and art in *Literature and Revolution*, he argued,

> Cosmism seems, or may seem, extremely bold, vigorous, revolutionary and proletarian. But in reality, Cosmism contains the suggestion of very nearly deserting the complex and difficult problems . . . on earth so as to escape into the interstellar spheres. In this way Cosmism turns out quite suddenly to be akin to mysticism . . . [and may] lead some . . . to the most subtle of matters, namely to the Holy Ghost.[112]

Interest in space, he argued, would lead enthusiasts from the useful to the useless, and from science to religion – what Lenin had scorned as the opiate of the masses. Trotskii's comment avoided underscoring the connection between science and religion, represented in the space fad by the technological utopians and the mystics respectively. Both rationales contributed in

[112] Trotsky, *Literature and Revolution*, 211.

wholly different ways in defining the contours and flavor of the space fad in the 1920s, but both also shared many deep-rooted rationales.

The approach of the technological utopians differed in important ways from their fellow mystics. Where technology-inspired space advocates looked to a future of many unknown possibilities for humanity, Cosmists looked to the past (the dead) as way station to a singular goal: the reanimation of humanity into a single universal organism. If the former tied their dreams of space exploration (however implausibly) with the modernizing exigencies of the day, the latter were not interested in modernization but the evolution of the species. It is tempting to argue that the tension between these seemingly contradictory ideas provided the charge for the creative outpouring on space exploration in the 1920s; or that both "old" and "new" appeal were necessary for mass interest in such an arcane idea as spaceflight. Besides being difficult to prove, such claims would, however, create artificial dichotomies.

A more analytically valuable perspective would be to view them as not altogether incompatible, especially because the boundaries between the two sensibilities were not always clear. The nearly invisible web of connections through friendship or acquaintance that linked disparate believers in the cause of space travel muddled distinctions between the differing rationales for space travel. Sometimes cold science and ill-defined mysticism existed in the same breath. The artists who emerged from the Suprematist umbrella embodied this duality without contradiction; they worked within the most avant-garde of artistic traditions – materialistic, forward thinking, urban – yet infused their work with Fedorovian views from the late nineteenth century that owed more to a pastoral and antimaterialistic aesthetic.

Technological utopianism and Cosmism shared a number of basic elements: Both were utopian, both relied on the notion that humanity needed complete control over nature, and both afforded technology a prominent role in the realization of their ultimate goal of transforming society. In their language and iconography, technological utopians spoke with the same evangelical tones as their spiritual compatriots. Like the cosmists, they were obsessed with the future imperatives of humanity and paid fealty to technology, travel, and Tsiolkovskii. In advocating the science of space exploration in the 1920s, "believers" not only used the language of mysticism – the most obvious meeting point between science and religion – but they also shared many of the same rationales, goals, and ideologies.

The case of spaceflight culture in the experimental climate of the NEP years provides a striking case in which the demarcations between science and mysticism were at best nebulous. Writing about Bol'sheviks' fascination with technology, Anthony J. Vanchu noted that "[w]hile science and technology had the power to demystify religion and magic, they themselves came to be perceived as the locus of magical or occult powers that could transform the material world."[113] In effect, science and technology became a new cosmology in the Marxist–Bol'shevik–Leninist context of the interwar years; they were both alternatives to religion and religions themselves. Spaceflight was one vibrant example of this conflation.

Through the decades after the 1930s, Soviet space advocates altered their strategies to fit the needs of practical science and industrialization. Still utopian, they abandoned the mystical for the technological. By the time that cosmonaut Titov declared that he found neither God nor angels in outer space, the religion of space travel could be distilled down to modernity, secularism, and progress. But statements such as Titov's obscured an alternate history of the Soviet space program that harked back to the 1920s, discarded and lost through much of the Soviet era. Titov's willful disengagement of Christ from the cosmos underscored the irony that his achievement had been made possible largely because of people like Tsiolkovskii who had set out to do the exact opposite, that is, to integrate them; the modern rocket with its new Communist cosmonaut was conceived as much in a leap of faith as in a reach for reason.

[113] Anthony J. Vanchu, "Technology as Esoteric Cosmology in Early Soviet Literature," in *The Occult in Russian and Soviet Culture*, 205–206.

4

Local Action, State Imperatives

Onwards to Mars!
Fridrikh Tsander, encouraging his factory coworkers to build rockets, 1931

INTRODUCTION

Kislovodsk is a health resort in southern Russia tucked away between the Black and Caspian Seas, famous for its clean mineral water. Just after the sensational launches of the first sputniks in 1957, fifty-year-old Sergei Korolev, the chief designer of the Soviet space program, took his wife there for a short vacation. While there, Korolev searched for the grave of an old friend who had passed away at the resort twenty-four years earlier. Unable to find it, he returned to Moscow frustrated but determined to locate the grave. He assigned a person in his design bureau to find the lost spot. It took a long while, but by combing through cemetery archives and town census reports, the friend's grave was eventually found, in a remote spot in neglected condition. Soon after, in the summer of 1958, Korolev petitioned a deputy chairman of the USSR Council of Ministers, Dmitrii Ustinov, for 60,000 rubles to erect at the grave a memorial to the man he considered the "successor to Tsiolkovskii," Fridrikh Tsander.[1] Korolev's efforts restored a nearly forgotten character to the historical fabric of Soviet rocketry and spaceflight.

Tsander was the most obvious link between the utopian cause of spaceflight in the 1920s and the practical work on rocketry in the 1930s. In the 1920s, he had communicated with spaceflight patriarch Konstantin Tsiolkovskii and actively promoted the cause of space exploration through publications and lectures. By 1930, however, Tsander's efforts moved beyond Tsiolkovskii to the practical sphere, especially organizational and technical work. In Moscow, Tsander founded the Group for the Study of Reactive Motion, a ragtag group of civilian space enthusiasts who through their own initiative and without any significant state support laid the foundation of Soviet rocketry. Along with the Gas Dynamics Laboratory in Leningrad, Tsander's group structured its goals and publicized its modest successes effectively so as to attract the interest of state organs, in particular the Red

[1] Korolev to Ustinov (June 22, 1958) in *SPKIED*, 255.

Army and *Osoaviakhim*, a mass voluntary society. The interaction between the government and amateur enthusiasts resulted in the formation of the world's first wholly state-subsidized project to design and build rockets in 1933.

The evolution from the utopian imagination of space travel to the state-sponsored work of developing rockets encompassed three critical and overlapping processes. Space enthusiasts formed the first amateur and civilian rocketry group in Moscow, finding a home under the aegis of the semigovernmental *Osoaviakhim*. Simultaneously, a parallel group of military engineers in Leningrad dedicated themselves to the cause of rocketry and found support from the research and development network of the Red Army during a period of acute military interest in new technologies. The work of the two groups already represented a conflicting agenda, the former aiming for space and the latter seeking better aerial weapons. Finally, the amateurs successfully sold their cause to the government by dovetailing their project with broader social and cultural trends related to industrialization. These included the national turn to more "practical" science as underscored by the First Five-Year Plan, strategic military needs to develop innovative weapons, and the state's propaganda project to eulogize the achievements of Soviet aviation. The amateur group's success in producing relatively innovative technology exemplified not only the vigor of non-state forums of scientific and technical work, but also the possibility of effective popular and local action in Soviet civil society in the early 1930s.

THE DREAMER

Like Konstantin Tsiolkovskii, Fridrikh Arturovich Tsander was often eccentric and naïve, but whereas the former was self-centered, pessimistic, and tired, Tsander was humble, optimistic, and full of life. He was also an indefatigable networker. Born in 1887 in the Latvian capital of Riga, Tsander grew up in a family of intelligentsia. In his youth, he was a dedicated fan of the many science fiction novels of the era and became interested in the topic of spaceflight by his twentieth birthday. Unlike Tsiolkovskii, who was concerned only with the theoretical aspects of space travel, Tsander engaged in rudimentary experimentation from an early age. His interest in space deeply affected his personal life: He named his two daughters Astra and Merkurii.

Through the 1920s, Tsander pursued the cause of space exploration with a persistence unmatched by most of his peers, and he actively participated in the space fad. He joined the Society for the Study of Interplanetary Communications in 1924 and contributed to the international exhibition organized by fellow enthusiasts in 1927.[2] At one point, Tsander quit his factory job

[2] Secondary Russian sources incorrectly ascribe the society's formation to Tsander's initiative, but archival sources suggest that Tsander joined the Society *after* V. P. Vetchinkin, a professor

to devote all his time to designing a spaceplane, surviving for food and rent on the generosity of his former coworkers, who donated 1% of their wages for his experiments.

Unlike many of his likeminded enthusiasts, Tsander was not a scientific dilettante dabbling in rocketry and space exploration; in fact, he had a masterful grasp of complex mathematics and developed groundbreaking ideas, some of which compared favorably with those of Tsiolkovskii. Although Tsander published only once in the 1920s, his frequent lectures in universities, factories, and party meetings in Moscow, Leningrad, Khar'kov, and Saratov – anywhere he found an audience – brought him to prominence among fellow space enthusiasts.[3] In their publications, spaceflight advocates such as Tsiolkovskii and Rynin singled out Tsander as an important scientist working in the field.[4] Like his peers, he was wholly driven by utopian ideals, believing that interplanetary flight would benefit all of humanity. He maintained that the only way to get to space was by using rockets.

After Tsander worked with scraps for several years, his experiments began to show results by 1930. By this time he drew up a plan to develop three rocket engines known as OR-1, OR-2, and OR-3 (where OR stands for *Opytnaia raketa*, or Experimental Rocket). For OR-1, he modified a blowtorch he found at a Leningrad factory and equipped it with a spark plug for ignition, a gauge to adjust fuel consumption, and a conic nozzle for exhaust. In October 1930, he began testing this rudimentary propulsion system, which worked on compressed air and benzene. It contained at least some of the basic elements of what engineers later called a liquid-propellant rocket engine.

Tsander was unable to interest his new employer, the recently formed Institute of Aviation Motors (*Institut aviatsionnogo motorostroeniia*, or IAM), to sponsor his work, partly because reactive engines were outside the institute's mandate, piston engines.[5] Tsander was used to rejection; through

at the Zhukovskii Air Fleet Academy, suggested that society members contact Tsander. ARAN, 4/14/197/32–35.

[3] F. A. Tsander, "Perelety na drugie planety," *Tekhnika i zhizn'* 13 (July 20, 1924): 15–16. Tsander tried repeatedly to publish a larger manuscript ("Flights to Other Planets and the Moon") in 1926 and 1927 but *Glavnauka*'s publishing house declined to sponsor its publication.

[4] K. Tsiolkovskii, *Issledovanie mirovykh prostranstv reaktivnymi priborami (pereizdanie rabot 1903 i 1912 g. s nekotorymi izmeneniiami i dopolneniiami)* (Kaluga: K. E. Tsiolkovskii, 1926), 126. In his encyclopedia, Rynin devoted sections to Tsander's winged rocket and also published his autobiography.

[5] Tsander was transferred to IAM in December 1930. For the interaction with IAM over the OR-1, see Tsander's diary entries for January 27 and 31, February 25, and March 21 and 28, 1930, ARAN, 573/3/38/1–17. For a summary, see G. S. Vetrov, *S. P. Korolev i kosmonavtika: pervye shagi* (Moscow: Nauka, 1994), 21–22. IAM was renamed the Central Institute of Aviation Motor Building (TsIAM) on July 29, 1932.

the 1920s, his several appeals to the state for support to build interplanetary ships had gone unheeded. Undeterred by yet another in a long line of disappointments, he continued to seek potential allies elsewhere.

On the advice of an acquaintance, a twenty-one-year-old space enthusiast named Nikolai Fedorenkov, Tsander decided to appeal for help from *Osoaviakhim*, the largest Soviet youth voluntary society.[6] Fedorenkov's suggestion struck a chord. Tsander had already approached *Osoaviakhim* for support in 1927 without any luck, but this time he recognized that popular Soviet interest in reactive motion might put his appeal in a different light. He could also demonstrate concrete results because he had already tested his crude OR-1 blowtorch. Fedorenkov's intervention focused Tsander's attention, in the summer of 1931, to *Osoaviakhim*.

OSOAVIAKHIM: SUPPORTING PEACEFUL LABOR AND DEFENSE

Osoaviakhim, the largest Soviet mass voluntary organization in the prewar era, was formed in January 1927 by combining two separate societies of the NEP period, OSO (Society for Assistance to Defense) and *Aviakhim* (Society of Friends of Aviation-Chemical Defense).[7] The Bol'sheviks established its predecessors amid high-level debates about the ways to modernize Soviet society in the face of endemic technical backwardness of both the urban and rural populations. Aviation and chemical warfare, considered two of the most obvious markers of technological modernity in the 1920s, were central to these discussions. *Aviakhim*'s goal was to bring ideas about aviation and chemical warfare to the masses, that is, to integrate the larger population with military and civilian aviation and chemical industry. The inculcation would span the gamut from educational outreach to learning about production and mastering how to use these technologies. OSO originally focused on technical education within the Red Army but later on became a mass volunteer society that accepted both civilians and soldiers for training in scientific and technical matters.[8]

[6] Fedorenkov to Tsander (May 12, 1931) in F. A. Tsander, *Iz nauchnogo naslediia*, ed. A. F. Tsander (Moscow: Nauka, 1967), 94–95.

[7] OSO's lineage went back to the Military-Scientific Society (VNO) established in 1920, which was reorganized in 1926 into OSO. *Aviakhim*'s lineage went back to two separate societies, the Society of Friends of the Air Fleet (ODVF) formed in 1923 and the Society of Friends of Chemical Defense and Chemical Industry (*Dobrokhim*) formed in 1924. The two were combined in 1925 to become *Aviakhim*. For a useful institutional history, see L. P. Borisov, "*Osoaviakhim*. Stranitsy istorii. 1927–1941 gody," *Voprosy istorii* no. 6 (1965): 45–60.

[8] William E. Odom, *The Soviet Volunteers: Modernization and Bureaucracy in a Public Mass Organization* (Princeton: Princeton University Press, 1973), 23–92. For ODVF's role in popularizing aviation in the early 1920s, see Scott W. Palmer, "Peasants into Pilots: Soviet Air-Mindedness as an Ideology of Dominance," *Technology and Culture* 39 (2000): 1–26.

Osoaviakhim's stated goal, iterated at its first all-union session in January 1927, was to "support peaceful labor and defense of the USSR."[9] If, in principle, the society sought to sponsor activities that would raise the technical competence of Soviet society at large, it also simultaneously tapped into a huge pool of "extra" labor – about 4 million people in 1928 – who in principle could be counted on to support the aviation, chemical, agricultural, and defense industries *and* serve as a mass reserve pool of mobilized labor in case of war. Leaders of the burgeoning Soviet air force, which was a major driving force behind the organization in the 1920s, invoked these rationales in justifying the society. To underscore the state's interest in these objectives, several influential Bol'sheviks in the party, government, and military, including Kliment Voroshilov, Sergei Kamenev, Sergo Ordzhonikidze, and Mikhail Tukhachevskii, sat on the society's Central Council during its first session in 1927.[10]

Although officially *Osoaviakhim* was to be self-supporting, one-third of its funding came from the state. The society accrued the remainder from membership dues and fund-raising from various campaigns. Dues included a membership fee and then an annual fee that in 1928 was about one-tenth of 1% of an average member's income (i.e., about twenty kopecks). As with most voluntary societies, the society faced difficulties in collecting dues; on average, 50% was the best rate of collection. To a large degree, the poor fee collection rates were offset by fund-raising efforts such as lottery campaigns. In 1931, for example, the society raised 10.7 million rubles, which it distributed across the *Osoaviakhim* structure. Because of lower than expected recruitment rates in its initial years, *Osoaviakhim*'s leaders focused primarily on recruiting and maintaining members. Although the society boasted as many as 12 million members in 1932, the actual figure was closer to 7 or 8 million, of whom about 35% each were either workers or peasants.[11]

Osoaviakhim's structure mirrored the Bol'shevik Party's hierarchy in that daughter organizations with carbon-copy structures were organized at the republic, *oblast*, and *guberniia* levels. The head organization was governed by a Central Council, which itself had a smaller Presidium. The chairman of the Central Council, who effectively served as the head of *Osoaviakhim*, defined and controlled its agenda by means of personnel staffed in the mid-levels of the society. Robert Eideman, the former chief of the Red Army's Frunze Military Academy, took over as *Osoaviakhim* chief in March 1932. Given his long involvement in developing military strategy, his appointment

[9] GARF, 8355/1/4/27.

[10] "Pervyi vsesoiuznyi s'ezd Aviakhima i TsSO," *Pravda*, November 11, 1927.

[11] Odom, *Soviet Volunteers*, 155–183; Borisov, "*Osoaviakhim*"; *Ustavnoi sbornik soiuza osoaviakhima sssr* (Moscow: *Osoaviakhim*, 1929), 20, 27; *Osoaviakhim* no. 16 (1929): 19; *Osoaviakhim* nos. 7–8 (1932): 5–12.

underlined a closer link to military needs than his predecessor, who was not a service officer.[12]

Initially, *Osoaviakhim*'s top-level Central Council oversaw nine sections (later expanded to sixteen) reflecting its thematic focus: agitation-propaganda, agriculture, chemical-scientific industry, aviation industry, aviation law, military-scientific research, air-chemical defense, riflery, and sports. Sections divided themselves according to more specific themes under bureaus, for example, for specific areas of agriculture. At the local levels, the working unit were cells (*iacheiki*) that were organized in factories throughout the country. Cell membership could vary from five to a hundred people who helped with production on factory floors. Cells operated under the jurisdiction of appropriate sections or bureaus, which funded their activities with money collected from membership dues, donations, lotteries, and revenues from publications and souvenirs.[13] William Odom has noted that "power to control outcomes [in *Osoaviakhim*] was diffused throughout the organization."[14] Such decentralization helped local cells tap into regional resources to fund activities ignored by the center.

Groups working within *Osoaviakhim*'s scientific-research section – one of its sixteen sections – failed to achieve any major advances in science and technology. Their small budget, 152,000 rubles out of *Osoaviakhim*'s total of nearly 50 million rubles for 1932, meant that they had few resources.[15] Their handiwork focused on "practical applications of technology" that emerged from crude trial and error rather than theory or extended investigations. One group, for example, made a winch system to pull gliders into the air by using a cable drum bolted to the back of a truck. Another modified gliders to train airplane pilots so that they could avoid expensive training on airplanes.[16] Here among the winch systems and gliders lay the interplanetary dreams of Fridrikh Tsander, who, having exhausted all other funding possibilities, thought he could find money to remake his broken blowtorch into a proper rocket engine.

GROUP FOR THE STUDY OF REACTIVE MOTION

Instead of going alone to *Osoaviakhim*, Tsander enlisted accomplices from different places. Some were interested coworkers from the Institute of Aviation Motor Building; the group included Fedorenkov, a young space enthusiast who had placed newspaper advertisements to invite people interested

[12] For biographies of Eideman, see D. V. Pankov, *Komkor Eideman* (Moscow: Voenizdat, 1965); A. I. Anokhin, *Oni byli pervymi (ocherk o rukvoditeliakh oboronnogo obshchestva)* (Moscow: Magistr-PRO, 2000), 39–49.

[13] Odom, *Soviet Volunteers*, 93–123; Vetrov, *S. P. Korolev i kosmonavtika*, 36–37.

[14] Odom, *Soviet Volunteers*, 275.

[15] Budget figures are from GARF, 8355/1/52/119–20.

[16] Odom, *Soviet Volunteers*, 231.

in the topic to form a group.[17] Tsander asked the invited to meet on July 18, 1931 and dubbed the assembled group the "Bureau for the Study of Reactive Engines and Reactive Flight." He tabled a plan for practical work that included development of rocket engines and installing them on airplanes "for the goal of super-aviation" (*superaviatsiia*), a contemporary euphemism for high-speed flight. The final goal would be to "develop an interplanetary spaceship."[18] Through the remainder of the summer, Tsander recruited more people to join this informal network, connected not by institutions but by a shared cause. Some came from the list of respondees to Fedorenkov's advertisements, a few were from a Moscow Aviation Institute rocket group where Tsander occasionally lectured, and still others were acquaintances from the Central Aerohydrodynamics Institute (TsAGI), the top Soviet airplane design institution. Along with a critical mass of supporters interested in practical work, he communicated with the *Osoaviakhim* cell in the Institute of Aviation Motors to sponsor the team's work.[19] In the first week of September, he changed the team's name to Group for the Study of Reactive Motion (*Gruppa izucheniia reaktivnogo dvizheniia*, GIRD), a name that would remain unchanged for the group's two-year existence. Although still short of a formal agreement with *Osoaviakhim*'s Central Council (necessary to obtain any money), Tsander and his friends sent missives, most notably to Tsiolkovskii, announcing GIRD's formation under *Osoaviakhim*'s scientific-research sector, specifically within its bureau of aviation technology.[20] At this time, in mid-September 1931, GIRD existed only as a local initiative, a volunteer cell attached to the Institute of Aviation Motors. Like many of *Osoaviakhim*'s other cells, it had no legal basis to engage in work that went beyond propaganda and education.

Although Tsander had only the vaguest of practical goals at that point, his diary entries from September 1931 show an interest in developing a rocket engine suitable to use on an aircraft, that is, to develop a rocket-plane. One of Tsander's favorite ideas was an aircraft that could fly into space; he had published a notable article on such an idea in 1924. His plane was a strange combination of two different propulsion systems: regular propellers to accelerate the vehicle and an innovative rocket engine that would use fuel from the melted remains of its wings to fly into space.[21] By the time of GIRD's formation, Tsander was thinking about a simpler concept, an

17 *Vecherniaia moskva*, December 12, 1930; *Rabochaia moskva*, February 12, 1931.

18 ARAN, 573/3/45/1; ARAN, 573/3/46/1–4. Among those who met on July 18 were N. K. Fedorenkov, M. P. Ogloblin (IAM), G. E. Blizniukov (IAM), Ruktishel' [Ruktishev] (*Osoaviakhim*), and Kanishchev (Zhukovskii Academy).

19 ARAN, 573/3/47/1–3 (September 20 and 23).

20 ARAN, 4/14/226/12–13 (September 20, 1931). This is the earliest preserved evidence noting *Osoaviakhim*'s acknowledgment of GIRD's existence.

21 Tsander, "Perelety na drugie planety."

aircraft using a single liquid-propellant rocket engine capable of testing various ideas in the air. In his first communication to GIRD, Tsiolkovskii also suggested a similar two-step approach, to develop first a "[high]-altitude aircraft using the products of [fuel] combustion" and then to move to a "pure reactive projectile."[22] Tsiolkovskii's blessing gave Tsander some direction in his work, but the latter still needed a concrete and realistic plan to propose to *Osoaviakhim*. The plan came from one of the young men who had joined up with GIRD in September, Sergei Pavlovich Korolev.

KOROLEV

Much has been written about the founding figure of the Soviet space program and chief designer of the *Sputnik* and *Vostok* spaceships.[23] In the West, historians have often compared Korolev's early life to that of Wernher von Braun, the German rocket engineer who was his most obvious Western counterpart and contemporary. Unlike von Braun, who committed fully to the idea of space travel from a very early age, Korolev had no discernible interest in such possibilities in his youth. A hardheaded and sometimes ruthless realist, Korolev most passionately believed not in space travel but in aviation. His ability to aim for realistic goals, his interest in aeronautics, and his skills as a leader, three qualities that Tsander lacked, allowed GIRD to move from aimless existence to directed action. One Russian historian described Tsander as being "too committed . . . to be objective."[24] Luckily for Soviet rocketry enthusiasts in the early 1930s, Korolev was both.

Korolev, about twenty years Tsander's junior, was born in 1906 to a family of working intelligentsia in Ukraine. His natural parents divorced at an early age, and he was shuffled between relatives until his mother remarried when he was ten. Inspired by the Bol'sheviks' promotion of aviation via ODVF (*Osoaviakhim*'s predecessor), Korolev became passionately interested in aeronautics, often to the great displeasure of his parents, who considered it a useless hobby. At seventeen he joined a glider club in Odessa and eventually became its leader. After early schooling in Kiev, in 1926 he enrolled at the Moscow Higher Technical School in the faculty of aeromechanics. Tensions between students of proletarian origin (about 13% in 1927) and others (such as Korolev) plagued the institution during his tenure. Korolev, however, remained markedly apolitical despite the turmoil in higher education in the late 1920s, which was exemplified by the

22 ARAN, 555/4/25/1–2 (September 23, 1931).

23 For the most comprehensive biographies, see Iaroslav Golovanov, *Korolev: fakty i mify* (Moscow: Nauka, 1994); Nataliia Koroleva, *S. P. Korolev: otets*, 3 vols. (Moscow: Nauka, 2007).

24 Golovanov, *Korolev*, 120.

changing curricula, the induction of the "trade union thousand" in engineering schools, and frequent interruption of classes.[25] Although still a student, he began working at one of the most famous aviation facilities in the country, Factory No. 22, in the Moscow suburb of Fili. He began his design career by working for the French airplane constructor Paul Richard, who had moved to Russia in the 1920s.[26]

Korolev's first claim to fame came from piloting gliders in several all-union rallies sponsored by *Osoaviakhim* in the late 1920s. By the turn of the decade, newspapers and journals frequently reported on the exploits of this young pilot who not only flew gliders but also designed and built them. His most famous creation was the SK-3 or *Krasnaia zvezda* (Red Star), a glider that brought Korolev's name to prominence at a rally in October 1930 when a pilot performed a spectacular maneuver known as the "death loop." Korolev combined his hobby with his studies by designing and building a two-engine light plane, the SK-4, for his diploma project, supervised by Andrei Tupolev, the famed Soviet airplane designer. In early 1931, the leading Soviet aviation journal in the country, *Vestnik vozdushnogo flota* (*Journal of the Air Fleet*), featured Korolev's SK-4 on its cover.[27] At about the same time, Korolev began publishing popular articles in many different journals on aviation.[28]

Precisely when Korolev began to show interest in space exploration remains unclear. Some of his biographers assert, based on a few of Korolev's statements made twenty-five years later, that he became devoted to the cause of space travel by 1929 after an alleged visit to see Tsiolkovskii in Kaluga. More than likely, Korolev fabricated the event to establish a direct connection to Tsiolkovskii at a time when such a link would help him escape the shadow of being a convicted felon.[29] Not one of his writings or actions before 1932 indicates the slightest inclination toward space travel. Instead,

[25] Sheila Fitzpatrick, "Professors and Soviet Power," in *The Cultural Front: Power and Culture in Revolutionary Russia* (Ithaca, NY: Cornell University Press), 37–64.

[26] Golovanov, *Korolev*, 5–81. Korolev began working at Factory No. 22 in May 1927 and then transferred to Factory No. 28 in March 1929.

[27] "Novyi sovetskii legkii samolet dal'nego deistviia konstruktsii S. Koroleva," *Vestnik vozdushnogo flota* no. 2 (1931). Articles about Korolev appeared between 1929 and 1931 in journals such as *Aviatsiia i khimiia* (*Aviation and Chemistry*), *Fizkul'tura i sport* (*Physical Culture and Sport*), *Nauka i tekhnika* (*Science and Technology*), *Samolet* (*Airplane*), *Vestnik vozdushnogo flota* (*Journal of the Air Fleet*) and newspapers such as *Izvestiia*, *Krasnaia zvezda*, *Pravda*, and *Vecherniaia moskva*.

[28] Korolev's first published work, "Legkii samolet dal'nego deistviia" [A Long-Range Light Aircraft], was published in *Vestnik vozdushnogo flota* no. 12 (1930). For an in-depth look at Korolev's contribution to glider and light-plane design, see G. S. Vetrov, *S. P. Korolev v aviatsii. Idei. Proekty. Konstruktsii* (Moscow: Nauka, 1988).

[29] Koroleva, *S. P. Korolev: otets: kniga pervaia, 1907–1938 gody*, 215–218; Golovanov, *Korolev*, 103–111.

news of German experiments with reactive motion at the turn of the decade profoundly affected his thinking.

For many, including Korolev, reactive motion, a catch-all term for both rocket and jet engines, implied a real engineering problem with a possible solution; it also promised immediate utility because such a principle could be used to propel airplanes. In the Soviet Union and abroad, some theoreticians speculated at the time that the conventional airscrew (propeller) powered by piston engines would eventually reach their limit in both altitude and speed. Reactive (or reaction) motion offered a tantalizing solution to these barriers.[30] A few in Europe were already trying to demonstrate the possibility. In 1928–1929, the "space fad" in Germany reached an intense peak of publicity associated with a variety of rocket-car and rocket-glider stunts orchestrated by the charismatic spaceflight enthusiast Max Valier, who joined forces with Fritz von Opel, the heir to the Opel automobile company. The fad culminated with the screening of the space fiction movie *Frau im mond* (The Woman in the Moon) in October 1929.[31] Simultaneously, the Soviet media was flooded with dozens of articles about the German exploits, suggesting that the reality of the rocket was at hand; reader interest in reactive motion reached a new high.[32] Mimicking German reports, one Soviet writer speculated on the feasibility of a rocket-bicycle while another announced that the "era of the rocket" had arrived.[33] The work of the two unassailable giants of astronautics, Robert Goddard and Herman Oberth, suggested that both were turning away from theory about space exploration to experimentation with rockets.

In this context, Korolev began to believe that the future of aeronautics lay in flying faster and higher and that the way to achieve those goals was to unite a rocket engine with an airplane. In December 1930, in a newspaper article, he highlighted the recent German tests and predicted that "a [rocket] flight with people" would be the next step in the development of modern aviation.[34] This idea, flying a man on an aircraft equipped with a rocket engine, came to dominate his thinking until, by the end of 1931, he began dedicating all his free time to it. Unlike Tsander, Korolev did not consider

[30] Edward Constant III, *The Origins of the Turbojet Revolution* (Baltimore: Johns Hopkins University Press, 1980).

[31] Michael J. Neufeld, "Weimar Culture and Futuristic Technology: The Rocketry and Spaceflight Fad in Germany, 1923–1933," *Technology and Culture* 31 (October 1992): 725–752.

[32] Literally dozens of articles on the Opel rocket-plane and the rocket-car were published in 1928 and 1929 in journals such as *Aviatsiia i khimiia*, *Khochu vse znat'*, *Khronika vozdushnogo dela*, *Nauka i tekhnika*, *Vestnik vozdushnogo flota*, and *Vestnik znaniia* and in newspapers such as *Krasnaia gazeta* and *Vecherniaia krasnaia gazeta*.

[33] "Era rakety," *Nauka i tekhnika* no. 23 (June 9, 1928): 22; "Velosipedy s raketami," *Nauka i tekhnika* no. 19 (April 5, 1930): 13.

[34] *Krasnaia zvezda*, December 22, 1930.

a rocket (or rocket engine) an end in itself but rather a means by which to achieve faster and higher flight – in other words, *superaviatsiia*. In pursuit of this goal, Korolev joined forces with Tsander.

FINDING A PLACE

Korolev's interest in gliding led him to make frequent visits to the *Osoaviakhim* main offices at Nikol'skaia Street. As a member of the society's small bureau of aviation technology, he ran into Tsander in September 1931 and soon added his name to Tsander's growing roster of volunteers in GIRD. Like Tsander, Korolev believed that *Osoaviakhim* might sponsor work on rockets. A few years previously, Korolev had received money from the society, with which he built a glider with the help of friends on the premises of an old church. He thought that perhaps he could use the same site to build something new – not a rocket-plane, which would require a real aircraft – but a rocket-*glider*, which would need only a cheaper glider. However, he recognized that it would be too difficult to fit a rocket engine to a regular glider because it would displace its center of gravity or perhaps burn the tail off.[35] His thinking led him to the simplest solution, a tailless glider.

In September and October, Korolev tracked down the most famous designer of tailless gliders in the country, Boris Cheranovskii, who let him start training on one of his gliders, the BICh-8.[36] On October 5, Tsander showed up at the *Osoaviakhim* airfield to see for himself how Korolev handled the glider in flight; they met again two days later to discuss a plan. Tsander would build a rocket engine named ORD-2, Cheranovskii would provide the BICh-8 glider, and Korolev would help design and test the new combination.[37] Based on this modest plan – a far cry from Tsander's earlier ideas of building spaceships – Tsander formally appealed to *Osoaviakhim*'s bureau of aviation technology for money. Bureau chief Iakov Afanas'ev, who was a protégé of society head Robert Eideman, found Tsander's appeal intriguing and chose to offer support. On November 18, 1931, Afanas'ev, on behalf of *Osoaviakhim*, signed an agreement with Tsander (as an individual) to disburse 1,000 rubles to produce the ORD-2 for a still-hypothetical rocket-glider named after "the Fourteenth Anniversary of October."[38] Although the men had no production space, no glider, and no promise of any further money, the 1,000 rubles, given from local cell

[35] S. P. Korolev, "Raketnyi polet v stratosfere," in *Pionery raketnoi tekhniki Vetchinkin Glushko Korolev Tikhonravov: izbrannye trudy (1929–1945 gg.)*, ed. S. A. Sokolova (Moscow: Nauka, 1972), 410, 427–431.

[36] S. P. Korolev, "Eksperimental'nyi planer BICh-8," *Samolet* nos. 11–12 (1931): 36. BICh stood for Bureau Named After Cheranovskii (*Biuro imeni Cheranovskogo*).

[37] ARAN, 573/3/38/1–17; ARAN, 573/3/57/1–10. Tsander first mentions the ORD-2 (or OR-2) in his diary on October 19, 1931.

[38] ARAN, 573/1/269/10 (November 18, 1931).

funds, was a turning point in the relationship between *Osoaviakhim* and the pursuit of rocketry research.

For the first few months, GIRD members worked out of Korolev's or Tsander's home, where, to the chagrin of Korolev's family, they performed calculations and drew up plans. They conducted experiments at Tsander's workplace at the Institute of Aviation Motors after the regular work day. Members brought hammers, files, pliers, and saws from their homes but depended on Korolev's resourcefulness to get lathes and other machinery by appealing to the generosity of others. One engineer remembered a day when they were unable to continue soldering a rocket combustion chamber because of a lack of silver:

> The next day, without any mention to each other, many brought silver from home: one a silver teaspoon, another a crucifix, another a silver thimble. All these silver 'details' were immediately melted down in a crucible, [and] the chamber was soldered and passed its hot tests well.[39]

In February 1932, glider designer Cheranovskii donated a new glider, the BICh-11, to GIRD. The new trapezoid-wing glider was similar in principle to its predecessor, but Korolev believed that the newer one would be more stable in handling a rocket engine. Although still without a working engine, GIRD members christened the glider the RP-1 (*Reaktivnyi pilotnii*, Reactive Piloted). The 470-kilogram vehicle had an odd, stubby fuselage about three meters long with wings spanning more than twelve meters. The development of the rocket engine proved to be the biggest hurdle in the months ahead, owing to both lack of equipment and working staff. But impatient to move ahead with the project, beginning February, Korolev flew the glider sans engine nine times at the Moscow Flying School's airfield near the Pervomaiskaia rail station. He even found a dilapidated old piston engine and with his colleagues installed it on the glider to simulate the behavior of a rocket engine, knowing full well that such an arrangement would be inefficient. He wrote "official" reports about these quite unexceptional flights as if to give a patina of formality to GIRD's work.[40]

These exercises in formality were not simply idiosyncrasies of Korolev's character but part of an image-making process to legitimize in the eyes of the state what was at that point little more than a project generated on voluntary and popular support. Korolev sought help not only from *Osoaviakhim* but also the one constituency that might plausibly be interested in GIRD's projected rocket-plane, the Red Army. As GIRD's leaders would soon discover, however, the Red Army's research and development branch had already committed to rocketry research, not in Moscow's GIRD but in a secret establishment in Leningrad. Unlike the GIRD enthusiasts, the

[39] Golovanov, *Korolev*, 139.

[40] The set of Korolev's "dispatches" on the RP-1 tests are stored in ARAN, 4/14/102/1–11.

Leningraders were more interested in rockets using solid rather than liquid propellants. They also came from an entirely different tradition of engineering, that of military artillery. Although they had little interest in utopian ideas such as spaceflight, their aspirations to build rockets coincided with those of the space dreamers from GIRD.

THE ARTILLERY TRADITION OF ROCKETRY

Like many areas of the history of Soviet rocketry, the events of post-Revolution work on solid-propellant rockets have been refashioned by those with the most to gain. The widely accepted story centers around the Gas Dynamics Laboratory (GDL), "the first Soviet scientific-research and experimental design organization to develop rocket engines and rockets... [which was] a state organization... founded in Moscow in 1921."[41] According to this narrative, the laboratory launched the first smokeless powder rocket in the world in 1928 and then played a major role in the development of *katiusha* salvo firing rockets made so famous during World War II. One of those who came from the Gas Dynamics Laboratory, Valentin Glushko, became both a collaborator and then a competitor of Sergei Korolev in the postwar years leading up to *Sputnik*. After Korolev's death in 1966, Glushko, by then the most influential and senior designer in the Soviet space program, singled out the contributions of the laboratory as being paramount for the cause of Soviet space exploration; he usually relegated GIRD's research to second place. In recounting this history, he emphasized that his own laboratory's work on rocketry began in 1921 – a decade before GIRD even existed.[42] Only part of this story is true. GDL members *did* contribute significantly to the evolution of Soviet rocketry but not because of their technical accomplishments (which were few) or because they were first (which they were not). Their true claim to importance lay in bringing the centuries-old tradition of artillery to the dream of spaceflight.

Like other European powers, Tsarist regimes from the time of Peter the Great had sponsored the production of gunpowder-propelled rockets. Although they may have initially been designed for fireworks or as flares, by the early nineteenth century the imperial army began using them as weapons. The Russians, for example, used black powder rockets extensively during the Russo-Turkish war of 1828–1829. Black powder, however, burned unevenly and was difficult to control in flight. It also possessed very low caloric content; in other words, it produced low discharge

[41] V. P. Glushko, *Razvitie raketostroeniia i kosmonavtika v sssr* (Moscow: Mashinostroenie, 1987), 23.

[42] All of Glushko's monographs on the history of Soviet space exploration devote considerable attention and first place to the role of GDL. See, for example, ibid., 23–32 (for GDL) and 32–34 (for GIRD).

velocity and thus did not provide much range. By the mid-nineteenth century, the major powers abandoned the use of black powder rockets because of several mechanical and chemical innovations, including the adoption of highly accurate, rifled, breech-loading guns and the introduction of high-energy nitrocellulose-based smokeless powder (for guns). Like other European powers, Russia began to favor traditional artillery and consigned the black powder rocket to history. The major Russian rocket factory shut down in 1887. Although there were sporadic research efforts to improve black powder rockets, the Russian government no longer used rockets as military weapons in the remainder of the Tsarist era.[43]

In the twentieth century, the resumption of research on solid rocketry in Russia was connected to the use of smokeless powder. Compared to black powder, smokeless powder, invented by the French in the mid-nineteenth century, had better performance characteristics. By borrowing the French formula, the Russians reproduced a type of smokeless powder called pyroxylin, which they produced in large quantities for their own guns.[44] Convinced that smokeless powder might be a potentially effective propellant for rockets, a lone sixty-year-old "inventor" named Nikolai Tikhomirov applied in 1919 for government support to design a "naval and aerial self-propelled mine" using smokeless powder. Tikhomirov sought to combine a rocket with an artillery cannon in which the projectile would be propelled not by the force of the explosion of gunpowder in a cannon but by the exhaust produced by burning powder within the projectile itself.

Tikhomirov had never conducted any research on rockets; in fact, his earlier vocation involved wool and sugar production, but after several rejections, in May 1921, the government issued him money to explore his idea. The Red Army's Main Artillery Directorate took over financing in December 1922.[45] Although latter-day Soviet histories place undue importance on

[43] Frank H. Winter, *The First Golden Age of Rocketry: Congreve and Hale Rockets of the Nineteenth Century* (Washington, DC: Smithsonian Institution Press, 1990); V. N. Sokol'skii, *Russian Solid-Fuel Rockets*, trans. H. Needler (Jerusalem: Israel Program for Scientific Translations, 1967).

[44] In 1846, the French opened the first gun cotton production plant near Paris. Four decades later, French ordnance engineer Paul Vieille created a new solution by gelatinizing gun cotton in a volatile solvent (ether-alcohol); this propellant was the first colloidal single-base powder, used widely in Europe in the late nineteenth century. Charles E. Munroe, *On the Development of Smokeless Powder* (1896); Byron Mac Cutcheon, *Smokeless Power, The Facts Stated* (Washington, DC: Gibson Brothers, 1899).

[45] From 1921, money came from a government office known as the Department of Military Inventions, which was part of the Committee of Invention Affairs (*Komitet po delam izobretenii, Kompodiz*) supervised by *Vesenkha*'s Scientific-Technical Department. *Kompodiz* was primarily a patent-registering body. In the early 1920s, its military department funded about 900 "inventors" like Tikhomirov. Robert Lewis, *Science and Industrialisation in the USSR* (New York: Holmes & Meier, 1979), 45.

Tikhomirov's work, his "laboratory" produced little that was either original or useful. For most of this time, he worked out of his apartment, aided by Vladimir Artem'ev, a former imperial army officer who had once worked in an artillery storehouse. Artem'ev was unexpectedly arrested in 1924 for alleged theft from the storehouse and spent three years in jail. By the time of his release, Tikhomirov had moved to Leningrad and tried to resume his experiments as part of a military-scientific society under the city's military district.

The work of these two men in the late 1920s was embellished to a large degree by Artem'ev's *ex post* memoirs (written in 1950), which in turn were exaggerated during the late Cold War by Soviet historians.[46] Among his many contentions, Artem'ev claimed to have launched the world's first smokeless powder rocket on March 3, 1928 using a "new" smokeless powder propellant that was a mixture of pyroxylin and TNT, that is, trinitrotoluene (known as PTP in Russia). These firings were, in fact, not "true" rocket firings; although the projectiles themselves were solid rockets, they were shot out of cannons much like a traditional mortar. In the parlance of the period, they were called "active-reactive" projectiles. Additionally, the two men actually appropriated the fuel mixture – which was grossly unsuitable for rocket flight – from scientists working in another institute.[47] Their exaggerated claims of successful rocket firings interested local representatives of the Revolutionary Military Council's Department of Military Inventions, who decided to provide new money to the men. In June 1928, Tikhomirov's motley group – which apparently numbered ten, if one includes "auxiliary" personnel – renamed themselves the Gas Dynamics Laboratory (*Gasdinamicheskaia laboratoriia*, GDL). In reality, the laboratory was essentially Tikhomirov's one-room apartment in Leningrad shared by Tikhomirov, his wife, and the unemployed Artem'ev, who depended on Tikhomirov for food. Because the two were not well versed in the theory of ballistics or chemistry, they made no progress whatsoever. On the other hand, because money for their research came from the Revolutionary Military Council, from 1929 they owed their livelihood to the research arm of the Red Army.[48]

46 ARAN, 4/14/148/1–8 (1950). What appears to be an earlier draft of the memoirs is in ll. 9–19.

47 ARAN, 4/14/148/3 (1950). PTP stood for *Piroksilino Trotilovyi Porokh* or "pyroxylin-TNT powder." Tikhomirov took the PTP solution from three other scientists, O. G. Filippov, S. A. Seriakov, and M. E. Serebriakov, who developed the mixture at the Red Army's Central Scientific-Technical Laboratory.

48 ARAN, 4/14/148/10 (1950); G. Alekseev, "Otets k lzheotsy 'katiushi'," *Molodaia gvardiia* no. 3 (1990): 142–145 and no. 4 (1990): 143–146; R. N. Kotel'nikova, V. M. Komarov, and G. A. Sadovoi, "Dokumental'nye materially o sozdanii i deiatel'nosti leningradskoi gazodinamicheskoi laboratorii (1919–1930 gg.)," *IIAIK* 61 (1990): 154–164.

MILITARY R&D UNDER TUKHACHEVSKII

After the Revolution and through the entire NEP era, most weapons research and development remained subordinated to the superministerial structure known as the Supreme Council of the National Economy (VSNKh or *Vesenkha*), that is, under civilian control. The *Vesenkha* managed applied research through its Scientific-Technical Department (NTO) set up in August 1918. By the mid-1920s, this body supervised institutes involved in both civilian and military research and development (R&D). The level of activity was low: about a dozen research institutes with a staff of 1,000 people worked on industrial research.[49] Until 1929, the NTO's primary forum for military weapons research was not through lone entrepreneurs such as Tikhomirov but through large R&D organizations such as the Central Aerohydrodynamics Institute, the seed of the Soviet aviation design bureau system that dominated the design and production of aircraft through the end of the Cold War. One NTO-supervised institution, known as *Ostekhbiuro* (*Osoboe tekhnicheskoe biuro po voennym izobreteniiam spetsial'nogo naznacheniia*, Special Technical Bureau for Special-Purpose Military Inventions), focused exclusively on military R&D and was formed in Petrograd after the Civil War in 1921. Although its original mandate was to develop military inventions for the Navy, eventually its work expanded to include research on aviation, explosives, and electrical devices.[50]

The organization of Soviet R&D underwent radical change during the years of the First Five-Year Plan and the Cultural Revolution before stabilizing in the mid-1930s. Two important elements of this transformation were growth and decentralization. Between 1928 and 1933, the number of industrial research institutes grew from 24 to 238, and their manpower increased tenfold. This growth mostly reflected the First Five-Year Plan's focus on the role of science and technology in supporting industrialization. Decentralization followed after December 1929 with dissolution of *Vesenkha*'s NTO. During the next three years, transitional bodies under *Vesenkha* – created specifically for managing R&D – supervised most research establishments. The reorganization culminated in January 1932 with the dissolution of *Vesenkha* into four smaller "commissariats," or ministry-level bodies, to oversee Soviet industrialization. The largest of these, the People's Commissariat of Heavy Industry (*Narkomtiazhprom*), inherited many of the military R&D bodies that *Vesenkha* previously supervised, including the major aviation research institutes.[51]

49 Lewis, *Science and Industrialisation in the USSR*, 20, 37–54.

50 E. N. Shoshkov, *Repressirovannoe ostekhbiuro* (St. Petersburg: NITs Memorial, 1995), 9–24.

51 Lewis, *Science and Industrialisation in the USSR*, 22–23, 55–64.

One dimension of the decentralization process was the emergence of military R&D institutions subordinate neither to the *Vesenkha* nor to industrial commissariats but to the Red Army itself. The military had managed some R&D, but the scope expanded dramatically in the early 1930s. The growth of military R&D occurred simultaneously with the major increases in national military spending that began in 1931, near the end of the First Five-Year Plan. Historians have variously attributed the causes for the enormous military buildup to the rise of the Red Army as a powerful faction invested in militarizing the Soviet economy, the need to prepare for a future "inevitable" war, the alarm caused by the "war scare" of 1927, and individual actors within the Red Army.[52] In the prelude to the buildup, in 1930–1931, the Red Army consolidated its influence over the defense industry by both "capturing" R&D institutions previously supervised by the civilian industry and also by organizing new R&D institutions dedicated wholly to developing weapons systems. For example, *Ostekhbiuro* was moved from *Vesenkha* to the People's Commissariat of Military and Naval Affairs on June 3, 1930.[53] Similarly, between 1931 and 1933, the military commissariat organized twenty-three new R&D centers in the form of design bureaus, laboratories, and independent "inventors' groups." Their profiles included developing better grenade launchers, aerial camouflage systems, electrical trouble-shooting systems, underground drilling machines, rail-based torpedoes, steam-powered turbine units, and air-launched bombs.[54] The Red Army's Directorate of Military Inventions (UVI), a body that reviewed innovative proposals from independent designers and managed projects once money was allocated, funded all of these R&D institutions.[55]

The Red Army leader most responsible for broadening the scope and size of military-funded R&D – including research on rocketry – was Mikhail Tukhachevskii, who served as Red Army chief of staff between November 1925 and May 1928. Russian historians have devoted much attention to Tukhachevskii, about his noble origins, his elitism, his ruthlessness (as he displayed when putting down the Kronstadt rebellion after the Civil War),

52 There is a vast literature on the prelude, motivations, and contours of the defense buildup of the First and Second Five-Year Plans. For a small sampling, see Lennart Samuelson, *Plans for Stalin's War Machine: Tukhachevskii and Military-Economic Planning, 1925–1941* (Basingstoke, UK: Macmillan Press, 2000); David R. Stone, *Hammer and Rifle: The Militarization of the Soviet Union, 1926–1933* (Lawrence, KS: University Press of Kansas, 2000); Sally W. Stoecker, *Forging Stalin's Army: Marshal Tukhachevsky and the Politics of Military Innovation* (Boulder, CO: Westview Press, 1998).

53 Shoshkov, *Repressirovannoe ostekhbiuro*, 41.

54 RGVA, 4/14/1171/1–14 (January 23, 1934).

55 Mikhail Tsypkin, "The Origins of Soviet Military Research and Development System (1917–1941)," Harvard University, PhD Dissertation, 1985, 40–118. The Red Army's Main Artillery Directorate also oversaw several design bureaus and institutes that developed weapons systems outside civilian control.

and his undoubted skills as a military theoretician and strategist.[56] After losing a dispute over the general staff's role in running the Red Army, Tukhachevskii resigned from his post and was reassigned as commander of the Leningrad Military District in May 1928. In Leningrad, Tukhachevskii took a hands-on approach to familiarize himself with the best in Soviet military R&D. He cultivated a good relationship with *Ostekhbiuro*'s staff and frequently attended weapons systems tests at its premises.[57] His interest in *Ostekhbiuro* was not frivolous but part and parcel of his plan for a massive military buildup of the Red Army that would include the most modern weapons in the world. His writings while in Leningrad show an interest in a wide range of technologies and processes that could be harnessed for the Red Army: modernizing artillery production, improving the design of submarines, enhancing military communications, and building modern roads for supplying matèriel to troops.[58] In the early 1930s, Tukhachevskii even sponsored research on using ultrashort waves (*porazhaiushchikh luchei*, strike rays) to destroy material objects.[59] In Leningrad, Tukhachevskii first became aware of GDL's modest work on solid-propellant rockets.

Tukhachevskii served in Leningrad for about three years. Despite Tukhachevskii's outspoken and unpopular stance on massive militarization – "Red militarism" as Stalin called it – the Soviet leader summoned him back to Moscow and in June 1931 appointed him Deputy Chairman of the Revolutionary Military Council with the portfolio of "chief of armaments."[60] In his new post, Tukhachevskii became responsible for rearming the Red Army, a task that included supervising military research and development. One of the bodies now under his control was the Directorate of Military Inventions.

In 1931, around the time of his return to Moscow, Tukhachevskii's attention gravitated to rockets and their military applicability. In "New Problems of War," an unpublished manuscript from 1931–1932, Tukhachevskii wrote glowingly on the possible applications of rocket-powered high-speed, high-altitude aircraft, believing that they would be invulnerable to anti-aircraft

56 There are, however, no comprehensive English-language biographies. For a brief treatment, see Shimon Naveh, "Tukhachevsky," in *Stalin's Generals*, ed. Harold Shukman (New York: Grove Press, 1993), 255–274.

57 David R. Stone, "Tukhachevsky in Leningrad: Military Politics and Exile, 1928–31," *Europe-Asia Studies* 48 (1996): 1365–1386; Shoshkov, *Repressirovannoe ostekhbiuro*, 140–141.

58 Many of Tukhachevskii's writings from the period (both draft and final versions) on weapons, organization, logistics, and strategy are stored in RGVA, f. 33988, op. 2, d. 693 and d. 700.

59 RGVA, 4/14/885/1–10b (January 9, 1933). Work on this project continued until at least mid-1934.

60 The chief of armaments post was established in November 1929 and initially occupied by Army commander Ieronim Uborevich.

fire.[61] The government's Defense Commission discussed these very qualities in December 1931 when reviewing the development of a new military airplane capable of reaching 15,000 meters in the air.[62] Tukhachevskii also keenly followed foreign work on rockets. In "New Problems of War," for example, he emphasized that Westerners were working "in extreme secrecy" on "creating reactive motors" and that "although flights into the stratosphere remain in the stage of early experiments, there is no doubt that a solution to this problem is not far off."[63]

The marshal's meditations on Western rocketry development were based on real information collected by Soviet spies and sympathizers abroad. In October 1931, a German rocket enthusiast, Rolf Engel, sent a secret report, "Historical Development of Rocket Technology," to the Red Army in which he described the concurrent German efforts of Hermann Oberth, Reinhold Tiling, and Johannes Winkler and even offered to bring a group of Germans to the USSR.[64] A Soviet engineer who worked with Oberth, Aleksandr Shershevskii, returned home in March 1932 with further reports on German experiments.[65] Some of this information was transmitted directly to engineers working on the ground. Based on Shershevskii's information about shapes of rocket engine combustion chambers, GDL designed and built two engines to reproduce Oberth's results in Germany; the Soviets, however, soon abandoned work on the Oberth-based designs and did not return to them. In another case, unnamed spies in Germany transmitted data on various German rockets that were sent to Tukhachevskii, including information on the work of Wilhelm Belz of Cologne, who claimed to have launched a liquid-propellant rocket to a distance of six kilometers. Tukhachevskii also had this information sent to engineers at GDL.[66]

EXPANSION AND SUPPORT

Between 1928 and 1931, GDL's staff hardly achieved any successes, continuing their elusive search to develop a "gas dynamic gun," that is, a combination of a rocket and a cannon that eventually proved to be a technological dead end. By September 1930, the laboratory employed at least twenty-three people, although only three occupied permanent staff positions.[67]

61 "Novye voprosy voiny," in M. N. Tukhachevskii, *Izbrannye proizvedeniia: t. 2, 1928–1937 gg.*, eds. G. I. Os'kin and P. P. Chernushkov (Moscow: Voenizdat, 1964), 182–184.

62 GARF, 8418/6/73/35–36 (December 19, 1931).

63 Tukhachevskii, "Novye voprosy voiny," 183.

64 *OIN*, 404–405.

65 GARF, 8355/1/370/4 (March 2, 1932). After his return, Shershevskii worked at GDL in Leningrad from March 1932 to December 1933.

66 GARF, 8355/1/370/18–18ob (February 20, 1932). Belz's claim later turned out be fraudulent. Neufeld, *Rocket and the Reich*, 19.

67 RGVA, 34272/1/40/60; G. Nazarov, "I vse zhe, kto izobrel snariad, dlia 'katiushi'?," *Izobretatel' i ratsionalizator* no. 10 (1988): 36–37 and no. 11 (1988): 36–37.

Tukhachevskii's reassignment to Moscow had profound consequences for their work. Less than two months after his new appointment, on August 15, 1931, Tukhachevskii transferred GDL under his subordination as chief of armaments. The following month, he assigned several qualified engineers from an important artillery institute to GDL. He also replaced the current laboratory chief – an active proponent of cannon-launched rockets rather than self-propelled rockets – and appointed one of his protégés from Leningrad, Nikolai Il'in, to serve as chief of the laboratory. As a result of Tukhachevskii's patronage, GDL became one of the most heavily funded R&D organizations under his purview, receiving a total of over 1.66 million rubles during its brief existence.[68]

According to staff recollections, the personnel at GDL increased rapidly. By December 1932, 120 researchers and staff worked there, a number that grew to 200 within a year. They worked in seven different subdivisions.[69] Most of them were not officially on staff but rather hired as contract workers. The majority of the full-time workers were recent graduates of artillery academies (i.e., members of the post-Revolution technical intelligentsia) who were in their early thirties. For example, Tukhachevskii assigned a group of twenty-seven engineers to the laboratory immediately after their graduation from the Dzherzhinskii Artillery Academy in 1933.[70] Many of them had fought in the Civil War. With a few notable exceptions, all had military ranks and were well versed in the science of artillery and warfare. In other words, they had entirely different backgrounds and interests than the amateur spaceflight enthusiasts of GIRD.

From late 1931, coincidentally at the same time as GIRD's formation, GDL's rocketry research took on a more productive turn. Within a year, the laboratory had facilities spread out over Leningrad. On Tukhachevskii's orders, the principal offices were split between the Main Admiralty building and the St. John Ravelin building in the Petropavlovsk (Peter and Paul) fortress south of the greater Neva river.[71] In an unusual move, in December 1932, Tukhachevskii tapped thirty-three-year-old Ivan Kleimenov, an aeronautical engineer and graduate of the Zhukovskii Military Air Academy, to head GDL. The appointment of an aviation specialist to lead an artillery-oriented laboratory apparently caused some friction, but Tukhachevskii believed that Kleimenov might have some

68 RGVA, 4/14/1171/16–34.

69 V. P. Glushko, "Rol' gazodinamicheskoi laboratorii (GDL) v razvitii raketnoi tekhniki," *Vestnik AN SSSR* no. 2 (1972): 100–108.

70 For the military pedagogical system, see Mark von Hagen, *Soldiers in the Proletarian Dictatorship: The Red Army and the Soviet Socialist State, 1917–1930* (Ithaca, NY: Cornell University Press, 1990); Roger R. Reese, *Stalin's Reluctant Soldiers: A Social History of the Red Army, 1925–1941* (Lawrence, KS: University Press of Kansas, 1996).

71 GDL facilities were also located at the Rzhevsk scientific-research artillery range, on Vasil'ev Island at a former pyroxylin powder laboratory belonging to the Navy, at the Commandant airfield where airplane testing was conducted, and at two other residential locations.

expertise with new technologies because he had served the previous three years as deputy chief of the engineering section of the Soviet trade mission in Berlin.[72]

Tukhachevskii's patronage from 1931 had two important effects. First, GDL turned its full attention to self-propelled rockets rather than cannon-launched rockets. Second, the volume of work dramatically increased. Between 1931 and 1933, GDL worked on ten different solid-propellant rocket systems, including two air-launched reactive projectiles, an 82-mm-caliber projectile with a range of 5.3 kilometers, and a 132-mm-caliber projectile with a range of 6.6 kilometers. The laboratory developed these weapons to fulfill prevailing military doctrine to attack heavy all-metal aircraft. Target accuracy remained a big problem, and after two years, few of the tested projectiles achieved their intended accuracy (one-twentieth to one-two-hundredth value of their range). In effect, they remained inferior to conventional artillery. The laboratory also developed auxiliary reactive projectiles such as a 132-mm-caliber "agitation" projectile to carry chemical weapons and an illumination flare for lighting areas during battle. Other projects included developing smaller agitation and lighting grenades, a signaling projectile, and a tracing projectile. Finally, they produced solid-propellant rockets that could be attached to a heavy bomber (the famous TB-1) to help it take off more easily and quickly.[73]

One of GDL's subdivisions, Department II, was an anomaly compared to the main work of the institute. Because its head, Valentin Glushko, later became the de facto head of the Soviet space program in the 1970s and 1980s, its contributions have been overstated. Glushko's adolescence is the stuff of legends. Born to a Ukrainian Cossack father and a Russian peasant mother in Odessa in 1908, he read Jules Verne at age twelve and discovered Tsiolkovskii's vision of space travel through a local astronomy club in Odessa. Tsiolkovskii's writings so captivated him that he wrote to the old man in September 1923 with a request for his monographs, an appeal to which Tsiolkovskii responded in less than two weeks. This tangible link to Tsiolkovskii was crucial during the 1970s and 1980s in legitimizing Glushko's claim as Tsiolkovskii's successor. During the Soviet space fad, in May 1924, Glushko published his first article – on the American rocketeer Robert Goddard – and followed it up two years later (when he was only eighteen) with an article on space stations in *Nauka i tekhnika* (*Science and Technology*), a major national publication.[74]

[72] I. Chutko, "'Katiusha' i drugie," *Znamia* no. 8 (1972): 172–195.

[73] RGVA, 4/14/1171/5–6. A tenth project, to develop an "automatic reactive cannon," was transferred out of GDL in 1933 to another artillery institute.

[74] V. P. Glushko, "Zavoevanie zemlei luny 4 iulia 1924 goda," *Izvestiia odesskogo glubkoma KPBU*, May 18, 1924, p. 3; V. P. Glushko, "Stantsiia vne zemli," *Nauka i tekhnika* no. 40 (October 8, 1926): 3–4.

After graduating with a bachelor's degree from the faculty of physics and mathematics at the Leningrad State University, Glushko moved quickly from speculation to engineering. In April 1929, he sent an idea for "metal as explosive matter" to the Bol'shevik government's Committee of Invention Affairs; to his surprise, the committee found the idea promising and gave him some money to pursue the project. The following month, he started paid work on an electric rocket engine in a laboratory at the Physical-Technical Institute in Moscow. In the spring of 1930, his three-man team moved to the GDL building, which it shared with another institute. By that time it was clear that electrical rocket engines had no immediate future. Instead, Glushko's team turned their attention to liquid-propellant rocket engines.[75]

Although Glushko's work at GDL was less expansive than Soviet histories would suggest, it was not trivial. He built and tested the world's first electrical or ion rocket engine, albeit a type of engine unsuitable for application within the Earth's atmosphere. His department also designed and constructed a series of liquid-propellant rocket engines that used nitrogen-based solutions as propellants. Such oxidizers were easier to obtain around Leningrad, and as Glushko discovered in March 1931, they ignite on contact with other fuels, eliminating the need for special ignition systems to start the engine. He designed a progression of rocket engines, each successive engine differing from its predecessor only slightly, as a means of perfecting a workable model. His research included identifying the best propellants and developing systems for cooling engines, ignition systems, and propellant supply systems. Many failures and abandoned engines led him to the ORM-50 and ORM-52, two relatively sophisticated engines that used nitric acid and kerosene as propellants but had different thrust levels (150 kilograms and 300 kilograms, respectively). They were fired during ground tests in November and December 1933, respectively.[76] None proved good enough for use in a rocket, and few tested with any success. However, the very *possibility* of liquid-propellant rocket engines was recognized by Tukhachevskii as a significant achievement. In a letter to a colleague in 1932, the marshal underlined the "special prospects" of GDL's liquid-propellant rocket engines. Tukhachevskii noted that "application of such engines in artillery and chemistry opens unlimited possibility in firing projectiles of any power and to any distance."[77]

[75] V. P. Glushko, "Rozhdenie mechty i pervye shagi (avtobiograficheskii ocherk)," in *Put' v raketnoi tekhnike: izbrannye trudy, 1924–1946* (Moscow: Mashinostroenie, 1977), 460–473. Glushko received a patent for an electrical rocket engine on March 23, 1931, by which time he had abandoned work on the idea.

[76] Forty technical documents on rocket engine development from Glushko's time at GDL in 1929–1933 are reproduced in *Put' v raketnoi tekhnike*, 12–190. ORM stood for *Opytnyi raketnyi motor* (Experimental Rocket Motor).

[77] RGVA, 34272/1/146/1–2 (1932).

APPRENTICES IN THE CELLAR

As GDL expanded under the Red Army's patronage, through early 1932, GIRD's work benefited from increased disbursements from *Osoaviakhim*. In February 1932, the society issued 13,000 rubles to GIRD for "testing of a rocket aircraft" followed by the promise of another 80,000 rubles in March.[78] But GIRD members, particularly Korolev, recognized that building rockets would require much more money – enormous amounts of money – beyond the capability of an organization like *Osoaviakhim*. To Korolev and Tsander, who were both aware of Marshal Tukhachevskii's interest in new military technologies, the Red Army was the obvious source for the necessary, massive funding. Immediately after GIRD's formation, the two men tried to contact various Red Army funding institutions, including the Directorate of Military Invention overseen by Tukhachevskii.[79] On February 1, 1932, Tsander gave a presentation on the prospects of liquid-propellant rocket engines to an Air Force representative who in turn alerted the top leadership of *Osoaviakhim* to the important work going on in one of its many hundreds of cells; a few days later, the paramilitary society's top leaders visited the GIRD premises to see a firing of one of Tsander's rocket engines.

The momentum of these contacts culminated with a meeting hosted by Tukhachevskii at the premises of the Revolutionary Military Council on March 3, 1932. For the first time in their nearly decade-long crusade, Soviet popular rocketry enthusiasts met with high-level government officials. Representatives of the Red Army and *Osoaviakhim* heard both Tsander and Korolev report in detail about their work, which perhaps belied the reality that GIRD was essentially still a ramshackle organization with only a handful of members and little to show in terms of results. Tukhachevskii took a risk and asked *Osoaviakhim* to continue to supervise GIRD's work, promising Red Army money to supplement funds from *Osoaviakhim*.[80]

Tukhachevskii's intervention had several immediate ramifications. If GIRD was a wholly voluntary organization surviving on *Osoaviakhim* funds, it was now at least partly funded by the government. GIRD's structure and organizational status also changed. The group determined to move out of Korolev's apartment. He took the initiative to find a more suitable place than his home and, along with his compatriots, went in search of empty or

78 GARF, 8355/1/52/86–88 (February 25, 1932). There is note of an award for 65,000 rubles early in December 1931, but it remains unclear if the money was actually delivered. ARAN, 555/4/652/12–12ob (December 8, 1931).

79 GIRD's point of contact in the Directorate of Military Inventions was Ia. M. Terent'ev, the chief of its second department, who relayed his impressions of GIRD to Tukhachevskii in early 1932. Ia. M. Terent'ev, "Iz istorii pervykh sovetskikh raketnykh organizatsii (1930–1935 gg.)," *Voprosy istorii estestvoznaniia* no. 2 (1984): 108–113.

80 ARAN, 573/3/48/14; GARF, 8355/1/63/70.

abandoned spaces in Moscow. Eventually he found an old wine merchant's cellar on Sadovo-Spasskaia Street, which not only was empty but also, as he later discovered, belonged to *Osoaviakhim*. GIRD members spent nights cleaning the cellar, painting the walls, and installing wiring for electricity. They salvaged a space of about 650 square meters. The basement's frosty chill and odor did not deter the young men and women, who started work with only one piece of machinery, a hand-operated grinder that a friend at an aviation institute had given them. On April 25, *Osoaviakhim* gave the basement a sheen of formality by naming it the "experimental factory" of GIRD.

A formal relationship with *Osoaviakhim* necessitated a hierarchical structure within GIRD. In late April, Tsander quit his job at the Institute of Aviation Motors and joined GIRD full time as its leader. He obtained permission to recruit several of his coworkers as well as new technicians from other places for work at GIRD.[81] Tsander had been the de facto head of GIRD, partly because he was the most theoretically and practically skilled of the group, but the younger Korolev had proved to be more energetic and innovative. Tsander remained at GIRD's helm for the short term while from March 20, 1932, Korolev served as head of its "technical council," a still-non-existent body that would determine future directions of work.[82] After receiving a report on GIRD's work to the top leadership in *Osoaviakhim* on July 10, the society's new chairman Robert Eideman decided that Korolev was a more suitable leader for the group. Four days later, he signed an order appointing Korolev head of GIRD and, more important, made GIRD an official "scientific-research and experimental-design" organization within the *Osoaviakhim* structure for "development of the national economy and strengthening the defensive capability of the USSR." Eideman's lengthy order from July 14, 1932 signaled the effective birth of GIRD as a formal organization charged with developing rockets. It established three primary goals: using reactive engines in the "technical reconstruction" of the Air Force; popularizing reactive engines and preparation of cadres; and involving working inventors in the work on reactive motion. To this end, GIRD would now have four functional departments: a secret unit for R&D work and three public units, for administrative affairs, propaganda work, and production (see Figures 11 and 12).[83]

At the time, a total of seventy-three men and women were officially listed in GIRD's ranks, a number that increased to about ninety within a year. These men and women came from many different backgrounds but most lacked higher education qualifications. Approximately 48% of the staff members were technical specialists, that is, graduates of vocational technical

81 ARAN, 573/1/269/15 (1932).
82 ARAN, 4/14/230/3–4 (March 20, 1932).
83 ARAN, 4/14/218a/5–11 (July 14, 1932).

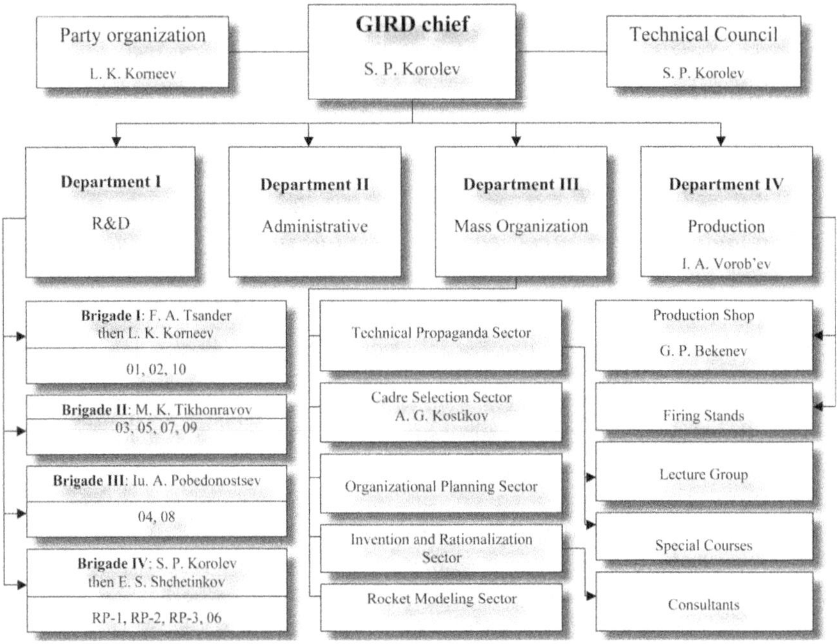

FIGURE 11. Organizational chart of GIRD, 1932–1933.

FIGURE 12. A studio photo of the core members of the Group for the Study of Reactive Motion (GIRD), taken in late 1932 when Sergei Korolev (center, sitting) had already assumed the leading role in the semi-amateur organization. Sitting on the right is Fridrikh Tsander, the spiritual guide of the group. Standing in the middle is Iurii Pobedonostsev, who would later go on to play an important role in the postwar Soviet missile program. [*Source*: Collection of Asif Siddiqi]

schools, of whom 15% to 20% were draftspeople. Most had finished specialized drafting courses, and some had already done similar work at major aviation enterprises.[84] About 80% were between the ages of twenty and thirty and about 85% were men. The women were split between rocket engineers and draftspersons; almost all the group's drafters were women.[85] Without exception, all came from the aviation industry, from low-level jobs in major airplane factories or institutes such as the Central Aerohydrodynamics Institute. Almost all members had been influenced by the writings of Tsiolkovskii, Perel'man, Rynin, and other popularizers of spaceflight during the 1920s. In this way, they were completely unlike the members of GDL, who were predominantly graduates of artillery academies, armed forces veterans, slightly older, and uninterested in spaceflight.

Recruitment in GIRD was an informal process. One man heard that the group was preparing for a flight to Mars and decided to quit his job at the aerodynamics laboratory of the Military Air Academy. One woman joined when she heard from a coworker at the Orgmetall factory about a group that was building an airplane that could fly without any lifting medium. Such interested men and women would typically show up at *Osoaviakhim*'s offices at Nikol'skaia Street in search of information. Korolev would then personally interview those interested, usually to gauge their commitment to rocketry given the low wages at GIRD, rates that were much lower than an average salary at an aviation factory or design bureau.[86] Work days were usually long, especially for those who had full-time day jobs elsewhere. Communist Party members were in the minority; in fact, Korolev was not a party member. However, legitimization of GIRD as a formal organization necessitated the formation of a party cell within the group, which was subordinated to the local *raikom* (*raionnyi komitet*, district committee). Communist Party members were also attached to each design brigade to maintain a strong party presence. By most accounts, most of the members were completely dedicated to the cause of rocketry. One man, Evgenii Moshkin, was expelled from the local Komsomol because he missed two of its meetings to finish a project at GIRD. When summoned to explain his absence, Moshkin failed to provide an adequate excuse because GIRD's R&D unit was a secret department whose existence could not be revealed.[87]

84 N. I. Efremov and E. K. Moshkin, "K piatidesiatiletiiu so vremeni organizatsii v moskve gruppy izucheniia reaktivnogo dvizheniia – GIRD," *IIAIK* 45 (1981): 3–43. The common interwar parlance for technical specialists was "engineering-technical workers" (*inzhenerno-tekhnicheskie rabotniki*, ITR).

85 "Sotrudniki gruppy izucheniia reaktivnogo dvizheniia (GIRD). Moskva, Sadovo-Spasskaia, d. 19," *IIAIK* 45 (1981): 44–48.

86 Although GIRD chief Korolev earned 900 rubles per month, the average wage for a GIRD production worker was about 300 rubles per month. GARF, 8355/1/374/73ob (May 1933).

87 Although GIRD's activities to support the popularization of rocketry remained public, the R&D unit was now considered a military institution and given the secret designation KB-8 (*Konstruktorskogo biuro-8*, Design Bureau No. 8). GARF, 8355/1/370/2–20b (March 20, 1932).

Despite Tukhachevskii's funding assurances, money posed a problem through 1932. The group's equipment remained at best second-hand left-overs thrown out by more well-funded factories. Group members joked that the letters GIRD stood for *Gruppy Inzhenerov, Rabotaiushchikh Darom* (group of engineers working for nothing).[88] As per Tukhachevskii's promise, from August 1932, the Red Army's Directorate of Military Inventions began funding GIRD's R&D activities, supplementing the money provided by *Osoaviakhim*.

Of the 189,269 rubles provided for GIRD's work in the remainder of 1932, about 70% came from the military. Conditions for the *girdovtsy* improved in 1933. Although *Osoaviakhim*'s share diminished to cover only GIRD's propaganda work (about 80,000 rubles), the military directorate granted more than 500,000 rubles, a sum that would have been unimaginable for the group's members a year before. From its two funding conduits, GIRD received about 900,000 rubles during its existence. This sum was quite low when compared to the larger aviation, tank, or artillery teams of the day, but for a small organization working on an entirely new field of R&D, it was noteworthy. GIRD ranked sixth in a list of nearly 100 new R&D projects funded by the Red Army's Directorate of Military Inventions.[89]

The year following GIRD's de facto birth in July 1932 was characterized by both advancement and crisis, including a scandal and the death of one of its leaders. The group appeared to be consistently on the brink of collapse, which was due to a lack of money and full-time workers and the bitter cold working conditions of the basement. In a letter to Tukhachevskii, Korolev listed problems with accommodations, production supplies, transportation, living conditions for workers, and getting qualified employees.[90] The group managed money so poorly that representatives of the Red Army conducted an investigation into its affairs in April 1933. They found inconsistencies in how GIRD accounted for funding between *Osoaviakhim* and the Red Army, misuse of credit, and unauthorized salary increases. The Directorate of Military Inventions issued a reprimand to Korolev with a warning to eliminate all mismanagement within two months or the military would take "more strict measures." These measures might have caused the certain dissolution of GIRD, especially given its lack of technical successes.[91] Korolev

[88] L. K. Korneev, "Zhizn', tvorchestvo i deiatel'nost' F. A. Tsandera (k 75-letiiu so dnia rozhdeniia)," in F. A. Tsander, *Problema poleta pri pomoshchi reaktivnykh apparatov*, ed. L. K. Korneev (Moscow: GNTI Oborongiz, 1961), 51.

[89] GIRD received a total of 750,825 rubles from the Red Army's Directorate of Military Inventions in 1932–1933, split between 135,700 rubles (in 1932) and 615,125 rubles (in 1933). The remainder (about 150,000 rubles) came from *Osoaviakhim*. Financial figures for GIRD were fairly inconsistent because the group received funding from two independent branches with their own accounting systems. For figures, see GARF, 8355/1/374/73–78 (May 1933); RGVA, 4/14/1171/33 (1934).

[90] ARAN, 4/14/242/14–17 (April 20, 1933).

[91] GARF, 8355/1/374/72–72ob (May 17, 1933).

responded to each accusation and asked that he be "cleared of this shameful accusation," accusing the auditors of not comprehending the difficulties that GIRD members dealt with daily.[92] Despite Korolev's defense, the team's reputation was marred.

The group also struggled to find the right balance between the goal of spaceflight and the practice of rocketry. Being the spiritual leader of the group, the space-obsessed Tsander naturally influenced many with his unwavering belief in the future of space exploration. His mantra during work was "Onwards to Mars!," a phrase that he used to encourage his younger coworkers during difficult days. Unlike some of the other members of GIRD who were outwardly reticent about their interest in spaceflight, Tsander was not shy. During one of Marshal Tukhachevskii's visits to their basement workshop, Korolev had instructed everyone to look and act as professional as possible. Tsander described his ORD-2 engine to the marshal but to everyone's alarm could not resist digressing into a discussion on flights to Mars, to which Tukhachevskii responded with polite interest. Korolev, who was capable of countering everyone at GIRD, did not interrupt Tsander and instead let him finish.[93]

Despite his idealism or perhaps because of it, Korolev considered Tsander a mentor and took great pains to make sure the older man's life was without trouble. For example, when Korolev noticed that Tsander was buying only the cheapest food items from the canteen for lunch, Korolev paid extra money without Tsander's knowledge so that the latter received a lunch worth thirty-five kopecks even though he thought he was paying for seven.[94] Tsander clearly influenced Korolev's thinking about rocketry and spaceflight. Before 1932, Korolev rarely, if ever, said a word about space travel. Yet one year after their first meeting, Korolev began occasionally talking about trips to the Moon, surprising his colleagues, who never expected such ideas from him. Where before he barely acknowledged Tsiolkovskii, in 1932, Korolev, on behalf of GIRD, sent the old man a congratulatory letter on his seventy-fifth birthday and also met him when he came to Moscow to accept an award.[95]

Korolev's public and private writings from the early 1930s show a marked but conflicted interest in spaceflight; on the one hand, he denigrated the cause of spaceflight and extolled the virtues of the rocket, while in the same breath he underscored that the rocket was the only true way to get to space. One of Korolev's letters to popular science writer Iakov Perel'man is emblematic of this tension:

[92] GARF, 8355/1/374/68–71 (June 25, 1933).

[93] For a participant recollection of the visit in December 1932, see Memoir of N. I. Efremov in *ASPK*, 157–158.

[94] Golovanov, *Korolev*, 147.

[95] Korolev met Tsiolkovskii on November 27, 1932.

I only wish that you in your future works, being a specialist in rocketry and the author of a number of excellent books, would pay more attention not to interplanetary issues, but to the rocket engine itself, to a stratospheric rocket, etc., since all this is now closer to us, more understandable, and more necessary. A great deal of nonsense has been written on interplanetary themes, and it is now hurting us badly.

But Korolev also added this: "I would very much like to see your excellent books in a series of studies to stir up enthusiasm for rocketry.... If this happens, then there will be a time when the first terrestrial ship will leave the earth. Granted, we may not live to see this, and may be destined to spend our life puttering about down below, but nevertheless, success is possible only on this foundation."[96]

Despite Korolev's ambivalent stance, Tsander continued to devote his energies to promoting space exploration. Tsander published a book on the topic in 1932 and also edited for release the selected works of Tsiolkovskii at the latter's request.[97] Because of overwork and poor eating habits, he became so haggard and emaciated that Korolev asked him several times to take a vacation at a sanatorium in Kislovodsk. Korolev took 1,300 rubles from GIRD's money fund and gave it to Tsander for a train trip. This error in judgment would come back to haunt Korolev when he would be accused of misappropriating a similar amount during the investigation into GIRD's financial matters.[98] Tsander, who was unenthused about taking a vacation from work, had to wait several months to get a pass to go on leave. By the time the pass came through, he was not in good health. In the spring of 1933, on March 2 – coincidentally just when one of his engines was undergoing ground testing – Tsander finally departed for Kislovodsk. Soon after he got to his destination, he fell ill and was taken to a local hospital where he was diagnosed with typhus. He apparently caught it by traveling third class to save money, which he left behind for his wife and children. In the hospital, he fell asleep and never regained consciousness. Tsander died on the early morning of March 28, 1933 at the age of forty-six. He was buried in the local cemetery.[99] The last letter he wrote to Korolev ended, "Forward, comrades, and only forward! Raise the rockets higher and higher, closer to the stars." When they received news of his death, many GIRD members, including Korolev, wept openly. Tsander, the dreamer, left behind 7,200

[96] St. Petersburg Branch of ARAN, 796/3/36/234–35 (April 18, 1935).

[97] F. A. Tsander, *Problem poleta pri pomoshchi reaktivnykh apparatov* (Moscow: Gosaviaavtoizdat, 1932); K. E. Tsiolkovskii, *Izbrannye trudy, kniga II. Reaktivnoe dvizhenie*, ed. F. A. Tsander (Moscow: Gosmashmetizdat, 1934).

[98] Korolev requested money from *Osoaviakhim* for Tsander's vacation as early as August 1932. GARF, 8355/1/58/28ob (August 15, 1932); GARF, 8355/1/58/35 (undated). Korolev apparently did not wait for the money to come through and took 1,300 rubles from GIRD's fund to give to Tsander. A GIRD worker, S. A. Rovenskii, complained about Korolev's actions to *Osoaviakhim*, which probably led to the investigation into financial improprieties.

[99] "Inzh. F. A. Tsander," *Tekhnika*, March 30, 1933.

pages of technical writings on almost every aspect of space exploration and rocketry, much of which has remained unpublished to this day.[100]

SELLING THE CAUSE: SCIENCE AS A MASS PHENOMENON

Being a locally generated enthusiast group, GIRD's rise to prominence cannot be explained only by military imperatives and Tukhachevskii's patronage. GIRD certainly used the defense of the USSR to sell its cause, but the group's "sales pitch" also had a public and nonmilitary dimension that resonated with broader national attitudes toward science and technology, especially about mastering modern technology as a mass phenomenon. By the end of the Cultural Revolution, at the tail end of the First Five-Year Plan, the public notion of science in the USSR became closely tied to practical science and, specifically, the needs of industrialization and modernization. The Bol'shevik Party issued a decree in August 1931 that focused the scientific resources of the country on technical literacy, echoing Stalin's phrase, "technology in the period of reconstruction decides all."[101] A second party decree in November 1931 reorganized the two important mass scientific organizations, the Scientific-Technical Society of the *Vesenkha* and *Tekhnika-massam* (Technology for the Masses) to focus "in all possible ways to encourage all kinds of personal, group, and social initiatives, moving ahead the matter of creation and development of technology and scientific-technological societies."[102] The party underlined the same idea at the Seventeenth Party conference in January to February 1932, when "shock-workers, inventors, and rationalizers" were singled out for support.[103]

GIRD members could hardly claim that rocket-planes were crucial to Soviet industrialization. But as articles on foreign work on reactive propulsion and stratospheric exploration flooded the Soviet media in the early 1930s, GIRD couched its development of such a rocket-plane – and rockets in general – as contributing to both education on and exploration of the

[100] To a large degree, Tsander's legacy was maintained by his daughter Astra Tsander. Because of her efforts, Tsander's papers are now deposited in the Russian Academy of Sciences. For a guide, see Iu. S. Voronkov et al., eds., *Rukopisnye materialy F. A. Tsandera v Arkhive AN SSSR: nauchnoe opisanie* (Moscow: Nauka, 1980). For collections of key works, see Tsander, *Problema poleta pri pomoshchi reaktivnykh apparatov*; Tsander, *Iz nauchnogo naslediia*; V. P. Mishin, ed., *F. A. Tsander i sovremennaia kosmonavtika* (Moscow: Nauka, 1976); F. A. Tsander, *Sobranie trudov*, ed. G. A. Teters (Riga: Zinatne, 1977).

[101] James T. Andrews, *Science for the Masses: The Bolshevik State, Public Science, and the Popular Imagination in Soviet Russia, 1917–1934* (College Station, TX: Texas A&M University Press, 2003), 130–134, 164–169.

[102] *Spravochnik partiinogo rabotnika, vyp. 8* (Moscow: Partizdat TsK VKP(b), 1934), 382–383.

[103] *Kommunisticheskaia partiia Sovetskogo Soiuza v rezoliutsiiakh i resheniiakh s'ezdov, ch. 3* (Moscow: Politizdat, 1954), 147–148.

stratosphere; the former was a mass phenomenon and the latter a heroic quest for knowledge.

The principal force behind popularization was GIRD's propaganda department. Under *Osoaviakhim*'s sponsorship, it joined forces with *Tekhnika*, the official newspaper of *Vesenkha*'s Scientific-Technical Department, to launch in March 1932 the "Storming the Stratosphere" (*Na shturm stratosfery*) campaign.[104] The campaign's goals were to inculcate a positive attitude among the populace toward the idea of stratospheric exploration, disseminate scientific information on the topic, encourage the formation of GIRD groups all over the Soviet Union, and collect donations for the work of these groups. Beyond publications, the campaign also involved lectures, planetarium shows, and radio programs such as *Komsomol'skaia pravda po radio* (*Komsomol'skaia pravda* on the radio). In 1932 alone, *Tekhnika* published about fifty articles on rockets and stratospheric flight, many written by GIRD members. Although the R&D unit of GIRD was a secret organization working with military money, members were allowed to make general claims about the existence of the broader group, especially its propaganda element.

Fascination with the stratosphere in the early 1930s was not a spurious phenomenon. In 1931, Frenchman Auguste Piccard's flight in a balloon to an altitude of sixteen kilometers had been reported throughout the world, including in Russia. Many other Westerners planned or performed increasingly daring feats high in the sky, including American aviator Charles Lindbergh, whose iconic status extended to the Soviet Union. Famed French aviator Louis Bleriot announced at the time that flight into the stratosphere was the second of four stages before conquering space. In effect, Piccard and others illustrated that the stratosphere represented a logical first destination, one that combined the adventure of space travel with the possibilities of current-day aviation.

Prompted by such international developments, the Soviet aviation industry used competition as a common strategy to declare itself on par with the capitalist world. Stratospheric exploration by means of balloons constituted one dimension of the public face of modern Soviet aviation, one that was focused on establishing new records and creating new heroes. Kendall Bailes and others have illustrated that setting aviation records served several ends for the emerging Stalinist state in the 1930s. These included establishing the might of new Soviet industry, creating the archetype of the new Soviet hero, countering the dour proceedings of the show trials later in the decade, and, most importantly, legitimizing harsh state policies. As part of this trend, beginning in 1933, the entire country celebrated Aviation Day every year

[104] "Na shturm stratosfery: my gotovy otdat' svoi sily etomu delu!," *Tekhnika*, March 30, 1932.

on August 18 as one of the most festive annual commemorations of early Stalinism.[105]

The coincidence of military need, in the form of high-speed aircraft that Tukhachevskii desired, and public imperatives to compete with foreigners generated attention at the highest levels of the Soviet government. In December 1931, materials on the "question of flight to the stratosphere" were sent directly to Stalin for review.[106] Through 1932, the government's Defense Commission issued memos to both military and industry on organization of work on stratospheric flight while Viacheslav Molotov asked that military and industry draw up a government decree that would steer work in that direction.[107] The discussions highlighted two paths of exploring the stratosphere, by balloon (a short-term solution) and by airplane (a long-term objective). As a result, in December 1932, the Revolutionary Military Council approved a plan to launch a spherical balloon up to the stratosphere to collect data necessary to develop an engine that would work at high altitudes.[108] *Osoaviakhim* played a central role in this effort, justifying Soviet efforts to explore the stratosphere by invoking the explorations of Piccard and other foreigners.[109]

Like their spaceflight advocates in the 1920s, the "Storming the Stratosphere" campaigners at GIRD used pronouncements from the heroes of the new frontier to legitimize their cause. For example, the inaugural *Tekhnika* issue of the campaign published congratulatory telegrams from Konstantin Tsiolkovskii, Iakov Perel'man, Nikolai Rynin, and others whose names were associated with reactive motion. The newspaper even reproduced a letter from the German popularizer of spaceflight, Willy Ley, wishing future success to GIRD. Letters also came from laypersons from all over the country, from students, factory workers, and artists. *Tekhnika* also announced a fund to support the work of building stratospheric airships, rocket-planes, and rockets, donating the first 110 rubles itself.[110] The phrase "gird movement" (*girdovskoe dvhizhenie*) was briefly in usage as a common way to refer to the practical aspects of the stratosphere campaign. As part of the drive, *Osoaviakhim* set aside money to publish a number of monographs on reactive propulsion by such luminaries as Tsiolkovskii, Tsander, Korolev, Tikhonravov, and others.[111]

105 Kendall E. Bailes, "Technology and Legitimacy: Soviet Aviation and Stalinism in the 1930s," *Technology and Culture* 17 (1976): 55–81; Jay Bergman, "Valerii Chkalov: Soviet Pilot as New Soviet Man," *Journal of Contemporary History* 33 (1998): 135–152.

106 GARF, 8418/6/74/38 (December 21, 1931).

107 GARF, 8418/6/74/42–44.

108 GARF, 8418/6/74/15 (December 11, 1932).

109 GARF, 8418/6/74/12–12ob (February 5, 1933).

110 "Sozdadim vsesoiuznyi fond 'shturm stratosfery'" and "Vnosim-vyzyvaem," *Tekhnika*, March 30, 1932.

111 GARF, 8355/1/75/74–81 (February 1933).

A testament to the power of the stratosphere campaign – and the widespread resonance of "reactive motion" as a forward-thinking technological idea in the early 1930s – was the number of registered groups studying rockets. By the end of the stratosphere campaign, amateurs had established GIRD groups in at least ninety locations beyond Moscow, including such distant locales as Arkhangel'sk, Perm, Odessa, and Khar'kov, supported and encouraged by *Osoaviakhim* cells in the periphery.[112] *Osoaviakhim* declared the Moscow GIRD to be the Central GIRD, that is, a central storehouse for information on reactive motion and stratospheric exploration. Excepting one or two GIRD teams, none of the outlier GIRDs achieved any technical success, although their ideas were passed to the center for discussion. The engineering work of the center, on the other hand, remained a secret to outsiders.

The stratosphere campaign peaked with the "shock month" of October 1932, when dozens of journals and newspapers joined in a chorus of articles on stratospheric exploration, timed partly to coincide with Tsiolkovskii's seventy-fifth birthday.[113] The excitement over the "Storming the Stratosphere" campaign in 1932 generated enough momentum for continuing favorable media treatment of stratospheric exploration through the mid-1930s. These articles and monographs, like their Western counterparts, shared general themes: the economic and scientific benefits of stratospheric research, the use of rockets for such exploration, and the idea that conquering the stratosphere was more beneficial than utopian ideas such as space travel.[114]

BUILDING ROCKETS

The public face of GIRD hid a varied and rich program of technical work. Although the group produced few substantive results, its work in the early 1930s laid the practical foundations of Soviet rocketry, giving a generation

[112] Groups were established in Arkhangel'sk, Baku, Briansk, Cheliabinsk, Erivan, Ivanovo-Voznesensk, Kazan', Khabarovsk, Khar'kov, Krasnodar, Leningrad, Minsk, Novocherkassk, Nizhnii Novgorod, Novosibirsk, Odessa, Ordzhonikidze, Perm, Rostov-na-Don, Simferepol, Sverdlovsk, Smolensk, Tiflis, and Tomsk. *Tekhnika*, September 9, 1932.

[113] Articles as part of the campaign were published in *Komsomol'skaia pravda*, *Krasnaia zvezda*, *Nauka i tekhnika*, *Nizhegorodskaia kommuna*, *Samolet*, *V boi za tekhniku*, *Vecherniaia moskva*, *Za industrializatsiiu*, and *Znanie-sila*. A sampling of articles from the campaign is stored in ARAN, r. 4, op. 14, d. 235.

[114] Notable Soviet monographs on stratospheric exploration included N. A. Rynin, *Zavoevanie stratosfery: k poletam sovetskikh vysotnykh aerostatov v stratosferu* (Leningrad, 1933); Korolev, "Raketnyi polet v stratosfere"; N. A. Rynin, *V stratosferu!* (Leningrad, 1934); A. Stivens, *Polet v stratosferu* (Moscow, 1936); and V. A. Sytin, *Stratosfernii front* (Moscow, 1936).

of engineers experience in postulating, designing, building, and then flying liquid-propellant rockets.

The group's R&D department began work on seven "themes" (or projects) in 1932, expanding to thirteen the following year. The enthusiasts picked projects according to decisions by a nine-member technical council that included both Korolev and Tsander.[115] By mid-1933, the R&D department had split into four brigades of about a dozen members each, headed by Tsander, Tikhonravov, Pobedonostsev, and Korolev. Each focused on different broadly defined goals and included team leaders, engineers, and mechanics.[116] All four brigades made important technical advances, but Brigade Two's work in particular displayed the kind of pragmatic innovation, both managerial and technical, that Soviet engineers would use many times in the future to gain support for their cause. Under Mikhail Tikhonravov, Brigade Two originally worked on three themes, a rocket engine for a rocket-glider known as RP-2 and two other small ballistic rockets.[117] Their work changed abruptly in early 1933. By that time, GIRD's fortunes had soured. Tsander had died, none of the group's projects had produced anything of note, and they were being accused of financial improprieties. Korolev reviewed the work of the brigades and decided that what GIRD needed was an immediate and visible success, not only for internal morale but to show something to his sponsors.

Earlier, a GIRD engineer visiting Baku had met a self-declared inventor who had stores of a jelly-like mixture composed of gasoline dissolved in resin. Seeing this solid gasoline, in late 1932, Tikhonravov conceived of a new simple rocket that he believed could successfully fly. The rocket would not have the complex engine pumps and propellant feeding systems that gave the engineers so much trouble. Instead, this solid jelly could be placed directly in the combustion chamber. Liquid oxygen fed into the chamber would be ignited by a regular spark plug, firing the engine. The whole rocket, which was a hybrid rocket because it used both "solid" and liquid propellants, weighed about nineteen kilograms. Korolev and Tikhonravov

[115] The members of the technical council were S. P. Korolev (chairman), F. A. Tsander, M. K. Tikhonravov, Iu. A. Pobedonostsev, A. I. Poliarnii, L. K. Korneev, A. V. Chesalov, E. S. Shchetinkov, N. I. Efremov, and N. A. Zheleznikov. The original seven themes included reactive engines (ORD-1, ORD-2, RD-V-1, RD-A, and RD-V) and rocket-gliders (RP-1 and RP-2).

[116] The brigades were established sequentially, not simultaneously. The technical divisions among the brigades reflected integrated solutions that the brigade chiefs chose rather than engineering subdisciplines such as materials, fuels, guidance, etc. Brigades 1 and 2 both focused on liquid-propellant rocket engines and rockets using them; Brigade 3 on ramjets; and Brigade 4 on rocket-planes.

[117] ARAN, 4/14/248/1–65 (1932–34). Brigade 2's original projects were themes 03 (the RD-A rocket engine), 05 (liquid-propellant rocket), and 07 (liquid-propellant rocket).

presented the rocket to the military as a possible replacement for a standard 122-mm-caliber artillery projectile, with which it shared a similar mass and range. Although both understood that the "hybrid" system might be only a short-term solution, they also recognized that this rocket might succeed where others had failed. Through March and April 1933, Tikhonravov's brigade conducted ground tests of the rocket, named "09," at a proving ground in Nakhabino outside of Moscow. The hopes of the group sagged through the summer as the project ground down in failure after failure. For a while, it seemed that their persistence was not paying off in kind. Much of the technology for the rocket was makeshift. For example, engineers used a special oxygen flask designed by Tsander to transport liquid oxygen to the firing range in a rented truck. These flasks leaked quite a bit of the oxygen, so that once engineers loaded them with oxygen, they had to race through the streets of Moscow to get to the firing ground to load their rocket before all the liquid oxygen boiled off into the air.[118]

In July, numerous ground tests of the 09 failed. By this time, Korolev suspended all other projects at GIRD and focused its entire attention on the rocket. Tikhonravov was so exhausted by the work that he and his engineers took a short vacation to go fishing. Korolev continued work on the project and invited a representative from the Red Army's Directorate of Inventions, Iakov Terent'ev, to witness 09's first launch on August 11. About thirty others were present. Unfortunately, the rocket did not go off as planned as a result of a short circuit in a spark plug. Another attempt on August 13 also failed.[119] By the third attempt on the night of August 17, the crowd had significantly dwindled. This time, however, the rocket lifted off, gradually gaining speed until it was about 400–500 meters above the ground, after which it sharply turned and came down in a nearby forest and hit the ground (see Figure 13). The entire flight lasted eighteen seconds. Although the rocket had been designed to fly higher, up to 5,000 meters (a gasket seal had broken, releasing gases that altered its trajectory), just the simple view of its flight transformed the mood of the engineers.[120] GIRD members quickly prepared the latest issue of the group's in-house news flier – called *Raketa* (The Rocket) – and included several testimonials from brigade members and production workers. Korolev wrote a short piece that was equal amounts bravado and pride:

> The first Soviet liquid propellant rocket has been launched. The day of August 17 will undoubtedly be a memorable day in the life of GIRD, and starting from this

[118] Golovanov, *Korolev*, 152–153.

[119] ARAN, 4/14/50/70 (August 11, 1933); ARAN, 4/14/50/75 (August 13, 1933).

[120] ARAN, 4/14/50/77 (August 17, 1933). Present at the launch were S. P. Korolev, N. I. Efremov, L. K. Korneev, Z. I. Kruglova, O. K. Parovina, N. I. Shul'gina, E. M. Matysik, L. A. Ikonnikov, A. S. Raetskii, and B. Shedko.

FIGURE 13. A photo taken of the launch in August 1933 of "09," the first Soviet rocket to use liquid propellants, launched about seven years after the first American one. Standing on the left is Sergei Korolev. This was probably a posed photo taken after the event to draw the attention of potential sponsors of their work. The rocket's main designer, Mikhail Tikhonravov, was not present, but on vacation, recovering from overwork. [*Source*: Collection of Asif Siddiqi]

moment, Soviet rockets should fly over the Union of Republics. The GIRD collective should exert all our forces to ... hand [the rocket] over for service in the ... Red Army.... Soviet rockets must conquer the expanse![121]

Technically speaking, Korolev's claim that it was the first Soviet liquid-propellant rocket was only partially true because the 09 was a hybrid rocket. The first true Soviet liquid-propellant rocket was designed and built by the

[121] S. P. Korolev, "Sovetskie rakety pobediat prostranstvo," *Raketa*, August 22, 1933.

late Tsander and used a relatively sophisticated liquid oxygen–ethyl alcohol engine.[122] The enthusiasts constructed the rocket out of aluminum alloy and steel, which they soldered together in their basement. The rocket, later known as GIRD-X, was launched on November 25, 1933, eight months after Tsander's death, and reached a height of eighty meters before the engine exploded as a result of high-frequency vibrations.[123] This first launch of a Soviet liquid-propellant rocket came about seven years after the first American flight and two years after the first German launch.

JOINING FORCES, MAKING AN INSTITUTE

The success of the 09 made a big impression on both *Osoaviakhim* and the Red Army. Korolev took advantage of the success to claim that GIRD could "deliver [such a rocket] to armaments and for peaceful uses" and eventually achieve a range of "a hundred, a thousand kilometers." He also trumpeted the need for a centralized and well-funded organization to pursue the development of rocketry.[124] Both *Osoaviakhim* and the Red Army had, in fact, proposed such a body since 1931. Marshal Tukhachevskii had raised the possibility of uniting GDL and GIRD as early as March 1932, a logical recommendation given that both were developing technologies based on reaction propulsion. Representatives from the two groups visited each other on a few occasions in 1932 and 1933, although they did not always see eye to eye. Beyond agreeing that the country needed rockets, they shared little else. During one visit to Leningrad in January 1933, Tsander expressed mixed opinions about the engine work at GDL.[125] The tension between the two groups, only latent at this point, manifested itself in their respective proposals for an institution to develop rockets that was directed by the Red Army. Initially, both supported an institute based on their *own* group. Later, after Tukhachevskii proposed uniting the two groups, the two sides cooled on the idea of uniting.[126] Korolev, for example, wrote to Tukhachevskii that GIRD should be directly subordinated to Tukhachevskii with no connection to GDL.[127]

[122] The rocket was to have used Tsander's favored metallic fuel engine, but once that idea fell by the wayside, the brigade redesigned the rocket for liquid propellants. Benzene, used early on as fuel, was replaced by ethyl alcohol, which allowed more stable combustion with liquid oxygen.

[123] ARAN, 4/14/49/1–23. Tsander's projects were themes 01 (ORD-1 rocket engine), 02 (ORD-2 rocket engine), and 10 (GIRD-X rocket). ARAN, 4/14/247/1–85 (1932–1934).

[124] GARF, 8355/1/374/143–143ob (August 22, 1933).

[125] V. A. Volodin, "2 sentiabria – 80 let so dnia rozhdeniia akademika V. P. Glushko (1908 g.)," *IIAIK* 59 (1989): 82–92.

[126] GDL had proposed a "gas-dynamics scientific-research institute" in 1932. ARAN, 4/14/243/1–5 (April 1932).

[127] ARAN, 4/14/242/14–17 (April 20, 1933).

Tukhachevskii was the prime mover in forcing the issue of a unified rocketry institute. In May, he wrote to Molotov about the issue, invoking "foreign achievements," particularly the work of Robert Goddard and Herman Oberth. Based on his belief that reactive engines would have important consequences for military technology, especially in areas of artillery, aviation, and chemical warfare, he set three goals for the new organization that were biased toward the liquid propellants of the GIRD team as opposed to the traditional solids of GDL.[128] In June, the Council of Labor and Defense created a subcommission to look into the matter, but remarkably, the issue bogged down in red tape for over a year as a result of inaction from Commissar of Defense Kliment Voroshilov, who had a well-known dislike of Tukhachevskii. There were also conflicting schedules of different commission members and disagreements over the proper role of the institute.[129]

In late February 1933, representatives from all parties met to discuss the R&D direction of a unified organization, but because GIRD and GDL members were unable to agree, the problem was assigned to yet another commission to arbitrate.[130] Through this period, the general consensus among all parties was that the newly formed institute would be subordinate to the Red Army's Revolutionary Military Council; in other words, GIRD would be moved out of *Osoaviakhim* and join up with GDL, which was already under military control.[131] As part of this agreement, two of GIRD's four departments, the propaganda and administrative departments, that is, the units that ran the "Storming the Stratosphere" campaign, would remain in *Osoaviakhim* because military leaders were not interested in publicity.[132]

At this time, however, Tukhachevskii appears to have changed his opinion about the need to directly control R&D organizations. If for a short period he cultivated military R&D, by mid-1933 he believed that R&D organizations were ineffective unless they had close contacts with broad industrial infrastructure that existed in civilian industry, principally in the giant superministry known as *Narkomtiazhprom*.[133] The chief of the Military Inspectorate of the Red Army, who was asked to resolve the whole mess regarding the new institute's organization, agreed with Tukhachevskii. He

[128] ARAN, 4/14/243/7–9 (May 16, 1932).

[129] The commission, created on June 22, 1932, included I. A. Akulov (chairman), I. P. Pavlunovskii, M. N. Tukhachevskii, and N. I. Bukharin. For summaries of the various turns and twists of this process, see RGVA, 4/14/885/8 (May 1933); ARAN, 4/14/243/33–35 (May 10, 1933). Akulov was replaced by Tukhachevskii as commission chairman on November 20, 1932.

[130] Terent'ev, "Iz istorii pervykh," 112; ARAN, 4/14/243/21 (March 1933).

[131] See, for example, the discussion on finalizing GIRD's transfer from *Osoaviakhim* to the Revolutionary Military Council in GARF, 8355/1/71/231–33 (April 10, 1933).

[132] GARF, 8355/1/374/19 (February 7, 1933); GARF, 8355/1/374/16 (March 5, 1933); GARF, 8355/1/71/234–35 (April 10, 1933).

[133] Tukhacheveskii noted as such in a letter to his boss Voroshilov. RGVA, 4/14/950/17–34 (May 21, 1933).

recommended that given "the meager cadre of research workers in reactive propulsion, and also the absence of a clear division of work and of parallelism" between GDL and GIRD, it would be best to unite them into a new institute and move it under *Narkomtiazhprom*. Tukhachevskii's boss Voroshilov concurred with this suggestion.[134]

Further twists nearly derailed the process of union, but finally, on October 31, the government belatedly issued a decree, "On organization of the Reactive institute," to unite GDL and GIRD under the civilian-controlled *Narkomtiazhprom*. The order gave the new institute, called the Reactive Scientific-Research Institute (*Reaktivnii nauchno-issledovatel'skii institut*, RNII), a new home: the vacated tractor laboratory of an agricultural research institute in the Likhobory suburb of Moscow.[135] In order to ensure strong military control over the new institute, Tukhachevskii stipulated that at least forty-six Red Army officers should be assigned to work there.[136] Deciding between Kleimenov (leader of GDL) and Korolev (leader of GIRD), Tukhachevskii chose the former because he was older (thirty-four), a Communist Party member, a military officer, a Civil War veteran, and a protégé of the marshal. Korolev was appointed deputy director of the institute, a not-inconsiderable honor for a twenty-seven-year-old man.

To commemorate the founding of the new institute, *Osoaviakhim* rented a club room on Kolkhoznaia Square in Moscow. All the GIRD members attended, dressed in their best formal wear. As the new deputy director of the institute, Korolev wore a jacket with two pips on tabs – the civilian equivalent to a lieutenant-general of engineers in the army. That night, *Osoaviakhim* gave awards to many GIRD members for their work over the past two years – badges, watches, even winter coats. After much drinking, Korolev gave a speech reflecting on the past two years of work in the basement. Fridrikh Tsander's dream of space flight was not forgotten, but the matter at hand now was to build stratospheric rockets – rockets for defense and for science.

CONCLUSIONS

Between 1931 and 1933, popular enthusiasts of spaceflight in the Soviet Union organized the first practical research organizations dedicated to developing rockets. Their achievement was particularly striking because

134 ARAN, 4/14/243/41–43 (June 4, 1933).

135 GARF, 8418/28/3/17–18 (October 31, 1933); RGVA, 4/14/885/13. *Narkomtiazhprom*'s order on the institute's creation was issued on November 4, 1933. RGAE, 8162/1/449/63 (April 25, 1941).

136 At one point earlier, on September 21, frustrated by slow action by the government, Tukhachevskii tried to unilaterally order the formation of the institute under his command in the Red Army, an order that was essentially rescinded by Voroshilov on October 5. These struggles underscore both a general ambivalence about the future of the institute as well as conflicts between Tukhachevskii and Voroshilov.

they accomplished their goal without significant support from the state or a high-level of technical expertise. Using money donated by a mass voluntary society, the activists initially built modest rockets. Their early practical experience provided them enough leverage to skillfully sell their cause to the state, in particular to the military. Subsequent state support, in the form of money and patronage, resulted in a potent union between activists working on their own initiative and the state intent on making use of their expertise. Their symbiotic union resulted in the formation of the world's first state-sponsored organization dedicated to developing powerful liquid-propellant rockets. As a result, advocates moved the idea of spaceflight in Russia from dreaming to doing; for the next twenty years, state and rocketry firmly displaced amateurs and spaceflight.

Two broader contextual factors helped Soviet rocketeers promote their cause. First, the popular fascination with stratospheric exploration prompted mass societies such as *Osoaviakhim* to redirect their attention to the lofty heights. Second, the Red Army discovered rocketry as a potentially powerful weapon of the future. If at first, in late 1931, the civilian-oriented GIRD rocket enthusiasts struggled to find direction in their work, by 1933 they began to use both stratospheric exploration and military need to sell their cause. Similarly, after years without any palpable mandate, the military-dominated GDL group also found a sponsor, Marshal Tukhachevskii, who believed that rockets would be an asset in the realities of modern-day war. The combination of stratospheric exploration (a public rationale) and military need (a secret one) provided the precise charge needed to justify the cause of practical rocketry in the early 1930s. Although GIRD and GDL did not share similar technical priorities, the immediate goal of developing rockets united them on the state's behalf.

The vibrancy of local and independent initiative in conceiving, designing, and then building rockets in the early 1930s sharply contrasts with historians' traditional view of the transformation of Soviet science and technology during the Great Break into a system controlled firmly from the center. At the time, the party "Bol'shevized" the Academy of Sciences so as to plan its entire scope of work in coordination with the five-year plans and use social utility as a metric of its research work. Similarly, the All-Union Association of Workers in Science and Technology for Cooperation in Socialist Construction (VARNITSO), the influential Marxist professional society of the period, launched a campaign to make the work of scientists and engineers "part of socialist construction and to criticize digressions from orthodox thought and expected behavior."[137] Yet, the GIRD members' modest successes in producing relatively innovative technology *outside* the traditional

[137] Alexander Vucinich, *Empire of Knowledge: The Academy of Sciences of the USSR (1917–1970)* (Berkeley: University of California Press, 1984), 126; Loren R. Graham, *Science in Russia and the Soviet Union: A Short History* (Cambridge, UK: Cambridge University Press, 1993), 93–98.

system of Soviet science suggests that despite the transformation into a centralized top-down controlled system of science, people on the ground could initiate and sustain vibrant, dynamic, and innovative scientific and technological work.

The union of amateur work with the state was symbiotic. The amateurs and enthusiasts, both in GIRD and GDL, required the state's resources to implement their ideas. The state, specifically the military, needed the expertise and innovative ideas of the amateurs to improve its fighting power. State intervention brought both benefits and risks to the now single group of rocketeers. Unfortunately for an unlucky few, it also brought incarceration and death.

5

"All of This Requires Investigation"

In Germany we realized that if there were no arrests, we would have reached a very high technical level as early as the late thirties. As a result of repressions in the army and the scientific community, the development of our rocketry stopped at powder rockets.[1]

G. A. Tiulin, a senior administrator in the Soviet space program, 1987

INTRODUCTION

On Monday, June 27, 1938, after a long day at work at the secret rocketry research institute, thirty-one-year-old Sergei Korolev walked home to his tiny one-room Moscow apartment in a drab five-story building on Koniushkovskaia Street near the U.S. Embassy. On his way home, he had picked up some fresh French bread and a copy of *Pravda*, which was filled with news about the previous day's historic elections to the Supreme Soviet. Korolev's three-year-old daughter Nataliia had been sent away to her grandmother's country house, so the apartment was unusually quiet that night. His wife Kseniia, a medical student, had noticed two men in dark suits lurking nearby when she returned from work, raising alarm bells. Several people from her building had disappeared in the past few months. After supper, as the two sat listening to music on their new phonograph, the doorbell rang. They both immediately sensed what was about to happen. Two men from the People's Commissariat of Internal Affairs (NKVD), the Soviet security police, walked in and directed Korolev to sit down while they searched the apartment. Then, as Kseniia later remembered, "They told Sergei Pavlovich to get dressed. He put on a leather coat he usually wore. I naively gave him two changes of underwear for the journey. We said goodbye and kissed each other. But when I wanted to go downstairs to see him off in the car, they prevented me quite roughly. I remained alone in the flat. I had golden hair and it went completely gray overnight."[2] Within a year, Korolev was digging for gold as a prison laborer in the depths of the Siberian Gulag.

[1] Maria Pastukhova, "Iarche liuboi legendy," *Ogonek* no. 49 (1987): 18–23.

[2] Kseniia Koroleva, interview, NOVA. *The Russian Right Stuff: Korolev*, Show 1808, WGBH-TV, PBS, February 20, 1991; Iaroslav Golovanov, *Korolev: fakty i mify* (Moscow: Nauka,

Korolev's arrest was the culmination of a remarkable series of events that few could have expected upon the formation of the Reactive Scientific-Research Institute (RNII) in 1933. For the many engineers, technicians, and factory workers who came from the GDL and GIRD teams to develop and build rockets, full state support to pursue their goals – especially patronage by Marshal Mikhail Tukhachevskii – fostered widespread optimism. State support meant not only more money to devote to rocket projects, but also higher status and easier access to influential military, state, and Party leaders. Yet, only five years after the institute's formation, the NKVD arrested several of its employees, including four of its top engineers, two of whom were shot.

These arrests, the culmination of the NKVD's attack on the institute, remain one of the most important turning points in accounts of state sponsorship of Soviet rocketry research. Both Russian and Western historians have treated the history of Soviet prewar rocketry as a linear technological evolution interrupted by the Great Terror of 1937 and 1938. Lacking a substantial archival record, the repression has been seen as the defining and singular break in rocketry work. In particular, explanations of the Soviet "lag" in rocketry at the end of World War II – especially compared to the unprecedented German development of the V-2 ballistic missile – have depended largely on the prewar Stalinist terror that appeared to have disrupted several years of sustained and innovative work on rockets.[3]

The purges were undoubtedly an important milestone in the evolution of the Soviet rocket and space programs, but were they a catastrophe for Soviet rocketry? Using this question as a starting point, I revisit not only the effect of repression on interwar research on rockets but also the effect of this research on the dynamic of the arrests within the community of scientists and engineers. In the shift from cosmic enthusiasm to practical work on rockets, engineers such as Korolev, Glushko, and Tikhonravov grappled with major technological questions and how to invest limited resources effectively. They could agree on few things. Bitter conflicts over the adoption of specific technologies plagued the institute before the Great Terror, disagreements that were inseparable from broader forces operating at a national level, especially fast-paced industrialization, rapid military rearmament, and weapons research and development in anticipation of war. As the deadly repercussions of *Ezhovshchina* – the horrific Stalinist purges of the late 1930s that took their name from Nikolai Ezhov, the chairman of the NKVD – began to envelop large swathes of Soviet society, these ostensibly

1994), 242–243, 248–249; M. Rebrov, "Lider: maloizvestnye stranitsy iz zhizni," *Krasnaia zvezda*, July 1, 1989.

[3] James E. Oberg, *Red Star In Orbit* (New York: Random House, 1981); Frank H. Winter, *Prelude to the Space Age: The Rocket Societies: 1924–1940* (Washington, DC: Smithsonian Institution Press, 1983); James Harford, *Korolev: How One Man Masterminded the Soviet Drive to Beat America to the Moon* (New York: Wiley, 1997); Golovanov, *Korolev*; G. S. Vetrov, *S. P. Korolev i kosmonavtika: perve shagi* (Moscow: Nauka, 1994); A. P. Romanov, *Korolev* (Moscow: Molodaia gvardiia, 1996).

technical disagreements became surrogate claims about one's location in Soviet society. The nebulous demarcations between technology and politics blurred as engineers took on the language of the state and vice versa. In that sense, the drama of the rocket purges was less an act of outside intervention than a self-immolation that has left a deep and dark legacy on the history of the Soviet space program.

INNOVATION IN THE INTERWAR YEARS

Once the Soviet rocketry effort passed from the amateur rumblings of such ramshackle groups as GIRD into the organizational infrastructure of RNII, it also became almost entirely subsumed under the institutional umbrella of the Soviet defense industry, which managed an important portion of the broader Soviet R&D system.[4] Earlier in the decade, Marshal Tukhachevskii had sought to organize weapons research and development directly under the military, but increased concerns about disconnecting R&D institutions from the factory system prompted key industrial managers such as Sergo Ordzhonikidze to favor situating most R&D institutions, both military and civilian in nature, under *Narkomtiazhprom*, the Soviet Union's superministry in charge of heavy industry.[5] Barring a few key R&D organizations such as *Ostekhbiuro*, most types of weapons research – especially those biased toward applied research – remained under Ordzhonikidze's control through most of the 1930s. He organized seven special directorates (*glavki*) within *Narkomtiazhprom* to manage different branches of weapons development. For example, the entire aviation industry, its design bureaus, research institutes, and factories, were managed through *Narkomtiazhprom*'s main directorate for aviation technology.[6] In 1937, the aviation industry comprised fifty-seven factories employing nearly 250,000 men and women.[7]

[4] For surveys of Soviet R&D and applied military research, see Ronald Amann and Julian Cooper, eds., *Industrial Innovation in the Soviet Union* (New Haven: Yale University Press, 1982); Matthew Evangelista, *How the United States and the Soviet Union Develop New Military Technologies* (Ithaca, NY: Cornell University Press, 1988); Jerry F. Hough, "The Historical Legacy in Soviet Weapons Development," in *Soviet Decisionmaking for National Security*, eds. Jiri Valenta and William C. Potter (London: Allen & Unwin, 1984), 87–115.

[5] In a February 1934 letter to his boss, K. E. Voroshilov, Tukhachevskii argued that most military R&D organizations should remain under his control, i.e., under the military. Voroshilov responded on April 28, 1934, rejecting Tukhachevskii's request, insisting that military R&D institutions should be under the control of *Narkomtiazhprom* because that commissariat could afford these organizations substantial industrial support. RGVA, 4/14/1171/54–59.

[6] The seven directorates supervised the aviation industry (GUAP), armaments and mortars (GUVP), the shipbuilding industry (*Glavmorprom*), the chemical industry (*Glavorgkhimprom*), the nitrogen industry (*Glavazot*), the electrical industry (*Glavesprom*), and precision instruments (VOTI). Two other "trusts" managed batteries and special-ordered steel. Civilian production was assigned to thirteen other directorates. Simonov, *VPK*, 94–96.

[7] RGAE, 4372/94/1863/29.

The lack of a strong individual to patronize the Soviet rocketry effort in the 1930s profoundly influenced the outcome of the project. For important sectors of military R&D, such as aviation, conventional artillery, and shipbuilding, influential sponsors at the highest levels of the government usually monitored and supported new projects. In his early work on Soviet military innovation, David Holloway underscored the importance of such individuals in fostering innovation that required new institutional arrangements.[8] The Soviet aviation industry, for example, enjoyed supporters at the very highest levels; Stalin, Voroshilov, and Ordzhonikidze kept close watch on the sector, often meeting with aviation designers or visiting airfields to witness test flights of new airplanes.

At the level of the research institution within the Soviet R&D system, innovation was driven by the so-called technical intelligentsia, which, to the extent that it existed as a separate social category, largely enjoyed an adversarial relationship with top-level state actors. As Kendall Bailes has noted, the technical intelligentsia did not simply execute demands from above but continually interacted with those in the top levels of the Party and government. Their work on innovation ultimately produced poor results that were due to a number of phenomena: Conflicts between the technical intelligentsia and the state, as well as internal conflicts based on cultural and class differences, contributed partly to the poor showing of Soviet R&D in the 1930s. The government demanded quantity and quality; given the economic exigencies of the day, industrial managers found these two goals contradictory and adopted new technology only under duress.[9] Like other R&D projects, the Soviet rocketry efforts of the period illustrate this inherent tension between short-term goals and new innovations that require long-term investment. Some have also seen the "failure" of Soviet rocketry as compared to the German program as being rooted in lack of intelligence about German efforts, resource shortages that prevented serious pursuit of rocketry, peculiarities in the Soviet R&D system that emphasized short-term goals, and pervasive technological conservatism that impeded innovation.[10]

[8] David Holloway, "Innovation in the Defence Sector: Battle Tanks and ICBMs," in *Industrial Innovation in the Soviet Union*, 388, 406–407.

[9] Kendall E. Bailes, *Technology and Society Under Lenin and Stalin: Origins of the Soviet Technical Intelligentsia, 1917–1941* (Princeton: Princeton University Press, 1978). In a similar but not identical vein, Robert Lewis attributes the poor showing of Soviet R&D in the 1930s to factors such as improper allocation of resources, an inefficient organizational structure, and the focus on quantity over quality. *Science and Industrialisation in the USSR*, 144–146.

[10] Mikhail Tsypkin, "The Origins of Soviet Military Research and Development System (1917–1941)," Harvard University, PhD Dissertation, 1985; Mark Harrison, "New Postwar Branches of Defence Industry (1): Rocketry," in *The Soviet Defence-Industry Complex from Stalin to Khrushchev*, eds. J. D. Barber and M. Harrison (London: Macmillan Press, 2000), 127–130.

Social pressures, particularly the threat of dismissal or arrest, also played a key role in the process of innovation, although discerning general patterns have proved difficult for historians and journalists. There are many anecdotal and biographical testimonies of the terrible toll inflicted upon weapons designers, especially aviation designers, by the Great Terror, and although these illuminate the tragic human costs, they typically fall back on gross generalizations, eliding, for example, the effect of terror on the work of those who managed to survive it unscathed.[11] Some have concluded that terror typically impeded military research and development because Soviet weapons designers frequently molded their design styles to negotiate a balance between the need for better weapons and the deadly repercussions of failing, which inevitably led to incremental innovation processes. All, however, have seen the terror and innovation as fundamentally independent and discrete processes that produced repercussions upon collision with each other.[12] A closer investigation, particularly in the case of rocket development, highlights how in the 1930s, the demarcation between the terrible social pressures of the Terror and arcane technological disagreements was often an indistinct one.

THREE CONFLICTS

Tukhachevskii had been the prime mover in uniting the two groups, GDL and GIRD, into a single institution (RNII) dedicated to the development of rockets. Although he had originally planned for RNII to be under his control within the Red Army, it was eventually formed under *Narkomtiazhprom*'s jurisdiction. Thus, having conceived and shepherded this merger, Tukhachevskii eventually relinquished control (see Figure 14). The new organization, the first governmental rocketry research institution in the world, would create its own mandate without his commitment to developing military rockets. The loss of his guidance set the stage for unprecedented discord between the former GDL faction (the solid-propellant experts interested in military rockets) and the former GIRD team (the liquid-propellant advocates interested in spaceflight).

Without Tukhachevskii's patronage, the new institute floundered. Although his original order had emphasized "the enormous prospects... of using reactive engines and especially liquid-propellant reactive engines in various areas of military technology," most engineers found the language

[11] D. A. Sobolev, "Repressii v sovetskoi aviapromyshlennosti," *Voprosi istorii estestvoznaniia i tekhniki* no. 4 (2000): 44–58; A. Pomogaibo, *Oruzhie pobedy i NKVD: Sovetskie konstruktory v tiskakh repressii* (Moscow: Veche, 2004).

[12] Golovanov, *Korolev*; Vetrov, *S. P. Korolev i kosmonavtika*; William P. Barry, "The Missile Design Bureaux and Soviet Manned Space Policy, 1953–1970," University of Oxford, DPhil. Dissertation, 1996.

FIGURE 14. Mikhail Tukhachevskii (1893–1937) was the most powerful sponsor of Soviet rocketry work in the early 1930s. His intervention into missile development in 1932 was critical for moving Soviet efforts from the purview of amateurs to formal state-directed activity in the form of the Reactive Scientific-Research Institute, the world's first governmental organization dedicated to the design of long-range rockets. As a result of changes in the organizational structure of military research and development, he was not deeply involved in this work after 1933. [*Source*: Collection of Asif Siddiqi]

of the mandate vague and confusing.[13] In establishing a final organizational structure, Tukhachevskii had approved a proposal from a senior GDL staff member who evidently never consulted anyone from the GIRD faction. The organizational structure firmly favored the GDL side because it put solid-propellant rockets under the jurisdiction of the institute's important "first department." In this climate, as the two teams moved their equipment to a single new location at Likhobory on the outskirts of Moscow, they quarreled over both management and technology.

The space enthusiasts from GIRD found the new arrangement unfavorable. Although they had eagerly supported the idea of a unified institute, they had not expected to be so marginalized. The division of responsibilities at the top of the institute paralleled the schisms and tensions between the factions. Ivan Kleimenov, one of Tukhachevskii's protégés from GDL who

[13] GARF, 8418/28/3/17–18 (October 31, 1933).

FIGURE 15. Ivan Kleimenov (1898–1938) was the director of the Reactive Scientific-Research Institute (RNII) during much of the 1930s. His particular management style, as well as specific technological preferences, contributed to enormous conflict within the organization. He was one of the first victims of the purges at RNII; he was shot by the Soviet security services in early 1938. [*Source*: Collection of Asif Siddiqi]

strongly supported the solid-propellant rocketeers from Leningrad, headed the institute and retained oversight of *all* the primary R&D divisions (see Figure 15). Sergei Korolev, the ambitious engineer from GIRD, served as his deputy and oversaw only some administrative departments, the manufacturing workshops, drafting teams, document copying, and the library.[14] Among the most creative engineers at the institute, Korolev chaffed at being cut off from design work. In his first three months as deputy, he repeatedly clashed with Kleimenov over the role of former GIRD engineers in the new setting. In January 1934, when Korolev sent a memo to his new boss complaining of the shoddy workmanship on the shop floor, Kleimenov lost his

[14] Vetrov, *S. P. Korolev i kosmonavtika*, 75; Golovanov, *Korolev*, 171. This institutional arrangement was partly accidental. In 1933, Tukhachevskii had established a commission to determine the institute's future structure. When the commission, composed of both GDL and GIRD representatives, failed to compromise, one of Tukhachevskii's subordinates, G. P. Novikov, stipulated a structure in which the director would supervise R&D activities and the deputy director would oversee production.

patience; he wrote to the local Party committee recommending Korolev's dismissal from the institute. As a compromise, Party functionaries demoted Korolev to a junior position in a design department.[15]

Upon the new institute's formation, Kleimenov stopped funding several research projects that had been fundamental to GIRD's work, including GIRD's coveted RP-1 rocket-plane effort, the original motivation for that group's existence. These cancellations fostered so much discord that Tukhachevskii, who hardly had any official connection with the institute, was besieged with letters and drawn into the conflict. In a May 1934 memo, for example, Korolev complained to Tukhachevskii that "the situation in the institute has become intolerable."[16] Tukhachevskii tried to have Kleimenov fired, but the effort failed despite widespread criticism of Kleimenov's managerial abilities.[17] Sergo Ordzhonikidze, the head of *Narkomtiazhprom*, evidently protected Kleimenov from further attacks. In the end, Kleimenov managed to get out of a difficult position with only a reprimand from the regional Party committee.[18] As a result of the infighting, many former GIRD members left, were fired, or were demoted in 1934. Remarkably, even one former GDL engineer complained about Kleimenov; as he explained to Tukhachevskii at the time, "[t]o characterize the general situation at RNII, one could point out that you could not find a single satisfied employee, [since all the] efficient workers, designers and engineers have run from [the institute]."[19]

In this environment, technology, or more precisely the choices among certain technologies, assumed a central role in the acrimony. Engineers focused their disagreements around three major technical issues. Opponents in one debate often supported each other in another dispute.

The first and most important disagreement involved the use of solid or liquid propellants. The GDL faction had been using solid propellants for over a decade; they worked in the same tradition of powder rocket development that stretched back two centuries in Russia. Due partly to institutional inertia, Kleimenov devoted the lion's share of the institute's personnel resources and production time to designing and manufacturing solid-propellant rockets. When he demoted Korolev in January 1934, Kleimenov replaced him with Georgii Langemak, a solid rocket pioneer; Kleimenov's order further

15 ARAN, 4/14/169/1–7 (January 17, 1934). He was demoted on January 25, 1934.

16 RGVA, 34272/1/177/17–19 (May 29, 1934); Golovanov, *Korolev*, 178.

17 RGVA, 4/14/1237/9–9ob (September 12, 1934). Tukhachevskii's aide, Ia. Terent'ev, who had played a key role in early military support for both GIRD and GDL, also recommended Kleimenov's dismissal in a scathing letter he wrote to his boss on the state of work at the new institute. RGVA, 4/14/1237/6–7 (September 5, 1934).

18 RGVA, 4/14/1237/10 (June 1934).

19 Golovanov, *Korolev*, 178–179. See ARAN, 4/14/150/38 for a list of engineers who left the institute.

fortified the solid-propellant faction. Unusual for a military institution in Stalinist Soviet Union, the two sides openly disagreed on the issue. For example, at a scientific conference held in the spring of 1934 in Moscow, Korolev enumerated all the drawbacks of solid propellants of the day, including their short firing times, low caloric content, and the need for heavy combustion chambers.[20] When *Pravda* favorably mentioned Korolev's presentation, Kleimenov wrote to the newspaper disavowing any connection to the young engineer.[21] Korolev also complained to the military. In his May 1934 letter to Tukhachevskii, Korolev opined that "powder reactive projectiles [may] have great significance as a new source for arming the [Red Army] today... but you can count on this – this is the disastrous politics of 'near sightedness.'"[22] Despite the complaints, the institute's GDL faction refused to compromise.

The second disagreement also dealt with propellant choice. Twenty years previously, Tsiolkovskii had predicted that rockets could travel most efficiently into space by using a specific combination of liquid propellants, supercooled (or cryogenic) liquid oxygen, and liquid hydrogen. Although engineers found liquid oxygen difficult to obtain and store, the oxidizer promised unprecedentedly high calorific energy content; in other words, a relatively small amount could impart sufficient energy to lift an object into space. Following in Tsiolkovskii's footsteps, the GIRD veterans had put all their energies into developing liquid-oxygen engines. Here again, they conflicted with the GDL faction who, in their limited interest in liquids, had chosen to spend money only on *storable* liquid-propellant rocket engines, which have less energy content. Their choice stemmed partly from circumstance and partly from operational military requirements. In their original location in Leningrad, GDL's head of storable rocket engines, Valentin Glushko, had found it easy to obtain nitric acid, a type of storable fuel, for his experiments. Nitric acid was in fact widely available and relatively cheap to produce, whereas liquid oxygen was much more difficult to obtain. Glushko published a monograph on the topic in 1936 that profoundly influenced the institute's preference for nitric acid. In it, he bluntly criticized liquid oxygen as inefficient and underscored nitric acid's better operational advantages.[23] Glushko's conclusions, as well as the need to conserve limited

[20] ARAN, 4/14/240/16–30. Korolev presented this paper at the First All-Union Conference for the Study of the Stratosphere held in March and April 1934.

[21] "Konferentsiia po stratosfere zakrylas'," *Pravda*, April 8, 1934; ARAN, 4/14/240/31–32 (April 11, 1934).

[22] RGVA, 34272/1/177/17–19 (May 29, 1934).

[23] V. P. Glushko, "Zhidkoe toplivo dlia reaktivnykh dvigatelei," in *Put' v raketnoi tekhniki: izbrannye trudy, 1924–1946* (Moscow: Mashinostroenie, 1977), 231–330 (see, especially, pp. 266, 271).

economic resources, prompted institute director Kleimenov to terminate all work on liquid-oxygen rocket engines in November 1936.[24]

The conflict over liquid oxygen and nitric acid fostered much more acrimony than the one over solids and liquids. Throughout the institute's existence, numerous individuals from the GIRD space faction wrote letters to the government and the Party – indeed to anyone who would listen – to air their grievances over the elimination of liquid-oxygen rockets. Two men, Leonid Korneev and Andrei Kostikov, independently led this attack, and both their charges would figure prominently in the terror that descended upon the institute in the late 1930s. Institute director Kleimenov had fired Korneev in May 1934 after a violent disagreement over the propellant issue. In a series of unusually bitter letters to Tukhachevskii and Stalin in 1934–1935, Korneev complained at length over the termination of work with oxygen.[25] None of these entreaties, however, convinced Kleimenov to back down. One senior engineer specializing in oxygen recalled that after the order, "documentation on oxygen engines and rockets was burned in the archives, and manufactured models [of oxygen missiles] and other components were thrown away in a dump."[26] In a remarkably prescient letter to his boss in early 1937, Kleimenov defended his action by arguing that liquid oxygen was notoriously difficult to store for long periods, thus compromising battle readiness.[27] For the GIRD space advocates, however, storability was far less important than energy characteristics.

The third technical debate concerned the choice to build winged or wingless missiles. When the old GIRD team had aimed for the cosmos, they built both types of rockets, unsure of which offered better performance. Many of the original GIRD engineers, such as Korolev and Tikhonravov, had come out of the aviation industry and had a natural predilection for wings. With the possibility of engines based on the reaction principle, their future anticipations saw a convergence between rocket engines and airplanes, that is, rocket-planes. The first logical step in building a manned rocket-plane was an unmanned one, in other words, a remote-controlled winged missile. There were also entirely technical and pragmatic reasons for the choice, particularly the limitations of engine technology. Because the Soviet Union had not designed powerful liquid-propellant rocket engines, Korolev believed that

24 On November 19, 1936, Kleimenov terminated work on the single liquid-oxygen engine still remaining in the work program, an engine known as "object 208." Subsequently, on December 4, 1936, liquid-oxygen engine expert M. K. Tikhonravov signed an order finalizing this arrangement. L. S. Dushkin, a liquid-oxygen engineer at RNII, attributes the cancellation specifically to Glushko's monograph: Gennadi Maksimovich, "Tak kto zhe est' kto," *Kryl'ia rodiny* no. 7 (1988): 28–31.

25 For excerpts from these letters, dated May 1934, April 17, 1935, and June 19, 1935, see *OIN*, 412, 415–416.

26 Maksimovich, "Tak kto zhe est' kto," 29. The oxygen engineer was L. S. Dushkin.

27 *OIN*, 422–423.

he could compensate by building missiles with wings. Thus, rockets using relatively weak engines could cover large distances because wings could provide additional lift. Wings might be a necessary stopgap measure until RNII developed more powerful liquid-fuel engines.

Through the 1930s, Korolev consistently worked on winged rockets for these reasons, although he expressed a certain amount of ambivalence in his writings. In his classic 1935 monograph, *Raketnii polet v stratosfere* (*Rocket Flight in the Stratosphere*), he highlighted the advantages of ballistic rockets – "instantaneous [and] light liftoff, a velocity of hundreds of meters per second and great altitudes." In contrast, rocket-planes could be "clumsy" and "heavy" at liftoff, flew only for a few minutes, and could not reach very high up, having to land immediately because of lack of propellants.[28] When leading engineers met in January 1935 to decide how to focus their limited resources on one path, winged or wingless (ballistic) missiles, Korolev recommended "not to terminate research into [ballistic] rockets... in the face of design failures."[29] Institute director Kleimenov shared Korolev's ambivalence, but both Korolev and Kleimenov had to defend their position against a vicious attack from Andrei Kostikov, a former GIRD engineer. He argued that ballistic rockets had no future as weapons of war; they could only be useful for scientific exploration of the upper atmosphere.[30] Through 1934, Kostikov had repeatedly asked his boss Kleimenov to eliminate work on such missiles. Kostikov had the blessing of a number of leading aeronautical engineers from academia, but Kleimenov refused to back down. Eventually, Kostikov and two associates decided to write a letter on the issue to *Narkomtiazhprom* commissar Sergo Ordzhonikidze. When Kleimenov found out, perhaps fearing for his job, he agreed to eliminate ballistic missiles from future plans, but only after dismissing Kostikov's two partners from the institute.[31]

These three technical disagreements within RNII stemmed from the strongly divergent visions of rocketry's future held by different groups at RNII. Some sought to satisfy short-term military imperatives; others aspired to the heavens. Unfortunately, the institute's engineers could not resolve the conflicts in a manner that fostered solutions to technical problems, partly because of external factors that profoundly influenced decision-making within the institute. The larger institutional setting for rocketry research not only exacerbated tensions within the institute, but it also impeded

[28] S. P. Korolev, "Raketnii polet v stratosfere," in *Pionery raketnoi tekhniki: Vetchinkin Glushko Korolev Tikhonravov: izbrannye trudy (1929–1945 gg.)*, eds. S. A. Sokolova and T. M. Mel'kumov (Moscow: Nauka, 1972), 381–451 (see p. 450). The original title of the book, changed at the last minute, was *Application of the Reaction Principle in Aviation*.

[29] ARAN, 4/14/171/150b (January 15, 1935)

[30] ARAN, 4/14/171/12–15.

[31] A. G. Kostikov, "V partkom VKP(b) NII No. 3 zaiavlenie ot chlena VKP/b/ s 1922 g No. 0050652," in *OIN*, 104–110.

the kind of radical innovation that was required to develop successful rockets.

THE BROADER PICTURE

Unlike almost all other Soviet R&D institutions of the 1930s, RNII dealt with what the Soviets called "new-in-principle" weapons, radically innovative armaments that had little connection with existing systems. Neither the armed forces nor the engineers grasped the potential of rockets in warfare. Holloway's observation, that influential individuals at the top and bottom can energize radical innovation in the Soviet R&D setting, rang particularly true for rocketry.[32] Both Tukhachevskii and Korolev had lobbied hard for establishing RNII. After 1934, Tukhachevskii hardly communicated with the institute, while Korolev's power declined with his demotion. By relinquishing control over the institute, Tukhachevskii inadvertently affected two external factors, the state and the military's commitment to such weapons. Both, combined with a third external factor, the lack of intelligence about foreign rocketry, fueled the internal discord.

State Commitment

For a brief period in the early 1930s, the Soviet government cultivated radical innovation, but by the middle of the decade, the pace had clearly slowed.[33] Robert Lewis has noted that "[b]y the late 1930s the Soviet R&D system was extensive. But its organisational structure, the pattern of resources and facilities, and the economic planning system all set up barriers to the widespread development of indigenous technology and its speedy innovation."[34] Ultimately, the institutional environment of the rocketry effort, that is, the national drive to militarize quickly in anticipation of war, acted as a countervailing force against funding radical innovation such as rockets, which required long lead times.

Narkomtiazhprom, the ministry overseeing RNII, did not consider the institute a priority and moved the organization to a poorly financed subdivision, its Scientific-Research Sector. Kleimenov repeatedly requested that the institute be moved under *Narkomtiazhprom*'s high-priority Main

[32] Holloway, "Innovation in the Defence Sector: Battle Tanks and ICBMs," 406–408.

[33] Sally Stoecker concludes that "the military as an independent institution . . . was capable of successful innovation during the First Five Year Plan (1928–33) with the aid of budgetary resources, reform-minded officers, foreign expertise, indigenous R&D programs and combat experience obtained in the Far East." *Forging Stalin's Army: Marshal Tukhachevsky and the Politics of Military Innovation* (Boulder, CO: Westview Press, 1998), 8.

[34] Robert Lewis, "Technology and the Transformation of the Soviet Economy," in *The Economic Transformation of the Soviet Union, 1913–1945*, eds. R. W. Davies, Mark Harrison, and S. G. Wheatcroft (Cambridge, UK: Cambridge University Press, 1994), 192.

TABLE 1. *RNII Funding, Expenditures, and Personnel*

Year	Funding	Expenditure	No. of Personnel
1934	3.075	—	251
1935	3.125	—	316
1936	3.420	3.377	446
1937	4.482*	4.482* (or 4.453*)	508
1938	—	6.111	514
1939	—	11.434	799
1940	11.725	11.233	—

Notes: Funding and expenditures are shown in millions of rubles; the total expenditures from 1934 to 1940 was 37.576 million rubles. The asterisk denotes planned, not actual, value. Data are missing for some years.
Sources: 1934–1935, ARAN, 4/14/171/46 and RGAE, 8162/1/16/4; 1936–1937, RGAE, 8162/1/16/1–6, 32–33; 1938–1939, RGAE, 8162/1/240/1–7, 32; 1940, RGAE, 7516/1/692/1–3 and 8162/1/449/2–12; total, RGAE, 7516/1/692/1–3.

Military-Mobilization Directorate, but the transfer never took place.[35] Throughout his tenure as institute director, Kleimenov complained to his superiors about insufficient funding. To some degree, Kleimenov's various appeals were strategies that many Soviet institutions of the period used to justify their existence; complaints about underfunding were the rule rather than the exception in Soviet bureaucracies of the period.[36] Yet, budget figures for RNII show that the institute was relatively poorly funded, at least from 1934 to 1937; funds increased very little from 3.075 million rubles to a planned 4.482 million rubles (see Table 1 and Figure 16). During the same period, the Soviet defense budget more than tripled, to over 17 *billion* rubles.[37] Although RNII expenditures increased about threefold in the late 1930s, they actually declined substantially when adjusted for inflation. The RNII budget also compared poorly with other military R&D institutions of the day. For example, in 1938, RNII's "sister" (conventional) artillery weapons institute, NII-24, received nearly four times the funding of RNII. Cumulative figures indicate that between 1934 and 1940 (inclusive), RNII spent 35.576

[35] RGVA, 4/14/1237/4–50b (August 27, 1934). *Narkomtiazhprom* moved RNII to its Scientific-Research Sector on April 4, 1934.

[36] For example, James R. Harris describes how industrial leaders in the Urals used complaints to the center about underfunding as a strategy for more attention. *The Great Urals: Regionalism and the Evolution of the Soviet System* (Ithaca, NY: Cornell University Press, 1999).

[37] Soviet defense budgets were 5.393 (in 1934) and 17.481 (in 1937) billion rubles. R. W. Davies and Mark Harrison, "Defence Spending and Defence Industry in the 1930s," in *Soviet Defence-Industry*, 73.

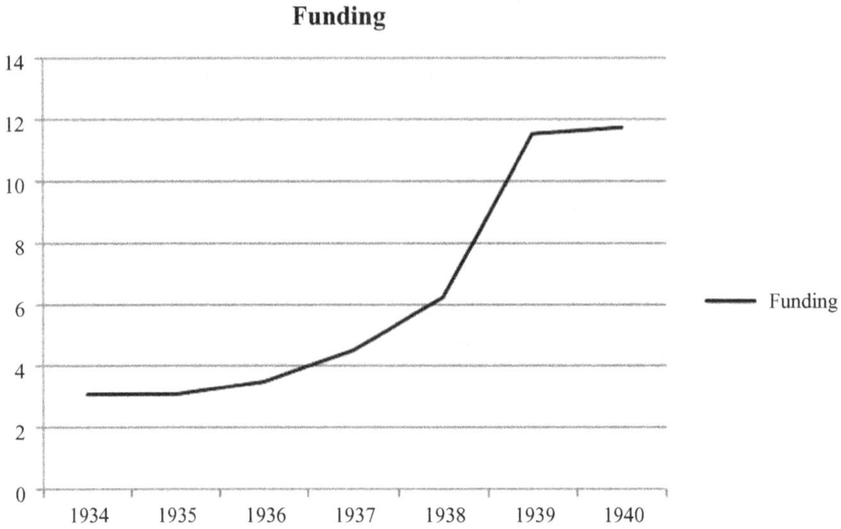

FIGURE 16. RNII Funding (in millions of rubles), 1934–1940. Note that the figures for 1938 and 1939 are estimated. [*Source*: see Table 1]

million rubles.[38] Kleimenov allocated about half of all money on solid rockets and one-third on liquids. Overall, the state invested a relatively miniscule amount of money on rockets and even less on liquid-propellant rockets.

Because, in Kleimenov's opinion, *Narkomtiazhprom* was unresponsive to the needs of the institute, he often bypassed ministry bosses and took his case directly to Stalin or Voroshilov.[39] In one letter dating from June 1935, Kleimenov tried to interest Stalin in the new field of rocketry, underlining Soviet achievements in both solid- and liquid-propellant missiles. Stalin never replied to any of his appeals.[40] This relationship contrasts sharply with the attention Stalin proffered other military R&D programs of the period by personally intervening and often deciding on a particular path of innovation. There is no evidence to suggest that Stalin, or indeed any industrial leader such as Sergo Ordzhonikidze or Kliment Voroshilov, ever expressed more than a cursory interest in rocketry after the mid-1930s. In 1935 and 1936, Tukhachevskii was invited to comment on a draft for a new government decree to drastically increase funding for RNII, especially for work on solid-propellant projectiles. Nevertheless, despite a flurry of letters back and forth,

[38] For comparative budgets of RNII, NII-24, and other institutes under *Narkomboepripasov*'s Thirteenth Main Directorate (specializing in artillery weapons) in 1938, see RGAE, 8162/1/299/9. For overall figures, see RGAE, 7516/1/692/1–6 (November 21, 1940).

[39] See, for example, the letter to Stalin, where Kleimenov complains about the "absence of sufficient material and technical resources at RNII." RGVA, 4/14/1398/54–55 (December 1935).

[40] ARPF, 3/47/179/1–7 (June 1, 1935).

including comments from Voroshilov, the government apparently shelved the plan because there were other, more pressing matters.[41] In fact, when the RNII leadership attempted to inform Viacheslav Molotov of the results of important tests of solid rockets in 1937, a mid-level bureaucrat intercepted the letter, claiming that such a report was "premature."[42]

Lack of commitment harmed rocketry research. The existing system could support technical innovation without top-level individual intervention, but it could not support *radical* technical innovation, partly because the latter was characterized by technological ambiguity. Sustained matériel and generous economic support could resolve such uncertainty by permitting scientists and engineers to pursue multiple paths of development, such as was possible with the rapidly growing and high-priority aviation industry, but RNII engineers had no such luxury because they were financially constrained, especially after 1935.[43]

Military Commitment

The military, the primary would-be operator of rockets in the Soviet Union, had an ambivalent attitude toward rockets. Jerry Hough has noted that despite the unprecedented Soviet military buildup in the 1930s, "[t]he leadership strongly emphasi[zed] the basic weapons – tanks, artillery, airplanes and (for a period) large ships – and peripheral weapons were neglected in the budgetary squeeze."[44] Within the military, the Air Force and the Main Artillery Directorate served as the primary conduits for issuing requirements for weapons to RNII, but because their leaders did not foresee using rockets, especially liquid-propellant rockets, in future wars, their connection to the institute remained tenuous at best. Before 1936, both issued a few contracts for battlefield solid-propellant rockets but none for liquid-propellant ones.[45] After 1936, the Air Force and the Red Army's Directorate of Communications assigned development of several liquid-propellant winged missiles. Unlike the solid rockets, however, all of these were experimental, that is, ordered to test new technologies.[46] Because the military exercised relatively little supervision over what the institute produced, RNII's managers

41 RGVA, 4/14/1398/45–79.

42 GARF, 8418/27/125/11–18 (April 23, 1939).

43 Lewis has argued that the Soviet aviation sector was one of the few successes in Soviet R&D in the 1930s precisely because of high-level commitment that allowed aviation engineers, among other things, to pursue multiple lines of research. Robert A. Lewis, *Science and Industrialisation in the USSR* (New York: Holmes & Meier, 1979), 132–142.

44 Hough, "The Historical Legacy," 100.

45 The Air Force issued orders to deliver an air-launched projectile, a tank-launched rocket, several types of chemical projectiles, illumination and signal flares, and rockets to aid heavy bombers during takeoff.

46 APRF 3/47/179/1–7 (June 1, 1935); ARAN, 4/14/87/1–23 (October 10, 1944).

developed their own requirements for weapons. Thus, Kleimenov could focus on nitric acid and shut down work on liquid oxygen without any accountability.

Military ambivalence characterized one of the major projects at the institute in the late 1930s. After RNII's formation in 1933, director Kleimenov had ensured that GIRD's main project under *Osoaviakhim*, a piloted rocket-plane, was not included in its future plans. Korolev, who was the prime mover behind the rocket-plane, never gave up the cause and in his free time continued to devote attention to the design of such a vehicle. He wrote frequently in prominent newspapers and journals about the need and feasibility of crewed rocket-planes, dovetailing its justification as part of the prevailing popular interest in stratospheric exploration.[47] Eventually, in late 1935, when Kleimenov finally agreed to fund a rocket-plane – swayed by Korolev's incessant publicity about its need – military involvement was essentially an afterthought. After getting the green light, in January 1936, Korolev wrote up a "tactical-technical requirement" for the rocket-plane, known as the "218."[48] This was an experimental two-seater aircraft theoretically capable of flying to an altitude of 25 kilometers and with at top velocity of 1,080 kilometers per hour (at 3,000 meters altitude). The idea originally was to fire the vehicle's rocket engine, solid or liquid propellant, after being towed into the air by a tug aircraft.

Normally, the military would dictate and define the necessity of such a weapon by issuing a tactical-technical requirement document. In this case, however, the military was barely interested, especially because Korolev seems to have had in mind a plane simply to break records, in line with the prevailing mania to present Stalin with evidence of the indisputable superiority of Soviet aviation.[49] Only much later, Korolev involved leading Air Force tacticians in the 218 project, obtaining the blessing of a commission of officers who thought the idea might have military utility.[50] Reversing the process of weapons development, that is, conceptualizing a weapons system and then asking the military if they needed it, led to further dispute because engineers never determined the original characteristics by using any standardized methods. Some supported the rocket-plane. Others opposed it.

47 Korolev may have been influenced by the work of Austrian theoretician Eugen Sänger, who published works in Germany on the development of rocket-planes in the 1930s. Sänger's rocket-plane inspired at least one other contemporaneous Soviet rocket-plane proposal. Engineer R. G. Sergeev, working at Factory No. 22 under the famous aviation designer A. A. Arkhangel'skii, wrote to the military in 1937 for permission to build a remote-controlled rocket-plane, the RI-1. The idea was funded from 1938 to 1940 but then abandoned. RGVA, 29/56/361/1–77.

48 ARAN, 4/14/105/221–34 (January 30, 1936).

49 K. E. Bailes, "Technology and Legitimacy: Soviet Aviation and Stalinism in the 1930s," *Technology and Culture* 17 (1976): 55-81.

50 ARAN, 4/14/103/75 (November 23, 1937); ARAN, 4/14/103/76–79 (December 1937).

Without firm military orders, the institute's commitment to different projects varied considerably through the late 1930s.

Intelligence on Foreign Efforts

The lack of high-level commitment and absence of military needs intertwined with a third factor, Soviet intelligence on foreign rocketry. Intelligence on German rocketry activities in the early 1930s, from both open and covert sources, had at least partly inspired Tukhachevskii's early exhortations to develop Soviet rockets quickly. Although security around German military programs tightened after Hitler came to power in 1933, recent evidence suggests that the Soviets had access to information from the top-secret German rocketry project through the late 1930s. Willy Lehmann, a communist sympathizer in the counterintelligence department of what became the Gestapo, had been passing information on German armaments to the Soviet security police since about 1930 under the code name *Breitenbach* (Wide Brook). In November 1935, Lehmann attended a ground firing of a large rocket engine at Kummersdorf in the presence of Wernher von Braun, one of the technical leaders of the German program. Lehmann's information, comprising six pages of data on the rocketry program, was then passed on to Stalin and Voroshilov on December 17, 1935 and to Tukhachevskii on January 26, 1936. Intelligence agents from the Red Army's General Staff responded with further questions including queries for Lehmann about "engineer Braun" and the possibility of "penetrating his laboratory." Although Lehmann appears to have sent no further information on rockets, he continued to transmit weapons information to the NKVD via intermediaries through the beginning of World War II. The Gestapo eventually discovered his activities and executed him in December 1942.[51] Tukhachevskii also expressed interest in the work of the American rocketry pioneer Robert Goddard and suggested to Voroshilov that the Soviets needed more intelligence information on his research. Probably as a result, in April 1936, the NKVD submitted more than fifty documents on foreign technology, including materials on Goddard, gathered from both open and covert sources, to Tukhachevskii.[52]

These recent revelations, although tantalizing, also raise some intractable questions because overwhelming evidence suggests that intelligence on German rocketry did *not* affect concurrent Soviet efforts. In fact, engineers

[51] V. S. Motov, "'Braitenbakh'," in *Ocherki istorii rossiiskoi vneshnei razvedki: tom 3, 1933–1941 gody*, ed. E. M. Primakov (Moscow: Mezhdunarodnia otnosheniia, 1997), 344. A. V. Pronin, "'Shtirlits' sluzhil pod nachalom . . . Miullera," *Voenno-istoricheskii zhurnal* no. 6 (1996): 22–31 and no. 1 (1997): 18–25.

[52] ARAN, 4/14/245/5–6 (July 23, 1935); B. V. Barkovskii, "Nauchno-tekhnicheskaia razvedka na sluzhbe sovetskogo gosudarstva (1917–1946 gg.)," *Voprosy istorii estestvoznaniia i tekhniki* no. 2 (1995): 76–87.

on the ground appear to have had little knowledge of the German project. Managers of the rocket program belatedly tried to learn something about foreign efforts. One plan was to send leading RNII engineers on a fact-finding mission to Germany.[53] They also translated several articles from the European and American media on rockets to acquaint themselves with contemporary work.[54] Foreign articles were often used to draw the attention of industrial managers to rockets.[55] Yet, as late as 1940, a key engineer at RNII asserted in an official report that he had no information on foreign work on long-range ballistic missiles.[56] The Soviet leadership's lack of interest in rocketry indicates either that intelligence on rocketry never reached top decision makers or that Soviet leaders failed to make proper use of this knowledge.[57] Tukhachevskii was certainly the person most likely to have made the best use of this information, but the information may have been too little too late. In April 1936, a few months after intelligence on rocketry reached the Red Army, Stalin fired Tukhachevskii as the Red Army's weapons procurement chief. Even if Tukhachevskii viewed the reports, he was no longer in any position to act on them. As one historian noted about Tukhachevskii, "it was clear [then] that he had lost his authority in matters of strategic force-building."[58] Ultimately, as a result of ineffective evaluation of intelligence information on German rocketry, the important data had very little effect on the Soviet rocketry project.

With weak state commitment, the military's lack of interest, and news of foreign efforts that was ineffectively used, Soviet engineers faced difficult choices on technology. In the three major debates over technology, Kleimenov and his allies tried to choose the path of least resistance and quickest returns, not surprising given the exigencies of the day. Their decisions, however, led to serious conflicts with those who preferred more ambitious options. Unfortunately for the institute, the internal discord and the Great Terror both peaked simultaneously. Technological debates now spiraled out of control.

53 RGAE, 8162/1/305/30 (April 11, 1940).

54 See the translation of a piece entitled "What Can We Expect of Rockets?" from the *Journal of Army Ordnance* 19 no. 112 (February–March 1939) stored in RGAE, 7516/1/323/2–18 (June 8, 1939).

55 See translation and attached letter dedicated to an article from the Italian journal, *Revista Maritima* no. 6 (1936): 421–139, stored in RGAE, 7516/1/324/1–4, 12–43.

56 RGAE, 8162/1/300/104. The engineer was L. S. Dushkin.

57 In an interview with a Russian newspaper in 1990, an unnamed person with access to the still-closed NKVD archives revealed that information on rocketry and other military technology from Germany was transmitted directly to the top, i.e., to Stalin, Molotov, Beriia, and others, but provided no evidence that these men had actually viewed the information. Lollii Zamoiskii and Iurii Nezhnikov, "U rokovoi cherty: Sovetskaia razvedka nakanune voiny," *Izvestiia*, May 5, 1990.

58 Shimon Naveh, "Tukhachevsky," in *Stalin's Generals*, ed. Harold Shukman (New York: Grove Press, 1993), 263–264.

THE ARRESTS

In the literature on the Great Terror, historians have devoted much attention to the Soviet security police's decimation of the upper layers of the Red Army in 1937–1938.[59] The NKVD set off its attack by arresting Marshal Tukhachevskii and seven other senior officers on May 26, 1937 for being part of an "anti-Soviet Trotskiite conspiracy." Among those arrested was Tukhachevskii's aide, Robert Eideman, the top-ranking military officer who, as the head of *Osoaviakhim*, had sponsored GIRD's rocketry works when the amateur group was barely on its feet. All were shot seventeen days later.[60] Those from the rocketry institute who had previously allied themselves with Tukhachevskii or Eideman immediately found themselves under scrutiny. No faction within the institute was beyond suspicion because, in the early 1930s, Tukhachevskii had supported GDL whereas Eideman had sponsored GIRD.

The engineers themselves took the lead in sealing their own fate. Just three days after the executions, Leonid Korneev, the oxygen engineer whom Kleimenov had twice fired from the institute, wrote to Stalin, contending that, "Only now, in the light of recent events, it has become clear that [RNII director] Kleimenov is also a saboteur, standing [with] the scum of humanity, extraordinary bastards of the twentieth century such as Piatakov, Tukhachevskii and others."[61] The letter spurred a local Communist Party commission to investigate; the commission sent a detailed complaint on Kleimenov to the commissar in charge of the rocketry institute on July 16.[62] Eight days later, Kleimenov responded to defend himself. Instead of writing to a Party commission or to the ministry, he took the matter directly to the NKVD:

As a supplement to the earlier message, I am reporting that 2 years ago a group was established in the institute that has been playing an active role in reducing the pace of work on reactive armaments. *They have demanded the reduction of work on powder rockets and [nitric acid] in favor of strengthening the oxygen sector.* Among others,

[59] For recent examples, see Roger A. Reese, "The Red Army and the Great Purges," in *Stalinist Terror: New Perspectives*, eds. J. Arch Getty and Roberta T. Manning (Cambridge, UK: Cambridge University Press, 1993), 198–214; O. F. Suvenirov, ed., *Tragediia RKKA: 1937–1938* (Moscow: Terra, 1998).

[60] Aleksei Khorev, "Kak sudili Tukhachevskogo," *Krasnaia zvezda*, April 17, 1991; J. Arch Getty and Oleg V. Naumov, eds., *The Road to Terror: Stalin and the Self-Destruction of the Bolsheviks, 1932–1939* (New Haven: Yale University Press, 1999), 444–448.

[61] RGVA, 4/14/1628/123–28 (June 15, 1937). The letter was passed on to Commissar of Defense Voroshilov from the Central Committee. Korneev also directly wrote to Voroshilov. RGVA, 4/14/1628/129–31 (July 14, 1937).

[62] The commission sent its report to M. L. Rukhimovich, the head of the People's Commissariat for Defense Industry (*Narkomoboronprom*), the ministry that oversaw RNII after December 1936. With the transfer, RNII was renamed NII-3 in January 1937.

the list of activists includes A. G. Kostikov, M. K. Tikhonravov, L. K. Korneev, L. S. Dushkin, and others. Outside of this institute, this group was led by a protégé of the executed spy M. N. Tukhachevskii [. . . including . . .] Ia. M. Terent'ev [who has been] expelled from the party and dismissed from the ranks of the [commissariat]. All of this requires investigation and bringing to account.[63]

Coming as it did when the internal terror in the Soviet Union began to escalate, a debate over rocket technology now threatened people's lives.

Despite Kleimenov's belated counterattack, in August, the ministry fired him and relegated him to a junior position at another institute.[64] His troubles were, however, only beginning. One of those whom Kleimenov had named as "activists," Andrei Kostikov, responded by writing a long letter to the local Party committee denouncing not only Kleimenov but also several others from the old GDL faction. His indictments ranged from incompetence to implicit sabotage.[65] In retrospect, Kostikov's letter proved to be the critical turning point of the entire affair. Unlike other letters of complaint, his statement held weight because Kostikov had a long history in local Party politics. He had been elected into the institute's *partkom* (Party committee), served as a delegate to *raion* (regional) Party conferences, and eventually became a member of the Party's local *raikom* (district committee), an honor that gave him authority that others in the institute lacked. Kostikov's statement provided the final spark to a powerful security police in the throes of losing control; the NKVD used the letter as the blueprint for its vendetta against the institute in the ensuing months. Every person whose name was on the letter became a top suspect.

The NKVD first came for Kleimenov, the closest link to the disgraced and deceased Tukhachevskii. Kleimenov lived with his wife and two daughters in a building where, night in and night out, people were being arrested. They could usually tell the name of the missing person the next morning by the identity of the orphaned pet dogs that were taken out for walks by neighbors. Inevitably, they came for Kleimenov too. At 3 a.m. on November 3, 1937, NKVD agents arrived at his apartment, told him to sit down, and ransacked his whole apartment, taking extra relish in humiliating him in front of his wife. Like many of his fellow Soviet citizens, he refused to believe that this was anything more than a misunderstanding, declining the money that his

63 Maksimovich, "Tak kto zhe est' kto," 28–29 (emphasis mine). Iakov Terent'ev had overseen funding for both GDL and GIRD as a ranking official in Tukhachevskii's Directorate of Military Inventions in the early 1930s. Kleimenov sent a second similar letter on July 25, 1937 to Rukhimovich, where he blamed commissariat officials for not helping the institute deliver rocket weapons to the Soviet armed forces and asked for an investigation into their negligence.

64 Kleimenov was dismissed on August 30, 1937 and given a mid-level appointment at the Central Aerohydrodynamics Institute (TsAGI) outside Moscow. Golovanov, *Korolev*, 232.

65 Kostikov, "V partkom VKP(b) NII No. 3 zaiavlenie ot chlena VKP/b/ s 1922 g No. 0050652," in *OIN*, 104–110; B. Viktorov, "Kto est' kto," *Nauka i zhizn'* no. 12 (1988): 74–76.

wife gave to him because he would, after all, be back by the next morning. The revelation that Kleimenov had once served as a member of a trade delegation in Germany made it relatively easy to build spying charges against him. Forty-three days after his arrest, Kleimenov, beaten viciously until he was barely conscious, admitted to a host of trumped-up charges, including membership in an "anti-Soviet Trotskiite spy-sabotage organization."[66] He later refused to sign his testimony, but the NKVD found another "member" of this organization and collected more "evidence" against the beleaguered former director.[67] The day after Kleimenov's arrest, the NKVD came for Georgii Langemak, the brilliant solid-propellant specialist and second-in-command at the institute; he was arrested and like his compatriot "confessed" under torture that Kleimenov was indeed a saboteur. Langemak's suspect past worked against him. His parents were German and Swiss and he himself had been married in a church in 1921, for which he had been excluded from the Bol'shevik Party.

On January 10, 1938, after a twenty-minute trial, the Military Collegium of the USSR Supreme Court condemned Kleimenov to death. Later the same day, the NKVD's on-duty commandant executed him. The following day, after another trial on similar charges, the Collegium sentenced Langemak to death along with thirty-five others. The sentences were carried out the same day.[68] It would be another fifty years before Kleimenov's wife, Margarita, found out the precise date of her husband's death during a journalist's interview; she was shocked to discover that her husband had been shot the day before she herself was arrested.

These executions did not occur in a vacuum. The NKVD fiercely attacked the top and middle levels of the commissariats that supervised the rocketry institute. Hundreds, if not thousands, of factory managers, senior staff members at institutes, and commissariat officials were arrested in a wave of horrific purges. Russian historian Nikolai Simonov speculates that the scale of the repression (arrested and/or purged from work) in *Narkomtiazhprom* and *Narkomoboronprom* was equal to that in the Red Army.[69] At the

[66] For an excerpt from the bill of indictment, see N. L. Anisimov and V. G. Oppokov, "Proisshestvie v NII-3," *Voenno-istoricheskii zhurnal* no. 10 (1989): 81–87.

[67] On November 14, 1937, another member of the Berlin trade delegation who had been arrested, M. A. Rubinchik, confessed under vicious torture that Kleimenov was a saboteur. The NKVD later also executed him. Ibid., 82.

[68] A. Glushko, "K 100-letiiu so dnia rozhdeniia I. T. Kleimenova," *Novosti kosmonavtiki* 9 no. 6 (1999): 70–72. In Langemak's case, the NKVD prepared the bill of indictment for his arrest on December 20, 1937, more than a month after his arrest. For excerpts from the indictment, see A. Glushko, "'Delo Eeorgii Erikhovich Langemaka': k 100-letiiu so dnia rozhdeniia," *Novosti kosmonavtiki* 8, nos. 15/16 (1998): 66–67.

[69] Simonov, *VPK*, 107–111. RNII was moved from *Narkomtiazhprom* (People's Commissariat of Heavy Industry) to *Narkomoboronprom* (People's Commissariat for Defense Industry) in December 1936 as part of an industry-wide restructuring plan. Recent research by historian Oleg Suvenirov suggests that about 20,000 officers were purged (discharged, arrested, and/or executed) in the late 1930s. *Tragediia RKKA*, 307–308.

rocket institute, the executions of two leading engineers led to more arrests. Before their deaths, both Kleimenov and Langemak had signed "confessions" implicating a number of other engineers. Kleimenov, for example, named Korolev, Glushko, and two others, Iurii Pobedonostsev and Leonid Shvarts, as counterrevolutionaries.[70] By including these names, he unwittingly expanded the pool of people originally under suspicion, that is, those that were on Kostikov's important letter to the Party committee in 1937 that the NKVD used as a guide.

All the accusations and counteraccusations narrowed focus on the most senior men still free at the institute. Those from the oxygen faction took advantage to vilify the leading engineer of nitric acid engines, Valentin Glushko. In February, the institute's new leadership held two meetings, attended by most of the senior engineering staff, whose ostensible goal was the "denigration of the personality" of Glushko. Those who had resented Glushko's influence at the institute took opportunity to blame him for all manner of unsubstantiated and sometimes ludicrous reasons, including not being vigilant enough to criticize the two men already arrested and having co-authored a book with one of them.[71] The matter was couched entirely in technical terms, full of arcane details about engine design. A month after these meetings, on March 23, 1938, the NKVD arrested Glushko, now the third member of the old GDL faction to be imprisoned.

The noose was closing in on Korolev by this time. He had already been under suspicion for over a year as a result of his associations with Tukhachevskii and Eideman. About two weeks after their executions, on June 28, 1937, at a meeting of the local (*raikom*) Moscow communist Party cell, Party functionaries called Korolev "politically unreliable" because he had had "close ties to enemy of the state Eideman." These accusations were serious, but Korolev continued to work at RNII for nearly a year. It took the testimony of his coworkers to seal his fate. In the interrogations of each of the men arrested before him, Korolev's name had been mentioned as a suspect "wrecker." Glushko, for example, in his initial testimony, implicated Korolev as a saboteur.[72] Kostikov, the architect behind many of the accusations against engineers at RNII, was particularly vigilant about uncovering any and every "plot" in the institute. At a Party meeting, Kostikov enthusiastically tried to get other engineers to point to conspiracies within the organization, especially about the unfinished plans of the already arrested institute managers. When Korolev noted bravely that "Everything that I have to say about the activities of Kleimenov and Langemak, I've already said to [them personally]," Kostikov was particularly irritated.[73]

70 Anisimov and Oppokov, "Proisshestvie v NII-3," 82.

71 ARAN, 4/14/171/130–36 (February 13, 1938); ARAN, 4/14/171/137–42 (February 20, 1938).

72 See the excerpt from Glushko's testimony from June 5, 1938 in *OIN*, 136.

73 Golovanov, *Korolev*, 115.

In this world of insanity, logic was at a premium: The chain of links from Korolev to the treasonous was as convenient or inconvenient as one would allow, and fortunes changed unexpectedly depending on who disappeared from work. At least initially, the arrests of solid-propellant engineers Kleimenov and Langemak put Korolev in a positive light; after all, Kleimenov had consistently attacked Korolev through the 1930s, so as an enemy of an "enemy of the people" he found himself insulated from criticisms. But after the arrest of nitric acid specialist Glushko, Korolev's standing again dropped, because he had cooperated with Glushko on a number of projects. Slowly, fellow engineers began to avoid Korolev at work, as if he was the plague. With one faithful colleague – Evgenii Shchetinkov – who refused to be cowed, Korolev continued work on his a rocket project, a winged torpedo named the 212, but he was injured in an accident that put him hospital for a couple of weeks. When he came back to work, his rocket-plane project was suspended without his knowledge. As Kostikov was closing the noose around him, Korolev recognized that his days were numbered, and he was proved right on that fateful night when he returned home with a copy of *Pravda* and some French bread.

Korolev's fate took a darker turn when, *after* his arrest in June 1938, four senior engineers – his former coworkers – signed an additional denunciatory statement, thirty-eight pages long, claiming that Korolev had sabotaged work at the institute.[74] In at least one interrogation, Korolev succumbed to brutal torture and admitted that he had been a member of an "anti-Soviet" organization that had also included Kleimenov, Langemak, and Glushko. The "investigators" broke both his upper and lower jaw so badly that later in life, Korolev grew to dislike visits to the dentist because he was never able to fully open his mouth. The final statement from his colleagues probably ensured that Korolev would receive a death sentence. On September 25, the NKVD placed him on a "death list," along with seventy-three others, for immediate execution. Stalin, Molotov, and Voroshilov personally signed this list. Two days later, fifty-nine persons from the roster (as well as others from other lists) were shot at Kommunark, the NKVD center on the Kaluga main road in Moscow. At the very last minute, for reasons still unclear, the NKVD spared Korolev and a few others.[75] Instead of execution, Korolev was brought in front of the judge and, after a fifteen-minute deliberation,

[74] The NKVD strong-armed the creation of this "expert committee" under the order of the institute's new director, B. M. Slonimer. Engineers A. N. Dedov, L. S. Dushkin, M. P. Kalianova, and A. G. Kostikov served on the committee. For excerpts from its final statement, dated July 20, 1938, see A. Glushko, "'Vrag naroda' Korolev," *Rossiiskii kosmos* no. 4 (2008): 68–72.

[75] Konstantin Tomilin, "Sovetskuiu kosmonavtiku spaslo chudo," *Izvestiia*, April 13, 2002. The "Stalin Execution List" was declassified in December 1999 and contains the names of 44,000 people who were part of the "first category" of convicted in 1937–1938, i.e., those whose deaths involved explicit sanction from Politburo members. According to records, about 80% to 90% of first-category persons were executed.

sentenced to ten years imprisonment with five years of "deprivation of political rights." Among the more absurd charges against him was of destroying his rocket-plane in 1935, an aircraft that in fact languished quite intact in the institute's main courtyard.[76] His lesser sentence meant that he would be sent to a labor camp in the far eastern Soviet Union.

ROCKETS AND REPRESSION

Undoubtedly, the arrests at the institute in 1937 and 1938 profoundly affected the community of the best and brightest rocket scientists, engineers, and technicians working in the Soviet Union. Kleimenov and Langemak were shot. At least five others, including Korolev and Glushko, arguably the most talented engineers in the institute, were incarcerated, losing, in some cases, six years of their lives to the deprivations of the Gulag.[77] Korolev and Glushko did not return to active work involving stand-alone missiles until after the war. We can never know what they may have produced in the intervening years had they not been imprisoned. But did the arrests, as historians have argued, significantly interrupt or change the nature of work at the institute?

Revisiting this episode with the benefit of archival evidence suggests that the Great Terror had much less impact on Soviet rocketry than previously believed. Debates *prior* to the arrests had already established technological priorities that the repression did not radically alter. After the arrests, the institute's overwhelming focus remained solid-propellant projectiles, the original primary mandate of RNII.[78] Among all the systems that had been developed and tested at the institute by the late 1930s, powder rockets were the most developed and close to their operational performance characteristics. In other words, management recognized that bringing them to the battlefield would not require significant amounts of further effort in research and development. After the arrests, the institute continued in the direction for which it had set out, benefiting from a spike in funding right after 1938 that doubled its budget in line with massive increases in national defense spending.

The many years of Soviet research on solid-propellant rocket research in the 1930s culminated in the technically modest but highly successful *Katiusha* system. By 1937, RNII had developed two types of short-range unguided solid-propellant rockets (of 82 and 132 mm caliber); these were

76 ARAN, 1546/1/25/1–4 (October 15, 1939).

77 Besides Glushko, Kleimenov, Korolev, and Langemak, at least three other RNII engineers were arrested: N. G. Chernyshev, V. I. Dudakov, and E. S. Petrov, all of whom eventually returned to work at the institute.

78 A list of the most productive work at the institute in 1938 included five solid-propellant projects and no liquid-propellant ones. RGAE, 8162/1/89/124. Similarly, for 1939, see RGAE, 8162/1/240/1–7 (1940).

used in the summer of 1939 as weaponry on Soviet fighters and bombers during the border war with Japan at the battle of Khalkhin Gol. Through the 1930s, institute engineers had fared poorly in trying to develop a ground-launched version, mainly as a result of an inability to design a proper launch system, relying instead on simple launching rods and wooden crossbars. At the height of the purges at RNII, on a modest assignment from the Red Army, the institute announced a competition to develop a ground-launcher system to simultaneously fire multiple solid rockets. Through a progressive series of iterations in 1938, a group under Ivan Gvai and Leonid Shvarts developed a simple but innovative system to that could fire sixteen improved 132-mm-caliber rockets in a volley from the back of a ZIS truck to a distance of about 8.5 kilometers. Although high-level Soviet artillery generals were at first uninterested in the system, the system was declared ready for battle operations just hours before the Nazi invasion, on June 21, 1941.[79] During the war, the Soviets used these multiple-firing launch systems extensively and effectively in thunderous volleys of firepower. Russian military historians consider these inexpensive rocket launch systems, affectionately called *Katiusha* (little Katy), one of the most effective Soviet weapons of the war.[80] Eulogized in many wartime battle hymns, the *Katiushi* assumed a kind of iconic status that few Soviet weapons before or since have attained. Undoubtedly, these short-range unguided solid rockets proved far more lethal and cost effective against the Nazis than the German liquid-propellant rocket, the V-2, was against the Allies.

In contrast, research on liquid-propellant rocket research, foretold by Tsiolkovskii as the first step to traveling through the cosmos, did not fare as well. The record of Soviet liquid-propellant rocket research in the 1930s, scattered through a number of different organizations, but largely conducted at RNII, was mixed, characterized by abandoned projects, rejected designs, sharp turns in development, and marginal successes (see Figure 17 and Table 2). At the institute, for example, engineers developed a variety of winged missiles, including the 212 (a surface-to-surface rocket with a range of 50 kilometers), the 216 (another surface-to-air rocket with a range of 15 kilometers), and the 301 (an air-launched missile with a range of 10 kilometers). Several of these projects faltered as a result of difficulties in developing automatic control systems, which had been deemed a low priority by the institute management. The 216 was canceled by 1937 whereas the 212, which elicited some lukewarm interest from industry, was delayed by

79 A. S. Koroteev et al., eds., *Issledovatel'skii tsentr imeni M. V. Keldysha: 70 let na peredovykh rubezhakh raketno-kosmicheskoi tekhniki* (Moscow: Mashinostroenie, 2003), 92–101.

80 P. A. Degtiarev and P. P. Popov, *'Katiushi' na pole boia* (Moscow: Voenno izdatel'stvo, 1991). For the *Katiusha*'s role in World War II, see David M. Glantz, *The Military Strategy of the Soviet Union: A History* (London: Cass, 1992), 65–69; Andrei A. Kokoshin, *Soviet Strategic Thought, 1917–91* (Cambridge, MA: The MIT Press, 1998), 160–163.

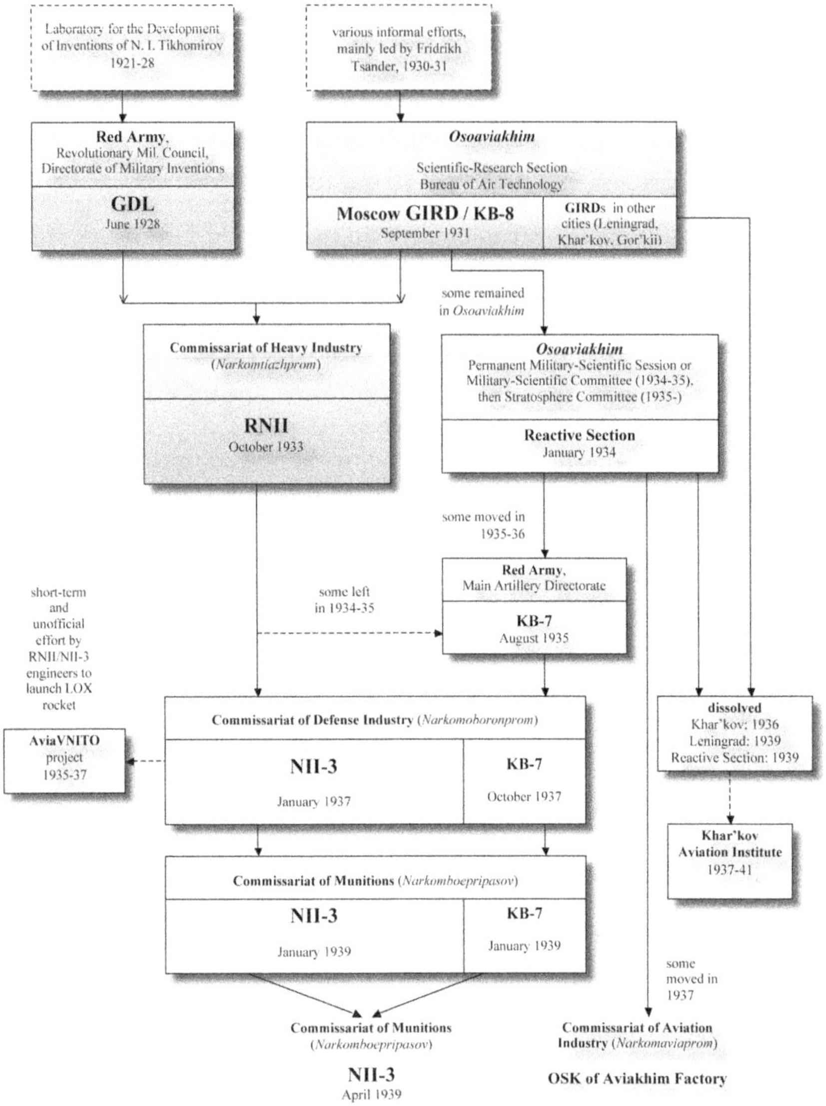

FIGURE 17. Institutional genealogy of Soviet rocketry propulsion efforts, 1930–1941.

years. Two were launched in 1939, after the arrest of Korolev, its principal designer; on both flights, the engine performance was inadequate, sealing the fate of the project.[81] Korolev's favorite rocket-plane, the 218, was never built. To develop technologies needed for this aircraft, he had designed and

[81] ARAN, 4/14/93/143–145 (June 19, 1939). Korolev's summary of the design and development of these winged missiles is in ARAN, 4/14/87/1–23 (October 10, 1944).

TABLE 2. *Soviet Rocket Projects, 1930–1941*

Designation	Range/ Alt.	Length/ Mass	Development Dates	Tests	Comments
GIRD					
Liquid and ballistic					
05	-/5.2	3.22/97	1932–1934	2	Basis for AviaVNITO
07	-/4.6	2.01/35	1932–1935	3	Dropped by RNII, 1935
09	-/5	2.4/18.95	1932–1934	5	Hybrid propellants; became 13a at RNII
10	-/5.5	2.2/29.5	1932–1934	1	First Soviet liquid rocket; became 10a at RNII
Liquid and winged					
06, 06/1		2.3/30	1932–1934	5	Led to 216 at RNII
Air-breathing					
08	5–12		1932–1934	21	Ramjet used on 76-mm artillery shell; 6 versions
Rocket-glider					
RP-1		-/470	1931–1934	–	Not pursued at RNII
LenGIRD					
Solid and ballistic					
Razumov flare	-/5	1.2/18	1932		
Razumov rocket	-/10	2.11/30	1932		Recording rocket
Liquid and ballistic					
Razumov-Shtern	-/5	2.565/90	1932–1937	1	Recording rocket; launched in solid version
GDL					
solid and ballistic					
68 mm			1930–1933		Signaling
68 mm			1930–1933		Tracing
74 mm	<1		1930–1933		Chemical warfare
74 mm	<1		1930–1933		Lighting flare
82 mm	5.3		1930–1933		
132 mm	6.6		1930–1933		
132 mm	6		1930–1933		Chemical warfare
132 mm	6		1930–1933		Lighting flare
245 mm			1930–1933		
410 mm			1930–1933		
takeoff rockets			1930–1933		
cannon rocket			1930–1933		
liquid and ballistic					
RLA-I		1.88/80	1931–1934	1	Not pursued at RNII
RLA-2		1.88/84	1931–1934	–	Became 22 at RNII

(continued)

TABLE 2 *(continued)*

Designation		Range/ Alt.	Length/ Mass	Development Dates	Tests	Comments
RNII						
solid and ballistic						
40 mm	agitation			1930s		
	tracing			1930s		
68 mm	agitation			1930s		
	tracing			1930s		
74 mm	flare			1930s		
82 mm	RS-82	6.2		1930s		Basic model
	ROS-82	5.9	-/6.7	1930s		Lighting
	RBS-82			1930s		Armor-piercing
	RZS-82	5.12	-/7.37	1930s		Airplane takeoff augmenting
132 mm	RS-132	7.2		1930s		Basic model
	ROS-132			1930s		lighting
	ROSV-132			1930s		
	ROFS-132	7.15	-/23.4	1930s		Explosive fragmentation
	RKhS-132	7.0	-/34	1930s		Chemical warfare
	RZS-132	6.0	-/22.4	1930s		Airplane takeoff augmenting
	RBS-132			1930s		Armor-piercing
	RSS-132			1930s		
140 mm	RS-140			1930s		
152 mm	signal			1930s		
	flare			1930s		
203 mm	ROFS-203	9.4	-/124	1930s		Explosive fragmentation
	flare			1930s		
	RKhS-203			1930s		Chemical warfare
	RBS-203		1930s			Armor-piercing
245 mm	RS-245		1933–1934			
M-8/*Katiusha*		c. 5.5	0.714/-	1938		Based on RS-82
M-13/*Katiusha*		c. 8.5	1.41/14.1	1938		Based on RS-132
solid and winged						
48				1935–1936		Testbed for 217
217/I		32/-	2.27/120	1935–1937		Airplane layout; anti-aircraft rocket
217/II		19/-	1.86/120	1935–1937		Four wings, tailless; anti-aircraft rocket

Designation	Range/ Alt.	Length/ Mass	Development Dates	Tests	Comments
liquid and winged					
201 (301)	10/-	3.2/200	1937–1939	–	Air-launched version (from TB-3) of 212
212 (312) (803)	80/-	3.16/210	1935–1939	4	Based on GIRD's 06/IV; 3-axis gyroscope
216	15.1/-	2.3/81	1935–1936	4	Based on GIRD's 06/III; 2-axis gyroscope
liquid and ballistic					
01		-/50	1935–1937	–	Test version of 209
10a (RBD-01)		2.42/34	1935–1937	1	Based on GIRD's 10
11a (RDD-11)		3.0/200	1935–1937	–	
13a (13)	-/4.5	2.46/20	1934–1935	5	Based on GIRD's 09
22		1.88/84	1934	1	Based on GDL's RLA-2
209	-/10–20	-/26	1936–1937	–	Based on GIRD's 10, stratospheric rocket
602	50/50		1939–1941	–	Based on KB-7's R-05
604	>20	3.12/184	1939–1941	>8	Combined solid + liquid rocket engine
521	>20	-/200	1939–1941	5	Air-launched 604
609/I		2.18/26	1937	–	Based on 209
609/II	-/15	2.75/34.8	1937	–	Based on 209; had gyroscope-based autopilot
rocket-plane					
218–1 (318–1) (601)	-/9–25	7.44/660	1936–1939	–	Transferred to OSK; testbed for 218 (318)
KB-7					
liquid and ballistic					
R-03	8.5	2.6/34	1935–1937	11	
R-04		1.1/25	1935–1939	–	spin-stabilized launch
R-05	-/50	2.25/69	1935–1939	–	Hybrid solid and liquid; given to MVTU in 1939

(continued)

TABLE 2 *(continued)*

Designation	Range/ Alt.	Length/ Mass	Development Dates	Tests	Comments
R-06 *Osoaviakhim*	0.65/5	1.7/10	1935–1939	11	Based on the Reactive Section's R-l
R-06/G		1.22/8.9	1935–1939	–	
ANIR-5	-/3	1.28/9.3	1936–1939	6	Based on R-05; gyroscope attitude control
solid and ballistic					
R-07/M			1935–1939	6	
AviaVNITO					
liquid and ballistic					
AviaVNITO	-/10.37	3.255/97	1935–1937	5	Based on GIRD's 05; stratospheric rocket
OSK of Aviakhim Factory					
ballistic					
VR-3	-/5–7	1.1/8.3	1937–1939	5	Based on the Reactive Section's R-3; second-stage ramjet
rocket-gliders					
G-14			1938–1940	–	
318–1 (601)	-/9–25	7.44/660	1939–1940	3	Same as RNII's 318–1
Reactive Section of Stratospheric Committee of *Osoaviakhim*					
liquid and ballistic					
R-1/*Osoaviakhim*	0.65/5	1.7/10	1934–1936	1	Led to R-06 at KB-7
R-2/TR-2		1.7/15	1934–1937		Triple-propellant rocket engine
solid and ballistic					
R-3/VR-3	-/2	1.1/8.3	1935–1937		Transferred to OSK; 2-stage, second-stage ramjet
Khar'kov Aviation Institute Named After N. E. Zhukovskii					
solid and ballistic					
	1.2/-	4/-	1937–1940	2	

Notes: I have included projects only if they reached the flight-testing stage, and thus I omit from the list the many projects that reached the drawing or model-building stage (such as GDL's RLA-100 or RNII's 318 rocket-glider). I have not included the few air-breathing reactive propulsion projects. Test flights include both failed launches and successes. Vehicles often changed designations as a result of reorganizations or transfers to other organizations. Altitude and range reflect design values. Where the range/altitude data are listed as "-/15.0," the vehicle was intended to reach the given altitude rather than attain range across territory. All data are from documents at ARAN.

built an experimental testbed known as the 218–1. Its design represented the marriage of a glider designed by Korolev and a rocket engine produced by Glushko. With Korolev close to arrest, the leadership at the institute wanted to wash their hands off the whole project, especially because Glushko's engine was notoriously unreliable and below specifications. Ultimately, they transferred the rocket-plane to another factory with barely any experience in such work.[82] Here, Aleksander Shcherbakov led a brave effort to salvage the project, using a new and better rocket engine developed by Leonid Dushkin, the liquid-oxygen specialist who had denounced both Korolev and Glushko at various points. Unknown to Korolev, who was already in prison, Shcherbakov orchestrated test flights of the 218–1 (by then named the 601) in 1940. After being tugged as dead weight to a specified altitude, a pilot fired its main rocket engine to accelerate the rocket-plane. Although these three flights were the very first rocket-plane tests in the Soviet Union, serious technical impediments related to its design ensured that there was no vested interest in improving its capabilities.[83] The project was abandoned soon after, and with it, Korolev's dreams of building a rocket-plane.

There were several small efforts to design and build ballistic missiles that operated outside of the RNII structure. Like their better funded peers at RNII, none of these groups produced anything of significance, although because they worked as part of public and voluntary groups, their sporadic efforts were afforded publicity – unlike Korolev's institute, which worked in secret. Groups like the Reaction Section of the Stratospheric Committee of *Osoaviakhim*'s Central Council were largely staffed either with amateur GIRD volunteers who had opted not to join RNII or those who had left RNII in the wake of the discord. Another amateur rocketry effort was based in AviaVNITO (Aviation All-Union Scientific Engineering-Technical Society), a professional society of technicians and engineers employed in the aviation industry, which had a membership of about 6,000 by 1935 spread through ninety locations in the country. At the height of the stratosphere craze in the early 1930s, the society created a Stratospheric Committee to devote attention to high-speed aviation.[84] The AviaVNITO project, exemplifying the last gasp of the amateur rocket ethos in the Soviet Union, owed its very existence to the strife at RNII. Because that institute would not fund research on liquid-propellant "stratospheric" rockets, a number of disgruntled RNII staff in their free time obtained leftover equipment from RNII and tabled a plan to launch a rocket on their own time and initiative. Korolev reviewed the project, which the RNII leadership only grudgingly tolerated.[85] Institute

[82] ARAN, 4/14/105/155–155ob (November 17, 1938).

[83] Protocols of the three flights are stored in ARAN, 4/14/106/43–45, 49–49ob, and 51–52.

[84] "Vsesoiuznoe soveshchanie AviaVNITO," *Avia promyshlenost'* no. 3 (1935); "Rabota AviaVNITO," *Samolet* no. 6 (1935): 8.

[85] ARAN, 4/14/57/2–2ob (May 16, 1935).

managers were not happy when the AviaVNITO group carried out two successful launches that were favorably reported in *Pravda*, in April 1936 and August 1937.[86] These launches – performed by engineers in their free time, unsanctioned by the government, and products of a shoestring budget using equipment tossed away by RNII staff – were the only rocket launches reported publicly by the Soviet press in the interwar years.

The Great Terror did not significantly affect the trajectory of any of these programs, either the officially funded ones at RNII or the unofficial efforts at places like AviaVNITO. In terms of priorities, already before the purges, Soviet engineers had set goals that were vastly different from their German counterparts who built the V-2. If anything, the crescendo of arguments among engineers played a much more substantive part in the character of Soviet rocket work in the interwar years than the Terror. That the RNII devoted considerable resources to solid-propellant research and winged missiles meant that, by the mid-1930s, the Soviets were already heading in a different direction than the German Peenemünde team. Ironically, the purges put key actors such as Andrei Kostikov and Leonid Dushkin in control of the Soviet rocket program, men who favored the kind of work that the Germans were doing. The new postpurge leadership at RNII resurrected funding for liquid-oxygen missiles that had been dropped from the agenda in 1936. In the immediate months after the arrests, Dushkin began work on a number of long-range liquid-propellant ballistic rockets, including one, object 602, theoretically capable of a range of fifty kilometers.[87] Later, in 1940, Dushkin designed and produced object 604, which the institute tested to a range of nearly twenty kilometers. The lightweight 3.1-meter-tall rocket used a hybrid propulsion system fed by both solid and liquid propellants (nitric acid and kerosene). After initial launch using solids, at altitude, the rocket shifted to using liquids. Although it was an unguided rocket, the vehicle was possibly the most advanced liquid-propellant rocket flight-tested by the Soviet Union before the Cold War.[88] The sudden onset of war in 1941, not the Terror, permanently ended development of the 604.

KOROLEV AND GLUSHKO

Korolev and Glushko each spent about six years as prisoners in the Gulag. Their fates differed starkly but eventually intersected. In the winter of 1938–1939, as Korolev mentally prepared himself for his transfer to a labor camp in the eastern Soviet Union, he clearly had no intention of succumbing to his

[86] L. Brontman, "Raketa idet v vozdukh," *Pravda*, April 9, 1936. Such rockets were launched on April 6, 1936 (failure), April 24, 1936 (success), August 2, 1937 (failure), and August 15, 1937 (success). See ARAN, 4/14/57/20–21, 25–26.

[87] ARAN, 4/14/18/16–20 (May 14, 1939).

[88] ARAN, 4/14/75/1–12 (February 15, 1940); GARF, 8162/1/240/50. At least eight 604 missiles were launched in January 1940. The institute also developed an air-launched version, object 521, with a range of about thirty kilometers.

fate. While languishing in a prison in Novocherkassk in southern Russian near the coast of the Black Sea, he wrote handwritten letters denying his accusations, to Nikolai Ezhov at the NKVD and several to the Supreme Court, in which he rejected his admission of guilt because it had been forced out of him.[89] He also asked for help. In one letter to his wife, he requested his family to give his best to "uncle Misha." His mother, Mariia Nikolaevna Balanina, correctly concluded that Korolev was hinting that she pay a visit to Mikhail Gromov, the famous Russian aviator who recently had set the world distance record by flying nonstop from Moscow to San Jacinto, California. Perhaps Gromov could help? Both Gromov and another famous Soviet aviator, Valentina Grizodubova, had known Korolev from his younger gliding days. At their own risk, both did much to help the imprisoned engineer.

In March 1939, Gromov wrote to the chairman of the Supreme Court, Ivan Goliakov, and a month later, Grizodubova contacted the chairman of the Military Collegium of the Supreme Court, Vasilii Ul'rikh, requesting a reinvestigation of Korolev's case. No doubt Gromov and Grizodubova's standing compelled authorities to review Korolev's sentence, but there was also a more pressing rationale: In late 1938, Nikolai Ezhov, the architect of the initial burst of the Great Terror, had been swallowed up by the process he set in action. Dismissed, censured, and eventually executed, he was replaced by a more loyal Stalinist lieutenant, the equally sadistic Lavrentii Beriia. In line with official statements claiming that the NKVD had misused its power during the Ezhov reign, Beriia wanted to show his "humanity" by revisiting, revising, and alleviating some of the sentences handed out under his predecessor. Korolev's case was one of these. On June 13, 1939, the Supreme Court met and decided that Korolev needed a retrial, and for him to be summoned to Moscow.[90] Korolev, unfortunately, was no longer in Novocherkassk; two weeks before, as part of his original sentence, he had been dispatched to Vladivostok on the Siberian coast to begin his term of hard labor at one of the most notorious and horrific Gulag camps in the Kolyma region.

Gold mining at Kolyma was initially run by *Dalstroi* (Far North Construction Trust), an industrial organization to develop transportation infrastructure in the Soviet far east, before being turned over to the NKVD in 1938. *Dalstroi* operated about fifty gold mines supported through the port of Nagaevo in Magadan, a city itself built by forced labor. Prisoners would arrive here after a perilous crossing over the Sea of Okhotsk and then be sent to camps scattered throughout the vast mining infrastructure along the Kolyma river. In 1939, the inmate population numbered close to 70,000, composed of both political prisoners and hardened "ordinary" criminals. Of the camps of the Gulag system, the ones at Kolyma were undoubtedly the

[89] Natalia Koroleva, *S. P. Korolev: otets: k 100-letiiu so dnia rozhdeniia: kniga vtoraia, 1938–1956 gody* (Moscow: Nauka, 2007), 42–46, 49–52.

[90] Koroleva, *Otets: kniga vtoraia*, 72.

most feared. One former prisoner of the *Dalstroi* complex later remembered "the complete contempt for people, for the most elementary human rights, and often for human life as well."[91] Conditions were abysmal, and camp superintendents did not expect prisoners to work at optimum levels for more than three months at best. Prisoners died through starvation, overwork from the twelve-hour work days, accidents, exposure, murder (by other inmates), or torture and execution by the guards. Korolev arrived here in July 1939 along with 5,000 new prisoners, many of whom did not survive the trip across the Sea of Okhotsk. He was assigned to work at a camp in Mal'diak, deep in Kolyma, only 350 kilometers south of the Arctic Circle. Summer soon turned to one of the worst winters on record. In the first few months, Korolev was so brutally treated that he was left with a huge scar on his head and lost fourteen teeth from scurvy. His single communication from Kolyma was a lengthy letter to the Supreme Procurator, smuggled out of the camp, once again requesting a retrial; he did not know that such a request had already been granted. Like his many other letters to high officials, including to Stalin, they invoked the name of Konstantin Tsiolkovskii as the beginning point of his career and ended by linking his fate to that of Soviet power:

> I have been here already 15 months, and been torn away from my life's work which has filled my whole life and was its sustenance and goal. I dreamt of creating the first technological super high-speed altitude rocket aircraft in the USSR being, for the time, a powerful armament and means for defense. I appeal for a review of my case and to remove my name from the profound charges of which I am absolutely not guilty. I appeal to You to give me the possibility to once again continue my work on rocket aircraft for strengthening the defensive capability of the USSR.[92]

By the end of the year, news came from Moscow in the form of a summons that his case was to be reexamined. Freed from the Mal'diak camp, Korolev made the 600-kilometer journey on his own by walking and hitching rides to the port city of Magadan to catch the next ship out. He was under a deadline as the review period would expire if he was not back in Moscow in time. He was naturally crushed that he missed the departing vessel, but he had reason to thank his fortunes when he learned that the ship, a steamer named *Indigirka*, ran aground in the Sea of Okhotsk and killed 700 people on board. His health was so frail by the time he made it on the next ship that doctors at Khabarovsk basically gave up on him as dead. Luckily, a doctor took care of him and nursed him back to life. Korolev finally arrived back in Moscow in February 1940. Five months later, to his shock, the result of the repeat investigation shattered his spirits: He was sentenced once again to eight years in a corrective-labor camp (with his sentence beginning

91 G. A. Ivanova, *Labor Camp Socialism: The Gulag in the Soviet Totalitarian System*, ed. Donald J. Raleigh (Armonk, NJ: Sharpe, 2000), 102. See also Robert Conquest, *Kolyma: The Arctic Death Camps* (London: Macmillan, 1978).

92 ARAN, 1546/1/25/1–4 (October 15, 1939).

retroactively in 1938). He would be expected to leave for another labor camp, *Sevzheldorlag*, where he would help to build railways in the bitter terrain of northern Russia.

A strange turn of events saved his life. Sometime in late 1937, as a large number of arrested prominent aviation designers awaited sentencing at the NKVD's infamous Lubianka, some of them put together a short proposal. Fearing that they would inevitably be sent to forced manual labor camps in Siberia, the authors enumerated a list of specific military weapons that they could develop if given resources, and sent the letter directly to defense industry manager Lazar Kaganovich in early 1938. Kaganovich was intrigued and passed the proposal onto then-NKVD chairman Nikolai Ezhov.[93] The idea appealed to the security services for several reasons. First, leaders such as Ezhov and especially his successor Beriia believed that the NKVD should have a strong institutional role in the general rearmament in anticipation of war with Germany; second, the control of leading scientists and engineers would reinforce the NKVD's expansion of its own vast economic infrastructure based in the Gulag penal system; and finally, the Great Terror that the NKVD had facilitated had so profoundly disrupted the functioning of scientific and technical organizations that some corrective work was required to bring the situation under control. In other words, in large measure, the NKVD needed to create a new institution to limit damage of their own doing.

The NKVD soon began rounding up designers in prisons for research work under a special department of the security services.[94] Beriia's appointment as NKVD chairman put the effort on a higher footing. In January 1939, only a month after his appointment, he renamed this department the Special Technical Bureau (*Osoboe tekhnicheskoe biuro*, OTB) and put it under his direct command. All scientists and engineers were initially transferred from their prisons to a sorting center at Bol'shevo on the outskirts of Moscow before being sent to various locations specializing in different weapons. Practically every prison in Moscow had a scientific group working within. Probably the most well-known and well-funded group operated under the patriarch of the Soviet aviation industry, Andrei Tupolev, who had been arrested in 1937 for being the "head of an anti-Soviet wrecking organization . . . and an agent of French intelligence."[95] Tupolev's group worked at Bol'shevo for a while but moved to larger facility, Factory No. 156 on Radio Street, in Moscow.[96]

[93] RGAE, 8044/1/408/78 (March 13, 1938).

[94] The name of the department changed over time from the Department of Special Design Bureaus of the NKVD (September 1938 to 1939) to the Special Technical Bureau of the NKVD (1939–July 1941) to the Fourth Special Department of the NKVD (July 1941–March 1953).

[95] V. Rigmant, "Tu-2 – Samolet-legenda," *AIK* 30 (September 1997): 1–16.

[96] Sobolev, "Repressii v sovetskoi aviapromyshlennosti."

In 1939, the NKVD asked Tupolev to compile a list of jailed engineers who he thought would be useful in developing military airplanes. Remembering Korolev as a bright young student from his days at the Bauman Moscow Higher Technical School, Tupolev put Korolev's name on a list of twenty-five that he gave to the NKVD. A year later, while Korolev was waiting for relocation to Siberia, the NKVD transferred him to Tupolev's care. In late 1940, Korolev arrived at the Tupolev *sharashka*, as the inmates called their prison laboratory.[97] According to one contemporary, Korolev "looked terrible. He was emaciated and exhausted." But "Tupolev showed a lot of care in his relationship with [him] which we could not understand. Apparently, he valued qualities of Korolev that we did not notice at the time."[98] The conditions at the *sharashka* were heavenly compared to those at Kolyma. When new prisoners arrived, they could hardly believe their eyes. Rumor has it that Korolev arrived at the prison camp carrying a ragged empty bag, a piece of bread, and a few pieces of sugar, all of which he adamantly refused to give up even when told that there would be well-rounded meals. The good conditions did little to change Korolev's mood. One fellow prisoner remembers Korolev as an inveterate pessimist who continued to believe that they "would all be shot."[99]

Besides Korolev, his old comrade-in-arms Glushko also ended up within the *sharashka* system. It took a very long time for Glushko's case to come to court due to a combination of institutional inertia and red tape. On August 15, 1939, more than a year after his arrest, he was sentenced to eight years in a corrective-labor camp for "participation in a counter-revolutionary organization" based on the testimony of those who went before him – Kleimenov, Langemak, and Korolev.[100] Unlike Korolev, Glushko was never sent to a labor camp but directly transferred to a *sharaskha*, first at a factory in Tushino and then finally to Kazan', about 900 kilometers directly east of Moscow in Tatarstan, where the NKVD supervised a group developing auxiliary rocket engines to aid planes to take off.[101] Glushko, a very proud man and a consummate engineer, was devastated by the trauma to his family during these years. His father was arrested in 1943 for "anti-Soviet

[97] The order for his transfer to the *sharashka* system was issued on September 18, 1940. See Koroleva, *Otets: kniga vtoraia*, 138–139.

[98] S. M. Eger, "Sila dukha," *Trud*, February 26, 1988. Recollections vary on the precise number of names on Tupolev's list. Eger quotes twenty-five whereas Kerber quotes "about 200." L. L. Kerber, *Stalin's Aviation Gulag: A Memoir of Andrei Tupolev and the Purge Era* (Washington, DC: Smithsonian Institution Press, 1996), 158.

[99] L. L. Kerber, Interview, Notebook No. 1, Papers of James Harford, December 10, 1991, 85–92.

[100] *OIN*, 135, 148.

[101] The NKVD's Special Department No. 28 (*spetsotdel no. 28*) supervised two engineering groups at Factory No. 16, one under Glushko to develop liquid-propellant rocket engines, and the other under B. S. Stechkin to create air-breathing jet engines. Stechkin was freed in 1943, and most of his former employees transferred to work for Glushko.

agitation" and died in prison five years later. His brother was fired from work after being denounced by others. His mother, writing to her son in prison, vented her anger at those of Glushko's colleagues who had let him down:

> Why such misfortune in our family?! Lord, save us.... What do people want from us? It's simply jealousy. But the hour of reckoning for them has come. Let them get their due. [Kostikov] and Poida and probably Shvarts and the whole... group should get the required punishment.[102]

After most of the Tupolev group were freed at the cusp of the war with the Nazis, the NKVD transferred Korolev to the *sharashka* in Kazan' to work for Glushko. Here, as a deputy to Glushko, Korolev designed systems to integrate Glushko's small rocket engines to airplanes. Although both men had, under duress, denounced each other a few years before during NKVD interrogations, there is no record that they had a bad relationship in Kazan'. They slept in the same room, separated by one bed. They were not close but they remained on friendly terms. Another inmate remembers that one of their favorite recreational activities was wrestling; perhaps tellingly, they always served on opposing teams.[103]

In 1944, at Beriia's urging, the bulk of the formal prison science system – the Special Technical Bureau (or the Fourth Special Department) of the NKVD – was dismantled. Thirty-five men from the rocket engine group at Kazan', including Glushko and Korolev, were freed in July. Beriia's true intentions for freeing the engineers remain unknown, but, to Stalin at least, he argued that "considering the importance of the work carried out, the NKVD considers it advisable to free... especially the distinguished incarcerated specialists... and direct them to work in the aviation industry."[104]

Although the men were technically "free," they remained in Kazan' and continued to work on their modest rocket projects. Because the Soviet Union lacked high-speed jet aircraft, the NKVD tasked Glushko and Korolev to develop small auxiliary liquid-propellant rocket engines to boost the performance of the older piston-engined fighters. The units they produced were successfully tested on many aircraft and generally fulfilled all their stipulated requirements. Glushko produced the engines (RD-1 and RD-1KhZ, both with a 300-kilogram thrust) and Korolev, the engine placement unit (RU-1), which were installed and tested on Petliakov's Pe-2 aircraft from 1943 to 1945. The group also experimented with the engines installed on several other aircraft produced by noted Soviet aviation designers Semen Lavochkin, Aleksandr Iakovlev, and Pavel Sukhoi.[105] The many problems

102 *OIN*, 159.
103 Testimony of A. I. Edel'man in *OIN*, 191–192.
104 GARF, 9401/2/65/385–92 (April 25, 1944); ARAN, 1546/1/28/1 (July 27, 1944).
105 ARAN, 4/17/124/3–10; RGAE, 8044/1/1182/114–17 (July 1, 1944).

associated with their use – such as short running times, the need for special propellant loading systems, and the danger to the pilot from toxic fumes – far outweighed the marginal improvements in speed that they provided. These experiments linking the airplane with the rocket proved to be the last involving Korolev and Glushko, and finally convinced both that this marriage was not the most efficient one. In the end, the Soviets were forced to accept that the airplane had a more efficient future with the jet engine. The rocket engine began to be more closely aligned with the ballistic missile, a linkage starkly on display with the latest fearsome German superweapon, the V-2.

CONCLUSIONS

The relationship between terror and Soviet rocketry was a complex not explicable simply by linear and unidirectional articulations. Soviet rocketry did not progress along a single line of evolution that the Great Terror interrupted abruptly. Rather, Soviet rocketry's dichotomous and oppositional nature – spaceflight advocates versus military promoters – profoundly affected the activities of RNII in the 1930s. Engineers pursuing competing technologies quarreled with each other through the decade. In a national climate of quick militarization and lack of information about foreign efforts, one faction favored simple technological solutions over the objections of others. On the one hand, these disagreements were simply about technology. But a deeper reading of the evidence and the context underscores how technology was not divorced from politics; indeed, that in the Soviet rocket project, one could not be understood without the other. In describing the accusations leveled against Valentin Glushko in 1938, one Soviet journalist's sly characterization that "Glushko's 'treason' was precisely in the fight against 'Bol'shevik' oxygen in favor of 'Trotskyite' nitrogen," perfectly illustrates this point.[106] These "technopolitical" disagreements not only served as pretexts for purging key engineers at the institute, but also affected the trajectory of Soviet rocketry more profoundly than the Terror.

The new evidence adds significantly to our understanding of the apparent Soviet "failure" to parallel the technical achievements of the Germans, especially given their comparable levels of expertise in the early 1930s. During Soviet times, historians explained this "failure" by suggesting that Soviet engineers had embarked on the "correct" path of technological development by producing short-range solid rockets, the *Katiusha*, instead of long-range liquid ballistic missiles such as the V-2. Given Soviet resource constraints, they argued – in many cases, convincingly – that developing the *Katiushi* was the most effective investment of resources, especially given the potency with which the Soviets used these battlefield rockets against the Nazis. Some

[106] Golovanov, *Korolev*, 239.

of this judgment was clearly influenced by hindsight and perhaps circumstance. During the Soviet era, native historians were in a bind. On the one hand, they were compelled to trumpet the prewar theoretical and practical achievements of Tsiolkovskii, Korolev, and Glushko. On the other hand, they had to reconcile these genuine successes with the "failure" to develop large liquid-propellant ballistic missiles such as the German V-2. The way out was to explain away development of the *Katiusha* as the most rational choice of development; in other words, Stalin made the right decision in the late 1930s.[107] In the post-Soviet era, with the revelations about the Great Terror no longer taboo for discussion, Russian (and Western) historians distinctly shifted their arguments. No longer shackled by the constraints of censorship, historians blamed the Stalinist terror for interrupting the Soviet rocketry program in its tracks. Had it not been for the Terror, they argued, Korolev and his associates might well have achieved the technical capabilities so dramatically demonstrated by the German V-2.[108]

In both interpretations, historians clung to the Whiggish notion that the "correct" path of development was that of the V-2 and that it was the standard by which all rocketry development was to be judged. They also substituted one argument (the repressions) for another (the optimal decision to develop solids) in order to explain the Soviet "failure" to build a rocket like the V-2. Finally, the key player in both explanations was Stalin. In the original reasoning, Stalin acted prudently. Now, after *glasnost'*, Stalin erred by arresting key engineers. New evidence undermines both lines of reasoning.

The case of Soviet rocketry in the 1930s is also instructive for a broader understanding of how radical innovation evolves under great social, political, and economic strain. The Soviet rocketry program's principal hallmark, unlike its German counterpart, was a lack of high-level commitment. But top-level patronage had both a positive and negative influence. Rocketry enjoyed the benefits of patronage when Tukhachevskii's influence was on the rise but suffered the worst of the repressions when Tukhachevskii's fortunes suddenly declined. In the initial stages of the effort, for only two years from 1932 to 1934, Tukhachevskii provided key leadership to accelerate R&D work on rocketry. Once he relinquished control over RNII, however,

[107] For a representative work with this line of reasoning, see V. M. Komarov, "30 let so vremeni priniatiia resheniia o sozdanii v Germanii issledovatel'skogo tsentra Peenemiunde (1936g.)," *IIAIK* 54 (1986): 32–43.

[108] From the Russian side, see Golovanov, *Korolev*; Vetrov, *S. P. Korolev i kosmonavtika*; Romanov, *Korolev*. From the Western side, see Harford, *Korolev*. See also the essay by space program veteran Boris Chertok entitled "On the Reasons for the USSR's Lagging Behind Germany in the Problem of Development and Creation of Rocket Technology in the Prewar Years," in E. Yu. Bashilova and T. A. Golovkina, "'Nam udalos' sdelat' ryvok'," *Istoricheskii arkhiv* no. 4 (2003): 46–53.

Soviet rocketry lost its primary sponsor. In many ways, Tukhachevskii's disassociation from the institute in the late 1930s may have actually insulated the institute from even more harm. In answer to a journalist's question on why only seven people were arrested from RNII during the purges whereas literally dozens disappeared from other organizations, Maria Kalianova, the secretary of the Komsomol organization at the institute, later tellingly replied, "[b]ecause, I think we were never taken seriously."[109] This lack of patronage, combined with an unfavorable industrial climate and limited resources, produced intractable conflicts. In the Stalinist era of the late 1930s, managers could not deal with such conflict in a productive manner. Instead, terror served as a tool for conflict resolution, albeit one that tragically destroyed the lives of several engineers and their families.

The case of Soviet rocketry in the interwar years echoes the recent accounts of social conflicts in factories, local Party meetings, peasant collectives, and trade unions, discord that was independent of and usually preceding the purges. There is compelling evidence to suggest that these internal tensions that undercut social cohesion within Soviet governmental, industrial, and Communist Party institutions may have significantly fueled the Great Terror.[110] Here, the existence of a powerful and lawless secret police and Stalin and his cohorts' self-sustaining paranoia were necessary prerequisites to the repression at the institute, but we must also consider the agency of engineers in the equation of repression.[111] Speaking of Soviet artists, historian Peter Kenez wrote this:

> [W]e are attracted to the image of the lone artist struggling against a repressive system and ultimately falling victim to the tyrant.... However, even a cursory examination will show that the artists were not simply victims but also architects of the system that destroyed them. The Soviet system succeeded in making... almost everyone into an accomplice.[112]

Much the same could be said of the scientists and engineers working at RNII, where the divisions between the technical intelligentsia and the political

[109] Golovanov, *Korolev*, 127.

[110] For works in this tradition, see Getty and Manning, *Stalinist Terror*; Getty and Naumov, *The Road to Terror*; Gabor Tamas Rittersporn, *Stalinist Simplifications and Soviet Complications: Social Tensions and Political Conflicts in the USSR, 1933–1953* (New York: Harwood, 1991); Peter Solomon, *Soviet Criminal Justice Under Stalin* (New York: Cambridge University Press, 1996); and Wendy Goldman, *Terror and Democracy in the Age of Stalin: The Social Dynamics of Repression* (New York: Cambridge University Press, 2007).

[111] For useful summaries of the debates on the often contentious scholarship on the purges, see Ronald Grigor Suny, "Revision and Retreat in the Historiography of 1917: Social History and Its Critics," *The Russian Review* 53 (1994): 165–182; I. V. Pavlova, "Contemporary Western Historians on Stalin's Russia in the 1930s," *Russian Studies in History* 40 no. 2 (2001): 65–91; Sheila Fitzpatrick, "Revisionism in Retrospect: A Personal View," *Slavic Review* 67 no. 3 (Fall 2008): 682–704.

[112] Peter Kenez, *Cinema and Soviet Society, 1917–1953* (Cambridge, UK: Cambridge University Press, 1992), 252.

structure were nebulous at best. Recent evidence from other fields in science – particularly, the development of radar, research in biology, and work in astronomy – suggests very similar patterns.[113] Consequently, our conventional understanding of the Soviet scientist as a victim of the state's ruthlessness appears far too simplistic. The scientist, it seems, was too often willingly doing the ruthless work of the state.

After the arrests in the late 1930s, many leading engineers engaged in military research and development ended up in the prison science system, where science and repression intersected in a highly unique setting. For many engineers, entry into the *sharashka* system meant not just continued incarceration but also a strategy for survival because it offered a better chance at life than at labor camps. Neither the "open" R&D system of the 1930s nor the wartime prison science system succeeded in producing radical technological innovations such as liquid-propellant rockets. It was the unexpected discovery of massive German liquid-propellant rockets at the end of the war that altered fundamentally the Soviet leadership's view on the need for such radically innovative weapons. Ultimately, the handiwork of Hitler's scientists succeeded in resolving technical ambiguity for their Soviet compatriots where Stalin's terror had failed.

[113] Asif Siddiqi, "The Rockets' Red Glare: Technology, Conflict, and Terror in the Soviet Union," *Technology and Culture* 44 no. 3 (2003): 470–501.

6

Russians in Germany

> We were to establish which [German] enterprises and companies cooperated in creating the missile weapon, and to recreate the system of mutual ties.[1]
>
> G. A. Tiulin, an artillery officer explaining his team's goals in Germany in 1945

INTRODUCTION

In the early twentieth century, space theorists such as Tsiolkovskii, Oberth, and Goddard had conjectured that access to space would be possible only if humankind could design and build rockets powerful enough to accelerate an object fast enough that it achieved "escape velocity." But such rockets did not exist during the first half the century; nor did any nation have plans to build any. Nazi Germany's wartime ballistic missile, the V-2, offered the first material evidence that, in the future, nations might develop rocket technology sufficiently powerful to breach the boundaries of space.[2] The goal of spaceflight, however, determined neither the rationale for building the V-2 (for Germany) nor the missile's value as an object of study after World War II (for the Allies). When, after the war, the victors scrambled to collect the detritus of the German rocket program, they did so not to explore space but because they believed that the V-2 possessed deadly military potential. Despite the evidently poor wartime effectiveness and high costs of the German missile project, the Allies recognized that German scientists and engineers had significantly advanced the possibilities of missile warfare.

German expertise and matériel, recovered at the end of World War II, served as the foundation for the first generation of Soviet long-range missiles. Although a small group of Soviet scientists, engineers, and technicians had acquired valuable experience in the design of rockets in the interwar

[1] G. Tiulin, "Semerka: gody, svershenii a, liudi," *Krasnaia zvezda*, April 1, 1989.

[2] The internal secret German designation for the missile was A-4. In open sources, the Nazis simply called the weapon *Vergeltungswaffe Zwei* (Vengeance Weapon Two, or V-2). In nearly all documentation, the Soviets referred to the rocket as Фау–2 (*Fau-2*), a transliteration reflecting the German pronunciation of the letter "V" as "fow." To eliminate confusion, I refer to the missile as the V-2 even if original Soviet documents use *Fau-2*.

years at the RNII rocket institute, the discovery of powerful German rockets fundamentally altered not only the state's view on the importance of rockets but also helped change the technological priorities of Soviet rocket engineers. This point, about the importance of German missiles, particularly the V-2, in the evolution of Soviet rocket and space programs has been emphasized by many.[3] But because the Soviet space program can largely be traced back to the V-2, these accounts have fallen prey to a kind of teleology that assumes without doubt that the long-range ballistic missile fueled by liquid propellants (such as the V-2) was the obvious and inevitable choice for a rocket weapon in the postwar years. All roads, in others words, led to the German rocket, and from the German rocket sprang the future.

Although it is true that the discovery of the V-2 was a turning point in Soviet efforts to build more powerful rockets, the events of 1945 and 1946 also encompassed continuity, contingency, and agency. Each of these requires some elaboration. Although a series of new institutions emerged from the experience in Germany, the postwar Soviet rocket program had deep connections with the interwar one, mediated by the *Katiusha* rocket launcher system, whose roots dated back to the 1930s and whose wartime users would go on to serve as clients for the Soviet space program. Contingency was also a fundamental part of postwar decision making. Stalin's sanction of V-2 development in 1946 was the outcome of an elaborate phase of indecision among Soviet industrial managers, who lacked adequate technical expertise to "fit" a ballistic missile into their a priori conceptions of weapons design. This ambivalence, combined with more important matters, deprived the missile program of a government commitment for almost a whole year. Finally, because our understanding of the Soviet search missions into occupied Germany has been based on memoir material, this episode comes to us through the narrow albeit overlapping narratives that communicate little sense of the agency of mid-level actors who were able to operate with relative independence to form coalitions across vocations, institutions, and nationalities that was critical to positioning German missiles as the key to postwar Soviet rocketry.[4] Teams of mid-level Soviet engineers and soldiers formed a strong informal social network in Germany – frequently without

[3] Matthias Uhl, *Stalin's V2: Der Technolgietransfer der deutschen Fernlenkwaffentechnik in die USSR und der Aufbau der sowjetischen Raketenindustrie 1945 bis 1959* (Bonn: Bernard & Graefe-Verlag, 2001); Mark Harrison, "New Postwar Branches (1): Rocketry," in *The Soviet Defence-Industry Complex from Stalin to Khrushchev*, eds. John Barber and Mark Harrison (New York: St. Martin's Press, 2000), 118–149; Steven J. Zaloga, *Target America: The Soviet Union and the Strategic Arms Race, 1945–1964* (Novato, CA: Presidio, 1993).

[4] For the memoir material, see Chertok, *RAP1*; Boris Konovalov, *Taina Sovetskogo raketnogo oruzhiia* (Moscow: ZEVS, 1992); V. S. Budkin, *Ot shturmovikov Il-2 do kosmicheskikh raket: vospominaniia* (Dnepropetrovsk: Vidavnitstvo DDU, 1993); "Vospominaniia Genrikha Naumovicha Abramovicha," http://www.sonbi.ru/tsiam/about/Anni/memoirs/gna.htm (accessed November 19, 2008).

the knowledge of the center – that served as the prototype of a systems approach to postwar Soviet innovation. In Germany, representatives from entirely different branches of Soviet industry and military bypassed standard bureaucratic barriers and communicated with each other. Their success in forming an effective network to produce missiles strikingly illustrated the possibility of local, flexible, and dynamic management in the immediate postwar period. This network provided the foundation for the Soviet missile program, which, ten years later, evolved into the Soviet space program.

THE ROCKET DURING WAR

During the war, the Red Army's ground forces fired 12 million unguided solid-propellant *Katiusha* "reactive projectiles" – as the Soviets called artillery rockets – in dozens of different versions. These rockets and their launch units had been developed by the RNII institute in the 1930s, with the involvement of Ivan Kleimenov and Georgii Langemak, both executed during the Purges. During the war, the Soviets measured the effectiveness of the *Katiushi* in both numbers and morale: The government extolled their success in official communiqués, awards to its designers, and, most famously, in poems and songs that mythologized the deadly power of Soviet rockets.[5] To make proper use of the *Katiushi* on the field, in August 1941, the Red Army created a special subdivision, the Guards Mortar Units (*Gvardeiskie minometnye chasti*, GMCh). In battle, armed divisions used them much like motorized cannons, driving them close to battle engagements, shooting them, and then advancing; their firing ranges were relatively short, between four and twelve kilometers. By early January 1945, the Guards Mortar Units had 519 divisions, each with twelve trucks.[6]

The Red Army not only operated these weapons on the field but also had a say in their development, testing, and acquisition. Recognizing the importance of reactive artillery, the State Committee of Defense (*Gosudarstvennye*

[5] The first operational *Katiusha* system was the BM-13, which used sixteen M-13 solid rockets (each of 132 mm caliber) fired from the back of a ZIS-6 truck. Each rocket had a theoretical range of about 8.5 kilometers. The initial test batch of launchers was manufactured at Factory No. 2 (or Komintern Factory, later Factory No. 723) in Voronezh, but throughout the entire war, most *Katiusha* launchers were manufactured at Factory No. 733 (or Kompressor Factory) in Moscow. A. N. Vasil'ev and V. P. Mikhailov, *Raketnye puskovye ustanovki v Velikoi Otechestvennoi Voine* (Moscow: Nauka, 1991); P. A. Degtiarev and P. P. Popov, *'Katiushi' na pole boia* (Moscow: Voenizdat, 1991); V. N. Novikov, ed., *Oruzhie pobedy*, 2nd ed. (Moscow: Mashinostroenie, 1987), 153–187.

[6] Iu. Maksimov, ed., *Raketnye voiska strategicheskogo naznacheniia: voenno-istoricheskii trud* (Moscow: RVSN, 1992), 22–23; A. I. Nesterenko, "Polevaia reaktivnaia artilleriia v voiakh za Rodiny," in *Nauka i uchenye Rossii v gody Velikoi Otechestvennoi Voiny 1941–1945: ocherki vospominaniia dokumenty*, eds. E. A. Beliaiev, N. M. Osipova, and E. A. Shitikov (Moscow: Nauka, 1996), 178–185.

komitet oborony, GOKO or GKO) – the highest wartime national governing authority, headed by Stalin – formed two bodies to coordinate *Katiusha* development, a Main Directorate of Armaments (to handle issues of development and acquisition) and a Military Council (to determine strategy and policy).[7] A generation of young artillery officers gained experience handling the *Katiushi* through both field operations and work in these new institutional structures. After graduating from artillery school (usually the L. B. Krasin First Red Banner Artillery School in Moscow), most officers were then screened for proper ideological qualifications for service in the Guards Mortar Units. Regiment commanders were normally in their mid-twenties and supervised by slightly older men, in their early thirties. The Mortar Units also had a strong Communist Party presence at top levels: Its Military Council included several high-ranking Party officials, including Artillery Major-General Lev Gaidukov, who simultaneously served as a department chief within the Bol'shevik Party's Central Committee; in other words, he not only had effective control over a wide variety of appointments in the *Katiusha* control structure but also represented reactive artillery interests directly to Stalin.[8] Many of these *Katiusha* men, both at the middle and the top, would go on to influential careers in the future Soviet space program.

If the wartime record of short-range solid rocket development was impressive, the same cannot be said of liquid-propellant rockets – or long-range rockets in general. Although some industrial leaders recognized the value of long-range liquid-propellant projectiles on the eve of the war, the Nazi invasion forced the topic to the background as the Red Army demanded weapons that were immediately available.[9] For this reason, no Soviet organization experimented with or developed liquid-propellant projectiles during the war.

Soviet military leaders showed much more interest in using liquid-propellant rockets on *airplanes* rather than projectiles. Already in the interwar years, forward-thinking engineers in both the Soviet Union and abroad recognized that the conventional airscrew propeller had reached its performance limits, prompting them to explore different modes of reactive

[7] The GOKO decree was issued on September 8, 1941. The Red Army appointed Lieutenant-General V. V. Aborenkov to head the Guards Mortar Units (GMCh) and Major-General N. N. Kuznetsov to head its Main Directorate of Armaments. Maksimov, *Raketnye voiska*, 22; Novikov, *Oruzhie pobedy*, 167.

[8] Novikov, *Oruzhie pobedy*, 167.

[9] In August 1939, after a discussion on the merits of long-range (fifty kilometers and higher) liquid-propellant projectiles, the technical council of the People's Commissariat of Munitions recommended developing them. ARAN, 4/14/180/24–25 (August 23, 1939). The government, however, abandoned the project after the war began. For a summary of liquid-propellant rocket engine work at NII-3 in the late 1930s and early 1940s, see RGAE, 8044/1/1182/44–45.

propulsion.[10] Just before the Nazi invasion, the commander of the Red Air Force noted in a letter to the government that "the problem of creating an aircraft with reactive engines is an extraordinarily important question [and] we have many organizations ... working in this field."[11] During the war, more than a half-dozen engineering teams, spread out in different design bureaus, research institutes, and factories, tried to develop aircraft using modern reactive propulsion engines, specifically liquid-propellant rocket engines. Most were fighter-interceptor aircraft designed to take off on short notice, fight incoming Nazi aircraft, and return to base. Although several projects reached the construction stage, only one such rocket-plane was ever tested in flight, Factory No. 293's so-called "BI" fighter-interceptor. Yet, already by 1944, it became clear that the BI could never be converted into a combat vehicle because liquid-propellant rocket engines posed major problems, not the least being that the plane barely took off before its propellant ran out.[12] The jet engine avoided this fundamental liability by using the atmosphere as its oxidizer, obviating the need to carry it on board. Despite the uncertain future of rocket technology, most of these wartime teams continued to work haphazardly on various rocket-powered planes, efforts that were hampered by uneven support from their ministerial managers.

REPARATIONS

The Soviet stance on the rocket technology altered fundamentally with the end of the war, as German war booty, captured as part of war reparations, began to trickle back to Moscow. As the war neared its end, Soviet officials began to speak of the right to reparations in the form of economic and human matériel from the defeated powers, particularly from Germany and Japan but also from Korea, Romania, Hungary, and Finland. Based on its own evaluation of the cost of material losses to the Soviet Union during the war (put at somewhere in the range of $128 billion), the Soviet government drew up plans to take advantage of areas under its control. In the postwar years, Soviet officials consistently quoted a figure of $10 billion worth of

[10] I. G. Sultanov, *Istoriia sozdaniia pervykh otechestvennykh turboreaktivnykh samoletov* (Moscow: Vuzovskaia kniga, 1998); Mark Harrison, "A Soviet Quasi-Market for Inventions: Jet Propulsion, 1932–1946," *Research in Economic History* 23 (2005): 1–59.

[11] TsAMO, 35/11280/36/108–117 (May 10, 1941).

[12] For the BI, see ARAN, 4/14/330/1–34 (1942). The Soviet aviation industry funded several other rocket-plane projects during the war, all chaotically and inefficiently distributed through various design bureaus (OKBs), factories, and research institutes (NIIs). These included the 302P (at NII-3), the *Maliutka* (at Factory No. 51), the R-114 (at OKB-86), the Iak-7R (at OKB-115), the 4302 (at OKB-207), and an unnamed rescue rocket-plane (at Factory No. 464). In addition, Sergei Korolev proposed two rocket-plane projects during the war, the RP (while at Factory No. 16) and the RP-1 (while at OKB-SD), although neither was approved by the government.

reparations owed by Germany.[13] Through 1945 and 1946, overseas teams known as "trophy brigades" – composed of scientists, soldiers, industrial managers, and Party representatives – scoured Europe and Asia, cataloguing and collecting a huge amount of material that was shipped back to the Soviet Union. Like the major Western powers, the USSR engaged in a systematic "exploitation and plunder" of Axis resources that was unrivalled in history.[14] The scientific and military component of this "reparation" was not trivial. Over a period of two years, teams representing the Soviet government collected and transported equipment from 4,786 German and Japanese enterprises, 655 of which were of an explicitly military nature.[15] Historian Norman Naimark speculates that, by 1948, the Soviets had transported about $2.68 billion dollars worth of material back to Russia; this was one-third of the Soviet-occupied zone's productive industrial capacity in 1945.[16]

Reparations took different forms: indiscriminate looting and "trophy" collecting in the last days of the war, more formal dismantling and transportation of industrial machinery, reparations in kind consisting of postwar economic exploitation of occupied Germany, and intellectual reparations in the form of German human expertise. For the Soviet military – and the rocketry industry in particular – factory deportations and intellectual transfers played the most critical roles in postwar research and development. Already by late 1944, the major Soviet industrial commissariats drew up detailed plans to collect reparations from abandoned factories that supported the war effort in German-occupied areas of Europe. By the Soviet government's calculations, its aviation industry had lost as much as $872 million as a result of the war, an amount that guided the Commissariat of the Aviation Industry's compilation of a list of nearly 200 German factories as targets for inspection.[17] Because of the Yalta agreements, the demarcation lines in Germany moved in such a way that about 600 German aviation facilities, that is, more than half of the entire German aviation industry, fell into Soviet hands by July 1945.

[13] According to the Yalta agreements in February 1945, the Soviets asked for 50% of $22 billion. *Foreign Relations of the United States: The Conferences at Malta and Yalta, 1945* (Washington, DC: GPO, 1955).

[14] John Gimbel, *Science, Technology, and Reparation: Exploitation and Plunder in Postwar Germany* (Stanford, CA: Stanford University Press, 1990); Matthias Judt and Burghard Ciesla, *Technology Transfer Out of Germany After 1945* (Amsterdam: Harwood, 1996); Christoph Mick, *Forschen für Stalin: Deutsche Fachleute in der sowjetischen Rüstungsindustrie 1945–1958* (Munich: R. Oldenbourg, 2000).

[15] For overall figures, see GARF, 5446/52/2/45–116. See also Bystrova, *VPK*, 30.

[16] Norman M. Naimark, Russians in Germany: A History of the Soviet Zone of Occupation, 1945–1949 (Cambridge, MA: The Belknap Press, 1995), 169.

[17] D. A. Sobolev, *Nemetskii sled v istorii sovetskii aviatsii: ob uchastii nemetskikh spetsialistov v razvitii aviastroeniia v sssr* (Moscow: Aviantik, 1996), 58.

Anticipating the need to coordinate the extraction of German resources, the Soviet government set up a mechanism to supervise the work at the highest level. Days after the Yalta Conference – which effectively divided up postwar Germany into American, British, French, and Soviet zones – the GOKO established a "special committee" tasked with coordinating all work on dismantling industry in areas of Germany and Poland occupied by Soviet troops.[18] Georgii Malenkov, the top GOKO official responsible for the development of Soviet aviation and mortars during the war, headed the committee.[19] On the ground itself, a separate GOKO decision called for the creation of "permanent commissions" as part of the four westward-moving Soviet fronts; these would be headed by mid-level industrial managers and include experts who could evaluate the worth of equipment found at factories. For example, as part of the first Belorussian front, the permanent commission included Major-General Pavel Zernov, an industrial manager in the tank industry.[20] Once survey operations in Germany began in late April 1945, members of the permanent commissions (such as Zernov) would find particular facilities, take a rough inventory, evaluate the usefulness of the equipment, and send a message back to the relevant commissariat. The commissar in question would then petition Malenkov's Special Committee for a top-level order from the GOKO to have a battalion of soldiers sent to that location to catalog, dismantle, pack, and send matériel back to Soviet territory. These military teams were subordinate to the Main Trophy Directorate headed by Lieutenant-General F. I. Vakhitov, also a key member of the Special Committee.[21] In early 1945, Vakhitov commanded as many as forty "trophy battalions" for capturing industrial equipment in Germany.

The circuitous process, whereby representatives from the commissariats communicated with the army through intermediaries in Moscow even though both might be at the same factory in Germany, was in theory seemingly reasonable but practically often chaotic. People on the ground frequently did not follow the rules to the letter, and few were ever certain of authority and subordination in occupied territory. The Soviet Military

[18] RGASPI, 644/1/373/48–51 (February 25, 1945).

[19] Other members were N. A. Bulganin, A. V. Khrulev, F. I. Vakhitov, and N. A. Voznesenskii. K. I. Koval', "Zapiski upolnomochennogo GKO na territorii germanii," *Novaia i noveishaia istoriia* no. 3 (1994): 124–47.

[20] The GOKO issued a decree (no. 7563ss) on the permanent commissions on February 21, 1945. Personnel assignments for the heads of these commissions were approved by forty separate GOKO decrees (nos. 7646 to 7685) issued on March 5, 1945. These commissions, assigned to the first, second, and third Belorussian fronts and the first Ukrainian front, were headed by P. M. Zernov, P. S. Kuchumov, G. I. Ivanovskii, and M. Z. Saburov, respectively. RGASPI, 644/1/376/84–88.

[21] See, for example, the cover letter and decree about moving equipment from a German factory in Mecklenburg that refers to information from a plenipotentiary of the GOKO and the request to have it moved by Vakhitov's Main Trophy Directorate. RGAE, 7516/1/1221/5–6 (May 24, 1945).

Administration in Germany (*Sovetskoi voennoi administratsii v Germanii*, SVAG), which after its formation on June 6, 1945 effectively controlled day-to-day life in occupied Germany in the postwar era, had little control over these trophy battalions and reparation teams, which, 70,000 strong, operated on direct orders from Moscow rather than Berlin.[22] As a result, in the three months before August 2, 1945 – the Allied deadline set for the end of "trophy removals" from occupied Germany – Soviet work in search of German industry was rather chaotic. Permanent commissions conflicted with "special" visiting scientific commissions while local military commandants who captured German towns viewed scientific teams with suspicion. Nevertheless, operating outside the standard institutional barriers of Soviet local governance allowed disparate constituencies, particularly engineering experts from various commissariats and military officers, to come into direct contact with each other in ways that would prove critical to the birth of the postwar Soviet rocketry program.

THE AVIATION ENGINEERS GO TO GERMANY

In 1945, two Soviet constituencies searched for German rocket technology – aviation engineers (who sought reaction propulsion technology such as rocket and jet engines) and artillery service officers (who sought projectiles that *used* reaction propulsion). Although each had its own agenda, the missions of both overlapped. Aviation engineers, largely under the employ of the Commissariat of the Aviation Industry (NKAP), took the lead in sending a number of highly qualified teams to German aeronautics centers. Their goal was to reach important facilities quickly, cordon them off from unwanted intruders, gather as much information as possible, and prepare equipment, archives, and drawings for shipping. Their technical focus was on advanced technologies such as wing design, reactive propulsion, guidance systems, radar, and electronics. Reaction (or reactive) propulsion was a major target, although at this early stage, the focus was on the aeronautical applications of reactive propulsion. Because aviation engineers classified rocket engines under this grouping, Soviet interest in aviation shaped early discoveries and evaluations of new German missiles.

Most engineers tapped to search out German reactive propulsion technology worked in the Moscow-based NII-1 institute, the wartime incarnation of the old RNII where the Soviets had developed rockets during the interwar years. In 1944, aviation industry managers had reorganized the old institute, renamed it NII-1 (*Nauchno-issledovatel'skii institut-1*, Scientific-Research Institute-1), and consolidated all work on reactive propulsion under one umbrella. Such redirection and reorganization was largely a response to information about the German Me 262 jet fighter and the perception that

[22] Naimark, *Russians in Germany*, 26, 179.

the jet engine would revolutionize postwar aviation. Despite a long history of theoretical work on jet propulsion, Soviet designers had failed to produce a workable design because of a lack of foresight at the managerial level, a poor technological base, and bad luck.[23] After 1944, the government increased NII-1's funding to develop reactive propulsion technology such as air-breathing jet engines, and liquid- and solid-propellant rocket engines.[24]

Initially, NKAP sent a high-level five-man commission headed by Major-General Nikolai Petrov, the director of the Moscow-based Scientific-Research Institute for Aircraft Equipment, to examine the topmost aeronautics R&D facilities (research laboratories, testing facilities, educational institutions, and airfields) located in Soviet-occupied Germany. The Petrov commission's written directive was typical of the ones issued to the many scientific teams that spread out through Germany:

> [Effect] the removal, safekeeping, and shipment to Moscow of all German experimental aircraft and engines of all types; aviation equipment, components, and all materials associated with their design and production; scientific research materials; laboratory installations; wind tunnels; instrumentation; libraries; and scientific archives. The commission must work on the scene immediately after Soviet troops capture appropriate locations, scientific centers, and industrial regions of Germany.[25]

Aided by eighty-eight "experts," the Petrov commission scoured more than a half-dozen German aeronautics facilities over three months, between April 24 and August 1, 1945. They arrived at their first target, the German Laboratory for Aviation (*Deutsche Versuchsanstalt für Luftfahrt*, DVL) at Adlershof to find a deserted town. In the offices of the DVL, all desk calendars stood frozen at April 13, the Germans having just abandoned their posts. On occasion, the Soviet team were fired upon and had to defend themselves in sporadic gunfights. Over the course of three months, they found models of jet fighters, jet engines, airborne radars, a V-1 winged missile, full technical reports on a wide range of equipment, wind tunnels, and aircraft belonging

23 I. G. Sultanov, *Istoriia sozdaniia pervykh otechestvennykh turboreaktivnykh samoletov* (Moscow: Vuzovskaia kniga, 1998); Mark Harrison, "A Soviet Quasi-Market for Inventions: Jet Propulsion, 1932–1946," *Research in Economic History* 23 (2005): 1–59.

24 APRF, 3/47/179/22–23 (February 18, 1944). As a result of the GOKO decree, NKAP issued a second order (no. 149ss) on February 28, 1944, effectively organizing the new NII-1 institute by combining the old RNII in Moscow and Factory No. 293 in Khimki. At NII-1, L. S. Dushkin, V. P. Glushko, and A. M. Isaev designed rocket engines while M. M. Bondariuk (ramjet) and A. M. Liul'ka (turbojet) designed air-breathing engines.

25 RGAE, 8044/1/6313/5–6. The members of this team included G. N. Abramovich (Deputy Director, NII-1), R. S. Ambartsumian (Deputy Director, VIAM), K. N. Surzhin (Deputy Director, TsAGI), V. D. Vladimirov (Deputy Director, TsIAM), and D. S. Zosim (Deputy Director, LII) and two professors from TsAGI, that is, A. K. Martynov and K. A. Ushakov.

to such industrial giants as Junkers, Daimler-Benz, Telefunken, Henschel, BMW, Siemens, and Askania.[26]

Because reactive propulsion constituted such a broad segment of advanced aeronautical research in Germany, Petrov detached a subgroup from his team under Dr. Genrikh Abramovich, a nationally renowned expert on jet propulsion and gas dynamics and deputy director of the NII-1 institute, to focus exclusively on the subfield. Ten other NII-1 employees – experts in rocket propulsion under Aleskei Isaev – arrived in Germany in early May 1945. They bolstered Abramovich's team as it made its way to Peenemünde, the famous base on the island of Usedom on the easternmost part of the German Baltic coast where the Nazis developed and tested the V-1, the V-2, the *Wasserfall*, and other liquid-propellant rocket projectiles.[27] Peenemünde had originally come under Soviet notice in early 1945 from interrogations of German prisoners of war captured by the advancing first and second Belorussian fronts.[28] Abramovich recalls that upon arrival at Peenemünde, they were met by a German man with two Scottish terriers, one black and the other white. Where almost everyone else had fled, he had remained behind to take care of the motel he owned on the island. Another German gave Abramovich a tour of the facilities. The Soviets carefully photographed everything, annotated the images, and sent information regularly back to NII-1, where a bureaucrat prepared an impressive album to show to ministers and their deputies.

The Abramovich/Isaev team's foray into Peenemünde allowed NKAP Commissar Shakhurin to report to the highest levels of the Soviet government by June 8, 1945. The scale of German wartime work clearly impressed Shakhurin, but he noted, almost with a tone of disappointment, that "[i]n spite of the great [production] power and the large workforce, [the institute] was only occupied with rocket artillery – rocket projectiles operating only on liquid fuel." The Germans' organization of work on rockets seemed only to confirm Shakhurin's suspicion that there was a fundamental difference between rockets with wings and rockets without. He noted that "[this difference] is underlined even more by the circumstances that... the testing station for the [V-1 winged projectile] located near the institute had no

[26] Konstantin Kosminkov and Nikolai Valuev, "Nemetskoie vliianie," *Mir aviatsii* no. 1 (1997): 23–32.

[27] The Abramovich team detached from the main Petrov group on May 1, 1945 and headed toward Peenemünde, arriving a few days later. Remarkably, Petrov had not heard from them as late as May 15. The "new" team under Isaev team traveled along the following route: Peenemünde to Wasdorf (near Berlin; the location of BMW company facilities) to Berlin to Nordhausen. Besides A. M. Isaev, the team included V. F. Berglezov, A. I. Cheshkov, A. S. Kosiatov, A. V. Pallo, A. S. Raetskii, I. I. Raikov, A. M. Smirnov, A. A. Tolstov, and L. I. Volkov. A. L. Loktev, *Nedavno eto bylo sekretom* (Moscow: Put', 2001), 78–79; Memoir of A. V. Pallo in *DVK2*, 42–43.

[28] RGAE, 8044/1/6313/131–32 (April 12, 1945).

relation to the [Peenemünde] institute system, and [that V-1 development] was subordinated directly to the control of the air force." He unequivocally recommended that:

> From the materials of the inspection of... Peenemünde, it is evident that work on the creation of the [V-2] and other types of rocket projectiles have an *artillery* profile, and therefore it is advisable to entrust [its development] to the People's Commissariat of Ammunitions, and transfer all the preserved equipment from... Peenemünde to it.[29]

In other words, the Soviet aviation industry wanted nothing to do with the V-2, because it seemed to be nothing more than a glorified artillery projectile.

FACTORY OF DEATH

Although there were a few things of interest at Peenemünde (mostly in the form of damaged equipment), the Soviets very quickly realized that there might be more valuable booty elsewhere. Earlier, in February and March 1945, about 4,000 members of the original Nazi rocket team had fled south from Peenemünde, carrying with them fourteen tons of documents encompassing more than a decade's worth of work. Most of what was left behind had been destroyed haphazardly by dynamite squads. The real riches, it transpired, were not at Peenemünde but in the giant underground *Mittelwerk* ("middle factory") facility near the city of Nordhausen in the Thuringia region (see Figure 18).[30] By late 1943, the Nazis had moved production of some of their most important weapons, including the V-2, to *Mittelwerk*; by the end of the war, 5,800 V-2 missiles emerged from the factory, which was built into the side of Kohnstein Mountain. The impressive facility contained two giant parallel tunnels, each nearly two kilometers long, that had railroad tracks running through it.

Mittelwerk was one node of a network that also included *Nordwerk* ("north factory"), for jet and piston engine production, and *Mittelwerk II*, for V-1 flying bomb production, integrated as part of a giant factory complex known as *Mittelbau*, whose history constitutes one of the darkest parts of the history of rocketry. Through its existence, the *Mittelbau* system was constructed and run by a combination of slave labor, foreign forced labor, and German civilians. Slave laborers "lived" in the associated Dora/*Mittelbau KZ* concentration camp, one of the most horrifying elements of the Nazi camp system, even by the repugnant standards of the Third Reich. Of the

29 APRF, 3/47/182/70–72 (June 8, 1945); the emphasis is mine.

30 Already, by May 11, the Petrov Commission had cabled Malenkov back in Moscow that it was urgent to reach *Mittelwerk* as quickly as possible. Koval', "Zapiski upolnomochennogo GKO na territorii germanii," 142–143.

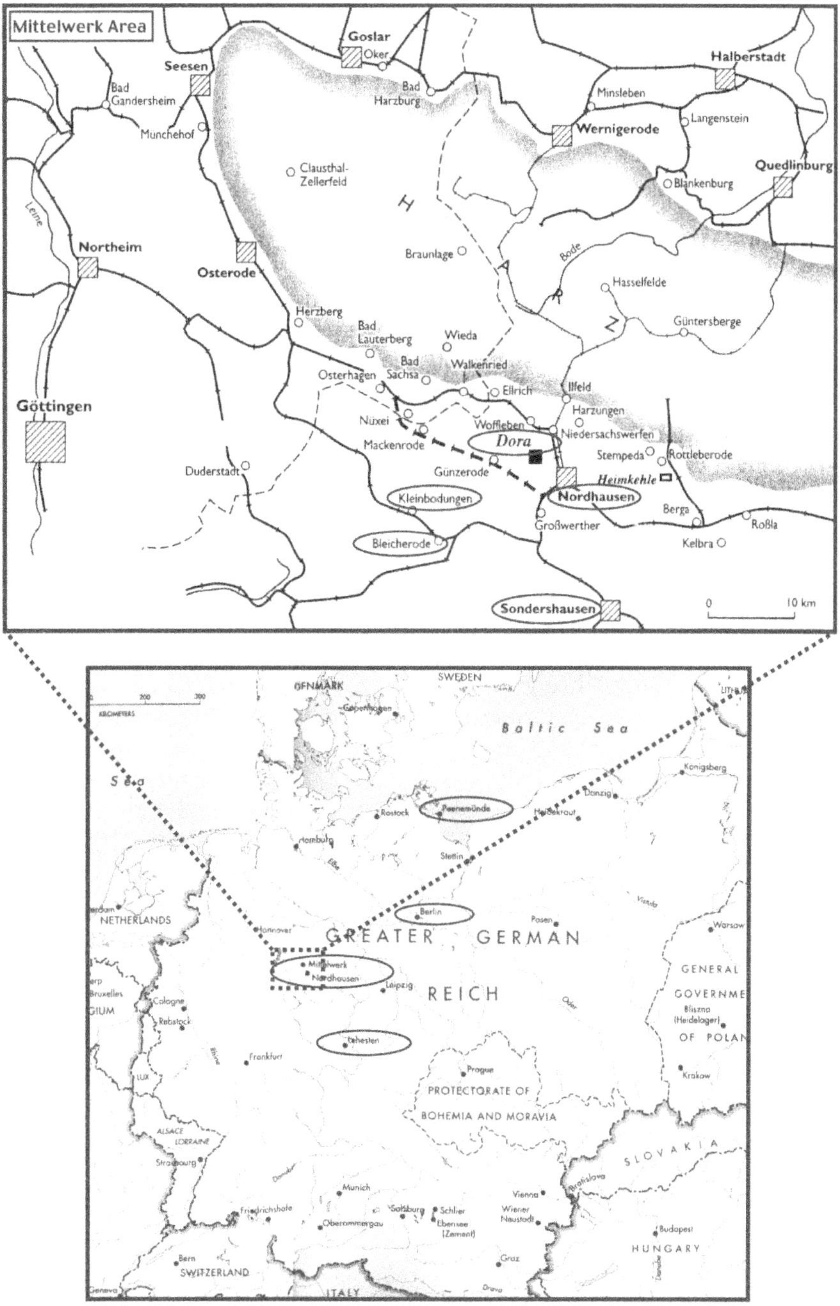

FIGURE 18. Key locations of the Soviet rocketry recovery efforts, in Germany, 1945–1946.

approximately 60,000 prisoners who passed through Dora, more than one-third perished from mass executions, starvation, torture, and overwork. In early 1944, as many as twenty to twenty-five laborers, mostly French and Polish, were dying per day. As historian Michael J. Neufeld astutely observed, "[the V-2] was a unique weapon: More people died producing it than died being hit by it."[31]

The first American battalions had arrived in the Nordhausen area in mid-April 1945, appalled by the conditions of the 14,000 prisoners remaining, most of whom were Soviet citizens. The Americans acted quickly to collect German technological know-how, and the U.S. Army's Ordnance Department had a technical team collect the booty from the factory. Because the Yalta Conference negotiations had stipulated that the entire area of Thuringia would be turned over to the Soviets by June 1, the Americans were in a hurry.[32] In late May, under a young Major William Bromley's authority, the Americans hired newly freed slave laborers who, aided by American soldiers and German civilians, packed 400 tons of equipment (including parts for 100 V-2s) in one week. These were quickly moved to Antwerp and then eventually to White Sands, New Mexico. The total American take included not only equipment, but also all of the technical documentation from both Peenemünde and Nordhausen and, under the top-secret Project Overcast, more than 100 of the best German scientists and engineers who had developed the V-2 missile. The transfer of the German Peenemünde team was carried out under another code name, Paperclip, which was an effort to bring German scientists and engineers to the United States and at the same time deny their expertise to any other country, including the other Allies. The group included Wernher von Braun, the Nazi engineer who served as technical director of the V-2 program at Peenemünde and participated in work at *Mittelwerk*, and who later headed the Saturn rocket project that helped put American astronauts on the Moon.[33] The last Americans left

31 Michael J. Neufeld, *The Rocket and the Reich: Peenemünde and the Coming of the Ballistic Missile Era* (Cambridge, MA: Harvard University Press, 1995), 211, 264. Foreign forced laborers ran *Nordwerk*, whereas labor at *Mittelwerk* was split half and half between concentration camp prisoners and German civilians. The Germans (about 10,000) were employed by industrial contractors such as AEG, Siemens, Rheinmetall-Borsig, Dinamit-AG, Krupp, and Telefunken. For Dora, see Yves Béon, *Planet Dora: A Memoir of the Holocaust and the Birth of the Space Age* (Boulder, CO: Westview Press, 1997).

32 Because of delays, the Allies agreed to postpone the date, at first to June 21 and then to late June 1945.

33 Clarence G. Lasby, *Project Paperclip: German Scientists and the Cold War* (New York: Atheneum, 1971); Tom Bower, *The Paperclip Conspiracy: The Hunt for the Nazi Scientists* (Boston: Little, Brown, 1987); John Gimbel, "Project Paperclip: German Scientists, American Policy, and the Cold War," *Diplomatic History* 14 no. 3 (1990): 343–366. For Project Overcast, see Gimbel, *Science, Technology, and Reparations*, 37–42.

the Thuringia region on July 1 with their booty, only hours before Soviet reconnaissance units reached the scene.[34]

ARRIVING AT *MITTELWERK*

Like the first forays into Peenemünde, the initial Soviet investigation teams at Nordhausen arrived under the delegated authority of Commissar Shakhurin. His deputy V. P. Kuznetsov oversaw the evaluation, aided by a number of teams, including the Abramovich/Isaev group from NII-1, which had performed in the same capacity at Peenemünde. A member later recalled that "[t]he sight of the camp, the remaining prisoners who were all skin and bones, and especially the furnaces for exterminating them, left us with a feeling of horror."[35] Another wrote that "I must honestly confess that we hurried to leave the [Dora] camp not because we had . . . run out of time [but because of the] horrors."[36] The group investigated not only the giant factory complex around Nordhausen but also the engine test stands near the village of Lehesten (130 kilometers southeast of *Mittelwerk*) and the Bleicherode area between July 1 and July 25, 1945. At Nordhausen, Kuznetsov's team found an impressive array of equipment related to both the V-2 and the V-1 missiles and also production lathes for the new BMW 003 jet engine and the *Taifun* surface-to-air missile. Although there were no functioning V-2 missiles, they found rockets in various states of disassembly, inspiring hope that whole missiles could be put together.[37]

At Nordhausen, many former Dora prisoners helped the Soviet teams. The Soviets converted the prison into a camp that housed about 6,000 former prisoners, most of whom were of Soviet origin. Initially, at least, the Soviet technical teams and the former prisoners helped each other. The teams provided employment while the prisoners helped engineers and military officers in their search for German equipment. One Russian ex-prisoner, who introduced himself as Shmargun and who had survived the horrors of Dora, led a team to a remote wooden hut where in a dark corner he unveiled a large spherical object, a gyrostabilized platform for missile guidance. Some Germans left behind by the Peenemünde team, typically low-ranking

[34] The U.S. side completed its withdrawal from Thuringia and Saxonia in accordance with the Yalta agreements by July 3–4, 1945. RGASPI, 17/121/395/28–31 (July 9, 1945). A reconnaissance team from the 47th Guard Army of the Soviet occupation forces arrived first at Nordhausen. TsAMO, 345/5487/335/198–201 (June 29, 1945).

[35] Memoir of Pallo in *DVK2*, 44.

[36] Chertok, *RAP1*, 279.

[37] By late July 1945, the Soviets had only two models of the V-2 in their possession, a very damaged crashed vehicle that was deposited at NII-1 in Moscow and a second one found by the Abramovich team at Peenemünde, handed over to the artillery team under Major-General A. I. Sokolov. RGAE, 8044/1/1318/235 (July 1945).

mechanics, led the Soviets through the labyrinths of *Mittelwerk* and explained its operation.

Soon after his arrival, Abramovich sent Isaev, accompanied by a few engineers, to Lehesten, the site of two giant stands (where the Germans test-fired rocket engine combustions chambers) and a liquid-oxygen production plant. The Germans erected the stands on a steep slope of a black slate quarry whose extracts the local population used to cover their roofs. In Lehesten, the Soviets found unprecedented riches: over fifty new rocket engine combustion chambers, fifteen railroad cars containing V-2 engines, flatcars with ground equipment, carriages for transporting missiles, and tanks for transporting liquid oxygen. The team also tracked down key Germans who had worked at the facility, which remained in remarkably good shape. Abramovich was so impressed by what his men found at Lehesten that in his summary report to Commissar Shakhurin, he confidently argued that, given sufficient resources, Soviet engineers could have at least five of the giant V-2 rocket engines ready for testing by early August, that is, within a week.[38]

THE ARTILLERISTS ARRIVE

The conflicting nature of the missions into Germany in the summer of 1945 underlined starkly the confusion about missiles, in particular the tensions between reactive propulsion (an aeronautics view) and projectiles (an artillery view). If aviation teams such as those under Petrov, Abramovich, and Isaev were the first to make useful evaluations of German rocketry, they worked in parallel – sometimes together, sometimes independently, and often in opposition – to artillery officers who fanned out across Soviet-occupied Germany. At both Peenemünde and Nordhausen, artillerymen had preceded the aeronautical engineers, accompanied by their own "experts" and under separate and frequently contradictory orders from various governmental branches. For example, one artillery team arrived at Peenemünde on May 5, 1945, simultaneously with Petrov's aeronautical team.[39] Headed by Artillery Major-General Andrei Sokolov, it consisted of engineers from different specialties. The artillery teams focused on *Katiusha*-type rockets; Sokolov, in fact, headed the team partly because he was involved in *Katiusha* development and procurement for the Red Army.[40] One of

[38] RGAE, 8044/1/1318/23–28 (July 25, 1945). A second group of NII-1 engineers (after the Isaev group), including L. S. Dushkin, A. A. Gukhman, G. F. Knorre, and N. G. Chernyshev, joined the Abramovich team in late July 1945.

[39] U.S. intelligence believed that the Soviets arrived on May 10. CIA, *A Summary of Soviet Guided Missile Intelligence*, US/UK GM 4–52, July 20, 1953, A8, NASA History Division, Historical Reference Collection.

[40] For a participant view of the work of this commission, see Tiulin, "Semerka." At the time, Major-General A. I. Sokolov was the Chief of the Main Directorate of Armaments of the Guards Mortar Units (GMCh). Other commission members included Lieutenant-Colonel

Sokolov's principal aides was Major-General Lev Gaidukov, the most vociferous supporter of long-range reactive projectiles in the Red Army who, even before the discovery of German rockets, had consistently lobbied for the development of such weapons. Gaidukov, called by many a "desk general" more comfortable in a managerial setting than on the battle front, had tabled a proposal in early 1944 to develop a long-range ballistic missile using the reaction propulsion expertise of the (then) newly formed NII-1. He proposed setting up a design bureau in the Commissariat of Munitions to manage the program. In effect, he suggested merging the two technological trends of aviation and artillery. Malenkov had rejected this proposal.[41]

Sokolov's second aide, Major-General Aleksandr Tveretskii, a battle-tested war veteran, ensured that artillery officers were indispensable to any effort to track down German rockets. Tveretskii was odd choice for such an important position, having once shot his driver at the war front in a paroxysm of anger, for which he had been excluded from the Communist Party. Because these troops were better equipped to travel freely and more safely than their civilian counterparts searching for the same prize, they were often on the scene before engineers. If they found a particular German factory or research facility, Tveretskii's troops would immediately inform the special commissions of the first Belorussian front. The Belorussian front would pay the favor back by providing Tveretskii's troops with key intelligence about where other rocket materials might have been hidden by the Germans before they fled.[42] In this way, within a few months, Guards Mortar Units artillery officers were situated firmly in the organizational matrix of the search for German rockets. Without them, the aeronautical teams would have been paralyzed.

Back in Moscow another constituency tried to react rapidly to the incoming information and put its stamp on the long-range missile. When formed in February 1945, Malenkov's Special Committee had divvied up sectors of German industry to various commissariats on the basis of their domestic profile. The Commissariat of the Aviation Industry (NKAP) naturally focused on aviation, whereas the Commissariat of Munitions (NKB), responsible at home for various artillery systems, got the job of looking for similar German

G. A. Tiulin (the senior aide to the chief of the scientific-technical department of Sokolov's directorate), V. P. Barmin, E. Ia. Boguslavskii, M. S. Riazanskii, and Iu. A. Pobedonostsev. Another participant engineer of the artillery search team, V. S. Budnik, points to May 24, 1945 as the arrival date at Peenemünde. According to him, the team included L. M. Gaidukov, A. I. Semenov, A. G. Mrykin, Iu. A. Pobedonostsev, V. S. Budnik, Shapiro, Timofeev, Vol'fovich, and others. S. Dverkov, "Rakety tret'ego reikha," *Rabochaia tribuna*, July 4, 1991.

41 RGAE, 8044/1/1182/1–2 (March 13, 1944).

42 G. V. Diadin, D. N. Filippovykh and V. I. Ivkin, *Pamiatnye starty* (Moscow: TsIPK, 2001), 44–45.

weapons. During the war, NKB head Boris Vannikov successfully supervised the development of ground and naval artillery munitions, mortars, aviation bombs, chemical substances for artillery weapons, infantry weapons, and, of course, *Katiusha*-type reactive projectiles.[43] Like many of his peers who ran other commissariats, Vannikov belonged to a generation of industrial managers who cut their teeth in the trenches of the defense industry by building up Soviet armaments to fight the Nazis. David Holloway described them as men who "worked under intense pressure and passed this pressure on to their subordinates. They did not enjoy political or personal security."[44] Like many of his colleagues, Vannikov had spent time in prison, in his case because of a disagreement with Stalin over weapons production at the beginning of the war.[45]

Vannikov showed initiative by making sure that his commissariat was at the center of any program to study long-range reactive projectiles such as the German V-2. In April, long before any Soviet team had set foot in a German aviation or rocket facility, he established an organization in Moscow, the State Central Design Bureau No. 1 (GTsKB-1), to "modernize existing and develop new designs of reactive projectiles."[46] With security police chief Lavrentii Beriia's help, the GOKO issued a decree on May 31 listing the GTsKB-1 design bureau as the final destination of all captured equipment from Peenemünde; the commissariat's old Crimean firing range would also temporarily receive similar materials. In effect, this decision made GTsKB-1 the de facto nerve center for long-range rockets in the Soviet Union.[47]

Through June, Vannikov also had his experts look for an appropriate place inside the USSR from which to test-fire V-2 missiles. On the basis of several criteria (e.g., sparse population, climate, a firing trace line of up to 200 kilometers, closeness to rail transportation), Vannikov proposed a site near the town of Makhach-Kala on the northwest coast of the Caspian Sea in the "autonomous" republic of Dagestan. By late June, his deputies had left on a mission to scout out the area.[48] Vannikov was able to move quickly on the matter partly because of the support of the Guards Mortar Units; General Gaidukov, who, on behalf of the units, had become the de facto coordinator of all information on reactive projectile factories in Germany, provided key information and support to Vannikov.

43 Simonov, *VPK*, 166–167.

44 David Holloway, *Stalin and the Bomb: The Soviet Union and Atomic Energy: 1939–1956* (New Haven: Yale University Press, 1994), 136.

45 M. F. Rebrov, "Chelovek iz epitsentr," *Krasnaia zvezda*, August 29, 1997.

46 RGASPI, 644/1/402/102 (April 19, 1945). The NKB order on the design bureau's creation was issued on April 27, 1945. RGAE, 7516/1/1636/36–39.

47 RGAE, 7516/1/1256/187 (June 11, 1945).

48 RGAE, 7516/1/1221/52 (June 6, 1945). The eventual site, finalized by June 22, was near the former Factory No. 182 belonging to the Commissariat of the Shipbuilding Industry in southern Makhach-Kala.

DEFINITION AND ALLOCATION

By mid-July 1945, the various Soviet constituencies operating in Germany recognized that their respective goals often contradicted each other's objectives. Some confusion stemmed from unclear definitions and undetermined allocations. The principal fissure lay between two groups, the aviation engineers and artillery officers, who cultivated a symbiotic relationship even though they had conflicting interests. The aviation engineers were interested in all forms of reactive propulsion, including jets and rockets, whereas the artillery officers were interested in artillery, that is, everything from guns to the giant V-2 rocket. Back in Moscow, two commissars, Shakhurin and Vannikov, were getting information from different sources, the former from his aviation engineers and the latter from artillery officers. Without clear definitions, reactive technology produced overlaps in claims that required resolution.

After the final evaluations of the various field commissions in Germany had come into Moscow, on July 20, the government formed an interagency Commission on Reactive Technology representing the major industrial players interested in this technology. Headed by Aviation Commissar Shakhurin, it included the seven top Soviet commissars and their deputies, representing the Commissariats of Aviation, Ammunition, Armaments, Electronics, Chemical Industry, Shipbuilding, and Mortars, as well as two military officers, one each from the artillery and air forces.[49] Its mandate was to determine the future of reactive technology in the Soviet Union, that is, to allocate tasks optimally to different branches of Soviet industry, to provide a recommendation on what to do in Germany, and ultimately to formulate the direction of future work on reactive technology in the Soviet Union given the vast German experience in the field.

Members of the Shakhurin Commission, especially Shakhurin and Vannikov, exchanged several letters in late July on how best to organize work. Both agreed that Vannikov should take over the development of wingless "reactive munitions" such as the V-2 because his commissariat had the most experience with artillery weapons. Vannikov tabled a plan that classified his projectiles into three categories ("mid-range" of 20 to 30 kilometers, "long-range" of 30 to 100 kilometers, and "super long-range" of more than 100 kilometers), each being assigned to a new "state central design bureau." The latter category would include the German V-2. All these design bureaus, as well as a "state central institute [firing] range"

[49] The members were A. P. Shakhurin (NKAP), P. V. Dement'ev (NKAP), N. N. Voronov (NKO), N. D. Iakovlev (NKO), L. M. Gaidukov (NKO), P. N. Goremykin (NKB), D. F. Ustinov (NKV), G. G. Kabanov (NKEP), I. G. Zubovich (NKEP), M. G. Pervukhin (NKKhP), I. I. Nosenko (NKSP), V. P. Terent'ev (NKSP), P. I. Parshin (NKMV), [initials unknown] Sloev (NKMV), A. K. Repin (VVS), and A. I. Berg (Council of Radar).

near the Caspian Sea, would be subordinate to Vannikov's Commissariat of Munitions.[50]

The discussions in late July were important for a marked change in the Soviet approach to the development of weapons systems. The "normal" process of Soviet weapons development, both in artillery and aviation, was very insular. That is, commissariats usually minimized relations with other commissariats and relied as much as possible on internal subcontractors. With machines such as the V-1, V-2, and jet planes that were far more complex than what Soviet industry had ever developed, such an approach would be unworkable. Although powerful commissars such as Shakhurin and Vannikov continued to view the ballistic missile as simply a bigger projectile shot out of a cannon, they also realized that the constituent parts of a missile system (guidance systems, electronics, launch platforms, liquid-propellant production, radio systems, and fuel tank manufacture) put them at an entirely different level of industrial expertise than what was required for making cannon shells. To his colleagues, Vannikov repeatedly argued that "a ministry alone cannot handle this problem," adding that what was needed was a network approach to innovation. Commission members – particularly Gaidukov – also came to recognize that the most difficult problem of developing long-range missiles would be the guidance system; according to Gaidukov, the V-2's guidance system still "remain[ed] a mystery."[51]

The Shakhurin Commission met on July 25, 1945 to deliberate on the problem of allocation. For the first time, members raised the question of mass producing the German V-2 rather than just studying and collecting information on these weapons. Such an approach was not an anomaly, especially during 1945. In the summer, Stalin had ordered reverse engineering of several foreign systems, including most famously the atomic bomb (based on intelligence on the Manhattan Project) and the American B-29 bomber (three of which landed on Soviet territory during the war).[52] At the meeting, Lieutenant-General Nikolai Iakovlev, the Commander-in-Chief of the Red Army's Main Artillery Directorate, proposed creating a special extraordinary institution, at a *higher* level than the commissariat and linked directly to Stalin, to coordinate work on reactive technology. Other attendees, however, did not consider the project to be necessary. Because neither Stalin nor Beriia had paid much attention to rockets, the attendees believed such extraordinary measures unnecessary. The meeting transcript suggests that the most important issue at hand was developing a network approach

[50] RGAE, 8044/1/1318/149–52 (July 23, 1945). Vannikov suggested the following locations for the design bureaus: GTsKB No. 1 (branch of Factory No. 568), No. 2 (at Factory No. 67), and No. 3 (at Factory No. 70).

[51] RGAE, 7516/1/1259/275–76 (June 26, 1945).

[52] Holloway, *Stalin and the Bomb*; Von Hardesty, "Made in the U.S.S.R.," *Air & Space* February/March (2001): 68–79.

to R&D. Each commissar, representing a different branch of industry, articulated his position on the responsibility of his respective branch. General Iakovlev cautioned that "at the present time there is no proper connection between [various branches] in the work on reactive technology."[53]

Based on their discussions, the commission members produced a report, "Materials to the Report on the Commission for the Study and Mastery of German Reactive Technology," which listed eighteen separate German reactive technology projects under scrutiny.[54] Using the report as a foundation, the commission put together two charts to serve as guidelines for future work, "Classification of Reactive Technology" and "Layout for the Organization of Work... on German Reactive Technology." Both detailed a complex web of subdivisions and classifications that reflected, in some sense, an important juncture in the decades-long struggle among engineers, managers, and defense industrialists in the Soviet Union to embrace the problem of reaction propulsion and projectiles. The discovery of such a wide array of German weapons forced a resolution to the problem of classifying such "hybrid" forms as the V-2 long-range ballistic missile, which reminded investigators of both artillery (as a projectile) and aviation (because it used reactive motion).[55]

A GOKO draft decree drawn up at the time, entitled "On Measures to Study and Master German Reactive Technology," directed the Soviet defense industry to undertake a broad R&D program to scrutinize and, in some cases, reproduce German reactive weapons. It tasked the Commissariat of Munitions with the "study and mastery" of everything resembling artillery, that is, reactive projectiles including the V-2 and the engines for them. In the same breath, the Commissariat of the Aviation Industry was assigned to study all things airplane related: German jet and rocket-planes, jet engines, liquid-propellant rocket engines for aircraft, and winged missiles such as the V-1. Some Soviet designers were explicitly ordered to copy German technology, as in the case of the Jumo 004 and BMW 003 jet engines. Various contractor commissariats were listed for subsystems for the missiles, including the Commissariat of the Electrical Industry and Commissariat of Armaments for guidance systems.[56] Although the drafters broke the traditional Soviet rule of R&D focused in single commissariats, their vision of a relatively small network of developers suggests that they underestimated the difficulty of developing constituent systems of guided missiles, a reflection of their continued equation of such weapons with artillery shells.

53 RGAE, 8044/1/1318/29–34 (July 25, 1945).

54 RGAE, 4372/94/1146/41a-29 (August 4, 1945). The document was formally issued the following day. For a nearly identical draft, see RGAE, 8044/1/1318/2–13 (late July 1945).

55 RGAE, 8044/1/1318/21 (July 1945); RGAE, 8044/1/1318/22 (July 1945).

56 RGAE, 4372/94/1146/28–22 (August 1945). The same can also be found in RGAE, 8044/1/1318/14–20.

Having apparently resolved the issue of definition and allocation, the next question was what to do with the various teams scouring Germany and the vast matériel they had collected. In late June, Gaidukov proposed to Malenkov the creation of an interbranch commission to "organize and head in the future, all the work . . . in German territory and on what we have collected, [and to] summarize and study models and materials on German reactive projectiles with subsequent reporting to the government." He suggested that a coordinating commission with representatives from all the commissariats would go a long way to streamline work.[57] In early August 1945, Stalin signed into law a decree forming such a body, the Special Technical Commission (*Spetsial'naia tekhnicheskaia komissiia*) headed by Gaidukov.[58] In essence, the decree gave Gaidukov, a ranking official in the Party's Central Committee, authority to take control of the entire network of rocketry operations in Germany.

Through the entire summer of 1945, the Soviets had been in a hurry to disassemble, pack, and transport to Russia as much material as possible, especially from areas that were to be turned over to the Americans. Once borders stabilized, the inertia of the original effort kept operations running at a fast pace; Gaidukov pushed for a total disassembly of the factories around Nordhausen, which, based on incoming reports, appeared to be the most valuable sites for reactive technology.[59] On August 3, the GOKO formally called for the packing and transport of all remaining equipment at the factories at Nordhausen to the appropriate factories of the NKAP (for reactive aviation) and the NKB (for reactive projectiles).[60] Within days, the second battalion of the sixth front trophy brigade, one of forty-eight trophy brigades operating in Germany, Poland, and Czechoslovakia, began dismantling and packing equipment at *Mittelwerk*.

Between May and August 1945, then, the Soviets had very capably spread out through Soviet-occupied Germany, evaluated the state of German reactive armaments, and begun the intensive process of sending what was valuable to the Soviet Union. Qualified experts, both military and civilian, had gleaned an enormous amount of information about German achievements in reactive technology despite the lack of technical documentation. By the

57 RGAE, 7516/1/1259/275–76 (June 26, 1945).

58 APRF, 3/47/179/29 (April 17, 1946). The new commission was an expanded version of a smaller commission formed by GOKO decree no. 9475ss issued on July 8, 1945 that included L. M. Gaidukov (GAU), P. N. Goremykin (NKB), Ia. L. Bibikov (NKAP), I. G. Zubovich (NKEP), and G. A. Uger (Council on Radar). RGAE, 4372/94/314/34.

59 Shakhurin's deputy commissar V. P. Kuznetsov reported in mid-July 1945 that *Mittelwerk* contained 1,900 metal-cutting lathes, seventy presses, thirty-nine pieces of mounting devices, eight electric welding machines, eighty other pieces of equipment, and seventy-five V-2 engines in various states of preparedness. He also noted that all technical documentation was gone from the factory, apparently taken by the Americans. RGAE, 8044/1/6313/1–2 (July 18, 1945); RGAE, 8044/1/6313/120 (July 31, 1945).

60 GOKO decree no. 9716 issued on August 3, 1945. RGAE, 8044/1/6313/156; RGASPI, 644/1/423/147.

end of August 1945, the official military printing press had issued a secret seventy-page monograph on the V-2, detailing every major system of the missile, its capabilities, and operational procedures.[61] The Soviet government had also authorized a body, the Special Technical Commission, under the direction of Gaidukov to coordinate and supervise all operations in Germany related to reactive technology. Finally, the commissars, principally Aleksei Shakhurin and Boris Vannikov, had resolved conflicts over allocation and definition of the long-range missile that had hobbled previous Soviet efforts to develop such weapons. They also laid the foundation of a network approach to developing reactive projectiles. Yet, Stalin never signed the August 1945 decree into law.

NOT A STATE PRIORITY

Three factors explain the inaction. Stalin's noticeable disinterest in the problem of German long-range missiles, at least in the immediate aftermath of the war, was the most important reason. Unlike advocates of nuclear, aviation, and jet technology, the backers of long-range rocketry were unable to meet with Stalin even once in 1945 to argue their case.[62] Although Stalin signed many decrees on deporting German reactive equipment back to the Soviet Union, he never approved a long-range plan of action on the issue. It is noteworthy that all of Shakhurin, Vannikov, and Gaidukov's appeals for organizing industrial development of rocketry were routed to Beriia, not to Stalin. Additionally, although anecdotal stories abound about Stalin's interest in atom bombs and jet planes, they are noticeably absent on the issue of rockets. Secondary literature describes one meeting between Gaidukov and Stalin in 1945 when the Soviet leader apparently entrusted the artillery colonel with picking a commissar – Vannikov, Shakhurin, or Ustinov – to oversee the missile project, but the evidence for this meeting is only anecdotal.[63] The mood among mid-level aviation engineers in 1945 reflected top-level indifference to missiles. When an engineer from the NII-1 aviation institute interrupted his search for rockets in Germany for a short visit to Moscow, his boss told him, "[n]obody needs the V2. We need jet aviation, and as fast as possible."[64]

[61] A. A. Vekser, *Raketa dal'nego deistviia Fau-2 (po trofeinym materialam)* [The Fau-2 Long-Range Rocket (Based on Trophy Materials)] (Moscow: Gosizoboronprom/NKAP, 1945). The monograph is stored in RGAE, 4372/94/314/90–57.

[62] The records of visitors to Stalin's office in 1945 do not indicate any personal meetings with Vannikov or Gaidukov in 1945, the two men most likely to lobby on behalf of long-range missiles. A. V. Korotkov, A. D. Chernev, and A. A. Chernobaev, "Alfavitnyi ukazatel' posetitelei kremlevskogo kabineta I. V. Stalina," *Istoricheskii arkhiv* no. 4 (1996): 40, 50.

[63] Gaidukov never met with Stalin in 1945. Korotkov, Chernev, and Chernobaev, "Alfavitnyi ukazatel'," 50. For accounts of this alleged meeting, see Chertok, *RAP1*, 12–13; Iaroslav Golovanov, *Korolev: Fakty i mify* (Moscow: Nauka, 1994), 361–362.

[64] Chertok, *RAP1*, 273.

Second, only days after the preparation of the decree assigning Vannikov responsibility for the long-range missile program, on August 6 and 9, 1945, the United States dropped atomic bombs on Hiroshima and Nagasaki. Almost overnight, the dynamic of power shifted irrevocably between the Soviet Union and the United States. Less than two weeks later, on August 20, 1945, Stalin signed a secret decree of the State Committee of Defense putting earlier Soviet work to develop atomic weapons at the highest national footing. For Vannikov's future career, the decision had profound consequences. Stalin and Beriia included him as a member of the top-secret "Special Committee" of the atomic bomb. They also assigned Vannikov to head a management body attached to the Special Committee that would control all "scientific research, development, and design organizations and industrial enterprises for the use of atomic energy . . . and the production of atomic bombs." Simultaneously, Vannikov was to be "discharged from his duties as People's Commissar of Munitions."[65] Although the latter stipulation of the edict was not carried out to the letter – Vannikov remained Commissar of Munitions for nearly another year – the sudden change of priorities impeded action on the draft decree on the rocket industry. Vannikov postponed further action on the issue of rockets until he could devote full attention to the matter.

Third, the widespread Soviet drive to demilitarize the economy slowed military R&D to a crawl, causing many problems, especially in those areas that were not considered of strategic importance. With the end of the war, Vannikov's commissariat was especially hard hit and had trouble adjusting to civilian conditions. Beginning May 1945, at about the time that teams were finding German missiles, the NKB began conversion activities aimed at moving significant resources from military to civilian production. As with other branches of the defense industry, Vannikov's genuine attempts to demilitarize created tensions for plant managers who remained unsure of how to restructure factories for "mixed production." Issues such as new machine procurement, "mixed" worker training, time management, priority allocation, and differential wages bogged plant managers down in a morass. Vannikov tried to embrace civilian production; in January 1946, several agricultural factories from other commissariats were attached to NKB, which now became the Commissariat (and soon the Ministry) of Agricultural Machine Building so as to indicate its mostly civilian profile. Through the first half of 1946, however, the ministry was unable to handle the transition as a result of gross mismanagement.[66]

[65] Holloway, *Stalin and the Bomb*, 129. The GOKO decree no. 9887ss/op, issued on August 20, 1945, is stored in RGASPI, 644/1/458/27–30.

[66] For demilitarization, see V. S. Lel'chuk, ed., *Poslevoennaia konversiia: k istorii 'kholodnoi voiny': sbornik dokumentov* (Moscow: IRI RAN, 1998).

In this context, Vannikov's only existing missile center, the GTsKB-1 design bureau, did not complete any fruitful work by the end of 1945 because of the lack of manpower and delays in both construction and deliveries.[67] By February 1946, over 700 railway cars of matériel from *Mittelwerk*, including parts for V-2, Rheintochter, Henschel Hs 293A and Hs 294, and Fritz X weapons, were on their way to NKB's Vladimir Il'ich Factory, which was to take over V-2 development, but the factory's design bureau was paralyzed because it effectively had no staff. By early May, only twenty-nine people worked there.[68] For the first quarter of 1946, the missile project, in effect, had no institutional foundation beyond the scattered outposts in Germany staffed by increasingly restless engineers who had little idea of the indecision prevailing in Moscow.

LOCAL NETWORKS

In late 1945, the top-level Soviet political leaders, especially those influencing defense policy such as Stalin, Beriia, Malenkov, and Voznesenskii, considered the long-range ballistic missile a low priority. In dealing with the security of the Soviet Union, they focused attention on joining the nuclear club by copying two recent American contributions to strategic warfare, the atomic bomb and its delivery system, the B-29 bomber. For understandable reasons – including cost, poor accuracy, and the dismal German wartime record – they believed the liquid-propellant, long-range missile an uncertain prospect at best. The two ineffectual attempts by Soviet industrialists to win support for missile development (in August and November 1945) exemplified the Soviet government's approach to long-range missiles: moderate interest on the part of industrial leaders (such as Vannikov and Shakhurin) followed by inaction from the top leadership (Stalin and Beriia).[69]

Meanwhile in Germany, in the eight months since the abandoned August 1945 decree on rocket technology, Soviet teams on the ground significantly

[67] Direct work on the design bureau's twenty-three thematic projects began only in July 1945, one month after the arrival of the first missile documentation from Germany. According to the organization's own accounting, by the end of the year, it finished 47% of its assigned work, which included fifteen design projects. RGAE, 7516/1/1636/36–37 (January 1946); RGAE, 7516/1/1256/136 (June 12, 1945). In 1945, GTsKB-1 focused on studying, reproducing, and testing German solid-propellant missiles, including the Rheinbote. RGAE, 4372/94/314/119–18 (1946).

[68] RGAE, 8495/1/1218/155–56.

[69] In November 1945, Vannikov and some associates, including artillery marshal Nikolai Iakovlev and *Gosplan* chairman Petr Kirpichnikov, once again sent a plan for postwar missile development to Beriia for approval. This time, they proposed that missile development be centered at a new institute, GSNII-70, headed by Valentin Glushko with Sergei Korolev as his deputy. Stalin never approved the proposal. For the cover letter, see RGAE, 4372/94/314/39–38 (November 22, 1945). For the decree draft, see RGAE, 4372/94/314/37–33 (November 1945).

altered the landscape of operations in Germany. Using his authority as chairman of the Special Technical Commission, Artillery General Gaidukov provided support to the men and women in the field but also permitted significant local initiative.[70] All over Soviet-occupied Germany, low-level aviation engineers and artillerymen, the two constituencies who had independently gone to Germany to search for missiles, fully integrated themselves into one large-scale framework that, by spring 1946, had moved from simply collecting information and materials about German rockets to establishing a vast and highly efficient scientific and technological network.

New Arrivals

Gaidukov played a critical role in reinforcing the intellectual strength of field teams by summoning a host engineers from the Soviet Union to occupied Germany, where they were assigned to various locations. Initially, Soviet authorities issued them two-month passes for field work in Germany, but most, helped by Gaidukov's intercessions, stayed for eight- to eleven-month stints. The first major intake arrived on August 9, 1945. The day before, the local party office in Moscow had summoned about a dozen employees from the NII-1 aeronautics institute, where they were told one by one that they would leave for Berlin immediately as members of a commission. Party officials told the engineers nothing about their mission but bestowed all with military ranks and uniforms effective immediately "to invest them with greater authority in the eyes of Germans and Red Army men who would be carrying out dismantling under their direction."[71] The next day, as they were driving to the airport, they heard on the radio that the Americans had dropped an atomic bomb on Hiroshima. Viktor Kuznetsov, one of those recruited for the trip to Berlin, remembers thinking, "Do we have this?"[72] All the men boarded a rickety Soviet Li-2 aircraft that took them directly to Berlin, from where, on Gaidukov's orders, they were told their missions and assigned to three groups to be based in Berlin, Nordhausen, and Prague.[73]

[70] For a brief period, between August and October 1945, Artillery Major-General N. N. Kuznetsov officially headed field operations of the Special Technical Commission in Germany. According to participant recollections, his role was minimal. At the time, Kuznetsov officially served as head of the Guards Mortar Units' Main Directorate of Armaments, i.e., as head of *Katiusha* development and procurement in the Red Army. Memoir of V. I. Chepa in *DVK2*, 76; Memoir of N. N. Iuryshev in *DVK2*, 115–116.

[71] V. L. Sokolov, *Soviet Use of German Science and Technology, 1945–1946*, Research Program on the U.S.S.R., Mimeographed Series No. 72, New York City, 1955, 2.

[72] M. Rebrov, "Sem' likov sud'by," *Krasnaia zvezda*, January 7, 1989.

[73] Passengers on August 9 included E. Ia. Boguslavskii, Florin, Goriunov, V. I. Kuznetsov, G. A. List, V. P. Mishin, N. A. Piliugin, M. S. Riazanskii, V. A. Rudnitskii, S. K. Tumanskii, and L. A. Voskresenskii. Most of these men moved up to high positions in the Soviet space program in the 1960s. V. P. Mishin, *Ot sozdaniia ballisticheskikh raket k raketno-kosmicheskomu mashinostroyeniiu* (Moscow: Informatsionno-izdatel'skii tsentr 'Inform-Znanie,' 1998), 16. For a list of the Soviet engineers in Germany in 1945–1946, see RGAE, 397/1/3/112–20.

Having heard that Czech insurgent forces near Prague might have captured a priceless set of V-2 technical drawings, the commission sent a team headed by young aviation designer Vasilii Mishin to search for the prize. In Prague, they heard that a Czech military unit had piled some documents in an old restaurant. Because Czech city authorities refused to help them access the booty, Mishin and his associates devised an elaborate plan that involved team member Aleksandr Berezniak's sister Marina, whom they had coincidentally found in a Prague POW camp. With the help of Marina – who infiltrated into the storehouse – they verified that the documents were indeed from the Peenemünde team. Eventually, with the help of Soviet soldiers, Mishin and his team carted off all the documents in a wagon pulled behind their car and drove all the way back to Berlin. They took with them several crates of Pilzen beer and a Tatra limousine as gifts for Stalin from the Czech army's General Staff.[74] The drawings – an incomplete set describing the V-2 – laid the foundation of a "theoretical-computation bureau" in Bleicherode where Mishin subsequently researched problems of missile ballistic trajectories, particularly systems to monitor and measure them from the ground.

Institute Rabe

In a striking example of local initiative, a few Soviet aviation engineers, who remained behind in Germany from the Abramovich/Isaev team, formed a local "institute" called *Rabe* at Bleicherode, a town a few kilometers southwest of Nordhausen.[75] Helped by twelve Germans, including Gunther Rosenplänter – a low-level employee from the Peenemünde rocket team – two junior Soviet engineers, Aleksei Isaev and Boris Chertok, set up headquarters at the formerly lavish Villa Frank where von Braun had once lived.[76] Instead of routing their actions to the center in Moscow, the Rabe engineers registered their institute with the regional branch of the Soviet military administration in Germany and operated under a local Soviet army commandant. In the beginning, they set out to collect material detritus and recruit German scientific personnel. They began with the gyrostabilized platform. Soon local miners led them to several sets of radio control systems for the

[74] B. Konovalov, "Iz germanii – v kapustin iar" (interview with V. P. Mishin), *Izvestiia*, April 6, 1991; V. P. Mishin, "Nekotory stranitsy istorii raketno-kosmicheskoi nauki i tekhniki v poslevoennyi period," in *IPIITR*, Vols. 8–10, eds. B. V. Raushenbakh et al. (Moscow: Nauka, 2001), 50–66. Others on the Prague mission included V. A. Bakulin, V. P. Barmin, E. Ia. Boguslavskii, and V. A. Rudnitskii.

[75] Different parties remember the origin of the word *Rabe* differently. Some claim it as an abbreviation for the German term *Raketenbau und Entwicklung Bleicherode* or "Missile Construction and Development in Bleicherode." The world *rabe* also means "raven" in German. Others claim that the name came from Frau Berta Rabe, who was the owner of a restaurant in Bleicherode frequented by Soviet military and civilian personnel. Chertok, *RAP1*, 289; Diadin, Filippovykh, and Ivkin, *Pamiatnye starty*, 69.

[76] *A Summary of Soviet Guided Missile Intelligence*, A2, A6–A7.

V-2's guidance system, hidden in a potassium mine. To communicate with the locals, they hired a language teacher and interpreter. Over a six-month period, despite the absence of any significant German documentation, the institute reconstructed a detailed layout of the V-2's guidance system. By the fall of 1946, using leftover German hardware, they produced at least thirty-five sets of the missile's autonomous guidance system and reconstructed entirely its complex telemetry system.[77]

In September, Gaidukov set up a group, similar to the Institute Rabe, who unlike their counterparts in Bleicherode who focused on the V-2, devoted their efforts to collect and study German surface-to-air missiles such as the *Wasserfall*. Because this group – later called the Institute Berlin – existed at the entry point into the German field operations, the *Wasserfall* anti-aircraft rocket assumed an important place in Soviet evaluations of German rocket technology.

Artillery Representatives

Apart from aviation engineers, artillery service representatives from the Main Artillery Directorate also settled into the local operations at Berlin and Bleicherode. These men and women – mid-level service engineers and active duty officers with experience handling the small *Katiusha* rockets – played a critical role in the work in Germany. They set up their main command in Oberschöneweide on the outskirts of Berlin. Under the command of Lieutenant-Colonel Georgii Tiulin, a postgraduate scholar in ballistics who had headed a *Katiusha* battalion during the war, the office distributed and assigned every Soviet specialist who arrived from Moscow into Berlin's airport. At "Tiulin's Enterprise," as it was called, incoming Soviet engineers were briefed on the state of field operations. Besides managerial duties, the many artillery service specialists who arrived in Germany in 1945–1946 contributed to theoretical research such as modeling aerodynamic and ballistic qualities of German missiles. Tiulin displayed expert managerial qualities. Being academically trained, scarred by battle, and a member of the *politboitsy* (political officer cadres), he also had the right qualifications for rising through the ranks. These qualities would lead him to one of the top managerial positions in the future Soviet space program. More than thirty years after his work in Berlin, he succinctly captured the network approach to the Soviet work in Germany: "We were to establish which [German] enterprises and companies cooperated in creating the missile weapon, and to recreate the system of mutual ties."[78]

Soldiers from the Guards Mortar Units, that is, the old *Katiusha* regiments, constituted the second major artillery presence in Germany. Under unit

[77] For a first-person account of the early days of Institute Rabe, see Chertok, *RAP1*, 287–298.

[78] Tiulin, "Semerka"; M. Rebrov, "Gde zhuravli letiat," *Krasnaia zvezda*, September 19, 1987.

commander General Tveretskii's leadership, these regular enlisted soldiers established the "Nordhausen Group." Like their civilian counterparts, they also organized teams to study German technology, particularly its electrical layout and the systems required to launch missiles such as the V-2. At *Werk 3* (Factory 3) at Kleinbodungen in the village of Berka six kilometers from Sondershausen, they mastered the use of the V-2's ground, transport, lifting, fueling, and power supply systems. Later, in the fall of 1946, the soldiers worked in Lehesten where the Germans had produced liquid oxygen (at the *Vorwerk-Mitte* factory) and used static-testing stands in deep pits to fire V-2 rocket engines. The soldiers conducted several rehearsal launches of the rocket by using a reconstructed V-2 installed on a firing table.[79] They were the first Soviet military units with the skills to launch liquid-propellant rockets. These former *Katiusha* regiments served as the seed of the formidable Strategic Rocket Forces that operated Soviet ICBMs throughout the Cold War.

Korolev and Glushko

Among the 284 Soviet experts who worked in Germany by late 1945, two men assumed leading roles, not by official appointment, but by force of will. Both served their apprenticeship in the nascent rocketry groups of the early 1930s, GDL and GIRD. Both had suffered deeply through the Great Terror, each spending at least six years in various prisons scattered throughout the Gulag. Although very different in temperament, both also shared one key personality trait: unfettered ambition. Valentin Glushko arrived in Germany on July 27 and eventually took over as head of operations at Lehesten, where he and a team of Soviet engine experts made use of the rich windfall of material left behind by the Germans, including fifty new combustion chambers and fifty-eight railroad cars packed with an enormous amount of engine parts. In a report to Gaidukov in November, Glushko confidently reported that he had taken control of the entire network of rocket engine production in Soviet-occupied Germany and provided his boss with a complete history of Peenemünde's work on rocket engines. He noted that, by that time, his team possessed the "basic layout, drawings... [and] notes... [and that the group] has carried out around 50 firing tests of the [combustion] chamber and engine units of the V2 [and] has the full complete drawings for the *Wasserfall*."[80] The experience provided an enormous boost to Soviet rocket engineering; Glushko's (and the Soviet Union's) most powerful engine in

[79] On these test launches, the soldiers filled the propellant tanks with water but fired the engine's turbopump with its propellants (hydrogen peroxide and sodium permanganate), thus ejecting the water from the engine nozzles. Maksimov, *Raketnye voiska*, 38; Diadin, Filippovykh, and Ivkin, *Pamiatnye starty*, 73.

[80] Glushko to Gaidukov (November 23, 1945) in *OIN*, 196–197.

1945 had a thrust of 1.5 tons, whereas the V-2 engine was rated at 25 tons. Glushko determined that by adjusting certain properties, he could potentially increase that thrust to an unprecedented 35 tons.

About six weeks after Glushko arrived in Germany, on September 8, 1945, Colonel Tiulin welcomed Sergei Korolev at Berlin's Tempelhof airport.[81] At the time, Korolev was officially employed at the same facility as Glushko back in Russia in the town of Kazan', where as Glushko's deputy, he developed rocket-assistance units for piston-engined planes. Like many engineers and technicians at Kazan', Korolev was assigned for a short term of fieldwork in Germany, but he stayed on much longer. On this, his first visit abroad, Korolev relished his new-found freedom to travel at will; using a "trophy" car, he drove from place to place – Lehesten to Nordhausen to Bleicherode to Berlin – trying to get a sense of the scale of the operation (see Figure 19). Gaidukov bestowed him with a "temporary" lieutenant colonel rank and ordered him to study launch equipment for Soviet missiles. Few in Germany had ever heard of Korolev, but within weeks, on his own initiative, Korolev moved beyond studying launch systems to take control of the somewhat chaotic network of engineering work in the field. Chertok was immediately impressed with Korolev's commanding presence wherever he went; according to Chertok, "[t]here was something about him like a boxer during a fight," a determination that compensated for his formal lack of authority.[82]

First, Korolev formed a group called *Vystrel'* (Shot) that included both civilian engineers and artillery officers for studying the entire process of preparing a V-2 rocket for launch. Second, he ensured that each of the major nodes of the network in Germany – the Institute Rabe in Bleicherode that worked on guidance systems, *Werk 3* (Factory No. 3) in Kleinbodungen where the Soviets initiated production of complete V-2 rockets, and the rocket engine group at Lehesten – had full communication with each other regarding operations. Korolev and Gaidukov established a leader at each location answerable to them, and common goals predicated on a single schedule toward which everyone worked. Korolev and Gaidukov also ensured that each location had the appropriate expertise. For example, to the new theoretical-computational bureau at Bleicherode (headed by Tiulin, who transferred from Berlin), they assigned military service engineers with academic credentials to prepare the necessary documentation for targeting, ballistics, and monitoring a flying V-2 rocket using ground-based optical systems.[83]

[81] ARAN, 1546/1/31/1 (January 12, 1947).

[82] Chertok, *RAP1*, 328.

[83] Mishin, *Ot sozdaniia ballisticheskikh raket*, 19; Memoir of Iu. A. Mozzhorin in DVK1, 136; *A Summary of Soviet Guided Missile Intelligence*, A14.

FIGURE 19. Sergei Korolev, shown here, standing on damaged parts of the V-2 rocket while visiting Peenemünde in September 1945. He relished his new-found freedom in Germany, having just left Kazan', where he had concluded a six-year long prison term in the Soviet Gulag system. [*Source*: Boris Chertok]

In Germany, Korolev and Glushko witnessed, for the first time, launches of the V-2. In October 1945, the British occupying forces in Germany invited a small Soviet delegation to observe "demonstration" launches of the V-2 from Cuxhaven near the coast of the North Sea in the British section of postwar Germany. The British Air Defense Division rounded up 1,000 German rocket specialists, including 274 POWs, to prepare and conduct the three launches. In response to an upper limit of three Soviet observers set by the British, the Soviets sent Artillery General Sokolov, involved in *Katiusha* development and procurement for the Red Army, Pobedonostsev, and Glushko. Korolev pleaded with Sokolov to take him along, even if it meant pretending to be the latter's chauffeur in front of the British. Sokolov agreed, but Korolev (and Tiulin) were forced to view the proceedings from outside the fence of the main British compound. The Russians attended the third launch on October 15.[84] The British launches, codenamed Operation Backfire, deeply affected the world view of the Soviet attendees, who, upon their return to Berlin, accelerated efforts to fire rockets from their territory.

Recruiting Germans

One major aspect of Soviet operations in 1945–1946, the recruitment of German scientific expertise, required action from both the top and the bottom. By mid-1945, the Soviets had already captured and relocated about a hundred German physicists, whom they put to work on the Soviet A-bomb project.[85] Later, in mid-July 1945, on orders from SVAG head Marshal Zhukov, the Soviets drew up a more formalized system of recruiting German scientific labor. Initially, Commissar of Aviation Shakhurin recommended that captured Germans should be held as prisoners in NKVD-controlled research organizations in Germany where they "must be isolated from [Soviet] scientific and development organizations."[86] In the end, SVAG decided to *employ* captured Germans rather than use them as slave labor, a decision based on the Soviet belief that wage labor might not only defuse any remaining hostilities but also entice undetected Germans to sign up. As a result, *Gosplan* (the national economic planning body) chief Mikhail Saburov drew up a detailed plan on the use of German scientific expertise that Zhukov signed into law on August 4, 1945. The order not only stipulated the capture of Germans, but it also called for establishing "closed" laboratories in Soviet-occupied Germany where Soviets and Germans would jointly work on a variety of scientific and technical problems.[87] The aviation industry took the lead in setting up four "special technical bureaus" in occupied Germany that employed about 1,000 Germans under Soviet supervision.[88] Most of the 3,000 German scientific workers in Soviet custody by 1945 had worked in low-level jobs during the war, but many of them had more skilled expertise.

[84] Memoir of G. A. Tiulin in *DVK1*, 156; Tiulin, "Semerka"; Jürgen Michels, *Peenemünde und seine Erben in Ost und West* (Bonn: Bernard & Graefe-Verlag, 1997), 194–201; Golovanov, *Korolev*, 344–349.

[85] Holloway, *Stalin and the Bomb*, 110–111, 178–180; Naimark, *Russians in Germany*, 207–214.

[86] RGAE, 8044/1/1267/287 (June 27, 1945).

[87] Diadin, Filippovykh, and Ivkin, *Pamiatnye starty*, 88–90. The August 4, 1945 decree was issued by SVAG and entitled "On the Organization of Work on the Use of German Technology for the USSR Industry."

[88] For detailed summaries of joint Soviet–German work on aviation in Soviet occupied Germany in 1945–1946, see RGAE, 8044/1/6335/3–12; Sobolev, *Nemetskii sled v istorii Sovetskoi aviatsii*, 62–88; Sokolov, *Soviet Use of German Science and Technology, 1945–1946*, 10–11.

For rocketry research, capturing Germans proved more difficult, and many of the disparate Soviet missions in Germany used local initiatives to find and hire them. For example, members of the Institute Rabe – Boris Chertok, Nikolai Piliugin, and Vasilii Kharchev – set up a system of recruiting Germans by using a combination of material enticements (such as alcohol) and outright coercion. In the initial months, most of the Germans who flocked to Bleicherode did so for food and housing. For Germans able to contribute to an understanding of Nazi rocket technology, the institute offered biweekly food rations and a monthly salary (1,400 marks).[89] The Soviets also developed a ranking system ranging from five cigarettes to a whole case of food to tempt Germans, especially those in Western zones who felt ignored by the Americans and the British. Conditions in Thuringia were so pitiful for most Germans that the promise of food and employment compelled many to put aside their reservations about working for the Soviets and offer their services to the local SVAG directorate.[90]

By the fall, rumors had spread throughout local areas about the generous Soviet treatment of German skilled labor, the good housing and working conditions, and perhaps most important, no requirement to undergo "de-Nazification" processes. These policies worked effectively. In the fall of 1945, the Institute Rabe recruited several accomplished German academics and industrial scientists. Although none had worked with the Peenemünde team, most had higher academic degrees and experience in Germany industry. They included Dr. Kurt Magnus, a specialist in theoretical mechanics, and Dr. Johannes Hoch, an expert in automatic control from Göttingen University. Dr. Manfred Blasing, a former employee of Askania, helped the Soviets in organizing a laboratory to test control surface actuators. The institute also recruited Professor Waldemar Wolff, the former chief ballistics expert for Krupp, and Dr. Werner Albring, an aerodynamics expert from Dresden.[91] These men played crucial roles in helping the Soviets fill gaps in both understanding the operation of German missiles and also setting up experiments to improve subsystems.

Albring, Wolff, and Otto assisted Tiulin's group by translating German documentation into Russian and by doing mathematical work to improve the V-2's range.[92] For modeling V-2 trajectories, the Soviets worked closely with Hoch, who laid critical groundwork for future Soviet work in the field.[93] Chertok later described how working with Germans was akin to "solv[ing] puzzles." They would first figure out how a device worked and then disassemble it "down to the last screw." They would then order the

[89] Naimark, *Russians in Germany*, 217, 525.
[90] Naimark, *Russians in Germany*, 218–219.
[91] RGAE, 397/1/3/36–39; Chertok, *RAP1*, 300; Michels, *Peenemünde*, 188–189.
[92] Memoir of Mozzhorin in *DVK1*, 138.
[93] Memoir of R. F. Appazov in *DVK1*, 28.

FIGURE 20. The German rocket engineer Helmut Gröttrup, shown here with his wife and children. Gröttrup proved to be the most important German specialist captured by the Soviets during the occupation missions in 1945 and 1946. He, like many of the other Germans, was kidnapped and brought to the Soviet Union, where he helped with the Soviet domestic rocket program in the late 1940s and early 1950s. In 1953, Gröttrup and his family returned to East, and then, West Germany. [*Source*: Boris Chertok]

Germans to make detailed drawings. From these, the Soviets would then rebuild the object themselves.[94]

Efforts to find former Peenemünde veterans proved difficult, but the Institute Rabe found some who joined the Soviet project. Fritz Viebach, an expert in V-2 launch systems, offered his services. Perhaps the most important find was Helmut Gröttrup, who served as a deputy for guidance, control, and telemetry at Peenemünde. Although approached by the Americans, Gröttrup communicated to the Soviets through his wife, Irmgard, that he would work for the Soviets if offered complete freedom.[95] Unlike most of the Peenemünde team, Gröttrup did not like the idea of relocating to the United States and hoped that working for Soviets would offer a modicum of stability for his family (see Figure 20). In late September, along with his wife and two children, Gröttrup moved from the American to the Soviet zone. He did not

94 Boris Chertok, interview by James Harford, Moscow, December 4, 1991, Notebook No. 2, Papers of James Harford.

95 "OMGUS Special Intelligence," March 20, 1947, National Archives (NA), RG 260, box 65.

disappoint. As head of the "Gröttrup Bureau" at the Institute Rabe, he wrote a "report in the middle of 1946 that was the most complete and objective account of Peenemünde and of the technical problems that were solved during the development of [the V-2]."[96] Gröttrup helped in other ways by telling the Soviets about further skilled Germans who might be useful to the Soviets as well as directing the Russians to find more material on the V-2. Chertok noted later, "I would say that we were right on the money with Gröttrup."[97] The Soviets compensated him accordingly, providing him with a mansion (owned by a rich German merchant who was thrown out) for his family and a salary of 5,000 marks per month, the highest among the Germans and higher than almost every Soviet engineer working in Germany. His wife got her own sports car and a riding horse.[98]

Local Labor

Through enticements of wages and food or sometimes by coercion, at least 1,200 skilled Germans worked on the rocketry program (at Bleicherode, *Mittelwerk*, Kleinbodungen, Lehesten, and elsewhere) by the end of 1945, compared to 248 Soviet employees. An additional 1,800 unskilled German laborers worked to disassemble the facilities at *Mittelwerk*, most of them young men from local families living in and around Nordhausen.[99] Within the research organizations, Germans and Soviets worked relatively harmoniously. Neither archival records nor personal reminiscences suggest any serious acrimony between the two sides working for the Special Technical Commission, despite the widespread complaints of rape and looting prevalent throughout Soviet-occupied Germany.[100] All German scientists and engineers, of course, labored under the watchful eye of MVD (the successor to the NKVD) "operative groups" that worked at each of the rocket control points in Germany. Thus, when the MVD's feared deputy chairman Ivan Serov reported to his boss that "the general mood of German specialists engaged in work in our institutes is completely satisfactory," it probably did not account for the fear that many Germans concealed.[101] Besides monitoring the Germans, MVD helped the rocketry project by scouring through German POW camps for men and women who had worked on the V-2. For example, in June 1946, Serov reported to his boss that his men had recently

96 Chertok, *RAP1*, 307.

97 Ibid., 302; Frederick Ordway and Mitchell R. Sharpe, *The Rocket Team* (New York: Cromwell, 1979), 318–319.

98 Ordway and Sharpe, *Rocket Team*, 320.

99 RGAE, 397/1/3/112–120; Memoir of Mozzhorin in *DVK1*, 137.

100 Chertok describes a single case of rape in 1945 connected to rocketry work. Chertok, *RAP1*, 313–315. For an in-depth look at the issue of rape in Soviet-occupied Germany, see Naimark, *Russians in Germany*, 69–140.

101 GARF, 9401/2/138/2–6 (June 1946).

found eighteen Germans in POW camps who were then immediately transferred to work for the Soviet program.[102]

Social relations in and around Nordhausen, especially in relation to the German *manual* laborers working to dismantle the factories, were very acrimonious. German historian Matthias Uhl has described how the Soviets began recruiting able German men from the area in late August 1945 when the Nordhausen city management sent out messages to round up all able-bodied German men from POW camps in and around the city. Through the fall, Soviet demands for labor widened from POWs to both men and women in the city of Nordhausen. In just one case, on October 3, the *Mittelwerk* disassembly teams requested 200 new workers. Five days later, they wanted another 1,000. The population strongly resented such calls because by the end of 1945 – with 2,400 German men and women involved in *Mittelwerk* disassembly work – the city no longer had any labor to devote to city operations, which remained paralyzed through the spring of 1946.[103] Their work usually consisted of using acetylene torches to cut hardware into pieces and loading the sections into railroad cars.[104] Women (about 20% of the labor force) usually did administrative tasks. By February 11, 1946, the Soviets and Germans had jointly spent about 80,000 person-hours of labor on the disassembly, of which the Germans contributed about 75%. From *Mittelwerk*, they had loaded 717 wagons carrying 5,647 tons of equipment back to the Soviet Union.[105]

Institutes Nordhausen and Berlin

In February 1946, the main actors operating in Germany – Gaidukov, Tveretskii, Korolev, and Pobedonostsev – consolidated all the disparate operations in Germany and set up two main institutes on rocket development, the Institute Nordhausen (for work on ballistic rockets) and the Institute Berlin (for work on everything else). The structures of both institutes reflected their vision of the network approach to innovation, which stemmed largely from the way the Germans had organized work on rockets during the war (see Figure 21). For example, the Institute Nordhausen was ultimately composed of about 3,000 people and was geographically spread at five "objects" – at Nordhausen, Sömmerda, Bleicherode (the site of the now defunct Institute Rabe), Kleinbodungen, and Lehesten.[106] Each site had a specific responsibility: Sömmerda (which included Factory No. 1) worked on production documentation and production of the V-2 mainframe; Montania

[102] Ibid.
[103] Uhl, *Stalin's V2*, 70–73.
[104] Memoir of Pallo in *DVK2*, 43.
[105] RGAE, 8044/1/6313/154–55.
[106] RGAE, 397/1/3/31–44.

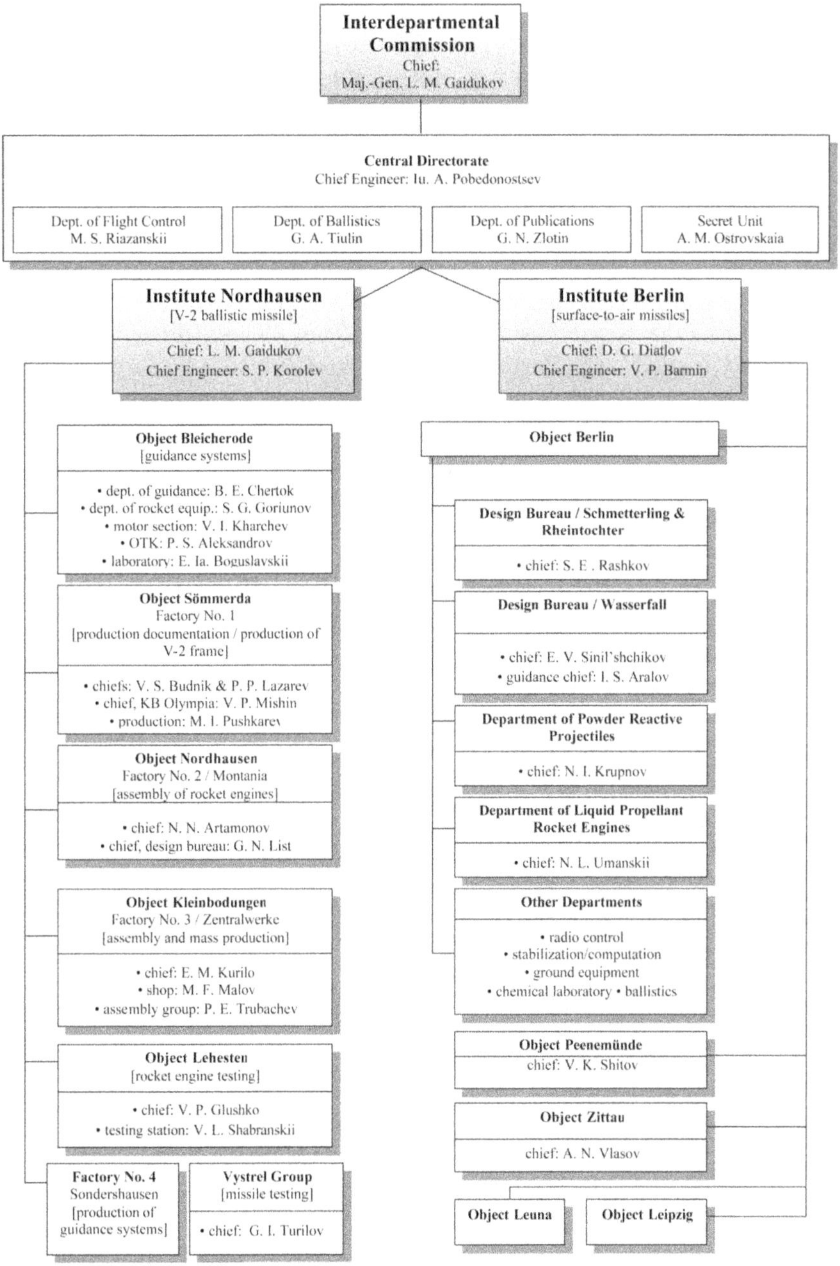

FIGURE 21. Institutional layout of Soviet work on missiles in occupied Germany, 1946, based on data from files in RGAE.

near Nordhausen (Factory No. 2) assembled rocket engines; Kleinbodungen (Factory No. 3) assembled V-2s for mass production; Sondershausen (Factory No. 4) manufactured guidance systems; Bleicherode developed guidance systems; and Lehesten tested rocket engines. At the center in Nordhausen, Gaidukov served as head of the institute and Korolev as its "chief engineer," a role that allowed him to coordinate all the engineering work of the various branches. Within the Institute Nordhausen itself, a launch group (*Vystrel*) worked with artillery soldiers under General Tveretskii.[107]

Gaidukov organized the smaller Institute Berlin similarly. Its structure centered around several design bureaus focusing on German winged missiles (such as the *Wasserfall*, *Schmetterling*, and *Rheintochter*) and solid-propellant rockets. The institute had departments on liquid-propellant rocket engines, solid-propellant rockets, chemical work, radio control, and ground equipment. Dmitrii Diatlov, a former deputy to Vannikov, headed the institute.[108]

A "central directorate" in Berlin monitored the two institutes' work in Germany. Here artillery service engineers worked hand in hand with civilian engineers and developed programs for ballistics and flight control. A veteran of the amateur GIRD days in the early 1930s, Iurii Pobedonostsev, served as the chief engineer of the directorate.

By April 1946, Lavrentii Beriia was able to report confidently to Stalin on the valuable work in Germany since August 1945. A year's work made a remarkable difference. He noted that, under Gaidukov's command, Soviet personnel had collected and translated into Russian a vast amount of German documentation on missiles; created a special rocket institute at Nordhausen as a nerve center for its operations; established five technological and design bureaus focusing on various areas of missile development; reconstructed the *Mittelwerk* factory sufficient to resume production of the V-2; refurbished various testing laboratories; and assembled seven V-2 rockets by using German components, of which four were ready for firing (see Figure 22).[109]

ENTER USTINOV

The success of the operations in Germany contrasted with the situation back in Moscow, where long-range rocket development still lacked an industrial advocate. Shakhurin had expressed little interest (and, besides, was fired as aviation commissar) while Vannikov was deeply immersed in A-bomb

[107] RGAE, 397/1/3/112–20; Memoir of Mozzhorin in *DVK1*, 137–138.

[108] RGAE, 397/1/3/112–20. The Institute Berlin also oversaw the Object Peenemünde and Object Zittau. For a participant description of the work at Institute Berlin, see Konovalov, *Taina Sovetskogo raketnogo oruzhiia*, 43–46.

[109] APRF, 3/47/179/28–31 (April 17, 1946); RGAE, 8495/1/71/115 (January 22, 1946).

FIGURE 22. A German V-2 missile being readied for launch. The V-2 rocket was the foundation of the postwar Soviet missile program. In reproducing a Soviet version of the rocket, Soviet engineers not only mastered a complex technological system but also quickly identified key drawbacks in the original German design that allowed them to move ahead to more advanced models such as the "indigenous" R-1 rocket. [*Source*: Matthias Uhl]

development.[110] Serendipity and circumstance allowed a third person to step in, Commissar of Armaments Dmitrii Ustinov, one of the architects behind the industrial powerhouse that provided guns and artillery for the Soviet war effort (see Figure 23). Raised in a working-class family, Ustinov represented a generation who graduated from higher technical schools in the wake of Stalin's "Great Break" in the late 1920s and early 1930s. A loyal Stalinist, he joined the Bol'shevik steel factory in Leningrad in 1937 as a junior engineer but, owing to the massive arrests during the Purges and the patronage of Leningrad Party secretary Andrei Zhdanov, became its director within a year. In 1941, about two weeks before the Nazi invasion, Georgii Malenkov summoned the thirty-two-year-old Ustinov to the Kremlin and told him that he was now in charge of the Commissariat of Armaments. He was the youngest defense manager in the Soviet war effort, in control of

[110] O. V. Khlevniuk et al., eds., *Politbiuro tsk vkp(b) i sovet ministrov sssr 1945–1953* (Moscow: Rosspen, 2002), 204. Shakhurin and many others were arrested in April 1946 for alleged negligence in developing Soviet military aviation. I. N. Kosenko, "Taina 'aviatsionnogo dela'," *Voenno-istoricheskii zhurnal* no. 6 (1994): 57–62.

FIGURE 23. People's Commissar Dmitrii Ustinov (1908–1984) was a late sponsor of the Soviet missile effort in occupied Germany, but once his ministry was granted control over the domestic project to build long-range missiles, he banked his career on it. For nearly forty years, Ustinov dominated the Soviet missile (and later space) programs, eventually becoming a Politburo member and Soviet Minister of Defense. [*Source*: Steven Zaloga]

some of the biggest and most famous Soviet plants such as the Bol'shevik, Arsenal, and Barrikady Factories. Ustinov demonstrated his expertise by managing huge increases in production within a year of his appointment. Through the war, his commissariat supplied most of the weapons, such as artillery cannons, machine guns, rifles, revolvers, and mortars, for Soviet ground, air, and naval forces.[111]

Like the other defense branches, the Commissariat of Armaments faced problems converting to "dual" civilian–military production after the war. Military contracts for weapons production declined dramatically after a major demilitarization order of August 1945. By the end of the year, the ambitious Ustinov was looking for something "big" to fill the vacuum developing in his commissariat. The appearance of new technologies such as jets, atomic bombs, radar, and missiles promised to revolutionize weapons design; he feared that this revolution would leave his manufacturing empire

[111] For a summary of the Commissariat of Armament's production activities during the war, see RGAE, 4372/77/255/108; Simonov, *VPK*, 158–162. For Ustinov's memoirs about the war, see D. F. Ustinov, *Vo imia pobedy: zapiski narkoma vooruzheniia* (Moscow: Voenizdat, 1988).

behind. Initially, he banked his commissariat's future on both radar and optics, particularly for future anti-aircraft artillery systems.[112]

Ustinov had been involved only peripherally with the nascent rocket program: in July 1945, in a communication to the Shakhurin Commission on Reactive Technology, Ustinov had announced his readiness to serve as a subcontractor for the reactive projectile effort by producing optical and targeting instruments, launch complexes, and fire control radars for anti-aircraft weapons.[113] He assigned the subcontractor work to one of his most famous plants, Factory No. 88 in the northeastern Moscow suburb of Kaliningrad, which had recently fallen on hard times. During the war, the plant had produced anti-aircraft artillery by the thousands, but from late 1945, Ustinov "converted" it to civilian drilling equipment and oil pumps, with which the factory coped badly. In early November, Ustinov singled out the factory for its poor-quality civilian work.[114]

If initially Ustinov found rockets only peripherally interesting, two interconnected factors forced him to look more closely. As demonstrated by Factory No. 88, he needed to guarantee high levels of military production in his factories at a time when demilitarization was causing havoc. To do that, however, he needed to maintain a strong relationship with the military, particularly the artillery forces that had been his commissariat's primary client during the war. Serendipitously, at the time, Artillery Marshal Nikolai Iakovlev, one of Ustinov's wartime military customers, enthusiastically supported the study of German long-range rockets, seeing in them the future of the Red Army's artillery forces. Apparently encouraged by Iakovlev and General Gaidukov, his rocket representative in Germany, Ustinov decided to learn more about the issue.

In April 1946, Ustinov sent his "first deputy" ("first among the deputies"), Vasilii Riabikov, to visit Berlin and the areas around Nordhausen to assess the work of the hundreds of Soviet and German engineers in the field.[115] On his trip, Riabikov saw, in effect, a small-scale version of the kind of intersectoral cooperation that would be required on an industrial level back in the USSR but that Soviet industry failed to implement a year earlier. He saw how Gaidukov, Korolev, and others had developed a horizontal approach to work that effectively bypassed the rigid, vertical, and insular

112 The GOKO issued a decree on June 10, 1945 on the production of fire control radars, optical systems to control anti-aircraft fire, and synchronization drives for ground anti-aircraft artillery. Most of the major factories for these systems were under Ustinov's Commissariat of Armaments, which created a special subdivision, the Fourth Main Directorate, on May 14, 1945. RGAE, 8157/1, introductory essay.

113 RGAE, 8044/1/1318/159–60 (July 1945).

114 RGAE, 397/1/5/3; *RKKE*, 21; Loktev, *Nedavno eto bylo sekretom*, 22–32, 41, 48. Ustinov issued warnings to several of his factory directors for their inability to produce civilian equipment. Simonov, *VPK*, 114, 118–119.

115 Diadin, Filippovykh, and Ivkin, *Pamiatnye starty*, 71.

system of Soviet R&D; each subsystem of a missile was represented by joint Soviet–German teams that worked toward common goals set by both the customer (artillerymen) and the producer (engineers).

By this time, in Germany, the Soviets selected two German missiles as the most worthy of their attention, the V-2 and the *Wasserfall* surface-to-air missile. Although the wartime effectiveness of the V-2 was questionable at best and the *Wasserfall* had never been deployed, they represented, at least in form, the most complex and powerful missile systems of the Soviet-controlled booty. During his visit, Riabikov also witnessed an engine firing at one of the remaining static test stands at Lehesten, which profoundly impressed him. Boris Chertok, a young guidance systems engineer, remembered that "[t]oward the end of the visit, we arranged a farewell dinner during which Vasilli Mikhailovich said very frankly that everything that he had seen and heard had significantly changed his technical world view."[116]

STATE INTERVENTION

An excited Riabikov conveyed his impressions to Ustinov, who acted quickly to take control of the long-range rocketry project. Factory No. 88, Ustinov's most productive wartime factory that was struggling with civilian production, seemed to be the ideal site for the missile project. Ustinov communicated with both Beriia and Malenkov as well as Marshal Iakovlev, who together compiled a report for Stalin, dated April 17, 1946, on the significant accomplishments of the Gaidukov commission and future prospects for long-range missiles. Noting that these impressive achievements could be reproduced on Soviet territory between Ustinov and Vannikov's commissariats, the drafters ended their report by requesting an audience with Stalin to "discuss all these issues."[117]

Twelve days later, Stalin hosted the first high-level meeting in the Soviet Union on a national strategy to deal with long-range missiles. For an hour and forty-five minutes on the late night of April 29, the Soviet leader met with the drafters of the April letter as well as several other interested parties. Generals Sokolov and Gaidukov, the two wartime *Katiusha* veterans who aggressively led the campaign in Germany to take control of German long-range missiles, also attended.[118] The thirty-six-year-old Ustinov was no

[116] Chertok, *RAP1*, 323.

[117] APRF, 3/47/179/28–31 (April 17, 1946).

[118] Korotkov, Chernev, and Chernobaev, "Posetiteli kremlevskogo kabineta I. V. Stalina," 123. The discussion with the big group extended from 9:30 p.m. to 10:45 p.m. on April 29, 1946 and included I. V. Stalin, L. P. Beriia (Minister, Internal Affairs), G. M. Malenkov, D. F. Ustinov (Minister, Armaments), B. L. Vannikov (Minister, Agricultural Machine Building), M. V. Khrunichev (Minister, Aviation Industry), I. G. Kabanov (Minister, Electrical Industry), M. G. Pervukhin (Minister, Chemical Industry), V. M. Riabikov (First Deputy Minister, Armaments), N. A. Bulganin (First Deputy Minister, Armed Forces),

stranger to the Kremlin, having visited frequently during the war to discuss the production of artillery pieces, but this was only his second meeting with Stalin after the end of the war. Ustinov knew the risks of taking on a new technological system such as long-range rockets, one whose wartime efficacy was still in doubt. Both during and after the war, Stalin, Beriia, and their security police surrogates considered ministers and commissars expendable. Later, Ustinov told one of his aides that upon seeing Beriia's cold stare that night, he knew that, "This was when I realized that this whole affair was no joke and became scared. Should anything go wrong, they would have my head."[119] In the two weeks after this meeting, Stalin's right-hand man Malenkov, in cooperation with *Gosplan*, Ustinov, and Iakovlev, prepared a draft decree that Beriia approved.

On May 13, 1946, Stalin signed into law as a Council of Ministers decree the document that Malenkov, Beriia, and *Gosplan* prepared. Entitled "On the Question of Reactive Armaments," the decree laid the foundation for the postwar Soviet (and later Russian) missile and space programs. The decree tied the long-range ballistic missile to artillery production culture and introduced a network approach to its development, based largely on the way engineers on the ground in Germany performed their work in 1945–1946. Stalin approved the creation of a network of three prime contracting ministries supported by four subcontracting ministries (with the prime ministries also managing some subcontracts). Each prime ministry would supervise a different type of missile: liquid-propellant reactive projectiles (such as the V-2 and *Wasserfall*) to the Ministry of Armaments, solid-propellant reactive projectiles to the Ministry of Agricultural Machine Building, and reactive airplane-projectiles (or winged missiles) to the Ministry of the Aviation Industry. Strikingly, the three men in charge of postwar missile development, Ustinov, Vannikov, and Khrunichev, had been managers of Soviet artillery during the war with little connection with either rockets or aviation. The subcontractor assignments largely reflected the organization of work in Germany; in other words, the supervising ministries of field engineers in Germany took those specializations that their engineers sought out in Germany.[120]

G. K. Zhukov (Commander, Red Army Ground Forces), A. M. Vasil'evskii (Chief of Staff, Armed Forces), N. N. Voronov (Commander, Artillery Forces), N. D. Iakovlev (Commander, Main Artillery Directorate), A. I. Sokolov (Chief, Main Directorate of Armaments, Guards Mortar Units), L. M. Gaidukov (Chief, Department of Reactive Armaments, Central Committee), and L. A. Govorov (Commander, forces in the Leningrad Military District).

119 Mikhail Pervov, *Zenitnoe raketnoe oruzhie protivovozdushnoi oborony strany* (Moscow: Aviarus-XXI, 2001), 32.

120 The Ministry of the Electrical Industry took over development of all guidance systems, the Ministry of the Shipbuilding Industry inherited work on gyroscope-based stabilization instrumentation, the Ministry of the Chemical Industry was assigned research on liquid

In terms of objectives, Stalin approved first-order goals as "the reproduction of rockets of the V-2 (long-range guided rocket) and *Wasserfall* (anti-aircraft guided rocket) type with the use of indigenous materials." Additional goals included the full reconstruction of technical documentation for the V-2, *Wasserfall*, *Rheintocher*, and *Schmetterling* rockets; the reconstruction of laboratories and stands necessary to test these and other rockets; and preparation of cadres of Soviet specialists who could "master the design of the V-2, anti-aircraft guided and other rockets, methods of testing, technologies of production,... and rocket assembly."[121] According to the decree, the nerve center for developing liquid-propellant reactive projectiles would be Ustinov's former artillery Factory No. 88 outside of Moscow. Here, a new research institute would copy and improve German missiles for the Soviet military.

CONCLUSIONS

In 1945 and 1946, various actors representing the Soviet government – industrialists, engineers, and artillery service persons – organized work in Soviet-occupied Germany to study German rocket technology. In the history of Soviet rocketry and spaceflight, this episode was the nation's most unambiguous interaction with foreign influence and expertise. From the 1920s to the early 1940s, foreign contact had decreased. Where direct and surrogate interactions with foreigners contributed to the sustenance of informal networks dedicated to the cause of spaceflight in the 1920s, the following decade the pendulum swung the other way as activists turned inward. The experience in Germany unquestionably returned a foreign presence to rocket development.

The "German engagement" in 1945 and 1946 compressed two interrelated processes that punctuated the development of rockets in the Soviet Union: setting up informal networks, and achieving state commitment. In search of reparations, various Soviet commissariats sent teams into Germany. Initially, they worked in a chaotic environment characterized by conflicting mandates from different branches of the Soviet government, including the Red Army and the Soviet Military Administration in Germany. Aviation engineers and artillery officers represented the two main

propellants, and the Ministry of Machine and Instrument Building was allocated development of ground-launch equipment. The decree also assigned additional subcontractor work to the following prime ministries: liquid-propellant rocket engines (Ministry of the Aviation Industry) and explosives and solid propellants (Ministry of the Agricultural Industry). Russian censors first permitted publication of the decree in "Voprosy reaktivnogo vooruzheniia," in *Khronika osnovnykh sobytii istorii raketnykh voisk strategicheskogo naznacheniia*, ed. I. D. Sergeev (Moscow: TsIPK, 1994), 227–234.

121 "Voprosy reaktivnogo vooruzheniia."

constituencies in search of reactive technologies such as rockets and jets. Their interests and activities overlapped, forcing them into a situation where they had to depend on each other's expertise. In Moscow, based upon incoming reports from the field, Soviet industrial managers prematurely put together a national plan to reproduce German reactive technology in August 1945. They struggled over how to define the new technology of long-range liquid-propellant missiles, eventually embracing an artillery viewpoint: that a rocket was nothing more than a complicated artillery shell.

Several factors – Stalin's disinterest, demilitarization, and the high-priority nuclear project – delayed the rocket plan's implementation. In the intervening period, those still in the field in Germany, on their own initiative, set up an informal organizational network to study and master German rocket technology. Taking advantage of the geographical and organizational distance from Moscow, network participants were able to act independently from the center (whether Berlin or Moscow), to engage in effective local action, and to indulge in flexible decision making. Such practice contrasted sharply with the highly centralized management structure in Soviet industry during the war. The men and women in Germany also operated relatively horizontally and informally; in fact, as memoirs testify, the scope and organization of the network was visible to most who worked within it, unusual for top-secret Soviet military endeavors with their extreme compartmentalization and strict hierarchies. Gaidukov's Special Technical Commission appears to have borrowed only the best attributes from wartime experience. For example, the commission appropriated the top-level State Committee of Defense's practice of delegating authority to plenipotentiaries for particular tasks but did not use the GOKO's centralized decision-making process, which involved Stalin's arbitration of all decisions.[122]

The informal network was a short-term solution that was made possible by a set of specific circumstances such as geographical distance from Moscow, the chaos that reigned in Germany after the war, and the alliance of key leaders representing different constituencies (Gaidukov, Korolev, Tveretskii, and others). Achieving the goals that they established in Germany – reconstituting the wartime German capacity and attracting the interest of Soviet leaders including Stalin – also ensured the termination of the network. Beriia's glowing report to Stalin in April 1946 on the success of the work in Germany proved critical. By this time, the rocketry project had important supporters, particularly Marshal Iakovlev and Commissar Ustinov. A month later, Stalin approved their proposed program, thus making the development of powerful liquid-propellant rockets an important

[122] Sanford R. Lieberman, "Crisis Management in the USSR: The Wartime System of Administration and Control," in *The Impact of World War II on the Soviet Union*, ed. Susan J. Linz (Totowa, NJ: Rowman & Allanheld, 1985), 59–76.

priority. Firm commitment replaced the ambivalence that characterized the government's stance in 1930s when it first financed work on rockets. The Soviet rocket project was about to enter a new phase, one fed by a new brand of postwar Soviet military reassertion driven by the shifting geopolitical winds of the Cold War. Here, the intersection of politics, technology, and professional ambition produced the conditions necessary for a wholly new kind of weapon, the intercontinental ballistic missile.

7

The Cold War and the Creation of the Soviet ICBM

> Considering the modern state of work on long-range missiles and the significance of this form of weapon for the defense of the country, it seems to us that the question has come to the fore on the necessity of revising our current existing posture and to adopt new decisions.[1]
>
> Viacheslav Malyshev, defense industry manager, arguing for the development of a Soviet ICBM, 1953

INTRODUCTION

The notion that the first human steps into the cosmos required a marriage between the utopian dreams of space and the military imperatives of war has become something of a cliché. The former, it is said, provided the vision, and the latter, the means to deliver an object into space. Since Tsiolkovskii, many space enthusiasts had correctly calculated that for humans to cast an object beyond the Earth's gravitational pull, one would have to impel it to travel at a velocity close to seven kilometers per second. Not by coincidence, this speed is close to that required for an intercontinental rocket to fly half way around the world and wreak destruction on others. In other words, the lethal intercontinental ballistic missile, with some cosmetic modifications, could also serve as an ideal rocket to launch a satellite into orbit around the Earth. Although no political leader had anticipated this dual capability, many space enthusiasts did. Moreover, some of the latter were seeded in key design positions within the Soviet military-industrial complex and responsible for creating the very thing that would help materialize their space dreams, an intercontinental ballistic missile.

Political leaders – and their military counterparts – were interested in the military potential of an intercontinental missile because it too was part of another marriage, one whose other party was the most fearsome weapon of the Cold War, the atomic bomb. The American use of nuclear weapons over Hiroshima and Nagasaki in 1945 signaled a qualitative change in the growing rift between the Soviet Union and the United States. The first Soviet atomic explosion in 1949 further altered the strategic dynamic between the

[1] APRF, 3/47/202/117–123 (October 19, 1953).

two superpowers, heightening the aura of nuclear anxiety that permeated polity and society in both the East and the West. Like their counterparts in Washington, Stalin and his coterie of advisors – Molotov, Beriia, and Malenkov – believed the atomic bomb to be the most important qualitative factor in the strategic balance between the two superpowers.

The possession of nuclear weapons was a necessary but not sufficient condition for creating a credible deterrent. Soviet leaders devoted attention to this question by exploring many different options for delivering atomic (and later, thermonuclear) bombs in the latter years of Stalin's rule. The most obvious option was to develop long-range strategic bombers that could carry such weapons across intercontinental ranges. Both the Soviet Union and the United States had established aviation industries and powerful lobbies who would support a prominent role for them in the new nuclear age. Other alternatives such as missiles became manifest in the early 1950s. That actors in our story eventually reached a consensus on the intercontinental ballistic missile (ICBM) as the most effective option was neither preordained nor obvious to those involved for a long time. The path from the birth of atomic program to the national commitment to produce the first Soviet ICBM was a long and circuitous one that was characterized as much by direction and willfulness as by accident and abandoned routes. And although the cosmos was not strictly a part of this narrative – in official papers, ICBMs and satellites are not mentioned in the same breadth until about 1955, well after the decision to build an ICBM – space exploration maintains a ghostly presence throughout the history of this rocket, insofar as the individuals who were responsible for conceiving an ICBM for Iosif Stalin and later Nikita Khrushchev were the same ones who had indulged in "fantasies" about space for over two decades.

The creation of the ICBM encompassed three different narratives: how the ICBM came to be seen as an effective way to deliver nuclear weapons; how it came to be designed; and how the government committed to building one. These three phases of its birth were not discrete and temporally sequential but rather intertwined, simultaneous, and difficult to isolate into distinct building processes. For example, engineers conceptually designed the ICBM while simultaneously trying to determine whether it was the most effective method to deliver atomic bombs. In each case, from selection to design to commitment, the outcomes were the result of complex negotiations between interested actors – engineers, bureaucrats, military officers, and Party leaders – who were influenced by a range of factors: power struggles in the Kremlin, the professional ambitions of engineers, Soviet military strategy, theoretical ideas rooted in the history of rocketry, and, of course, technical considerations. We see that at different phases, different actors (and factors) were more important than others, their importance in the matrix of the Soviet missile program changing according to broader changes in Soviet society, particularly the death of Stalin and the subsequent political and institutional equivocations that followed.

During the first phase of the history of the ICBM, from 1947 to 1953, when there was little state interest in the ICBM, Soviet missile designers essentially set the agenda for research. Top state actors did not afford the missile program undue high priority, and when they did, it was to establish V-2 production in a domestic setting. In this context, missile designers were able to establish a certain amount of "creative latitude," especially in terms of the long-term agenda, by pushing for a vast number of modestly funded research projects to explore the technologies of future missile design. In carefully tracing their design decisions through iterations of missiles, we see how the designers' method was to explore as many options as possible and then narrow down to the ones that worked best given the constraints of Soviet industry. Here innovation encompassed both incremental steps to rationalize a design but also large programmatic leaps that were much more risky. This creative phase – what we might recognize today as applied research and design – lasted about six years, and it was unique in Soviet weapons development in the early Cold War because it did not result from a government mandate; instead the government mandate emerged as a result of the research, which had substantiated the specifics of a weapon that could satisfy an urgent need to deliver an atomic bomb to the continental United States.

Once the missile designers had reached a consensus on the conceptual foundation of an intercontinental missile, the demarcations between technological innovation and political action became more nebulous. In this second phase, discussions about the missile, elevated to a "higher" policy level than the gross engineering level, drew in new actors besides designers – industrial bureaucrats, Party leaders, and especially military officers. In this period, roughly from 1953 to 1955, innovation was not simply about inventing a better rocket engine or designing a new guidance system but rather a more broadly understood activity that involved institutions, strategies, and technologies. Here, technology was not in the "driver's seat," as some have argued; on the contrary, the final shape of the weapon was shaped by social, institutional, and technological constraints.[2] Without these constraints, the ICBM, later given the name R-7, would have looked entirely different, and in fact, might have arrived much later than when it did, in 1957, about the same time that the United States also began testing its own first ICBM, the Atlas. The dizzying and Byzantine changes in the defense industry between 1953 and 1955, driven largely by the conflicting ambitions of managers in the nuclear sector and a rising constituency of service officers fresh from service in World War II, created an opening for the emerging missile lobby to put the ICBM as foremost on the strategic agenda. Their efforts put the missile program – and particularly the ICBM – square and center as representing the future of strategic weapons.

[2] John F. Guilmartin, Jr., "The ICBM and the Cold War: Technology in the Driver's Seat," *Quarterly Journal of Military History* 9 no. 3 (Spring 1997): 52–61.

THE ATOMIC BOMB

Stalin's view of the future of Soviet military strategy after World War II evolved in line with the fracture of the grand alliance over the question of Europe. His position, evident in both public speeches and internal deliberations, betrayed a mixture of patient *realpolitik* combined with the older Leninist sensibility of the inevitability of world revolution in the indefinite future.[3] Stalin's minimal and obvious goal was a security buffer in eastern Europe – guaranteed through a combination of diplomacy and de facto reality on the ground – but he also articulated a view best described as unilateralist and not a bit expansionist, a kind of "socialist imperialism."[4] Although he did not foresee war as an impending reality, he did believe that it was inevitable, a point that underlay his famous speech at the Bolshoi theater in February 1946. Touching on the successes of the war, Stalin argued that in the postwar era, economic policy would echo that of the interwar years when the focus on heavy industrial development mobilized the Soviet Union in anticipation of war, principally through the use of "mobilization plans" in the defense industry. Hand in hand with continuing sacrifices to be made by ordinary people, the preparation for war would involve having the most modern and deadly weapons, chief among them the atomic bomb. Although the terrifying devastations wrought by the American atomic bombs at Hiroshima and Nagasaki had a profound psychological effect on Soviet Party and government leaders, most did not believe that the atomic bomb had changed the fundamental nature of warfare overnight. Stalin correctly assumed that the American bomb was no immediate threat to the Soviet Union – the Americans had few bombs and, after all, war weariness had set in. As David Holloway has argued, to Stalin "the danger was not the atomic bomb as such, but the American monopoly of the bomb. The obvious solution to this problem, in Stalin's mind, was a Soviet atomic bomb."[5]

Stalin put the Soviet nuclear bomb program on an emergency footing on August 20, 1945, less than two weeks after Hiroshima, with the creation of a top-level governmental body to supervise the development of a Soviet atomic bomb. Within the context of the Soviet defense industry, the atomic

[3] Stalin's motives at the beginning of the Cold War have been the subject of a vast canon of literature. For some recent examples, see Vladislav M. Zubok, *A Failed Empire: The Soviet Union in the Cold War from Stalin to Gorbachev* (Chapel Hill: University of North Carolina Press, 2007); Gerhard Wettig, *Stalin and the Cold War in Europe: The Emergence and Development of East-West Conflict, 1939–1953* (Landham, MD: Rowman & Littlefield, 2008); Geoffrey Roberts, *Stalin's Wars: From World War to Cold War, 1939–1953* (New Haven: Yale University Press, 2006); Vojtech Mastny, *The Cold War and Soviet Insecurity: The Stalin Years* (New York: Oxford University Press, 1996).

[4] Zubok, *A Failed Empire*, 6–11.

[5] David Holloway, *Stalin and the Bomb: The Soviet Union and Atomic Energy, 1939–1956* (New Haven: Yale University Press, 1994), 166.

bomb decision was an extraordinary one, and in many ways unique. First, it created institutional structures that were later replicated for other important weapons systems. Second, it created a powerful lobby of managers who dominated the Soviet defense industry as a whole for a decade. Their purview extended far beyond atomic (and later, thermonuclear) bombs, and their managerial duties frequently bled over into policy definition. Both of these features would have a profound effect on the project to develop an intercontinental ballistic missile.

In signing the August 20, 1945 decree, Stalin sanctioned the creation of a nine-member "Special Committee" under the direction of Lavrentii Beriia, the notorious secret police bureaucrat who headed the People's Commissariat of Internal Affairs (NKVD).[6] The Special Committee for the atomic bomb was not the first such interdepartmental body to have been created; it appears to have been patterned after a similarly named committee under Georgii Malenkov that operated in 1945 to oversee the location, dismantling, and transport of German industry to the Soviet Union.[7] Beriia's Special Committee, however, was of an entirely different stature, given that it enjoyed unlimited authority, was not subject to funding ceilings, and worked outside the formal conduits of the Soviet defense industry. Although the decree itself says little about the role of the security services, Beriia made sure that the NKVD (and after 1946, the Ministry of Internal Affairs, the MVD) was deeply enmeshed in the project. Although the MVD was not represented directly on the Committee itself, MVD representatives flooded organizations involved in atomic bomb development at all levels. Such integration not only allowed Beriia to control and monitor the project, but it also ensured that, eventually, the Soviet security agencies were indispensable to the program.

Following the precedent of the atomic bomb, Stalin sanctioned the creation of two other special committees in 1946, the Special Committee for Reactive Technology (for missiles) and the Special Committee for Radar.[8] Superficially, the establishment of two subsequent "special committees" subordinate directly to the USSR Council of Ministers would suggest that all three programs – atomic, missile, and radar – were on the same footing; historians and veterans have long assumed that all three strategic programs were "extraordinary" projects operating at a much higher priority than the conventional weapons industry. The rocket Special Committee was, in fact,

[6] "O spetsial'nom komitete pri GKO" (August 20, 1945), reproduced in *Voenno-istoricheskii zhurnal* no. 4 (1995): 65–67. Beriia relinquished his position as chairman of the NKVD in January 1946 but retained control of security services as a deputy chairman of the Council of Ministers.

[7] RGASPI, 644/1/373/48–51 (February 25, 1945).

[8] A Council of Ministers decree (no. 1529–678) on July 10, 1946 entitled "Problems of Radar" established the Committee for Radar of the USSR Council of Ministers, headed by G. M. Malenkov. See Simonov, *VPK*, 254.

renamed Committee No. 2 in May 1947, suggesting that it might be the second major weapons effort behind the atomic bomb.[9] In reality, during the postwar period under Stalin, the Soviet long-range missile program was not a national military priority, was only episodically paid attention to by Stalin, and largely escaped the attention of Lavrentii Beriia, who brought a single-minded and cold efficiency to the atomic bomb project. By all measures, from cost to infrastructure to top-level attention, the atomic bomb project completely overshadowed every single other weapons development project in the late 1940s. The atomic bomb Special Committee was given unlimited access to state funds, at a level that proved troubling to even some of the project's participants. Recent estimates of the cost of the nuclear project in the period 1947–1949 fall in the range of 14.5 billion rubles, nearly seven times the amount spent on missiles. Work on the atomic program, conducted in deep secrecy, not only created a countervailing pressure against the move to demilitarize the Soviet armed forces, but also, some have suggested, significantly mitigated any move to ameliorate the dismal lives of Soviet citizens after the devastations of the war. Academician Aleksandr Aleksandrov, a leading scientist in the atomic bomb project, noted many decades later that "a major part of the difficulties" that the nation experienced in the postwar years was due to the extraordinary resources devoted to the atomic bomb project.[10]

That a special committee existed to supervise the missile program was less a reflection of unanimity among the top leadership of the urgent need for long-range missiles than it was the result of bureaucratic jockeying. In at least five of the first drafts of the postwar plan to develop a missile industry, composed over nearly a year in the fall of 1945 and the spring of 1946, there was, in fact, no mention of an extraordinary organ such as the Special Committee, appearing only in the last minute in the sixth draft that was finally signed in May 1946.[11]

There were also differences in supervision. Stalin had assigned the atomic bomb project, that is, the chairmanship of the Special Committee, to Lavrentii Beriia. On the other hand, for the Committee No. 2, Stalin put Georgii Malenkov in charge. Malenkov had been a major figure in wartime governance, having been the Central Committee Secretary in charge of the aviation industry during the war. However, he had been involved in the postwar "aviation affair" that ended the careers of a number of industrialists and

[9] See, for example, Chertok, *RAP2*, 1–23. The Special Committee for Reactive Technology was renamed Committee No. 2 on May 10, 1947.

[10] A. P. Aleksandrov quoted in V. N. Mikhailov et al., eds., *Sozdanie pervoi sovetskoi iadernoi bomby* (Moscow: Energoatomizdat, 1995), 65. For estimated costs of the atomic bomb project, see Simonov, *VPK*, 242.

[11] Drafts were prepared in August 1945, November 1945, January 1946, February 1946, and early April 1946. The last one, prepared in late April, was the one that was signed. See Vladimir Ivkin, "Reshenie na proryv," *Voenno-promyshlennyi kur'er* 19 (135) (May 24–30, 2006).

military officers. In early May 1946, Malenkov lost his coveted place in the Secretariat of the Central Committee for, among other shortcomings, his "moral" failings.[12] Yet, nine days later, on May 13, Stalin put him in charge of Committee No. 2, that is, the missile program. During his short tenure as chair of this organ, Malenkov evidently had little to do with the actual supervision of the project, rarely running meetings and devoting only "occasional" attention it the Committee's work.[13] Most strikingly, Stalin's presence in the missile project, at least in the late 1940s, was rather minimal. In the last seven years of his life, from the spring of 1946 to 1953, Stalin met thirteen times with Dmitrii Ustinov, the minister in charge of the missile program. In the same period, Stalin met Mikhail Khrunichev, the minister in charge of the Soviet aviation industry, at least forty times.[14] Similarly, Stalin met only once with the chief designer of the Soviet version of the German V-2 ballistic missile, Sergei Korolev, whereas he received Andrei Tupolev, the leading aviation designer, at least six times. Eventually, institutional changes were made commensurate with national priority: Conceding that the development of missiles was not urgent on a national scale, Committee No. 2 was officially dissolved on September 15, 1949, just three years following its formation.[15] Its duties were transferred to the "normal" system of the Soviet defense industry.

The "normal" tempo of weapons production in the postwar era was not insignificant. The move to demilitarize in the immediate aftermath of the war proved to be extremely short lived. By 1949, the Soviet defense budget (excluding expenditures for the atomic program) began to expand, steadily rising from 6.6 billion rubles in 1948 to 10.9 billion rubles in 1952.[16] Defense industry managers who had been wholly resistant to Stalin's initial moves to demilitarize and demobilize were rewarded by reducing the amount of civilian production tasked to their factories and siphoning resources back to military work. New programs, particularly in shipbuilding, aviation, rocketry, and radars, necessitated the creation of a massive industrial infrastructure. For example, between 1945 and 1950, the aviation industry produced more than twenty types of aircraft, of which nine were declared operational, and thirty new engines, including two jet engines that were put into series

[12] "Postanovlenie politbiuro ob aviatsii i aviatsionnoi promyshlennosti" (May 4, 1946) in Khlevniuk, *Politbiuro TsK VKP(b)*, 205–206.

[13] Iaroslav Golovanov, *Korolev: fakty i mify* (Moscow: Nauka, 1994), 394.

[14] A. V. Korotkov, A. D. Chernev, and A. A. Chernobayev, "Posetiteli kremlevskogo kabineta I. V. Stalina," *Istoricheskii arkhiv* no. 4 (1998): 16–203 (see, especially, pp. 177 and 184).

[15] I. A. Tiulina, ed., *Arkadii Aleksandrovich Kosmodem'ianskii* (Moscow: Nauka, 2003), 11.

[16] Iu. D. Masliukov and V. S. Glubokov, "Planirovanie i finansirovanie voennoi promyshlennosti v sssr," in *Sovetskaia voennaia moshch' ot Stalina do Gorbacheva*, ed. A. V. Minaev (Moscow: Voennyi parad, 1999), 86. Although the amounts invested in defense increased, the portion for defense as a percentage of the state budget declined from 12.2% in 1947 to 7.9% in 1960 as a result of a higher growth rate of the state budget.

FIGURE 24. Sergei Korolev, shown here at the remote launch range in Kapustin Iar in 1953 while directing launch tests of new missiles. At the time, Korolev's future was still uncertain. His fortunes changed dramatically by the fall, after his induction as a full member of the Communist Party and his election as a Corresponding Member of the Academy of Sciences. These honors were important markers in his professional life, and they laid the groundwork for future access to the top levels of Soviet power in the late 1950s. [*Source*: Collection of Asif Siddiqi]

production. The creation of jet engines – of both foreign and indigenous origin – required massive investments. At least twelve facilities with 520,000 square meters of workspace and 40,000 workers were transferred to pilot production to support jet aviation.[17]

RESEARCH

In this period of growing defense budgets, Soviet industry took important steps in the development of domestic long-range missiles. Already in the fall of 1947, Soviet engineers had launched several V-2 rockets assembled from parts collected in Germany. Within a year, under the direction of "chief designer" Sergei Korolev, and with not inconsiderable help from captured German engineers, they completely reproduced the German rocket using Soviet-made components (see Figure 24). In building this missile,

[17] Simonov, *VPK*, 202–203. These data are from a Party report prepared in 1952 analyzing the Soviet defense industry between 1938 and 1950.

known as the "R-1," Soviet managers achieved several qualitative milestones. They established a vast network of contractors and subcontractors spanning dozens of institutes, design bureaus, and factories that could serve work on more capable of missiles. They also created an industrial base for many new materials, such as high quality metals and propellants, which were largely nonexistent in the Soviet Union. And they organized a group of talented engineers, technicians, and factory workers who quickly outgrew German technology and could investigate much more ambitious designs.[18]

The talents and ambitions of Soviet rocket engineers proved to be critical between 1950 and 1953 when they not only brought older German-derived short-range missiles such as the R-1 and R-2 onto service duty, but also engaged in a sustained effort to conceptualize the future of long-range missile design. This work was valuable because it helped designers narrow the design of an intercontinental missile and it established a connection between the design bureaus in the defense industry and applied research institutions outside of it, a relationship critical to both the development of the R-7 ICBM and the first *Sputnik* satellite. The polity and military were hardly involved in this work; the designer constituency almost entirely alone drove this process until, by 1953, they had defined the basic contours of an intercontinental missile, just at the point when state actors began discussing the possibility of using missiles to deliver atom bombs half way across the world.

The basic directions of research on future directions of missile development were initiated by several decrees of the Council of Ministers in the late 1940s. These were typically prepared by *Gosplan*'s Department No. 2, responsible for economic supervision of the missile sector and headed by Georgii Pashkov until June 1951, in consultation with ministry bureaucrats who depended on input from chief designers such as Korolev. These drafts were then circulated to the various ministries involved in research and development who signed off on, or often disagreed with, particular provisions. The disagreements would then be ironed out at *Gosplan* before heading up to the top-level Committee No. 2.[19] Here, further deliberations would ensure that all parties were aware of their responsibilities, with Nikolai Bulganin, chair of the Committee in the late 1940s, agreeing to all the provisions. After a brief report to Stalin on the general directions of research, Stalin would sign the decree, thus making it fully binding to all parties enumerated within. The three major decrees on missile development in the late 1940s, issued in May 1946, May 1947, and April 1948, show a marked evolution from addressing issues related to establishing an infrastructure to support V-2 production to advanced studies projecting several years into the

[18] Asif A. Siddiqi, *Challenge to Apollo: The Soviet Union and the Space Race, 1945–1974* (Washington, DC: NASA, 2000), 49–50, 53–57, 61–63. For a recent study on the fate of German scientists and engineers kidnapped to work on the postwar Soviet missile program, see Asif A. Siddiqi, "Germans in Russia: Cold War, Technology Transfer, and National Identity," *Osiris* 24 (2009): 120–143.

[19] See, for example, RGAE, 4372/94/1827/169.

future.[20] On the one hand, this evolution reflected the increased mastery over German V-2 technology, but on the other, it underscored the modest but growing influence of Soviet missile designers, who made use of their near-monopoly of information on arcane engineering to advance research projects without often demonstrating a substantive return on investment. Designers were able to set the agenda in terms of long-term research because of their leverage with information sharing but also because of the lack of close supervision of the missile project at the highest levels.[21]

The designers, spearheaded by Korolev and his first deputy, Vasilii Mishin, pushed hard for more advanced designs than the V-2. Their ambitions are underlined by the inclusion of a section in the May 7, 1947 decree committing the missile industry to develop a draft plan (*eskiznyi proekt*) – documentation that would lay out the basic design elements of a missile, with associated substantiations of all incorporated design choices – for a missile with a range of 3,000 kilometers, that is, *ten* times greater than the V-2.[22] Korolev's engineers had already begun exploratory work on this missile, known as the R-3, the moment they had returned from Germany earlier in the year. In the initial years of the operation of the NII-88 institute, roughly 85% of funds were allocated for ongoing programs such as the V-2, R-1, and R-2, while the remainder were dedicated to downrange research work; for example, in the first nine months of 1948, a little over 6% of resources were focused on the highly ambitious R-3 design.[23] This portion increased significantly after another decree on April 14, 1948, which not only put the development of a draft plan for the R-3 as a central goal for NII-88 but also initiated several dozen research projects (or "themes") on aspects of missile design, ranging from the development of antiballistic missiles (Theme I-31) to determining the trajectory of payloads released by long-range missiles (Theme I-13). One theme (I-22) involved analyzing and synthesizing and all the experimental data from tests of the early V-2-derived missiles.[24] These themes typically

[20] The May 1947 decree, for example, approved "concrete assignments and specializations of ministries and branches of reactive armaments, enumerating the [institutes, design bureaus], and experimental and other factories involved in this technology, questions of capital construction ... material-technical supplies, financing labor and preparation of specialists." See RGAE, 4372/96/680/59–53 (September 1949).

[21] In Soviet-era parlance, engineering work focused on developing a prototype was known as "experimental-design work" (*opytno-konstruktorskaia rabota*, OKR) whereas applied research focused on long-term goals was known as "scientific-research work" (*nauchno-issledovatel'skaia rabota*, NIR).

[22] For the basic points of the decree, entitled "On a Plan for the Most Important Scientific-Research and Experimental Work on Reactive Armaments in 1948–1949," see RGAE, 4372/95/437/19–15 (April 1948). The decree called for the development of thirteen missile weapons systems for delivery to the industry. For reference to the 3,000-kilometer-range missile, see RGAE, 8044/1/1612/5–7 (September 29, 1947); RGAE, 4372/94/1827/179–173 (November 11, 1947).

[23] Calculated from RGAE, 4372/95/439/24–2.

[24] S. P. Korolev, "Ob issledovaniiakh uslovii raboty raket dal'nego deistviia ikh agregatov i apparatury v polete" (October 1949) in *SPKIED*, 128–130. Theme I-22 was officially

involved integrated teams with members from both the secret design bureaus and research institutes as well as from universities and the USSR Academy of Sciences, a relationship that effectively gave the missile industry access to a vast infrastructure of fundamental research. Boris Chertok, describing an agreement at this time with the Moscow Power Institute to develop telemetry systems, notes that such contracts underscored "the quest to integrate three elements of our scientific and industrial infrastructure – the Academy's fundamental research in various fields of science, the scientific potential of institutes of higher learning, and the most leading-edge industrial technology – into a single, systemic statewide program."[25]

In terms of priority, the R-3 proposal eclipsed all other research profiles. Korolev structured the development of the draft plan in a pragmatic way: It was not only a project to develop a missile with a range of 3,000 kilometers but one to define the basic directions of future work to produce a much more capable missile. As he noted in the introduction to the twenty-volume draft plan:

> It's especially necessary to note that if we're speaking of future prospects, then in that case, the flight range equal to 3,000 kilometers can be viewed only as the first stage, making it possible to solve certain problems envisaged in the tactical-technical requirement [i.e., the initial specifications] for the R-3. The costs and the whole set of technical steps necessary for attaining a flight range of 3,000 km are so great that it would be unacceptable to isolate this work from the prospects of further development. Therefore, as part of the subsequent stage ... a range on the order of 8,000 km was projected with a [consequently] increased payload mass.[26]

In other words, all the work devoted to the R-3 project was assumed to be a direct investment in the development of an intercontinental missile.

In defining the form of the R-3, Korolev had different teams independently trying to solve the same problem, an approach that reflected Korolev's philosophy of design. As one of his junior designers later remembered, "Usually ... in different situations, we'd [choose] the simplest path [because] it was the optimal path but Korolev used all paths, even the most difficult, to get redundancy. For example, he ordered a number of different people to solve the same problem."[27] Engineers settled on four different R-3 configurations as a way to conceptually establish the advantages and liabilities of certain design choices, thus opening the door to the best design in the future. These included a single-stage vehicle and three different two-stage variants. The multistage designs were innovative for the times. One involved the use

entitled "On Research on the Work Conditions of Long-Range Missiles, Their Elements and Instruments in Flight."

25 Chertok, *RAP1*, 108.

26 S. P. Korolev et al., "Printsipy i metody proektirovaniia raket bol'shoi dal'nosti" (1949), in *TNASPK*, 291–318 (see p. 292). This is a published (and edited) version of the introduction to the draft plan for the R-3 missile.

27 Interview with G. Iu. Maksimov, December 1991, Collection of James Harford, Notebook No. 2, leaf 52.

of large external tanks attached to the central core of the rocket, which would be discarded once they were empty of propellant, thus lightening the overall mass and increasing the ascent velocity of the rocket. Another involved a standard two-stage vehicle with one rocket mounted on top of another in tandem. The bottom stage would burn out and separate as the second stage fired to accelerate the payload faster. A final variant saw the use of stages strapped together in parallel, like a bunch of pencils in a rubber band. The advantage here was that all the engines could fire at liftoff, providing a huge amount of thrust. All the engines would be furnished with propellant from tanks in the external strapons, which would be cast off at propellant depletion. After a thorough analysis of all the options, Korolev's engineers decided that for the R-3, the most rational choice would be a single-stage missile, largely because of the inefficient mass-to-thrust ratios of the multistage versions given the prevailing state of Soviet rocket engine technology. Besides ballistic missile designs, Korolev's OKB-1 organization also studied two different winged (or cruise) missile options, one a single-stage variant, essentially a ballistic missile with wings, and the other a multistage version, whose first stage would be a ballistic rocket and whose second would be a cruise missile. The analysis clearly showed that for very long distances, the latter model, equipped not with a rocket engine but an air-breathing ramjet, was the preferable one.[28]

Although Korolev selected a single-stage vehicle for the final design of the R-3, in his comments at a plenary session of the NII-88 institute's scientific-technical council on December 7, 1949, he singled out the third ballistic option, the one with the strapons, as the "most realistic layout... for *very* great distances." Korolev seemed to believe that the R-3, which with a range of 3,000 kilometers was at the extreme limit for a single-stage ballistic missile, could then be used "as part of one of the more complex multi-stage designs," that is, it could be the building block for a more powerful ballistic missile with strapons.[29] In the R-3 draft plan, Korolev wrote several unusually praiseworthy paragraphs on the advantages of this particular design layout, which they called a "package" (*paket*).[30]

The package idea would eventually give birth to the Soviet ICBM. As a design concept, it did not emerge out of a vacuum but could be traced back through individuals and ideas to the 1920s; even at the height of the Cold War, missile engineers inherited sensibilities forged during the shadow of the Soviet "space fad" of the post-Revolutionary era. The key figure here was Korolev's old comrade-in-arms Mikhail Tikhonravov, who, after

[28] The analysis of all these variants are laid out in Korolev et al., "Printsipy i metody," 291–318.

[29] S. P. Korolev, "Doklad na plenarom zasedanii NTS NII-88 po eskiznomu proektu rakety R-3" (December 7, 1949), in *SPKIED*, 130–140 (see, especially, pp. 134–135).

[30] See his comments in Korolev et al., Printsipy i metody," 314.

World War II, had found a job at a military research institute known as NII-4 based in the northeastern Moscow suburb of Bol'shevo. Although Tikhonravov's work day was devoted to assessments of the types and uses of ballistic missiles for the Soviet armed forces, in his free time he also devoted time to bringing to light obscure books on the history of rocketry and space exploration. Unlike Korolev, Tikhonravov had been a passionate advocate of space exploration from their early days working together in the 1930s. In 1947, Tikhonravov edited two collections of selected works, one of Tsiolkovskii and the other of the late Fridrikh Tsander, founder of the amateur GIRD where both Korolev and Tikhonravov had served their apprenticeship. Their titles, *Works on Rocket Technology* and *The Problem of Flight with the Aid of Rocket Apparatus*, underscored that these were focused on rocketry, but both included meditations on the technical feasibility of spaceflight.[31]

While putting together Tsiolkovskii's papers for publication, Tikhonravov serendipitously came upon some old essays in which Tsiolkovskii had described two forms of multistage rockets, a "rocket train" (*raketnyi poezd*) and a "rocket squadron" (*eskadry raket*), that each could allow a rocket to reach a high enough velocity sufficient to launch a satellite into orbit.[32] The former was essentially a tandem-type rocket with a rocket divided into successive stages, one behind the other. The latter involved connecting rockets in parallel, where each constituent would exchange propellant during flight and mutually control each other's trajectories. Tikhonravov was deeply struck by these very old ideas, and, unable to let go of them, organized an informal group at the institute to study them in more detail. Research on these multistage concepts led his team at NII-4, which included several young and bright university graduates, to explore different variations of a missile that he called a "rocket package," that is, a collection of identical rockets attached together side by side like a cluster.

Tikhonravov strongly believed that package designs offered several important advantages over other multistage designs such as successively staged missiles. With a rocket package, engineers could develop smaller, less powerful rockets instead of one huge one, an option that would be undoubtedly

[31] K. E. Tsiolkovskii, *Trudy po raketnoi tekhnike*, ed. M. K. Tikhonravov (Moscow: Oborongiz, 1947); F. A. Tsander, *Problema poleta pri pomoshchi raketnykh apparatov*, ed. M. K. Tikhonravov (Moscow: Oborongiz, 1947).

[32] The bulk of Tsiolkovskii's work on multistage rockets was featured in K. E. Tsiolkovskii, *Kosmicheskie raketnye poezda. Reaktivnyi dvigatel'* (Kaluga: K. E. Tsiolkovskii, 1929). He introduced additional ideas on multistage rockets ("rocket squadrons") in Chapter 10 of an unpublished manuscript, "Osnovy postroeniia gazovykh mashin, motorov i letatel'nykh priborov" ["Principles of Constructing Gas Machines, Motors, and Flying Instruments"], written in 1934 and 1935. Tikhonravov included both these essays in the collection of Tsiolkovskii's works he edited in 1947. Tsiolkovskii, *Trudy po raketnoi tekhnike*, 215–243, 348–360.

challenging given that Soviet industry had barely mastered the older V-2 technology. Furthermore, for most package designs, there would be no need to create rocket engines to ignite in vacuum – an as yet unsolved problem involving sophisticated nozzle design – because all engines could fire simultaneously on the ground. Additionally, if all the rockets in the package combination were of the same type, mass production could be easier and benefit from economies of scale. Finally, the capabilities of package rockets could be adjusted by altering the number of rockets in the package, thus incorporating great flexibility to the design.

Tikhonravov presented his initial considerations on the package issue at two meetings in 1948, one hosted by the scientific council of the NII-4 institute and the other by NII-4's parent body, the Academy of Artillery Sciences.[33] Korolev attended both lectures and found himself intrigued by this work, and drawn especially to the idea of the "simplest package," a version with identical boosters strapped together mechanically, all firing at liftoff. He visited the NII-4 premises – an adjacent suburb next to his own workspace at Kaliningrad – in July 1949 to familiarize himself firsthand with Tikhonravov's work, offering support where there was little from within Tikhonravov's own institute. Later in the year, Korolev sent Tikhonravov a formal assignment to continue this work, using the R-2 missile as one of the constituents of his rocket package. The goal was to conduct "research on the possibility and feasibility of creating multi-stage long-range missiles of the 'package' type."[34] Tikhonravov's team, on their own initiative, also conducted similar studies using the still-on-paper R-3 missile – much more powerful than the R-2 – and showed that a two-stage package with three R-3s strapped together could not only fly intercontinental distances but also deliver an object into *orbit* around the Earth, results that Tikhonravov presented at a scientific conference in March 1950, once again to hostility, or at best indifference.[35]

All of these studies of the Tikhonravov group, which were essentially conducted informally without significant supervision from the top levels of the Soviet government, were critical to moving ahead with conceptions of an intercontinental missile. Their results were integrated into the second long R&D plan on missiles formulated by engineers and scientists, formally

[33] The text of Tikhonravov's lecture in July 1948, entitled "Paths to Accomplishing Great Ranges by Firing Missiles," has been published as M. K. Tikhonravov, "Puti osushchestvleniia bol'shikh dal'nostei strel'by raketami (doklad v akademii artilleriiskikh nauk 14 iulia 1948 g.)," *IIAIK* no. 67 (1995): 3–26.

[34] S. P. Korolev, "O rabotakh po sostavnym raketam tipa 'paket'," in *SPKIED*, 149–150.

[35] For participant testimonies of the Tikhonravov group's work, see I. M. Iatsunskii, "O deiatel'nosti M. K. Tikhonravova v period s 1947 po 1953 gg. po obosnovaniiu vozmozhnosti sozdaniia sostavykh raket," *IIAIK* no. 42 (1980): 31–38; I. K. Bazhinov and G. Iu. Maksimov, "Ob issledovaniiakh vozmozhnostei sozdaniia v sssr pervykh moshchnykh sostavnykh raket i iskusstvennykh sputnikov zemli," in *IPIITR*, Vol. 7, 13–25.

approved in a major government decree in December 1950. Like the predecessor decree in May 1947, over 100 applied research programs were funded. Three of them focused on specific options for the future of Soviet missile design:

- Theme N-1, which subsumed the R-3 missile program, involved research on a missile with a range of 3,000 kilometers;
- Theme N-2 focused on producing a missile using not cryogenic propellants, such as those used on the V-2, but storable propellants that would allow greater flexibility in battle operations; and
- Theme N-3 focused on exploratory research on developing an intercontinental missile.

The latter theme, carried out simultaneously at several organizations spread out within the Soviet military-industrial complex, but led by Korolev's OKB-1, extended the studies originally done as part of the R-3 framework by looking at concrete options.[36] Like the earlier studies, scientists and engineers looked at both ballistic and cruise missiles, and also like the earlier work, the military was not involved; the official customer was not the armed forces but Ustinov's Ministry of Armaments.[37]

In the ballistic case, Korolev and his colleagues focused on creating a multistage missile that would use liquid oxygen and kerosene and be capable of carrying a three- to five-ton payload over 7,000 kilometers.[38] Here again, the central focus was on developing Tikhonravov's package concept. Early mathematical studies by Tikhonravov's group at NII-4 had proved that the "simplest package" favored by Korolev, despite its elegance, would be much heavier, perhaps 30% to 50% heavier, than other more sophisticated package designs, because each booster would basically be designed as an independent rocket with all of its own systems capable of flying independently of the package. When Tikhonravov's team completed their work in support of

[36] Organizations involved in theme N-3 included those from the Ministry of Armaments (NII-88, OKB-456, and GOI), the Ministry of the Aviation Industry (TsAGI and TsIAM), the Ministry of Defense (NII-4, NII-3, and GKNII VVS), the Ministry of the Shipbuilding Industry (NII-49 and NII-10), the Ministry of Agricultural Machine Building (NII-6, NII-504, NII-137, NII-125, and KB-3), the Ministry of the Communications Industry (NII-885), and the USSR Academy of Sciences (the Institute of Applied Mathematics). See RGAE, 4372/99/1104/154–155 (1952). The official title of the theme was "Research on the Prospects of Creating [Long-Range Missiles] of Various Types with a Flight Range of 5,000–10,000 km with a Warhead with a Mass of 1–10 tons."

[37] RGAE, 4372/99/1104/154–155 (1952).

[38] The principal designers reporting on the results of the research were S. P. Korolev, V. P. Mishin, and A. N. Oleinik (for super long-range missiles), V. P. Glushko and Z. B. Borshchevskii (for rocket engines), M. M. Bondariuk and A. G. Galanov (for ramjets), and M. S. Riazanskii, N. A. Piliugin, and B. M. Konoplev (for guidance systems). See RGAE, 4372/99/1112/3–4 (1952).

FIGURE 25. This famous picture, dating from July 1959, shows the "Three Ks" of the Soviet military-industrial complex, (from the left) Sergei Korolev, Igor' Kurchatov, and Mstislav Keldysh. Kurchatov was considered the "father" of the Soviet atom bomb project, whereas Keldysh provided much of the applied scientific power behind a number of important strategic weapons programs, including the thermonuclear program, the missile program, and the air defense project. On the right is Vasilii Mishin, Korolev's senior deputy who contributed to the conceptual design of the R-7 ICBM. [*Source*: Collection of Asif Siddiqi]

the N-3 theme, they issued two reports studying various combinations of R-2 and R-3 missiles, but Tikhonravov declined to devote any more attention to trying to optimize the so-called simplest package because he believed that any hopes of improving its properties would basically undercut the advantages of the package concept as a whole. Korolev was bullheaded about the value of the simplest package and invited another group of young scientists, ones at the V. A. Steklov Mathematics Institute of the Academy of Sciences (*Matematicheskii institut Akademii nauk*, MIAN), to do the optimization. Here, the nuclear program's star mathematician, Mstislav Keldysh, had created a brilliant team of applied mathematicians ("Keldysh's Boys") led by twenty-eight-year-old Dmitrii Okhotsimskii, alumni of the TsAGI, to do work on the physics of nuclear explosions (see Figure 25). Korolev's request brought, for the first time ever, the Academy of Sciences firmly into the orbit of missile design, fortifying an increasing connection between design and applied science.

Keldysh's team summarized the results of this optimization work in a long report entitled "Ballistic Possibilities of Multi-Stage Missiles," which examined a variety of configurations for intercontinental missiles including simple single-stage models and Tikhonravov's package schemes. In investigating the package design, the team carried out detailed comparisons using the R-2 or R-3 missile as the basic building block of each package. Keldysh and his colleagues found that Korolev's favored simplest package (of three or five R-3 missiles) could achieve the necessary velocity of 7,500 meters per second, sufficient for intercontinental distance, and very close to orbital velocity. In their synopsis, the authors concluded that the simplest package would indeed be the most efficient path of development, given the relatively minimal modifications required of an already existing "standard" missile such as the R-3. Development of such elements as guidance systems, the authors predicted, would be an easier proposition. Although the report was largely exploratory in nature, Keldysh's team recommended the most favored variant for an ICBM as being a two-stage missile utilizing two strapon boosters, each essentially an R-3 missile.[39]

In the winter of 1951–1952, the NII-88 institute hosted several meetings to discuss the results of the N-1, N-2, and N-3 themes. Two days after Christmas 1951, Korolev reported to a large group of representatives from industry, academia, and the scientific community on the integrated research on Theme N-3, synthesizing all the work done by various institutions including that by Keldysh's Boys and in-house research at NII-88 under his direction. The goal was to decide on an optimal design of an intercontinental missile given the constraints of Soviet industry. The scope of in-house work at NII-88 had been extremely wide, encompassing rocket design, guidance systems, rocket engine design, and flight dynamics. In summarizing the work done, Korolev described five different missile designs, the favored one being the fifth, partly because it was the simplest package. This version had a central booster with a 34-ton thrust engine combined with two strapons, each having a sea-level thrust of 115 tons.

Although the results of the research work of Keldysh's Boys deeply influenced Korolev's thinking, his recommendations also betrayed a keen understanding of *practical* limitations that moved from the specific to the general: the envelope of rocket engine design, the level of Soviet industry, money, and time. In each case, the available options seemed to suggest that the simplest package was the most favorable design even though it would not be as elegant or light as other designs. The goal, however, was not sophistication or grace but whether the rocket could perform its mission. Korolev, especially, but also Keldysh strongly believed that the simplest package could if a few critical obstacles – particularly related to engine design – could be overcome. In the conclusion of the report, Korolev cautioned that, "[i]t must be noted that these investigations of ballistic and long-range missiles may only serve

39 M. V. Keldysh, S. S. Kamynin, and D. E. Okhotsimskii, "Ballisticheskie vozmozhnosti sostavnykh raket" (1951), in *MVKIT*, 39–140.

as a basis for the establishment of primary directions to be followed by detailed elaborations of definite projects and proposals."[40]

Selecting a particular type of ballistic missile was one subset of a larger problem: Should the intercontinental missile be ballistic or cruise? Simultaneously with their investigations of potential ballistic missiles, various groups also studied possible cruise missiles. After a preliminary exploration, Korolev had settled on a two-stage cruise missile. Unlike the ballistic design, however, the cruise missile was to use a traditional rocket engine on the first stage, and a supersonic ramjet engine on the winged second stage. Like concurrent American cruise missiles such as the Navaho XSM-64, the Soviet vehicle was designed to travel its entire flight within the atmosphere, using the air itself as its oxidizer.

A few weeks after the meeting on the ICBMs, in January 1952, Korolev presented the NII-88's research on intercontinental cruise missiles to an audience of reviewers. Korolev's engineers believed that the best design would be a two-stage cruise missile with a mass of about 90–120 tons and a range of 8,000 kilometers. The first stage would accelerate the second stage to an altitude of 15–20 kilometers and a velocity of 900 meters per second, that is, fast enough for ignition of the ramjet engines, which could only fire at certain speeds. The second stage would then fly at about Mach 3 on a horizontal trajectory to its target and deposit its warhead. As with the ICBM conceptions, one of the primary challenges was developing sufficiently powerful liquid-propellant rocket engines for the first stage. NII-88's analysis indicated that engines with thrusts of the order of 100–165 tons would be required. Ramjet engine thrusts could be limited to 8–10 tons. Engineers also examined three different launch configurations for the cruise missile: horizontal launch, air launch, and vertical launch. Given time and technological limitations, the latter would prove to be the best option.[41]

The debate over prioritizing ballistic or winged missiles was not new – Soviet rocket engineers, including Korolev, had been debating the issue since the early 1930s when camps favoring one or the other option refused to compromise. As the choice depended on many factors – technology, resources, objectives, military strategy, and entrenched cultural predilections – it also had wide-ranging repercussions on many of those same considerations. In the 1930s, Korolev firmly believed in the future of winged missiles for a number of reasons. Rocket engines from the 1930s had relatively low thrust (a few hundred kilograms), and thus rockets equipped with wings could

[40] S. P. Korolev et al., "Tezisy doklada po rezul'tatam issledovanii perspektiv razvitiia ballisticheskikh raket dal'nego deistviia" (1951), in *TNASPK*, 319–327 (see, especially, p. 327). The N-3 theme was officially finished on July 16, 1952. Theme N-2 was finished on June 9, 1952. See RGAE, 4372/99/1104/154–155 (1952).

[41] An edited version of the report has been published as S. P. Korolev at al., "Tezisy doklada po rezul'tatam issledovanii perspektiv razvitiia krylatykh raket dal'nego deistviia" (January 16, 1952), in *TNASPK*, 328–341.

deliver the same payload as much as four or more times further than rockets without. In addition, for engineers steeped in aviation culture, winged missiles were artifacts resembling their world view; to many, such missiles were no more than aircraft with autopilots and rocket engines. Ballistic missiles, launching straight up and harder to control, were unfamiliar and promised fewer returns, especially from a military perspective.

These considerations began to shift with the Soviet discovery of German rocket engines with thrusts several orders higher than contemporary Soviet models. The V-2's alcohol and liquid-oxygen engine, for example, had a thrust of approximately twenty-five tons. Such engines meant that missiles (both ballistic and winged) could fly must faster and further, but they also raised their own set of challenges, particularly in terms of guidance and navigation.

Given the constraints of Soviet defense industry in the 1950s, each option had advantages and liabilities. ICBM warheads, for example, required special thermal shielding to protect them during reentry. They would also require either radio or inertial guidance systems to navigate the missile through its powered phase before ballistic flight. Cruise missiles, on the other hand, needed highly sophisticated guidance systems that could navigate the missile through thousands of kilometers within the atmosphere during either day or night. They had operational differences, too. An ICBM had the advantage of flying at altitudes of 1,000 kilometers and at velocities of almost 25,000 kilometers per hour, making it virtually invulnerable to any kind of defense. It would take a missile minutes to reach its targets across the globe. Cruise missiles, on the other hand, flew relatively slowly and at low altitudes, taking several hours before reaching the American landmass. They were much more vulnerable to defensive measures.

Both industrial officials and designers were unwilling to come out unequivocally in favor of one approach, ballistic or cruise, although by the late 1940s, Korolev was beginning to favor ballistic missiles. His preference was based not only on genuine technical and industrial considerations, but also on the issue of control. He reasoned that if the cruise missile option proved to be the most effective way to deliver a warhead to the United States, then more than likely, its development would be transferred to another design bureau with the Ministry of the Aviation Industry, that is, out of NII-88.[42] Korolev had already taken a gamble by ejecting all cruise missile development from NII-88 by 1951; a national commitment to develop an intercontinental cruise missile might deprive NII-88, and Korolev, in particular, of its livelihood. There may have been one other consideration: Cruise missiles could not fly into space, whereas powerful ballistic missiles could. This notion was never spelled out anywhere but circumstantial evidence suggests that, already from the late 1940s, Korolev and Glushko were thinking not

[42] Chertok also makes this point. See *RAP2*, 231.

only of the military applications of what they built but also of their cosmic applications.

INNOVATIONS, SMALL AND LARGE

All of these plans depended on the fate of the still-on-paper R-3 missile. The principal challenge in that project was its engine, a mammoth contraption with a thrust of 120 tons, compared to the V-2's 25 tons. At the time of Korolev's reports on missile design in the winter of 1951–1952, Valentin Glushko's team at Khimki was struggling to create this monster, putting the entire R-3 project into jeopardy. The missile had been conceived as an evolution of previous Soviet missiles derived from German ones, moving from the German V-2 to its Soviet copy (the R-1) to an improved version (the R-2) to a vastly improved version (the R-3). In the late 1940s, Soviet designers under Korolev and Glushko had introduced four relatively small but critical improvements to the original R-1 (the Soviet copy of the V-2) to produce the R-2, thus doubling the range of the original but keeping the missile roughly in the same mass category. First, one of the two propellant tanks of the missile, the one carrying ethyl alcohol, was incorporated as an integral part of the overall structure of the rocket, significantly lightening the mass of the vehicle. Second, they introduced a separable warhead making it possible to have a much lighter rocket body, given that heavy thermal insulation would now be unnecessary for the main body after separation of the warhead from the missile. Third, the R-2 had a much improved guidance system that allowed increased targeting accuracy and also easier access during prelaunch operations to decrease the time required for preparing launches. Finally, the missile used an uprated version of the original engine, with a thrust of 35 tons, as compared to the R-1 engine, which offered 25 tons of thrust. This increase was largely achieved by increasing the concentration of ethyl alcohol and raising combustion pressure.[43]

Further innovations were introduced to the ambitious R-3. These included using a separating warhead, integral pressurized propellant tanks, a lighter aluminum-magnesium alloy for the main structure, a more streamlined internal layout that made effective use of unused volume, and bolted joints instead of welded ones; designers also deleted the old graphite steering vanes. The principal bottleneck in the project had, however, been the development of an engine with a thrust of 120 tons, significantly exceeding the best rocket engine of the day, rated at 35 tons of thrust. At Khimki, Glushko had opted to scale up the old V-2 design in the hopes of achieving this leap in capability. During tests of the engine, the unit was subjected to extremely high frequency oscillations that threatened to literally shake it apart. In a letter to his boss, Minister of the Aviation Industry, Mikhail Khrunichev, Glushko wrote that

[43] "Rakety R-2E, R-2R, R-2 (8Zh38)," in *SPKIED*, 548–551.

"the creation of an engine [with a thrust of] 120–140 tons is connected with a number of problems, which are... at the limits of available modern science and technology."[44]

Because of the serious problems with the development of the R-3, by late 1951, it was clear to Korolev that they had reached a turning point in missile development. The hitherto path of scaling up the V-2 had reached a dead end. The cluster-type package arrangement appeared to be the *only* optimal path to developing very-long-range ballistic rockets. It was also evident that the constituent parts of the package had to be less ambitious than the R-3, as Keldysh's Boys had suggested. Should they continue to invest resources in bringing the R-3 to life, or should they work on developing less powerful rockets that could one day fit as part of an intercontinental missile? This conundrum was solved by Korolev's first deputy ("first among the deputies"), Vasilii Mishin, a bright and somewhat brash young engineer (he was 34 at the time) who Korolev depended on as a "generator of ideas." Mishin suggested abandoning the R-3 program and committing to a full-scale project to develop an ICBM, with a range of about 6,000 to 7,000 kilometers. At the same time, using already invested work in the R-3, he felt confident that they could develop an intermediate rocket, known as the R-5, with a range of about 1,200 kilometers. Both Korolev and Glushko strongly resisted Mishin's idea because many organizations had invested two years of work in the R-3. They had reasonable objections: If Glushko had failed to develop an engine for the R-3, what was the sense in abandoning the missile and moving to an even more ambitious weapon? But Mishin's suggestion had a persuasive logic to it: Why not scale everything down and put *more* of them together to make a bigger missile?

Mishin arrayed a number of supporters within the Ministry of Armaments who would be crucial to making his case, including Deputy Minister Ivan Zubovich, who convinced his boss, Minister Dmitrii Ustinov, of the value of the plan.[45] There is some evidence to suggest that the military opposed the move to cancel the R-3 project. The military's objections, which focused on the downgraded version of the R-3, were not entirely without justification; they justifiably argued that Korolev could not simply break an agreement to produce a 3,000-kilometer missile and start producing one with a range of 1,200 kilometers; the military, after all, had waited two years for this

44 *OIN*, 454. Another engine designer, A. I. Poliarnii, working at the NII-1 institute, was also invited to develop an engine for the R-3 missile but his design also ran into similar problems.

45 V. P. Mishin, *Ot sozdaniia ballisticheskikh raket k raketno-kosmicheskomu mashinostroeniiu* (Moscow: Inform-Znanie, 1998), 27. Mishin has also written that a mid-level bureaucrat in the Ministry of Armaments, A. V. Zaitsev, was one of the co-authors of this idea. See V. P. Mishin, "Problemy pervogo poleta cheloveka v kosmos," in *Gagarinskie nauchnye chteniia po kosmonavtike i aviatsii, 1991* (Moscow: Nauka, 1992), 18–26.

rocket.[46] Ustinov's support of Mishin's plan, undoubtedly a risk for his career, proved to be crucial in resolving a stalemate.

Mishin's suggestion to leapfrog ahead, although promising, still did not free the Soviets of dependence on the limits of engine design. After all, there would be no intercontinental missile unless Valentin Glushko's engineers could design powerful engines. Original conceptions of the ICBM had incorporated two strapons, each with a thrust of about 115 tons, a limit now beyond reach given Glushko's inability to scale the V-2 design up to the R-3's required 120 tons. To circumvent this problem, Korolev's designers chose the option of *reducing* the thrust of the engines and *increasing* the number of strapons. Thus, through 1952, the layout of the ICBM changed such that it had a core booster and *four* strapons, each equipped with single-chamber engines of 50 to 60 tons of thrust.[47]

Glushko believed that 50 to 60 tons would be possible, but only if the engines incorporated innovations amassed from a variety of sources: other Soviet engine designers, Glushko's own work in the interwar years, and German advances from the same period. For many years, rocket engineers had been well aware that one of the possible ways of increasing rocket engine performance was to raise pressure in the combustion chamber. Increased pressure, however, resulted in increased heatflow through a chamber's cooled firewall. To protect the chamber from overheating, one solution was to have thinner chamber walls. But thinner walls in turn would not be able to withstand the higher chamber pressures required, leading to a conundrum. Conventional regenerative cooling solutions would not be effective in breaking this vicious cycle. Glushko's engineers found a solution to the problem by using what was later known as an "integrated solder-welded design," in which the chamber had relatively thin walls but with numerous thin ribs for coolant to pass through. Glushko benefited from both antecedent work and German help. Back in 1933, Glushko had developed an engine called the ORM-48 that used ribbed steel walls for its nozzle for water cooling. Almost simultaneously and independently, the German Eugen Sänger, in 1934, also tested (and later patented) a combustion chamber with a similar design.

Soviet industry faced significant problems in manufacturing such chambers because they were unable to produce *firmly* interconnected shells (an inner and outer one) with ribs within them. These shells needed to be firmly interconnected because differing thermal stresses in the constituent shells of the chamber could cause major failures in the chamber. The answer came from Aleksei Isaev, a contemporary of Glushko, as talented but less ambitious, who absent Glushko's headstrong personality, might have ended up in the driver's seat for designing the ICBM engines. In 1944, at the

[46] RGAE, 4372/99/1103/148 (March 3, 1952).

[47] Mishin, "Problemy pervogo poleta cheloveka v kosmos," 20–21. In another source, he says eighty-ton thrust engines. See Mishin, *Ot sozdaniia*, 28.

NII-1 institute, Isaev had pioneered a new integrated solder-welded method. Glushko's engineers, with the active help of captured German scientists based at Glushko's design bureau, resurrected the old ribbed wall design, but this time using Isaev's welding method to produce, in the late 1940s, two experimental combustion chambers, the KS-50 and ED-140. Describing the KS-50, one Soviet historian recalled:

> In such [an integrated solder-welded design] with frequent connections, the walls could have a small width, since, thanks to the numerous thin ribs, the individual conduits obtained for the passage of the coolant were narrow. Thus, the combustion wall could be produced from a relatively flimsy, but still highly heat-conductive copper alloy.[48]

In other words, efficiently solder-welded designs allowed increasing operating pressures, while reducing relative dimensions and specific masses of the new engines. The ED-140 experimental chamber was built to improve methods of mixing propellants in the combustion chamber; it used special flat injector "mixing heads" for injecting propellants into a cylindrical combustion chamber. The flat injector head design as well as the introduction of so-called "film cooling" were new innovations in Soviet rocket design.

Using the experience with these two combustion chambers, Glushko's engineers introduced a variety of further innovations into the next generation of Soviet rocket engines. For example, Glushko replaced the old spherical combustion chamber favored by the Germans with a cylindrical one, an idea that probably came from captured German scientists who had worked at his design bureau in the late 1940s. Glushko's engineers, in cooperation with other scientific-research institutes, developed improved welding methods (including vacuum soldering of chamber joints in a neutral protective medium such as nitrogen) and introduced corrugated walls (as opposed to ribbed walls) for cooling engine nozzles. With these experimental chambers, he also switched from alcohol to kerosene as fuel, thus making a conscious departure from the German antecedents of alcohol.[49] The change was motivated by the promise of better performance with kerosene.

Individually, these modest alterations and innovations in missile and engine design were not significant. There was no singular watershed of "breakthrough" innovation that moved the project from one footing (is this possible?) to another (yes). Collectively, however, they represented the ability of Soviet designers to master a large-scale technology and improve it at a fundamental level such that the new system was a qualitative rather than a quantitative improvement over its predecessor. Here, beyond the cumulative

[48] V. I. Prishchepa, "Iz istorii sozdaniia pervykh kosmicheskikh raketnykh dvigatelei (1947–1957)," in *IPIITR*, Vol. 1 (1981), 123–137 (see, especially, p. 127).

[49] The fuel for the earlier RD-100 was a solution of 75% ethyl alcohol and 25% water. For later engines such as the RD-101 and RD-103, Glushko used a 92% ethyl alcohol solution.

notion of small innovations representing a larger one, there was also a second aspect of the innovation process: the willingness to take risks on a systemic level. Mishin's suggestion (and ministerial support for it) to abandon the R-3 and move directly to the creation of an intercontinental ballistic missile was not typical of the Soviet defense industry, particularly during the Cold War. By and large, engineers and managers were used to incremental steps that secured rather than disrupted habits in bureaucracies, design bureaus, and factories. This type of anomalous action – or agency – was crucial at key points in the history of the ICBM, sometimes from designers and sometimes from bureaucrats. We can ascribe some but not all of this behavior to ambition. Some designers wanted the benefits that had accrued to their colleagues in the nuclear weapons industry and were willing to take the risk. But beyond ambition, there was also a relative lack of supervision over the missile project from the very top, and not inconsiderable institutional chaos at the middle levels, especially between 1949 and 1953. This lack of direct control afforded designers "creative latitude," in which they managed to consistently push the envelope on missile capabilities in numerous research studies. Such research profiles were relatively inexpensive, unobtrusive, and, by dint of their links with academia and the Academy of Sciences, enjoyed a patina of scientific esotericism. This creative latitude would face a severe trial in 1953 as the missile program was subjected to deep scrutiny.

THE NUCLEAR INDUSTRY TAKES OVER

Between Stalin's death in 1953 and the launch of *Sputnik* in 1957, control over the long-range missile program was in deep flux as institutions and managers rotated through various permutations so bewildering that the precise evolution of these changes still eludes even surviving veterans (see Table 3). The goal of building an ICBM was one of the many proposals caught in the crossfire of the postwar Stalinist succession among Lavrentii Beriia, Georgii Malenkov, and Nikita Khrushchev. We see, in particular, how as the possibility of the ICBM grew in promise, multiple constituencies sought to lay claim to it.

Stalin's death on March 5, 1953 set off a chain reaction of changes at the highest levels of the power structure, manifested in a struggle for influence among Beriia, Malenkov, and Khrushchev. At first, Beriia and Malenkov, in charge of the security services and Council of Ministers, respectively, faced a standoff. Beriia enjoyed a much superior position with regard to control over the Soviet defense industry, particularly the two most important strategic programs, the nuclear and air defense projects, both of which he ran out of his Special Committee out of sight from even the Politburo. Other more "normal" programs, such as aviation and missile development, had been subordinated to special organs of the Council of Ministers. Since 1949, these institutions changed name and subordination but they were run

TABLE 3. *Individuals and Organizations Coordinating Soviet Missile Programs in the Postwar Era*

From	To	Individual	Institution
	Coordinator of the Soviet defense industry in the postwar era (except the atomic bomb and air defense programs)		
3/20/46	Early 1947	L. P. Beriia	Bureau of the Council of Ministers
Early 1947	3/26/49	V. M. Molotov	Bureau of the Council of Ministers
3/26/49	2/16/51	N. A. Bulganin	Bureau of the Council of Ministers
2/16/51	10/18/52	N. A. Bulganin	Bureau of Military and Military-Industrial Questions of the Council of Ministers
10/18/52	1/26/53	N. A. Bulganin	Permanent Commission on Defense Questions of the Presidium of the Central Committee
1/26/53	3/16/53	L. P. Beriia	Troika
3/16/53	6/26/53	L. P. Beriia	Special Committee
6/53	1/54	N. A. Bulganin	Department of Defense Industries of the Council of Ministers
1/54	2/28/55	N. A. Bulganin	Department within the Council of Ministers
2/28/55	5/25/55	M. V. Khrunichev	Department within the Council of Ministers
5/25/55	12/25/56	M. Z. Saburov (via M. V. Khrunichev)	Department within the Council of Ministers
12/25/56	5/10/57	M. G. Pervukhin (via M. V. Khrunichev)	State Economic Commission on Current Planning of the National Economy (*Gosekonomkomissiia*) of the Council of Ministers
5/10/57	12/14/57	M. V. Khrunichev	Department within the Council of Ministers
12/14/57	3/13/63	D. F. Ustinov	Military-Industrial Commission
	Coordinator of the Soviet missile programs in the postwar era		
5/13/46	5/10/47	G. M. Malenkov	Special Committee for Reactive Technology
5/10/47	8/29/49	N. A. Bulganin	Committee No. 2
9/15/49	8/9/50	A. M. Vasil'evskii	4th Directorate of the Ministry of the Armed Forces
8/9/50	6/51	?	?
6/51	1/26/53	L. P. Beriia (via G. N. Pashkov)	Department within the Council of Ministers
1/26/53	3/16/53	L. P. Beriia (via G. N. Pashkov)	Troika
3/16/53	6/26/53	L. P. Beriia (via G. N. Pashkov)	Special Committee
7/29/53	4/14/55	V. M. Malyshev (via M. V. Khrunichev)	Ministry of Medium Machine Building
4/14/55	12/14/57	V. M. Riabikov	Special Committee

by Nikolai Bulganin, a loyal Stalinist with a long background in military affairs. Stalin's confidence in Bulganin was underscored when the latter was appointed to replace Stalin as USSR Minister of Defense in February 1947, to the chagrin of many in the service elite who saw Bulganin as a civilian who had no business in this post. Four years later, Stalin appointed Bulganin into a special post within the Council of Ministers, putting him charge of the Soviet defense industry; he was thus head of both the client and customer side of the Soviet military, that is, at the apex of the postwar Soviet military-industrial complex.[50]

Bulganin's control over the Soviet military-industrial complex did not extend to the high-priority nuclear and air defense projects run by Beriia, but this arrangement changed in 1953. In his last years, Stalin had increasingly become inaccessible, and he withdrew from close supervision of the Soviet defense industry. In the final months of his life, he appears to have relinquished full control of these matters to Beriia, who engineered the formation in January 1953 of a Troika, a three-person body including Beriia, Malenkov, and Bulganin to supervise all "special work," that is, nuclear, air defense, and missile development.[51] Two aspects of this reorganization warrant scrutiny. First, with the formation of the Troika, Bulganin had entered the most inner circle, quite possibly to serve as Stalin's eyes and ears on strategic weapons development. Second and more important, for the first time, missile development was elevated to parity with nuclear weapons work. Since the postwar rocket program was founded in May 1946, it had been an important project of the Soviet defense industry but it had hardly enjoyed the purposeful commitment such as the atomic program, and later the air defense project. The change was brought about by a confluence of factors: the slow and tenuous progress of the strategic bomber program,

50 Bystrova, *VPK*, 161–162. Management mechanisms for the Soviet defense industry were restructured several times in the postwar years. Typically, in the early period, a single person in the Bureau (later Presidium) of the Council of Ministers supervised the defense industry. This position was held by L. P. Beriia (1946–1947), V. M. Molotov (1947–1949), and N. A. Bulganin (1949–1951). Other junior members were responsible for particular industries and ministries. On February 16, 1951, Stalin appointed Bulganin to head the new Bureau for Military-Industrial and Military Issues of the Council of Ministers, whose job was to manage the entire defense industry. Members on this body included M. V. Khrunichev, D. F. Ustinov, A. M. Vasil'evskii, and I. S. Iumashev. This body was abolished in October 1952, although Bulganin retained control of the defense industry through the new Commission on Defense Problems of the Presidium of the Central Committee until January 1953. These myriad and confusing changes in the control over the defense industry reflected an increasing ambivalence about both the concentration of power and the duality of power (shared by the Party and the government). For many primary documents on these changes, see *Politbiuro TsK VKP(b) i Sovet ministrov sssr 1945–1953*, eds. O. V. Khlevniuk et al. (Moscow: Rosspen, 2002).

51 "Vypiska iz protokla No. 7 zasedaniia Biuro Prezidiuma TsK KPSS ob organizatsii 'Troiki' dlia nabliudeniia za spetsial'nymi rabotami" (January 26, 1953), in *APS*, 505–506.

the development of deliverable nuclear weapons, and principally, the missile designers' claim that they were ready to move rapidly ahead and build an intercontinental missile.

On February 9, 1953, Beriia, Malenkov, and Bulganin held the Troika's first meeting in the Kremlin attended by key figures in the missile project: Ustinov, Pashkov, and Khrunichev from industry, Marshal Vasil'evskii and Colonel General Nedelin from the armed forces, and Korolev, representing the designers.[52] On the agenda was the plan of research and development work on long-range missiles (which took the code name "R") in the period 1953 to 1955. The discussions were not without disagreements. For example, Korolev strongly resisted the proposal to build a second missile development nerve center in Ukraine, one that would develop missiles using storable propellants that could be kept ready for much longer than those with Korolev's preferred liquid oxygen.[53] The attendees approved the development of several new long-range missiles and also committed resources to two new themes, T-1 and T-2, efforts that represented the convergence of several years of work on the search for an optical intercontinental missile.[54] Theme T-1 involved the design of an intercontinental ballistic missile whereas T-2 focused on an intercontinental cruise missile. Each would have a range of 8,000 kilometers. According to a plan drawn up at the meeting, seven models of the T-1 ICBM would be ready for static and flight testing by the first quarter of 1955, while designers would produce eight experimental cruise missiles with an initial range of 700 kilometers for flight testing by the second quarter of 1954. These research projects, the first top-level decision on intercontinental missiles, were formalized by Stalin's signature on February 13, 1953.[55] Like the earlier themes, several organizations were involved in the studies, including Korolev's OKB-1 and Keldysh's department at MIAN.

Twenty days later Stalin died. Like the rest of Soviet society, polity, and culture, the men and women of the Soviet defense industry also faced

[52] "Iz protokola No. 2 zasedaniia Troiki po rukovodstvu spetsial'nymi rabotami" (February 9, 1953), in *APS*, 126–128.

[53] Korolev lost this battle. A new design bureau, OKB-586, was established on April 10, 1954 at a large automobile factory in the Ukrainian city of Dnepropetrovsk. The factory had already been manufacturing R-1 and R-2 missiles from Korolev's design bureau but now moved into design work under M. K. Iangel', a talented aviation designer from NII-88.

[54] These new missiles were the R-11 (a missile with a range of 270 kilometers fueled by storable propellants to replace the R-1), the R-5 (a "strategic" missile with a range of 1,200 kilometers derived from a test variant of the abandoned R-3), and the R-12 (another storable propellant missile with a range of 1,500 kilometers). The first two were tasked to Korolev's OKB-1 in Kaliningrad, and the latter to Iangel's OKB-586 in Dnepropetrovsk.

[55] "Postanovlenie soveta ministrov sssr No. 443–213ss: 'o plane nauchno-issledovatel'skikh rabot po raketam dal'nego deistviia na 1953–1955 gg.'" (February 13, 1953), in *SKI*, 40–42. The official title of theme T-1 was "Theoretical and Experimental Research on the Creation of a Two-Stage Ballistic Missile with a Range of 7000–8000 km."

unprecedented changes. A wave of institutional changes cascaded through the Soviet defense sector through the rest of 1953, putting the T-1 and T-2 programs into the hands of the most unexpected group, those in charge of the nuclear weapons project. For a brief period, Beriia resurrected the old Special Committee, this time subsuming all work on the nuclear, air defense, and missile programs under its structure.[56] Beriia's subsequent fall from power opened the door to another set of reforms. The highest security programs had essentially been run out of Beriia's personal secretariat beyond the purview of Politburo members. Upon Beriia's fall (and his execution later in the year), only a few Party or government officials had any inkling about the inner workings of this vast empire. One of them was Viacheslav Malyshev, a defense industry alumnus who had served his apprenticeship in the sector during the war. Displaying the necessary iron will to create a mammoth tank industry, his ministry produced nearly 25,000 tanks before the end of the war. After 1945, Malyshev had been recruited to work in the atom bomb project. For helping to develop a domestic competence in the technology of gaseous separation of uranium isotopes, a process that helped the Soviet Union produce highly enriched uranium-235, he was awarded the Stalin Prize in 1951. Malyshev was also deeply involved the creation of a Soviet nuclear submarine force in the early 1950s.[57] In political terms, Malyshev was, in the words of physicist Andrei Sakharov, "Malenkov's man."[58] His allegiance to Malenkov immediately put him at the apex of governmental power and simultaneously at odds with the Party power structure headed by Nikita Khrushchev. Technically, Malyshev's position obligated him to report to both Malenkov and Khrushchev on strategic programs, but in reality Malyshev only reported to Malenkov, who was, in Malyshev's words, surprised by the scale of the deceased Beriia's vast nuclear empire.

Malyshev acted quickly to consolidate control, which he was able to do partly because few in the top political leadership had a clue about the size or scope of Beriia's atomic program. Georgii Malenkov, for example, did not even know that there was a hydrogen bomb project. Malyshev immediately merged the three main directorates under the Special Committee that had hitherto managed the atomic bomb and air defense projects, and put them under a single new "super" ministry, the Ministry of Medium Machine Building (*Minsredmash*), using the old staff of the Beriia's Special

[56] This Special Committee, reestablished on March 16, 1953, hosted at least three meetings, on March 28, April 11, and May 6. Missiles were discussed at all these meetings but only relatively short-range ones such as the R-1, R-2, and R-5 projects. See "Postanovlenie sm sssr No. 697–355ss/op: 'o rukovodstve spetsial'nymi rabotami' " (March 16, 1953), in *APS*, 532–534 for the reformation of the Special Committee.

[57] V. Chalmaev, *Malyshev* (Moscow: Molodaia gvardiia, 1978); Arkadii Kruglov, *Shtab atomproma* (Moscow: TsNIIAtominform, 1998), 137–141.

[58] Andrei Sakharov, *Memoirs* (New York: Knopf, 1999), 169.

Committee, now purged of those who might still owe their loyalty to the feared former secret police chief.[59]

Few Soviet governmental institutions before or since would have the size and power of *Minsredmash*. Formed officially on June 26, 1953, the ministry employed over 3,000 people, including a vast number of representatives from the security services.[60] Malyshev established a superstructure, whereby each of his deputies was responsible for one single profile of strategic weapons. To ensure continuity of competence, a number of key officials from Beriia's reign were retained, including Boris Vannikov, who kept his old profile of nuclear weapons development. Vasilii Riabikov remained with the air defense project. On July 29, Malyshev transferred all guided long-range missile development, meaning in particular the ICBM project, to *Minsredmash*, thus consolidating all strategic weapons development programs under him.[61] Physicist Andrei Sakharov later singled out Malyshev for praise, noting that "Malyshev was by no means a conservative who resisted all innovation. On the contrary, he actively supported new ideas, and he deserves much credit for the priority given to missile technology."[62]

Malyshev delegated day-to-day management of these projects under each of his new deputies. The most obvious choice for the missile program would have been Dmitrii Ustinov, but remarkably, Malyshev appointed Mikhail Khrunichev, the former minister in charge of the aviation industry, to take over the ICBM project.[63] Ustinov retained his post as Minister of the Defense Industry, and thus technically still oversaw the main design bureaus involved in the intercontinental project, but his authority was curbed significantly, made even worse by his subordination to Khrunichev.[64] The sources are sparse for this period but the choice of Khrunichev to head the long-range missile program suggests that there were deep fissures in the control structure of the rocket project just as the ICBM project was beginning to take off.

59 The First and Second Main Directorates, for producing the atomic bomb and procuring uranium respectively, were united into one single First Main Directorate on March 16, 1953 just after Stalin's death. See "Postanovlenie sm sssr No. 697–355ss/op: 'o rukovodstve spetsial'nymi rabotami' " (March 16, 1953), in *APS*, 532–534.

60 "Vypiska iz protokola No. 10 zasedaniia Prezidiuma TsK KPSS 'ob obrazovanii Ministerstva srednego mashinostroeniia sssr' " (June 26, 1953), in *APS*, 558–561.

61 The profile of *Minsredmash* included "atomic energy" as well as "anti-aircraft guided missiles, guided aircraft-projectiles [i.e., cruise missiles, and] long-range missiles." See "Postanovlenie sm sssr No. 2006–822ss 'O zadachakh i pravakh Ministerstva srednego mashinostroeniia' " (July 29, 1953), in *APS*, 573–575.

62 Sakharov, *Memoirs*, 183.

63 "Pis'mo V. A. Malysheva G. M. Malenkovu . . . " (July 30, 1953), in *APS*, 793–794.

64 Some evidence suggests that Ustinov may have been completely sidelined from involvement in the long-range missile program during this period, and that Khrunichev only dealt with Ustinov's deputies (in particular, A. V. Domrachev and K. N. Rudnev). At the time, the two principal organizations within Ustinov's ministry involved in missile design were Korolev's OKB-1 and Glushko's OKB-456.

Where missile development had essentially been run through the normal channels of the defense industry, the promise of a truly strategic weapon, the intercontinental ballistic missile, raised the stakes, leading to a scramble for control over rockets. In this battle, Ustinov found himself on the weaker side. In *Minsredmash*, Khrunichev ran the missile program through a special secret department under Georgii Pashkov, the *Gosplan* bureaucrat who was technically far junior to Ustinov but whose new-found authority put him in direct control over the missile designers as they were beginning to vocalize their aspirations to use the still-on-paper ICBM as a launching vehicle for a space satellite.[65]

One of Malyshev's initial duties as head of the giant *Minsredmash* was to oversee the explosion of the first Soviet thermonuclear device. As chair of the State Commission for the bomb trial, he was on hand at Semipalatinsk on August 12, 1953 to witness the test, confidently taking an entourage to visit ground zero soon after the explosion.[66] Possession of a hydrogen bomb informed the process of choosing an intercontinental weapons delivery systems for the same reason it played into the calculus of delivery in the United States: The potent power of the thermonuclear weapons obviated the need for high-precision delivery because destruction could be wreaked upon much a larger area. The military had been hesitant to integrate ballistic missiles into war strategy partly because of the imprecision of such weapons, but the hydrogen bomb put the issue into a new light. There was, however, a qualitative difference between having a bomb and having one that was *deliverable*. In a report to Malenkov a few weeks after the H-bomb test, Malyshev informed his boss that he would host several meetings in the late fall to discuss the marriage between the bomb and deliverable systems. In September, they would discuss "the goal of creating new aircraft and reequipping existing aircraft to deliver atomic and hydrogen bombs." Two months later, there would be further meetings to discuss "a plan of work on the creation of a small scale [bomb], and also missiles, torpedoes, and... [cruise missiles] with atomic [bombs]."[67]

MISSILES OR BOMBERS?

At this point, the options for strategic offense were confined to three choices: ballistic missiles, cruise missiles, and bombers. Ranked in terms of potential

[65] Pashkov's missile department was known as the Directorate of Transport Machine Building (*Upravlenie transportnogo mashinostroeniia* or UTM). It was formally established on July 18, 1953. See Kruglov, *Shtab atomproma*, 106; Nikolai Dombkovskii, "Oktiabr'-aprel'-vselennaia," *Sovetskaia rossiia*, April 12, 1989.

[66] The bomb, known as RDS-6s, was technically a boosted fission weapon and not a true "superbomb" with a very large mass of thermonuclear fuel. The Soviet thermonuclear effort was initiated by two government decrees on June 10, 1948 and February 26, 1950.

[67] "Voprosy Ministerstva srednego mashinostroeniia" (August 31/September 1, 1953), in *APS*, 798–800.

effectiveness at the time, bombers appeared to be the least promising. Soviet military officials were well aware that the increasingly capable American Air Defense Command, which was in the process of setting up operation of several lines of radar defense in the North America, would be very effective against the slow and lumbering Soviet bombers of the time. If, by the mid-1950s, a number of key officials within the Soviet military – principally Marshals Georgii Zhukov and Mitrofan Nedelin – began to believe strongly that, in the long run, ballistic and cruise missiles offered the most cost-effective and promising way to deliver nuclear weapons, there remained many within the Party and government – such as Nikita Khrushchev – who continued to believe in the future of strategic bombers. Their argument was bolstered by the institutional momentum of a technological system with powerful actors, such as aviation designer Andrei Tupolev, who had the ears of the topmost leaders of the country.

Soviet theories on strategic bombing dated back to the mid-1930s, although they played only a minor role in World War II. The capture of an American B-29 Superfortress in 1944 changed all that as Stalin instructed Andrei Tupolev to reproduce the American aircraft, the most advanced bomber in the world, part by part. The Soviet leader's son Sergei later noted that "[i]t is no exaggeration to say that an entire modern aircraft industry had to be built in the effort to carry out Stalin's order to make an exact copy."[68] Tupolev's copy, the Tu-4, first flew in May 1947 and was declared operational in May 1949, just three months before the atomic bomb explosion. About 850 airplanes came off the lines before production was discontinued in 1952.[69] Although some of these were equipped to carry atomic bombs, by the time the aircraft was accepted for series production, it was painfully obvious that its relatively slow speed (558 kilometers/hour) and short range (6,200 kilometers) – it could barely only fly one-way missions to the extremities of the American landmass – would be inadequate for a strategic nuclear bomber.[70] Tupolev developed further turboprop bombers such as the Tu-95 but the need for a high-speed bomber, that is, one with jet engines, eclipsed these efforts. When Tupolev declined to develop a new jet engine strategic bomber, favoring the development of a turboprop aircraft, Stalin gave the task to Vladimir Miasishchev, who, like Tupolev, had served time in the same prison workshop (*sharashka*) as Sergei Korolev in the early 1940s.[71] A

[68] Sergei Khrushchev, *Nikita Khrushchev and the Making of a Superpower* (University Park, PA: Penn State University Press, 2000), 46.

[69] V. Rigmant, "B-4 (Tu-4, samolet 'R')," *Aviatsiia i kosmonavtika: vchera, segodnia, zavtra* (July 1998): 41–43; Steven J. Zaloga, *Target America: The Soviet Union and the Strategic Arms Race, 1945–1964* (Novato, CA: Presidio, 1993), 69–79.

[70] These shortcomings were spelled out in a letter to Stalin from Commander-in-Chief of the Air Force Marshal Pavel Zhigarev on February 28, 1951. See N. V. Iakubovich and V. N. Lavrov, *Samolety V. M. Miasishcheva* (Moscow: Rusavia, 1999), 45–46.

[71] In 1951, Tupolev wrote to Stalin, personally laying out his position on turboprop engines. See Iakubovich and Lavrov, *Samolety V. M. Miasishcheva*, 47. See also A. A. Bruk et al.,

highly original and creative aviation designer, Miasishchev was also prone to flights of fancy and extremely ambitious designs; at the time of his appointment to head the jet bomber program, not one of his designs had been accepted for series production by the Soviet armed forces. He was, however, one of the first Soviet aviation designers to propose a strategic bomber design during the war, and he also had the strong support of Minister of the Aviation Industry Mikhail Khrunichev. And like Korolev, Miasishchev inspired total loyalty and hard work in his team of engineers.

In March 1951, Stalin put one of the largest manufacturing facilities in the Soviet aviation industry, Factory No. 23 in the Moscow suburb of Fili, at Miasishchev's disposal and opened a new design bureau, OKB-23, to develop new strategic bombers capable of delivering nuclear warheads to the United States. Its history tracing back to imperial times, the Fili factory was the site where the German Junkers company had produced all-metal aircraft in the 1920s before complete nationalization. Tupolev, the patriarch of Soviet aviation, got his start here too, and produced the famed TB-3 bomber that had given the Soviet Union many aviation records in the 1930s. Such was the priority of the new bomber program that almost the entire graduating class of the Moscow Aviation Institute in 1951 was transferred wholesale to Miasishchev's design bureau; many from other aviation design bureaus were reassigned to work for the resurgent designer. By 1953, at least 10,000 men and women worked at the factory and design bureau, undoubtedly the largest defense conglomeration in the Soviet defense industry barring "special" sectors such as nuclear weapons.

The Air Force's requirements were ambitious: They wanted a bomber that could fly 12,000 kilometers while carrying a five-ton nuclear fission bomb. In response, OKB-23 produced the M-4 bomber, which first flew in January 1953, just two months before Stalin's death, and about nine months after the first test flight of its most obvious rival, Boeing aircraft's B-52 Stratofortress.[72] It had a speed of about 1,000 kilometers per hour and a range of about 9,000 kilometers, higher than Tupolev's bombers but still far short of a requirement issued by the Soviet Air Force in 1947 for a bomber with a range of 12,000–13,000 kilometers. Worse, it was still several years from service duty.[73] Tupolev's Tu-95 was even further behind schedule, although it promised longer ranges with its nuclear cargo.

These considerations were paramount when, in anticipation of the November 1953 meetings, Malyshev and Khrunichev sent a lengthy letter a

Illiustrirovannaia entsiklopediia samoletov OKB V. M. Miasishcheva, t. 2, ch. 1 (Moscow: Aviko Press, 2001), 16–17.

72 Like many Soviet weapons systems, the bomber had a variety of designations, depending on which organization was involved: The design bureau called it 2M, the military called it the M-4, and the factory called it "product 25."

73 For detailed histories of the M-4, see Iakubovich and Lavrov, *Samolety V. M. Miasishcheva*, 48–66; P. Ia. Kozlov, *Konstruktor* (Moscow: Mashinostroenie, 1989), 32–120.

month early to Georgii Malenkov on the topic of delivery systems. Beyond simply providing information, the letter appears to have been a full-on critique of Dmitrii Ustinov's management of the program since 1945. They first lamented the fact that Ustinov's ministry had produced only the R-1 and R-2 missiles in the previous "7–8 years," while "almost all branches of the defense industry had not only created and developed many models of new technology, but [also] carried out full refurbishment of some of the armed forces." They blamed this situation on "the weakness of the scientific base of [Ustinov's] Ministry of the Defense Industry because the work [had] not been based on new scientific achievements, but mainly on the method of copying German models and their future modifications." The rest of the letter laid out the most compelling case made so far at the top levels of the Soviet government to move to a posture focusing on strategic missiles as the backbone of nuclear forces. After laying out the weaknesses of bombers to air defenses, they noted that

> The loss of bombers [due to American air defenses] would undoubtedly be very great, and if we take into account such factors as cost of one modern long-range bomber, which are calculated to be approximately 50–60 million rubles, then it's evident that at the present time long-range missiles are more invulnerable and more suitable for delivering atomic bombs. One of the primary shortcomings of ballistic missiles – the comparatively low precision to the target... could be partially compensated by equipping rockets with atomic bombs, the explosive force of which is many thousands of times greater than normal explosives.... We cannot exclude the possibility that in the next 7–10 years because of the development of electrical vacuum and radio technology, rockets of all forms (short-range, medium, and long-range) will become the primary armaments and could in significant measure replace interceptors, bombers, and large-caliber long-acting artillery. Considering the modern state of work on long-range missiles and the significance of this form of weapon for the defense of the country, it seems to us that the question has come to the fore on the necessity of revising our current existing posture and adopt new decisions.[74]

Malyshev and Khrunichev concluded the letter with several proposals to realign the defense industry to focus on the development of intercontinental ballistic and cruise missiles, including developing a wide range of missiles, lighter atomic bombs, and more powerful hydrogen bombs (of more than 100 megatons of charge). From an institutional perspective, they also wanted to move the missile program out of Ustinov's ministry and to the aviation industry.

The report prompted two Politburo meetings in November 1953 to discuss changes in the nuclear and missile projects. Andrei Sakharov was present at

[74] APRF, 3/47/202/117–123 (October 19, 1953).

the first meeting, for which he had been invited to present a new idea for a hydrogen bomb. He recalled that, in preparing for the meeting,

> Malyshev [had...] asked me to submit a brief written report on my conception of a second-generation [thermonuclear] device, its principles of operation, and its approximate specifications.... I had an idea which at the moment seemed promising (it later turned out to be neither very original nor successful).... I nevertheless wrote a report on the spot and gave it to Malyshev."[75]

At the meeting, Malyshev introduced Sakharov's idea to the rest of Politburo. At a second meeting, on November 20, missile designers, undoubtedly including Sergei Korolev, were present, to discuss whether they could build a missile to deliver Sakharov's new bomb as well as the issue of whether to remove the project from Ustinov's ministry to the aviation industry. On the latter issue, the status quo appears to have been maintained: Ustinov's ministry institutionally retained the main missile organizations but overall control remained with Malyshev and Khrunichev. The more important outcome was the firm marriage between the hydrogen bomb and the ballistic missile; the former, especially the mass of Sakharov's still-on-paper idea, indelibly laid its stamp on the latter. Two new secret resolutions from the government were issued immediately, one to develop the bomb and the other to build a missile for it. Sakharov made this note:

> In essence, this meant that the weight of the thermonuclear charge, as well as the dimensions of the missile, had been fixed on the basis of my report. The program for an enormous organization was set in this manner for many years to come. The rocket designed for that program launched the first artificial satellite into orbit in 1957, and also the spacecraft with Yuri Gagarin aboard in 1961. The thermonuclear charge that provided the original rationale for all this, however, fizzled out, and was replaced by something completely different.[76]

This small "mistake" meant that the first Soviet ICBM was able to carry a heavier mass than was actually necessary, much heavier, in fact, than any comparable American rocket, a difference that would make a glaring public impact in a few years.

REDESIGNING THE ICBM

For missile designers, the decision to link the hydrogen bomb with the ICBM was both a blessing and a curse, the former because their intercontinental project had finally received the fullest commitment of the Soviet leadership and the latter because they were asked to go back to the drawing board. When the T-1 and T-2 research themes had been approved in February 1953, the ICBM took on a particular design that was determined to a

75 Sakharov, *Memoirs*, 180.
76 Sakharov, *Memoirs*, 181. The decrees were probably issued on November 27, 1953.

large degree by the expectation that its payload would have a mass of about 3,000 kilograms, just enough to carry a small atomic bomb.[77] At this point, engineers, benefiting from the N-3 design studies, had narrowed down their conception of the ICBM to a two-stage vehicle with a core and four attached boosters on the side, somewhat similar to Tikhonravov's package concept, but with rockets attached only mechanically and not hydraulically. Unlike some of the early conceptual designs in which each of the strapon boosters were classic cylinders, in the new design the boosters were slightly conical. Engineers gravitated to a conical shape primarily because of the aerodynamic advantages over a standard cylindrical design but also for three other reasons: the large size of the engines at the tail end, the possibility of imparting additional thrust to the central sustainer by the shape of the booster, and the opportunity of decreasing tank wall thickness. All five engines would fire simultaneously at liftoff, being separated at altitude, leaving the central one, now serving as the second stage, firing until final cutoff. Each of the boosters would be equipped with a single-chamber liquid-oxygen and kerosene engine with a thrust of about 45 to 50 tons. The end result was four conical-shaped boosters attached to a central element that widened in its diameter to meet the apexes of each of the four cones. Overall launch mass and launch thrust would be of the order of 190 tons and 270 tons, respectively.[78]

Sakharov's plan to produce a new thermonuclear bomb changed everything. His hasty report put the new mass of the payload at about 5,500 kilograms, nearly *twice* the amount missile designers had expected. Malyshev, on a visit to see OKB-1's work on a shorter-range missile, casually mentioned the new figure to Korolev, almost as if it was a joke. For a week, Korolev's top designers labored over this problem, reporting to the chief designer every evening on the course of their work. Sergei Kriukov, one of the main conceptual designers in charge of the ICBM program, kept coming back to Korolev, saying that given the design layout of the missile – the strapons, the engines, the dynamics – this would be impossible to do. Korolev had no reason to doubt Kriukov, one of the most dependable on his senior staff. When Malyshev came back the following week to inquire about the work, Korolev replied that engineers would need to redesign the machine completely, and they would need a lot of money to do this. Malyshev sanguinely told Korolev to ask for anything they needed; the *Minsredmash* budget for 1954 was, after all, over 2.25 billion rubles, an astronomical

[77] M. V. Keldysh et al., "O perspektivakh sozdaniia raket s bol'shoi dal'nost'iu poleta" (1953), in *MVKIT*, 144–145.

[78] The original specifications for the T-1 concept included the following: launch thrust at sea level (270 tons), launch mass (190 tons), mass of fuel (43.5 tons), mass of oxidizer (117 tons), empty mass (18.5 tons), accuracy to target (±15 kilometers), maximum velocity at engine cutoff (6.5 kilometers/second), maximum altitude of trajectory (1,270 kilometers), flight duration (35 minutes), and range (7,000–8,000 kilometers).

sum for the Soviet government. Witnesses remember the minister's exact words: "it is better to spend too much and do something worthwhile than to save and have nothing. Don't you agree with me?"[79]

Korolev's designers went back to the drawing board and within a few weeks produced a remarkable transformation of the original ICBM without altering its basic conceptual design. The primary changes were in engine design. In the original conception, each of the boosters had a single engine with a sea-level thrust of about 55 tons. These engines were essentially scaled up and improved versions of Glushko's experimental combustion chambers that combined cylindrical chambers with flat injector heads.[80] Unfortunately, ground tests of these engines were less than successful because of high-frequency instabilities in the combustion chambers; in other words, they basically shook apart violently. In light of Malyshev's instructions to significantly raise the lifting weight of the ICBM, the failures of these engines seriously jeopardized any future plan to build an intercontinental missile.

Once again, an idea came from Aleksei Isaev, the modest but highly innovative engine designer overshadowed by Glushko in the early postwar years. In the late 1940s, Isaev had produced a small rocket engine by combining multiple combustion chambers fed by a single turbopump. Each combustion chamber had relatively small thrust (2 tons), but combined they produced 8 tons of thrust.[81] The advantages were obvious: One could combine smaller thrust chambers to build a big engine and avoid the risks of building a big engine, risks that included the likelihood that high pressure would cause thrust chambers to explode as a result of excessive vibrations. Korolev himself had alluded to such an approach to engine design as early as 1949, but the continuing problems with engine development as well as Malyshev's insistence on a redesigned missile forced the issue.[82] As a result, in late 1953, Glushko put together a design for a new engine that grouped together four 23-ton thrust combustion chambers, each a scaled up and modified version of the experimental ED-140, powered by a single turbopump. This was safe territory for Glushko because the low thrusts of each chamber were manageable, but combined they could produce nearly 100 tons of thrust. The new design also meant that the length of the engine was significantly reduced, lowering the mass of the rocket. Additionally, the philosophy of modular

79 Golovanov, *Korolev*, 472–474. *Minsredmash* budget figures are from Simonov, *VPK*, 246.

80 These engines were known as the RD-105 (55 tons of thrust) and RD-106 (53 tons). They were essentially identical engines, except that the latter was an altitude variant and was equipped with lengthened exhaust nozzles for operation in vacuum.

81 This engine was the SO9.29, developed for a Soviet variant of the German *Wasserfall* anti-aircraft missile. Mikhail Pervov, *Zenitnoe raketnie oruzhie protivovozdushnoi oborony strany* (Moscow: Aviarus-XXI, 2001), 42. Mishin notes that Isaev actually built a forty-ton engine based on this design. See Mishin, "Problemy pervogo poleta cheloveka v kosmos"; Mishin, *Ot sozdaniia*, 28.

82 S. P. Korolev, "Annotatsiia rabot po teme N-3" (August 11, 1952), in *SPKIED*, 172–173.

construction of each chamber would enable mass production without significant changes to factory machinery. Based on this design, Glushko produced two nearly identical engines, each with four main chambers, the RD-107 and the RD-108. The latter differed from the former in having four (instead of two for the RD-107) additional steering chambers and a different design of the throttle.

In December 1953, on Malyshev's instructions, Korolev and his senior staff prepared a draft of a government decree on the development of the vehicle, laying out the participation of all involved enterprises, their specific roles, and delivery dates for items. There were a series of intense meetings at the designer level in the following two months as events began to move at a dizzying pace. On January 5, 1954, the major chief designers involved in the project, that is, Korolev, Glushko, Pilyugin, Riazanskii, Kuznetsov, and Barmin, met and agreed to issue a final draft plan for the R-7 ICBM by May 1. On January 30, these men met again to discuss, debate, and agree on the final technical changes to the missile as a result of Malyshev's request to increase the missile's lifting mass. They also gave the missile a name, the R-7. Three days later, at another meeting, they agreed to a reasonable schedule to build and test the missile. Finally, two days later, Korolev sent to his governmental bosses a list of 27 applied research themes necessary to carry out in order to produce the ICBM.[83]

Discussions during this period also touched on the role of cruise missiles as delivery weapons for nuclear weapons. Keldysh's Boys had already conducted detailed research on the feasibility of such a rocket, while Korolev's design bureau had even begun work on an experimental testbed.[84] By this time, it was clear to Korolev that his organization, OKB-1, had the resources to focus on only one path. His first deputy Vasilii Mishin recalled that

> In spite of the fact that S. P. Korolev was an admirer of cruise missiles given that he developed similar [ones] in the prewar years at RNII, he gave his preference to a two-stage ICBM.... Sergei Pavlovich was a realist and understood that the achievement of intercontinental distances with the required target precision at that time could be accomplished in a shorter time with an ICBM.[85]

On Korolev's recommendation, the responsibility for developing an intercontinental cruise missile was transferred to an institute in the aviation industry, NII-1, the successor organization to the interwar RNII where Korolev himself had served his apprenticeship. Here, the cruise missile project would be directed by Mstislav Keldysh, arguably the most important Soviet scientist involved in weapons research. The actual engineering work on the missiles

[83] *SPKIED*, 661.

[84] M. V. Keldysh et al., "Teoreticheskie issledovaniia dinamiki poleta sostavnykh krylatykh raket dal'nego deistviia" (1953), in *MVKIT*, 147–196.

[85] Mishin, *Ot sozdaniia*, 26–27.

was contracted to two aviation design bureaus headed by famous Soviet designers Semen Lavochkin and Vladimir Miasishchev. All these arrangements were finalized in two decrees issued by the Soviet Council of Ministers on May 20, 1954.[86] The first one approved the development of the R-7 intercontinental ballistic missile at Korolev's design bureau and enumerated various schedules for its implementation. The second one did the same for two intercontinental cruise missiles, one by Lavochkin known as *Burya* (storm), and the other by Miasishchev known as *Buran* (snowstorm). Both would be supervised by Keldysh. In effect, the Soviet government simultaneously committed to the development of three intercontinental missile programs, each capable of delivering nuclear weapons to the United States.

The new ICBM came with many different designations, as was common in a Byzantine Soviet bureaucracy obsessed with maintaining secrecy through a proliferation of nondescript names. To the designers, it was the R-7; to the military, it was "product 8K71." Most people who worked on it, however, simply called it the *semerka* ("number seven"), an informal moniker that has stuck with it for over half a century. Soon after the government commitment, on July 24, 1954, Korolev's engineers completed the missile's draft plan – a document detailing every aspect of its design – which spanned a total of fifteen volumes. Unwilling to commit to something that might prove to be a colossal waste of money, the Soviet government established an "expert commission" of independent scientists, chaired by Academician Keldysh, to study the plan and approve its choices. A host of scientists, engineers, and industry managers representing the academic community, the designer constituency, the defense industry, and the military staffed the commission. Their evaluations were overwhelmingly positive, clearing the way for full-scale industrial work on the missile. On November 20, 1954, in an unusual step, the Council of Ministers officially approved the draft plan for the R-7 missile, a decision that would have been normally left in the hands of engineers or scientists.[87]

MAKING A NATIONAL COMMITMENT

Industrial bureaucrat Viacheslav Malyshev, who had presided over the marriage of nuclear weapons with rockets, and, at a key moment, had set in

[86] *RKKE*, 74.

[87] Members of the expert commission included designers: S. A. Lavochkin (OKB-301) and A. M. Liul'ka (OKB-165); applied research scientists from industry: M. V. Keldysh (NII-1), A. A. Dorodnitsyn (Central Aerohydrodynamics Institute, TsAGI), A. I. Makarevskii (TsAGI), B. S. Stechkin (OKB-300), and A. P. Vanichev (TsAGI); service officers: A. G. Mrykin (Directorate of the Deputy Commander of Artillery, UZKA) and N. N. Smirnitskii (UZKA); military scientists: G. A. Tiulin (NII-4); and scientists from academia and the Academy of Sciences: B. N. Petrov (Institute of Control Problems of the Academy of Sciences) and Kh. A. Rakhmatulin (Bauman Moscow Higher Technical School, MVTU). See *RKKE*, 74–75.

motion a chain of events that defined the final shape of the first Soviet ICBM, would not live to see it fly. First sacked and then sick, he had a precipitious fall from grace resulting from a power struggle at the Kremlin. For two years, Malenkov, Bulganin, and Khrushchev had been jockeying for power in the post-Stalin era. Malenkov appeared to be an early favorite but came under increasing fire for his famous speech in August 1953 arguing for more investments in consumer goods rather than heavy industry. Those who advocated a more confrontational approach to the West used this speech and another one in March 1954, in which Malenkov declared that thermonuclear war "would mean the end of world civilization," to undermine his position. These conflicts culminated in his ousting from the position of chairman of the Council of Ministers in February 1955. Bulganin replaced Malenkov while Marshall Georgii Zhukov replaced Bulganin as Minister of Defense.

These changes produced deep ripples in the management of strategic weapons industry. They reinforced the position of Nikita Khrushchev, who, as First Secretary of the Central Committee, helped to shift the locus of Soviet power from the government to the Party, while consolidating his control over the domestic and foreign policy, the military-industrial complex, and the security services.[88] Furthermore, with Malenkov's departure from the top, Malyshev, one of Malenkov's most visible servants in the defense industry, also lost his job. He was moved out to the defense industry to an innocuous position as head of a state organ to introduce new technology into the civilian economy; this was a significant demotion that was obvious to all. A highly ambitious and sharp-witted industrial manager, Malyshev was devastated by the "banishment," eventually falling into ill health. He died less than two years later from acute leukemia, a condition probably stemming from his exposure to radiation during nuclear testing.[89]

After his fall, Malyshev's moves to centralize all weapons programs under *Minsredmash*, that is, the nuclear industry, were reversed. Khrushchev immediately took control of long-range missile development out of *Minsredmash* and established a new structure to supervise strategic rocket programs. Echoing the postwar urgency of the nuclear program when a special committee under Beriia had directed atomic weapons development, Khrushchev created a similar organ, the officially titled Special Committee for Rocket and Reactive Weapons (*Spetskomitet*, for short), and put it directly under

[88] Zubok, *A Failed Empire*, 95–101.

[89] Sakharov, *Memoirs*, 184. For a brief period between February and May 1955, Malyshev served as a deputy chairman of the Council of Ministers with a portfolio to supervise a number of civilian industrial ministries. From May 1955 to December 1956, Malyshev was chairman of the State Committee for New Technology and from December 1956 to February 1957, a first deputy chairman of the State Economic Commission on Current Planning in the Economy (*Gosekonokomissii*), a body that focused on economic planning for the state's Five-Year Plans.

his and Bulganin's control. Unlike so many other Soviet governmental bodies with dull names and confusing subordinations, this committee, almost unmentioned in the history of Soviet missile and space programs, did live up to its name, for it was extremely special. Its creation on April 14, 1955 finally meant that the development of long-range missiles was now an urgent national priority on the level of nuclear weapons and air defense missiles. Its job was to "coordinate all work on the creation of rocket and reactive weapons" under the broad policy directives issued down from the Politburo, but in practice its actions bled into the policy arena.

The backbone of the *Spetskomitet* comprised the group of managers who had directed, through various institutional incarnations, affiliations, and names, the Moscow air defense project from 1950 to 1955.[90] The air defense program, known as *Berkut* (Golden Eagle), had swallowed up an enormous amount of defense industry resources in the early 1950s, some of it clearly siphoned off from the missile program. In effect, like the atomic program before it, *Berkut* effectively had left the missile program playing second fiddle in terms of resource allocation. After 1949, much of the staff of the old Committee No. 2 (for missiles) was reassigned to work in the air defense project. Both Sergei Korolev and Vasilii Mishin, the top missile designers, were considered to lead design of the *Berkut*'s missile, and only after the intervention of Minister of Armaments Dmitrii Ustinov, who oversaw the missile program, did the job go to the well-known aviation designer Semen Lavochkin.[91] Ustinov was, however, not able to retain his most senior ministerial deputy, Vasilii Riabikov, a protégé from his days directing a weapons factory in the 1930s, who Beriia took out of the missile program and appointed head of the massive organizational structure in charge of *Berkut*. Riabikov brought with him several veterans of the missile program who had worked with him on long-range missiles.[92] Eventually, they amassed vast experience in initiating, managing, and putting into operation one of the most complex technological systems fielded by the Soviet armed forces. Their experience in managing large programs in the early 1950s – a Soviet version of systems engineering – proved to be critical to the ultimate success of the Soviet ICBM project in the late 1950s.

[90] "Postanovlenie TsK KPSS i Soveta Ministrov sssr No. 720–435ss: 'voprosy raketnogo i reaktivnogo vooruzheniia'," in *SKI*, 47–55; Kruglov, *Shtab atomproma*, 107, 117; Kisun'ko, *Sekretnaia zona*, 305, 367. From February 1951 to June 1953, the air defense project was supervised by the Third Main Directorate of the Council of Ministers, and then from June 1953 to April 1955 by subdepartments (*Glavspetsmash* and *Glavspetsmontazh*) of the nuclear *Minsredmash*.

[91] Pervov, *Zenitnoe raketnie oruzhie*, 60.

[92] Riabikov's connection to Beriia predates the formation of TGU; already on July 14, 1949, Beriia had tapped Riabikov to be the nuclear program's liaison within Ustinov's Ministry of Armaments. See Kruglov, *Shtab atomproma*, 90–91.

FIGURE 26. As head of the extraordinary *Spetskomitet*, Vasilii Riabikov (1907–1974) served as the manager of the Soviet ICBM project during the most critical period in its development, from 1955 to 1957. During this time, he was closely involved in all the major decisions in the project, including the launch of the *Sputnik* satellite. Since his passing, he has all but been forgotten in the grand narrative of Soviet space history. [*Source*: Peter Gorin]

The man picked to head the new *Spetskomitet* was not an obvious choice. Vasilii Riabikov had managed to negotiate his way through the dizzying and dangerous minefields of the Soviet defense industry through several different patrons, but nothing in his career had suggested such a precipitous rise to power (see Figure 26). His life story had all the touchstones of a postwar industrialist. He had been an early and ardent communist, having served as the secretary of the Komsomol cell at the famous Bol'shevik Factory in the 1920s. He was schooled at the Leningrad Military-Mechanical Institute, served briefly in the Red Army, and then went for higher studies at the K. E. Voroshilov Naval Academy. After his education, he rejoined the Bol'shevik Factory, where his Party activities caught the attention of influential apparatchiks in the Central Committee. In January 1939, only 33 at the time, he was picked out to serve as a deputy people's commissar of armaments in the Kremlin. He displayed enormous reserve during the war in marshalling the production of artillery under his boss Dmitrii Ustinov. One of Riabikov's decisions during wartime communicates a sense of his philosophy. The Soviet Union lacked good automatic weapons during the war, and Marshall Grigorii Kulik decided to produce a new model, but Riabikov accurately gauged wartime conditions and argued that it should produce in mass numbers the old Maksim mounted machine guns instead of untested new weapons. The decision proved propitious for the Soviet army, because it put guns – albeit outdated – quickly in the hands of those that needed them.[93]

Through the war, Dmitrii Ustinov cultivated and supported his junior colleague and later assigned him with key duties in the postwar ballistic missile program. When Lavrentii Beriia needed someone capable to direct the top-secret Moscow air defense program, he tapped Riabikov for the job, making him, in some sense, more powerful and influential than Ustinov. Remarkably, Riabikov survived Beriia's fall and eventual execution partly because he had a new patron, Soviet war hero Marshal Georgii Zhukov, who was instrumental in positioning Riabikov in the post-Malenkov era as the best candidate for managing the development of the ICBM.[94] Thus, just two weeks after he oversaw the last test trial of the air defense system in April 1955, Riabikov switched jobs and returned to the ballistic missile sector. He brought with him almost the entire managerial staff of the air defense project as well as some key administrators, such as Georgii Pashkov, who had shepherded the ballistic missile program through the early 1950s.[95] Riabikov's rise continued to outshine that of his former patron, Dmitrii Ustinov, who, while nominally remaining the minister in charge of the missile industry, now reported to Riabikov on those issues. In comparing Ustinov and Riabikov, Grigorii Kisun'ko, the leading Soviet anti-ballistic missile designer, later wrote that "Riabikov in his character was less tough [and] more lenient towards people than Ustinov; if Ustinov was more feared than loved, then Riabikov was more loved than feared."[96]

Riabikov's climb to the apex of the missile program was also an outcome of the rising influence of military control over Soviet defense policy, a role in which the military typically had very little input. Through the late 1940s the service chiefs had been in a relatively weak position, but by the late 1950s, with increasing links between strategic weapons and Cold War policies, "the professional military's influence on the forced development of new military programs was . . . growing."[97] A central figure in this rising

[93] "Proizvodstvennoe ob'edinenie 'Tulamashzavod'," http://www.tulamash.ru/pagenews.php?id=148 (accessed October 28, 2008).

[94] Evgenii Zhirnov, "'Eti ser'y pidzhaki budut nami komandovat'!'," *Vlast'* no. 45 (November 14, 2005).

[95] The original members of the Riabikov's *Spetskomitet* included first deputy chairman G. A. Titov, deputy chairmen A. K. Repin and A. N. Shchukin, and members G. N. Pashkov, V. V. Illiuviev, P. I. Kalinushkin, and B. A. Kiasov. A Council of Ministers decree on June 3, 1955 created a "scientific-technical council" of the Committee staffed by forty-six prominent scientists and designers to advise the body on strategic decisions.

[96] Kisun'ko, *Sekretnaia zona*, 367.

[97] Irina Bystrova, *Soviet Military Policy in the Early Cold War Period*, The Kurt London Papers, Institute for European, Russian and Eurasian Studies, Elliott School of International Affairs, George Washington University, 1999, 11.

coterie was Soviet World War II hero Marshal Georgii Zhukov, one of the most vociferous opponents of the atomic industry's stranglehold over a vast range of weapons systems; Zhukov reserved a particular animus to *Minsredmash*'s former chief Malyshev, and was evidently one of the architects behind the latter's fall from grace.[98] Zhukov personally canvassed for Riabikov's appointment to head *Spetskomitet* because he recognized that many influential service leaders saw Riabikov as sympathetic to military concerns as the Cold War began to heat up. Paradoxically, the mid-1950s were one of the few periods in Soviet history when military spending declined and the share of consumer goods as part of the GNP actually increased, moves largely shepherded by Malenkov, Bulganin, and Khrushchev in the immediate post-Stalin years. They *reduced* the defense budget by an estimated 200 million rubles between 1955 and 1958, precisely during the period when Riabikov was overseeing the creation of the R-7 ICBM.[99] The reductions were, however, largely focused on conventional forces, particularly on troop reductions, and evidence suggests that spending on strategic weapons such as bombers and missiles continued to increase dramatically.[100]

The evidence suggests that Zhukov was one of the principal architects behind the palpable shift in favor of missiles, and not as he is commonly seen in the West, as one who favored the outdated tactics of World War II and resisted the incorporation of nuclear weapons into military doctrine. Zhukov commanded the first Soviet military exercise using nuclear weapons in the early 1950s and at key points provided impetus to the growing strategic missile program. He was instrumental in helping establish the third major center for missile development in the Soviet Union (after Sergei Korolev's OKB-1 in Kaliningrad and Mikhail Iangel's OKB-586 in Dnepropetrovsk). Because of Zhukov's influence, in 1955, Korolev spun off a new design organization, SKB-385, based in Miass in Siberia.[101]

Besides Riabikov, Zhukov assigned another forceful individual to the ICBM project. In 1955, simultaneously with Riabikov's appointed at *Spetskomitet*, Zhukov created a new deputy under him responsible for the testing and procurement of long-range ballistic missiles for the Soviet armed forces; to this post he appointed Marshal Mitrofan Nedelin, one of the rising military service stars of the postwar era, who consistently supported advanced strategic projects in the 1950s.[102] A veteran of the Spanish civil war, Nedelin

[98] Sakharov, *Memoirs*, 193; Bystrova, *VPK*, 202.

[99] Masliukov and Glubokov, "Planirovanie i finansirovanie voennoi promyshlennosti v sssr," 86. Other sources suggest a reduction of 1 billion rubles in the same period. See Bystrova, *VPK*, 47–48.

[100] Bystrova, *VPK*, 105.

[101] V. Ivkin and A. Dolinin, "S imenem marshala Zhukova," *Krasnaia zvezda*, July 25, 1997.

[102] Nedelin's official title was Deputy Minister of Defense for Special Armaments and Reactive Technology. He was appointed to his position on March 21, 1955. See V. Tolubko, *Nedelin: pervyi glavkom strategicheskikh* (Moscow: Molodaia gvardiia, 1979), 216.

started World War II as the commander of an artillery brigade and ended it as the commander-in-chief of all artillery forces of the third Ukrainian Front. Nedelin was the most obvious successor to the tradition of military innovation founded by the late Marshal Tukhachevskii; he was forward thinking, able to pick out the most important path among many, and blessed with a large ego that often ran slipshod over even his superiors. Yet, he managed to establish good relations with Korolev, who said this about Nedelin:

> I think it's a great fortune that during the development and realization of the ambitious projects to build the first ballistic missiles, together with me was a smart military leader, erudite in all respects, with an understanding of the subtleties of science and technology. It was a pleasure to work, to talk, even to argue. When dealing with the quality and timing of the manufacture of our products, Mitrofan Ivanovich was an especially principled and demanding customer.[103]

Nedelin's active interest in ballistic missiles fortified the already firm stranglehold of the artillery sector over operational aspects of the missile program, forged a decade before, beginning with their job of dragging around captured V-2 missiles in occupied Germany.

The changes in 1955 – the formation of *Spetskomitet* under Riabikov, the appointment of Nedelin to lead missile procurement, and Zhukov's support of nuclear-tipped ballistic missiles – put the R-7 missile project on a firm standing. But the most important support came from Nikita Khrushchev. As late as 1955, at the Central Committee plenum in June, Khrushchev extolled the value of strategic bombers. He noted that "it's not possible to bridle madmen, to bring them to order, without [using] well-developed and powerful aviation – one can only contain them with long-range aviation."[104] His belief in strategic bombers was shaken at least partially by the unsatisfactory performance of the leading lights of the Soviet Air Force, Tupolev's Tu-4 and Miasishchev's M-4. Sergei Khrushchev remembers his father's visit to see Miasishchev, when the aviation designer confided that his new bomber would only be able to reach Mexico on a one-way trip, at which point the pilot would have to bail out. Khrushchev incredulously asked, "Did the Mexican government agree to this plan? Or maybe your mother-in-law lives there?"[105]

Informing Khrushchev's view on the rising importance of rockets was a display of stark power. In early 1956, Korolev's design bureau prepared a new model of their R-5M missile, a long-range rocket whose creation had been made possible by some of the early research work done in support of the intercontinental missile in the early 1950s. What was unique about the R-5M was not its range – which was sufficient to reach all of mainland

[103] Tolubko, *Nedelin*, 176.
[104] Khrushchev quoted in Bystrova, *VPK*, 88.
[105] Khrushchev, *Nikita Khrushchev*, 56.

Europe – but that this time, they had prepared the rocket with a live nuclear warhead. Launched on February 20, the missile flew 1,190 kilometers in a little over ten minutes and deposited its twenty-kiloton nuclear warhead over a target area in the Semipalatinsk range, where it exploded in a spectacular dazzle. It was the first such missile test in the history of nuclear weapons. The experiment, spearheaded by Marshall Zhukov and leading scientists from the nuclear industry, was a watershed moment for the rocket designers, for it brought them, for the first time, squarely in the sights of the top Party and government leadership. More than honorific titles (such as being elected Corresponding Members of the Academy of Sciences or being accepted into the Communist Party, milestones that Korolev passed in 1953), the visible demonstration of naked power brought the missile designer constituency into the upper echelons of power. In cooperating with famous nuclear project managers such as Igor' Kurchatov and Avramii Zaveniagin, missile designers managed to invert or at least equalize the power relationship with the nuclear empire, having been considered subordinate and less important for at least a decade. Remembering the initial collaboration with the high-profile nuclear physicists, one of Korolev's senior test engineers noted this:

> At the start of this work Sergey Pavlovich [Korolev] gathered the project leaders to make a speech concerning the program. This was a meeting before the start of work with the atomic people, with *Minsredmash*. The first thing he said was that we ought to be very careful in our activities. Because they had been spoilt, first, due to publicity and second, because they considered themselves superior to everybody else... after developing the atomic bomb.... S. P. Korolev said that at least in the beginning we should pander to them. But pander very precisely and carefully such that in the end we would prove to them that we were in the driver's seat and they were merely passengers.[106]

The success of the R-5M test swiveled the center of gravity of influence away from the nuclear elite for the first time since they began their work in 1945. After 1956, missile designers, especially Sergei Korolev, began to have increased access to the top levels of the Kremlin. This was reflected both in symbolic and practical terms. A week after the nuclear test, Nikita Khrushchev, Nikolai Bulganin, Viacheslav Molotov, and several other Politburo members graced Korolev's design bureau with their presence, a rare honor accorded to few design organizations.[107] In his memoirs, Khrushchev conceded that the visitors were bewildered by the rocket, "walked around [the missile] like peasants at a bazaar ready to buy some calico, poking it and tugging to test its strength," but that "[t]he leadership was soon filled with

[106] Memoir of A. I. Ostashev in *NKE*, 69.

[107] Besides the above named, the entourage also included L. M. Kaganovich, N. K. Kirichenko, and M. G. Pervukhin. The visit took place on February 28, 1956. See *SPKIED*, 663. Sergei Khrushchev has a long description of this visit based on his personal recollections. See Khrushchev, *Nikita Khrushchev*, 101–112.

confidence in [Korolev]."[108] On April 20, the Supreme Soviet bestowed three nuclear scientists, Andrei Sakharov, Iulii Khariton, and Iakov Zeldovich, for the second (for Sakharov) and third times with the highest civilian honor in the nation, the Hero of Socialist Labor. What was special about the occasion was that for the first time missile designers were among the honored. They included the six main chief designers involved with the R-7 project, Korolev, Glushko, Piliugin, Riazanskii, and Barmin, as well as Korolev's right-hand man Mishin. Many other junior designers at OKB-1 were simultaneously given less prestigious but notable national awards. These events significantly elevated the authority of missile designers, especially Sergei Korolev, within the Soviet defense industry. Nikita Khrushchev's son Sergei notes that "[f]rom then on [Korolev] could phone Father directly, bypassing numerous bureaucratic obstacles.[109] This new-found authority, established on the basis of missile development, and in particular, the promise of an intercontinental ballistic missile, would prove critical in firmly pulling together two entirely different sensibilities among the missile designers – the job of designing powerful missiles for the Soviet armed forces and the dream of breaching the cosmos. To realize this connection, the line to the Kremlin was one of paramount importance.

CONCLUSIONS

During the latter part of the Cold War, Western observers, not having the benefit of archival Soviet sources, assumed that Stalin committed to the development of an ICBM soon after the end of World War II. This belief was fed by tangible evidence that the Soviets tested their first ICBM before its American counterpart, the Atlas, whose development had been underway since about 1951 but did not become a national commitment until 1954.[110] Other evidence in the form of information from a Soviet defector suggested that Stalin and his cohort may have met as early as 1947 to decide in favor of a "transatlantic missile."[111] Yet, evidence suggests that in the late 1940s,

108 Nikita Khrushchev, *The Memoirs of Nikita Khrushchev, Vol. 2: Reformer (1945–1964)*, ed. Sergei Khrushchev (University Park, PA: Penn State University Press, 2006).

109 Khrushchev, *Nikita Khrushchev*, 106.

110 Edmund Beard, *Developing the ICBM: A Study in Bureaucratic Politics* (New York: Columbia University Press, 1976); Thomas P. Hughes, *Rescuing Prometheus* (New York: Pantheon Books, 1998), 69–139.

111 The defector was one Georgii Aleksandrovich Tokatev (née Tokaty), an aeronautics academic who was briefly involved in the Soviet search for aviation technology in occupied Germany just after World War II, and who later defected to Great Britain in 1948. After his move to the West, Tokaty wrote a number of memoirs claiming that he attended meetings with Stalin in 1947 where ICBMs were discussed. Although he exaggerated his role in the postwar missile industry (which was insignificant), declassified documents show that he did indeed meet with Stalin once, not to discuss ICBMs, but on the matter of kidnapping the prominent German aeronautics expert, Eugen Sänger. For two of his many memoirs,

long-range missiles were not proffered the kind of attention that the atomic bomb or air defense programs enjoyed, and that it was not until in 1953, just before Stalin's death, that the Soviet Communist Party and government leadership committed to the development of an intercontinental missile. It took another two years before the program was elevated to one of national priority.

The one defining characteristic of this phase was repeated points where actors had to choose between two or more options to commit resources in one direction. We see how in the early phases of long-range missile development, these choices were made entirely by rocket designers or applied scientists who benefited from a relative lack of scrutiny at the highest levels of Soviet power afforded the missile program in the late Stalin years. But as the ICBM project matured and intersected with state imperatives, at the time of Stalin's death, state actors intervened to put their imprint on the missile. From then on, the architecture of the missile was narrowed down through a long and complicated process of consensus-making that involved not only designers but also managers, government officials, and Party leaders. By 1953, the Soviet missile industry had sufficiently matured to take on the ambitious task of producing an intercontinental missile, having reproduced German models and built upon those to mass produce improved variants. Two other high-priority strategic weapons programs, nuclear weapons and a Moscow air defense system, had also passed critical milestones, freeing up important resources, including personnel, institutions, and money, for the intercontinental program.

From a conceptual standpoint, the R-7 missile, as eventually built, represented the union of several disparate technical legacies, spanning both time and space (Figure 27). German wartime rocket design was crucial for Soviet industry to learn design approaches and master production processes. Nevertheless, buried in *its* design was Konstantin Tsiolkovskii's rocket squadron that first appeared in a 1920s booklet, as well as Mikhail Tikhonravov's appropriation of that idea in the postwar years into novel "rocket packages." The missile was powered by massive four-chamber engines from the design bureau of Valentin Glushko, who had developed some of the earliest Soviet liquid-propellant rocket engines in the early 1930s. German rocket engine technology had allowed Glushko's engineers to skip from designing modest 1.5-ton thrust engines to 25-ton thrust engines within two years, but innovations from a variety of sources, including another Soviet engine designer, Aleksei Isaev, provided the jump to 50-ton thrust chambers. At the Academy of Sciences, Keldysh's Boys provided the raw mathematical support to optimize the design of the rocket.

see *Stalin Means War* (London: Weidenfeld & Nicolson, 1951) and *Comrade X* (London: The Harvill Press, 1956). For documents on Tokatev's meeting with Stalin, which took place on April 17, 1947, see RGAE, 8044/1/1647/162–163.

FIGURE 27. The R-7 ICBM, shown here during one of its early launches in 1957, before the launch of *Sputnik*. A special missile launch base was constructed to test the rocket, in the remote area of Tiura-Tam in Kazakhstan, far from prying eyes. [*Source*: Timofei Varfolomeyev]

Soviet missile designers were forced to consider a number of technological limitations while simultaneously catering to requirements from the primary client, the nuclear weapons estate. Their work was framed by an acute awareness of the relationship between innovation and risk, that a burst of the former inevitably increased the latter. They tried to control this relationship by incorporating small bursts of innovation that collectively delivered qualitative gains. For example, Soviet engine designers lacked confidence to build engines designed to ignite at a high altitude, that is, in relative vacuum, and thus resorted to clustering many engines at the bottom of the rocket, all firing at liftoff. They were also unable to build chambers with thrusts higher than fifty tons, leading to them to group multiple chambers fed by unitary turbopumps. The requirements were often counterintuitive or unexpected. The development of thermonuclear weapons, many orders more destructive than atomic bombs, obviated the need for highly accurate missiles. When the nuclear weapons designers suggested that the missile would have to lift a very heavy bomb, something of the order of five tons, the missile experts were forced to retool the rocket into a very powerful vehicle, one that would eventually prove to be a boon for the Soviet space program.

There was, however, nothing inevitable about the development of the R-7, neither in the early years of research nor in the later years when the idea was converted to metal. Human agency was critical at every stage – technology was merely the outcome of a negotiated series of compromises by actors invested in one choice or another. At a most critical point, for example, designers lobbied hard for a major and risky gamble, moving from a modest missile (the R-3) to a truly intercontinental missile (the R-7), driving the program into a substantively new phase. Further, support from the top political elite (Khrushchev and Bulganin) and influential military brass (Zhukov and Nedelin) ensured that the program was bestowed a high level of support, but the program was under peril from the limitations of industry, competing options (bombers and cruise missiles), and the finite patience of the military, who wanted quick returns. Ultimately, the work of missile designers and industrial managers was elevated to a new footing with the Soviet government's firm commitment in 1955. As a result, the relationship between the state and rocketry entered a new phase. For space enthusiasts such as Korolev and Tikhonravov, the next goal was to introduce the cosmos into the equation.

8

Fellow Travelers

> "[T]he problem of creating an artificial satellite of the Earth is being given special attention in the U.S.A."[1]
>
> Sergei Korolev, in a letter asking the Soviet government to approve a Soviet satellite project, 1955

INTRODUCTION

It was rare, even unheard of, for a prominent designer in the Soviet defense industry to give a public talk, especially in the 1950s. But this was a special occasion, the 125th anniversary of the establishment of the famed Bauman Moscow Higher Technical School, and although each member of the audience required permission to attend, the talk was technically open to all students. Sergei Korolev, the erstwhile chief designer of long-range ballistic missiles, had, however, received permission from the ministry to give a talk at his alma mater. Most students and faculty attending the lecture, held on September 25, 1955, had little or no idea of Korolev's true profession. The chief designer gave a spirited and long talk, noteworthy not only for his passion for the topic, the use of rockets to explore the upper layers of the atmosphere, but also for the explicit link he made between the Soviet past and the Soviet future. Korolev noted with emphasis that, "in his works Konstantin Eduardovich [Tsiolkovskii] has shown the path to solving the goal of creating an artificial satellite of the Earth." In concluding his talk, Korolev lapsed almost into an incantation, repeating each of five sentences with increasing emphasis:

> Our goal should be to have Soviet rockets fly higher and earlier than before this is done elsewhere! Our goal should be to have a Soviet citizen be the first to fly on a rocket! Our goal should be to create a new type of super-speed transport for passengers and cargo, the creation of rocket ships! Our goals should be that the first artificial satellite of the Earth be Soviet, created by the Soviet people! And our goals should be to have Soviet rockets and rocket ships be the first to fly in the limitless expanse of the universe![2]

[1] APRF, 3/47/272/41-43 (August 5, 1955).

[2] S. P. Korolev, "K voprosu o primenenii raket dlia issledovaniia vysokikh sloev atmosfery" (September 25, 1955), in *SPKIED*, 190–200.

Few in the audience knew that Korolev's claims were invested with authority. Just forty-eight days before, the Soviet Politburo had approved a plan to launch an artificial Earth satellite into space. Korolev's exhortations were one of a carefully orchestrated series of missives sent out from the secret world of the defense industry to the public world, complementing the vibrant popular discourse in Soviet culture on the impending reality of space exploration.

This link between past and future, between imagination and engineering, and between private and public, framed the birth of the Soviet space program. In the 1950s, simultaneously with the development of the R-7 intercontinental ballistic missile, advocates of space exploration, both within and outside of the defense industry, successfully convinced the Soviet government to support their proposal for a space program. Serendipity, coincidence, and context greatly helped their cause, but the launch of *Sputnik* would not have been possible without deliberate action to popularize the notion of space exploration within the Soviet Union. The first step for space advocates was resurrecting Konstantin Tsiolkovskii and canonizing him as the founder of spaceflight theory. In this process, their success depended to a large degree on the broader turn to a more nationalistic discourse within Soviet culture. Reestablishing Tsiolkovskii's place in the history of science reintroduced the idea of space travel into popular dialogue after a long interruption. A widespread resurgence of technological utopianism played a crucial role in accelerating the popularization of spaceflight. Simultaneously, in the early 1950s, space advocates working secretly on military missiles established a web of connections with public popularizers of spaceflight in a joint project to underscore the benefits and inevitability of spaceflight. This vibrant informal network's actions had unexpected consequences in the international arena. Engineering leaders of the ICBM project seized on these unanticipated repercussions to bolster their case for a Soviet project to launch a satellite. Their successful lobbying eventually led to the launch of *Sputnik* in 1957.

TIKHONRAVOV'S SECOND WIND

The primary conceptual architect behind *Sputnik* was someone barely known in the West, Mikhail Tikhonravov, who, through coincidence and agency, had a hand in some of the most important turning points in the Soviet drive for space.[3] In the pre-1945 years, he helped found the amateur

[3] For biographies, see Aleksandr Zuzul'skii, *Stupeni v nebo* (Iaroslavl': DIA-Press, 2000); B. E. Chertok, A. V. Brykov, and Iu. V. Biriukov, "M. K. Tikhonravov – pioner raketnoi tekhniki i kosmonavtiki," in *IPIITR*, Vols. 8–10, 32–49. Many of his writings from the interwar period are collected in S. A. Sokolova and T. M. Mel'kumov, eds., *Pionery raketnoi tekhniki: Vetchinkin Glushko Korolev Tikhonravov: izbrannye trudy (1929–1945)* (Moscow: Nauka, 1972).

GIRD group (1931), designed the first Soviet rocket using liquid propellants (1933), worked on the *Katiusha* rockets (1938), and served on the first Soviet team to inspect captured German V-2 rockets (1944). Later, during the early Cold War, he contributed immensely to a remarkable series of Soviet successes: the first Soviet ICBM, the first *Sputnik*, the first Moon probes, and eventually the flight of Iurii Gagarin, the world's first space voyager. No less important were his critical contributions to the mass popularization of spaceflight in the Soviet Union, especially in the postwar era.

Tikhonravov was born in 1900 in Vladimir, one of the oldest cities in Russia, located a little about 175 kilometers east of Moscow. His parents were teachers, and thus inculcated the young boy with a love for learning. Even as a precocious young man, he was known to his friends as unusually intelligent – he mastered Latin and ancient Greek, and he loved ancient mythology. His passion for Latin endured throughout his life, and for relaxation, he read ancient Roman poets and philosophers such as Ovid and Seneca.

After finishing among the first graduating class of the prestigious Zhukovskii Military Air Academy, he worked as an aeronautical engineer in the late 1920s. In his free time, he indulged in his love for gliders. At a regional glider competition, Tikhonravov met for the first time, another young and aviation enthusiast, Sergei Korolev. Tikhonravov was the older of the two but Korolev, barely twenty years old, was much more vocal and assertive. In an apt metaphor of their later relationship, Tikhonravov designed a famous glider named *Firebird*, which Korolev decided to use to get his pilot's license, thus bringing Korolev's name to greater prominence within the glider community. Besides his day job and his gliding pastime, Tikhonravov was a prolific writer. Among many different topics, he wrote frequently on the mechanics of bird and insect flight. In the hope of mechanically replicating bird flight, Tikhonravov spent years immersed in mathematical arcana and experimentation. Friends remember serving as guinea pigs for strange experiments, which soon convinced Tikhonravov that human muscles augmented by mechanical wings were simply incapable of flight. He published monographs on the topic, and, to the end of his days, he collected flies and beetles from all over the world to study them under a microscope, a collection later donated to a major Soviet museum.[4] After a 1934 visit to see Tsiolkovskii in rural Kaluga, Tikhonravov fully committed himself to the cause of rocketry and space exploration and hailed Tsiolkovskii as a visionary.[5]

[4] M. K. Tikhonravov, *Polet ptits mashiny* (Moscow, 1949). A first edition was published in 1936.

[5] ARAN, 555/2/52/7; M. K. Tikhonravov, "Takoe ne zabyvaetsiia," in *K. E. Tsiolkovskii v vospominaniiakh sovremennikov*, ed. V. S. Zotov (Tula: Priokskoe knizhnoe izdatel'stvo, 1971), 82–85.

During the postwar years, Tikhonravov had no formal connection to the NII-88 institute that produced long-range missiles and did not participate directly in the various rocket projects of the day. Instead, at the age of forty-six, he began work in 1946 at a new institute known as NII-4 in Bol'shevo, a Moscow suburb close to Kaliningrad. Unlike most other organizations involved in defense R&D, NII-4 was not subordinate to Soviet industry but reported directly to the military; its army designation was "military unit 25840." The military assigned the institute to formulate "methods of testing, acceptance, storage, and combat application of missile weaponry."[6] In other words, NII-4 did not build missiles but served as an institutional forum for the military to decide what kind of rockets it needed and how such weapons could best serve the security needs of the country. It performed as a uniquely Soviet version of the American think tank RAND, studying issues related to the innovation, management, development, operation, and future of ballistic missiles.

Tikhonravov, Korolev, and their associates worked in the secret world of the Soviet military-industrial complex, a network comprising the defense industry ministries and the armed forces. The former designed and produced weapons for the latter under the supervision of the top party and government elite. With few exceptions, in the 1940s and 1950s, almost no one from the defense industry – from the lowest mechanic to the highest chief designer – was allowed to write publicly under his or her own name or to reveal the place of his or her employment. Weapons research institutes or design bureaus were openly identified only with a post office box number. Korolev, who wrote frequently in the Soviet press in the 1930s, published only one article in the open media under his own name in the last twenty years of his life.[7] In a few cases in the 1950s, the Communist Party allowed some designers to write publicly but only when the publication in question had no military implications and did not reveal any data on Soviet weapons. Tikhonravov belonged to this select group. He published on arcane scientific phenomena and on general topics related to rocketry. Those who were not allowed the luxury of writing in public usually wrote for classified in-house journals. For example, Committee No. 2, the top-level governmental body overseeing the postwar long-range rocket program, issued the secret journal *Raketnaia tekhnika* (*Rocket Technology*) in the late 1940s that published the scholarly works of Soviet researchers. Another journal, *Voprosy raketnoi tekhniki* (*Problems of Rocket Technology*), was issued from 1952 and

[6] RGVA, 4/11/83/229-32 (May 24, 1946); Iu. Mozzhorin and A. Eremenko, "Ot pervykh ballisticheskikh do . . . ," *AIK* no. 7 (1991): 40–41.

[7] Korolev's single article commemorated Tsiolkovskii's one hundredth birthday. S. P. Korolev, "Osnovopolozhnik raketnoi tekhniki: k 100-letiiu so dnia rozhdeniia K. E. Tsiolkovskogo," *Pravda*, September 17, 1957.

included translated reproductions of Western articles, book reviews, and news items about Western rocketry.[8]

ZHDANOVSHCHINA AND NATIONALIST SCIENCE

Tikhonravov took up his job at NII-4 at the same time that the postwar Soviet Union was struggling to rebuild after the devastation of World War II. Apart from the very real problems of economic reconstruction and increased repression, the early postwar years were characterized by social and cultural ramifications of a nationalist campaign launched in 1946, part of the Communist Party leadership's drive to foster a national identity rooted in rehabilitating individuals and symbols from the Russian national past and reconciling them with more recent Marxist-Leninist statist ideology. Glimpses of this seemingly paradoxical campaign of rhetoric had appeared in the late 1930s but, in the early years of the Cold War, the experience of the war added a powerful and recent dimension to the notion of a particularly Soviet (as opposed to Russian) national identity. Besides a rejection of non-Russian republican claims to Soviet identity and a valorization of the uniqueness of the Soviet wartime experience, a fundamental constituent of this ideological campaign was a complete repudiation of foreign influences in Soviet culture.[9] The campaign began in 1946 as the first Cold War tensions were mounting, when Communist Party secretary and former Leningrad Party boss Andrei Zhdanov demanded stricter ideological regulation of two publications that had dared to include works by writers considered "apolitical," "bourgeois," and "individualistic." Eventually, Zhdanov's ideas, which distilled cultural production down to two camps, imperialistic and democratic, were applied to all forms of intellectual activity, including literature, art, music, and finally, science. Actions considered bourgeois or those intellectuals accused of "servility to the West" were severely penalized, often with tragic outcomes. The campaign, known popularly as *Zhdanovshchina* (loosely translated as "the time of Zhdanov"), became a surrogate for rooting out any and all vestiges of "Western" influence in Soviet culture; it eventually acquired a distinctly anti-Semitic character in its critique of "cosmopolitanism."[10]

[8] Iu. Biriukov, "Dolgii put' k kosmicheskomu zhurnalu," *NK* no. 9 (2001): 5–6. The editorial board of *Raketnaia tekhnika* included A. A. Kosmodem'ianskii, N. I. Belov, S. P. Korolev, A. S. Predvoditelev, and N. G. Chernyshev; Predvoditelev also served as editor of *Voprosy raketnoi tekhniki*. All of them were members of Committee No. 2.

[9] David Brandenberger, *National Bolshevism: Stalinist Mass Culture and the Formation of Modern Russian National Identity, 1931–1956* (Cambridge, MA: Harvard University Press, 2002), 183–225.

[10] Kees Boterbloem, *The Life and Times of Andrei Zhdanov, 1896–1948* (Montreal: McGill–Queen's University Press, 2004); Laurent Rucker, "La 'Jdanovshchina': une campagne antisemite (1946–1949)?," *Bulletin de l'Institut d'Histoire du Temps Present* 35 (1996): 83–94.

The *Zhdanovshchina* campaign affected several Soviet scientific and social scientific disciplines such as physics, biology, cybernetics, linguistics, psychology, and philosophy. In many cases, scientific communities took the initiative to reform their particular disciplines, often with chaotic or contradictory results that didn't always conform to the Party's relatively simplistic demarcations of what was acceptable (class-based science) and what was not (science without context). Scientists frequently used the campaign to bolster their own professional positions, helping to foster more discord. Most famously, Party intervention, combined with internal professional conflicts, nearly ended the practice of at least two disciplines, Mendelian genetics – of Lysenko fame – and cybernetics.[11]

Zhdanovshchina explicitly linked science with national identity by deifying dead and living Russian intellectuals precisely for their Russian heritage. These claims were generated largely as a response to increasing Cold War tensions and the rise of the United States (which represented a generic "West") as a global superpower. Soviet writers declared that Russians invented the steam engine, bicycle, airplane, electric light bulb, radio, insulin, vitamins, synthetic rubber, and even the game of baseball. The campaign was orchestrated and sanctioned at the highest levels; in a secret letter to the Communist Party Central Committee, both Zhdanov and Stalin provided examples of Russian inventions and discoveries that were now "misappropriated" by foreigners.[12] In 1949 the Academy of Sciences hosted a conference on the history of Soviet science, the goal of which was to eliminate a "contemptuous attitude" toward national achievement in science. The following year, the academy issued a volume, *Iz istorii otechestvennoi tekhniki* (*From the History of Native Technology*), whose explicit goal was to highlight "the grandeur and diversity of the fatherland's scientific thought."[13] Attempts to direct attention to native Russian scientists brought to prominence a number of scholars who had written about rocketry and space travel decades before, including Konstantin Tsiolkovskii. As a result, after nearly twenty years in oblivion, Tsiolkovskii's legacy passed into a new phase.

[11] Kirill Rossianov, "Editing Nature: Joseph Stalin and the 'New' Soviet Biology," *Isis* 84 no. 4 (1993): 728–745; Peter Kneen, "Physics, Genetics and the *Zhdanovshchina*," *Europe-Asia Studies* 50 no. 7 (1998): 1183–1202; Alexei Kojevnikov, "Rituals of Stalinist Culture at Work: Science and the Games of Intraparty Democracy circa 1948," *Russian Review* 57 (1998): 25–52; Slava Gerovitch, *From Newspeak to Cyberspeak: A History of Soviet Cybernetics* (Cambridge, MA: MIT Press, 2002); Ethan Pollock, *Stalin and the Soviet Science Wars* (Princeton: Princeton University Press, 2006).

[12] Nikolai Krementsov, *Stalinist Science* (Princeton: Princeton University Press, 1997), 139.

[13] V. V. Danilevskii, ed., *Iz istorii otechestvennoi tekhniki: issledovaniia i materialy* (Leningrad: gazetno-zhurnal'noe i knizhnoe izdatel'stvo, 1950), 3; Alexander Vucinich, *Empire of Knowledge: The Academy of Sciences of the USSR (1917–1970)* (Berkeley: University of California Press, 1984), 230.

RESURRECTING TSIOLKOVSKII

By paying lip service to *Zhdanovshchina*, a few key spaceflight advocates used the campaign's tenor to bring Tsiolkovskii back into the public eye. This was not the first time that such an attempt had been made. In the years leading up to the war and right after Tsiolkovskii's death, several of his protégés wrote glowing reviews of the deceased scientist's life. At least five superficial biographies of Tsiolkovskii appeared, and the Soviet airline *Aeroflot*'s publishing house sponsored a tribute volume in 1939.[14] *Aeroflot*, which held the rights to Tsiolkovskii's papers, also began a project to publish his collected works in eight volumes, and invited Mikhail Tikhonravov to edit the fifth volume dedicated to Tsiolkovskii's meditations on rocketry. Although Tikhonravov finished editing the work, the project was permanently postponed with the onset of war in 1941.[15]

Advocates for Tsiolkovskii's canonization – including some involved in the prewar *Aeroflot* project – regrouped after the war. His ninetieth birthday in 1947, near the height of *Zhdanovshchina*, provided a perfect milestone to commemorate a homegrown and self-educated genius. The new Academy of Artillery Sciences, formed only a year before in July 1946 under the Ministry of War, took the lead in the celebrations. The academy was established after leading artillery officers argued that the military needed a unique educational and research institution for fundamental and applied research on artillery weapons, now including long-range rockets.[16] The first president of the academy, Anatolii Blagonravov, was a ballistics scientist who held the honorary rank of lieutenant-general in the artillery forces. During the war, Blagonravov had plucked the young Mikhail Kalashnikov out of obscurity, recognizing the value of his new idea for a submachine gun. Now, as the head of the Academy of Artillery Sciences, Blagonravov presided over several new military institutions, including NII-4 where Tikhonravov worked. Korolev and Tikhonravov knew Blagonravov well, because both had recently been elected junior members of Blagonravov's academy.[17]

With Blagonravov's help, Tikhonravov orchestrated a "closed" function to commemorate Tsiolkovskii's ninetieth birthday. He recruited several speakers, including his former coconspirator from GIRD, Sergei Korolev,

[14] The collection of tributes was published as N. A. Islent'ev, ed., *K. E. Tsiolkovskii* (Moscow: Aeroflot, 1939).

[15] ARAN, 555/7/40/1 (July 15, 1939); ARAN, 555/7/40/4 (November 24, 1939); ARAN, 555/7/42/27 (June 14, 1941).

[16] A. V. Minaev, ed., *Sovetskaia voennaia moshch' ot Stalina do Gorbacheva* (Moscow: Voennyi parad, 1999), 412–413; V. I. Ivkin, "Iz istorii vooruzheniia i tekhniki," *VIZ* no. 12 (2001): 40–47.

[17] The junior rank was known as Corresponding Member. Pobedonostsev was elected on September 10, 1946; Korolev on April 14, 1947; and Tikhonravov in 1947. See ARAN, f. 1546/1/30/1.

who had just been appointed to create a Soviet version of the German V-2 rocket at the neighboring NII-88 institute. For Korolev, devotion to Tsiolkovskii was a relatively recent phenomenon. He had neither participated in the 1920s space fad nor visited Tsiolkovskii in Kaluga as had many other GIRD members, although he had not hesitated to use the old man's name in the name of expediency, as in his letters from prison.[18] After the war, many remember that Korolev showed an overt interest in space topics in contrast to the interwar years: judging by his writings and the memories of his contemporaries, he seemed to have genuinely become a convert to the cause of cosmic travel by the late 1940s.[19] In November 1946, prior to *Zhdanovshchina*'s advent, Korolev began working on a long article on Tsiolkovskii's legacy. He soon joined forces with Tikhonravov to celebrate the late scientist's ninetieth birthday and prepared his article for reading during the commemoration, held at the Central Hall of the Soviet Army on September 17, 1947 (see Figure 28). Korolev's speech was one of the first in the postwar years to return to the main theme of the prewar discussion about Tsiolkovskii, the latter's claim to be *first* in the field of astronautics. The overtly patriotic tone of the speech reflected Korolev's acknowledgment of *Zhdanovshchina*'s ideological tenor; he touched on the campaign specifically by referring to a recent article in *Pravda* with the awkward title "Russian Inventors in the Crooked Mirror of the History Textbook" by Professor A. A. Zvorykin, who parroted Zhdanov and Stalin's take on Soviet science by suggesting that world science was an "abstraction" whereas national science was a "reality."[20]

Korolev gave his speech in secret and few outsiders were aware of it, but for many of the postwar scientific intelligentsia who attended, it was the first tribute to Tsiolkovskii at a prominent gathering. Significantly, Korolev drew attention to Tsiolkovskii's ideas about space travel rather than rocketry or airships, thus beginning the process of relocating Tsiolkovskii within space research rather than aeronautics.[21] On the same day, Tikhonravov published a piece for the general public in *Izvestiia* that shared the same hagiographic tone of his friend's talk and also touched on space themes. Other laudatory articles appeared in many other newspapers in September.[22]

[18] S. P. Korolev, *Raketnyi polet v stratosfere* (Moscow: Gos. voennoe izd-vo, 1934). ARAN, 1546/1/25/1–4 (October 15, 1939).

[19] Kurt Magnus, *Raketensklaven* (Stuttgart: Deutschen Verlags-Anstalt, 1993), 29–30; Memoir of G. I. Ioffe in *DVK2*, 19.

[20] A. Zvorykin, "Russkie izobretateli v krivom zerkale uchebnikov istorii," *Pravda*, August 26, 1947. See also his "O sovetskom prioritete," *Bol* no. 22 (1948): 23–42.

[21] MDMK, KP 3053/164, ll. 191–212. An edited version is reproduced in *TNASPK*, 197–207.

[22] M. Tikhonravov, "Znamenityi deiatel' nauki," *Izvestiia*, September 17, 1947. Tributes to Tsiolkovskii appeared in *Komsomol'skaia pravda*, *Krasnaia zvezda*, *Krasnyi flot*, *Nauka i zhizn'*, *Trud*, and *Vecherniaia moskva*, all in September 1947, commemorating his ninetieth birthday.

FIGURE 28. The ninetieth birthday of Konstantin Tsiolkovskii in 1947 proved to be the first major step in resurrecting Tsiolkovskii's legacy from oblivion. In the fall of the year, Mikhail Tikhonravov (third from the left), and Sergei Korolev (right) orchestrated a major ceremony to commemorate the late Tsiolkovskii's work. They recruited important members of the Soviet academic and scientific community and also refocused attention on Tsiolkovskii's writings on rockets and space rather than aeronautics. Standing on the left are Arkadii Kosmodem'ianskii and Boris Vorob'ev, who both became custodians of Tsiolkovskii's legacy in the 1950s and 1960s. The image was taken at the anniversary celebration in September 1947. Note the bust of Tsiolkovskii behind the attendees. [*Source*: Collection of Asif Siddiqi]

TSIOLKOVSKII, SPACE EXPLORATION, AND THE ACADEMY OF SCIENCES

Blagonravov, Tikhonravov, Korolev, and others were not simply paying lip service to the codes of *Zhdanovshchina*. They used the campaign skillfully for their own agenda, legitimizing space exploration as a useful and achievable goal. A central component of this strategy was to promote Tsiolkovskii in the eyes of the elite Soviet scientific community, that is, the USSR Academy of Sciences, whose members had consistently ignored Tsiolkovskii throughout his life. Tikhonravov's statement that "there are some skeptics who in one way or another stand in the way of Tsiolkovskii's technical ideas and who still call them untimely" was aimed as much at the Academy as it was to "bourgeois capitalists." Building on the publicity over Tsiolkovskii's birthday celebrations, and invoking the needs of *Zhdanovshchina*, the strategy to legitimize both Tsiolkovskii and spaceflight worked effectively. The Academy of Sciences took note.

On April 23, 1948, the USSR Council of Ministers issued an official decree transferring all of Tsiolkovskii's papers from *Aeroflot*, where they had languished for the past decade, to the Academy of Sciences.[23] A year later, in February 1949, the academy established a "Commission for the Development of the Scientific Contributions and Preparation for Publication of the Works of K. E. Tsiolkovskii." The four-member body – later expanded to six – defined and maintained Tsiolkovskii's legacy in the Academy of Sciences for the next forty years. Two members, Anatolii Blagonravov and Arkadii Kosmodem'ianskii, became de facto curators of Tsiolkovskii's papers and his legacy during the remainder of the Soviet era. The Soviet government permitted both men the rare honor to publish openly in the media. Between them, they published books, monographs, and articles, numbering into the hundreds, on Tsiolkovskii and his often-exaggerated contributions to world science. Like Blagonravov, Kosmodem'ianskii had deep connections to the "black" world of Soviet science and technology. An expert in the field of mechanics, Kosmodem'ianskii served on Committee No. 2, the top-secret body that supervised the Soviet long-range missile project under Malenkov and Bulganin's watchful eyes.[24] Soon, Tikhonravov joined the Tsiolkovskii legacy commission, adding another link between the public presentation of Tsiolkovskii's memory and the secret world of building missiles.[25]

In *Zhdanovshchina*'s backdrop, the Academy of Sciences republished numerous works of prominent Russian scientists; the Tsiolkovskii commission was tasked to do the same for the late scientist by publishing twelve volumes of his collected works. In bringing Tsiolkovskii's works to light, the editors struggled over and resolved a number of important issues whose outcome defined the way the Russian and Western public have perceived Tsiolkovskii in the following fifty years. For example, in contrast to the plans for publishing Tsiolkovskii's writings in the late 1930s when rocketry

[23] "O peredache arkhiva K. E. Tsiolkovskogo iz Aeroflota v Akademii nauk sssr i ob izdanii ego trudov," April 23, 1948, USSR Council of Ministers decree.

[24] Kosmodem'ianskii served as deputy chairman of Committee No. 2's scientific-technical department between May 1947 and September 1949, i.e., until the committee's dissolution. A. A. Kosmodem'ianskii, "Avtobiografiia," in *Arkadii Aleksandrovich Kosmodem'ianskii*, ed. I. A. Tiulina (Moscow: Nauka, 2003), 11.

[25] The commission, created on February 14, 1949, originally included four members: Academician B. N. Iur'ev (chairman), Professor A. A. Kosmodem'ianskii, Professor V. A. Semenov, and "engineer" B. N. Vorob'ev (secretary), who was not an engineer but a friend of the late scientist. It later expanded to include Academician A. A. Blagonravov and M. K. Tikhonravov. Commission chairman Academician Iur'ev, who was a prominent specialist in aerodynamics and helicopter design, also served as chairman of the Academy's Commission for the History of Technology between 1944 and 1950.

and space travel were consigned to Volume 5 – *after* aeronautics, dirigible design, natural sciences, and astronomy – the new editors "moved" spaceflight and rocketry to Volume 2, thus subtly shifting cosmic travel to the center of Tsiolkovskii's legacy. The commission also sought to locate Tsiolkovskii not only internationally but also nationally. As commission chairman Academician Boris Iur'ev wrote to one of his fellow editors, "it is absolutely necessary to show the native role of K. E. Tsiolkovskii in relation to our other rocketeers and workers in interplanetary travel." Furthermore, the goal was not only to make Tsiolkovskii the best and first in space travel in Russia and the world, but also, as Iur'ev noted, to show "his priority in any and every branch of reactive technology."[26] The editors also ensured, at each step of the way, that publication of Tsiolkovskii's works – some of them eighty years old – would not compromise state secrets. They consulted engineers in the defense industry, who "cleared" each of the essays for public consumption.[27]

In anticipation of the inaugural volume of Tsiolkovskii's collected works, in 1950, the editorial commission issued a blitz of popular articles on Tsiolkovskii's role as one of the greatest Russian scientists in history. Commission members wrote most of these articles; the remainder were split between Tsiolkovskii devotees in his hometown village of Kaluga and missile engineers in secret institutions from the defense industry.[28] The Academy of Sciences also devoted special articles and issues of its journals to the undertaking. In September 1950, the academy organized a public memorial to commemorate the fifteenth anniversary of Tsiolkovskii's death. Its proceedings – a series of lectures by eminent academicians – appeared in print soon after.[29] The academy published the first volume of Tsiolkovskii's memoirs in 1951 followed by the second devoted to rocketry and space exploration in 1954. In this volume, editor Anatolii Blagonravov took up the cause of establishing Tsiolkovskii's priority, echoing many of the same arguments that Tsiolkovskii used in the 1920s when the lack of official recognition from the Bol'sheviks compelled him to write about the travesty of being ignored. In 1954, Blagonravov hinted that foreigners might have stolen Tsiolkovskii's ideas, writing that "the founders of the theory of long-range rockets [such as] Goddard, Oberth, von Braun and others deliberately concealed the name

[26] ARAN, 555/7/45/22 (October 25, 1951).

[27] See, for example, ARAN, 555/7/45/23 (April 7, 1952).

[28] In 1950, over thirty articles on Tsiolkovskii appeared in newspapers (*Izvestiia*, *Komsomol'skaia pravda*, *Krasnaia zvezda*, *Krasnoi sokol'*, *Leningradskaia pravda*, *Pravda*) and journals (*Nauka i zhizn'*, *Ogonek*).

[29] B. N. Iur'ev, "Zhizn' i deiatel'nost' K. E. Tsiolkovskogo: doklad na zasedanii otd-niia tekh. nauk. akad. nauk sssr, posviashch. 15-letiiu so dnia smerti K. E. Tsiolkovskogo. 18 sent. 1950 g.," *Trudy po istorii tekhniki* no. 1 (1952): 7–19; A. A. Kosmodem'ianskii, "K. E. Tsiolkovskii, osnovopolozhnik sovremennoi raketodinamiki," *Trudy po istorii tekhniki akademii nauk* no. 1 (1952): 20–34.

of Tsiolkovskii" in the 1920s while also implying that others "to this day" continue to do so.[30]

Academy construction of Tsiolkovskii's "proper" place in the pantheon of science and technology fundamentally altered its stance on the idea of space travel. For thirty years, the Academy had ignored the possibility of spaceflight, but now, at least publicly, embraced it. The Academy's new position was most visibly underlined by its sponsorship of a medal named after Tsiolkovskii to honor "distinguished service in the area of interplanetary travel." In a meeting on September 24, 1954, the Academy's Presidium, that is, its governing body, stipulated that the gold medal would be awarded once every three years. Initially, the Academy reserved the Tsiolkovskii gold medal for Soviet citizens, but two years later, in the midst of the first thaw of the Khrushchev era, it decided that both foreign and Soviet citizens would be considered for the award.[31] Popular writers publicized widely the establishment of this award; one went so far as to say that "[s]uch high encouragement of scientific work in this very complicated field of knowledge will undoubtedly be conducive to the speedy solution of the problem of space flight."[32] Ironically, despite all the publicity, the first Tsiolkovskii medal awards – to chief rocket designers Korolev, Glushko, and Piliugin in February 1958 after the launch of *Sputnik* – were hidden from the public because the identities of all three were considered state secrets.

SCIENCE AND TECHNOLOGY IN THE POPULAR IMAGINATION

Beyond the secret world of military missiles, in broader Soviet civil society, there was a resurgence of widespread fascination in space exploration in the early 1950s. Like the space fad in the 1920s, the spark that set off the new boom was related to Tsiolkovskii – in this case, the state's appropriation of Tsiolkovskii as a symbol of the prescience of Soviet science. The various celebrations of the late theoretician's birthday in the late 1940s and early 1950s – instigated by Korolev, Tikhonravov, and likeminded enthusiasts – brought the possibility of space exploration to the foreground. Popular scientific media served as the most important forum for promoting the cause and benefits of spaceflight. And if Tsiolkovskii provided the catalyst and the

30 A. A. Kosmodem'ianskii, "K. E. Tsiolkovskii – osnovopolozhnik sovremennoi raketodinamiki," in *K. E. Tsiolkovskii: sobranie sochinenii, tom vtoroi: reaktivnye letatel'nye apparatury*, ed. A. A. Kosmodem'ianskii et al. (Moscow: AN SSSR, 1954), 18.

31 ARAN, 2/6/176/151-152 (September 24, 1954); ARAN, 2/6/221/191-95 (June 22, 1956). According to the rules, an "expert commission" attached to the academy's department of physical-mathematical sciences would carry out secret deliberations for the award.

32 A. A. Shternfel'd, "Problemy kosmicheskogo poleta," *Priroda* no. 12 (1954): 13–22; "Utverzhdenii zoloti medali...," *Pravda*, September 25, 1954; "Soiskanie zolotoi medal imeni K. E. Tsiolkovskogo," *Izvestiia*, September 28, 1956.

popular scientific media the vehicle for the new space fad, a new kind of technological utopianism allowed it to flourish in the postwar years.

In the aftermath of the war, utopia was the furthest thing from people's minds. The devastations wrought upon the Soviet populace by the war – death on a massive scale, destruction of infrastructure, and displacement of the population – were on a level almost unimaginable. What natural euphoria that emerged in the wake of the victory over the Nazis was mitigated by the new postwar social and economic order; resurgent repressions, labor shortages, poor housing, food rationing, and the mobilization of a new forced labor regime sapped the hopes of most of the population, especially those without access to the levers of power. The government lifted food rationing in 1947, but life beyond Moscow and Leningrad improved only marginally. The postwar economy recovered relatively slowly, and the average citizens could not discern any substantive improvements until about 1950. Although consumers could depend on low prices for basic food items, household products remained in chronic short supply until the late Stalin years.[33]

A modicum of economic stability returned to Soviet life only in the early 1950s, particularly after Stalin's death, when a less fearful population could enjoy the fruits of their economic stability. Vera Dunham has pointed out that the Soviet "middle class," that is, factory managers, engineers, administrators, and Party officials, became the new conservative establishment whose goal was social stability and material rewards in exchange for obedience and conformity.[34] The middle class, who were both the producers and consumers of the new Soviet space fad, differed from their predecessors in the 1920s, who were more eager for social and cultural experimentation. The two periods, the 1920s and the 1950s, however, shared one common characteristic, a popular interest in the transformative and positive role that science and technology could play in improving Soviet life. The renewed broad interest in science and technology was rooted deeply in the wartime experience, with new weapons and technologies such as the atomic bomb, the jet engine, the rocket, and radar having replaced older ones in the popular imagination. Few could ignore that science and technology had helped to fundamentally alter the nature of war, and now, with the arrival of a stable lifestyle for most Soviet citizens, it promised to transform the nature of peace.

[33] E. Iu. Zubkova, *Russia After the War: Hopes, Illusions, and Disappointments, 1945–1957* (London: Sharpe, 1998); *Donald Filtzer, Soviet Workers and Late Stalinism: Labour and the Restoration of the Stalinist System After World War II* (Cambridge, UK: Cambridge University Press, 2002).

[34] Vera Dunham, *In Stalin's Time: Middleclass Values in Soviet Fiction* (Cambridge, UK: Cambridge University Press, 1976).

As in the 1920s, an explosion of popular scientific media in the 1950s served as the primary vehicle for spreading a uniformly uplifting and futuristic view of science and technology to the Soviet masses. Having quickly recovered from wartime interruptions, the media focused much of its attention on atomic power and jet aviation as harbingers of new technologies for a glorious communist future. The message was unabashedly technologically utopian but without the millenarian and international dimensions from the 1920s. Instead, the role of technology in Soviet society was presented as evolutionary (like the gradual introduction of nuclear power stations) and national (to benefit Soviet citizens rather than a global borderless humanity). According to this view, after achieving its status as a modern (and peaceful) state, the Soviet Union would finally be able to compete on an international stage.

New popular science journals joined already existing publications such as *Tekhnika-molodezhi* (*Technology for Youth*), *Znanie-sila* (*Knowledge is Power*), and *Nauka i zhizn'* (*Science and Life*), while the market was flooded with biographies of great Russian scientists written for popular consumption. *Science and Life* alone had monthly print runs into millions, comparable to lifestyle magazines such as *Ogonek* (*Spark*). Unlike the 1920s, radio and television played a prominent role in disseminating scientific ideas, with shows such as "Nauka i zhizn'," the half-hour radio program sponsored by the journal of the same name.[35]

The resurgence of Soviet science fiction complemented the popular interest in modern technologies such as spaceflight. After the war, Soviet science fiction had an uneven path to its "golden age," from 1956 to the early 1970s. In the late Stalinist era, writers were explicitly ordered to adhere to the law of the "near target" (*blizkaia tsel'*), that is, that all stories depict scenarios that were nearly at hand so as not to divert readers' attention to indefinite utopian futures. The passing of Stalinism precipitated a gradual rebirth of the genre; over 100 novels were published in the three years before *Sputnik*, many of them devoted to space topics. If not respected within elite literary circles in the 1950s, writers such as Aleksandr Kazantsev, Ivan Efremov, Georgii Martynov, and Vladimir Nemtsov contributed to the increased visibility of the idea of spaceflight in the Soviet Union.[36] Ironically, the ideology of the so-called near target, which remained a rhetorical tool for many science fiction writers after 1953, helped to promote the notion that spaceflight was

[35] Mark Kuchment, "Bridging Two Cultures: The Emergence of Scientific Prose," in *Science and the Soviet Social Order*, ed. Loren R. Graham (Cambridge, MA: Harvard University Press, 1990), 325–340.

[36] A. F. Britikov, *Russkii sovetskii nauchno-fantasticheskii roman* (Leningrad: LO Nauka, 1970), 179–219; Patrick L. McGuire, *Red Stars: Political Aspects of Soviet Science Fiction* (Ann Arbor: UMI Research Press, 1985), 15–18.

close to being a reality. Martynov's *220 dnei na zvezdolete* (*220 Days in a Starship*), for example, described expeditions to Mars sponsored by both the United States and the Soviet Union in the very near future.[37]

Echoing the themes of the 1920s, the message of all these works was of technology as a value-neutral force that could be harnessed for the good of Soviet society, especially by using it to "control" nature. Fetishization of the atom occupied a central role in this ethos. Nuclear power promised a brave new future in which the Soviet state would master this "magnificent" source of energy to solve a panoply of social and economic problems. Russian scientists promised to develop nuclear reactors for rockets, planes, trains, and even automobiles. Soviet nuclear culture of the 1950s had its own icons, including Igor' Kurchatov, Lev Artsimovich, and Igor' Tamm, all public figures who traveled internationally. Popularization of nuclear power in the 1950s owed much to the authority of physicists involved in the atomic bomb program and their influence over public policy.[38]

In the field of space travel, most of its principal advocates – and the individuals who could do the most transform the idea into a reality – worked in a secret world without recourse to public action. Being responsible for building missiles within the defense industry, they had some leverage, but they also enjoyed much less authority than the nuclear physicists. They could not directly mount a public campaign to spread the cause of space exploration like their physicist colleagues did for atomic power. They could, however, use intermediaries and circumvent the barriers of secrecy. They had done just that to legitimize Konstantin Tsiolkovskii as a scientist worthy of the respect of the Academy of Sciences. By the time of Stalin's death in 1953, this constituency of designers and engineers began to use some of the same strategies to popularize the cause of cosmic travel. They were helped in this mission not only by the prevailing popular mood of technological optimism and the veneration of Tsiolkovskii, but also by a new generation of space popularizers in voluntary societies who worked openly, without the constraints of secrecy.

THE DOSAAF POPULARIZERS

In the early 1930s, *Osoaviakhim* had sponsored societies to popularize the cause of rocketry. The mass voluntary society did the same for spaceflight in the 1950s, serving as the central clearing point for bringing the idea to the Soviet masses. *Osoaviakhim* had survived through tumultuous times. The Great Terror wreaked havoc on the organization; hundreds of upper-

37 Georgii Martynov, *220 dnei na zvezdolete* (Leningrad: Detgiz, 1955).

38 Paul R. Josephson, "Atomic-Powered Communism: Nuclear Culture in the Postwar USSR," *Slavic Review* 55 no. 2 (1996): 297–324; Paul R. Josephson, "Rockets, Reactors, and Soviet Culture," in *Science and the Soviet Social Order*, 168–191.

and middle-level staff members had been arrested. The NKVD shot Robert Eideman, the society's longtime chairman, and also purged his successor. As a result, the society postponed its nationwide conference. Yet, after the Purges, membership continued to increase, partly due to coercion. The ranks swelled from 9.56 million in January 1939 to 12.89 million in January 1940.[39] Pre-1941 wartime preparations helped the society to regroup to some extent, and once the war began, over 7 million civilian *Osoaviakhim* members with military training moved immediately to wartime duty in the Red Army and partisan groups. Over 100,000 who had learned to fly airplanes and gliders and to parachute in the society's airclub system played a crucial role in augmenting the Red Air Force. Remaining *Osoaviakhim* members provided support to the war effort by defusing mines in recaptured territory or by operating radios.

In the postwar years, *Osoaviakhim* briefly split into three separate mass societies focusing on aviation, army, and the navy, before reuniting into one organization, the Voluntary Society for Assistance to the Army, Aviation, and Navy (*Dobrovol'noe obshchestvo sodeistviia armii, aviatsii i flotu*, DOSAAF) in 1951. At that point, it had about 15 million members. DOSAAF remained an influential civil defense organization in the 1950s, with branches in factories, farms, and schools. Its primary sponsors and leaders came from the Red Army and Red Air Force, who invested heavily in the society because it was an extremely effective recruiting tool. Soviet youth (over fourteen years of age) participated in war games and contests and trained in a wide array of activities such as motorcycling, fencing, riflery, grenade throwing, and parachute jumping. Generations of young Soviet boys and girls learned to fly planes, operate radio equipment, and scuba dive as paying members of DOSAAF.[40]

As a result of action by some university students, DOSAAF soon became a sponsor for space-themed publications in the Soviet Union. Already by the late 1940s, with more free time for recreation activities, groups of students began to form societies and associations in various institutions such as the Moscow State University, the Bauman Moscow Higher Technical School, and Moscow Aviation Institute.[41] Some of them went on to work in the classified world but retained connections with student activities; Oleg Gurko, for example, after graduating from the Moscow Aviation Institute, worked at NII-4 under Mikhail Tikhonravov and helped with many of the preliminary ICBM concept studies in the early 1950s (see Figure 29).

[39] GARF, 8355/1/197/8.

[40] For an official and sanitized history of DOSAAF, see A. L. Getman, ed., *Krasno-znamennoe oboronnoe* (Moscow: DOSAAF, 1971).

[41] Documents related to student activity focused on space exploration in the 1940s and early 1950s are stored in ARAN, r. 4, op. 14, d. 284.

FIGURE 29. Mikhail Tikhonravov's biography shadows the history of Soviet rocketry and space exploration in uncanny ways. He contributed to Soviet successes in rocketry during a period spanning more than sixty years, from designing the nation's first rocket to use liquid propellants (in 1933) to designing the first lunar landing probes (in the early 1960s). Perhaps his most important contributions were the conceptual design of the first Soviet ICBM and then producing the groundwork for *Sputnik*. He is shown here in 1970, standing behind two of his team members who worked on *Sputnik*, Oleg Gurko (left) and Igor' Iatsunskii (right). [*Source*: Oleg Gurko]

When some university students decided to set up an open forum to discuss and popularize the topic, they naturally gravitated to DOSAAF but decided to contact Gurko, hoping that he could pull some strings with his boss Tikhonravov, knowing that he had a keen interest in representations of space exploration in popular culture. In 1951, for example, when a group at the Moscow Aviation Institute tracked down a copy of the German science fiction film *Frau im Mond* (*Woman in the Moon*, 1929), Tikhonravov had his entire staff watch it.[42] In late 1953, Tikhonravov and Gurko arranged an audience with Academy of Sciences President Aleksandr Nesmeianov. An organic chemist by profession, Nesmeianov enjoyed a reputation for being open to new ideas. During a lecture at the World Peace Council in Vienna in November 1953, he unexpectedly claimed that "[s]cience has reached a state when it is feasible to send a stratoplane to the Moon, [and] to create

[42] ARAN, 4/14/284/191–194.

an artificial satellite of the Earth."[43] Nesmeianov supported the idea of a popular space society, and he interceded so that DOSAAF's Central Airclub, the Moscow headquarters of its national airclub system, sponsored a new "section on astronautics." A group of students from the Moscow Aviation Institute became the core of the DOSAAF club's new Astronautics Section.[44]

Through contacts, the DOSAAF Section recruited prominent commentators on space travel, including one Ari Shternfel'd, who became a successor of sorts to the late Iakov Perel'man, the most influential public advocate for space travel in the Soviet Union in the interwar years. Like many fellow-minded space travel popularizers in the 1950s, Shternfel'd's roots went back to the Soviet space fad of the NEP era. Born in Sieradz (not far from Lodz) in Poland in 1905, he moved to Paris for higher education in mechanical engineering in the 1920s. Captivated by information about Tsiolkovskii transmitted to France during the late 1920s, Shternfel'd began systematically studying a wide array of problems related to spaceflight. Although the Sorbonne declined to give him doctorate, having found the topic too impractical, in 1933, Shternfel'd finished a 490-page work in French summarizing his research, which included innovative solutions to finding optimal elliptical trajectories for spaceships traveling between planets. His lectures in Paris enthralled the French scientific community, which feted the young Polish scholar and gave him many honors. Shternfel'd established regular contact with Tsiolkovskii during the Soviet scientist's final years and popularized the work of Soviet enthusiasts in the French press.[45] During a visit to the Soviet Union in May 1935 to meet with Tsiolkovskii, Shternfel'd and his wife decided not to return to France and settled in Moscow, where they became Soviet citizens the following year.

For a brief period, Shternfel'd enjoyed a rare honor for a foreigner, employment at the secret Reactive Scientific-Research Institute (RNII), where he worked closely with Korolev, Tikhonravov, Glushko, and others developing rockets. The institute's chief engineer, Georgii Langemak, helped Shternfel'd secure a contract for his manuscript and translated it from French into Russian. The book, *Vvedenie v kosmonavtiki* (*Introduction to Cosmonautics*), appeared in print in 1937, but soon after, Langemak was arrested and shot, while Shternfel'd was fired from the institute because of his association with the deceased.[46] Few read Shternfel'd's technically

43 "Sessiia vsemirnogo soveta mira," *Pravda*, November 28, 1953.

44 O. V. Gurko, interview by Asif Siddiqi, July 25, 2002, Bol'shevo, Russia; A. I. Zuzul'skii, *Vperedi svoego vremeni* (Moscow: SIP RIA, 2000), 76–77. The Central Airclub, formed in March 1935 and named after famed Soviet aviator V. P. Chkalov, served principally as a forum for Soviet pilots to register daring aviation records on the international stage. In the postwar years its mandate shifted to aviation sports.

45 Shternfel'd's letters to Tsiolkovskii from 1930 to 1934 are in ARAN, 555/4/708/1-30.

46 A. Shternfel'd, *Vvedenie v kosmonavtiki* (Leningrad: ONTI, 1937); N. S. Narovlianskii, *Shturman kosmicheskikh trass Ari Shternfel'd* (Moscow: SVSKS, 2006), 40.

complex book, but it introduced the term *cosmonautics* into the Russian language, a word describing travel through space that he believed was more appropriate than the common Western *astronautics*. For many years, Shternfel'd was unable to find work, his foreign origins being a liability. After the war, Shternfel'd continued to write serious works and also produced popular treatments of his more arcane research, including a 1949 book, *Polet v mirovoe prostranstvo* (*Flight into Cosmic Space*), one of the few published on the topic in the late Stalin era.[47]

The DOSAAF publicizers invited Shternfel'd and two other popular science writers to their first meeting on the evening of January 9, 1954 at Tushino, the base of the airclub. Shternfel'd gave a talk on "The Contemporary State of the Problem of Flight into Cosmic Space."[48] At a second meeting in February, the section defined its primary mission as "[a]ssisting the accomplishment of space flights in our country for peaceful goals." To achieve its mission, the group believed it needed to promote the "popularization of the problem of interplanetary flight."[49] The members elected a chairman, Nikolai Varvarov, and a deputy chairman, Vladimir Dobronravov, and filled other posts. They organized five committees specializing in different fields related to space travel: astronomy, rocket technology, space navigation, space biology, and radio control. Beyond the few science popularizers, the section's members were either students or young workers. They also made contact with the Party authorities, both to ask for support and to ensure that that their work was properly vetted through the censorship system. By February 1956, the DOSAAF Section had nearly 420 members specializing in a variety of outreach programs that reached literally millions of Soviet citizens.[50]

VISIONS OF THE FUTURE

In the four years leading up to the launch of *Sputnik*, from 1954 to 1957, the members of the DOSAAF Section were the most important popularizers of spaceflight in the Soviet Union. They were the symbolic and real successors to Iakov Perel'man and Nikolai Rynin who did much the same for fostering cosmic enthusiasm among the Soviet populace in the 1920s and 1930s. Both had tragically died in 1942, the former from starvation during the siege of Leningrad and the latter from cancer. Now, twenty years later, the DOSAAF Section's efforts not only introduced the idea of space travel as an impending reality to the urban masses but also contributed to

[47] A. A. Shternfel'd, *Polet v mirovoe prostranstvo* (Moscow: Gostekhizdat, 1949).

[48] I. I. Krasnoiurchenko ("Targets and Goals of the Astronautics Section") and K. P. Staniukovich ("Works of Native Scientists in the Creation and Development of the Science of Astronautics") read the other lectures. S. Gushchev, "Entuziasty mezhplanetnykh poletov," *Komsomol'skaia pravda*, January 13, 1954.

[49] "Sektsiia astronavtiki v 1954 godu," *Komsomol'skaia pravda*, February 19, 1954.

[50] RGANTD, 31/6/473/1-7; RGANTD, 31/6/580/11.

unanticipated intersections with the secret community that was building missiles in the defense industry. Excepting Shternfel'd, none of the popularizers had a history of research or outreach on the topic, but all were well versed in the basic technical ideas behind the science of space exploration. Kirill Staniukovich, one of the most prolific writers in the section, was the author of a number of noted textbooks on mechanics and explosives, and Dobronravov was an expert on asynchronous machines. Both worked as professors at the Moscow Aviation Institute.[51] Iurii Khlebtsevich was an electronics expert in an industrial institute. A couple of members worked in the defense industry and thus connected the secret and public worlds. For example, Igor' Merkulov, a veteran of GIRD from the early 1930s, directed factory production of the *Buria* intercontinental cruise missile designed to carry nuclear bombs to the United States. Another, Aleksandr Seriapin, worked in a secret Air Force institute designing biological systems for high-altitude rocket flights carrying dogs.

The popularizers of the DOSAAF Section remained in close, if often indirect, contact with the designers working in the secret world. The relationship between the two communities, one secret and one public, was less exploitative than symbiotic. Both parties shared common goals but brought different qualities to the coalition. Only the missile engineers could produce actual hardware to make their dream come true, but only the popularizers could write openly about those dreams. Mikhail Tikhonravov, involved in the early 1950s in defining requirements for the first Soviet ICBM, served as a key link between the communities.[52] Because of the connections between the two constituencies, the basic technical themes of the public writing of Shternfel'd and others reflected the priorities of men such as Korolev and Tikhonravov. For example, in nearly all the writing on spaceflight in the 1950s, two ideas – artificial Earth satellites and spacecraft designed to reach the Moon – were prominent. These two ideas were also central to Korolev and Tikhonravov's early vision of a space program as articulated in May 1954, just months after the DOSAAF Section's formation, in a report to senior industrial managers.

Members of the DOSAAF Section produced the lion's share of the numerous publications on spaceflight between 1954 and 1957 (inclusive). During that period, nearly forty books and about 200 articles on rocketry and space exploration appeared in the Soviet media.[53] Journals such as *Kryl'ia*

[51] K. P. Staniukovich, *Neustanovivshiesia dvizheniia sploshnoi sredy* (Moscow: Gos. izd-vo tekhniko-teoret. lit-ry, 1955). The book was later translated and published in English as K. P. Staniukovich, *Unsteady Motion of Continuous Media* (New York: Pergamon Press, 1960).

[52] Tikhonravov, for example, co-wrote an article with one of the most prolific publicizers of spaceflight, B. V. Liapunov, for the *Great Soviet Encyclopedia* in 1955. M. K. Tikhonravov and B. V. Liapunov, "Raketa," *Bol'shaia sovetskaia entsiklopediia*, 2nd ed., t. 35 (Moscow: BSE, 1955), 665–668.

[53] For an indispensable translated collection of many of these works, see the RAND-sponsored book by F. J. Krieger, *Behind the Sputniks: A Survey of Soviet Space Science* (Washington, DC: Public Affairs Press, 1958).

rodiny (*Wings of the Motherland*), *Nauka i zhizn'* (*Science and Life*), *Priroda* (*Nature*), *Radio* (a journal for amateur radio enthusiasts partly sponsored by DOSAAF), and *Tekhnika-molodezhi* (*Technology for Youth*) published dozens of articles by the DOSAAF Section (see Figure 30). In 1954, *Technology for Youth* issued the text of a roundtable discussion on space travel organized to "meet... readers' interest in the problem of space travel."[54] Seven of the leading lights of the DOSAAF Section participated in the panel, which proved to be a hugely popular event. Daily newspapers also carried articles on the topic, whereas more serious theoretical works appeared in the various journals of the Academy of Sciences. Among the many popular books on spaceflight, two works by Shternfel'd ended up selling tens of thousands of copies.[55] His book *Isskustvennye sputnik zemli* (*Artificial Satellite of the Earth*), published a year before the launch of *Sputnik*, was a remarkably accurate description of what lay ahead. After *Sputnik*, several Western publishers immediately translated and issued his books.[56]

The DOSAAF Section also used weekly lectures to disseminate its message. Usually held on Sundays at Moscow's Polytechnic Museum, they featured popular writers such as Dobronravov, Khlebtsevich, and Merkulov. The texts of these lectures were later issued as short (about thirty-page) monographs.[57] Another lecture series, "Contemporary Problems of Astronautics," was sponsored as part of a broader series of lectures for the Soviet public by the All-Union Society for the Propagation of Political and Scientific Knowledge, a nationwide voluntary body whose stated goal was to create a new postwar Soviet intelligentsia versed in the matters of modern science and knowledge. Established in 1947 at the height of *Zhdanovshchina*, the society's original objective was to emphasize the contributions of native scientists. By the mid-1950s, the society conveyed easy-to-digest information on science and technology via its own journals (six), museum, planetaria, and publishing house, Znanie (Knowledge), which issued the text of the Sunday lectures by the space advocates.[58]

Besides the society's obvious and stated mandates, the group also sought to disseminate antireligious, "rational" knowledge to the masses, thereby

[54] N. A. Varvarov et al., "Na puti k zvezdam," *Tekhnika-molodezhi* no. 7 (1954): 1–7.

[55] A. A. Shternfel'd, *Mezhplanetnye polety* (Moscow: Gostekhizdat, 1955); A. A. Shternfel'd, *Iskusstvennye sputniki zemli* (Moscow: Gostekhizdat, 1956). A second edition of the former work was published in 1956.

[56] A. Sternfeld, *Interplanetary Travel* (London: Central Books, 1957); Ari Shternfeld, *Soviet Writings on Earth Satellites and Space Travel* (New York: Citadel Press, 1958).

[57] V. V. Dobronravov, *Kosmicheskaia navigatsiia* (Moscow: Znanie, 1956); Iu. S. Khlebtsevich, *Radioteleupravlenie kosmicheskie raketami* (Moscow: Znanie, 1955); I. A. Merkulov, *Reaktivnaia aviatsiia* (Moscow: Znanie, 1954); I. A. Merkulov, *Kosmicheskie rakety* (Moscow: Znanie, 1955).

[58] A. I. Lukianov and B. M. Lazarev, *Sovetskoe gosudarstvo i obshchestvennye organizatsii*, 2nd ed. (Moscow: Gosudarstvennoe izdatel'stvo iuridicheskoi literatury, 1961), 178–179.

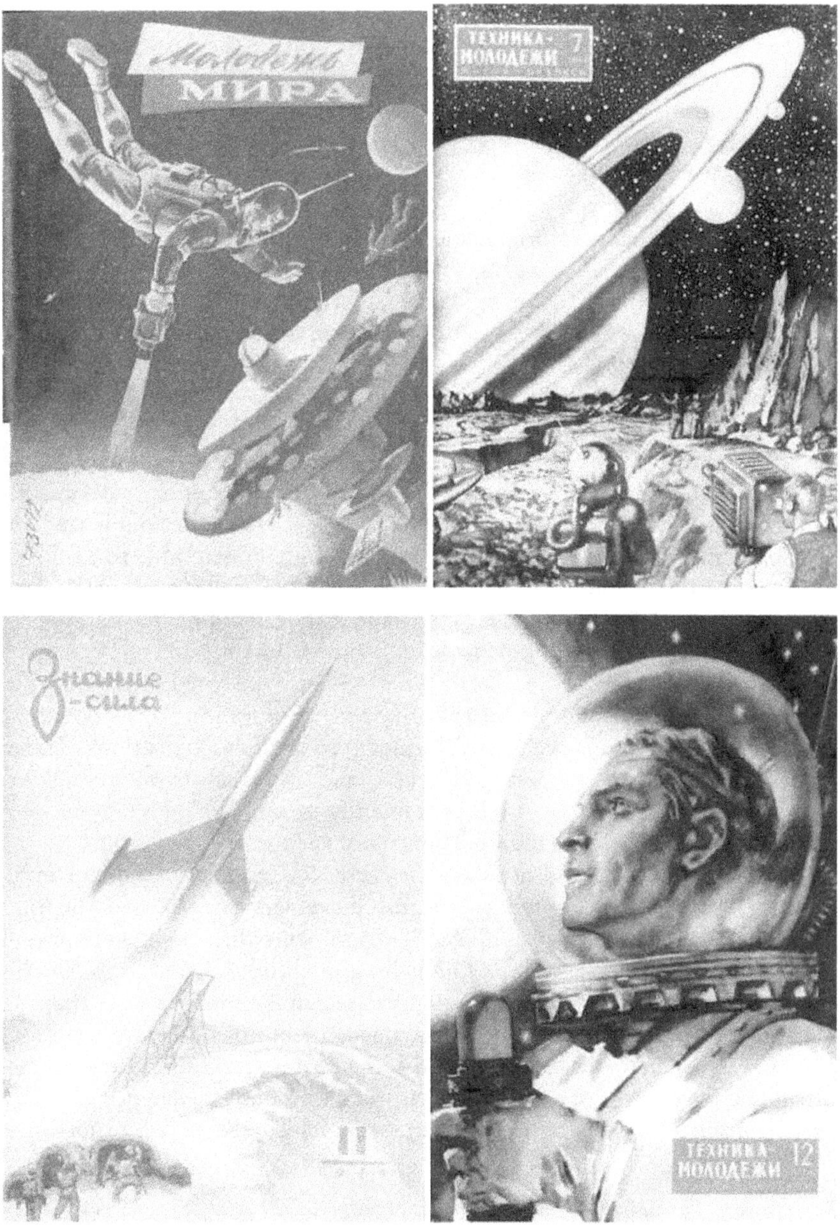

FIGURE 30. Four magazine covers from the mid-1950s illustrate the visions of space exploration as propagated by Soviet popularizers. The magazines, clockwise from top left, are: *Molodezh' mira* (*Youth of the World*), two covers from *Tekhnika-molodezhi* (*Technology for Youth*), and *Znanie-sila* (*Knowledge is Power*). The latter is a special issue from 1954 styled as a magazine from twenty years in the future. [*Source*: Collection of Asif Siddiqi]

discouraging superstition. The explicit union of spaceflight with atheism in the 1950s discourse starkly contrasted with that of the first Soviet space fad in the 1920s, when Cosmism and other spiritual ideas were an integral part of the motivation to reach space. In the 1950s, spaceflight in the Soviet Union was denuded of such superstitious ideas, as pointedly underlined by the whitewash of Tsiolkovskii's legacy as a scientist who actively dabbled in mysticism and the occult.

DOSAAF's publicity efforts inculcated a generation of young Soviet men and women with the idea that spaceflight was not only imminent but also completely inevitable. The Soviet discourse broadly mirrored the American media treatments of spaceflight in the 1950s but differed in some important details. In his important work on the relationship between space advocacy and public policy in the early American space program, *Space and the American Imagination*, Howard C. McCurdy identified how influential space activists promoted space travel as the obvious next step in the human urge to explore, based around human (as opposed to robotic) spaceflight and necessity (because of military needs).[59] For Soviet publicizers, a national cultural imperative (rather than the innate human urge to explore) was a more important benchmark. Nikolai Varvarov, for example, noted in 1955 that "[t]ales and ballads, songs and fairy tales, which arise in deep Russian antiquity, show that the Russian people from time immemorial have dreamed of mastering the ocean of air."[60] Writers devoted attention to a second theme, the economic benefits of space exploration to the country, ranging from travel and weather forecasting to telecommunications. These rationales were also common in the discourse over nuclear power and jet aviation, both of which featured prominently in most of the space-related discussions as part of a triad of harbingers of the future.[61]

Because publicists could not describe secret Soviet efforts in the defense industry, they often recounted American achievements in rocketry. The topics ran the gamut from the results of U.S. experiments with monkeys to physicist S. Fred Singer's proposal for a launching satellite, all taken from American books or conference papers. In many cases, illustrations from American magazines were reproduced without proper attribution to describe certain ideas or concepts. In one case, the DOSAAF Section devoted an entire article discussing the efficacy of a futuristic American idea published in *Popular Science Monthly*.[62] Highlighting only American achievements put writers in a

59 Howard C. McCurdy, *Space and the American Imagination* (Washington, DC: Smithsonian Institution Press, 1997).

60 Varvarov at al., "Na puti k zvezdam," 1.

61 N. Varvarov, "Problemy poleta v kosmicheskoe prostranstvo," *Sovetskii flot*, May 29, 1955; R. Perel'man, "Atomnye dvigateli," *Nauka i zhizn'* no. 1 (1956): 26–32; K. Staniukovich, "Problemy mezhplanetnykh polet," *Krasnaia zvezda*, August 10, 1954.

62 V. G. Fesenkov, "Zvezdnye miry," *Tekhnika-molodezhi* no. 3 (1954): 5–10; I. Kucherov, "Radioupravliaemye rakety," *Radio* no. 8 (1955): 50–53; V. Petrov, "Na puti v kosmos,"

bind because it implicitly reflected poorly on native developments. Publicizers got around this problem by attributing militaristic intentions to American advances in rocketry and spaceflight. The criticism of American intentions waned from the late Stalin years to the thaw era but never completely disappeared. For example, Soviet writers criticized the series of articles published by *Collier's* magazine in the early 1950s in which former German rocket scientist Wernher von Braun and famous space artist Chesley Bonestell introduced fantastic ideas about the future of space travel to a broad segment of the American public. One Soviet writer argued that the series showed space exploration "only in terms of U.S. military potentialities."[63] Soviet commentators also criticized American science fiction, both movies and books, and singled out for opprobrium *Destination Moon*, an early genre film.

America set up a new finish line that they thought they could get to first.

SPACE RESEARCH IN THE SECRET WORLD

In parallel to the vigorous popularization of spaceflight in the open Soviet media, space activists within the defense industry sought to implement the goal of spaceflight, a project that would require major state support. Until 1954, however, the Soviet government neither sponsored work on space exploration nor expressed any interest in the idea. Initially, the possible military uses of satellites altered that view. Two additional factors moved the discussion of spaceflight from idle thinking to a topic of serious consideration: the impending reality of an ICBM capable of launching a satellite and growing interest from the Soviet scientific community.

A number of actors from different constituencies working in coalition brought the idea of space exploration to the government, but the process depended critically on the reception of the DOSAAF publicity work, both at home and especially abroad. The central figure here was, once again, Mikhail Tikhonravov, who since the late 1940s, on his own initiative and in his free time, had continued to study possible ways to launch satellites into orbit. By 1951, he had formed a small team of young university graduates at his institute, the NII-4, who pursued this work, research that eventually evolved into studying not only how to get to space but what to do once arrival was ensured. They produced three memoranda between 1952 and 1954 that answered a variety of problems related to the creation of an artificial satellite and the possible tasks one could accomplish with them. With the tacit support of a high official in the Ministry of Defense, Tikhonravov and

Krasnaia zvezda, May 19, 1957; L. Vasil'evskii and M. Tarnopol'skii, "Gorod v mezhplanetnom prostranstve," *Iunost'* no. 8 (1956): 102–106.

63 K. P. Staniukovich, "Rendezvous with Mars," *News: A Soviet Review of World Events*, October 16, 1956, 25–26. In a similar vein, see N. Varvarov, "Problema poleta v kosmicheskoe prostranstvo," *Sovetskii flot*, May 29, 1955; V. Borisov, "Doroga k zvezdam," *Znanie-sila* no. 4 (1990): 7–8.

his coworkers began a two-year pilot study dedicated to the study of artificial Earth satellites, the first of its kind in the Soviet Union. They would produce a classified and comprehensive report on the topic, much like the secret satellite reports that RAND issued in the United States in those same years. They hoped that they could use such a report to appeal to the government for support.

On September 16, 1953, the leadership at NII-4 approved a "scientific-research theme" entitled "Research into the Problems of Creating an Artificial Satellite of the Earth." The R&D project, with the code name "Theme No. 72," would begin the following January and last two years. Tikhonravov's young protégé Igor' Iatsunskii oversaw the project under his mentor's guidance.[64] The group included the same young students – ten men and one woman – who earlier studied ICBM design concepts and, some, like Oleg Gurko, who communicated with the DOSAAF Publicity Section. The team explored a variety of engineering problems, including placing a satellite in orbit, changes in a satellite's orbit, returning to Earth, radio communications, and optical tracking of satellites from the ground. They developed a preliminary model of a satellite they called "the simplest satellite" (*prosteishii sputnik*), which could serve as a technology-proving concept launched by the still-on-paper R-7 ICBM.[65]

Military applications were the central *raison d'être* for the 442-page report issued by the team by March 1955. In the report's conclusion, Tikonravov noted that

> The simplest satellite will have great scientific importance. Its military significance will be the possibility of testing the operation of a number of systems necessary for other more complex and heavier satellites carrying military payloads. Besides, it is likely that it will be possible to systematically photograph the enemy's territory from the simplest satellite.[66]

The team also researched the possibility of using a satellite to drop bombs to hit ground targets ("maximum deviation will be less than 15 kilometers from the target"), crewed military spaceships, and orbital stations.

A second modest effort on satellite research began within the Academy of Sciences' Mathematics Institute under the prominent mathematician Mstislav Keldysh, who would play a crucial role in the genesis of *Sputnik*. By

64 Igor' Iatsunskii, "O deiatel'nosti M. K. Tikhonravova v period s 1947 po 1953 gg. po obosnovaniiu vozmozhnosti sozdaniia sostavykh raket," *IIAIK* 42 (1980): 31–38; Valerii Baberdin, "Zdes' nachinalsia voennyi kosmos," *Krasnaia zvezda*, April 30, 1994.

65 The team members included M. K. Tikhonravov, I. M. Iatsunskii, G. Iu. Maksimov, A. V. Brykov, L. N. Soldatova, I. K. Bazhinov, O. V. Gurko, V. T. Garibian, Iu. S. Shukshin, E. V. Korol'kov, A. A. Zakharov, and K. A. Biantovskii.

66 M. K. Tikhonravov et al., "Predvaritel'nyi otchet No. 571: Issledovaniia po voprosu sozdaniia iskusstvennogo sputnika zemli," April 2, 1955, cover, table of contents, and conclusion in possession of the author.

adding Keldysh to the network of space activists, Korolev and Tikhonravov opened access to the most powerful ranks of the Soviet scientific community. A Latvian by birth, Keldysh completed his higher education under the famous Nikolai Luzin, who educated a generation of brilliant Soviet mathematicians. In recognition of Keldysh's research on the aeronautical problems of flutter and shimmy, in 1946 the academy elected the thirty-five-year-old to its membership. He was one of the youngest inductees in the 300-year history of the institution.[67]

After the war, Keldysh ended up managing a high-profile aeronautics research institution, the NII-1 institute, the new incarnation of the old RNII where Korolev and Glushko had worked in the 1930s. By the late 1940s, on the recommendation of one of the greatest Soviet mathematicians, Ivan Vinogradov, he was drawn into highly classified work on the new thermonuclear weapons project for which he headed a "mathematical-computational bureau" to support mathematical modeling. He also oversaw the development of high-speed computers for the project. Keldysh's contribution, essential to the explosion of the first true Soviet hydrogen bomb in late 1955, was so valued that when president of the Academy of Sciences, Aleksandr Nesmeianov, wanted Keldysh to take over a senior post in the academy, Lavrentii Beriia refused to let Keldysh be taken from the nuclear program and firmly rejected the academy's request.[68] Keldysh's mathematical bureau was eventually transferred to the academy and reorganized as a Department of Applied Mathematics, but only after Stalin's death and with the considerable clout of Kurchatov.[69]

Keldysh's stature steadily rose through the decade, largely because of his close working relationships with influential scientific elites such as Igor' Kurchatov and Andrei Sakharov. With rising clout, Keldysh's portfolio diversified; by the mid-1950s, Keldysh was directly involved in thermonuclear weapons development, ICBM design, the intercontinental cruise missile project, and the development of supercomputers. One of the projects that his team of scientists ("Keldysh's Boys") took on involved the study of how to ensure that nuclear warheads, having been lobbed onto their intercontinental trajectories, could survive the reentry back into the atmosphere. This problem also had a dual application, as scientists would need to solve the same problem if they ever intended to recover orbiting satellites from space. This first, albeit peripheral, dabbling into space-related research steadily

[67] A. V. Zabrodin, ed., *M. V. Keldysh: tvorcheskii portret po vospominaniiam sovremennikov* (Moscow: Nauka, 2001). "Shimmy" describes self-induced oscillations of aircraft landing gear whereas "flutter" denotes undesirable wing surface oscillations on aircraft.

[68] See the letters back and forth between Nesmeianov, Beriia, and Zaveniagin dating from September 1952 reproduced in *APS7*, 765–767.

[69] The department was formally established on April 18, 1953. See "Rasporiazhenie SM SSSR No. 6111-rs," April 18, 1953 in *APS7*, 542–544.

drew Keldysh's interest to the cosmos; subsequently, by 1955, he sponsored research at NII-1 into satellite orientation systems.[70]

Keldysh did not share the passion for space exploration that by this time was almost instinctual in men such as Korolev, Tikhonravov, and Glushko, but his support for the cause, given his influence in the Soviet military-industrial complex and his standing in the Academy of Sciences, proved to be crucial. Korolev recognized this and in early 1954, although busy with a host of ballistic missile projects, invited Keldysh to attend a series of meetings to discuss a possible plan to launch a satellite into orbit.[71] Two meetings in the Academy of Sciences, on March 16 and May 25, brought together important scientists curious about the scientific benefits of the satellite project. The former was attended by Academician Petr Kapitsa, the world famous Soviet nuclear physicist (and future Nobel Prize winner). The biggest coup was attracting the attention of the president of the academy, Aleksandr Nesmeianov, who agreed to host the second meeting in his own office. The assembled, including Korolev, Tikhonravov, and Keldysh, spent three hours discussing a possible satellite proposal that could be sent to the government for approval; Nesmeianov agreed, at least in principle, to support exploratory work on an artificial Earth satellite.[72]

Not everyone supported the effort. In his diaries, Tikhonravov noted that the deputy director of his institute, Georgii Tiulin, "didn't 'get' anything, and Korolev got the impression that he won't be offering any help, even though he had [been] promised [such help before]. I should have expected it."[73] But Korolev's boss, Minister of Armaments Dmitrii Ustinov, expressed interest in the idea and asked to see the proposal. The men acted very quickly. On May 26, 1954, just six days after the Soviet government approved full-scale work on the R-7 ICBM, Korolev sent high officials in the defense industry a preliminary and short version of Tikhonravov's study on satellites, along with translations of a number of articles on space exploration from the American media. In his cover letter, Korolev wrote,

[70] For the Keldysh's role in nuclear weapons and missile development in the 1950s, see Iu. A. Trutnev, "M. V. Keldysh i ego kollektiv v reshenii atomnoi problemy" and V. A. Avduevskii and T. M. Eneev, "O rabotakh M. V. Keldysha po raketostroeniiu i kosmonavtike," in *M. V. Keldysh*, 66–78.

[71] In his diaries, Tikhonravov noted at least a dozen meetings from January to March 1954 on the satellite proposal, most of them at Keldysh's office at the Academy of Sciences. M. K. Tikhonravov, Diary Notes, 1950–1966, daily entries for January, February, and March 1954.

[72] Tikhonravov Diary, daily entries for March 16 and May 25. For a summary of the meetings in early 1954, see Iu. V. Biriukov, ed., *Materialy po istorii kosmicheskogo korablia 'Vostok'* (Moscow: Nauka, 1991), 208–210. Besides P. L. Kapitsa, scientists involved in these discussions included S. E. Khaikin (physics), I. A. Kibel' (geophysics), B. V. Kukarkin (astronomy), and S. N. Vernov (physics).

[73] Tikhonravov Diary, daily entry for March 14, 1954. Korolev had met Tiulin the day before.

> I draw your attention to the memorandum of Comrade M. K. Tikhonravov, "On an Artificial Satellite of the Earth," and also to the forwarded [media] materials from the U.S.A. on work being carried out in this field. The current development of [the R-7 ICBM] makes it possible for us to speak of the possibility of developing in the near future an artificial satellite.... It seems to me that at the present time it would be timely and feasible to organize a scientific-research department [in NII-88] for performing the initial exploratory work on a satellite and more detailed work on the set of problems associated with this goal.

He ended the letter with a simple phrase: "I await your decision."[74]

In the attached report, a *tour de force* of foresight and elegance, Tikhonravov suggested beginning the Soviet space program with work on three simultaneous goals:

- launching a "simplest satellite" weighing about three tons and orbiting around the Earth at altitudes varying between 170 and 1,100 kilometers;
- developing the capability to launch a human on a suborbital flight; and
- recovering a capsule from Earth orbit.

Future goals would include a piloted orbital spaceship, a space station, and research on lunar flights.[75]

Keldysh and Nesmeianov's involvement in this proposal prompted Soviet industrial managers to pay attention. In August 1954, Viacheslav Malyshev, then at the apex of the military-industrial complex as head of *Minsredmash*, the nuclear ministry, along with a number of associates, sent a request to Georgii Malenkov asking for approval "to work on scientific and technical questions related to space flight," that is, not to build a satellite but to consider whether such an idea had any value, scientific, military, or otherwise.[76] Malenkov, in his capacity as chairman of the Soviet Council of Ministers, signed an official decree on August 10, 1954 and approved the following:

- research and development on a satellite (at OKB-1, NII-4, and the Academy of Sciences);
- creation of a commission in the Academy of Sciences for scientists to discuss the potential scientific benefits of an Earth satellite[77]; and
- establishment of an award in honor of Konstantin Tsiolkovskii to be given to individuals who have made important contributions to astronautics.

[74] S. P. Korolev, "O vozmozhnosti razrabotki iskusstvennogo sputnika Zemli," in *TNASPK*, 343. Various reliable sources cite different dates (May 26 or May 27) and recipients (D. F. Ustinov in most sources; V. M. Riabikov, G. N. Pashkov, and D. F. Ustinov in others) for this important letter.

[75] M. K. Tikhonravov, "Dokladnaia zapiska ob iskusstvennom sputnike zemli," in *Materialy po istorii*, 5–15.

[76] *RKKE*, 86. Besides Malyshev, the request was signed by B. L. Vannikov, M. V. Khrunichev, and K. N. Rudnev.

[77] ARAN, 472/1-ch. II/380/22 (January 12, 1956).

Although the work focused only on paper studies, it moved the slow movement of Soviet cosmic aspirations, begun nearly a century before, to an entirely new footing. For the first time since Konstantin Tsiolkovskii dreamt of floating free of gravity above his home, the government had intervened in the idea of space exploration. The Academy of Sciences, for so long hostile or at best indifferent to such concepts, issued a formal decree nine days later asking Korolev's design bureau to develop some basic concepts for a scientific satellite weighing about 1.5 tons.[78]

IN THE PUBLIC EYE

As per the government edict, in December 1954, Keldysh established a commission to discuss space travel within the academy. The commission, formally under the academy's Astronomy Council, had a name that was almost comical in its sheer length: the "Permanent Interdepartmental Commission for the Coordination and Monitoring of Scientific-Theoretical Work in the Field of Organization and Accomplishment of Interplanetary Developments and of the Thematics of Research Problems and Analysis of the Possibilities of the Practical Realization of Interplanetary Communications." For much of the Cold War, even the American Central Intelligence Agency had barely any inkling of the *raison d'être* of this commission. Declassified records from the academy's archives show its activities in 1955 included the following:

> the clarification of first priority scientific research tasks [possible to solve] with the aid of an artificial earth satellite; analysis of the contemporary state of problem; [and] formulating the [most] promising problems to a number of scientific-research institutions in our country.[79]

In other words, the most important goal for the interplanetary commission was to serve as a place for academy scientists to deliberate on the scientific and applied scientific problems associated with both the creation of a satellite and the goals it could solve. Unlike the DOSAAF Section, the academy would give scientific legitimacy to the topic and allow academy scientists – especially those without any knowledge of or contact with the secret military world – to participate in the discourse on spaceflight. The commission, however, had another equally important task that was not officially enumerated. According to a scientist working at the time for Keldysh on satellite problems, the commission

> served the USSR as an official face to the community (Soviet and global) for the results of secret work on the creation of space technology [which was] carried out by the

[78] V. V. Molodtsov, "Pervye kosmicheskie proekty (k 40-letiiu zapuska 1-y ISZ)," *Zemlia i vselennaia* no. 4 (1997). The Academy issued a decree on August 19, 1954 on satellite research.

[79] ARAN, 472/1-ch. II/380/22 (January 12, 1956).

Academy of Sciences in cooperation with [secret scientific-research institutes, design bureaus] and factories. The members of the commission (and primarily its chairman and scientific secretary) visited foreign countries as representatives of Soviet space science, although they almost never participated in [secret] work.[80]

Undoubtedly the driving force behind the creation of the commission was Mstislav Keldysh, who made sure that key members on it included people who had little or no knowledge of the top-secret ICBM program but if necessary could be counted upon for their expertise. To chair the interplanetary commission, Keldysh appointed Academician Leonid Sedov, a colleague who knew nothing of the missile program, but worked as a respected aeronautics scientist specializing in hydrodynamics, gas dynamics, and mechanics.[81] Those on the inside, that is, Korolev, Keldysh, and others, closely monitored and controlled the commission's public pronouncements via the one member of the commission who *did* have close connection to the secret world of missile development, Mikhail Tikhonravov.[82] Keldysh also had one of his closest assistants, Gennadii Skuridin, serve as an "associate" of the body. Korolev visited the commission's offices once in late 1954 – soon after its formation – to discuss its plan of publicity work.[83] One result of the collusion between the secret and public worlds was publicizing the commission's work in the Soviet media.

(UN)INTENDED CONSEQUENCES

The unusually intense publicity afforded the topic of space travel by the DOSAAF Section in the 1950s was followed with keen interest by observers in the West. This ambience surrounding space drew the attention of many abroad who suspected that the sheer volume of media attention underscored a deep and abiding interest in space travel among the Soviet populace, if not the Soviet government. One news item, a public announcement on the work of the academy's interplanetary commission, issued in early 1955, caught the eye not only of the Western media but also those responsible for advising the American president on Soviet intentions. This public announcement set off a chain of events that connected three hitherto disparate phenomena: public advocacy for spaceflight in the Soviet Union, secret Soviet work on missiles, and the U.S. government's own interest in an Earth satellite. The intersection of these strands created an unanticipated and international link

80 V. A. Egorov, "Iz vospominanii o M. L. Lidove," *Kosmicheskie issledovaniia* no. 5 (2001): 451–453.

81 V. P. Lishevskii, *Ocherki o deiateliakh rossiiskoi nauki i tekhniki* (Moscow: Nauka, 1999), 222–225.

82 Tikhonravov Diary, daily entry for September 20, 1954.

83 For Korolev's visit, see Memoir of G. A. Skuridin in *ASPK*, 453.

between Soviet and U.S. plans for the cosmos, thus sparking the creation of *Sputnik* and ultimately the Soviet space program.

In February and March 1955, Korolev and Tikhonravov worked behind the scenes to orchestrate a detailed public announcement about the existence of the academy's interplanetary commission.[84] The article, in dry and uninspiring prose, appeared on April 16, 1955 in the Moscow newspaper *Vecherniaia moskva* (*Evening Moscow*).[85] Western wire services picked up the story and reported it prominently in the American press.[86] A *New York Times* article in July, for example, noted that "[i]intense Soviet interest in achieving priority over all other nations in regard to all aspects of interplanetary flight has been evident for some years." The *Times* went on to recount the various public pronouncements by the DOSAAF advocates and then described the *Evening Moscow* statement. "The United States and the Soviet Union now appear to be in a race for the glory of making the first step toward interplanetary flight," the article concluded.[87] In his "Matter of Fact" column, one of the most widely syndicated columns in the United States, journalist Stewart Alsop noted that the "bland [Soviet] announcement... caused much dismay at least among the more sensible men in the Pentagon.... [T]his kind of before-the-fact boasting by the Soviets must be taken very seriously indeed as the Pentagon has learned to its sorrow, conspicuously in the case of the atomic and hydrogen bombs."[88]

Alsop, a former Office of Strategic Services officer with strong ties to the American intelligence community, was not simply conjecturing; within the black world of the American security establishment, the relatively innocuous announcement had deep repercussions. A CIA National Intelligence Estimate prepared for U.S. President Dwight D. Eisenhower and issued later in 1955 singled out the Soviet interplanetary commission and cited the *Evening Moscow* article as well as other recent writings from the DOSAAF Section as evidence "of a coordinated survey of the theoretical problems involved in establishing a space satellite."[89]

In May 1955, the U.S. government's National Security Council issued a top-secret policy document known as NSC 5520, which recommended that

[84] On February 1, 1955, Tikhonravov met with commission chairman L. I. Sedov, noting in his diary that "another report is needed [for the commission]." Later, on March 11, Tikhonravov called Korolev to discuss specifically the work of the commission. Tikhonravov Diary, daily entries for February 1 and March 11, 1955.

[85] "Komissia po mezhplanetnykh soobshchenii," *Vecherniaia moskva*, April 16, 1955.

[86] "Interplanetary Commission Created: Russians Planning Space Laboratory for Research Beyond Earth's Gravity," *Washington Post*, April 17, 1955.

[87] Harry Schwartz, "Russians Already Striving to Set Up Space Satellite," *New York Times*, July 30, 1955.

[88] Stewart Alsop, "Debate on the Satellite," *Washington Post*, May 25, 1955.

[89] CIA, National Intelligence Estimate Number 11-12-55, Soviet Guided Missile Capabilities and Probable Programs, December 20, 1955, NASA HQ Archives, Box for CIA NIEs.

the Eisenhower Administration approve development of a small scientific satellite to be launched as part of the International Geophysical Year (IGY), a broad-scale international program to study the Earth and its upper atmosphere set for 1957–1958, a predicted period of intense solar activity.[90] The decision, an important milestone in the birth of the American space program, had cascading consequences, eventually leading to several early space projects such as the civilian Vanguard program and the highly classified CORONA project. The Eisenhower Administration's decision had a hidden agenda known only to a handful of individuals at the time. The authors of NSC 5520 sought to establish the precedent of "freedom of space" with a peaceful scientific satellite, that is, the right to fly over other nations' territories in space, thus clearing the way for military reconnaissance satellites that could later spy on the Soviet Union with impunity.[91] NSC 5520 was, in fact, issued as a result of an earlier recommendation from the Technological Capabilities Panel (TCP), a high-level scientific body headed by MIT President James R. Killian, Jr. that was asked to study the issue of a surprise attack by the Soviet Union. Among its many influential recommendations, the TCP advocated that the United States immediately start developing a spy satellite.[92]

Although establishing the precedent of so-called freedom of space might have served as the main impetus for the American decision to launch a small scientific satellite, it was not the only one. Prestige – specifically preempting the Soviet Union in launching the first satellite – also figured prominently. Here again, the *Evening Moscow* article served as a catalyst. Days after its publication, Joseph Kaplan, chairman of the U.S. National Committee on the IGY, wrote an urgent letter to Alan T. Waterman, the National Science Foundation's director who was involved in the deliberations leading to NSC 5520, about the immediate need to approve a satellite project. To emphasize the urgency of his request, Kaplan attached a copy of the

[90] In October 1954, IGY scientists had proposed launching satellites as part of the program. Harold Spencer Jones, "The Inception and Development of the International Geophysical Year," in *Annals of the International Geophysical Year, Vol. I: The Histories of the International Polar Years and the Inception and Development of the International Geophysical Year*, ed. M. Nicolet (London: Pergamon Press, 1959), 392–393.

[91] Walter McDougall, *... the Heavens and the Earth: A Political History of the Space Age* (New York: Basic Books, 1985), 119–121; R. Cargill Hall, "The Eisenhower Administration and the Cold War: Framing American Astronautics to Serve National Security," *Prologue* 27 (Spring 1995): 58–72.

[92] James R. Killian, Jr., *Sputnik, Scientists, and Eisenhower: A Memoir of the First Special Assistant to the President for Science and Technology* (Cambridge, MA: The MIT Press, 1977), 11–12, 70–82; Dwayne A. Day, "Cover Stories and Hidden Agendas: Early American Space and National Security Policy," in *Reconsidering Sputnik: Forty Years Since the Soviet Satellite*, eds. Roger D. Launius, John M. Logsdon, and Robert W. Smith (Amsterdam: Harwood, 2000), 161–195.

Washington Post's report on the Soviet newspaper article.[93] As evidence of Soviet pursuit of a satellite project, NSC 5520 singled out *Evening Moscow*'s announcement on the interplanetary commission as well as the Soviet press statement announcing the establishment of the Tsiolkovskii gold medal the previous September.[94]

Eisenhower's assistant secretary of defense for research and development Donald A. Quarles, the principal architect behind NSC 5520, "seized ... on the Soviet threat" to push through his hidden agenda to establish the freedom of space principle under cover of a civilian satellite.[95] As Michael J. Neufeld has noted, "the Soviet factor played a critical role" in the Eisenhower's satellite decision of May 1955, a point explicitly underlined in NSC 5522, a follow-up report to NSC 5520 issued in June 1955, in which the authors noted,

> There is an increasing amount of evidence that the Soviet Union is placing more and more emphasis on the successful launching of the satellite. Press and radio statements since September 1954 have indicated a growing scientific effort directed toward the successful launching of the first satellite. Evidently the Soviet Union has concluded that their satellite program can contribute enough prestige of cold war value ... to justify the diversion of the necessary skills.... The nation that first accomplishes this feat will gain incalculable prestige and recognition throughout the world.[96]

On the same day that NSC 5522 was issued, the Department of Defense tasked Quarles with making the American scientific satellite a reality.

The freedom of space rationale gained particular urgency following President Dwight D. Eisenhower's return in July from the summit in Geneva of the four former wartime allies. At the meeting, Eisenhower had tried unsuccessfully to convince Soviet leaders Nikita Khrushchev and Nikolai Bulganin to agree to an "open skies" policy, that is, a proposal to facilitate mutually supervised reconnaissance flights over each other's territories. After the Soviets refused the offer, Eisenhower met with Waterman and Quarles to convey his full support for an American satellite project for IGY. The satellite

93 Kaplan to Waterman, May 6, 1955, reproduced in *Exploring the Unknown: Selected Documents in the History of the U.S. Civil Space Program, Vol. 1*, ed. John M. Logsdon (Washington, DC: NASA, 1995), 302–303. For the attachment see p. 308.

94 "National Security Council NSC 5520, 'Draft Statement of Policy on U.S. Scientific Satellite Program,' May 20, 1955," in *Exploring the Unknown*, 309.

95 Michael J. Neufeld, "Orbiter, Overflight, and the First Satellite: New Light on the Vanguard Decision," in *Reconsidering Sputnik*, 239.

96 Comments on the Report to the President by the Technological Capabilities Panel of the Science Advisory Committee, June 8, 1955, White House Office, Office of the Special Assistant for National Security Affairs: Records, 1952-61, NSC Policy Papers, Box 16, Folder NSC 5522 Technological Capabilities Panel, A55-A56, Dwight D. Eisenhower Library, Abilene, Kansas. Historian Dwayne Day notes that by late 1956, the NSC deemphasized the need to be first in favor of other rationales such as establishing the "freedom of space" principle and the need to produce substantive scientific results. Day, "Cover Stories and Hidden Agendas," 179–180.

FIGURE 31. Leonid Sedov (1907–1999) played an important role in advertising Soviet intentions in space exploration in the pre-*Sputnik* era and during the early years of the Soviet space program. His press conference in Copenhagen in early August 1955 was a critical factor in moving the Soviet satellite project from one that was conjecture to one that demanded the attention of the Soviet Politburo. [*Source*: NASA]

would fulfill both rationales: freedom of space and prestige by beating the Soviet Union into space. Days later, on July 29, 1955, Eisenhower's Press Secretary, James C. Hagerty, publicly revealed that the United States would launch "small Earth-circling satellites" as part of its participation in the IGY.[97]

The Eisenhower Administration's announcement set off a round of publicity over the possibility of an American satellite. Although the Soviet government never officially responded – it, after all, had no official plans to do the same – Soviet spaceflight enthusiasts working both in secret and in public took the American announcement as an ideal opportunity to intensify their quest to attract the attention of the Soviet government. Four days after the Eisenhower announcement, Academician Leonid Sedov, the erstwhile chairman of the Soviet interplanetary commission, rather spontaneously announced at an international conference in Denmark (see Figure 31) that "[i]n my opinion, it will be possible to launch an artificial Earth satellite

97 "Statement by James C. Hagerty, The White House, July 29, 1955," in *Exploring the Unknown*, 200–201; "Plany sozdaniia 'iskusstvennogo sputnika Zemli'," *Pravda*, August 3, 1955.

within the next two years." He added that "[t]he realization of the Soviet project can be expected in the comparatively near future. I won't take it upon myself to name the date more precisely."[98] Being only a public figurehead, Sedov knew nothing of the behind-the-scenes lobbying but, more than likely, Keldysh and others in Moscow, that is, those actively proposing a Soviet satellite, had prepared Sedov's statement for public consumption.[99]

The day after Sedov's press conference, the major Western press outlets ran front-page stories that considerably exaggerated his claims. Other Soviet scientists had made similarly vague statements in public before, but because Sedov's announcement immediately followed the Eisenhower statement, the Western media found a story too big to ignore. The *Washington Post* headlined its story "Russians Say They Intend to Beat U.S. In Launching First Unmanned Satellite," while the *Los Angeles Examiner* screamed, "We'll Launch 1st moon, and Bigger, Says Russ."[100] Sedov later objected to the characterization of a satellite race between the two countries, but Western publications, at least for a few weeks, parroted the notion of international competition.[101]

The public statements of the DOSAAF Section and the Academy of Sciences' interplanetary commission – particularly the April 1955 article in *Evening Moscow* – significantly accelerated American plans to pursue a satellite project. The Eisenhower Administration's stated purpose in its July 1955 announcement of U.S. plans to launch a satellite during IGY was partly a response to the alarm about Soviet intentions. The American announcement then prompted the Soviet interplanetary commission's Sedov to comment publicly on the possibility of a Soviet satellite. The American announcement and Sedov's garbled response to it – as well as the Western media's reportage of both – provided the final weapon, international prestige, that Korolev, Tikhonravov, and others needed to convince the top leadership of the importance of a Soviet satellite project.

POLITICAL SIGNIFICANCE

Those advocating a Soviet space program – designers such as Korolev, Tikhonravov, and Glushko – had allied themselves with a powerful member

98 "Mezhdunarodnyi kongress astronavtov," *Pravda*, August 5, 1955.

99 G. A. Skuridin, Keldysh's secretary who worked in Sedov's interplanetary commission (and also knew about Korolev's work), implies as much. Memoir of G. A. Skuridin in *ASPK*, 453; G. A. Skuridin, "S. P. Korolev i pervyi iskusstvennyi sputnik Zemli," *Zemlia i vselennaia* no. 5 (1982): 57–61.

100 "Russians Say They Intend to Beat U.S. in Launching First Unmanned Satellite," *Washington Post*, August 3, 1955; "We'll Launch 1st Moon, and Bigger, Says Russ," *Los Angeles Examiner*, August 3, 1955; John Hillary, "Soviets Planning Early Satellite," *New York Times*, August 3, 1955.

101 "Manned Space Ships Will Reach Moon by End of Century, Scientists Predicts," *Washington Post*, August 4, 1955; Lindsay Parrott, "U.N. Role is Urged in Satellite Race," *New York Times*, August 4, 1955; Alsop, "The Real Satellite Story"; Herman Oberth, "Why the Race to the Moon?," *Washington Post*, October 2, 1955.

of the scientific community, Mstislav Keldysh, to bolster their case. Military rationales were also important, for Tikhonravov's early research had shown the importance of satellites for both reconnaissance and combat actions. International political dynamics, as exemplified in the flap over Soviet public announcements on space travel, proved to be the third important factor. Here, the space advocates used an effective tool – Western news clippings about the importance of spaceflight, many of which were alarmist reports in the West reporting on DOSAAF's popular articles on space travel – to convince their government to go forward with a space program. As early as 1954, Korolev had amassed, in Tikhonravov's words, a set of "interesting translations" from the Western media about space exploration.[102] When Tikhonravov visited the offices of Georgii Pashkov, the powerful defense industry administrator specializing in the missile program, to convince him of the need to approve a satellite project, Tikhonravov tried a similar tack. Pashkov recalled that, in 1955, Tikhonravov appeared "with two albums in his hands." Pashkov continued,

> One had a large number of excerpts from the foreign press describing the American project on an [artificial Earth satellite]. The other contained computations and layouts, convincingly showing that we were already... in a situation to put into orbit an artificial satellite ten times more [heavy] than the American one.[103]

Through early 1955, Korolev and Tikhonravov sent Pashkov several reports and letters on the satellite issue, all appealing for a government decision to build one and enclosing foreign news clippings on satellites. Excerpts from Western press reports proved particularly effective in convincing Pashkov to push the matter to a higher level, that is, to his boss, Vasilii Riabikov, the chair of the powerful *Spetskomitet* in charge of managing the development of Soviet long-range missiles, including the ICBM project. Riabikov and his boss Mikhail Khrunichev reported directly to Nikita Khrushchev on all matters related to missiles; Korolev and his associates were acutely aware that without their assent, there would be no satellite because they controlled work on the ICBM, the satellite's ride into space. The Eisenhower announcement and the hoopla surrounding it provided the perfect opportunity. In the days following the announcement of an American satellite project, Korolev quickly and efficiently marshaled all his resources: He put together a dossier of media reports from the United States, distilled Tikhonravov's ideas on satellites into a compact plan, and moved the idea of international prestige to the center of his argument. Very quickly he was able to mobilize the support of Riabikov and Khrunichev, both of whom had been

[102] Tikhonravov Diary, daily entry for February 7, 1954.

[103] Nikolai Dombkovskii, "Oktiabr' – aprel' – vselennaia" (interview with G. N. Pashkov), *Sovetskaia rossiia*, April 12, 1989; N. Dombkovskii, "Korolev: k 80-letiiu. Biografiia v dokumentakh," *Sovetskaia rossiia*, January 10, 1989; Zuzul'skii, *Stupeni v nebo*, 186–188.

"softened up" for months with a stream of letters. Both men agreed with Korolev that his satellite idea had merits, and not only scientific and military ones.

Exactly a week after the announcement by the Eisenhower Administration, on August 5, Korolev sent a formal letter to the Politburo asking for permission to launch a satellite. Although the letter had been drafted by Korolev, Khrunichev and Riabikov signed off as co-authors. Exploiting the publicity over the recent Eisenhower announcement, Korolev got right to the point in the first sentence, mentioning, "the appearance of announcements in the American press that in 1957–58, small artificial Earth satellites will be created." In repeatedly noting that "the problem of creating an artificial satellite of the Earth is being given special attention in the U.S.A.," he elaborated at length on two projects of Wernher von Braun (whom he referred to as simply "Braun") – one a forty-five-kilogram satellite and another a launch vehicle with a mass of 7,000 tons ("25 times greater than the mass of the R-7"). The letter was rather technical for a document intended for politicians – in it, Korolev described the mechanics of orbital flight, the kinds of scientific experiments possible with a satellite, as well as the details of the rocket required for such a feat. In asking for a Soviet satellite, Korolev provided some raw data: the satellite would weigh 1.5 to 2 tons, it would orbit at altitude of 200 × 700 kilometers, it would cost up to 250 million rubles (in 1955 costs, without the expense for the launch vehicle), and it could be launched within two to three years, that is, in 1957 or 1958, during IGY. He concluded the letter by noting that,

> Considering that the creation of an artificial satellite of the Earth will open new prospects in the development of science and military technology, it is considered advisable in the nearest future to begin work on its creation. A list of necessary steps [for its implementation] can be submitted within one-and-a-half and two months.[104]

The Politburo had much more serious issues on its mind at the time. With the rise of Nikita Khrushchev to the apex of the Party structure in 1955, Kremlin leaders were struggling to define a stable post-Stalin foreign policy, one that encompassed a contradictory mix of both intransigence and conciliation. The Geneva Summit in July 1955, the first postwar meeting between the four former wartime allies, was to have opened the first glimmer of hope of rapprochement between the new Khrushchev leadership and the Eisenhower Administration at a time of very high tensions between the two superpowers. Yet, Khrushchev resolutely rejected Eisenhower's so-called open skies proposal for allowing aerial monitoring of each other's weapons systems as a way to manage the fear of nuclear war. For understandable reasons, Khrushchev, Bulganin, and others saw this as a pretext for American espionage of the black world of Soviet weapons development,

104 APRF, 3/47/272/41-43 (August 5, 1955).

production, and deployment. At the same time, the Soviet leadership began to adopt policies that departed from the Stalinist mode. They opened up to foreign trade, paid lip service to the possibility of international disarmament, and engaged in "public diplomacy," that is, authorizing trips of Soviet intelligentsia such as artists, scientists, writers, musicians, and journalists to the West as a strategy to dispel preconceptions about life in the Soviet Union.[105] By early 1956, Khrushchev publicly articulated the idea of "peaceful coexistence" strategy, which officially disavowed the belief in the inevitability of revolution beyond Soviet borders.

In this context, when on August 8, less than a month after the meeting in Geneva, the Politburo met to deliberate on a number of issues, one of the points on the agenda was to discuss the request to launch an artificial satellite of the Earth. On Korolev's orders, Tikhonravov had quickly prepared a summary report, entitled "Primary Data on the Scientific Significance on the Simplest Satellite and Projected Expenses," that was used for the discussions.[106] The outcome of the deliberations was unambiguous: A short memo entitled "On the Creation of an Artificial Satellite of the Earth" was issued. Graded "Top Secret," the document simply noted the following:

> To approve the idea for the creation of an artificial satellite of the Earth. To entrust Comrades Khrunichev and Riabikov to go ahead in working to create an artificial satellite of the Earth and in a month-and-a-half's time submit to [the Central Committee of the Communist Party of the Soviet Union] a draft for the necessary steps on this question and also to submit to [the Central Committee] the text of a communiqué for the press on work being carried out on the creation of an artificial satellite of the Earth.[107]

Public perception of the event was paramount from the very beginning, bolstered by Khrushchev's new approach to international contacts, that scientists (and science) were one conduit for introducing the Soviet Union to the outside world. An official communiqué on the satellite was hastily prepared, discussed at a subsequent Politburo meeting, revised by chief Party ideologue Mikhail Suslov, and finalized by August 23. The final line in the draft noted that "It's impossible to overestimate the difficulties existing on the road to creating the first artificial Earth satellite, but the USSR has

105 Vladislav Zubok, *A Failed Empire: The Soviet Union in the Cold War from Stalin to Gorbachev* (Chapel Hill: University of North Carolina Press, 2007), 105–109; John Prados, "Open Skies and Closed Minds: American Disarmament Policy at the Geneva Summit," in *Cold War Respite: The Geneva Summit of 1955*, eds. Günter Bischof and Saki Dockrill (Baton Rouge: Louisiana State University, 2000), 215–233; Konstantin Ivanov, "Science After Stalin: Forging a New Image of Soviet Science," *Science in Context* 15 no. 2 (2002): 317–338.

106 *SPKIED*, 662.

107 APRF, 3/47/272/40 (August 8, 1955).

a real scientific and technological base for the successful solution of this problem."[108]

Despite the Politburo decision, there were some who strongly opposed the project. In attendance at a meeting with Riabikov on August 30 was Major-General Aleksandr Mrykin, an artillery officer in charge of strategic missile procurement for the Red Army. Like the others, Mrykin had participated in the search missions in Germany in 1945 and 1946, where he first began working together with Korolev, Glushko, and others. To their audience, Korolev and Keldysh explained that the satellites would have both political and military significance. They described Tikhonravov's work on "the simplest satellite" known as Object D (*Ob'ekt D*), which they wished to launch as part of the Soviet scientific participation during the impending International Geophysical Year. Despite the various rationales for launching a satellite, General Mrykin, a man with a legendary temper that many feared, resisted all of Korolev's arguments. To those assembled, he exclaimed, "What are we talking about here?! When we launch the R-7, *then* we can think about this satellite." Hearing Mrykin's tirade, Korolev scribbled one word in his notes next to Mrykin's name: "Later!"[109]

The Politburo approval in August was supposed to have led to a formal decree of the Central Committee and the Council of Ministers, but for several months, Korolev, Keldysh, and Tikhonravov waited in vain for such a decision. When a draft of a formal government decree was sent to the Central Committee for approval on September 14, the document remained unexamined for four months, prompting another full offensive to obtain the final go-ahead for their project. In one document circulated to both designers and to Georgii Pashkov, Korolev emphasized the political significance of a satellite by underlining the phrase three times with a pencil.[110] To Marshal Mitrofan Nedelin, the deputy minister of defense in charge of operating and procuring all Soviet missiles, Korolev pointed out that the Americans would also launch a satellite during IGY and that "without doubt, it is impossible not to consider the significance of priority in . . . creating the first artificial satellite of the Earth."[111] Finally, via Gennadii Skuridin, Keldysh's pointman in the public Soviet interplanetary commission, as well as through contacts in the DOSAAF Section, the "inner" group stimulated a new wave of publications in the Soviet media in late 1955 on the benefits of artificial satellites. The authors of these articles – Sedov, Shternfel'd, Karpenko, Liapunov, Pobedonostsev, and Skuridin himself – all had close links to those

[108] APRF, 3/47/272/48-51 (August 23, 1955).

[109] G. S. Vetrov, interview with James Harford, October 21, 1992, Notebook No. 3, Papers of James Harford, Princeton, New Jersey; Golovanov, *Korolev*, 520.

[110] Cover letter to S. P. Korolev, "Predvaritel'nye dannye o prosteishem sputnike" (September 3, 1955), in *SPKIED*, 189.

[111] Korolev to Nedelin (December 27, 1955), in *SPKIED*, 204.

working in the black world and essentially paraphrased their secret compatriots' messages.[112]

The strategy – both in private and in public – paid off. In November 1955, Korolev, Keldysh, and Tikhonravov met several times with Pashkov to iron out the details of the final document. They lined up each of their rationales – defense, science, and prestige – and received support from a wide circle of scientists.[113] After Riabikov and several powerful industrial managers signed off on the plan, the drafters sent the party and government a second draft on January 11. On January 30, 1956, the Council of Ministers issued a decree (no. 149–88ss) approving the launch of the Object D satellite in 1957 in time for IGY. The military agreed to donate two test ICBMs for the satellite launches because they could be used to verify and test certain flight capabilities of the rocket. Apart from the Academy of Sciences, five industrial ministries would be involved in the project.[114] All future Soviet space projects, including the current-day Russian space program, emerged as a result of this government decision.

CONCLUSION

The story of the last lap to the birth of the Soviet space program was a complex one, full of surprising twists and intersections, beginning with *Zhdanovshchina* in 1947 and ending with the launch of *Sputnik* ten years later. An informal network of space enthusiasts working inside and outside the Soviet defense industry played the central role in this process, first by popularizing and then implementing the project of space exploration. Popularization and implementation of other Soviet scientific projects in the postwar era required a coalition of interests acting to promote specific goals, but spaceflight discourse differed from them in one significant aspect: It lacked patrons who were *both* public and powerful in the scientific and political communities. In advancing a positivist notion of nuclear culture, powerful and influential scientists such as Kurchatov, Sakharov, and Aleksandrov, as

[112] These included A. A. Shternfel'd, "Polet na lunu," *Kryl'ia rodiny*, no. 9 (1955): 19–20; A. A. Kosmodem'ianskii, "Konstantin Eduardovich Tsiolkovskii," *Nauka i zhizn'* no. 9 (1955): 53–55; Iu. S. Khlebtsevich, "Doroga v kosmos," *Nauka i zhizn'* no. 11 (1955): 33–37; P. K. Isakov, "Problemy nevesomosti," *Nauka i zhizn'* no. 12 (1955): 17–20; A. G. Karpenko and G. A. Skuridin, "Problemy mezhplanetnykh poletov," *Oktiabr'* no. 9 (1955): 140–147; L. I. Sedov, "O poletakh v mirovoe prostranstvo," *Pravda*, September 26, 1955; B. Liapunov, "U poverkhnosti vozdushnogo okeana," *Tekhnika-molodezhi* no. 12 (1955): 9–13; A. G. Karpenko and G. A. Skuridin, "Sovremennye problemy kosmicheskikh poletov," *Vestnik akademii nauk sssr* no. 9 (September 1955): 19–30; and Iu. Pobedonostsev, "Ob iskusstvennom sputnike zemli," *Vestnik vozdushnogo flota* 38 no. 9 (1955): 87–96.

[113] Tikhonravov Diary, daily entries for November 23, November 24, November 26, and December 29, 1955.

[114] S. P. Korolev, "Tezisy doklada o razrabotke eskiznogo proekta iskusstvennogo sputnika Zemli" (September 25, 1956), in *TNASPK*, 362–368.

well as political leaders Nikita Khrushchev, defined and drove the discussion in the media.[115] In the case of spaceflight, its primary advocates were missile designers working in anonymity within the defense industry. To bypass the curtain of secrecy, they formed a very effective alliance with spaceflight enthusiasts on the "outside," who shared with them a sincere belief in the inevitability and benefits of space technology. Outsiders included many science popularizers, who had been deeply influenced by the space fad of the 1920s, and like their predecessors from the interwar years, were genuinely gripped by technological enthusiasm, this time steeped in the postwar celebratory discourses on nuclear power and aviation. Whereas the space advocates of the 1920s could only dream about space travel, the new generation in the 1950s – both insiders and outsiders – believed that they could combine their ideals with the new technology of ICBMs, thereby creating the basis for a space program. Luckily for them, rocket design had matured significantly, aided by the large-scale appropriation of German rocket technology after the war. The maturation finally made the possibility of spaceflight a topic of serious consideration.

The first step in bringing spaceflight to reality in the Soviet Union was its legitimation. The network did this by first resurrecting Konstantin Tsiolkovskii's legacy from near oblivion in the postwar years. Members skillfully used the prevailing ideologies of *Zhdanovshchina* to their benefit in canonizing Tsiolkovskii as a great scientist in the Russian tradition. Tsiolkovskii's deification opened the door for the Academy of Sciences to treat space exploration as a legitimate topic of study and discussion, which in turn helped to open the floodgates to many eminent scholars and scientists to weigh in on the topic for the first time in Soviet history. In this respect, at least, *Zhdanovshchina* – which negatively affected so many Soviet scientific disciplines – helped to create a new one, space technology.

In one period, however, the insiders very skillfully orchestrated activities of the outsiders, and their actions had unexpected repercussions in a discourse played out internationally. When the insiders released information about a public (and essentially powerless) Soviet commission to study space science, Western media picked up the news item. In the context of increasing Soviet publications on spaceflight sponsored by DOSAAF, American intelligence services saw the announcement as the first serious intention by the Soviet Union to explore space. This perception was a potent force in the decision to initiate to an American satellite project, a program that the Eisenhower Administration publicly announced in July 1955.

A few space enthusiast missile Soviet designers, such as Korolev, Tikhonravov, and Glushko, had, since 1954, struggled to convince the Soviet government to fund a satellite project. They had used the rationales of both defense and science, but the Eisenhower Administration's announcement

[115] Josephson, "Atomic Powered Communism."

(among many others) presented them with a golden opportunity. By skillfully using evidence of publicly stated American interest in a satellite project, the designers, now involving a coalition of missile designers, academy scientists, and defense industry managers, were able to convince a reluctant government to fund their project. As a result, in August 1955, just days after the Eisenhower Administration announced its plans for a satellite, the Soviet Politburo approved a Soviet satellite project. In the end, a few designers in the military world and a handful of space enthusiasts working in popular clubs combined their forces to convince the Soviet government to accomplish one of the most defining moments of the Cold War.

9

Launching *Sputnik*

"Nobody back then was thinking about the magnitude of what was going on: everyone did his own job, living through its disappointments and joys."[1]

Oleg Ivanovskii, the deputy lead designer for *Sputnik*

INTRODUCTION

On the early morning of September 20, 1956 – just before 2 a.m. – the U.S. Army launched a Jupiter C intermediate-range ballistic missile from Launch Pad 5 at Cape Canaveral. The missile was a modified version of the Redstone, a direct descendent of the German V-2, built in Huntsville, Alabama by the team led by the famous (but not yet infamous) Wernher von Braun, former German rocket engineer in the pay of the Third Reich, and more recently transplanted American citizen. The Jupiter C, which had a dummy fourth stage loaded with sand, lifted off successfully, generating a thrust of over thirty-five tons from its first stage engines, which burned for 150 seconds. The upper stages continued to arc over the Atlantic, reaching an altitude never reached before by any manmade object, nearly 1,100 kilometers. The sand-filled package tumbled about 5,400 kilometers downrange from the launch site before burning up in the Earth's atmosphere. As radio systems beamed back information to the blockhouse on the record-breaking flight, von Braun was said to have "danced with joy."[2] It had been quite a feat – one of the longest flights ever by a rocket. Although the Army did not publicly announce the launch or the results of the flight, information about the event leaked out to the mainstream press within a week.[3]

Quite unexpectedly, the V-2 and its German creators once again cast a shadow over Soviet intentions. This barely remembered and somewhat obscure event, registered only by missile buffs, had a rather unexpected effect on a few Soviet men and women halfway across the world. Rather

[1] Aleksei Ivanov [Oleg Ivanovskii], *Vpervye: zapiski vedushchego konstruktora* (Moscow: Moskovskii rabochii, 1982), 35.

[2] Michael J. Neufeld, *Von Braun: Dreamer of Space, Engineer of War* (New York: Knopf, 2007), 304.

[3] "Army Test Reported on 'Jupiter' Missile," *New York Times*, September 27, 1956.

than making them "dance with joy," it threw them into fright, paving the way for a series of unexpected decisions that, within a year, introduced the lexicon of cosmic travel, particularly the word *sputnik*, to a global audience.

A number of recent histories communicate the political – especially the geopolitical – context of the creation of *Sputnik*, interspersed as they are with the obligatory references to the two central characters of the received story: the omniscient and omnipresent chief designer Sergei Korolev and the first secretary of the Communist Party's Central Committee, Nikita Khrushchev.[4] The two men, especially Korolev, were the driving forces behind the project, but our urge to distill complexities down to hagiographies has produced a distorted narrative imbued with a kind of false importance to the preamble to *Sputnik*, as if all the actors recognized the weightiness of their work. On the contrary, memoirs, documents, and contemporaneous testimonies on the design, manufacture, and launch of *Sputnik* suggest not only a curious disconnect from the broader political climate of the Cold War but a distinct lack of awareness that the making of *Sputnik* was anything special at all. This chapter, then is a recovery of the disappointments and joys, a revisiting of the twists and turns within a relatively small community of designers, factory managers, workers, soldiers, and operators who were most closely involved in an event that the late Soviet journalist Iaroslav Golovanov succinctly described as "the first time on Earth something that had been thrown upwards had not come down again."[5] Recasting the story as one at the micro level underscores how the *Sputnik* event was an ordinary tale made extraordinary by the passage of time but not so fundamentally different from the work of others who came of age in the late 1950s Soviet Union – a time that imbued the ordinary with a patina of hope for a better future.

WHY NOT SOMETHING SIMPLER?

Von Braun's launch of the Jupiter C rocket was largely left uncommented on in the Western press. It was, however, noticed across the Iron Curtain. By the time that news of the flight reached Moscow, a somewhat mundane military launch was perceived by some in the Soviet Union as an "attempted launch of a satellite" by Americans. This clearly garbled piece of information shook both Sergei Korolev and Mikhail Tikhonravov, the two architects behind the Soviet satellite project. At this time, they were mired deep in

[4] Paul Dickson, *Sputnik: The Shock of the Century* (New York: Walker, 2001); Matthew Brzezinski, *Red Moon Rising: Sputnik and the Hidden Rivalries that Ignited the Space Age* (New York: Times Books, 2007); Michael D'Antonio, *A Ball, A Dog, and a Monkey: 1957, the Space Race Begins* (New York: Simon & Schuster, 2007).

[5] Iaroslav Golovanov, *Korolev: fakty i mify* (Moscow: Nauka, 1994), 544.

technical problems in producing a massive scientific observatory – weighing 1.3 tons – known rather cryptically as Object D. Ground tests had also showed that the launch vehicle slated to launch this behemoth, the R-7 ICBM with some improvements, would not have the necessary efficiency required to launch into orbit. If before, Korolev and his associates were concerned about losing first place to the Americans, now, with the garbled news of von Braun's launch, they were seriously anxious. Korolev had long complained about all the delays with the Object D to Tikhonravov; usually Tikhonravov remained quiet, pondering over all the problems. Korolev had often seen this as indifference on Tikhonravov's part but, in fact, the latter had been devising an alternate plan, a "Plan B."

In mid-November 1956, Tikhonravov suddenly piped up to Korolev: "What if we make the satellite a little lighter and a little simpler? Thirty kilograms or so, even lighter?"[6] Korolev quickly pondered over the suggestion, weighing all the options carefully. One of the main problems with the development of Object D had been the many delays in delivering its component scientific instruments. Having never designed instruments to operate in space, the subcontractors were facing numerous intractable problems during production and testing. As a solution, Tikhonravov suggested reducing the satellite down to its most essential components: one or two radio transmitters and a power source to feed them. Finding this plan more and more attractive, Korolev decided to cut out almost all of the subcontractors and rely instead on two people he could count upon. He asked Mikhail Riazanskii of the NII-885 institute to provide the radio equipment and Nikolai Lidorenko of the Scientific-Research Institute of Current Sources to supply the batteries to power the former. Everything else would be built in-house under his direct command at the modest "experimental" factory located right next to Korolev's design bureau, OKB-1, in Kaliningrad near Moscow. True to its elementary nature, the new satellite was called PS-1 (*Prosteishyi sputnik-1*, Simplest Satellite-1). It was so simple, the idea went, that it could be built and tested in a month or two, time enough to "beat" the Americans to the launch pad. The satellite would not only be simple but also cheap – if it was destroyed on launch, they could quickly ready another one without much ado.

Not everyone supported the PS-1 plan. In fact, although Korolev and Tikhonravov firmly believed in the idea, the third man in the original satellite proposal, Academy scientist Mstislav Keldysh, strongly opposed it. He had good reason to do so: Keldysh was, after all, the scientific head of the original Object D project. He had committed the resources of the Academy of Sciences into the massive scientific observatory and was reluctant to have to tell his scientists that their beloved satellite would not be the first. Others in Korolev's design bureau also opposed the new plan. Il'ia Lavrov, one of

[6] Golovanov, *Korolev*, 532.

Korolev's engineers who had invested an enormous amount of energy into bringing the Object D satellite project to fruition, was one of the most vocal. Speaking of the "simplest satellite," he told his colleagues that "this sphere is nonsense and a disgrace to the design bureau," and that they should finish the original job that they set out to do on Object D.[7]

More than quelling internal dissension, Korolev also needed to convince the government that this was the right thing to do. He knew the military would be problematic. They had already committed to handing over a military weapon, the R-7 ICBM, to launch the "useless" Object D satellite. Now, Korolev wanted more ICBMs to launch another satellite. On January 5, 1957, he sent a letter to the government with his revised plan, asking for permission to launch two "simplest satellites," each weighing about forty to fifty kilograms, between April and June 1957, that is, before the beginning of the International Geophysical Year (IGY), the 18-month-long sustained international program to study the Earth and its environs.[8] Korolev's thinking on the schedule was based on a simple premise: If Americans were planning to launch a satellite during IGY, then the Soviets should launch *before* the IGY. Knowing that government leaders would respond more strongly to competition with Americans than any rationale of scientific research, Korolev prominently highlighted the possibility that the Americans might easily preempt the Soviets. As in previous lobby efforts, Korolev was able to marshal top-level support for the plan. A second letter, with important co-authors, including Ustinov, Riabikov, and Keldysh, reached the Politburo on February 12. Riabikov apparently pushed the idea most strongly at the top.[9] Three days later, on February 15, at a regular meeting, the Politburo signed off on a decree approving the new plan. Two identical satellites, PS-1 and PS-2, would be launched in April and May 1957 on retooled R-7 rockets.[10] According to the Politburo decision, the goals of the PS satellites would be rather simple: "Deliver the simplest unoriented Earth satellite (the object PS) into orbit, [and] verify the possibility of observing the PS in orbit and receive signals, transmitted from the object PS."[11]

A BALL IN SPACE

What should this first simplest satellite look like? In the beginning, designers were not sure. Long before official approval of the PS-1 plan, on

7 Golovanov, *Korolev*, 533.

8 S. P. Korolev, "Predlozheniia o pervykh zapuskakh iskusstvennykh sputnikov zemli do nachala mezhdunarodnogo geofizicheskogo goda," in *TNASPK*, 369–370.

9 A. A. Maksimov, "Iz istorii sozdaniia komandno-izmeritel'nogo kompleksa," *IIAIK* no. 60 (1990): 12–19. The co-authors were D. F. Ustinov, S. P. Korolev, V. M. Riabikov, I. P. Bardin, I. S. Konev, and V. D. Kal'mykov.

10 Memoir of M. K. Tikhonravov in *ASPK*, 447.

11 *SPKIED*, 666.

November 25, 1956, Korolev had tasked a young antenna specialist in his design bureau, Nikolay Kutyrkin, to make the initial drawings for the satellite.[12] Early on, the designers working on the satellite settled on a cone shape for PS-1, echoing the cone chassis for the much larger Object D. They reasoned that a cone would fit well and naturally with the shape of the R-7 rocket's payload fairing. But when Tikhonravov's deputy, Evgenii Riazanov, met with Korolev to show him some draft sketches of the satellite, Korolev flipped through all of them and didn't like any. Cautiously, Riazanov asked, "Why?" Korolev mysteriously answered, "Because it's not round."[13] As one designer later remembered, "there were weighty scientific considerations" in favor of a sphere.[14] Two factors were crucial for picking a ball. First, a sphere was an ideal geometric shape with maximum volume in ratio to minimum surface area, giving it a favorable trade-off between packing as much equipment into as possible while limiting surface area exposure to changes in temperature. Second, a spherical shape (as opposed to a more irregularly shaped object) was ideal for determining atmospheric density on its orbital path. Korolev also apparently believed that a shiny metal *spherical* object would better reflect light and thus have a better chance of visibility with telescopes. It was, however, clear that such a small object would not be visible to the naked eye. Visually tracking a moving object at a range of about 1,700 kilometers (the distance of the satellite from an observer as the satellite was above the horizon) was practically impossible. Initially, the sphere was quite small, weighing in at about 40 to 50 kilograms. At some point in January 1957, the satellite's design mass doubled to about 80 kilograms (although the mass margin was about 100 kilograms). Based on the new calculations, on January 25, Korolev signed off on the specifications for the PS-1.[15]

The satellite, as it eventually took shape, was a pressurized sphere, fifty-eight centimeters in diameter and made of a 2-mm-thick aluminum alloy (see Figure 34, page 351). The sphere was constructed by combining two hemispherical casings ("front" and "rear" half-casings) together along a ring-like rubber seal. The overall pressurized sphere was held together by thirty-six bolts. The internal volume of the sphere was filled with nitrogen (at 1.3 atmospheres), which maintained three silver-zinc batteries, two radio transmitters, a thermal regulation system, a fan, a commutator, temperature and pressure sensors, and associated wiring. Of the three batteries (each shaped like a rectangular block), two provided power to the radio equipment while the third supplied power to the ventilation fan, which regulated the temperature within the satellite, and also the commutator. By means of

[12] Golovanov, *Korolev*, 532.
[13] Memoir of M. L. Gallai in *ASPK*, 63.
[14] I. Miniuk, "Ot pervogo sputnika . . . ," *AIK* no. 9 (1987): 46–47.
[15] Memoir of Tikhonravov in *ASPK*, 447; V. Poroshkov, "Sozdanie i zapusk pervogo sputnika zemli," *NK* no. 10 (2002): 56–60.

a switch operated by a temperature sensor (a thermocouple), the fan was designed to operate when temperatures were higher than 30°C and turn off when values were between 20°C and 23°C.

The two radio transmitters operated on frequencies of 20.005 and 40.003 megacycles at wavelengths of 15 and 7.5 meters. These transmitters (which obviously used vacuum tubes) each had a power intake of one watt and provided the famous "beep-beep-beep" sound to *Sputnik*. The signals on both the frequencies were spurts lasting 0.2 to 0.6 seconds, and carried information on the pressure and temperature inside the satellite; one set would transmit during the "pauses" of the other. The frequency of the signal, as well as the relationship between the length of the signals and the pauses in between, would change according to changes in temperature and pressure within the satellite hull. The satellite had simple pressure and temperature pickups that would close a circuit, given certain ranges of temperatures (>50°C or <0°C) and pressures (<0.35 atmospheres), thus changing the signals' parameters.[16]

Four antennae were installed outside of the main body of the ball, two with a length of 2.4 meters each and the remaining two with a length of 2.9 meters each. All four would spring open into their unfurled position at separation from the launch rocket, at an angle of 35° with the satellite's main axis. The total mass of the satellite was 83.6 kilograms, of which 51.0 kilograms was simply the power source.[17]

The development of *Sputnik*'s radio transmitter package was fraught with uncertainty. Korolev visited Riazanskii's institute several times in the late winter and early spring of 1957 to discuss the nature of the instrument. Korolev was adamant that signals from the transmitters should be picked up by "the most dilapidated receiver, [and] that the whole world should hear them!" Yet, Korolev was also well aware that there was really no way to predict the behavior of radio waves, let alone the lifetime of the satellite in orbit. Riazanskii resisted, putting a firm limit on the working lifetime of the radio transmitter, but he eventually guaranteed that it would provide a "decent signal" for at least two weeks. Based on these discussions, on February 15, 1957, the two signed an agreement (which included the technical specifications) for Riazanskii to deliver a functioning radio transmitter unit for use on PS-1.[18]

[16] Tikhonravov notes that the signals were between 0.2 and 0.6 seconds but doesn't specify if these were nominal or off-nominal values. Poroshkov notes that the original beeps were 0.3 seconds in length but that the beeps would "change from 0.2 to 0.4 seconds" when temperature or pressure parameters were out of range. See M. K. Tikhonravov, "Provozvestnik kosmicheskoi ery: iz istorii sozdaniia pervogo sputnika," *AIK* no. 10 (1974): 40–41; Poroshkov, "Sozdaniie i zapusk pervogo sputnika zemli."

[17] The technical details of *Sputnik* are based on the following sources: "Pervyi iskusstvennyy sputnik zemli," in *SPKIED*, 574–575; Tikhonravov, "Provozvestnik kosmicheskoi ery"; *RKKE*, 89–90.

[18] Memoir of Tikhonravov in *ASPK*, 447.

In conceiving the basic design of the transmitter, Korolev and Tikhonravov took the advice of many, including Academician Vladimir Kotel'nikov, the director of the Academy of Sciences' Institute of Radiotechnology and Electronics, as well as scientists from other academy institutes such as the Institute of Earth Magnetism and Propagation of Radio Waves and the P. N. Lebedev Physical Institute. The actual hardware was built in a subdivision of Riazanskii's NII-885 institute, the Laboratory for the Propagation of Radio Waves, headed by Konstantin Gringauz. Not everyone agreed with Gringauz' vision of the instrument; despite objections from everyone (including Korolev), Gringauz insisted that PS-1 carry a high-frequency transmitter (i.e., the 20.005 MHz transmitter operating in the decameter waveband) in addition to the VHF transmitter (which had been commonly used on Soviet ballistic missiles). Many believed that having a high-frequency transmitter would delay the satellite launch because it would have to be much larger than its twin. In the end, Gringauz won over his opponents, partly because everyone agreed that a high-frequency transmitter would ensure that the radio transmissions would be heard around the world.[19]

The transmitter hardware was built by one of Gringauz' youngest engineers, Viacheslav Lappo, who worked day and night trying to make the deadline. Lappo later confided in Soviet journalist Iaroslav Golovanov that he built the system without really knowing whether it would function in outer space. Because a radio transmitter had never been in space before, there was no hard data on what to protect against; there was only conjecture. Lappo tried to account for sharp temperature fluctuations, cosmic radiation, even meteorites, but without much confidence. In the end, designers under Tikhonravov decided to sheath the radio transmitter within the battery system, almost as if to "protect" it from the elements.

Once, Korolev showed up suddenly at Lappo's laboratory late at night and asked to listen to the signals from the satellite. The young designer described the operation of the transmitter to Korolev, explaining how the "beep-beeps" would change in frequency and length according to the internal pressure and temperature of the satellite. Lappo told Korolev, "You understand, Sergei Pavlovich, that in the hour of its death, it will squeak differently." Korolev seemed very pleased with this, and afterwards, almost bashfully added, "Couldn't you make it squeak a word of some kind?"[20] Testing on this radio transmitter system was completed by May 5, 1957, ten days before the first attempted launch of the R-7 ICBM.

For every project at Korolev's design bureau, there two major phases: design and production. For PS-1, Tikhonravov had led the design phase (although many others had participated). When transitioning from design

[19] Mikhail I. Verigin and Norman F. Ness, "Konstantin Iosifovich Gringauz, 1918–1993," *Space Science Reviews* 64 (1994): 1–3; Golovanov, *Korolev*, 536.

[20] Golovanov, *Korolev*, 536.

to experimental production, Korolev usually appointed a "lead designer," a mid-level engineer who would be responsible for converting the designers' drawings into metal. They would also be Korolev's "eyes and ears" in the production shop, reporting back any glitches to the chief designer himself. For PS-1, Korolev appointed Mikhail Khomiakov as lead designer; Khomiakov, on his initiative, asked another man, Oleg Ivanovskii, to serve as his deputy.

Unlike Khomiakov, who has remained largely silent, Ivanovskii, an active Communist in local Party politics in the 1950s, has written a memoir of his time as a designer, which has been published in many editions in Russian.[21] Yet, strangely, Ivanovskii's memoirs provide only glimmers of the development of *Sputnik* – a few random details and generalized descriptions that say little. Vagueness seems to characterize the recollections of many with regard to the world's first artificial satellite. The journalist Iaroslav Golovanov later remembered:

> I have had occasion to speak about our first satellite with many of the assistants at S. P. Korolev's experimental design bureau, and also with specialists from the factories that were producing accessory components. It is strange but they don't remember it clearly. The work on the rocket [i.e., the R-7 ICBM] was so voluminous and intensive that in people's memory, it overshadowed the little sphere with the "feeler" antennas.[22]

The few extant details do, however, provide a fairly colorful picture of the preparations leading up to the launch of *Sputnik*. A number involve Korolev. At some point, probably in the late summer of 1957, when many of the satellite components had been manufactured and tested, Korolev convened a meeting of the leading *Sputnik* designers and announced that the satellite had to be larger – that the diameter had to be increased from 0.6 to 1 meter. Evidently, he was concerned that the satellite would not be visible with the naked eye. Naturally, many designers were upset, not the least because they had spent months bringing the project to fruition. One of Korolev's senior deputies, Sergei Okhapkin, was most upset because he was afraid that a change in the design so late would mean they would miss the launch date. A bigger satellite would also mean a more powerful launch vehicle, meaning more changes and more time. Eventually, even the mighty Korolev was convinced that this was a bad idea.[23]

[21] During the Soviet era, Ivanovskii wrote under the pen name "Aleksei Ivanov." His memoirs were published as Aleksei Ivanov, *Pervye stupeni* (Moscow: Molodaia gvardiia, 1970). Subsequent updated editions were published in 1975 and 1982. An unexpurgated version of his memoirs appeared in 2005 as O. G. Ivanovskii, *Rakety i kosmos v sssr: zapiski sekretnogo konstruktora* (Moscow: Molodaia gvardiia, 2005).

[22] Golovanov, *Korolev*, 534–535.

[23] Miniuk, "Ot pervogo sputnika"; Golovanov, *Korolev*, 533–534.

PS-1 was assembled at Factory No. 88 located right next to Korolev's design bureau in Kaliningrad (or Podlipki). Most factory engineers involved in the creation of *Sputnik* did not perceive it as anything more or less important than any other object created at the plant. The factory's chief engineer, Viktor Kliucharev, later recalled that constructing PS-1, especially in comparison to the immensely complicated R-7 ICBM, was a relatively painless job for the workers. For the factory foremen, the most challenging job proved to be manufacturing and assembling the hemispherical casings of the hull of the satellite. These half-shells were made by "stamping," which produced many defects (or folds) typical of "deep drawing." They took great skill to eliminate from the final operational models. Technologists also had to ensure that the satellite was as shiny as possible to fulfill particular coefficients of absorption and reflection (to make it as visible as possible). Shop workers spent a lot of time "finishing" the aluminum outer shell of the satellite. In the summer of 1957, Korolev and Academician Kotel'nikov had discussed ways to increase the reflectivity not only of the satellite but also the core booster, which would also be inserted into orbit and fly along with the satellite. Kotel'nikov, the director of the Academy of Sciences' Institute of Radiotechnology and Electronics, assigned one of his scientists, V. M. Vakhnin, to develop a deployable angular reflector to be installed on the core.[24] The use of this reflector made it possible for Soviet ground-based radar stations to track the rocket for several weeks after launch.

Before launch, engineers thoroughly tested the satellite and its associated systems. Full dry-run static tests of PS-1 in conjunction with an R-7 booster were carried out at the factory in Kaliningrad on August 31, 1957, not coincidentally just ten days after the first successful long-range flight of the R-7 ICBM. Once all the assembly and testing operations on PS-1 had been finished, in early September 1957, Korolev invited all those involved in the satellite's assembly and testing – about forty people, including his deputies, department chief, and factory shop foremen – to discuss the status of the satellite. He asked Khomiakov to give a report; he indeed provided a detailed status summary but twice mistakenly referred to "PS" as "SP." The latter was the nickname many at Korolev's bureau used to informally refer to the chief designer ("SP" for "Sergei Pavlovich"). Korolev rudely interrupted Khomiakov, saying that "I know that many of you call me 'SP' but this is not our... simplest satellite, that's 'PS'! Don't confuse the two."[25]

PUBLICIZING *SPUTNIK* BEFORE LAUNCH

As many have noted over the years, the Soviets were not shy about announcing the fact they would launch a satellite during IGY. Between 1953 and

[24] Memoir of G. A. Skuridin in *ASPK*, 459.
[25] Ivanovskii, *Rakety i kosmos v sssr*, 30.

1957 – peaking especially in the latter years – several hundred articles on space travel flooded the popular Soviet media, largely driven by the highly organized publicists at DOSAAF. Most appeared in popular science journals such as *Nauka i zhizn'* (*Science and Life*), *Kryl'ia rodiny* (*Wings of the Motherland*), *Tekhnika-molodezhi* (*Technology for Youth*), and *Priroda* (*Nature*); others appeared in popular general issue journals such as *Ogonek* (*Zest*) or daily papers such as *Pravda*, *Izvestiia*, and *Krasnaia zvezda* (*Red Star*). Although none of these articles contained any specific details about *Sputnik*, its launch vehicle, its designers, or its schedule, the prolific nature of these articles suggested a deep and persistent interest in space exploration in the Soviet Union.[26] Designers in the "secret world" of the Soviet military-industrial complex (such as Korolev and Glushko) directly and indirectly passed information to public writers for public consumption, but the process was not always easy.

Soviet participation in IGY, although marred by a certain ambivalence, was the most visible and effective vehicle for publicizing a possible satellite launch in the near future. About two years after the International Council of Scientific Unions invited the Soviet Union to participate in IGY, on July 19, 1954, the Soviet government issued a decree approving the formation of a Soviet "interdepartmental" committee to coordinate Soviet activities during IGY.[27] Hampered primarily by secrecy and the remnants of the postwar insularity of Soviet science, Soviet scientists were slow to embrace the IGY program. Eventually, Soviet participation proved quite significant despite early complaints about projected costs.[28]

Soviet scientists were well aware that their public statements were closely monitored abroad but frustrated that they could say very little. In July 1956, an exasperated Academician Ivan Bardin, the reputed Soviet metallurgist and chairman of the Soviet IGY committee, wrote directly to Nikita Khrushchev after the academy leadership had ignored his requests for some guidelines about what was appropriate to say. Bardin noted that, "Not having appropriate authority, Soviet delegates participating at meetings on ... the International Geophysical Year have naturally avoided responding to questions [about Soviet plans to launch a satellite] which was met with bewilderment by the foreign press."[29] Korolev was explicit about the need to publicize the impending Soviet space program. In response to Bardin's request, he had told fellow chief designers that "the results of the true situation [with the satellite project] needs to be communicated at [international] conferences

[26] For a useful English-language collection of these articles, see F. J. Krieger, *Behind the Sputniks: A Survey of Soviet Space Science* (Washington, DC: Public Affairs Press, 1958).

[27] ARAN, 2/6/189/21–22 (April 8, 1955).

[28] At a meeting on April 8, 1955 approving the Soviet IGY program, some complained about the excessive cost of the Soviet contribution to IGY, then projected at 200 million rubles. See ARAN, 2/6/189/41 (April 8, 1955).

[29] APRF, 3/33/204/157–158 (July 4, 1956).

not by direct participants of the work but by major scientists, [who are] able to understand what they're talking about."[30] Korolev specifically singled out upcoming IGY conferences in Barcelona and Rome. Bardin's request prompted industrial managers Khrunichev and Riabikov to put together a set of rules dictating what Soviet scientists could talk about and what they couldn't, which was formalized in a government decree issued in late August 1956.[31] A couple of weeks later in Barcelona, Bardin officially confirmed that the Soviet Union would launch a satellite during the IGY. Bardin, of course, knew only superficial details of Korolev's satellite plans, but enough that he could talk in broad generalities. Four months before the launch of the satellite, in June 1957, Bardin provided more information to the international community, although he did not elaborate on timing for the launch.[32]

Korolev and Tikhonravov also disseminated information about the planned satellite launch in other ways. In one particular case, they managed to galvanize the energies of thousands of young amateur radio enthusiasts all across the Soviet Union to help the engineers track the satellite once it was in orbit. Beyond its public relations dimension, such a campaign could also support the *Sputnik* designers' own hopes of tracking the satellite in orbit. At the time, there were few professional observation posts spread across the Soviet landmass – the few existing ones belonged either to the Air Defense Forces or some scattered astronomical observatories; making use of amateurs was a clever and effective way to "fill in the blanks."

Here, Academician Kotel'nikov, who had counseled Korolev's engineers in the creation of PS-1's radio transmitters, played a key role. On Korolev's instructions, some of Kotel'nikov's scientists at his institute passed on details of the satellite's radio transmitters, including its transmission frequencies, to the Central Radio Club of the major Soviet paramilitary youth organization, DOSAAF. Soon, DOSAAF, in coordination with Kotel'nikov's scientists, delivered special tracking instruments (tape recorders, signal generators, etc.) to twenty-six separate amateur radio clubs across the country, who all reported to the Central Club back in Moscow. The particular clubs were chosen according to their location, spread along a line from the Baltic states all the way to Chukotka in eastern Siberia. Nikolai Kazanskii, president of the Soviet Amateur Radio Federation, remembers that he actually attended a meeting where Korolev was present, at which they asked him how many minutes it would take for the DOSAAF people to relay information on positive identification of the satellite to Moscow. Kazanskii assured them

30 G. S. Vetrov, "Pervyi sputnik: istoricheskii rubezh," *NK* no. 16 (1997): 2–8.

31 *SKI*, 71.

32 "The USSR Rocket and Satellite Program," in *Annals of the International Geophysical Year, Vol. IIA: The International Geophysical Year Meetings*, ed. M. Nicolet (London: Pergamon Press, 1959), 310–311; "USSR Rocket and Earth-Satellite Program for the IGY," June 10, 1957, U.S. National Academy of Sciences, IGY Archives, Drawer 19, File: TPESP Sat. Corr. June 1957.

that he could get news from any of the outlying clubs to the central location at Rastorguevo (in Moscow) within 15 minutes.[33]

Simultaneously, in the summer of 1957, DOSAAF published information about the satellite in its amateur ham journal, *Radio* (which had a circulation of about 200,000). There was no information on the actual satellite nor about when or how it would be launched, but there was data useful to amateur radio enthusiasts: how the satellite might fly, how its signals might transmit through the ionosphere, and of course, the transmission frequencies. DOSAAF also funded test runs on the equipment delivered from Kotel'nikov's institute: at the Central Club, they used an Iak-12, a tiny single propeller airplane capable of carrying one or two extra passengers, to send out signals from a makeshift transmitter that radio hams tracked from the ground. By October, there were many thousands of young Soviet citizens who were ready for the "real" thing.[34]

Evgenii Riabchikov, a journalist for the popular Soviet journal *Ogonek* who was one of the few in his profession with access to the "secret" world, also contributed to public anticipation for *Sputnik*. Riabchikov, who had spent time in Antarctica with the Soviet expedition working under the auspices of impending IGY, wanted to do a series of articles on space exploration. He met with Tikhonravov, who eventually arranged for Riabchikov to talk directly to Korolev. As a result of these discussions, Riabchikov published two major *Ogonek* articles in the summer of 1957 that included very general details about *Sputnik* without mentioning either Korolev or Tikhonravov. Official state censors allowed such articles to be published once they were approved for public consumption by Academy of Sciences Corresponding Member Evgenii Fedorov, a meteorologist charged with approving the dissemination of scientific information to the public and who ironically knew very little about the satellite effort.[35]

SUCCESS WITH THE R-7?

Although Korolev had obtained permission to launch PS-1 earlier in February, the launch was not a foregone event. In his letter to the government in January, he had noted that "two rockets upgraded for [satellite] launches could be ready in April-June 1957 and launched immediately after the first successful launches of the intercontinental missile."[36] In other words, the

[33] N. Grigor'ev, "Radioliubiteli i kosmos," *Radio* no. 10 (1982): 5–7.

[34] Grigor'ev, "Radioliubiteli i kosmos." For the 1957 articles in *Radio*, see nos. 6, 7, and 8; Rip Bulkeley, "Harbingers of Sputnik: The Amateur Radio Preparations in the Soviet Union," *History and Technology* 16 (1999): 67–102.

[35] E. Riabchikov, "Shturm kosmosa," *Ogonek* no. 23 (1957): 6–7; E. Riabchikov, "Sputnik zemli," *Ogonek* no. 24 (1957): 25–26. For Riabchikov's recollections, see "Zaria kosmicheskoi ery," *Ogonek* no. 40 (1987): 1–3.

[36] Korolev, "Predlozheniia o pervykh zapuskakh."

military would allow Korolev to indulge his fantasies only after *two* successful launches of the R-7 ICBM. There were, however, several consecutive failures of the missile in the summer of 1957: One missile exploded 104 seconds into its ascent on May 15; a second rocket never left the pad despite three consecutive attempts on June 9, 10, and 11; a third R-7 was destroyed 33 seconds after launch on July 12.[37] If there had been hope of launching two satellites in the summer, that expectation was quashed. The mood at the launch range was at a nadir by the time that a fourth R-7 was brought out to the pad. Engineers, soldiers, and even government bureaucrats were all desperate for a success. One of Korolev's principal deputies, Anatolii Abramov, later remembered,

> Now, if ever, was the time to despair, to lose faith in the whole program. However S. P. Korolev's composure and the absence of any attempt to find "scapegoats" made people realize that we had embarked on a new level of scientific-technical complexity where no one had gone before. To have fallen into confusion or become mired in apportioning blame would have destroyed the team, its unity and self-confidence. The weight of responsibility resting on S. P. Korolev's shoulders was enormous, especially when you consider that he had still not been formally rehabilitated [after his imprisonment]. Arrest, prison and exile were still fresh in his mind.[38]

Luck favored them in this dark hour. An R-7 lifted off on its first (relatively) successful flight on August 21. To the delight of thousands of engineers, the R-7's engines, combustion chambers, strapon boosters, hybrid guidance system, and launch complex worked with clockwork precision. The missile flew 6,500 kilometers, and its warhead entered the atmosphere over the Kamchatka peninsula in the far-eastern coast of the Soviet landmass. Although the actual warhead container disintegrated about 10 kilometers above the target, the flight was considered a major step forward in the R-7 program. Korolev was so animated by the event that he kept his deputies awake until three in the morning, talking almost nonstop about the possibilities of the future.

As for the missile, a quickly dispatched search party of about 500 men spent almost a whole week gathering the remains of the dummy warhead and its thermal coating. It was only after the search party returned, on August 27, that the official Soviet media issued a public statement:

> A few days ago a super-long-range, intercontinental multistage ballistic missile was launched. The tests of the missile were successful; they fully confirmed the correctness of the calculations and the selected design. The flight of the missile took place at a very great, hitherto unattained, altitude. Covering an enormous distance in a short

[37] Riabikov and Nedelin to the Central Committee (July 19, 1957) in S. Dereviashkin and I. Baichurin, "Trudnye starty znamenitoi 'semerki'," *NK* no. 10 (2000): 66–69.

[38] Memoir of A. A. Abramov in *NKE*, 21.

> time, the missile hit the assigned region. The results obtained show that there is the possibility of launching missiles into any region of the terrestrial globe. The solution of the problem of creating intercontinental ballistic missiles will make it possible to reach remote regions without resorting to strategic aviation, which at the present time is vulnerable to modern means of antiaircraft defense.[39]

It was extremely unusual for Soviet authorities to publicize successes in any military field at any point during the Cold War, let alone in the 1950s. The ICBM was, however, a special case. The statement was undoubtedly intended for a foreign (i.e., American) audience, given that there were armaments reductions talks ongoing in London at the time, focusing on means of verification.[40] Yet Politburo records show that more than a year before the first test, at a meeting in March 1956, Soviet leaders had suggested publishing an announcement of the launch; some had even suggested publishing one *before* a launch.[41] The announcement, then, must be seen in the broader context of Khrushchev's increasing urge to position the Soviet Union as a power equal to the United States, particularly in the military arena. In 1956, the Soviet Union still lacked a credible intercontinental delivery system but an announcement of the existence of such a means fit in line with Khrushchev's pattern of nuclear brinkmanship and aggressive bluffing.[42] A domestic audience for the announcement cannot also be discounted; the missive was certainly also aimed for those officials high up in the Communist Party, the government, and especially in the military, who had strongly expressed doubt about the massive amounts of resources that Khrushchev diverted from conventional forces to strategic (particularly missile) weapons.

Korolev returned briefly to Moscow on August 31 before heading back to the launch range at Tiura-Tam on September 5 for his fourth trip that year to the missile base in Kazakhstan. The subsequent launch of the R-7 two days later was as successful as its predecessor, and the missile flew across the Soviet Union before depositing its dummy warhead over the skies of Kamchatka. Like the previous time, the warhead container disintegrated. It was clear that although the rocket itself was performing without fault, it could still not effectively deliver a warhead to any target. The problem required some serious research on the dynamics (shape, angle of entry, materials, and aerodynamic quality) of the warhead container. Nevertheless, the second

39 "Soobshchenie TASS," *Pravda*, August 27, 1957.

40 "Russians Caution West over Arms," *New York Times*, August 29, 1957.

41 A. A. Fursenko, ed., *Prezidium TsK KPSS, 1954–1964, T. 1* (Moscow: Rosspen, 2003), 110–111.

42 *Pravda* published excerpts from international media response to the ICBM launch in a special article published a day after the original announcement.

failure of the warhead container actually helped Korolev's case in launching a satellite. Korolev's "first deputy" Vasilii Mishin later noted this:

> To determine the reasons for the destruction [of the warhead containers] required time, and on S. P. Korolev's suggestion, a decision was taken on launching [the satellite] in the course of... testing the R-7 missile and gather statistic[al data] on the flight of this rocket on the powered portion of its trajectory.[43]

In other words, it would take weeks, perhaps months, to determine the precise cause for the destruction of the warhead containers. Engineers might have to produce an entirely new container (which is what they did). In the meantime, might not Korolev and his engineers continue to fly R-7 missiles to gain more data on its other systems? Launching a satellite would be an ideal test in that sense, for the warhead would be replaced by the satellite, but most everything else would largely be the same. For this reason, military representatives allowed Korolev to indulge his space dreams and handed over a perfectly "good" ICBM to launch a space satellite.

At a meeting on September 26, the Politburo discussed a report prepared by Riabikov, Korolev, and others on the impending satellite launch. The deliberations were short but focused on the possible hazards posed by the reentering central core of the R-7 rocket as well as the possibility that returning fragments could allow Western agencies to determine the shape of the secret rocket. Riabikov assured all present that there was little to worry about. A draft of a TASS communiqué was approved with spaces empty for specific data about the launch and the satellite's orbit. The launch was set for mid-October.[44]

TSIOLKOVSKII TO *SPUTNIK*

In the months leading to the launch of the first satellite, the primary actors revisited the past, underscoring the deep connections between the 1920s and the 1950s in the complex panorama of Soviet space history. On September 10, weeks before the planned satellite launch, Korolev and others took a break from their work in remote Kazakhstan – the site of their launch base – and returned to Moscow.[45] A major anniversary was approaching: the one hundredth birthday of Russian cosmonautics pioneer Konstantin Tsiolkovskii, who was born on September 17, 1857. The tributes to Tsiolkovskii attained a crescendo around the time of his centennial celebrations, orchestrated by an Academy committee that included Korolev as one of its

[43] V. P. Mishin, "Nekotorye stranitsy istorii raketno-kosmicheskoi nauki i tekhniki v poslevoennyi period," in *IPIITR*, Vols. 8–10, 2001, 50–66.

[44] APRF, 3/47/273/9–16 (September 24, 1957).

[45] Korolev's movements in 1957 are detailed in L. A. Filina, "Istoriia odnogo eksponata," *IIAIK* no. 75 (2000): 9–18.

FIGURE 32. In the final days leading to the launch of *Sputnik*, the USSR Academy of Sciences sponsored several functions dedicated to celebrating the one hundredth birthday of Konstantin Tsiolkovskii. Here on September 15, 1957, in Kaluga, where Tsiolkovskii lived during most of his later life, the leading architects behind *Sputnik* were in attendance, with vague claims about launching satellites in the near future. Standing on the left are Valentin Glushko, Sergei Korolev, (unknown), and Anatolii Blagonravov. On the right, behind the lamp, is Mikhail Riazanskii, whose institute designed *Sputnik*'s radio transmitters. [*Source*: Collection of Asif Siddiqi]

members. On September 15, Korolev and a number of major designers and scientists (including Glushko, Tikhonravov, Riazanskii, and Blagonravov) traveled by train to Kaluga, the town south of Moscow from where Tsiolkovskii had sent out his prolific missives on the cosmos during the last few decades of his life. In the regional (*oblast'*) theater in town, there was a function (see Figure 32). Later, the guests all made their way to Peace Square (*Mirnyy ploshchad'*), where a stone was laid for a future monument to the now-revered scientist. Finally, the procession walked to School No. 9 where Tsiolkovskii had taught for many years. One striking photograph from the day shows Korolev and Tikhonravov uncharacteristically smiling, almost happy (see Figure 33). They, the two primary authors of *Sputnik*, knew what few of their colleagues in attendance knew: that the space age would begin within a few weeks.

The ceremonies in Kaluga were merely a prelude to a major event in Moscow two days later, on Tsiolkovskii's actual birthday. At 7 p.m., in the Hall of Columns at Union House in Moscow, hundreds of eminent

FIGURE 33. The celebrations for Tsiolkovskii's one hundredth birthday coincided with the final preparations leading up to the launch of *Sputnik*. Here we see Mikhail Riazanskii, Mikhail Tikhonravov, Sergei Korolev, his wife Nina Koroleva, and Konstantin Trunov, during a light moment after the function in Kaluga on September 15, 1957. The three men on the left flew back to the launch range in Kazakhstan soon after this, to direct the *Sputnik* launch. This was Korolev's last public appearance. After *Sputnik*, he disappeared from view completely in the secret world of the Soviet military-industrial complex. [*Source*: Collection of Asif Siddiqi]

scientists and designers arrived to pay tribute. Academy President Aleksandr Nesmeianov opened the conference with a typically hagiographic lecture that set the tone for the continuing decades of hero worship associated with Tsiolkovskii. Both Korolev and Glushko gave prominent speeches, hailing Tsiolkovskii as not only one of the greats of Russian science but as a luminary on par with the greatest names in the history of science. In his lecture, Korolev noted pointedly that "in the near future, for scientific purposes, the first trial launches of artificial satellites of the Earth will take place in the USSR and the USA."[46] Only a few in the audience really knew that these words, far from being bluff and bluster, represented very reasonable expectations. Perhaps Korolev relished alarming the censors: In his paper, he noted that Soviet scientists were currently working on problems of sending probes to the Moon, circling the Moon, and even human spaceflight. The presentation ended with a slide show that began with photographs of Tsiolkovskii and ended with rare pictures of recent

[46] ARAN, 1546/1/4/1–28 (September 17, 1957)

Soviet suborbital flights that carried dogs to the upper atmosphere. Few who attended the function knew the true jobs of Korolev and Glushko – they were simply introduced as "Corresponding Members of the Academy." Nevertheless, their speeches were given widespread publicity.[47] On the morning of the anniversary, *Pravda* published a full-page spread dedicated to Tsiolkovskii that included an abridged version of Korolev's speech.[48] It was the *only* article he published under his own name during the last three decades of his life. Soon an even darker shroud of secrecy would descend over his life. Having made their connection to the past, Korolev and Glushko returned to Kazakhstan in Soviet central Asia, now looking to the future.

THE LAUNCH

On September 30, a six-day conference opened at the National Academy of Sciences in Washington, DC, focusing on rocket and satellite research during IGY. Representatives from six countries, including the Soviet Union, attended. Korolev kept tabs on the proceedings via cables from the Soviet embassy in Washington. Seeing that the title of one of the papers was "A Satellite over the Planet [sic]," he concluded that this meant only one thing: that the Americans were timing a secret launch during the conference and that the paper would essentially be an announcement of the event. The fact that the paper was by John P. Hagen, manager of the U.S. Naval Research Laboratory's Vanguard satellite program, seemed to confirm his fears. Hagen was apparently familiar to Korolev, who "read [Hagen's papers] attentively."[49] Korolev contacted KGB representatives to verify if the Americans were planning a launch, but the security agency reported back that there was no evidence to suggest a launch was in the offing. Stubborn to the core, Korolev refused to take a chance. Now panicked about being preempted by Americans at the last minute, he insisted that the satellite launch be brought forward by two days, from early morning October 7 to late night October 4. As a result, at 4 p.m. on the afternoon of October 2, he signed an order for the *new* launch date and sent it to Moscow for final approval. Launch would be in two days; he didn't bother to wait

47 "Velikii russkii uchenyi," *Pravda*, September 18, 1957.

48 The spread was under this general title: "Velikii sovetskii uchenyi" ["A Great Soviet Scientist"], *Pravda*, September 17, 1957. Korolev's article was titled "Osnovopolozhnik raketnoi tekhniki" ["The Founder of Rocket Technology"]. Other pieces included those by E. Glushkova (secretary of the Izhevsk Party committee), P. Nikitin (a senior official at a public science institute), and O. Tretiakova-Zubkova (a schoolteacher).

49 Golovanov, *Korolev*, 537–538. The specific paper that so alarmed Korolev was Hagen's "The Satellite Launching Vehicle; Placing the Satellite in Orbit," which he presented on September 30. See M. Nicolet, ed., *Annals of the International Geophysical Year, Vol. IIB: The International Geophysical Year Meetings* (London: Pergamon Press, 1959), 640–665.

for official confirmation to begin the long sequence of actions required to launch. In the predawn twilight of October 3, a diesel train carrying the rocket and its delicate payload emerged out of the assembly building and slowly headed for the launch pad at Site 1. Witnesses remember Korolev saying, "Well, have a good trip... let's accompany our first-born."[50] Scores of people lined the railway track to the pad. With Korolev at the front, everybody slowly escorted the vehicle all the way to its launch site. (The signed document from Moscow approving the launch was returned on the morning of October 4, launch day).

It was warm at the time, unusual for October at Tiura-Tam. On the morning of the launch, a Friday, testers at the pad were concerned that the high temperatures might overheat the tiny satellite, rendering its systems useless. A quick test seemed to indicate that temperatures were in fact rising underneath the payload fairing. A young military officer, Vladimir Kobelev, assigned to work with the designers at the firing range, took the initiative to go up the service platform and cover the payload fairing with a large white fabric while other tests were going on. This proved ineffective. Eventually, Kobelev set up a hose that released cold air into the fairing, which reduced temperatures down to tolerable levels.[51]

Fueling of the rocket had already begun at 5:45 a.m. local time. Korolev, under pressure, remained cautious throughout the proceedings. He told his engineers, "Nobody will hurry us. If you have even the tiniest doubt, we will stop the testing and make the corrections on the satellite. There is still time." Evgenii Shabarov, one of Korolev's deputies in charge of flight testing, later remembered that the launch preparations for the satellite were conducted at "a slower pace" than was usual.[52] Most personnel at the launch range, understandably enough, did not have time to ponder over the historical value or importance of the upcoming event.

The men and women on hand at Tiura-Tam were a mix of people from Korolev's design bureau and those from various rocket and artillery divisions in the Soviet armed forces. On behalf of Korolev, the launch preparations were directed by his deputy, forty-four-year-old Leonid Voskresenskii, already a legend in his own time, known for his fearlessness, colorful personality, and lack of respect for rules. Korolev relied on the trustworthy Voskresenskii to fix any situation at the pad, who sometimes disregarded even Korolev's own edicts. Commanding the launch with Voskresenskii was Lieutenant-Colonel Aleksandr Nosov, the same age as his colleague, whose official title was deputy commander of the launch range, which in effect meant that he was personally responsible for all missiles that took off from any pad. A World War II veteran, Nosov had gained considerable experience

50 Golovanov, *Korolev*, 538; Memoir of Tikhonravov in *ASPK*, 447–448.

51 Ivanovskii, *Rakety i kosmos v sssr*, 33.

52 Golovanov, *Korolev*, 538; Memoir of E. V. Shabarov in *NKE*, 63.

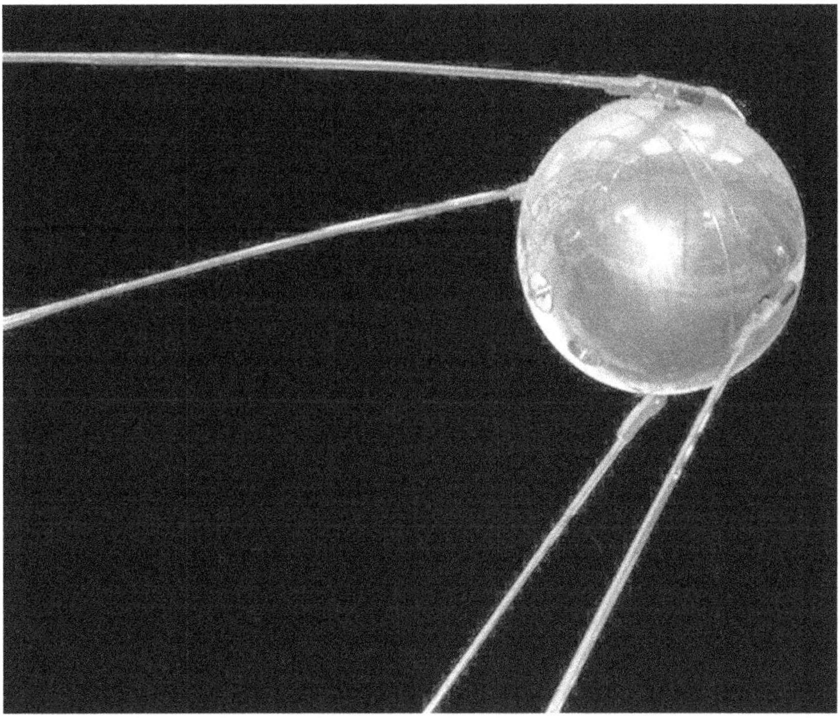

FIGURE 34. The now-iconic visage of the *Sputnik* satellite with its elegant round shape. The four antennae stretching back from the ball seem to be imploring the ball ahead to some unknown future. [*Source*: NASA]

firing rockets during long tours of duty at Kapustin Iar near the Volga river where the Soviets had tested their first German V-2s back in the late 1940s.

For the satellite launch, a young artillery captain, Vladimir Nikulin, was put in charge of maintaining the paperwork – filling out the mission goals and flight logs. Unsure of what to fill in for "goal of the launch," Nikulin turned to Korolev's first deputy Vasilii Mishin who told him to dispense with such entries as "target," and instead write out the launch azimuth (the angle between "true north" and the direction of the launch) as 34° 37′ 59.2″.[53] The value was calculated based on the desired orbital inclination of 65.1°, which would ensure that the satellite would pass over almost all inhabited areas of the globe, including, most importantly, both the eastern portion of the Soviet Union and the United States.

Nikulin's job was to get the key military testers responsible for each system of the launch vehicle and the satellite to sign off that "their" system was ready for launch. Such rituals had long been part of tradition with military rocket

[53] N. L. Semenov, "Kak zapuskali pervyi sputnik," *Zemlia i vselennaia* no. 5 (2002): 49–55.

launches, now made doubly important with the very critical test flights of the R-7 ICBM. The R-7 was an expensive and massive piece of machinery; to lose one of these as a result of a junior army officer's negligence was unacceptable. One by one, Nikulin got his signatures: Senior Lieutenant Iurii Chalykh in charge of programming the rocket's launch azimuth, Lieutenant-Colonel Aleksei Dolinin on the readiness of all the engines of the rocket, and Captain Semen Grafskii and Lieutenant Vladimir Ganushkin for the propellants. All the chief designers involved in the operation – in particular, the "big six" from the famed Council of Chief Designers of the 1940s – signed off on the launch: Korolev, Glushko, Piliugin, Riazanskii, Barmin, and Kuznetsov. The latter two, Vladimir Barmin and Viktor Kuznetsov, were in charge of the launch complex and the rocket's gyroscope systems respectively. Another chief designer, Aleksei Bogomolov – responsible for the R-7's telemetry systems – was listed as a "technical supervisor" rather than a chief designer because historically he had not been part of the original "big six" but was a new entrant to the big leagues. Nikulin remembers finding Korolev very close to the rocket; he signed off on the launch log pensively, in silence.[54]

On the night of the 4th, huge flood lights illuminated the launch pad as servicemen crowded around the rocket and completed their various tasks. Korolev was clearly anxious. About an hour before launch, Korolev abruptly ordered satellite lead designer Khomiakov and a military tester from the launch team to go up to the very top platform and check everything. This was highly unusual and probably quite dangerous, but Khomiakov obliged without hesitation.[55] Back in the bunker there were six command and control panels, each manned by one or two individuals responsible for a particular aspect of the rocket: two panels, each controlling two of the strapons, a control panel for the core booster, a panel for charging the onboard batteries of the rocket, a panel controlling fire extinguishing systems on the pad, and a control panel for monitoring the deployment of satellite at the end of the R-7's long skybound trajectory.

Fifteen minutes before launch, the whole area around the pad was evacuated. Five minutes later, finally, Korolev, Voskresenskii, Nosov, and a few others joined the rest of the command crew in the bunker. Voskresenskii and Nosov, in charge of the launch, took their places at periscopic sights. A loudspeaker echoed the announcements in the now-deserted and dark area around the launch pad: "Ten minutes readiness!" Voskresenskii's deputy Shabarov, also in the bunker, had a vivid memory:

> With the exception of the operators, everybody was standing. Only N. A. Piliugin and S. P. Korolev were allowed to sit down. The launch director [Nosov] began issuing commands. I kept an eye on S. P. Korolev. He seemed nervous although he tried

[54] Semenov, "Kak zapuskali pervyi sputnik."
[55] Memoir of Kavyzin [Khomiakov] in *ASPK*, 451.

to conceal it. He was carefully examining the readings of the various instruments without missing any nuance of our body language and tone of voice. If anybody raised their voice or showed signs of nervousness, Korolev was instantly on the alert to see what was going on.[56]

Boris Chekunov, the twenty-four-year-old lieutenant in charge of pushing the ignition button for the central core booster, later described the final moments as the clock ticked down to liftoff: "When only a few minutes remained until liftoff, Korolev nodded to his deputy Voskresenskii. The operators froze, awaiting the final order. Aleksandr Nosov, the chief of the launch control team, stood at the periscope. He could see the whole pad. 'One minute to go!,' he called."[57] As the seconds counted down to zero, an operator announced "Key to launch!" (*Kliuch na start!*). Chekunov turned a key on his panel clockwise from left to right. He would do this nearly 600 more times in a career spread over thirty years, but this was the very first time for a launch into space.[58]

For Soviet launches, there was no countdown, only an occasional voice announcing "X minutes readiness" punctuated by the announcement of sudden commands. The next command, "Key to drainage!" (*Kliuch na drenazh!*), meant that the drainage valves were closed after disconnecting from the rocket's propellant tanks. Operators then waited the few seconds until the second hand of the clock approached the precise time for engine ignition indicated on their launch cards. As the word "Launch!" (*Pusk!*) rang out, Chekunov decisively pressed the launch button on his panel to begin the engine firing cyclogram. There was a little over a minute now left to the actual departure of the rocket from the pad, perhaps the most anxiety-inducing seconds of the whole launch. Voskresenskii and Nosov's eyes were glued to their periscopes as they watched the launch vehicle vent steam around it. A panel indicator lit up: "Preliminary" (*Predvaritel'naia*), meaning that the engines had ignited and were revving up to their preliminary thrust regime. All in the bunker began to sense the growing rumbling vibrations. An operator yelled, "Main!" (*Est' glavnaia!*) and almost immediately "Contact of Liftoff! (*Est' kontakt pod'ema!*), Liftoff! (*Pod'em!*)"[59]

It was exactly 2,228 hours 34 seconds Moscow Time, about an hour-and-a-half after midnight local time. Flames from the base of the rocket cut through the darkness of the Kazakhstan desert steppes as the arms of the launch complex pulled back, allowing the graceful rocket to lift off from its pad. One participant remembered, "At the moment [of liftoff] it seemed to onlookers that the rocket would burn where it was, on the launch pad,

[56] Memoir of Shabarov in *NKE*, 63.

[57] Ivan Borisenko and Alexander Romanov, *Where All Roads Lead to Space Begin* (Moscow: Progress, 1982), 66.

[58] Mikhail Rebrov, "Kliuch – na start!," *Krasnaia zvezda*, July 2, 1995.

[59] Semenov, "Kak zapuskali pervyi sputnik."

FIGURE 35. There are no clear still photographs of the launch of *Sputnik*. All of the images are stills from a movie camera that captured the moment of launch. Because of the time of the launch, close to midnight local time, the quality of the film was, unfortunately, rather poor. [*Source*: Collection of Asif Siddiqi]

without taking off."[60] First slowly, but then quickly, almost too quickly, the nearly 273 ton mass of metal, oxygen, and kerosene, gathered speed and shot up into the warm night sky (see Figure 35). The five engines, the children of Glushko's genius, generated a total of nearly 400 tons of thrust.

There were problems on the outbound flight, in both the engines and in the inertial guidance system. At liftoff, telemetry noted that the engine in one of the strapon boosters (Block G) reached its "intermediate" stage late; that is, it took longer than usual to reach the desired level of thrust. Because of this, there were moments of anxiety, a fear that the rocket might fly off-kilter at a dangerous angle because of the unequal thrust spread across the bottom. Fortunately, the engine completed its thrust buildup, and the rocket "returned" to its correct attitude within 18 to 20 seconds.[61] A more serious problem occurred soon after, at T + 16 seconds, when the system that regulated how much propellant was being used for each engine, failed. The malfunction led to a higher consumption of kerosene than planned, and as a result, the booster did not have enough propellant to reach the original

60 Golovanov, *Korolev*, 540.
61 "Osnovnye rezul'taty puska."

burnout point (296.4 seconds after launch). The main core engine, in fact, shut down 1 second earlier than planned, that is, at 295.4 seconds.[62]

These details were not known at the time of the launch. In the bunker, only the major events were reported back. Controllers were informed that 116.38 seconds after launch, the four strapon boosters separated as planned, as the rocket made its way across the Soviet landmass, gaining altitude and velocity. At main core engine burnout – which was reported back in the bunker with an exclamation of "Main Command!" – the core and its satellite payload were traveling at 7,780 kilometers per second at a height of 228.6 kilometers above the Earth. As planned, 19.9 seconds later, precisely 314.5 seconds after launch, the satellite successfully separated from the core booster. Simultaneously, the nose fairing over the satellite was discarded (using a spring system). At the moment of separation, the satellite's commutator switched on its own power supply as well as its internal pressurization system. Less than 11 seconds later, the angular reflectors on the core deployed.[63]

From the data streaming into the bunker – principally a signal that was received from the booster core's telemetry system (known as *Tral*) by a ground station at Tiura-Tam that indicated that the engines had shut down – it seemed that Earth orbit had been achieved. Shabarov recalled that "everyone breathed a sigh of relief, and there was [finally] a minute of silence. And suddenly, everyone began talking to each other, and people began to go up. The launch chief and I were even allowed to smoke inside the bunker."[64]

While Korolev was in the bunker, another group of people had begun crowding around a van stationed near a house at Site 2, the main living area of the launch range. Inside, Viacheslav Lappo and Konstantin Gringauz, the men who had built the radio transmitters, were sitting with headphones to their ears, waiting for a sign from the heavens.[65] People were persistently trying to shove their way into the van, to the irritation of the two, who repeatedly told people to be quiet. Suddenly, there was weak "beep-beep-beep" that slowly grew in volume, becoming louder and louder each second. There was a round of "hurrahs" outside the van. Riazanskii, Lappo and Gringauz' boss, immediately got on the phone and called Korolev, who was still back at the bunker: "There it is! There's a signal!"[66] This was apparently a tape recording, transmitted from one of the tracking stations in the far

[62] Poroshkov, "Khronika vazhneishikh sobytiy," 111–112; *RAP2*, 386–387.

[63] "Pervyi iskusstvennyi sputnik zemli."

[64] Memoir of Shabarov in *NKE*, 64.

[65] Sources differ on the location and personnel involved. Ivanovskii (echoed by Golovanov) refers to Lappo and Gringauz at Site 2 whereas Semenov refers to Junior-Lieutenant V. G. Borisov, who was stationed in the Finnish houses at IP-1. For the latter, see Semenov, "Kak zapuskali pervyi sputnik."

[66] Golovanov, *Korolev*, 540.

eastern Soviet landmass in Kamchatka.[67] Korolev was not impressed. He dryly commented, "This could be a mistake. Until we hear the signals after the satellite comes back after its first orbit... it's too early to celebrate."[68]

In general, people urged caution. There was, after all, a chance that the satellite was heading on a ballistic trajectory into the Pacific Ocean, helplessly transmitting its beep-beep-beeps for all to hear. There was only one thing to do now: Wait an hour or so for the satellite to come around again. Korolev, Riabikov, Keldysh, Glushko, Barmin, Voskresenskii, Nosov – all of them made their way out of the bunker and headed to the van of the radio operators. It took about an hour and a half for the satellite to return back around the Earth. Once again, Lappo picked up the signals, the insistent "beep-beep-beep." He screamed: "It's there! It's there! Turn on the tape recorders!"[69] Ballistics experts brought in their data: According to their calculations, the satellite was in an orbit with an apogee (high point above the Earth) of 939 kilometers and a perigee (low point) of 215 kilometers.[70] These figures would be adjusted later, but at the time, the numbers seemed like a revelation, even if the apogee was much lower than expected; compared to the original planned apogee of 1,450 kilometers, the high point appears to have been far below its the target range, by as much as 500 kilometers.

These were minor considerations, because the first object made by humans was in a freefall trajectory – an orbit – around the Earth. According to calculations revised over the night – sharpened by scientists back at the Computation Center at the NII-4 institute near Moscow – the satellite was in a 947 × 228 kilometer orbit. The "orbital period," that is, the time it took to make one complete circuit around the Earth, was a little over 1.5 hours, more precisely, 96 minutes 10.2 seconds. The satellite was circling at an angle of 65.1° to the equator, giving it surface coverage over an enormous portion of the Earth's inhabited surface.[71]

As had been agreed, the State Commission, the ad hoc body overseeing the launch, decided to inform Khrushchev after the first orbit, with Commission Chairman Riabikov making the critical call to the Soviet leader. There are conflicting reports about the conversation. Khrushchev's son, Sergei, who was with his father, recalls that the older Khrushchev was on a trip to Kiev to discuss economic issues with the Ukrainian Party leadership. Around 11 p.m. – it was already past 2 a.m. at Tiura-Tam – these negotiations were

[67] Ivanovskii, *Rakety i kosmos v sssr*, 35. Semenov makes no mention of the signal being a recording.

[68] Memoir of Shabarov in *NKE*, 64.

[69] Ivanovskii, *Rakety i kosmos v sssr*, 35.

[70] Golovanov, *Korolev*, 541.

[71] These data are according to the TASS announcement of October 5. An internal OKB-1 report issued on November 1 states parameters at orbital insertion as 223 × 950 kilometers with an orbital period of 96.2 minutes, but these refer to the core stage of the booster. See "Osnovnye rezul'taty puska"; "Pervyi iskusstvennyi sputnik zemli."

interrupted by a telephone call. Khrushchev left the large meeting hall to take the call, and then returned without saying anything – at least at first. His son described the scene:

> He finally couldn't resist saying [to the Ukrainian officials]: "I can tell you some very pleasant and important news. Korolev just called (at this point he acquired a secretive look). He's one of our missile designers. Remember not to mention his name – it's classified. Korolev has just reported that today, a little while ago, an artificial satellite of the Earth was launched."[72]

The Ukrainian Party leaders were not a bit bewildered as Khrushchev continued to ramble on about the satellite. They, after all, had important economic issues to discuss. The younger Khrushchev claims that the Soviet leader was animated the rest of the evening, speaking in glowing terms about the new era of missiles that could "demonstrate the advantages of socialism in actual practice" to the Americans. Contemporaneous accounts paint a very different picture, suggesting that Khrushchev had little or no idea of the impact that the satellite would make on the international stage. A few days after the launch, an American journalist who spoke to Khrushchev noted that the Soviet leader told him that "the engineer in charge of the project, whom he did not name, had telephoned to say that the satellite had been launched and was on course. Then, said Mr. Khrushchev, we congratulated each other and went off to bed."[73]

For the engineers, scientists, soldiers, workers, and bureaucrats responsible for the achievement – in Moscow, in Bolshevo, at Kaliningrad, at Tiura-Tam, and at tracking stations all over the country – the feeling was one of elation and exhaustion. As night turned to day – the first daylight of the space age – people arranged an impromptu meeting at which Korolev climbed onto an improvised rostrum and gave a speech that was unusually flowery for him:

> Dear comrades! Today, that which the best human minds have dreamed of has taken place! The prophetic words of Konstantin Eduardovich Tsiolkovskii that mankind would not always remain on the Earth have come to pass. Today the first artificial satellite in the world has been injected into circumterrestrial orbit. With its injection into orbit, the conquest of space has begun. And the first country to open the road to outer space has been our country – the land of the Soviets! Allow me to congratulate all of you on this historic occasion. And allow me to especially thank all the junior specialists, technicians, engineers, and designers who took part in the preparation of the [rocket] and the satellite, for their titanic labor.... Once more I give to you a hearty Russian thanks![74]

[72] Sergey N. Khrushchev, *Nikita Khrushchev and the Creation of a Superpower* (University Park, PA: Penn State University Press, 2000), 260.

[73] James Reston, "Khrushchev Asks World Rule of the Satellite and Missiles if Part of Wide U.S.-Soviet Pact," *New York Times*, October 8, 1957.

[74] Golovanov, *Korolev*, 541.

Soon, Voskresenskii's deputy Shabarov ordered the chief of the mission at Tiura-Tam to express thanks in a different way by handing out alcohol. So that people would not come back for more, he stipulated that each man would get a whole teapot of spirits. Meanwhile, radio transmitter designer Lappo extended one of his speakers right out into the street and set it at full volume; all over Site 2, one could hear the enigmatic "beep-beep-beep," – a tape that ran over and over again. Later in the day, there was a celebration in a small movie theater in at Site 10, the main living area at the launch range; Riabikov gave a speech congratulating all, followed by Korolev and Keldysh.

After nightfall, Korolev and a small group of his coworkers took off in an Il'iushin Il-14 aircraft from Tiura-Tam to head for Moscow. Despite the two massive piston engines that roared through the flight, most of the men were exhausted and slept through the trip – some, after all, were sleeping the alcohol off. Soon after takeoff, the pilot of the airplane, Tol'ia Esenin, came out of the cockpit and bent over Korolev's seat to tell him that "the whole world was abuzz" with the launch – "in all languages you can hear, 'Russia' and 'satellite'." Korolev quickly got up and went into the pilot's cabin. Returning back to the passenger's area, he announced gleefully to everybody, "Well comrades, you can't imagine – the whole world is talking about our satellite," adding with a huge smile, "It seems that we have caused quite a stir."[75]

At about 1:30 a.m. Moscow Time on the early morning of October 5 – just after 7:30 p.m. in Washington, DC, the night before – the official Soviet news agency TASS released the communiqué on the launch that Riabikov and others had authored in late September. Published in the morning edition of *Pravda*, it was exceptionally low key and was not even the headline of the day – the main headline "above the fold" on October 5 was "Preparation for Winter is an Urgent Task."[76] Even the text of the satellite launch was understated. When the authors wrote the original text, they were clearly being rather modest:

> For several years scientific research and experimental design work have been conducted in the Soviet Union on the creation of artificial satellites. As has already been reported in the press, the first launching of the satellites in the USSR were planned for realization in accordance with the scientific research program of the International Geophysical Year. As a result of very intensive work by scientific research institutes and design bureaus the first artificial satellite in the world has been created. On October 4, 1957, this first satellite was successfully launched in the USSR. According to preliminary data, the carrier rocket has imparted to the satellite the required orbital velocity of about 8,000 meters per second. At the present time the satellite is describing elliptical trajectories around the Earth, and its flight can be observed in

[75] Memoir of Skuridin in *ASPK*, 457–458.

[76] "Podgotovka k zime – delo neotlozhnoe," *Pravda*, October 5, 1957.

the rays of the rising and setting Sun with the aid of very simple optical instruments (binoculars, telescopes, etc.).[77]

In the announcement, there was no detail on the actual orbit of the satellite, just a general comment that it was traveling at "altitudes of up to 900 kilometers above the Earth's surface." The only individual named in the communiqué was Konstantin Tsiolkovskii who "already in the 19th century first substantiated the possibility of accomplishing space flight with the aid of rockets." The Soviet media did not ascribe a specific name for the satellite (like the Americans would with *Explorer-1*), but generically called it "the artificial satellite of the Earth" (*iskusstvennyi sputnik Zemli*). Because the word for satellite in Russian was *sputnik*, that word acquired a greater resonance than perhaps intended. In the West, *Sputnik* became a synonym for the satellite, although in Russia even to this day, the satellite is still simply called "the first Soviet artificial satellite of the Earth" (*Pervyi sovetskii iskusstvennyi sputnik Zemli* or *Pervyi sovetskii ISZ*).

A CODA

Sputnik's factory manager Mikhail Khomiakov underscored that "frankly speaking, many of us did not understand the full significance of this event."[78] Not one of the Soviet designers, including Korolev, Tikhonravov, and Keldysh, the three principal architects of *Sputnik*, nor the bureaucrats in the government such as Riabikov, Khrunichev, and Ustinov, nor the workers on the shop floor directly involved in the events truly anticipated the scale of the response, both at home and abroad. Oleg Ivanovskii, who was one of the leading production managers for the satellite, later recalled that "Nobody back then was thinking about the magnitude of what was going on: everyone did his own job, living through its disappointments and joys."[79] For engineers, the event was largely seen as the end result of a set of planned operations involving the R-7 missile, that is, just another launch, a day's work. Almost no one had expected anything more than moderate publicity, maybe domestically, but certainly nothing on an international scale. They were focused entirely on the job itself. Their anticipations were also colored by the fact that nothing like this had ever happened, anywhere or anytime. Without precedent, expectations were that much more nebulous and uncertain.

At the top levels of the Soviet leadership, Khrushchev and others were initially not a bit bewildered. In an interview with *New York Times* correspondent James Reston four days after *Sputnik*, the journalist noted that

[77] "Soobshchenie TASS," *Pravda*, October 5, 1957.
[78] Memoir of Kavyzin [Khomiakov] in *ASPK*, 451.
[79] Ivanov [Ivanovskii], *Vpervye*, 35.

"Mr. Khrushchev was almost casual in his references to the Soviet earth satellite that has created such a sensation in its lightning course around the globe."[80] Yet, as the global response, particularly the hoopla in the American media, began to seep into the halls of the Kremlin, the Politburo began to galvanize and exploit the opportunity. On October 10, at a Politburo meeting, Riabikov, Korolev, Nedelin, and others reported to Khrushchev on the results of the launch. Discussion focused on both the international response as well as tasking Riabikov with assigning appropriate honors and prizes for the participants, including new dachas for the most senior designers.[81] By a secret decree, about 500 designers, engineers, and workers involved in the development of the R-7 ICBM and *Sputnik* were handed out awards in late December, a few of them with the nation's highest civilian honor, the Hero of Socialist Labor.

At the Politburo meeting, Khrushchev was unusually animated, and asked if Korolev could launch another satellite, in time for the impending fortieth anniversary of the October Revolution in early November. Korolev replied that not only could he launch another one, but could even put a dog on board, an idea that seemed to please the First Secretary. Korolev's deputy Mishin remembered this:

> After [*Sputnik*] we disbanded for a break. Korolev, Voskresenskii and I with our two deputies, and a group of the main workers from the special design bureau obtained travel authorization. We stayed at Bulganin's big dacha [at the resort of] Sochi. We rested for exactly 5 days... then we got a telephone call....: "Fly back urgently. We have been tasked to make a new satellite." So we did. It turned out that Khrushchev had been pleased with the political effect of the first *Sputnik* and he ordered another one on a priority basis.... Only after that did we go off for a real rest.[82]

This time, Khrushchev, through Politburo member Frol Kozlov, kept daily tabs on the work. After another Herculean effort – many of the workers remember hardly sleeping – another satellite, this time with a dog, reached orbit on November 3, setting off another paroxysm of self-congratulations at home and public soul searching in the West.[83] In Moscow, a large stuffed dog's head was installed so it almost comically poked out of a model satellite outside of the TASS office's building on Gorkii Street. The dog, whose name was revealed as Laika a few days later, became the first deliberate instrument of Soviet power in space, signaling the full combination of geopolitics, media hoopla, and technology in the new emerging Soviet space program.

[80] Reston, "Khrushchev Asks World Rule."

[81] Fursenko, *Prezidium TsK KPSS*, 268. All six members of the Council of Chief Designers (Korolev, Glushko, Piliugin, Riazanskii, Barmin, and Kuznetsov) received dachas by a government edict issued on December 18, 1957.

[82] A. Tarasov (interview with V. Mishin), "Polet vo sne i naiavu," *Pravda*, October 20, 1989.

[83] "Vtoroi sovetskii iskusstvennyi sputnik sovershaet polet vokrug Zemli," *Pravda*, November 4, 1957.

The Soviet media was quick to pick up on the hysteria in the West, and mobilized in the days after the launch of the first *Sputnik*. On October 6, the first three pages of *Pravda* were dedicated to the satellite launch; the day after, a full page was dedicated to excerpts from a wide range of Western accounts on the satellite.[84] Every day following the launch, newspapers published detailed numbers on the location of the satellite so it could be followed by those on the ground. Surprised by the media reaction in the United States, one of Keldysh's assistants at the Academy of Sciences, Gennadii Skuridin, met with a small group to hammer out a more informative description of the satellite. Although the principal author was Mikhail Tikhonravov, others included the young scientists led by Dmitrii Okhotsimskii from the Department of Applied Mathematics who had developed the basic equations for orbital flight earlier in the decade and a number of Korolev's representatives. Their draft was passed around to Korolev, Glushko, Keldysh, and others before being sent to *Pravda*, where Skuridin and *Pravda*'s science editor A. G. Azizian smoothed out any sensitive information. The article was typeset and then published as a major story in *Pravda* on the morning of October 9. Given the constraints that its authors were working with, the article was rather informative, chock full of technical information, especially about the satellite itself, and included the first published photograph of the satellite as well as its ground track.[85] The parties responsible for this great deed were, of course, not named.

Soon, as more chest-beating pieces in the Soviet media began to appear, *Sputnik*, the event, became inseparable from the Western response to it. On October 16, Academician Aleksandr Topchiev, a well-known Soviet chemist who had some cursory knowledge of the satellite project, wrote a long piece on *Sputnik* that encapsulated the rhetoric that suffused the Soviet media in the late fall of 1957. He wrote,

> The whole world's press have devoted much attention to this event. Given the enthusiastic response, many organs of the bourgeois press could not hide their concern about the new remarkable success of Soviet science and technology. Objective people see this as a great victory of socialism in competition with capitalism. Enemies of the Soviet Union, in an attempt to diminish the significance of the event have declared it casual, minor. But is an Earth satellite launched for the first time on record a minor success? No!... The advance of science and technology in our country moves on a broad front.[86]

[84] "Mir voskhishchen grandioznoi pobedoi sovetskoi nauki i tekhniki," *Pravda*, October 7, 1957.

[85] "Sovetskii iskusstvennyi sputnik Zemli," *Pravda*, October 9, 1957; Memoir of Skuridin in *ASPK*, 458.

[86] A. V. Topchiev, "Velikaia pobeda Sovetskoi nauki," in *Stantsii v kosmose: sbornik statei*, ed. A. A. Mikhailov (Moscow: AN SSSR, 1960), 15–24 (see p. 15).

We hardly question this point, of *Sputnik* as a symbol of Soviet power, and how it fits into the matrix of Cold War superpower confrontation at a number of levels – political, economical, social, and cultural. This interpretation coalesced very quickly in the days after *Sputnik* as Western responses to the satellite launch were translated and reproduced galore in Soviet newspapers and magazines, especially after Korolev and his team launched a second satellite into orbit just a month later.

Beyond the global ramifications, from the perspective of the ones who had labored to produce this achievement, hesitation about pride was replaced with a sense of relieved delight. After the *Sputnik* launch, but before he left the launch range to head back to Moscow, Korolev had asked Mikhail Khomiakov, the satellite's main production manager, to stay back to pack up and bring back the spare model of the satellite, "an exact copy of the one which was now in orbit around the Earth." When Khomiakov returned to the design bureau near Moscow, he checked in with Korolev, saying that he was back from his "business trip." This was the usual way engineers spoke about going to the launch range – an assignment to Tiura-Tam was a "business trip," one of many bland euphemisms that were accepted as part of the culture of intense secrecy surrounding the missile industry. Korolev responded "what business trip?," confusing Khomiakov. The chief designer raised his voice: "What's this you say, a business trip, a business trip.... Tell your comrades that you have participated in the preparation and launch of the world's first artificial satellite of the Earth."[87] Khomiakov walked away, thinking about history for the first time; no longer embarrassed to think of the big picture, he smiled for the first time in weeks.

[87] Memoir of Kavyzin [Khomiakov] in *ASPK*, 451.

Conclusion

> [I]n time utopia becomes actual social consciousness; it invades the consciousness of a mass movement and becomes one of its essential driving forces. Utopia, then, crosses over from the domain of theoretical and moral thought into the field of practical thinking, and itself begins to govern human action.[1]
>
> Leszek Kolakowski

Sputnik was not a triumph of Soviet science. This is not to say that Soviet scientists did not contribute to the feat, but that it emerged from a complex milieu in which the state's sponsored science – "Soviet science" – was but one in a constellation of factors. The term *Soviet science* itself is, of course, somewhat of a misnomer. During the Cold War, influenced by the obvious fetish with all things Soviet, historians subsumed all scientific phenomena in Russia (geographical) under the sharper and circumscribed contours of post-1917 Soviet science, thus occluding deep continuities between the imperial and Bol'shevik eras. Others, both during and after the Cold War, sought to identify the vagaries of the even more specific *Stalinist science*. Some obvious touchstones color our understanding of these terms, particularly the attack on genetics exemplified by the Lysenko episode and the making of the first Soviet atomic bomb.[2] If some argued that Soviet (and Stalinist) science was inarguably and dialectically linked with ideological considerations, others sought to situate these and other episodes as part of broader processes emblematic of Soviet society and culture, or the intellectual trajectories of particular disciplines.[3] My point about *Sputnik* is that its life history suggests a much more expansive reading than the reductive and received notion of "Soviet science": *Sputnik* was, for example, both Soviet *and* Russian, its ideological underpinnings had as much to do with Marxism as mysticism,

1 Leszek Kolakowki, "The Concept of the Left," in *Marxism and Beyond: On Historical Understanding and Individual Responsibility* (London: Pall Mall, 1969), 89.

2 David Holloway, *Stalin and the Bomb: The Soviet Union and Atomic Energy, 1939–1956* (New Haven: Yale University Press, 1994). Nikolai Krementsov's *Stalinist Science* (Princeton: Princeton University Press, 1997) explicitly conflates the Lysenko episode with "Stalinist science."

3 For a useful critique of the literature, see Michael D. Gordin, "Was There Ever a 'Stalinist Science'," *Kritika* 9 no. 3 (Summer 2008): 625–639.

its history is littered with exchanges with foreign factors, and – perhaps most important – it encompassed phenomena not typically associated with the state. It was a type of "Soviet science" completely at odds with our received understanding of the notion.

The example of *Sputnik* suggests that the history of Russian and Soviet science and technology comprised phenomena beyond those driven by a symbiotic relationship between elite scientific communities and the state. The half-century-long origin of the Soviet space program provides evidence of a kind of "science from below" that could operate without significant support from the state, at least for a while. The prehistory of *Sputnik* contrasts strikingly with the other major post-Cold War project of Soviet science, the development of the atomic bomb, which grew out of the interests of a community of physicists operating in elite academic, industrial, and educational institutions in the 1930s.[4] The project of spaceflight, on the other hand, grew out of the musings of a half-deaf, lone autodidact in rural Russia, the work of amateur societies, and the handiwork of men and women who built rocket engines out of broken blowtorches in factory workshops. Ideas – some innovative, some not – bubbled up from people with no more than a secondary school education and influenced decades of work. They were aided by a pool of starry-eyed utopians so committed to the cosmic cause that their ardor inspired generations of young Soviet citizens to anticipate the coming of the space age not with surprise but with expectation.

The project of spaceflight would, of course, not have been possible without state intervention. It required the massive personnel, financial, and material sources of the state to build powerful rockets, particularly the intercontinental ballistic missile (ICBM) that launched *Sputnik* into orbit. In the postwar years, spurred by the discovery of German advances in missile design, Party and government officials committed to developing indigenous rockets, a process that created a vast infrastructure within the defense industry dedicated to missile production. Cold War imperatives, particularly the articulation of a new military strategy tied to the development of the atomic bomb, eventually led the post-Stalinist leadership to use this industrial foundation to fully commit to the development of an ICBM, a program that dwarfed most other weapons projects in the 1950s. The creation of this missile, the R-7, was a central episode in the history of *Sputnik*, but it assumed its critical role not because of state-driven motives but because the same community of designers responsible for the missile were the architects of the two interconnected campaigns, one to foster a public enthusiasm for all things cosmic, and the other to convince the government to invest in a satellite project.

In the four decades prior to *Sputnik*, the Soviet government had an ambivalent relationship to both rocketry and space exploration. The government remained largely indifferent to the vibrant space fad of the 1920s and sponsored the development of rockets with great ambivalence in the 1930s.

[4] Holloway, *Stalin and the Bomb*.

Still, the latter period signaled a turning point in rocketry work as amateur rocketry enthusiasts successfully convinced the state to sponsor their activities. Ironically, this new relationship led to the terrible purges among rocket designers in the late 1930s, when the NKVD arrested and shot several engineers.

The anticipation of confrontation with the Nazis had a pronounced impact on the development of rockets as the Soviet government focused on creating weaponry that offered more immediate returns; powerful liquid-propellant rockets were abandoned in favor of the crude and short-range *Katiusha* projectiles. Not until exposure to extremely powerful German rocket weapons after the war did the state finally commit to massive spending in support of building rockets. In the postwar era, the two strands of independent action – one, an often public campaign to explore space and the other, a state-sponsored intervention to build rockets – intersected. At this time, the state could take advantage of an experienced cadre of engineers who had been influenced by the utopian space culture of the 1920s and who subsequently learned and mastered the design of complex rocket systems in amateur societies in the early 1930s. They included Sergei Korolev, Mikhail Tikhonravov, and Valentin Glushko, the three main engineering minds behind *Sputnik*.

Although *Sputnik* was not a triumph of Soviet science – at least as the notion is typically understood – it became one, *post facto*, as commentators both in the Soviet Union and abroad conflated the perceived caesura of 1957 with Cold War anxieties about nuclear Armageddon. Nikita Khrushchev's grandstanding about space achievements in the late 1950s and early 1960s communicated two powerful and interconnected messages: that Soviet science and technology was on par if not ahead of the capitalist camp, and that the missiles that launched the satellites into orbit could also deliver bombs to the other side of the world. *Sputnik*, in fact, profoundly accelerated the Soviet ballistic missile program. A few weeks after *Sputnik*, at a plenum of the Central Committee, Khrushchev did not equivocate: "We have good bombers . . . but bombers flying to America – for now, this is a difficult task. On the other hand – the intercontinental ballistic missile. This is an absolute weapon."[5]

As missiles assumed a central role in Soviet military doctrine, those who had banked their careers on rockets rose to the apex of the Soviet military-industrial complex. In the wake of *Sputnik*, missile experts convinced Khrushchev to establish a new branch of the armed forces to operate ballistic missiles, leading to the formation of the Strategic Rocket Forces in December 1959, headed by Marshal Mitrofan Nedelin, one of the prime movers behind the development of the R-7 rocket.[6] Similarly, the special committee (*Spetskomitet*) that had overseen development of the R-7 was

[5] Khrushchev quoted in Bystrova, *VPK*, 91.

[6] N. E. Solovtsov and V. I. Ivkin, "Mezhkontinental'naia ballisticheskaia raketa – eto absoliutnoe oruzhie," *VIZ* no. 12 (2004): 2–7.

used as foundation to establish a new state organ, the Military-Industrial Commission, to supervise the entire Soviet defense industry; as a result, managers of the missile industry such as Dmitrii Ustinov, Vasilii Riabikov, Georgii Pashkov, and Leonid Smirnov found themselves at the top of the Soviet military-industrial complex, dominating it for close to thirty years.[7] The rise of these men to the top of Soviet power created, in effect, a Soviet version of what historian Dale Carter (invoking Thomas Pynchon) described as a "rocket state," a place where the demands of the missile industry dominated and subsumed all other concerns of the Soviet economy.[8]

Enthusiasm for the cosmos, which began in pre-Revolutionary times and surged in the 1920s and 1950s, peaked to a crescendo in the aftermath of *Sputnik*, and particularly during the halcyon days of Soviet space achievements in the 1960s. As hero after hero cosmonaut circled the Earth, the state sponsored a massive industry to promote Soviet space exploits, distinguishing the new popular enthusiasm from its antecedent periods which was largely ignored at the top. Yet, there were some continuities with the earlier space fads, for example, in the way in which the media – through newspapers, popular science magazines, and monographs – was the most important vehicle to foster a cosmic consciousness for a new generation of Soviet citizens. This new upsurge began to fade in the early 1970s when the Soviets suffered major setbacks and American space achievements eclipsed Soviet ones. Soon, fascination with space exploration assumed a wistful flavor, and cosmic enthusiasm became mired in nostalgia for the future rather than an aspiration for it.[9]

The spectacular Soviet successes in space, particularly *Sputnik*, became calcified in a story of statist initiative even though the state's central institution for scientific research, the Academy of Sciences, played only a minor role in the genesis of *Sputnik*. Through the NEP and early Stalin eras, the academy ignored the vibrant space activism and contributed little to the burgeoning rocketry efforts of the 1930s. Leading space theorists such as Konstantin Tsiolkovskii were denied access to the academy, partly because many of them had no higher education. The postwar move to canonize Russian scientists prompted the academy to substitute its indifference to Tsiolkovskii with a vigorous campaign to claim him as a great scientist. Space activists, now working deep within the defense industry, used the campaign skillfully to legitimize the idea of spaceflight in the eyes of the academy. The success of their efforts contributed in large part to the academy's creation of a forum to discuss space exploration in 1954, thirty years after students

[7] The Military-Industrial Commission was formed on December 6, 1957. RGAE, 4372/76/320/33–38 (December 6, 1957).

[8] Dale Carter, *The Final Frontier: The Rise and Fall of the American Rocket State* (London: Verso, 1988).

[9] For nostalgia and the Soviet space program, see Svetlana Boym, "Kosmos: Remembrances of the Future," in Adam Bartos, *Kosmos: A Portrait of the Russian Space Age* (New York: Princeton Architectural Press, 2001), 83–97.

and space activists had done so in their amateur societies. In both cases, Konstantin Tsiolkovskii served as the central touchstone for inspiration and activism.

At various points in the preamble to *Sputnik*, Soviet citizens – some ordinary, some powerful, and some neither – used informal social networks as important vehicles to advance the cause of rocketry and space exploration. These social networks were leveraged on state infrastructure but operated often independently of state mandates or resources. Beyond popularizing the idea of spaceflight among the urban reading public – a not insignificant accomplishment – such networks achieved other significant goals that contributed to the reality of spaceflight in the Soviet Union. During the NEP era, for example, informal networks successfully linked the utopian notion of space exploration with science and, by consequence, with "being modern." An explosion of artistic exuberance, some rooted in occult ideas about the cosmos, was fundamental in energizing these communities and their visions of the future. These networks allowed the first amateur spaceflight societies to organize; later, in the 1930s, they served as the foundation for the first amateur research and development groups to study reactive motion. The informal space activist network disintegrated by the onset of World War II, but a new network reconstituted in Soviet-occupied Germany. Here, away from the center, aviation designers, military artillery officers, and industrial managers formed important connections – both weak and strong – for exchanging information, engendering innovation, and generating influence on top decision-makers back in Moscow.[10]

Another informal network in the postwar era exemplified the way in which designers working in the secret military-industrial complex were able to establish connections with those on the "outside" to create a community that could collectively affect state policy on the possibility of space exploration. One of the rationales for forming this alliance was the inability of missile designers to speak publicly like their nuclear and aviation counterparts, who, as David Holloway notes, possessed "unprecedented authority among the political leaders."[11] In 1956, for example, on a visit to Britain, Nikita Khrushchev introduced to Winston Churchill, "Academician Kurchatov who makes our hydrogen bomb" and "Academician Tupolev... who produces the plane that delivers it."[12] Because the rocket designers did not enjoy such status in the early 1950s, they were unable to disseminate directly to the public their views on the future of space travel. Instead, using informal social connections, now including a new generation of younger activists working in semigovernmental voluntary societies, they sustained a

[10] I draw on some of the work of Mark S. Granovetter and his claim about the resilience of "weak" connections in networks. "The Strength of Weak Ties," *American Journal of Sociology* 78 no. 6 (1973): 1360–1380.

[11] Holloway, *Stalin and the Bomb*, 366.

[12] Holloway, *Stalin and the Bomb*, 360.

vibrant and informative discussion in the Soviet media on the merits of space travel. Like its predecessors in the 1920s, the networks of space activists in the 1950s promoted a technologically utopian view of space exploration, thus inculcating a generation of Soviet citizens that space exploration was both an inevitability and a necessity.

Foreign factors played an important role in the realization of the project of spaceflight. At its very origins, in the late nineteenth century, Frenchman Jules Verne's works inspired Tsiolkovskii to pursue the idea of using rockets to explore space. From the emergence of Tsiolkovskii's first theories to the realization of *Sputnik*, foreign factors manifested themselves in four broad patterns: popular international discourses, intelligence information, intellectual reparations, and material technology.

Popular international discourses played out through the nodes and pathways of the informal networks that existed in the 1920s and 1950s. One of important contributions to the international conversation was news of foreign work – such as by Oberth and Goddard – that catalyzed the first generation of interest on the topic in Russia. Bolstered by the vibrancy of the international network centered around Tsiolkovskii, Perel'man and Rynin the space fad grew as a truly international exchange of ideas that often generated substantive debate on the technical options available for building rockets and spaceships of the future. The NEP era's popular scientific media played an enormous role in fostering this conversation. International exchanges significantly impacted events later, in the 1950s. By generating enough "noise" in the Soviet media, the secret missile designers were able to communicate to both the Soviet public and the American media about their intentions. The publicity had unintended consequences by contributing to the American government's plans to build a satellite. In turn, Soviet missile designers used the publicity over the American project to justify their own proposal for a Soviet satellite, which they sent to the government. The specter of international competition provided the critical necessary ingredient for the Soviet government to approve a satellite project in the summer of 1955.

A comparison with the Soviet physics community that built the atomic bomb highlights some differences with the rocket and space activists. In his study, Holloway concludes that the physicists in the 1930s "were part of an international community, competing with research groups in other countries to make discoveries and win recognition for their work."[13] Soviet space enthusiasts acted in the same manner in the 1920s, competing and cooperating with their foreign counterparts, but diverged in important ways. The "science" that space activists produced was equal parts amateurish science and groundbreaking research. Without the formal standards of an academic community, such as refereed journals and conferences, spaceflight enthusiasts produced a mixed bag of work that they circulated by informal means.

[13] Holloway, *Stalin and the Bomb*, 364.

The ultimately questionable quality of the science does not, however, diminish the community's commitment to exchanging information and advancing the cause of spaceflight. This space research community was the true parallel to the physics community of Kurchatov and Kapitsa, who frequented Oxford and Cambridge in the 1930s, for it produced the basic theoretical contributions that led to *Sputnik* in 1957.

Intelligence information from spies abroad in the 1930s served much the same function as the international discourse did in the 1920s. Several factors accounted for the evolution from open exchanges to covert spying, including the national Soviet turn to cut off contacts with outside, the progressively "closed" nature of rocketry research in both Germany and the United States, and the relocation of the original space advocacy community into a secret institute dedicated to military rockets. In the early 1930s, the Soviet military used secretly obtained information about foreign work on rocketry to initiate and then justify its own funding of similar research. By the end of the decade, intelligence information began to dry up. What little that arrived did not alter established government priorities for deemphasizing the development of liquid-propellant rockets in favor of low-tech solid-propellant ones. I show, in particular, how the Great Terror was much less important in affecting Soviet work on rocketry than previously assumed; instead, the onset of war had a more profound impact on this research.

The most tangible foreign influence on the Soviet rocketry and space program was the appropriation of German expertise and technology at the end of the war. German scientists and technicians who worked as part of the informal, flexible, and dynamic network in Soviet-occupied Germany contributed to studying and reconstructing the operations of the wartime technological system that produced German missiles. Similarly, German rocket technology served as the foundation of the Soviet postwar missile program. With the help of German reparations, the Soviet design team led by Sergei Korolev successfully reproduced the V-2 but then quickly outgrew the German roots. In rapid succession, Korolev's team developed missiles that owed more to indigenous technology than to the German lineage, finally producing the R-7 ICBM, which launched *Sputnik* into orbit. This missile was a mélange of streams of innovation, comprising the work of Tsiolkovskii in the 1920s, German wartime V-2 technology, advances produced by Soviet designers in the 1940s and 1950s, and, finally, the genius of Soviet managers and designers of the 1950s.

These three dimensions of the prehistory of *Sputnik* – the relationship between the state and the project of spaceflight, the action of informal scientific networks, and the influence of foreign factors – raise some broader concerns about the history of science and technology in twentieth-century Russia.

The accepted notion that Soviet science was essentially state science merits rethinking. In one of the most visible and known projects of Soviet science, the creation of *Sputnik*, those outside the formal levers of state power, connected by social networks, contributed the most. Recasting the origins of the Soviet space program as a mix of both science inside and outside the state apparatus contrasts strikingly with the received wisdom about its origins as a wholly state-subsidized project from 1917. The evidence of rich activity of space activists in Soviet civil society in both the early 1930s and the early 1950s counters the largely unquestioned axiom of Stalinist science as a monolithic social reality that disallowed local initiative. Such conclusions suggests that other areas of Soviet science – especially fields of applied "big science and technology" like the development of the atomic bomb, aeronautics, and computing – merit reassessment, particularly the ways in which the work of elite scientific and technical communities intersected with the popular advocacy for (or resistance to) these science and technologies.

Mass enthusiasm and public support was necessary for the Soviet Union to break through to the cosmos. This is perhaps the most striking conclusion of this project, especially given that most of the events described occurred during Stalin's time. Public advocacy took specific forms that mixed utopian aspirations with practical considerations, a strategy that also held wide resonance in the United States. In his groundbreaking study *Space and the American Imagination*, Howard McCurdy noted that "[t]he ability of policy advocates to advance their agendas [of space exploration in the United States] depend[ed] to a considerable extent upon their skill at constructing models that [were] familiar, easy to understand, and desirable."[14] In the Soviet quest to breach the boundaries of the cosmos, utopian proponents invoked two familiar and easily understood ideas. The first appealed to the future, specifically the power of modern technology to remake the universe around us. The second appealed to the past, in particular to the hallowed ghost of the patron saint of cosmonautics, Konstantin Tsiolkovskii. This synthesis of the past and the future is also characteristic of other utopians, who often romanticize a past that never existed and hope for a future that never will. The cosmic utopians were particularly effective in their fusion of past with future, and of imagination with engineering.

Tsiolkovskii's role in the birth of the Soviet space program cannot be overstated. Both during his life and after, he served an important inspirational role, as a mandatory rite of passage for those imagining utopia and those doing engineering. Already during his life, space enthusiasts deployed pseudo-religious lexicon to describe their engagement with the old man: He was a "patriarch" to his "followers," who were required to make "pilgrimages" to Kaluga. After his death, Tsiolkovskii loomed like a ghost over each painful step towards the cosmos, appearing in Korolev's letters from the

[14] Howard E. McCurdy, *Space and the American Imagination* (Washington, DC: Smithsonian Institution Press, 1997), 6.

Gulag, in nationalist campaigns in the late Stalin years, and in the centennial celebrations in the preamble to *Sputnik*. Like the Soviet space program, he embodied all its contradictions. The mythology of his life became as important as his material accomplishments; they rarely coincided but frequently fed each other and, like imagination and engineering, eventually became indistinguishable.

The connection between thought and action maps onto other dichotomies. In his book *Preserving the Self in the South Seas, 1680–1840* on sea voyagers who mapped the South Pacific, Jonathan Lamb suggested that utopia is something that cannot be seen or categorized properly because distinctions and language fall apart the more we consider the notion.[15] So it was with the utopia of space exploration. At different times activists invoked different rationales on the continuum from reason to faith, often conflating utopia with reality, and reason with faith.

That this dichotomy existed within a unified whole was perhaps expressed best by Tsiolkovskii himself in one of his most oft-repeated phrases, which he used in an article published in 1911 and which Westerners have quoted endlessly. It is almost always translated as "The earth is the cradle of humanity, but one cannot forever live in the cradle."[16] The original Russian word *razum*, however, translates not only as "humanity," but also as the "human mind" and most literally as "reason." The latter conveys an entirely different and darker motif:

> The Earth is the cradle of reason, but one cannot forever live in the cradle.[17]

Tsiolkovskii was, in effect, saying that we must fully abandon reason in order to explore the cosmos. Those who carried his torch to the end proved him at least partly correct. Through four decades of activism, space enthusiasts had to merge the hard and cold realities of Soviet life with an often inexplicable and irrational urge to leave the Earth. When *Sputnik* finally reached the heavens, it encapsulated not only mathematics and reason but also utopia and yearning, and most important, hope for a new era that would forever separate those who came before from those who came after.

[15] Jonathan Lamb, *Preserving the Self in the South Seas, 1680–1840* (Chicago: University of Chicago Press, 2001).

[16] William Shelton, *Soviet Space Exploration: The First Decade* (New York: Washington Square Press, 1968), 12–13; Roger D. Launius, *Space Stations: Base Camps to the Stars* (Washington, DC: Smithsonian Books, 2003), 9.

[17] K. Tsiolkovskii, "Issledovanie mirovykh prostranstv reaktivnymi priborami (1911–1912 gg.)," in *Izbrannye trudy*, ed. B. N. Vorob'ev and V. N. Sokol'skii (Moscow: Nauka, 1962), 196. The original phrase was "Планета есть колыбель разума, но нельзя вечно жить в колыбели," or "*Planeta est' kolybel' razuma, no nel'zia vechno zhit' v kolybeli.*"

Notes about Abbreviations in Citations

Russian archives are typically organized according to the following convention:

fond	collection
opis'	subgroup within a collection
delo	file
list	leaf

Thus, a reference in the main text to ARAN, 555/4/10a/12–17 (January 24, 1935) refers to Archives of the Russian Academy of Sciences, *fond* 555, *opis'* 4, *delo* 10a, *listov* 12–17. The date denotes the date that the document was first authored or issued. In many cases, dates are absent in archival documents. In those cases, either the date is omitted or approximated. Occasionally, the last number (for leaves) will also have the form "450b," with "ob" standing for *obratnaia* or obverse of the main page. Some leaf numbers are in reverse (e.g., 17–12) because this is the way they appeared in the original.

I have also used abbreviations for a number of published sources. They are as follows.

AIK	*Aviatsiia i kosmonavtika* (journal).
APS	L. D. Riabev, ed., *Atomnyi proekt sssr: dokumenty i materialy, tom II: atomnaia bomba, 1945–1954, kniga 7* (Moscow: Nauka-Fizmatlit, 2007).
ASPK	A. Iu. Ishlinskii, ed., *Akademik S. P. Korolev: uchenii, inzhener, chelovek* (Moscow: Nauka, 1986).
DVK1	Iu. A. Mozzhorin et al., eds., *Dorogi v kosmos: I* (Moscow: MAI, 1992).
DVK2	Iu. A. Mozzhorin et al., eds., *Dorogi v kosmos: II* (Moscow: MAI, 1992).
IPIITR	*Issledovaniia po istorii i teorii razvitiia aviatsionnoi i raketno-kosmicheskoi nauki i tekhniki* (book in series).
IIAIK	*Iz istorii aviatsii i kosmonavtiki* (book in series).
MVKIT	V. S. Avduevskii and T. M. Eneev, eds., *M. V. Keldysh: izbrannye trudy: raketnaia tekhnika i kosmonavtika* (Moscow: Nauka, 1988).
NK	*Novosti kosmonavtiki* (journal).
NKE	Iu. A. Mozzhorin, ed., *Nachalo Kosmicheskoi ery: vospominaniia veteranov raketno-kosmicheskoi tekhniki i kosmonavtiki, vyp. 2* (Moscow: RNITsKD, 1994).
OIN	V. F. Rakhmanin and L. E. Sterpin, eds., *Odnazhny i navsegda...: dokumenty i liudi o sozdatele raketnykh dvigatelei i kosmicheskikh system akademike Valentine Petroviche Glushko* (Moscow: Mashinostroenie, 1998).
RAP1	Boris Chertok, *Rockets and People, Vol. I*, ed. Asif A. Siddiqi (Washington, DC: NASA, 2006).
RAP2	Boris Chertok, *Rockets and People, Vol. II: Creating a Rocket Industry*, ed. Asif A. Siddiqi (Washington, DC: NASA, 2007).
RKKE	Iu. P. Semenov, ed., *Raketno-kosmicheskaia korporatsiia 'Energiia' imeni S. P. Koroleva* (Korolev, Russia: RKK Energiia, 1996).

TNASPK	M. V. Keldysh, ed., *Tvorcheskoye naslediye akademika Sergeya Pavlovicha Koroleva* (Moscow: Nauka, 1980).
SKI	Iu. M. Baturin, ed., *Sovetskaia kosmicheskaia initsiativa v gosudarstvennykh dokumentakh, 1946–1964 gg.* (Moscow: RTSoft, 2008).
SPKIED	B. V. Raushenbakh and G. S. Vetrov, eds., *S. P. Korolev i ego delo: svet i teni v istorii kosmonavtiki: izbrannye trudy i dokumenty* (Moscow: Nauka, 1998).
Bystrova, VPK	I. V. Bystrova, *Voenno-promyshlennyi kompleks sssr v gody kholodnoi voiny* (Moscow: IRI RAN, 2000).
Simonov, VPK	N. S. Simonov, *Voenno-promyshlennyi kompleks SSSR v 1920–1950-e gody: tempy ekonomicheskogo rosta, struktura, organizatsiia proizvodstva i upravlenie* (Moscow: Rosspen, 1996).

List of Abbreviations in the Main Text

AIIZ	*Assotsiatsiia izobretatelei-izobretateliam* [Association of Inventors to Inventors, or Association of Inventors]
Aviakhim	*Obshchestvo sodeistviia aviatsii i khimicheskoi oborone* [Society of Friends of Aviation-Chemical Defense]
AviaVNITO	*Aviatsionnoe otdelenie Vsesoiuznogo nauchno-tekhnicheskogo obshchestva* [Aviation Department of the All-Union Scientific-Technical Society]
BICh	*Biuro imeni Cheranovskogo* [Bureau named after Cheranovskii]
Cheka	*Chrezvychainaia komissiia po bor'be s kontrrevoliutsiei i sabotazhem* [Extraordinary Commission for the Struggle with Counterrevolution and Sabotage]
ChK	see *Cheka*
CIA	Central Intelligence Agency
DOSAAF	*Dobrovol'noe obshchestvo sodeistviia armii, aviatsii i flotu* [Voluntary Society for Assistance to the Army, Aviation, and Navy]
GDL	*Gasdinamicheskaia laboratoriia* [Gas Dynamics Laboratory]
GIRD	*Gruppa izucheniia reaktivnogo dvizheniia* [Group for the Study of Reactive Motion]
GKO	see GOKO
Glavnauka	*Glavnoe upravlenie nauchnykh, muzeinykh i nauchno-khudozhestvennykh uchrezhdenii* [Main Directorate of Scientific, Museum, and Scientific-Artistic Organizations]
GOKO (or GKO)	*Gosudarstvennye komitet oborony* [State Committee of Defense]
Gostekhizdat	*Gosudarstvennoe tekhnicheskoe izdatel'stvo* [State Technical Publishing House]
GAU	*Glavnoe artilleriiskoi upravlenie* [Main Artillery Directorate]
GMCh	*Gvardeiskie minometnye chasti* [Guards Mortar Units]
Gosplan	*Gosudarstvennaia planovaia komissiia* [State Planning Commission]
GTsKB	*Gosudarstvennoe tsentral'noe konstruktorskoe biuro* [State Central Design Bureau]
Guberniia	province
Gubsovnarkhoz	*Gubernskii sovet narodnogo khoziaistva* [*Guberniia* Council of the People's Economy]
GULAG	*Glavnoe upravlenie lagerei* [Main Directorate of Camps]
IAM	*Institut aviatsionnogo motorostroeniia* [Institute of Aviation Motor Building]

IGY	International Geophysical Year
ICBM	intercontinental ballistic missile
ISZ	*isskustvennyi sputnik zemli* [artificial Earth satellite]
KB	*konstruktorskoe biuro* [design bureau]
Malyi sovnarkom	*Malyi sovet narodnykh komissarov* [Small *Sovnarkom*]
MIAN	*Matematicheskii institut Akademii nauk* [Mathematical Institute of the Academy of Sciences]
Minsredmash	*Ministerstvo srednego mashinostroeniia* [Ministry of Medium Machine Building]
MOLA	*Moskovskoe obshchestvo liubitelei astronomi* [Moscow Society of Astronomy Enthusiasts]
Narkomaviaprom	see NKAP
Narkomboepripasov	see NKB
Narkomoboronprom	*Narodnyi komissariat oboronoi promyshlennosti* [People's Commissariat of Defense Industry]
Narkompros	*Narodnyi komissariat prosveshcheniia* [People's Commissariat of Enlightenment]
Narkomtiazhprom	*Narodnyi komissariat tiazheloi promyshlennosti* [People's Commissariat of Heavy Industry]
NEP	*Novaia ekonomicheskaia politika* [New Economic Policy]
NII	*nauchno-issledovatel'skii institut* [Scientific-Research Institute]
NKAP	*Narodnyi kommissariat aviatsionnoi promyshlennosti* [People's Commissariat of the Aviation Industry]
NKB	*Narodnyi komissariat boepripasov* [People's Commissariat of Munitions]
NKTP	see *Narkomtiazhprom*
NKVD	*Narodnyi komissariat vnutrennikh del* [People's Commissariat of Internal Affairs]
NSC	National Security Council
NTO	*Nauchno-tekhnicheskii otdel* [Scientific-Technical Department]
ODVF	*Obshchestva druzei vozdushnogo flota* [Society of Friends of the Air Fleet]
OGPU	*Ob'edinennoe glavnoe politicheskoe upravlenie* [Unified Main Political Directorate]
OIMS	*Obshchestva izucheniia mezhplanetnykh soobshchenii* [Society for the Study of Interplanetary Communications]
OKB	*opytno-konstruktorskogo biuro* [Experimental-Design Bureau]
OSO	*Obshchestvo sodeistviia oborone* [Society for Assistance to Defense]
Osoaviakhim	*Obshchestvo sodeistviia oborone i aviatsionno-khimicheskomu stroitel'stvu sssr* [Society for Assistance to Defense and Aviation-Chemical Construction of the USSR]
OST	*Obshchestvo khudozhnikov-stankovistov* [Society of Easel Painters]
Ostekhbiuro	*Osoboe tekhnicheskoe biuro po voennym izobreteniiam spetsial'nogo naznacheniia* [Special Technical Bureau for Special Purpose Military Inventions]
OTB	*Osoboe tekhnicheskoe biuro* [Special Technical Bureau]
OTK	*otdel tekhnicheskogo kontrolia* [Department of Technical Control]
partkom	party committee
PS	*Prosteishyi sputnik* [Simplest Satellite]
raikom	*raikom raionnyi komitet* [district committee]
RKKA	*Raboche-krest'ianskaia Krasnaia Armiia* [Workers' and Peasants Red Army or Red Army]

RNII	*Reaktivnii nauchno-issledovatel'skii institut* [Reactive Scientific-Research Institute]
ROLM	*Russkoe obshchestvo liubitelei mirovedeniia* [Russian Society of Enthusiasts for the Study of the Universe]
SNK	see *Sovnarkom*
Sovnarkom	*Sovet narodnykh komissarov* [Council of People's Commissars]
STO	*Sovet truda i oborony* [Council of Labor and Defense]
SVAG	*Sovetskoi voennoi administratsii v Germanii* [Soviet Military Administration in Germany]
TCP	Technological Capabilities Panel
TsAGI	*Tsentral'nii aerogidrodinamicheskii institut* [Central Aerohydrodynamics Institute]
TsIAM	*Tsentral'nii institut aviatsionnogo motorostroeniia* [Central Institute of Aviation Motor Building]
UVI	*Upravlenie voennykh izobretenii* [Directorate of Military Inventions]
VARNITSO	*Vsesoiuznaia assotsiatsiia rabotnikov nauki i tekhniki dlia sodeistviia sotsialisticheskomu stroitel'stvu* [All-Union Association of Workers in Science and Technology for Cooperation in Socialist Construction]
Vesenkha	*Vysshii sovet narodnogo khoziaistva, VSNKh* [Supreme Council of the National Economy]
VKP(b)	*Vsesoiuznaia kommunisticheskaia partiia (bol'shevikov)* [All-Union Communist Party (Bol'sheviks)]
VNO	*Voenno-nauchnoe obshchestvo* [Military-Scientific Society]
VSNKh	see *Vesenkha*
VTsIK	*Vserossiiskii tsentral'nyi ispolnitel'nyi komitet* [All-Russian Central Executive Committee]
ZhRD	*Zhidkostnyi reaktivnyi dvizhenie* [liquid (propellant) reactive engine]

Notes on Usage

All Russian names appearing in the text have been transliterated from Cyrillic into the Latin alphabet of modern English by using the Library of Congress system. When referring to secondary sources in the footnotes, the spellings used in these sources (e.g., *Tsiolkovsky*) have been retained even if they were not in the Library of Congress system (i.e., *Tsiolkovskii*).

A Note on Primary Sources

For historians studying the Soviet space program, limited access to primary sources has always been an impediment. Such restrictions were significantly loosened when, in the immediate postsocialist years, many state archives made large collections of documents available for public use. For those interested in the roots of Soviet cosmonautics, the most important archival resource is the Archive of the Russian Academy of Sciences (ARAN) in Moscow. ARAN holds (in *fond* 555) a vast majority of the papers of K. E. Tsiolkovskii, making it an indispensable stop for scholars delving into the early history of Soviet cosmic enthusiasm. These papers include not only all of his own works, much of it unpublished, but also his massive corpus of correspondence with enthusiasts across the world. The Academy archive also holds a vast collection of materials from numerous space activist groups operating in the pre-1945 era (held in the *razriad* 4 collection). These include many documents from both GIRD and RNII, the two major rocket development organizations active in the 1930s, as well as the very early enthusiast societies of the 1920s. ARAN stores much evidence of popular Soviet interest in the cosmos, in the form of newspaper and journal articles and monographs from the early twentieth century, including the papers of Ia. I. Perel'man, the indefatigable popularizer of cosmonautics whose documents are stored (in *fond* 796) in the St. Petersburg branch of ARAN.

As Soviet rocketry development became intertwined with state and specifically military concerns, ARAN's documents become less useful. For state imperatives, scholars need to explore the Russian State Military Archive (RGVA), which houses documents dealing with the tumultuous work of the RNII in the 1930s, many of which shed light on the deadly repercussions of the Great Terror. Here, one will also find many documents related to M. N. Tukhachevskii's sponsorship of rocketry work in the early 1930s, including the work at GDL in Leningrad.

As RGVA's collection is limited only to 1941, for wartime and postwar developments involving rockets, one needs to make use of the Russian State Archive of the Economy (RGAE), which houses documents at the ministerial levels on all aspects of Soviet industry. Here, one will find large numbers of documents from the two ministries, aviation and armaments, that closely directed rocket development during the war and the early Cold War years. These documents are in *fond* 8044 and *fond* 8157, respectively. State policy on missile development can be discerned also by closely following the planning documents of *Gosplan*, which are housed in *fond* 4372. Researchers should be aware that all of the documents related to the Soviet defense industry are not housed at the main RGAE complex at ul. Bol'shaia pirogovskaia but rather at a nondescript branch located in a building at an entirely different location at ul. Profsoiuznaia. This building also houses the Russian State Archive of Scientific-Technical Documentation (RGANTD), which technically purports to be the singular archive on the history of the Soviet space program. As those who have worked there have no doubt found, access to documents at RGANTD is notoriously limited, and it requires the explicit permission of the original owner of the documents, which in many cases is impossible to obtain. The holdings of RGANTD are, however, useful for their undeniably vast and rich collection of imagery associated with the entire vista of the Soviet space program.

I also consulted documents from other archives, including the State Archive of the Russian Federation (GARF) and the Archive of the President of the Russian Federation (APRF). Access to documents is severely restricted at the latter, but this facility houses the original ministerial decrees related to all postwar missile and space programs. I was fortunate to get access to a few documents here through intermediaries. Finally, I used supplementary documents on Tsiolkovskii's life from the K. E. Tsiolkovskii State Museum on the History of Cosmonautics based in Kaluga.

The long sections of the book dealing with popular enthusiasm for cosmonautics, both in the 1920s and the 1950s, were based on extensive research on published Soviet materials, most of which I located either at the Library of Congress in Washington, DC or at Widener Library at Harvard University. These publications are listed in the bibliography of primary sources. Many of Tsiolkovskii's most rare early works are stored in the archives of the Smithsonian's National Air & Space Museum in Washington, DC. A most useful English-language collection of Soviet media pieces on space exploration, *Behind the Sputniks: A Survey of Soviet Space Science* (1958), was an important touchstone for reconstructing the nature of cosmic enthusiasm in the Soviet Union in the 1950s. Wherever I could, I interspersed information from interviews and personal papers to deepen the understanding afforded by records issued directly by state organs.

One of the advantages of scholarship on this topic has been the availability of a plethora of published collections of primary documents. Although one must exercise the obvious prudence in the use of published documents – particularly, the problem of selection bias – these volumes are excellent starting points for the study of the Soviet space program. The most important in this regard include *Sovetskaia kosmicheskaia initsiativa v gosudarstvennykh dokumentakh, 1946–1964 gg.* (*The Soviet Space Initiative in Government Documents, 1946–1964*), which includes many declassified documents from APRF, *S. P. Korolev i ego delo: svet i teni v istorii kosmonavtiki: izbrannye trudy i dokumenty* (*S. P. Korolev and His Affairs: Light and Shadow in the History of Cosmonautics: Selected Works and Documents*), an absolutely indispensable collection of documents on the early history of the Soviet space program, *Put' v raketnoi tekhniki: izbrannye trudy, 1924–1946* (*Path to Rocket Technology: Selected Works, 1924–1946*), on the works of Glushko, *K. E. Tsiolkovskii: Genii sredi liudi* (*K. E. Tsiolkovskii: Genius Among the Masses*), which collects most of Tsiolkovskii's philosophical works, *Tvorcheskoe nasledie Akademika Sergeya Pavlovicha Koroleva: izbrannye trudy i dokumenty* (*The Creative Legacy of Sergei Pavlovich Korolev: Selected Works and Documents*), a pre-*glasnost'* volume that has held up remarkably well, *M. V. Keldysh: Izbrannye trudy: raketnaia tekhnika i kosmonavtika* (*M. V. Keldysh: Selected Works: Rocket Technology and Cosmonautics*), which has important documents on early ICBM development, *Pionery raketnoi tekhniki: Vetchinkin Glushko Korolev Tikhonravov: izbrannye trudy (1929–1945)* (*Pioneers of Rocket Technology: Vetchinkin Glushko Korolev Tikhonravov: Selected Works*), which contains many documents on the early years, and *Sobranie sochinenii: t. 2, reaktivnye letatel'nye apparatury* (*Collected Works: Vol. 2, Reactive Flying Vehicles*), which includes most of Tsiolkovskii's technical works on rockets.

Two further works on Tsiolkovskii are worth mentioning. The first, *Rukopisnye materialy K. E. Tsiolkovskogo* (*Manuscripts on K. E. Tsiolkovskii*) is somewhat dated but still useful as a detailed listing of the holdings of the Tsiolkovskii collection in the Archive of the Russian Academy of Sciences. The second, *Konstantin Eduardovich Tsiolkovskii (1857–1935): bibliograficheskii ukazatel'* (*Konstantin Eduardovich Tsiolkovskii (1857–1935): Bibliographic Guide*), is an extremely handy annotated bibliography of all published works by and about Tsiolkovskii published until 1983.

Since the late 1990s, the Russian publishing house Rosspen has issued a number of useful collections of documents that touch upon disparate dimensions of Soviet history. Most useful for this project were *Politbiuro tsk vkp(b) i sovet ministrov sssr 1945–1953* (*Politburo of the CC of the CPSU and USSR Council of Ministers, 1945–1953*), *Prezidium TsK KPSS, 1954–1964,*

T. 1 (*Presidium of the CC of the CPSU, 1954–1964, Vol. 1*), and *Poslevoennaia konversiia: k istorii 'kholodnoi voiny': sbornik dokumentov* (*Postwar Conversion: On the History of the Cold War: A Collection of Documents*). Perhaps the most important series of volumes focused on Soviet security in the Cold War era have been the ongoing series of volumes entitled *Atomnyi proekt sssr: dokumenty i materialy* (*The USSR Atom Project: Documents and Materials*). So far, at least nine volumes have been published, containing thousands of documents declassified from the Archive of the President of the Russian Federation. Book 7 of Volume 2, published in 2007, proved especially useful as it detailed the intricate institutional changes in the missile program during the early 1950s during a critical period of ICBM development.

The vast list of published memoirs should also not be ignored. Absolutely essential are Boris Chertok's four-volume memoirs, published between 1994 and 1999, under the general title *Rakety i liudi* (*Rockets and People*). These are now being published in English in significantly updated form by the NASA History Division. Three collections of recollections are essential: the three-volume *Dorogi v kosmos* (*Roads to Space*), published in 1992 and 1994, and *Akademik S. P. Korolev: uchenii, inzhener, chelovek* (*Academician S. P. Korolev: Scientist, Engineer, Man*), published in 1986. These priceless volumes were compiled by conscientious Russian archivists who transcribed lengthy interviews with many key participants of the Soviet space program, most of whom are no longer living. A similar volume, *V vospominaniiakh sovremennikov* (*In the Recollections of Contemporaries*), proved equally useful in understanding the popular perception of Tsiolkovskii during his lifetime.

Archival Sources

Archives of the Russian Academy of Sciences (Arkhiv rossiiskoi akademii nauk, *ARAN*)

fond 2	papers of the Presidium of the Academy of Sciences
razriad 4, *opis'* 14	files on pre-1945 rocketry
fond 472	papers of the Astronomy Council of the Academy
fond 555	papers of K. E. Tsiolkovskii
fond 573	papers of F. A. Tsander
fond 1546	papers of S. P. Korolev

Memorial House-Museum of Academician S. P. Korolev (Memorial'nyi dom-muzei akademika S. P. Koroleva, *MDMK*)

Russian Military-State Archive (Rossiiskii gosudarstvennyi voennyi arkhiv, *RGVA*)

fond 4	Affairs Directorate of *Narkomvoenmor*
fond 29	Directorate of the Air Force
fond 34272	

Russian State Archive of Sociopolitical History (Rossiiskii gosudarstvennyi arkhiv sotsial'no-politicheskoi istorii, *RGASPI*)

fond 17	documents of departments of TsK VKP(b), 1920–1939
fond 74	papers of Voroshilov
fond 85	papers of Ordzhonikidze
fond 644	documents of GOKO

Russian State Archive of the Economy (Rossiiskii gosudarstvennyi arkhiv ekonomiki, *RGAE*)

fond 397	documents of seventh GU of *Minvooruzhenie*
fond 4372	documents of *Gosplan*

fond 7297	documents of *Narkomtiazhprom*
fond 7515	documents of *Narkomoboronprom*
fond 7516	documents of *Narkomboepripasov*
fond 8044	documents of *Minaviaprom*
fond 8157	documents of *Minvooruzhenie* and *Minoboronprom*
fond 8159	documents of *Narkomtiazhprom*
fond 8162	documents of *Narkomoboronprom*

State Archive of the Kaluga Region (Gosudarstvennyi arkhiv kaluzhskoy oblast, _GAKO_)

fondi R-112 and R-156	various topics

State Archive of the Russian Federation (Gosudarstvennyi arkhiv Rossiiskoi Federatsii, _GARF_)

fond R-130	documents of Council of RSFSR People's Commissars
fond 3316	documents of USSR Central Executive Committee
fond 3415	documents of Communist Academy of the TsIK SSSR
fond 8355	documents of *Osoaviakhim*
fond 8418	documents of Defense Committee of *Sovnarkom* SSSR

Central Archive of the Ministry of Defense of the Russian Federation (Tsentral'nyi arkhiv Ministerstva oborony Rossiiskoi Federatskii, _TsAMO RF_)

fondi 35 and 345	various topics

Archive of the President of the Russian Federation (Arkhiv presidenta Rossiiskoi Federatsii, _APRF_)

fond 3, op. 47, *delo* 179 and 272	documents on missile and space programs

United States Archival Sources

NASA History Division Archives, NASA Headquarters, Washington, DC
National Air & Space Museum Archives, Smithsonian Institution, Washington, DC
National Archives, College Park, MD
Robert H. Goddard Papers, Clark University, Worcester, MA

Personal Papers

James Harford, Princeton, NJ
Mikhail Tikhonravov, notes from diary

Books in Series

History of Rocketry and Astronautics (1977–)
Issledovaniia po istorii i teorii razvitiia aviatsionnoi i raketno-kosmicheskoi nauki i tekhniki (1981–)
Trudy chtenii, posviashchennykh razrabotke nauchnogo naslediia i razvitiiu idei K. E. Tsiolkovskogo (1967–)
Zagadki zvezdnykh ostrovov (1982–)

Published Primary Sources

Anisimov, N. L., and V. G. Oppokov, "Proisshestvie v NII-3," *Voenno-istoricheskii zhurnal* no. 10 (1989): 81–87 and no. 11 (1989): 65–71.

Armand, A. A., *Nauchno-issledovatel'skie instituty tiazheloi promyshlennosti* (Moscow: ONTI, 1935).

Avduevskii, V. S., ed., *K. E. Tsiolkovskii: kosmicheskaia filosofiia* (Moscow: URSS, 2001).

Bashilova, E. Iu., "Iz Nordkhauzena – v Podlipki," *Istoricheskii arkhiv* no. 6 (2001): 79–96.

Baturin, Iu. M., ed., *Sovetskaia kosmicheskaia initsiativa v gosudarstvennykh dokumentakh, 1946–1964 gg.* (Moscow: RTSoft, 2008).

Bazhinov, I., "O rabotakh M. K. Tikhonravova po sostavnym raketam i iskusstvennym sputnikam zemli v 1946–1956 gg.," *Novosti kosmonavtiki* no. 8 (2003): 68–71.

Bazhinov, I. K., and G. Iu. Maksimov, "Ob issledovaniiakh vozmozhnostei sozdaniia v sssr pervykh moshchnykh sostavnykh raket i iskusstvennykh sputnikov zemli," in *Issledovaniia po istorii i teorii razvitiia aviatsionnoi i raketno-kosmicheskoi nauki i tekhniki*, Vol. 7, eds. B. V. Raushenbakh et al. (Moscow: Nauka, 1989), 13–25.

Biriukov, Iu. V., ed., *Materialy po istorii kosmicheskogo korablya 'vostok': k 30-letiiu pervogo poleta cheloveka v kosmicheskoe prostranstvo* (Moscow: Nauka, 1991).

Bogdanov, Alexander, *Red Star: The First Bolshevik Utopia*, eds. Loren R. Graham and Richard Stites (Bloomington: Indiana University Press, 1979).

———, *Krasnaia zvezda: roman-utopiia* (St. Petersburg: Tvorchestvo khudozhestvennoi pechati, 1908).

Budnik, V. S., *Ot shturmovikov Il-2 do kosmicheskikh raket: vospominaniia* (Dnepropetrovsk: Vidavnitstvo DDU, 1993).

Brykov, A. V., *U kosmosa v plenu* (Moscow: TsPT MIA, 2000).

———, *Piat'desiat let v kosmicheskoi ballistike* (Moscow: SIP RIA, 2002).

Central Intelligence Agency (CIA), National Intelligence Estimate Number 11–6–54: *Soviet Capabilities and Probable Programs in the Guided Missile Field* (October 5, 1954).

———, National Intelligence Estimate Number 11–12–55: *Soviet Guided Missile Capabilities and Probable Programs* (December 20, 1955).

———, National Intelligence Estimate Number 11–5–57: *Soviet Capabilities and Probable Programs in the Guided Missile Field* (March 12, 1957).

———, Special National Intelligence Estimate Number 11–8–57: *Evaluation of Evidence Concerning Soviet ICBM Flight Tests* (September 18, 1957).

———, National Intelligence Estimate Number 11–10–57: *The Soviet ICBM Program* (December 10, 1957).

———, Office of Scientific Intelligence. Scientific Intelligence Research Aid OSI-C-RA/60–2. *Scientific Research Institute and Experimental Factory 88 for Guided Missile Development, Moskva/Kaliningrad* (March 4, 1960).

———, U.S. Guided Missiles Working Group. *A Summary of Soviet Guided Missile Intelligence*. US/UK GM 4–52 (July 20, 1953).

Chertok, Boris, *Rockets and People*, Vol. I, ed. Asif A. Siddiqi (Washington, DC: NASA History Office, 2005).

———, *Rockets and People, Vol. II: Creating a Rocket Industry*, ed. Asif A. Siddiqi (Washington, DC: NASA History Division, 2006).

Diadin, G. V., D. N. Filippovykh, and V. I. Ivkin, *Pamiatnye starty* (Moscow: TsIPK, 2001).

Fursenko, A. A., ed., *Prezidium TsK KPSS, 1954–1964, T. 1* (Moscow: Rosspen, 2003).

Gacheva, A. G., and S. G. Semenova, eds., *N. F. Fedorov: sobranie sochinenii v chetyrekh tomakh* (4 vols. plus a fifth supplement) (Moscow: Progress and Traditsiia, 1995–2000).

Glushko, V. P., *Put' v raketnoi tekhniki: izbrannye trudy, 1924–1946* (Moscow: Mashinostroenie, 1977).

Goddard, Esther C., and G. Edward Pendray, eds., *The Papers of Robert H. Goddard, Volume I: 1898–1924* (New York: McGraw-Hill, 1970).

Golovanova, L. V., *K. E. Tsiolkovskii: Genii sredi liudi* (Moscow: Mysl', 2002).
Iatsunskii, I. M., "Obosnovanie M. K. Tikhonravovym idei mnogostupenchatoi rakety skhemy (k 30-letiiu doklada M. K. Tikhonravova)," *Iz istorii aviatsii i kosmonavtiki* 36 (1979): 185–188.
_____, "O deiatel'nosti M. K. Tikhonravova v period s 1947 po 1953 gg. po obosnovaniiu vozmozhnosti sozdaniia sostavykh raket," *Iz istorii aviatsii i kosmonavtiki* 42 (1980): 31–38.
Isaev, A. M., *Pervye shagi k kosmicheskim dvigateliam* (Moscow: Mashinostroenie, 1979).
Ishlinskii, A. Iu., ed., *Akademik S. P. Korolev: uchenii, inzhener, chelovek* (Moscow: Nauka, 1986).
Islent'ev, N. A., ed., *K. E. Tsiolkovskii* (Moscow: Aeroflot, 1939).
Ivanovskii, O. G., *Naperekor zemnomy pritiazhen'iu* (Moscow: Politizdat, 1988).
_____, *Rakety i kosmos v sssr: zapiski sekretnogo konstruktora* (Moscow: Molodaia gvardiia, 2005).
_____ [pseudonym, Aleksei Ivanov]. *Vpervye: zapiski vedushchego konstruktora* (Moscow: Moskovskii rabochii, 1982).
Ivkin, V. I., "Kak sozdavalis' raketnye voiska v sssr," *Voenno-istoricheskii zhurnal* no. 1 (1995): 53–57.
_____, "Pervyi pusk," *Voenno-istoricheskii zhurnal* no. 6 (1997): 42–50.
_____, "Posle Khirosimy i Nagasaki" *Voenno-istoricheskii zhurnal* no. 4 (1995): 65–67.
_____, "Raketnoe nasledstvo fashistkoi germanii," *Voenno-istoricheskii zhurnal* no. 3 (1997): 31–41.
_____, "U istokov otechestvennogo raketostroeniia," *Voenno-istoricheskii zhurnal* no. 2 (1996): 35–43.
Keldysh, M. V., *Izbrannye trudy: raketnaia tekhnika i kosmonavtika*, eds. V. S. Avduevskii and T. M. Eneev (Moscow: Nauka, 1988).
_____, *Tvorcheskoe nasledie Akademika Sergeya Pavlovicha Koroleva: izbrannye trudy i dokumenty*, ed. M. V. Keldysh (Moscow: Nauka, 1980).
Kerber, L. L., *Tupolev* (St. Petersburg: Politekhnika izdatel'stvo, 1999).
Khlevniuk, O. V. et al., eds., *Politbiuro tsk vkp(b) i sovet ministrov sssr 1945–1953* (Moscow: Rosspen, 2002).
Khrushchev, Nikita S., *Khrushchev Remembers: The Glasnost Tapes* (Boston: Little, Brown, 1990).
_____, *Khrushchev Remembers: The Last Testament* (Boston: Little, Brown, 1974).
_____, *Memoirs of Nikita Khrushchev* (3 vols.), ed. Sergei Khrushchev (University Park, PA: Penn State University Press, 2004–2008).
Khrushchev, Sergei, *Khrushchev on Khrushchev: An Inside Account of the Man and His Era* (Boston: Little, Brown, 1990).
_____, *Nikita Khrushchev: Creation of a Superpower* (University Park, PA: Penn State University Press, 2000).
_____, *Nikita Khrushchev: krizisy i rakety: vzgliad iznutri* (2 vols.) (Moscow: Novosti, 1994).
Kisun'ko, Grigorii, *Sekretnaia zona: ispoved' general'nogo konstruktora* (Moscow: Sovremennik, 1996).
Kleimenov, I. I., "Proisshestviia posle 'proisshestviia . . . '," *Voenno-istoricheskii zhurnal* no. 3 (1991): 78–81.
Kondratiuk, Iu. V., *Zavoevanie mezhplanetnykh prostranstv* (Novosibirsk: Iu. V. Kondratiuk, 1929).
_____, *Zavoevanie mezhplanetnykh prostranstv*, 2nd ed., ed. P. I. Ivanov (Moscow: Oborongiz, 1947).
Korolev, S. P., "O prakticheskom znachenii nauchnykh i tekhnicheskikh predlozhenii K. E. Tsiolkovskogo v oblasti raketnoi tekhniki," in *Issledovaniia po istorii i teorii razvitiia aviatsionnoi i raketno-kosmicheskoi nauki i tekhniki*, eds. B. V. Raushenbakh. et al. (Moscow: Nauka, 1981), 39–49.

———, *Raketnyi polet v stratosfere* (Moscow: Gos. voennoe izd-vo, 1934).
Koval', K. I., *Poslednii svidetel': 'germanskaia karta' v kholodnoi voyne* (Moscow: Rosspen, 1997).
Kramarov, G., *Na zare kosmonavtiki: k 40-letiiu osnovaniia pervogo v mire obshchestva mezhplanetnykh soobshchenii* (Moscow: Znanie, 1965).
———, "Pervoe v mire obshchestvo kosmonavtiki," *Novoe v zhizni nauke i tekhnike, IX seriia, fizika i khimiia* 15 (1962): 5–31.
Krieger, F. J., *Behind the Sputniks: A Survey of Soviet Space Science* (Washington, DC: Public Affairs Press, 1958).
Krylov, A. N., *Moi vospominaniia* (Moscow: AN SSSR, 1945).
Langemak, G. E., and V. P. Glushko, *Rakety, ikh ustroistvo i primenenie* (Moscow: ONTI, 1935).
Lel'chuk, V. S., ed., *Poslevoennaia konversiia: k istorii 'kholodnoi voiny': sbornik dokumentov* (Moscow: IRI RAN, 1998).
Logsdon, John M., et al., eds., *Exploring the Unknown: Selected Documents in the History of the U.S. Civil Space Program. Vol. I: Organizing for Exploration* (Washington, DC: NASA, 1995).
Maksimovich, G., "Tak kto zhe est' kto!," *Kryl'ia rodiny* no. 7 (1988): 28–31.
Mikhailov, A. A., ed., *Stantsii v kosmose: sbornik statei* (Moscow: AN SSSR, 1960).
Mishin, V. P., ed., *F. A. Tsander i sovremennaia kosmonavtika* (Moscow: Nauka, 1976).
———, "Istoriia otrasli i sovremennyi spetsialist (iz zapisok ochevidtsa)," *Vestnik vysshei shkoly* no. 1 (1989): 62–65.
———, "Nekotory stranitsy istorii raketno-kosmicheskoi nauki i tekhniki v poslevoennyi period," in *Issledovaniia po istorii i teorii razvitiia aviatsionnoi i raketno-kosmicheskoi nauki i tekhniki*, Vols. 8–10, eds. B. V. Raushenbakh et al. (Moscow: Nauka, 2001), 50–66.
———, "Ot sozdaniia ballisticheskikh raket k raketno-kosmicheskomu mashinostroeniiu," *Problemy mashinostroeniia i nadezhnosti mashin* no. 3 (1996): 3–14.
———, *Ot sozdaniia ballisticheskikh raket k raketno-kosmicheskomu mashinostroeniiu* (Moscow: Informatsionno-izdatel'skii tsentr 'Inform-Znanie,' 1998).
Molodtsov, V. V., "Pervye kosmicheskie proekty (k 40-letiiu zapuska 1 isz)," *Zemlia i vselennaia* no. 4 (1997).
Mozzhorin, Iu. A., et al., eds., *Dorogi v kosmos: Vospominaniia veteranov raketno-kosmicheskoi tekhniki i kosmonavtiki: I i II* (Moscow: MAI, 1992).
———, eds., *Nachalo kosmicheskoi ery: vospominaniia veteranov raketno-kosmicheskoi tekhniki i kosmonavtiki: vypusk vtoroi* (Moscow: RNITsKD, 1994).
Nicolet, M., ed., *Annals of the International Geophysical Year, Vol. I: The Histories of the International Polar Years and the Inception and Development of the International Geophysical Year* (London: Pergamon Press, 1959).
———, ed., *Annals of the International Geophysical Year, Vol. IIA & IIB: The International Geophysical Year Meetings* (London: Pergamon Press, 1959).
Obert, G. [H. Oberth], *Puti osushchestvleniia kosmicheskikh poletov*, ed. B. V. Raushenbakh (Moscow: Oborongiz, 1948).
Odoevskii, V. F., *4338 god: Peterburgskie pis'ma* (Moscow: Ogonek, 1921).
Perel'man, Ia. I., *Mezhplanetnye puteshestviia* (Petrograd: P. P. Soikin, 1915).
———, *Mezhplanetnye puteshestviia: polety v mirovoe prostranstvo i dostizhenie nebesnykh svetil*, 4th ed. (Petrograd: Akad. izd.-vo., 1923).
———, *Mezhplanetnye puteshestviia*, 5th ed. (Leningrad, 1924).
———, *Mezhplanetnye puteshestviia*, 6th ed. (Leningrad: Priboi, 1929).
———, *Mezhplanetnye puteshestviia*, 10th ed. (Leningrad: ONTI, 1935).
———, *Polet na lunu. Sovremennye proekty mezhplanetnykh pereletov* (Leningrad: Seiatel', 1925).
———, *Puteshestviia na planety* (Leningrad: P. P. Soikin, 1929).

———, *Raketoi na lunu* (Moscow: Gosizdat, 1930).
———, *Tsiolkovskii: ego zhizn', izobreteniia i nauchnye trudy* (Leningrad: Gostekhizdat, 1932).
———, *Zanimatel'naia fizika* (kn. 1) (St. Petersburg: P. P. Soikin, 1913).
Rakhmanin, V. F. and L. E. Sterpin, eds., *Odnazhdy i navsegda... : dokumenty i lyudi o sozdatele raketnykh dvigatelei i kosmicheskikh sistem akademike Valentine Petroviche Glushko* (Moscow: Mashinostroenie, 1998).
Raushenbakh, B. V., ed., *Iz istorii Sovetskoi kosmonavtiki: sbornik pamiati Akademika S. P. Koroleva* (Moscow: Nauka, 1983).
Riabev, L. D., ed., *Atomnyi proekt sssr: dokumenty i materialy, tom II: atomnaia bomba, 1945–1954, kniga 7* (Moscow: Nauka-Fizmatlit, 2007).
Rodnykh, A. A., *Rakety i kosmicheskie korabli*, 2nd ed. (Leningrad: Gosmashmetizdat, 1934).
Rynin, N. A., *Mezhplanetnye soobshcheniia* (9 vols. in 3 parts) (Leningrad: various publishers, 1928–1932).
———, *V stratosferu!* (Leningrad, 1934).
———, *Zavoevanie stratosfery: k poletam sovetskikh vysotnykh aerostatov v stratosferu* (Leningrad, 1933).
Sakharov, Andrey, *Memoirs* (New York: Knopf, 1990).
Saukke, M. B., *Neizvestnyi Tupolev* (Moscow: KTsNTI 'Original,' 1993).
Semenov, Iu. P., ed., *Raketno-Kosmicheskaia Korporatsiia "Energiia" imeni S. P. Koroleva* (Korolev: RKK Energiia, 1996).
Sergeev, I. D., ed., *Khronika osnovnykh sobytii istorii raketnykh voisk strategicheskogo naznacheniia* (Moscow: RVSN, 1994).
Shakhurin, A. I., *Kryl'ia pobedy* (Moscow: Politicheskoi literatury, 1990).
Shternfel'd, A. A., *Iskusstvennye sputniki zemli* (Moscow: Gostekhizdat, 1956).
———, "Istoriia moei pervoi knigi," *Voprosy istorii estestvoznaniia i tekhniki* no. 3 (1981): 134–139.
———, *Mezhplanetnye polety* (Moscow: Gostekhizdat, 1955).
———, *Polet v mirovoe prostranstvo* (Moscow: Gostekhizdat, 1949).
———, *Vvedenie v kosmonavtiki* (Leningrad: ONTI, 1937).
Skuridin, G. A., "S. P. Korolev i pervyi iskusstvennyi sputnik zemli," *Zemlia i vselennaia* no. 5 (1982): 57–61.
Sokolova, S. A. and T. M. Mel'kumov, eds., *Pionery raketnoi tekhniki: Vetchinkin Glushko Korolev Tikhonravov: izbrannye trudy (1929–1945)* (Moscow: Nauka, 1972).
Solovtsov, N. E. and V. I. Ivkin, "Mezhkontinental'naia ballisticheskaia raketa – eto absoliutnoe oruzhie," *Voenno-istoricheskii zhurnal* no. 12 (2004): 2–7.
Terent'ev, Ia. M., "Iz istorii pervykh sovetskikh raketnykh organizatsii (1930–1935 gg.)," *Voprosy istorii estestvoznaniia i tekhniki* no. 2 (1984): 108–113.
Tikhonravov, M. K., "The Creation of the First Artificial Earth Satellite: Some Historical Details," *Journal of the British Interplanetary Society* 47 (1994): 191–194.
———, *Raketnaia tekhnika* (Moscow: ONTI, 1935).
Tikhonravov, M. K. et al. *Osnovny teorii poleta i elementy proektirovaniia ISZ* (Moscow: Mashinostroenie, 1967).
Tokaev, G. A. [G. A. Tokaty], *Comrade X* (London: The Harvill Press, 1956).
——— [G. A. Tokaty], *Stalin Means War* (London: Weidenfeld & Nicolson, 1951).
Tolstoi, A., *Aelita (zakat Marsa)*. (Moscow: Gosizdat, 1923).
Trotsky, Leon, *Literature and Revolution* (Ann Arbor: University of Michigan Press, 1975).
Trudy vsesoiuznoi konferentsii po izucheniiu stratosfery 31 marta – 6 aprelia 1934 g. (Leningrad: AN SSSR, 1935).
Tsander, F. A. *Iz nauchnogo naslediia*, ed. A. F. Tsander (Moscow: Nauka, 1967).
———, "Perelety na drugie planety," *Tekhnika i zhizn'* no. 13 (July 20, 1924): 15–16.
———, *Problema poleta pri pomoshchi reaktivnykh apparatov* (Moscow: Gosaviaavtoizdat, 1932).

———, *Problema poleta pri pomoshchi reaktivnykh apparatov*, ed. L. K. Korneev (Moscow: GNTI Oborongiz, 1961).
———, *Sobranie trudov*, ed. G. A. Teters (Riga: Zinatne, 1977).
Tsiolkovskii, K. E., *Budushchee zemli i chelovechestva* (Kaluga: K. E. Tsiolkovskii, 1928).
———, *Gore i genii* (Kaluga: K. E. Tsiolkovskii, 1916).
———, *Grezy o zemle i nebe i effekty vsemirnogo tiagoteniia* (Moscow: A. N. Goncharov, 1895).
———, "Issledovanie mirovykh prostranstv reaktivnymi priborami," *Nauchnoe obozrenie* no 5 (1903): 45–75.
———, "Issledovanie mirovykh prostranstv reaktivnymi priborami," *Vestnik vozdukhoplavaniia* no. 19 (1911): 16–21, no. 20 (1911): 29–32, nos. 21–22 (1911): 31–37, no. 2 (1912): 2–7, no. 3 (1912): 15–16, no. 5 (1912): 2–5, nos. 6–7 (1912): 6–9, and no. 9 (1912): 7–11.
———, *Issledovanie mirovykh prostranstv reaktivnymi priborami (dopol'nenie k I i II chasti truda togo zhe nazvaniia* (Kaluga: K. E. Tsiolkovskii, 1914).
———, *Issledovanie mirovykh prostranstv reaktivnymi priborami (pereizdanie rabot 1903 i 1911 g. s nekotorymi izmeneniiami i dopolneniiami)* (Kaluga: K. E. Tsiolkovskii, 1926).
———, *Izbrannye trudy*, eds. B. N. Vorob'ev and V. N. Sokol'skii (Moscow: AN SSSR, 1962).
———, *Izbrannye trudy, kniga II. Reaktivnoe dvizhenie*, ed. F. A. Tsander (Moscow: Gosmashmetizdat, 1934).
———, *Kosmicheskaia raketa. Opytnaia podgotovka* (Kaluga: K. E. Tsiolkovskii, 1927).
———, *Kosmicheskie raketnye poezda. Reaktivnyi dvigatel'* (Kaluga: Sektsii nauchnykh rabotnikov, 1929).
———, *Liubov' k samomu sebe, ili istinnoe sebialiubie* (Kaluga: K. E. Tsiolkovskii, 1928).
———, *Monizm vselennoi* (Kaluga: K. E. Tsiolkovskii, 1925).
———, *Na lune* (Moscow: I. D. Sytin, 1893).
———, *Nauchnaia etika* (Kaluga: K. E. Tsiolkovskii, 1930).
———, *Novyi aeroplan. Za atmosferoi zemli. Reaktivnyi dvigatel'* (Kaluga: K. E. Tsiolkovskii, 1929).
———, *Otkliki literaturnye* (Kaluga: K. E. Tsiolkovskii, 1928).
———, *Prichina kosmosa* (Kaluga: K. E. Tsiolkovskii, 1925).
———, *Proshedshee zemli* (Kaluga: K. E. Tsiolkovskii, 1928).
———, *Raketa v kosmicheskoe prostranstvo* (Kaluga: K. E. Tsiolkovskii, 1924).
———, *Reaktivnyi aeroplan (vziato iz bol'shoi rukopisi)* (Kaluga: K. E. Tsiolkovskii, 1930).
———, *The Science Fiction of Konstantin Tsiolkovsky*, ed. Adam Starchild (Seattle: University Press of the Pacific, 1979).
———, *Selected Works*, ed. A. A. Blagonravov (Moscow: Mir, 1968).
———, *Sobranie sochinenie: t. 1, aerodinamika*, eds. B. N. Vorob'ev, B. N. Iur'ev, and N. Ia. Fabrikants (Moscow: AN SSSR, 1951).
———, *Sobranie sochinenii: t. 2, reaktivnye letatel'nye apparatury*, eds. A. A. Blagnoravov et al. (Moscow: AN SSSR, 1954).
———, *Soprotivlenie vozdukha i skoryi poezd* (Kaluga: K. E. Tsiolkovskii, 1927).
———, *Stratoplan polureaktivnyi* (Kaluga: K. E. Tsiolkovskii, 1932).
———, *Tiazhest' ischezla, fantasticheskii ocherk* (Moscow: Gosmashmetizdat, 1933).
———, *Trudy po raketnoi tekhnike*, ed. M. K. Tikhonravov (Moscow: Oborongiz, 1947).
———, *Tseli zvezdoplavaniia* (Kaluga: K. E. Tsiolkovskii, 1929).
———, *Um i strasti* (Kaluga: K. E. Tsiolkovskii, 1928).
———, *Vne zemli* (Kaluga: KOIPiMK, 1920).
———, *Zvezdoplavateliam* (Kaluga: K. E. Tsiolkovskii, 1930).
Tukhachevskii, M. N. *Izbrannye proizvedeniia: t. 2, 1928–1937 gg.*, eds. G. I. Os'kin and P. P. Chernushkov (Moscow: Voenizdat, 1964).
Ustinov, D. F. *Vo imia pobedy: zapiski narkoma vooruzheniia* (Moscow: Voenizdat, 1988).

Vetrov, G. S., ed., *S. P. Korolev i ego delo: svet i teni v istorii kosmonavtiki: izbrannye trudy i dokumenty* (Moscow: Nauka, 1998).
Vorob'ev, B. N., "Iz perepiski K. E. Tsiolkovskogo," *Voprosy istorii estestvoznaniia i tekhniki* no. 6 (1958): 46–49.
Vorob'ev, B. N., and V. N. Sokol'skii, eds., *Pionery raketnoi tekhniki: Kibal'chich Tsiolkovskii Tsander Kondratiuk: izbrannye trudy* (Moscow: Nauka, 1964).
Zabrodin, A. V., ed., *M. V. Keldysh: tvorcheskii portret po vospominaniiam sovremennikov* (Moscow: Nauka, 2001).
Zenger, E. [Eugen Sänger], *Tekhnika raketnogo poleta*, 2nd ed., ed. V. A. Shtokolov (Moscow: Oborongiz, 1947).
Zotov, V. S. et al., eds., *V vospominaniiakh sovremennikov*. Tula: Priokskoe knizhnoe izdatel'stvo, 1971.

Newspapers

Izvestiia
Kommuna
Krasnaia gazeta
Krasnaia zvezda
Literaturnaia gazeta
Pravda
Rabochaia moskva
Raketa
Sovetskaia rossiia
Tekhnika
Vecherniaia izvestiia
Vecherniaia moskva

Journals

Aviatsiia i khimiia
Aviatsiia i kosmonavtika
Bor'ba mirov
Chelovek
Elektrichestvo i zhizn'
Istochnik
Istoricheskii arkhiv
Istoriko-astronomicheskie issledovaniia
Iz istorii aviatsii i kosmonavtiki
Izobretatel' i ratsionalizator
Khochu vse znat'
Khronika vozdushnogo dela
Krasnaia mirov
Kryl'ia rodiny
Mir aviatsii
Mir prikliuchenii
Molodaia gvardiia
Moskva
Nauchnoe obozrenie
Nauka i tekhnika
Nauka i zhizn'
Nauka v rossii
Novaia i noveishaia istoriia

Novosti kosmonavtiki
Ogonek
Pioner
Priroda i liudi
Radio
Rech'
Rodina
Samolet
Sovremennoe slovo
Svet: priroda i chelovek
Svobodnaia mysl'
Tekhnika i zhizn'
Tekhnika-molodezhi
Trudy instituta istorii nauki i tekhniki
Trudy po istorii tekhniki akademii nauk
Vestnik akademii nauk sssr
Vestnik vozdukhoplavaniia
Vestnik vozdushnogo flota
Vestnik znaniia
V masterskoi prirody
Voenno-istoricheskii zhurnal
Voprosy filosofii
Voprosy istorii
Voprosy istorii estestvoznaniia i tekhniki
Vsemirnyi sledopyt'
Znamia
Znanie-sila

Index

CPSIA information can be obtained
at www.ICGtesting.com
Printed in the USA
LVHW111751020420
652036LV00001B/11

9 781107 639324